Economic Reforms and Perspectives

Recent Developments in Indian Economy

Economic Reforms and Perspectives

Recent Developments in Indian Economy

Edited by
Boppana Nagarjuna
Department of Economics
University of Hyderabad
Hyderabad (India)

SERIALS PUBLICATIONS
New Delhi

First Published–2004

ISBN: 81-86771-28-X

Published by

Head Office : **SERIALS PUBLICATIONS**
4, B.S.S. Hall, Khyber Pass Market
Civil Lines, Delhi–110054 (India)
Phone: 23245225
Fax: 91-11-23272135
E-mail: serials@satyam.net.in

Branch Office : *4830/24, Prahlad Street, Ansari Road*
Darya Ganj, New Delhi-110002 (India)

Printed at : R. K. Offset Process, Naveen Shahdara,

PRINTED IN INDIA

This volume is
brought out
in Honor of
Prof. V. V. N. Somayajulu
on the eve of his
relinquishing
the office.

Acknowledgements

In preparing this volume, I have received very valuable papers from academicians, economists, researchers and also from policy makers.

I take this opportunity to thank all of them who responded positively, timely to my request for contributing their papers in honor of Prof. V. V. N. Somayajulu. It is their kind cooperation and encouragement that have helped me to complete the task successfully.

I am highly indebted to Prof. B. Kamaiah who provided the real inspiration for undertaking this project, with his timely guidance and help I could finish the job beyond expectations.

I am delighted for the preface written by Prof. D. L. Narayana and grateful to him.

Also, I am obliged to Serials Publications for printing the book within the anticipated time schedule.

Acknowledgements

Preface

It gives me a great pleasure to congratulate Dr. Boppana Nagarjuna, Faculty, Department of Economics, University of Hyderabad, Hyderabad for undertaking this task to honour Prof. V.V.N. Somayajulu, who retired from the Department in April 2003.

Prof. V.V.N. Somayajulu is an eminent academician who developed the Economics Department and rendered valuable services to the University of Hyderabad. His good qualities of head and heart need no assertion, he is a self-made man and versatile economist, he helped the poor and needy students and encouraged the students who are having abilities and talent. His democratic way of administration endeared one and all, and maintained harmony in running the department. He is quite conscious of values which make a person true educationist and humanist, he never compromised with principles and ideals that made him a personality that enabled to be a perfect humanist under the Indian circumstances.

His contribution to research in Economics is quite valuable, and contributed on research works on the Planning Techniques, Economic Development, while his research interests were also spread to Industrialisation, Privatization and Industrial Development. His performance as an economist and researcher was on par with the work of any reputed international economist. For the preparation of this volume the well known reputation of Prof. V.V.N. Somayajulu has facilitated to secure valuable papers from academicians, economists, and research scholars. The wide range of issues with great depth are presented in the book "Economic Reforms and Perspectives" as per anticipated Schedule. As the papers are in large number and their importance facilitated their appreciation as policy problems.

Dr. Boppana Nagarjuna prepared a model of "Memorabilia" on the contributors and their papers which is worthy of imitation in to, in the case of big books dealing with wide range of problems. It gives knowledge of policy problems in a nut shell, before going through different chapters in detail.

The book deserved to be in all the libraries of Indian Universities and other important libraries in the country, not to speak of relevant significant libraries elsewhere. The Overwhelming response of wide range of contributors from different parts of India has facilitated this valuable publication.

It would be a good tradition if the other departments and universities in India emulate publications to honour their great academicians. it would be quite rewarding for the efforts of Dr. Boppana Nagarjuna's model stimulates the undertaking of such works.

Prof. D. L. Narayana
Chairman-Second & Third State Finance Commission
Government of Andhra Pradesh.

Founder Chairman–A.P. Economic Association,
President – The 8th World Economic Congress,
New Delhi–1984-85.

Memorabilia

This volume is aligned to honor Prof. V.V.N. Somayajulu with great respect and the contents are dearer to him as a teacher, a researcher and also as an intellectual with nationalism at the core of his heart. The response to this effort is overwhelming from all parts of India, abroad and all the contributors are felt very glad to contribute in honoring him.

The book is classified into eight chapters each one focuses on specific areas.

I. Macro Economic Policy Issues

II. Monetary Policy Issues

III. Trade Policy and WTO issues

IV. Financial Sector Issues

V. Industrial Policy Issues

VI. Privatization and Foreign Investment Issues

VII. Educational Economics Issues, and

VIII. Agriculture, Forestry, Tourism and other Issues

Chapter one deals with the **Macro Economics Policy Issues,** paper one is "*Trends in Central Government Expenditure, Revenue, Fiscal Deficit and Domestic Debt: 1980-2000*" by D. Brahma Reddy and B. Nagarjuna. The structure of public finances in an economy is defined by the level and composition of expenditure of the Government and the instruments relied upon to finance them, viz., the tax and non-tax revenue sources and borrowings. The excess of Government expenditure over current revenues and non debt capital receipts gets reflected in fiscal deficits financed either by way of borrowings from internal and external sources and seignorage. If expenditure persistently exceeds revenue, fiscal deficit to the extent is not covered by seignorage, steadily adds to outstanding debt resulting in increasing interest payments. Unless met with larger revenue receipts, this gives rise to a self-perpetuating spiral of debt and deficit. the study period is 1980 to 2000.

The Second paper is on *"A Decade after India's Economic Reform.. 'Finance driven' model must give way to Keynesian activism "* by D.Sambandhan Post independent India witnessed two major currency convulsions. The first acute foreign exchange crisis ended up with a massive devaluation of rupee occurred on June6, 1966. Nevertheless, that did not result in reversing of the command model of development; instead, it underlined the imperative of indigenous way of economic development. Despite a hostile international financial and economic climate of 1970s characterized by transition from fixed to floating exchange rates and the twin oil shocks triggered world wide stagflation, India could still manage all the shocks and disturbances of world economy. It continued to remain as an insular economy, reasonably protectionist and increasingly reluctant to embrace the market based supply side Economics of Thatcherism and Reagonomics variety.

Third paper is on "*Export led growth in India evidence from VARs*" by Geethanjali and Pravakar Sahoo. This paper attempts to test the long run relationships among exports, imports, gross domestic capital formation, trade policy and GDP in India using annual data from 1965-66 to 1997-98, within the empirical framework of Vector Auto-regressions (VAR) augmented with an error correction mechanism in the presence of a structural break. The forecast error variance decomposition (FEVD) technique is employed to account for error variance in each of the variables in the VAR system, to innovations in own as well as other variables in the system. The FEVD test reveals that exports and imports are largely explained by their own innovations. On the whole, the findings of the study do not lend support to the export-led growth hypothesis but at the same time brings out the fact that there exists a strong relationship among imports, exports, trade policies, investment and GDP in India.

The chapter Two discusses the **Monetary Policy Issues**, it's having three papers. The first one is "A Test of Monetarist model of imported Inflation: A comparison of India's case with open economies" by Kishore Kulkarni and Meenakshi Rishi from USA. The paper discusses the theory of monetary approach to balance of payments and constructs an empirically testable model of imported inflation from it. There are some unique features of the monetary approach to balance of payments such as its focus on capital flows as a source of disturbances in balance of payments and the assumed stability of demand for money of an economy. While few economists in recent years have tested monetary approach to balance of payments, there is a need of investigating the phenomenon of imported inflation by using monetary approach to balance of payments.

The process in which the importation of inflation occurs is as follows: An increase in worldwide inflation can make an increase in capital inflow of an open economy. In the absence of successful sterilization process by the domestic monetary policy, (and under fixed exchange rates) the economy may end up with increase in broadly defined money supply as the foreign reserves in it go up. This increase in money supply can be inflationary. The paper is divided into three sections. Section 1 is the introduction that sets the problem of imported inflation. Section 2 reviews the relevant literature as well as surveys the similar studies on this topic. It also includes the explanation and construction of monetarist model of imported inflation. Section 3 uses the data of six countries: India, Malaysia, the Netherlands, Mexico, Singapore and Belgium to test the model and makes summary and conclusion. The sample of countries is expected to represent diversity of regional and structural characteristics of the countries to find out the relevance of monetary model.

The Second paper titled as *"Do Fiscal Deficits and Money Supply determine Interest rate in India?"* by Hrishikesh Mallick and P.C.Parida. This paper examines the relationship of interest rates with fiscal deficits and money supply in the Indian context, which has not received much attention in the past. It uses monthly data from 1997:4 to 2001:6. Employing the Johansen co-integration technique, the study concludes that interest rates have a stable long run equilibrium relationship with fiscal deficits and money supply. Further, using the error variance decomposition analysis, it finds that rate of interest is not influenced by other two variables such as money supply and fiscal deficit rather it influences money supply.

M. Ramanjaneyulu titles the third paper as "Impact of EURO on Indian Economy". A historic decision has been taken by European Union summit, which was taken place in Brussels on May1, 1998 for implementation of European Economic and Monetary Union with 11 countries from January 1st 1999. They are Austria, Finland, France, Belgium, Germany, Ireland, Italy, Luxembourg, Nederland, Portugal, Spain and Greece has participated in the Euro from 1st January 2001, which increases to 12 the number of Member states of the Euro zone. Electronic and non-cash transactions in the new common European Currency has been made, then the Euro conversion to notes and coins has also been taken place from January 2002 .It is a unique currency in monetary history. It has become the first international currency without backing of bullion or any national government and became the legal tender in participating countries of the European Union. It is an unprecedented experiment for a single currency across national borders of countries.

Indian Economy is predominantly agrarian one. Indian corporates entered into manufacturing activities, which were in the nature of import substitutes. Industrial sector is acquiring a degree of sophistication in its manufacturing base, which is becoming a manufacturing base for components for global corporations. It is evident that Indian Software companies are providing a competitive edge for their clients through cost and quality advantages, state of the art capabilities, technical trained professionals and high reliability. Large number of organizations is already gaining significant benefit from outsourcing Information Technology work to organizations in India, which is undoubtedly the leading provider of offshore IT services. India has the second largest pool of scientific manpower in the world, low manpower cost, and its democratic and legal systems provide significant advantages over the countries in attracting western business. The Indian I T industry has grown at an annual compound rate of almost 52 per cent over the last five years and exports already exceed to the worth £ 2.5 billion pounds by the year 2000.

The Chapter Three is on **Trade Policy and WTO issues**. It has four papers, the first paper is "*SAPTA and India's Trade performance with SAARC*" by M. Pradeep, V. Vijay and Boppana Nagarjuna. This paper addresses an important question of what happened to India's trade performance after the SAPTA Agreement with other South Asian Countries, which are the members of the SAARC. Employing three time series structural break techniques of Perron (1989), Banerjee et al., (1992) and Perron (1997) on the monthly data (1985:1 – 2001:12) of India's Exports to and Imports form SAARC Countries, it has been found that exports exhibit a more dynamic profile overtime when compared to imports.

The Second paper titled as *"Did Economic Reforms Reform the Indian Export Performance*? by T. Gopinath. This paper attempts to explore the role of economic reforms in imparting sustained dynamism to Indian exports, the key to success of such reforms. Based on the evidence collected and complied, involving 23 select export commodities (at 3-digit SITC level) accounting for 46 per cent of the total value of exports, the paper finds that the contribution of reforms to export promotion appears ambiguous, as 57 per cent of the commodities either suffered erosion of or stagnation in their global markets in the post reform period. It identifies 10 commodities – where potential for increased market penetration exists – for focused attention. It also identifies 3 commodities for building up potential for future growth. Further, the paper observes that world demand, as it evolves, appears to be drafting away from the leading Indian exports and that FDI inflows into the country are basically domestic-market-oriented.

The third paper is on *"International Negotiations on Transfer of Technology"* by C. Niranjan Rao. In the post reform period Technological development has been identified as an important source of growth of countries. Soon after regaining their independence many developing countries[1] saw technology as the key input into the development process. They had two choices (not mutually exclusive), one to develop technology indigenously and the other to acquire technology from developed countries. As they were in a hurry to catch up they followed the latter option that of acquiring technology from developed countries. They looked at it not only as short term solution for acquiring technology for immediate production needs but also as a way of acquiring technological capability. Some of these countries introduced incentives for technology generation by domestic firms. It is interesting to note that these same countries thought that initial transfer technology would lead to long-term technological capability. There are two ways of acquiring technology from developed countries, either through licensing or by foreign direct investment.

The regaining of independence by a large number of countries in the 1950s and later generated a euphoric atmosphere in which countries could have a choice in choosing their development paradigm. Independence restored the ability of these countries to take greater control over their development process. While the developing countries were trying to do what ever they could within their countries, they also had access to a sympathetic attitude of the international community. This international community in the form of the United Nations system helped these countries in articulating their perceived needs. The atmosphere till the 1980s was to listen to the articulations of developing countries. The situation changed in the 1980s and later to that of hardening of attitudes. The successive development decades starting in the 1960s and the 'New International Economic Order' provided the necessary background.

The fourth paper is about the *"One Year China's entry into World Trade Organization: Implications for China and India"* by Pradeep Agrawal and Pravakar Sahoo. China's accession to WTO is likely to have the following effects: (i) China's exports would be affected positively due to a more steady access to world markets and negatively due to the elimination of export subsidies, dual pricing practices, etc. - the overall long term impact is expected to be positive; (ii) China's imports would increase due to reduction in tariff and non-tariff trade barriers and in government regulations; and (iii) Foreign investment inflows into China will increase in export activities due to a more steady access to world markets and for domestic production due to the opening up of many additional sectors. Thus accession to WTO provides economic benefits to China, while reducing its vulnerability on foreign policy and other issues by eliminating the need for numerous bilateral trade agreements that have to be renewed frequently. This explains China's eagerness to join the WTO. Further, the one-year experience of WTO accession shows that China has gained in terms of output growth, exports and imports and also in attracting more FDI. Since India and China compete in the exports of many labour intensive manufactures, China's accession to WTO would have a significant negative impact on India's exports and foreign investment inflows. This can be overcome if we further strengthen our economy by improving infrastructure and undertaking additional reforms.

The chapter Four cares about the **Financial Sector Reforms**, and it has five papers. The first one titled as "*Fiscal Autonomy of states in a Federation: a case study of India*" by Achal Kumar Gaur. States and other political units, which join their hands together in a federation, are primarily interested to reap the socio-economic advantages along with some extent of autonomy, especially in financial affairs. Thus, states usually prefer to retain some degree of autonomy (especially fiscal autonomy) in federation. Contrary to it, at least in financial matters, states are in an Oligopolistic situation as compared to the federal government which enjoys a monopoly. Consequently, demand for higher fiscal autonomy by the federating units has become a prominent and complex feature for not only Indian federation but for almost all the federations in the world today.

A new model based upon decentralized theorem has been developed for which Herfindahl indices of revenue and expenditure has been calculated. The crux of the theoretical modeling is that the states may be autonomous when centralization in expenditure and revenue are identical. Otherwise, they may be either 'under autonomous' or 'over autonomous' according as centralization in revenue is greater than or less than centralization in expenditure. Empirical results, which are based on 23 units (22 states and central government) reveal that states were financially 'under autonomous' during the period 1985-86 to 2000-2001. It is interesting to observe that the degree of 'under autonomy' was higher during pre-liberalization (1985-91). Thus, it may be inferred that the introduction of Structural Adjustment Programmes (SAPs) in 1991 has succeeded in redressal of incidence of 'under autonomy' of states in Indian federation during post-liberalization era i.e. 1991-2001.

The second paper in this chapter is "*Some aspects of modeling Stock return behavior: a review of issues and evidence*" by Puja Padhi. Markowitz had given one of the prominent contributions to the theory of finance in the year 1952. He analyzed the individual's investment decision under the condition of uncertainty using mean-variance analysis. Individual choose among risky investments as if they were maximizing the expected value of their utility. In mean- variance analysis maximizing the expected return for a given variance or minimizing the variance in return for a given expected return is consistent with expected utility paradigm. This states that the individual will choose those alternatives as if he or she were maximizing expected utility. An individual preference for risky assets can be evaluated in terms of each assets expected utility. The quadratic utility function is of particular interest in financial theory because it helps to calculate the expected utility of return on risky assets as a function of the mean and variance of their probability distribution.

The evolution of efficient market is synthesized by Fama (1970). The efficient market literature had provided finance with its own research methodology, the "event study". Fama utilized three broad categories for test of market efficiency based on the "relative availability" of subsets of information underlying the tests. There are three forms of information set in the context of efficient market hypothesis. The weak form asserts that current prices fully and instantaneously reflect all information implied by historical sequence of prices. The semi-strong form asserts that the current price fully and instantaneously reflect all public information about companies including the information set on past price series. The strong form asserts that information by monopolistic access (privately held information).

The excess of expected return over risk free return is known as 'volatility'. Volatility of return is one aspect of stock return behavior. The theory of rational bubbles is an example of a model in which expectations are formed rationally and market is informationally efficient but there are large deviation between market prices and fundamental values. If the market value is greater than the fundamentals this indicates an excess volatility. The rational market hypothesis shows positive relationship between excess return and expected and ex-ante volatility. In almost all financial models, variance is used as a proxy for variability. The measure of variability that is based on past prices that conforms to the present variability has been conceptualized as 'volatility' in financial market. Thus volatility, as concept, can be treated as synonymous with variability in general or variance in particular. Broadly speaking there exist two broad canvases, under which stock market volatility can be modeled, viz, 'conditional volatility' approach and 'stochastic volatility' approach. There are various aspects, associated with volatility in stock return such as: shocks and noise trading, fads, seasonality, co-movement or volatility transmission, price limit, margin trading, circuit breakers and transaction tax.

Empirical research has identified a significant amount of volatility in stock prices that cannot be easily explained by changes in fundamentals (Poterba and Summer 1988). One interpretation of the result is that asset prices respond not only to news but also to irrational demand, or "noise trading" (Black 1986). Fads interpretation of volatility test, noise trading by naïve investors plays a significant role in stock price determination explained by West (1988) and Campbell and Kyle (1986). An asymmetry reaction of conditional volatility to the arrival of news was induced both by the sign of past shocks and the size of unexpected volatility (Engle and Ng 1993). There are factors other than the sign of past shocks are responsible for the asymmetric behavior of volatilities. To examine this (Fornari and Mele 1997) proposed a model – the Volatility – switching ARCH – that captures asymmetries via the impact of past shocks on the level of volatility, rather than through the unexpected returns. Not only shocks and noise trading but also seasonality in asset behavior affects stock return. Weekend effect, January effect is some of the important factor for explaining the seasonality in stock return. The cross-sectional differences in January return of selected securities are systematically related to their returns in previous 1 to 5 years, reported by Branch (1977) and Bondt De et al (1987). All size – based portfolios exhibit significant January mean-reversion in the post War period explained by Jegadeesh (1991). To analyze the "week – end" for daily stock return, Jaffe and Wasterfield (1985) examined the daily stock returns for four foreign countries. Volatility transmission means, to know the role of measurable economic variable in explaining the magnitude and changes in asset price co movement. It tried to explain the "price of risk" associated with different asset prices are same or different across countries and the inter-temporal behavior of the stock price indices (King et al 1994). Stock exchange often employ four measures to curb stock price volatility, namely, margin, price limits, circuit breakers, transaction taxes. Price volatility has been the subject of intense debate for many decades. The purpose of price limit was to prevent stocks from excessive volatility. Margin trading was found to be an effective tool in restricting the activity of new entrants in the stock market. Circuit breakers are primarily used on a stock index. The basic purpose of the circuit breaker is to curb volatility. Transaction taxes can also be used to curb volatility. The tax is aimed at curbing the instincts of 'wild' speculators (information-less). Many studies have been conducted abroad on issues concerning return behavior of the stock market. However no significant efforts have been made in India to examine the issues related to the return behavior of the stock market. Some of the important issues related to the return behavior such as noise trading, size and sign of shocks, week - end effect, January effect, co movement, regulatory measures, etc. This present study attempts to fill this void. In the back drop of the above discussion, this essay presents a discussion as to how the concept of stock market volatility has been treated in the literature and the developments to model volatility. Section ii, would discuss, in brief, the return behavior of the stock market: section iii, presents factors that are responsible for creating seasonality in stock return. Section IV, tries to link changes in co - movement or volatility transmission between different stock market. In section V, the regulatory measures to curb stock price volatility have been presented. The concluding remarks are followed by the last section .VI. different models of volatility.

The th*ird paper titled as* "Interest Payment Expenditure in Southern States during 1990-91 to 2000-01" by M. Seenuvasan. Interest payment expenditure of the government comprises of interest charges on public debt and other obligations. They are interest charges on internal debt and small savings and Provident Fund, interest on loans and advances from Central Government and interest charges on reserve funds. Interest payments on internal debt consists of interest on market loans and other internal debts such as loans from LIC, NABARD (National Bank for Agriculture and Rural Development), loans from SBI and other banks, Special Securities issued to NSSF (National Small Saving Funds) and others. The expenditure incurred on the management of debt is also included under interest payments. Interest payments incurred on Small Savings and Provident Fund includes interest paid on State Provident Fund, Incentives and Bonus to Provident Fund subscribers. Interest on trusts and Pension Fund, Interest on Insurance and Pension Funds and interest on special Deposits and Accounts. Interest payments on loans and advances from Central Government consists of interest on loans for State Plan Scheme, interest on loans for centrally sponsored plan schemes, interest on loans for non-plan schemes, interest on ways and means advances and other State loans.

A serious concern was raised about the growing interest liabilities of the governments in recent years. Increasing interest payments exacerbates the stress on revenue as a significant portion of the funds went towards interest payments leading to perennial revenue deficits. While the major rigidities on the expenditure side of the center is interest liabilities, subsidies and defense, on the state side it is interest liabilities and salary bill (Mundal and Rao, 1991). In Uttar Pradesh, bulk of the revenue expenditure is of a committed nature and the entire borrowings are used in paying interest and repayment of debts (Shankar 1998). A continuous revenue deficit leads to large interest burden and as a consequence, states are pushed towards borrowing more to meet their repayment needs (Jalan 1998). The emergence of a fiscal crisis at the state level as a consequence of expenditure outpacing revenue have been brought out in studies on state finances such as Guhan (1986) on Tamil Nadu, Jetha (1985) on Gujarat and Govinda Rao and Sen (1999) on Kerala finances. The deterioration in Kerala State finances has been caused by faster growth of interest payments and administrative expenditure. The repayment liabilities on account of borrowings, especially interest liability, are a fast growing item of expenditure for all the states (X Finance Commission). Tenth Finance Commission observed that interest payments and salaries and wages have emerged as the major components of expenditure as a direct result of the mode of financing of expenditure and the expansionary policies pursued by government. The Tenth Commission further observed that it is the burden of interest payments arising out of none too prudent use of borrowings that lies at the root of the fiscal problem. (P.5.1994). In the case of states, the rising revenue deficit has also cut into maintenance expenditure in the revenue budget. In order to accommodate the rising interest payments and the growth of wages and salaries, which have come to be regarded as committed expenditure, maintenance expenditure has been treated as a residual item. The adverse impact of increasing debt service payments on capital expenditure growth was seriously noted in recent years. (Mohan R. 2000) The implication of increasing interest burden was recognized at different levels. Gopalakrishan and Rangamannar (1996) while examining the shortfalls in States plan outlays pointed out that the interest burden can fuel non-plan expenditure growth that can cause a reduction in the government savings available for plan financing.

The fourth paper in this paper is on Mutual Funds, the exact title of the paper is *"Performance Evaluation of Mutual Funds in India: an Empirical Analysis"* by Kedar Nath Mukherjee. This paper presents the performance of mutual funds in India and evaluates 53 sample schemes of the Unit Trust of India, empirical data have been taken to examine their performance based on different ratios of return, such as, total return, expense ratio, expense to income ratio, income ratio and portfolio turnover rate. The study covers a period of three years – April, 1997 to March 2000. Through applying various measures based on return, the study concluded that though most of the schemes were not performing well during the initial study period, they turned out to be good performers after passing of time. Some of the schemes show negative performance over the years. Though there are both good as well as bad performers in the mutual fund industry, neither scheme has been find out as the best and worst performer as per all the measures consider jointly.

The last paper in this chapter is "*Credit Risk Measurement and some Issues*" by Manoj Kumar Barik. This paper highlights some of the issues relating to credit risk measurement. The author argues that bad or defaulted loans, if unchecked, may leads to insolvency of a financial institution, including banks. It concludes that though there is risk management system in the banks or Financial Institutions, more sophistication is needed to contain credit risk.

The Chapter Five is named as **Industrial Policy Issues**; this chapter presents three papers, all these papers covers the Small Scale, Large scale and Telecom industry too. The first paper refers to the Karnataka state case study, paper titled as "*Factors contributing to Sales Turnover of Small Scale Industries in the Era of Globalization: Empirical Evidence and Policy Implications for Karnataka State*" by M. Jaya Krishna. The main focus of this paper is to identify the factors contributing to sales turnover of SSIs. It is estimated using 2001-02 data on sample SSIs in Bangalore districts of Karnataka. The study has used descriptive statistics and multiple regressions for analysis.

The important results of the estimation are as follows: First, sales turnover of the SSIs is contributed significantly by the investment on technology, working capital and workers. Secondly, generations of the entrepreneurs are also relatively better contributors of the sales turnover of SSIs. To rise sales turnover and compete successfully with internal or/and external industries; SSIs should use quality raw material, improve productivity, and reduce costs the study suggests government (i) should provide good infrastructure, and technology up-gradation. (ii) Invite foreign investment for better technological transfer and improve skill of the labourers. (iii) Encourage old generation entrepreneurs to invest and extend marketing support for new generations entrepreneurs. (iv) encourage diversified export base, and promote role of association and non-government organizations in setting up of common facilities in technology, marketing, infrastructure and other support services through private-public partnership.

The second paper examines the *Decomposition of total factor productivity growth in Indian Industrial machinery by using data envelopment analysis* this paper is contributed by Mukhesh Kumar and Partha Basu.

This paper uses the frontier technique of Data Envelopment Analysis (DEA) to measure the Malmquist productivity indexes for the industry of industrial machinery in India during the period spanning 1988-89 to 1997-98. These indexes are decomposed into several components under the variable returns to scale, obstructed from the distance functions as solutions to different linear-programming problems. Included here are productivity fluctuations due to technological change, technical efficiency change and the change in scale efficiency. The results reveal that most of the firms experience loss in technical as well as scale efficiency, thereby resulting in slow growth rate in TFP during the period studied. As expected, the technological change is found to be the only source of productivity change in this industry. An investigation to the sources of variations in TFP change and its components shows that both R & D and import have positive and significant impact on technological change as well as TFP change. The demand factors have favorable impact on scale efficiency change. Finally, capital utilization and catching-up factor shows the expected sign on technical efficiency change.

The last paper in this chapter is on Telecommunications, the title of the paper is "*Telecommunications Infrastructure and Economic Growth: An Input Output Analysis*" by Ashish Dash. This paper is an attempt to analyze the role of telecommunications on economic development through interdependence between producing sectors. Using the standard linear static Input-Output technique to assess the role of telecommunications in economic development, the study identifies three key sectors of Indian economy, which are the major users of telecommunication services, and also estimate their contribution to the National Income. In addition the key sectors are ranked in terms of six different types of linkages and compared with the overall degree of interdependence of the Indian economy.

The chapter Six discusses the **Issues related to Privatization and Foreign Investments** in Indian Economy. It's having three papers. The first one discusses the issues like, *Public sector reforms dis-investment and Privatization in India.* Satish and Boppana Nagarjuna contribute this.

In India public sector reforms is synonymous with public enterprise reforms, which include 'Attempts to improve performance', 'Privatization' and 'Liquidation'. Attempts to improve performance while retaining public ownership include: restructuring of existing financial, technical and organization structures; clarifying enterprise objectives and goals; streamlining the relationship between the Government and the managers of the public enterprises so as to bring in the required levels of managerial autonomy and accountability, imposing financial discipline, creating a market and thereby competition, and improving the performance monitoring systems. This paper presents in detail the public sector reform policy process, also discusses the Disinvestment policies and progress and presents the privatization scenario in India.

The second paper in this chapter presents *"Foreign Direct Investment and Export competitiveness in India"* written by Pravakar Sahoo. Foreign Direct Investment (FDI) has contributed in a big way in improving export competitiveness and volume of exports particularly technology intensive manufacturing exports in China and Singapore. India has also made earnest efforts in recent years to sell itself as an attractive destination for FDI not only to acquire advanced technology but also to enhance its export potential and export competitiveness with emphasis on technology intensive exports. The note highlights the fact that by emulating the policies followed by China and Singapore and also with the right mix of domestic policies for FDI by the government, India can substantially enhance its export competitiveness in the international market.

M. Jaya Krishna and J. Venugopal contribute the last paper in this chapter. The main focus of this paper is to identify various determinants of private foreign investment, *foreign direct investment and foreign portfolio investment inflows in post reform India,* using quarterly data of the variables over the period September 1991 to June 2001 using multiple regressions. The study found that Index of share prices, exchange rate, foreign institutional investment, infrastructure, London Inter Bank Offered Rate and stock of science and engineering personnel's are found to be the superior and formed a robust combination for attracting more private foreign investment into liberalized India. Likewise, in the case of direct foreign investment, share prices, index of industrial production, infrastructure, London Inter Bank Offered Rate and man-days lost are found to be the superior combinations. Finally, turning to FPI, share prices, exchange rate, infrastructure, London Inters Bank Offered Rate and treasury bills are found to be the important determinants of foreign portfolio investment during the reform period in post-reform India. In conclusion this paper compliments some of the reform policies of the government with regard to foreign investment have been successful in attracting private foreign investment inflows to India. However, it could be inferred from the results of this study that foreign investment would flow only if the investment policies are considered investor-friendly. More than one factor would be responsible in creating an investor-friendly environment. Thus, the paper offers inputs to policy makers in attracting foreign investment on sustainable basis. Further, the study suggests that the government needs to concentrate on specific policies as the findings indicate to attract more private foreign investment in future either in the form of direct or portfolio investment. The study recommends to strengthen the existing infrastructure and amendment of the existing labour laws in turn will attract more investment. The study also recommends the strengthening of market institutions and implementation of transparent regulations will increase inflow of foreign capital in high technology industries. This would call for some hard reform measures.

The chapter seven deals with **Educational issues**, the first paper presents the *"Economics of Schooling in India"* by J. Srinivasan. This paper tries to develop a household choice model, based on the new theory of consumer behavior, to analyze the determinants of household demand for schooling for their children. For this purpose, both secondary level and higher-secondary level education have been considered in rural and urban areas separately. A primary household survey (covering both rural and urban areas) has been generated and used as the data set for this work. The empirical results, in general, support the theoretical expectations of the model and also suggest that the monthly consumption expenditure is important in deciding the demand for schooling. Further, the paper confirms that, the parental schooling, wife's age and number of school going children in the family are the other factors in deciding their children's schooling. The average amount spent on boys schooling is more than that of girl's schooling in the case of rural areas. This only reminds that, both the Central government and the State government should make sustained efforts to upgrade women's schooling in our country.

The other paper is a study on *"Information Technology Education and Training in the era of Economic Reforms: Implication of Accessibility"* by G. Nagaraju and E. Hari Babu. This paper presents the socio-economic analysis; Information Technology has become a potent force in transforming various sectors of production, services, and culture. Economic and cultural change is taking place not only in the developed countries but also in the developing countries with the application of IT. To sustain the IT centered economy it is necessary to develop software, hardware, appropriate organizational innovations and highly skilled manpower with technical expertise. In the Indian context, the IT industry and IT education has grown mostly in response to the developments brought about by economic reforms of the 90's. Over the last one-decade, thousands of IT education institutes proliferated across the country particularly in the private sector in response to the growing demands of the economy. Due to the social prestige, monetary benefits and number of perks associated with IT jobs, members of diverse social groups have begun to attach a great deal of significance to IT education. The paper focuses on the following questions: firstly, how IT education expanded in private sector in the era of liberalization? Secondly, which sections of the society are gaining access to IT education? And who are marginalized from IT education. The data indicate that although the private sector expanded at a phenomenal rate, still several regions and marginalized social groups seem to be excluded from the private sector. The study reveals that while particular social groups such as upper castes, backward castes and urban background students are included in this process of IT education, while the Dalits and scheduled tribes are excluded from this process. The study argue that the state should take proactive role in imparting IT education to the rural and backward regions and excluded comminutes.

The last chapter presents **Agriculture, Forestry, Tourism and other issues**, it's having five papers. The first paper presents *"An Empirical Validity of Complementarities between Public and Private Investment in the Indian Agricultural sector"* by K. Shambhat, Tripura Sundari and I. Mohamudha Begum. This paper tries to handle the issues related to public and private investment in Agriculture. Modern agriculture capital includes all those forms of capital, which are made in the industrial sector under factory conditions; it includes all types of machinery from irrigation pumps to tractors, from sprayers to combine harvesters, as well as various inputs into current production such as chemical fertilizers, pesticides and herbicides. Traditional agricultural capital, by contrast is produced largely if not entirely by labour alone within the agricultural sector. The obvious type of traditional capital is land itself. The theme that 'land is man-made' (Simon, 1997) and that 'the soil of today, owes as much to nurture as to nature'(Lakdawala, 1946) has been stressed by many writers. Boserup (1981) lists a number of labour investment activities associated with land, such as clearing, leveling, terracing, building, irrigating and draining.

The second paper is a case study of West Bengal state, India, the Exact title of the paper is "*A Decadal performance of Food Grains Productivity in West Bengal – an inter district analysis*" by Kakali Majumdar and Partha Basu. West Bengal is predominantly a food grains producing state. Unfortunately for a long time the growth of food grains production of the state remained low with a bit of silver lining during green revolution at the all-India level around 1964-65. Productivity change being an important component of output change, the present paper analyses the growth pattern of the productivity (valued at constant average prices for the period 1987-89) of food grains in West Bengal during 1970-71 to 1999-2000. Goodness of fit has been assessed for a number of alternative functions of time including linear, parabolic, and exponential also log quadratic both in their simple and kinked (double kink) forms. Results indicate that in West Bengal and in most of the districts, linear form with kinks at 1983-84 and 1991-92 gives the best fit.. After relative stagnation of 1970s, in the next decade growth rate of food grains productivity was remarkable. Both technological and institutional factors seem to be responsible for this remarkable growth, which was once again short lasting. Performance during the 1990s is a matter of concern not only because of a sharp decline in the absolute growth in 1991-92 but also a continuous fall in the relative growth rate over the decade in view of the linearity of the growth rate.

The third paper in this chapter is "*Distress diversification into non-farm activities among poor rural female, workers in Pondicherry region*", by V. Nirmala and Mogana Sundari. In most of the developing countries, agricultural transformation is characterized by technological changes and sectoral diversification. More scientific and productive technologies are gradually replacing human labour, besides the sector losing its cultivable areas to the fast expanding industries, housing and commercial activities. As a consequence, there are evidences of shrinkage in the sector's contributions to gross national product and its share of workforce (Bhadhuri, 1993;Jeemol, 1997; and Parthasarthy, et. al., 1998). The analysis of modern economic growth in the recent developed countries by Simon Kuznets supported this trend in the context of countries that have achieved successful and sustained economic growth. This was partly attributed to the supply-side effects of the improvement not only in the whole economy but in agricultural sector as well, and partly to the demand-side due to the operation of Engel's law resulting in low growth rate in demand for food compared to non-agricultural goods and other services (Chaudhuri, 1993). The process of economic growth has also widened income inequalities, thus compelling the rural workers to diversify into non-farm activities or to migrate from the low-income traditional sector to higher income industrial sector. Besides, the incidence of drought or flood, the seasonal nature of agricultural employment and a rise in educational level have also contributed to a tendency among the rural workers to shift into non-agricultural activities. The increasing supply of casual labour in the Indian rural labour market has been exerting pressure on agricultural and non-agricultural wage employment, thus depressing real wages in the rural sector. This has led to a diversification of wageworkers into self-employment activities, which further lowers labour productivity in the sector. This in turn lowers earnings and increases poverty, resulting in a vicious circle with a decline in real wages leading to a decrease in demand for labour and further depressing the wage rates. The slow transfer of labour from farm to non-farm activities, however, indicates the inability of the latter to rapidly create employment opportunities (Jeemol, 1997).

In India, the rural areas bore the burden of workforce restructuring during the 1990s, by acting as the residual sector for the workers who were unable to find non-farm employment either in the rural or urban labour markets. Women workers in the region were the worst affected in the process. The favorable trends of low poverty, real wages and workforce structure of the 1980s reversed during the 1990s, with improved employment elasticities in some of the sub-sectors. However, despite a sharp fall in labour productivity, the post-1990 period witnessed a disturbing new development of de-linked trends in rural poverty from the trends in agricultural performance and growth rates in per capita income (Sheila, 1997).

The fourth paper is on Forestry area a case study from Orissa state, India, i.e. *"Comparison between Government Forestry Projects and Social Forestry Projects: Case Studies from Orissa"* by Sabita K. Acharya and Binayak Rath. Studies on environmental conservation/protection ensuring better quality of life are the urgency and fashion of the modern World in the 21st century. The environmental subjects, e.g., the global climatic changes, green house effect with carbon-dioxide increase in the atmosphere, loss of biological diversity or extinction of animal and plant species, critical conditions of tropical rain forests, etc. are the major problems that are often highlighted in various international forums, academic discussions/debates, and also in the mass media. It is realized that most of these problems are inherited from the loss of forest area due to degradation and deforestation. Thus, forest has a great role in the environmental conservation. In addition to this role forest as a form of renewable natural resource has remarkable contribution in the development of an economy. This means role of forest is complex- at one end it is a source of revenue and hence exploitation is natural; at the other end it is needed for environmental conservation and hence should be properly maintained.

After independence, the Government of India had has been undertaking great care for protecting the environment in terms of plans, programs and policies. In order to solve the problems of forest development, it is argued that to draw proper policies and efficient schemes/program, there should be projection of forest development programs. This argument is based on the premise that in a planned economy like India, where the investment allocations are by and large predetermined at the national level, there is an urgent need to utilize the scarce resources in such a fashion that the targets set in the national plans are fully achieved. Once the overall plan allocation is made, the problem to be tackled is how to maximize the net benefits from investment, which in turn envisages the problem of ranking the alternative projects. Hence, here lies the importance of the Social Benefit-Cost Analysis (SBCA) in a planned economy. The literature on forestry management also portrays the need of SBCA in the forestry sector for establishing their viability. In view of these arguments, in this study we have attempted to evaluate few plantation schemes from a selected region, viz., Orissa. In accomplishing such exercises, we have adopted the approach suggested by the UNIDO Guidelines for project evaluation with proper modifications and some improvements.

The last paper of this chapter is on Tourism, viz., *"Economic development through Rural Tourism in India: Challenges and Strategies"* by J.B.Komaraiah. Basic definitions of tourism ware established at the United Nations (Conference of Tourism and International Travel, Rome 1963) and by the United Nations Commission on Statistics (April 1968). Later on these definitions were revised and updated at the World Tourism Organization (WTO) conference at Ottawa in June 1991 and certain recommendations were formulated. These have been adopted by most of the countries. The W.T.O. distinguishes between three basic forms of tourism:

Domestic tourism: involving residents of the given country traveling only within the country:

Inbound tourism: involving non-residents traveling in another country

Outbound tourism: involving residents traveling in another country

Tourism has become an integral part of modern life. Tourism works as a force for socio-economic, cultural, educational and environmental changes, and it has had an impact of the same order as the industrial revolution.

Boppana Nagarjuna
Department of Economics
University of Hyderabad
Hyderabad 500 046

Contributors

Achal Kumar Gaur, Reader, Department of Economics, Banaras Hindu University, Varanasi, Utter Pradesh.

Ashish Dash, Doctoral Fellow-Economics, Institute for Social and Economic Change, Nagarbhavi, Bangalore.

Boppana Nagarjuna, Faculty, Department of Economics, University of Hyderabad, Hyderabad.

Binayak Rath, Professor, Indian Institute of Technology (IIT), Kanpur, Utter Pradesh.

C. Niranjan Rao, Associate Professor, CESS, Hyderabad.

D. Brahma Reddy, Research Scholar, Department of Economics, University of Hyderabad, Hyderabad.

D. Sambandhan, Reader, School of International Studies, Pondicherry University, Pondicherry.

E Haribabu, Professor, Department of Sociology, University of Hyderabad, Hyderabad.

Geetanjali Natarajan, Asst. Professor, Indian Institute of Foreign Trade (IIFT) New Delhi.

Hrishikesh Mallick, Doctoral Fellow-Economics, Institute for Social and Economic Change (ISEC), Nagarbhavi, Bangalore.

I. Mohamudha Begum, Research Scholar, Department of Economics, Pondicherry University, Pondicherry.

J.B.Komaraiah, Lecturer, Department of Economics, Banaras Hindu University, Varanasi, Utter Pradesh.

J. Srinivasan, Lecturer, Department of Economics, R.K.M. Vivekananda College, Chennai.

J. Venugopal, Doctoral Fellow-Economics, Institute for Social and Economic Change (ISEC), Nagarbhavi, Bangalore.

Kakali Majumdar, Research Scholar - Economics, Department of Humanities and Social Sciences, Indian Institute of Technology (IIT), Kharagpur, West Bengal.

Kedarnath Mukherjee, Research Scholar, Department of Economics, University of Hyderabad, Hyderabad.

Kishore G. Kulkarni, Professor of Economics, Metropolitan State College of Denver, P.O. Box 173362, Campus Box 77, Denver, CO 80217-3362, USA.

K. Sham Bhat, Professor and Head, Department of Economics, Pondicherry University, Pondicherry.

M. Jaya Krishna, Economics Unit, Institute for Social and Economic Change (ISEC), Nagarbhavi, Bangalore.

Meenakshi Rishi, Associate Professor of Economics, Ohio University, Ada, Ohio, USA.

M. Seenuvasan, Assistant Adviser, Department of Economic Analysis and Policy, Reserve Bank of India (RBI), Hyderabad.

Mukesh Kumar, Faculty Member, ICFAI- Business School, Nagarjuna Hills, Hyderabad.

Manoj Kumar Barik, Research Scholar, Department of Economics, University of Hyderabad, Hyderabad.

Mogana Sundari, Department of Economics, Pondicherry University, Pondicherry.

M. Ramanjaneyulu, Reader, Department of Economics, Bangalore University, Bangalore.

M. Pradeep Kumar, Research Student, Department of Economics, University of Hyderabad, Hyderabad.

Nagaraju Gundemeda, Research Scholar, Department of Sociology, University of Hyderabad, Hyderabad..

Partha Basu, Professor of Economics, Department of Humanities & Social Sciences, Indian Institute of Technology (IIT), Kharagpur, West Bengal.

Pradeep Agrawal, Professor and Head, RBI Chair Unit, Institute of Economic Growth (IEG), Delhi University Enclave, Delhi-110007.

Pravakar Sahoo, Faculty, RBI Endowment Unit, Institute of Economic Growth (IEG), North Campus, Delhi University Enclave, Delhi-110007.

Puja Padhi, Research Scholar, Department of Economics, University of Hyderabad, Hyderabad.

Purna Chandra Parida, Research Fellow, RBI Endowment Unit, Institute for Social and Economic Change (ISEC), Nagarbhavi, Bangalore-72

Sabita K. Acharya, Faculty, Birla Institute of Technology & Science (BITS), Pilani, Rajasthan.

T. Gopinath, Assistant Adviser, Department of Economic Analysis and Policy, Reserve Bank of India, Mumbai.

Tripura Sundari. C. U, Research Scholar, Department of Economics, Pondicherry University, Pondicherry.

V. Nirmala, Reader, Department of Economics, Pondicherry University, Pondicherry.

V. Vijay, Research Student, Department of Economics, University of Hyderabad, Hyderabad.

V. V. M. Satish Reddy, Research Scholar, Department of Economics, University of Hyderabad, Hyderabad.

CONTENTS

VIII. AGRICULTURE, FORESTRY, TOURISM AND OTHER ISSUES

Part—I

Macro Economic Policy Issues

1

Trends in Central Government Expenditure, Revenue, Fiscal Deficit and Domestic Debt: 1980-2000

*Boppana Nagarjuna**

*D. Brahma Reddy***

Introduction

The structure of public finances in an economy is defined by the level and composition of expenditure of the Government and the instruments relied upon to finance them, viz., the tax and non-tax revenue sources and borrowings. The excess of Government expenditure over current revenues and non debt capital receipts gets reflected in fiscal deficits financed either by way of borrowings from internal and external sources and seignorage. If expenditure persistently exceeds revenue, fiscal deficit to the extent is not covered by seignorage, steadily adds to outstanding debt resulting in increasing interest payments. Unless met with larger revenue receipts, this gives rise to a self-perpetuating spiral of debt and deficit.

* Lecturer, Department of Economics, University of Hyderabad.

** Research Scholar, Department of Economics, University of Hyderabad.

Plan of the Paper

Section I deals with introduction, Section II deals with Plan of the Paper, Section III deals with Trends in Expenditure, Section IV deals with trends in Revenue, Section V deals with Sustainable Fiscal Deficit and Debt in a theoretical perspective, Section VI deals with Trends in fiscal deficit, Section VII deals with Fiscal Deficit financing Scenario, Section VIII deals with trends in domestic debt, Section IX deals with the trends in the ownership pattern of outstanding Government securities and Section X deals with Concluding remarks. The Study Period is 1980 to 2000.

Trends in Expenditure

The average growth rate (chart 1) of total expenditure in1980s (18%) has been much higher than the average growth rate in 1990s (11.5%). Total expenditure as a percentage of GDP, which was 16.61 in 1981-82, reached to peak level by 1986-87 (22.61%) and started declining secularly reaching 16.96 percent by 2000-01(chart1). The impact of expenditure compression measures that were implemented as a part of over all economic reform programme largely fallen on the growth rate of capital expenditure. The average growth rate of capital expenditure declined to 8.5% during the period 1991 to 2001 compared to 13% during the period 1982 to 1991.

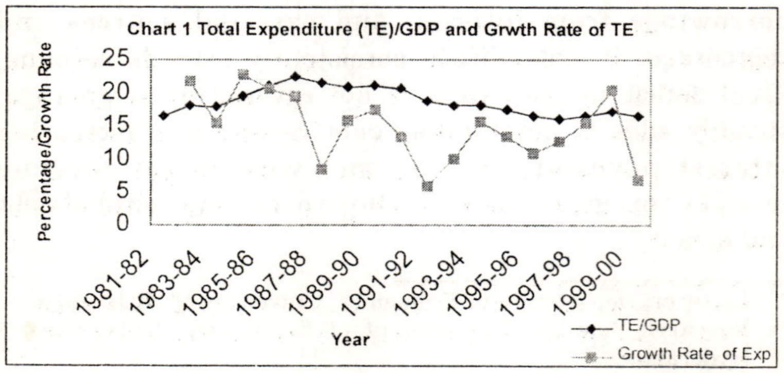

(Chart1a). On the other hand the average growth rate of revenue expenditure declined to 14.4% during the period 1991 to 2001 from 17.8% during the period 1982 to 1991(chart 1a). An other important development is the increasing share of revenue expenditure in the total

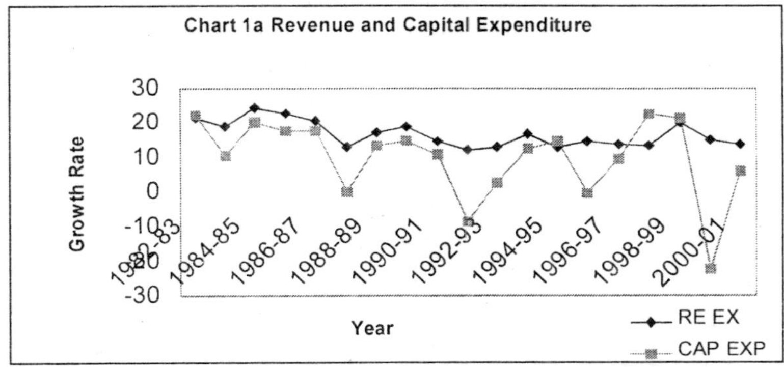

expenditure. Revenue expenditure as a percentage of total expenditure increased to 84.5%by 2000-01 from 60.9% in1981-82 as a result capital expenditure as a percentage of total expenditure declined to 15.5% by 2000-01 from 39.1% in 1981-82 (chart 2).

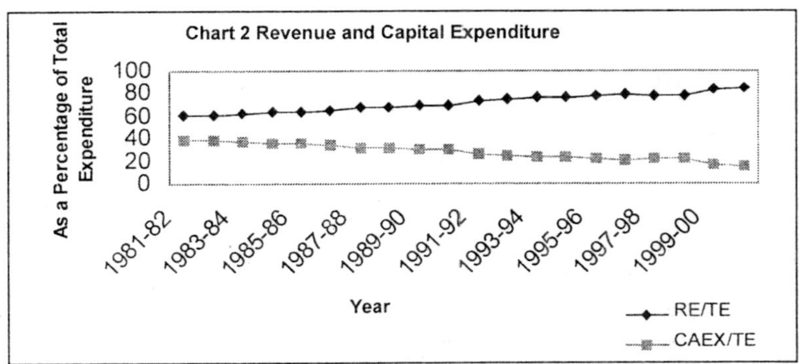

The share of interest payments as a percentage of total expenditure increased to 30% by 2000-01 from 12.64% in 1981-82(chart 3). Similarly interest payments as a percentage of revenue expenditure increased to 35.5% by

2000-01 from 20.7% in 1981-82 (chart 3) and as a percentage of net tax revenue and net revenue receipts increased to 69.71% and 48.82% by 2000-01 from 27.68 and 21.66% in 1981-82 (chart 3a) and as a percentage of GDP[1] increased from 2.1% in 1981-82 to 5.05% by1999-2000 (chart 3). The three important components of revenue expenditure namely interest payments, defence and subsidies constitute 59% of revenue expenditure and 49% of total expenditure in the year 2000-01(chart 3b).

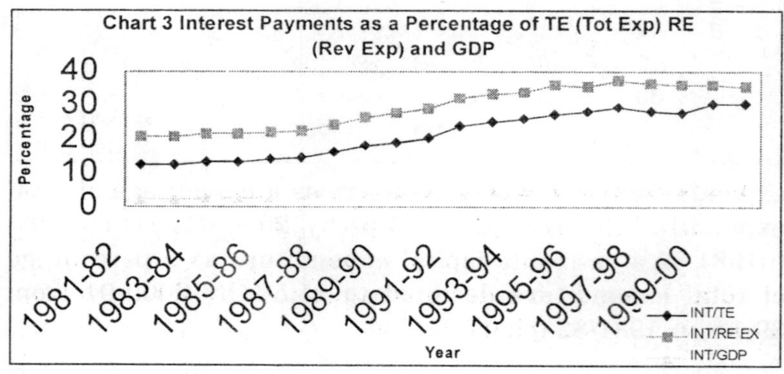

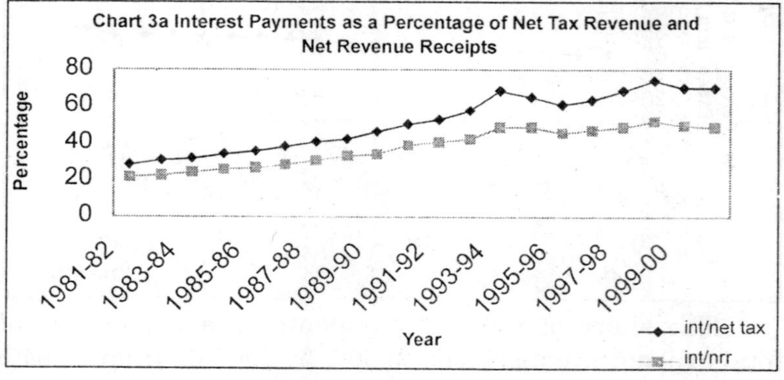

1 GDP is defined as GDP at factor cost at market prices (base 1993-94).

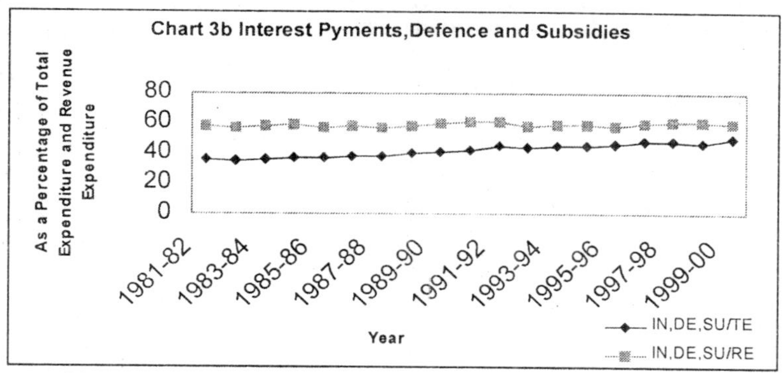

Trends in Revenue Receipts

The average growth rate of net tax revenue[2] receipts declined to 13.4% during the period 1991-2001 from 16.2% during the period 1982-1991(chart 4) as a result the average Net Tax-GDP ratio declined to 6.9 percent during the period 1991-2001 from 8.3% during the period 1982-1991 (chart 4a). Similarly the average growth rate of net revenue receipts (net tax revenue plus non tax revenue receipts) declined to 14.8% during the period 1991-2001 from 15.7% during the period 1982-1991(chart 4) as a result the average Net Revenue Receipts-GDP ratio

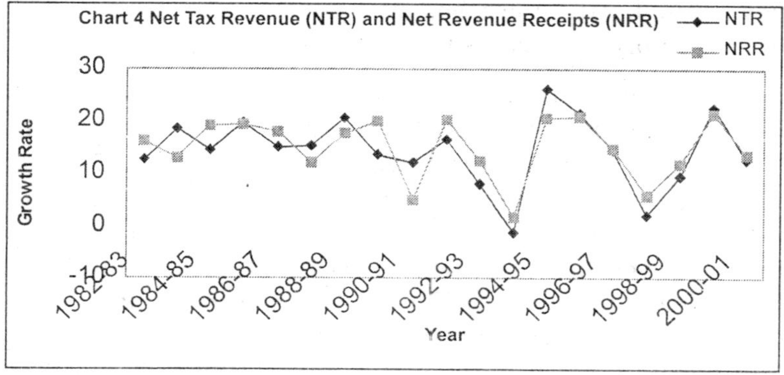

2 Net Tax Revenue is defined as Gross Tax Revenue less states share in the Gross Tax Revenue.

declined to 10.3% during the period 1991-2001 from 11.1% during the period 1981-1991(chart 4a).

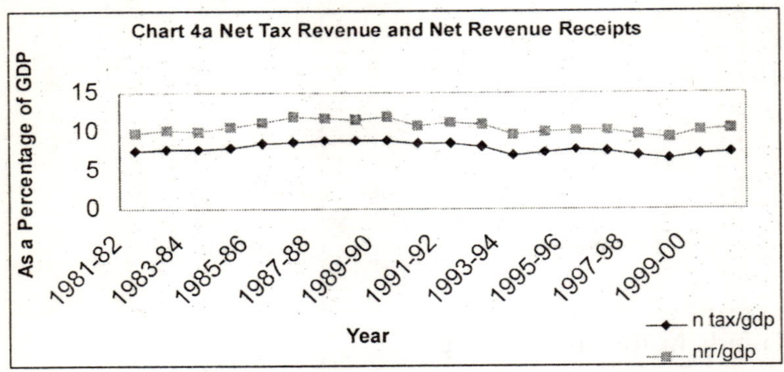

Sustainable Fiscal Deficit and Debt: A Theoretical Perspective

Government's fiscal stance as reflected in the size of the fiscal deficit and the manner of financing it plays a critical role in macro-stabilisation. The apparently cheapest source of finance for governments is seignorage, which adds to base money or high-powered money. As the economy grows, the demand for money also grows, and depending on the elasticity of the demand for money, some increase in money supply can be absorbed without inflation. But beyond a limit, increases in base money can result in unacceptably high rates of inflation.

Borrowing from foreign sources, the other alternative for financing deficits tends to appreciate the exchange rate. However, by its very nature the flow of foreign funds depends on many factors, not all economic. The economy's aggregate external borrowings (public and private) have to be managed by the central bank taking into account the safe limit to the current account deficit, the structure of existing external debt and their time profile. The government's external borrowings should be limited considering that its vulnerability to external shocks increases if external debt servicing requirements are too large.

Domestic borrowings are the other main source for financing deficits in government budgets. However, it has implications for the rate of interest and the availability of savings for the private sector. A critical issue that we need to consider is whether government borrowing and debt are sustainable at the present level. For their sustainability over a period of time, an essential condition is that the ratio of debt to GDP does not grow beyond a point. The debt ratio may, however, remain stable even while there is a primary deficit (i.e., the excess of expenditure excluding interest payments over receipts), as long as the rate of interest does not exceed the rate of GDP growth. This is known as the budget constraint rule. However, the level of primary deficit relative to GDP should not exceed the threshold derived from the difference between growth rate and the effective interest rates on government borrowing. Unless the present trends are reversed and the deficits are brought down, the debt-GDP ratio will keep growing undermining the solvency of the public sector. From the angle of sustainability, it is necessary not only to contain the deficits to levels permissible under the budget constraint rule but also to bring down the debt ratio from its present level, which is rather high. The need to reduce the debt level also arises from difficulties in debt servicing associated with high levels of indebtedness. When debt-servicing liability is large - as it happens when the level of debt is high and a large chunk of the revenue receipts is used up in servicing the debt-the budgets should either cut down non-interest expenditure to the barest minimum or generate adequate revenue to finance the essential expenditure of the government after meeting the interest liabilities or do both.

Ultimately the right size of fiscal deficit relative to (full employment) GDP depends on how the borrowed resources are used. If borrowing is for consumption or current expenditure, borrowed resources will not create any assets that can yield a return to service the additional liability in the future. Hence, the dictum that there should be no deficit on the revenue account; rather the revenue budget should generate surpluses for government investment. An exception can be considered for revenue expenditure that fosters human capital formation. The sustainability of fiscal deficit would depend on the expected rate of return on government investment, including expenditure on human capital, and the efficacy of the revenue system to finance the resulting debt servicing needs. Other things remaining the same, if the rate of return on government investment financed by deficit is lower than the interest rate at which the incremental debt to finance the deficit is incurred, then debt and fiscal deficit will tend to spiral. In comparing the rate of return on government investments against the interest rates, it is necessary to look at not only the financial returns on government capital but the social return as well. Fiscal deficit may be sustainable to the extent it helps to support government expenditure so that GDP growth warranted by full employment of available resources becomes possible, provided the revenue sources are also buoyant enough to take care of the requirements of debt servicing. However, there are clear limits to increasing full employment output growth rate by continuously running a high fiscal deficit because of the solvency question. Further, if the debt level is high, interest payments will pre-empt an unduly large share of current receipts leaving too little for expenditure on other essential heads of the budget. There are also limits to the extent to which the rise in the tax level that may be required to meet mounting expenditure commitments, would be acceptable to the community.

Trends in Fiscal Deficit

The gap between expenditure growth and revenue growth resulted in high levels of revenue deficits and fiscal deficits. Revenue deficit as a percentage of GDP reached to 3.9 by 2000-01 from 0.25 in 1981-82 (chart 5). Similarly fiscal deficit reached to 8.73% of GDP by 1990-91 from 5.69% in 1981-82 (chart 5). The expenditure compression measures that were implemented as a part of over all economic reform programme resulted in the decline of Fiscal deficit-GDP ratio to 5.6% by2000-01 (chart 5). The primary deficit[3]-GDP ratio declined to 0.57% by 2000-01 from6.4% in 1986-87(chart 5). Revenue deficit as a percentage of fiscal deficits reached to 69% by 2000-01 from 4.5% in 1981-82 (Chart 5a). This indicates that most part of the fiscal deficit is unproductive and unsustainable.

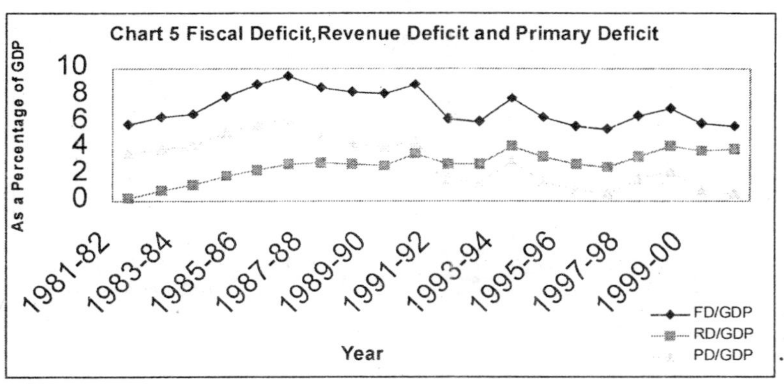

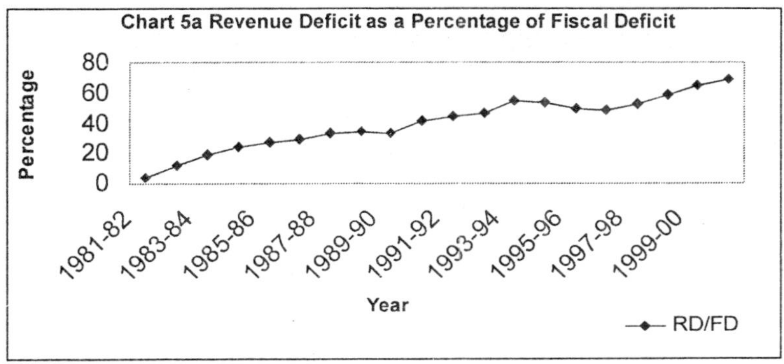

3 Primary Deficit is defined as Fiscal Deficit less Interest Payments.

Fiscal Deficit Financing Scenario

The different instruments that are used to finance fiscal deficit are external finances, market borrowings, and other liabilities and budget deficit[4]. In 1980-81 the ratio of external finance-GFD, market borrowings-GFD, other liabilities-GFD, and budget deficit-GFD were in the order of 11.21%, 33.61% (Table 6, chart 6), 39.1% and 16.15 percent (Table 6a, chart 6a). Over a period of time the dependency over external finances declined gradually. It has declined to 7.12% by 1990-91 and further to 1.12% by 1999-2000 (chart 6). On the other hand the dependency

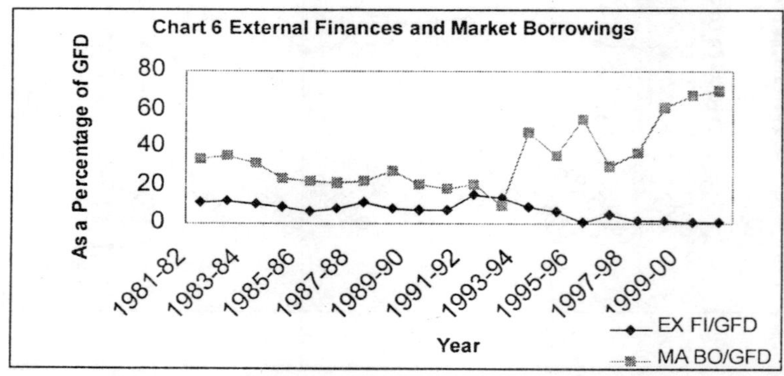

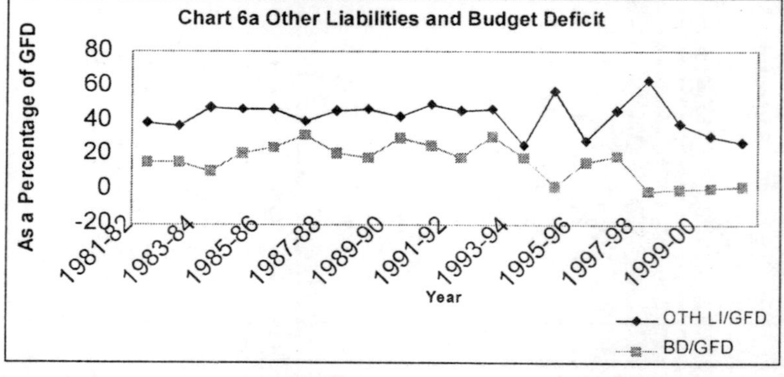

4 Budget Deficit is defined as that part of fiscal deficit financed by issuing 91 day Treasury Bills to RBI.

on market borrowings increased from 33.6% in 1980-81 to 67% by 1999-2000 (table 6, chart 6) and other liabilities increased from 39.1% in 1980-81 to 45.53 by 1990-91 and declined to 27.54% by 2000-2001(chart 6a). The budget deficit as a percentage of fiscal deficit increased to 30.64% by 1992-93 from 16.15% in 1980-81 declined to 1.66% by 1994-95 (chart 6a). Since April 1 1997 the Ad-hoc Treasury Bills system was abandoned and Ways and Means Advances[5] system was implemented. As a result budget deficit recorded a negative of –1.02% in 1997-98 and –0.18% by 1998-99 (chart 6a).

Trends in Domestic Debt

The heavy dependency on market borrowings and other liabilities resulted in accumulation of Domestic debt. Domestic debt as a percentage of GDP reached to 55.87% by 2000-2001 from 36.73 percent in 1981-82 (chart 7). This has resulted in heavy interest payments and Interest payments emerged as the single largest expenditure item in 1990s.Interest payments as a percentage of total expenditure increased to 30% by 2000-01 from 12.64% in

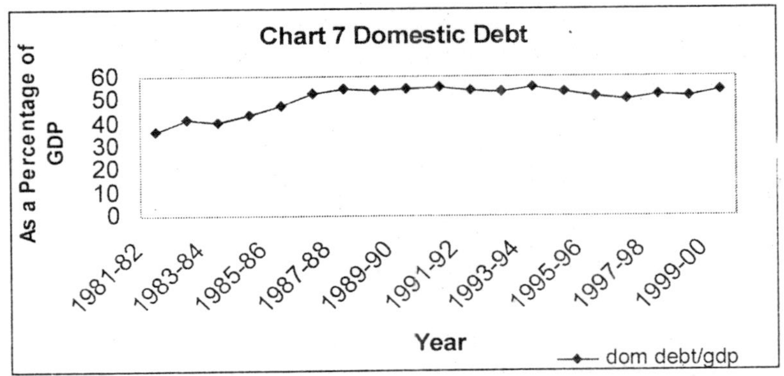

5 In Ways and Means Advances system the quantum of credit available and interest rate on such credit from RBI to the Central Government is decided by RBI in consultation with Central Government from time to time.

1981-82.Similarly interest payments as a percentage of revenue expenditure increased to 35.5% by 2000-01 from 20.7% in 1981-82 and as a percentage of net revenue receipts increased to 49.7% by 2000-01 from 21.66% in 1981-82 and as a percentage of GDP increased from 2.1% in 1981-82 to 5.05% by1999-2000 and the weighted average interest rate on government securities increased from 7.29% in 1980-81 to 11.4% by 1989-90 and further to 13.75% by 1995-96 and declined to 11.77% by 1999-2000 (chart 8).

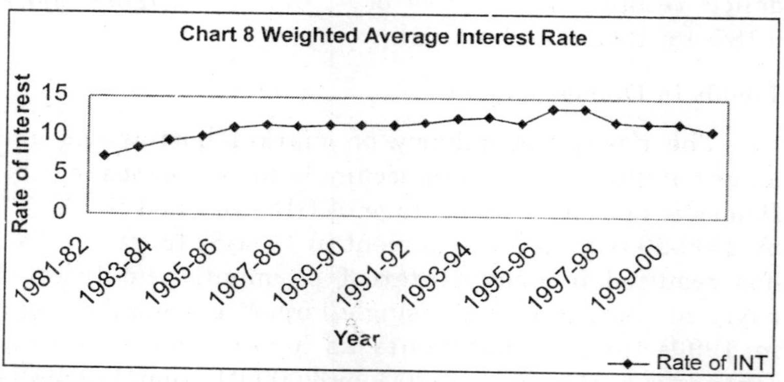

The growth rate of domestic debt during 1980s is 17.7% much higher than the growth rate of nominal GDP at 13.1% (chart 9). In 1990s it seems the difference between the growth rates of domestic debt (14.7%) and nominal GDP (14.5%) narrowed down (chart 9).

Trends in Ownership Pattern of Outstanding Domestic Debt

Domestic debt constitutes Internal Debt plus Other Liabilities. Internal Debt includes Treasury Bills and Dated Government Securities. If we look at the trends in ownership pattern of the outstanding government securities we observe that the outstanding government securities held by the RBI declined from 24.79% in 1990-91 to 2.5% by 1994-95 and increased to 12.7% by 1997-98 and again declined to 8.32% by 1999-2000 (chart 10).

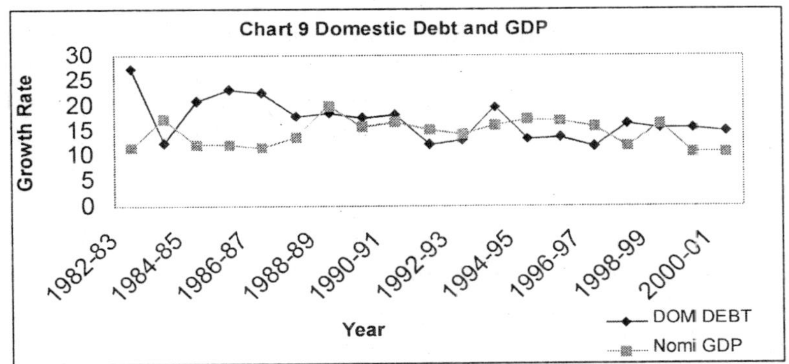
Chart 9 Domestic Debt and GDP
Growth Rate
30
25
20
15
10
5
0
1982-83
1984-85
1986-87
1988-89
1990-91
1992-93
1994-95
1996-97
1998-99
2000-01
Year
DOM DEBT
Nomi GDP

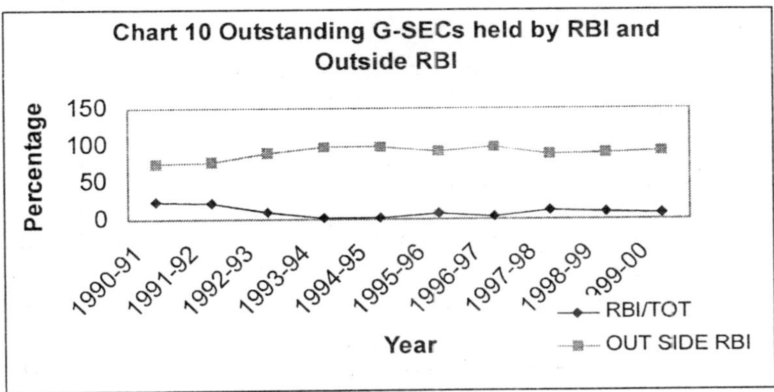
Chart 10 Outstanding G-SECs held by RBI and Outside RBI
Percentage
150
100
50
0
1990-91
1991-92
1992-93
1993-94
1994-95
1995-96
1996-97
1997-98
1998-99
?99-00
Year
RBI/TOT
OUT SIDE RBI

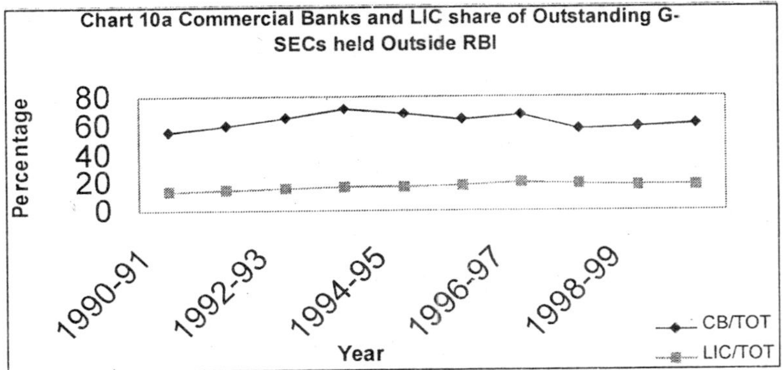
Chart 10a Commercial Banks and LIC share of Outstanding G-SECs held Outside RBI
Percentage
80
60
40
20
0
1990-91
1992-93
1994-95
1996-97
1998-99
Year
CB/TOT
LIC/TOT

Similarly out standing government securities held outside the RBI increased from 75.21% in 1990-91 to 91.67% by 1999-2000.Out of 91.67% held outside the RBI, commercial banks hold 60% (chart 10a) and LIC hold 18% (chart 10a).

Concluding Remarks

The concerns about domestic debt sustainability in India essentially arises from (1) The high stock of domestic debt (2) Its changing composition from low cost to high cost constituents (3) Interest rates on such borrowings (4) Increasing stock of domestic debt held outside the RBI.

REFERENCES

1. Handbook of statistics on Indian Economy 2001, RBI.
2. Reddy .D.B. "Analysis of Central Government Expenditure, Revenue and Fiscal Deficit 1980 – 2000" M.Phil Dissertation submitted in March 2002 to Department of Economics, University of Hyderabad.
3. Report of the Eleventh Finance Commission, Government of India.
4. Tahir Mohammad "Managing Public Debt- Issues and Challenges", ED, RBI speech delivered at the seminar on Managing Public Debt organized by ASSOCHAM at New Delhi on September 3, 2002.

Appendix -Tables

Table 1 (Chart 1) **Table 1a (Chart 1A)**

Year	*TE/GDP*	*Growth Rate of Exp*	*Year*	*RE EX Gro Rate*	*CAP EXP Gro Rate*
1981-82	16.61559				
1982-83	18.1631	21.8721552	1982-83	21.63811	22.23800345
1983-84	17.88954	15.4038518	1983-84	18.72265	10.24151382
1984-85	19.59184	22.7894411	1984-85	24.44834	20.01053979
1985-86	21.10464	20.7049872	1985-86	22.50912	17.57104322
1986-87	22.61067	19.4622717	1986-87	20.4457	17.68221108
1987-88	21.60206	8.49545426	1987-88	13.00538	0.140551324
1988-89	20.90169	15.8948741	1988-89	17.1785	13.21139132
1989-90	21.2109	17.4400526	1989-90	18.67445	14.76904619
1990-91	20.60812	13.335773	1990-91	14.49307	10.74639348
1991-92	18.91303	5.80827746	1991-92	11.93754	-8.36951734
1992-93	18.21363	10.0561868	1992-93	12.65008	2.726461095
1993-94	18.15498	15.6869301	1993-94	16.68465	12.59526675
1994-95	17.52768	13.3137826	1994-95	12.89001	14.67462297
1995-96	16.61044	10.9096112	1995-96	14.53502	-0.55142776
1996-97	16.16402	12.7510868	1996-97	13.6364	9.527776332
1997-98	16.69396	15.4452333	1997-98	13.46605	22.92151923
1998-99	17.28554	20.3776723	1998-99	20.03272	21.58049422
1999-00	16.68575	6.71010238	1999-00	15.08262	-22.1123109
2000-01	16.96233	12.559547	2000-01	13.81965	6.15007657

Table 2 (Chart 2)

Year	*RE/TE*	*CAEX/TE*
1981-82	60.9855531	39.01444686
1982-83	60.8684356	39.13156442
1983-84	62.6189002	37.38109979
1984-85	63.4648882	36.53511184
1985-86	64.4134736	35.58652641
1986-87	64.9437345	35.0562655
1987-88	67.6433102	32.35668976
1988-89	68.3925118	31.60748821
1989-90	69.111379	30.888621
1990-91	69.8170905	30.18290946
1991-92	73.8614537	26.13854632
1992-93	75.602277	24.39772301
1993-94	76.2542914	23.74570859
1994-95	75.9691176	24.03088236
1995-96	78.452391	21.54760903
1996-97	79.0683907	20.93160935
1997-98	77.7128501	22.28714992
1998-99	77.4901554	22.50984463
1999-00	83.5700675	16.4299325
2000-01	84.505636	15.49436401

Table 3 (Chart 3)

Year	*INT/TE*	*INT/RE EX*	*INT/GDP*
1981-82	12.64595	20.73598131	2.101199558
1982-83	12.78945	21.01163163	2.322961215
1983-84	13.49412	21.54959328	2.414036148
1984-85	13.69179	21.57379654	2.682472329
1985-86	14.26347	22.14361514	3.010254581
1986-87	14.69578	22.62848752	3.322815517
1987-88	16.48233	24.36652662	3.56052191
1988-89	18.04806	26.38894023	3.772348616
1989-90	19.11246	27.65457094	4.053924478
1990-91	20.41634	29.24261385	4.20742376
1991-92	23.87133	32.31905896	4.51479071
1992-93	25.34293	33.52139112	4.615869083
1993-94	25.90076	33.96629349	4.702276203
1994-95	27.4109	36.08162998	4.804494372
1995-96	28.0718	35.78195494	4.662848433
1996-97	29.59001	37.42331674	4.782935251
1997-98	28.28535	36.39726065	4.721943654
1998-99	27.88072	35.97969149	4.819332278
1999-00	30.27637	36.22871916	5.051837182
2000-01	30.34	35.50425873	5.089224597

Table 3a (Chart 3a)

Year	*Int/Net tax*	*Int/NRR*
1981-82	27.681511	21.2659744
1982-83	30.2527464	22.5880463
1983-84	31.0536882	24.3265182
1984-85	33.8451079	25.4581096
1985-86	35.5345317	26.7950776
1986-87	38.0196554	27.9478886
1987-88	40.1606282	30.3777304
1988-89	42.3039317	32.7544677
1989-90	46.3036846	33.9547958
1990-91	50.0209409	39.1199913
1991-92	53.1186962	40.2786612
1992-93	57.4994449	41.9207317
1993-94	68.7402945	48.6938889
1994-95	65.3185875	48.3734616
1995-96	61.0759223	45.4417507
1996-97	63.476377	47.100468
1997-98	68.6062798	49.0245433
1998-99	74.4199824	52.1002107
1999-00	70.35807	49.7204057
2000-01	69.7125406	48.8281288

Table 3b (Chart 3b)

Year	*IN, DE, SU/TE*	*IN, DE, SU/RE*
1981-82	35.54324	58.28141225
1982-83	34.73093	57.05901185
1983-84	36.26386	57.91200395
1984-85	37.44041	58.99389693
1985-86	36.7011	56.97736116
1986-87	37.94901	58.43367597
1987-88	38.22388	56.50799151
1988-89	39.90343	58.34473071
1989-90	41.35812	59.84270363
1990-91	42.2895	60.57184831
1991-92	45.13885	61.11286638
1992-93	44.04574	58.25980022
1993-94	44.64058	58.54172637
1994-95	45.00463	59.24069706
1995-96	45.74506	58.3093214
1996-97	47.7466	60.38645215
1997-98	47.55422	61.19222558
1998-99	47.01654	60.67420921
1999-00	50.37875	60.2832495
2000-01	49.86201	59.00435572

Table 4 (Chart 4)

Year	*NTR*	*NRR*
1982-83	12.7794143	16.041
1983-84	18.6218023	13.06069
1984-85	14.3125445	19.05028
1985-86	19.7665855	19.47072
1986-87	15.037843	18.00606
1987-88	15.1979933	11.95176
1988-89	20.4747457	17.69582
1989-90	13.6233001	19.96972
1990-91	12.0707189	5.082607
1991-92	16.4991391	20.15504
1992-93	7.93904412	12.26412
1993-94	-1.1009548	1.787449
1994-95	26.2025482	20.71488
1995-96	21.4738933	20.9117
1996-97	14.3545808	14.66358
1997-98	2.10349943	6.023963
1998-99	9.38623631	11.65096
1999-00	22.5690861	21.42556
2000-01	12.5764982	13.58195

Table 4a(Chart 4A)

Year	*N TAX/GDP*	*NRR/GDP*	*TE/GDP*
1981-82	7.59062451	9.88057032	16.615589
1982-83	7.67851349	10.2840289	18.1631028
1983-84	7.77375019	9.92347581	17.8895434
1984-85	7.92573135	10.5368088	19.5918367
1985-86	8.47135009	11.2343567	21.1046416
1986-87	8.73973075	11.8893257	22.6106707
1987-88	8.86570272	11.7208293	21.6020608
1988-89	8.91725299	11.5170506	20.9016859
1989-90	8.75507968	11.9391809	21.2109036
1990-91	8.4113247	10.7551756	20.6081174
1991-92	8.49943811	11.2088897	18.913028
1992-93	8.0276759	11.0109459	18.2136327
1993-94	6.84064018	9.65680973	18.1549764
1994-95	7.35547806	9.93208717	17.5276809
1995-96	7.63451169	10.2611549	16.6104367
1996-97	7.53498463	10.154751	16.1640181
1997-98	6.88266973	9.6317953	16.693956
1998-99	6.47585786	9.25012051	17.2855381
1999-00	7.18018158	10.1604907	16.6857454
2000-01	7.30029999	10.4227312	16.9623294

Table 5 (Chart 5)

Year	*FD/GDP*	*RD/GDP*	*PD/GDP*
1981-82	5.6992161	0.257799758	3.59801652
1982-83	6.2686919	0.771567615	3.94573072
1983-84	6.5599356	1.278759503	4.14589941
1984-85	7.8202106	1.897128488	5.13773826
1985-86	8.7590714	2.359876095	5.74881686
1986-87	9.4667539	2.794888197	6.14393836
1987-88	8.5584174	2.891519749	4.99789552
1988-89	8.1700754	2.778137393	4.39772676
1989-90	8.1347884	2.719967125	4.08086389
1990-91	8.7350329	3.632812347	4.52760914
1991-92	6.1663323	2.760377941	1.65154154
1992-93	5.9672827	2.758975136	1.35141358
1993-94	7.7119582	4.187138844	3.00968202
1994-95	6.2921865	3.383537355	1.48780121
1995-96	5.6130278	2.770129818	0.9501794
1996-97	5.3663475	2.625877933	0.58341227
1997-98	6.398152	3.341553708	1.67620834
1998-99	7.0140276	4.144469822	2.19469528
1999-00	5.8617074	3.783798005	0.80987025
2000-01	5.6607494	3.911393186	0.57152477

Table 5a(Chart 5a)

Year	*RD/FD*
1981-82	4.52342488
1982-83	12.3082714
1983-84	19.4934766
1984-85	24.2593018
1985-86	26.9420807
1986-87	29.5231949
1987-88	33.7856826
1988-89	34.0038159
1989-90	33.4362371
1990-91	41.5889944
1991-92	44.7653131
1992-93	46.2350335
1993-94	54.2941069
1994-95	53.773634
1995-96	49.3517919
1996-97	48.9323123
1997-98	52.2268572
1998-99	59.0883025
1999-00	64.5511235
2000-01	69.0967385

Table 6 (Chart 6) | **Table 6a (Chart 6a)** | **Table 7 (Chart 7)**

Year	*EX FI/GFD*	*MA BO/GFD*	*Year*	*OTH LI/GFD*	*BD/GFD*	*Year*	*Dom Debt/GDP*
1981-82	11.12393261	33.6141242	1981-82	39.10685437	16.15509	1981-82	36.73515021
1982-83	11.83777171	35.4850852	1982-83	37.09419403	15.58295	1982-83	41.99380622
1983-84	10.2686109	30.990023	1983-84	47.86646201	10.8749	1983-84	40.3468761
1984-85	8.337161231	23.5128617	1984-85	46.6467616	21.50322	1984-85	43.46736714
1985-86	6.629151798	22.3442218	1985-86	46.70601153	24.32061	1985-86	47.81904812
1986-87	7.683547187	21.0006833	1986-87	39.95520462	31.36056	1986-87	52.55805763
1987-88	10.69738204	21.6757876	1987-88	46.12113593	21.50569	1987-88	54.5385499
1988-89	7.95524367	27.2224558	1988-89	46.57698153	18.24532	1988-89	53.90484846
1989-90	7.282779524	20.779075	1989-90	42.21205658	29.72609	1989-90	54.75754532
1990-91	7.127173329	17.9265997	1990-91	49.52276394	25.42346	1990-91	55.39304908
1991-92	14.92360633	20.6744666	1991-92	45.53062629	18.8713	1991-92	53.93338154
1992-93	13.24023598	9.15042441	1992-93	46.96188983	30.64745	1992-93	53.42302156
1993-94	8.420598437	48.0077004	1993-94	25.38294306	18.18876	1993-94	55.11304225
1994-95	6.207649516	35.2252049	1994-95	56.90172088	1.665425	1994-95	53.17897014
1995-96	0.527862158	54.9225636	1995-96	28.27050446	16.27907	1995-96	51.70949369
1996-97	4.476046334	29.9881618	1996-97	45.77944945	19.75634	1996-97	49.97298049
1997-98	1.226711043	36.5415969	1997-98	63.25488829	-1.0232	1997-98	52.01008315
1998-99	1.693883493	60.8633512	1998-99	37.62715154	-0.18439	1998-99	51.64201474
1999-00	1.126846644	67.1113573	1999-00	30.93671515	0.825081	1999-00	53.88268077
2000-01	0.513521237	69.6129389	2000-01	27.54706534	2.326474	2000-01	55.87378832

Table 8 (Chart 8) **Table 9 (Chart 9)**

Year	*Rate of INT*	*Year*	*DOM DEBT*	*Nomi GDP*
1981-82	7.29			
1982-83	8.36	1982-83	27.44817	11.488531
1983-84	9.29	1983-84	12.5734	17.168559
1984-85	9.98	1984-85	20.7921	12.120526
1985-86	11.08	1985-86	23.27073	12.052715
1986-87	11.38	1986-87	22.55575	11.505248
1987-88	11.25	1987-88	17.84037	13.561155
1988-89	11.4	1988-89	18.38654	19.778286
1989-90	11.49	1989-90	17.55863	15.727983
1990-91	11.41	1990-91	18.00466	16.650838
1991-92	11.78	1991-92	12.25334	15.291396
1992-93	12.46	1992-93	13.20087	14.282295
1993-94	12.63	1993-94	19.73224	16.060699
1994-95	11.9	1994-95	13.25034	17.369152
1995-96	13.75	1995-96	13.80018	17.034146
1996-97	13.69	1996-97	11.97406	15.865052
1997-98	12.01	1997-98	16.33713	11.780505
1998-99	11.86	1998-99	15.43511	16.257854
1999-00	11.77	1999-00	15.34236	10.545948
2000-01	10.95	2000-01	14.81573	10.724176

Table 10 (Chart 10) **Table 10a (Chart 10a)**

Year	*RBI/TOT*	*OUT SIDE RBI*	*Year*	*CB/TOT*	*LIC/TOT*
1990-91	24.79538	75.20461521	1990-91	55.13527	13.45913
1991-92	22.29547	77.70453009	1991-92	59.85593	14.68508
1992-93	10.57985	89.42014616	1992-93	64.63957	16.34534
1993-94	2.994185	97.00581474	1993-94	71.90385	16.851
1994-95	2.506636	97.49336436	1994-95	68.78377	17.18503
1995-96	8.980386	91.01961363	1995-96	64.3268	17.82156
1996-97	3.455802	96.54419808	1996-97	67.50375	19.84935
1997-98	12.84098	87.15901744	1997-98	57.7011	18.6786
1998-99	10.89492	89.10508209	1998-99	58.92383	18.22538
1999-00	8.32563	91.67436976	1999-00	60.66969	18.43271

2

A Decade after India's Economic Reforms

'Finance driven' model must give way to Keynesian Activism

*D. Sambandhan**

Introduction

Post independent India witnessed two major currency convulsions. The first acute foreign exchange crisis ended up with a massive devaluation of rupee occurred on June 6, 1966. Nevertheless, that did not result in reversing of the command model of development; instead, it underlined the imperative of indigenous way of economic development. Despite a hostile international financial and economic climate of 1970s characterized by transition from fixed to floating exchange rates and the twin oil shocks triggered world wide stagflation, India could still manage all the shocks and disturbances of world economy. It continued to remain as an insular economy, reasonably protectionist and increasingly reluctant to embrace the market based supply side Economics of Thatcherism and Reagonomics variety.

The Premature liberalisation of the economy through '80s without exposing the domestic industry even to internal competition combined with fiscal imprudence and

* The author is Reader, School of International Studies, Pondicherry University, Pondicherry - 605 014.

monetary disequilibrium, eventually accelerated inflation rate, and deepened the twin deficits namely current account and budgetary deficits. Confronted with this unprecedented payments and fiscal crisis, began the second major economic crisis with the two stage devaluation of rupee in July 1991. This step was only a beginning for a series of trade, industry and external sector related reforms to follow in full swing which at one stroke dismantled the import substitution led industrialisation strategy model dominated and frustrated fully by the state over the years in a highly protectionist environment. To understand the state of economy prior to liberalisation process, consider the following comment by George P. Shultz, the U.S. ex-secretary of State in his foreword to a recent book "Economic Policy Reforms and the Indian Economy" edited by Anne O. Krueger (Oxford University Press, 2002).

> *"In a country with the second largest population in the world and the largest democracy in the world as measured by numbers of people, the economy was becoming less and less important to the world. India's rate of growth in real per capita income remained stubbornly low at around 1.5 to 2.0 percent per annum, while its share of world trade fell from 1.8 percent in the early 1950s (a share larger than Japan's) to 0.6 percent by the late 1970s (a share smaller than Algeria's). Although progress was made in reducing poverty, 330 million people more than half of the population were still living in desperate poverty in 1974. By 1999 the record was better but, even so, estimates are that about 270 millions people, over one-fourth of the population, live in poverty. Thus, the pressing need to bring better living standards increased literacy, and improved health to this enormous population make this economic performance very disappointing....*
>
> *"When crisis struck in the early 1990s the Indian government began to reform its economic policies. Protection was reduced; quantitative restrictions on trade were dismantled; the financial sector was partially*

liberalised. Private economic activity was permitted in a number of areas previously reserved to the public sector and the extent of controls was reduced...

"The resulting acceleration of growth in India during the 1990s reaching an average level of almost seven percent per annum in the latter part of the decade was not surprising, but was surely gratifying. All friends of Indian students of India are watching the current pace of reforms with cautious hope. What should we expect in the future?"

Economic Reforms: A Check List

To understand the flavour and essence of reform process and fix ideas, in the following we provide a checklist of a series of measures undertaken since 1991 to place the country on high growth trajectory. They are:

- *Remove* all inhibiting restrictions on industry and trade via elimination of industrial licensing, capacity controls and capital issues controls
- *Relax* MRTP regulation and replace FERA by FEMA
- *Reduce* government expenditure and redirect it away from subsidies
- *Carryout* a fiscal and financial sector reform to contain inflation, current account deficit and wipe out NPA
- *Reform* Money, Credit and Capital Market via reduction in CRR, SLR and deregulation of interest rates
- *Inculcate* price discipline and productivity criteria in PSUs and gradually phase out administrative prices and bureaucratic management of foreign exchange rate
- *Ensure* current account convertibility and make attempts towards at least partial capital account convertibility

- *Allow* the twin prices-namely exchange rate and interest rate to respond to market forces rather than to the dictates of the state.
- *Accelerate* the pace of Dis-investment and privatization process to free the government from doing business
- *Usher* in import liberalisation for export promotion through dismantling of quantitative restrictions and eventually replacing them by tariffs
- *Reduce* tariff duties in conformity with WTO guidelines and the average rate prevailing in south east Asian nations
- *Liberalise* trade and FDI flows to attract capital, technology and managerial skills
- *Open* up capital market to augment foreign exchange and also improve country's access to international money and capital market
- *Adopt* freely flexible exchange rate mechanism which will help ensure a competitive real exchange rate in tune with the requirements of the real sector of the economy.
- *Guarantee* a flexible labour market, and ensure an exit route and so on.

Tracking Down of Reform Period: Reliance on the latest RBI Report

Into the twelfth year of economic reform, India is comfortably sitting on a mountain of foreign exchange reserves and a huge buffer stock of food grains. Macro economic management as revealed by low inflation rate, better money supply management, confidence in the external sector, stable rupee and so on, might indicate that the report card of Reform era is reasonably good. And yet, the behaviour of the real sector is not that vibrant and the effect of reforms are also inadequate from the point of view of vulnerable segment of the community including the agricultural sector. At a time when the Tenth Plan is on course towards an ambitious 8% growth target, we begin our review by asking the question: How did the Indian Economy perform during the reform period?

Has the market based shift in economic paradigm and the resulting finance driven capitalist ideology done any miracle to enhance saving and investment, accelerate growth, reduce poverty levels and help create an economic environment to exploit the full potentials of growth? This essay attempts to evaluate and assess India's decade old romance with reform process, laying emphasis only on the nature of growth process experienced.

To follow the major trends in the growth trajectory of Indian economy, the latest RBI report on Currency and Finance for 2001-02, but published in April 2003 (hence forward called Report) has been of immense help and form the basis for our review and interpretation. Given the space constraint, no exhaustive review is attempted.

What's the purpose of reviews and comments while they are available in abundance by eminent professional experts? Proliferation of comments and criticism are called for, as they essentially arouse and excite besides illuminating some hard economic truth. There are certain facts we need to know if we are to understand and appreciate properly and objectively about the success areas and failure zones of reform period. A critic by his selective discourse, some passing reference to long forgotten passage or phrase might offer an imaginative and speculative reconstruction of reality, though an unbiased picture of economic truth will be as rare as durable peace on the desert soil of Arab world.

The embarrassing question however is how far can critical comments and constructive criticism, inclusive of creative appreciation go? Where does interpretation end and nonsense begin? Why is one interpretation hailed, while others get brick bat? Eventually, it boils down to one's own intellectual training, ideology, quality of knowledge and sense of perception towards society, while examining economic issues which really touch the lives of millions of people with all social ramifications.

Growth Fundamentalism gives way to GDP Gloom: Service and External Sectors lend a helping hand

India may have registered 6 percent plus growth rate in the initial years of euphoria of reform period, (shall we call it growth fundamentalism) but the decelerating trend during the second half, (especially in the recent years) has given way to "GDP gloom".

While admitting that "the country has gained significantly from policy reform", the RBI report makes it abundantly clear that GDP growth has slowed down and that India is saving less and investing less. This simply means, the impact of decade old economic reform on the real economy is inadequate and that very growth process is not only becoming unsustainable but also very fragile and increasingly volatile. Despite booming exports, rising foreign exchange reserves, competition in telecom sector and the national highway projects, GDP growth rate of less than 5%, to be specific 4.4% for 2002-03, the first year of the Tenth Plan is far below the wishful target of 8 percent of the plan projection. Though the failed monsoon of 2002-03 the worst in many years, has been cited as one among the prime villain of the piece, it must be underlined here that both industry and services sector have not made adequate contribution so as to fill the vaccum left by the declining role of agriculture as the important contributor to GDP. Now agriculture just accounts for one third of GDP and a very bad monsoon would make the economy slip to that extent; the food grains output is lowest in seven years and oil seed production lowest in 15 years. But for the contribution from service sector, growth statistics would have been more dismal.

The lapse on the part of industrial and manufacturing sector to sustain growth momentum, has been amply reflected in the overall trend rate of growth of 6.1% during reform period (92-93 to 2002-03) which is only marginally higher than 5.6 % rate achieved during the pre-reform decade. It must be remembered that in other emerging markets, growth momentum has been led by industrial sector. Relentless marches of software and IT service sectors have only lent a helping hand to sustain a semblance of high growth (?) trajectory, in our country. This contribution from the service sector, as we all know is independent of the reform process.

Besides the country specific structural factors such as infrastructure gaps, labour market rigidities, lack of appropriate reforms in the agricultural sector, weak bankruptcy and exit procedures cyclical factors have been also at work and they are accentuated by global recession convulsions leading to a fall in aggregate demand. Again even during the period of global economic sluggishness exports did rise and in the absence of matching imports caused by low investment activity, current account surplus has emerged as a marginal propeller of aggregate demand. But for this pleasant turn around in favourable current account surplus, the growth scenario would have been still worse in the recent years.

Having been accustomed to a variety of sops and government goodies in a highly protective environment, the manufacturing segment of the economy is yet to make its mark on global competitive map. By Asian yardstick, its share in GDP (currently at 27% as against 45% in China) is not only very low, but palpably inadequate as an engine of growth in both stimulating exports and employment.

Unlike China which is both export oriented and domestic driven, Indian economy is largely domestic driven, the marginal current account surplus being an exception in the recent years. Failure on the part of government to provide quality infrastructure has also added more strains on the already ailing industrial sector.

The decade long neglect of government investment in infrastructure is now, felt keenly by everyone but there's no firm resolve to translate the sentiment into reality due to paucity of resources. The drastic cut in capital expenditure by the government has had a disastrous consequence for growth in general and private sector confidence in particular during reform period. Private sector investment has received a jolt from the sluggish government investment. RBI report clearly underlines how the steep fall in public sector investment in the 1990s, caused by deterioration in public sector saving rate, had its share in derailing private investment still further. Ever rising interest payments, ballooning fertilizer and food subsidies and rigidity in wages have always enlarged revenue account deficit, leaving very little for any kind of worthwhile capital expenditure.

The corporate sector for long demanded a low interest rate regime and various fiscal/budgetary concession for boosting capital market. But lower interest rate regime has failed so far to boost industrial output and investment or exports for that matter; low cost of credit is necessary but not a sufficient condition. We should remember, still a small farmer has to pay minimum 12% or double that rate in unorganized monetary transactions whereas a highly rated corporate entity could mobilize funds at 8 or 9%. There must be many other factors missing in the real economy for lower interest rate to have the desired impact.

Now that the pressure exerted on RBI and government for lower interest rate has failed to revive industrial economic activity, it's time the corporate sector understood some home truth. To quote Dr. S.S.Tarapore, former Deputy Governor RBI:

> *"The problem with the Indian system is that entrepreneurs have got habituated to unsustainable huge borrowings with minimal owned funds. Any successful entrepreneur must realise that borrowing should only be the icing on the cake and internal generation should form the predominant element. Thus, the question which needs to be posed is not how to stimulate the flow of funds from intermediaries to industry but how industry can become self financing. Making the interest rate too attractive and credit too easy to obtain is a sure path to disaster".*

Understanding the Anomalies in Agricultural Sector and Streamlining the Asymmetry in the Reform Process

Furthermore a careful perusal of the Report on the contours of growth path traversed, especially in the second half of reform period, provides an additional insight into the nature of deceleration. During the six years from 1997-98 to 2002-03, as many as three years recorded a growth rate of only 4.5 percent and the decline in agriculture and allied activities is more pronounced. In so far as agriculture is concerned, the trend rate of growth stagnated at 2.5% during the entire reform period of ten years, which is far lower than the over all post independent long run trend rate of 3%. It should not be a surprising factor because, agriculture has never merited any serious attention that it deserved in the scheme of things encompassing trade, industry and external sector related reform package; Agriculture was just left to weather gods and decisions of micro farmers. The state did not actively involve itself in raising public investment and making any net addition to irrigated area and also not strengthening sufficient flow of institutional credit in rural areas; to add insult to the injury the over all effect of trade liberalisation also helped keep many crop prices down even when domestic output falls. Agricultural sector, not fully revamped could not insulate itself from the onslaught of globalisation effects.

The story of artificially keeping farm prices low - be it food grains, oil seeds or cotton, soon after harvest and raising it to sky high levels during the lean period by the vested interests is all too known to be narrated here. RBI report faults the minimum support price mechanism (MSP) for the distortion in the relative price mechanism leading to wrong composition of agriculture output, tilted in favour of food grains and thus falling short of full potentials of the economy. To quote the report,

> *"A factor contributing to the below potential performance of agriculture is failure to sufficiently diversify the cropping pattern. The minimum support price (MSP) policy has distorted the relative prices between rice and wheat on the one hand, and other food and non-food crops on the other giving rise to a distorted cropping pattern. There is a need to re-examine the price support mechanism to eliminate the distortion of agricultural product composition in line with diversification of the consumption basket of a representative Indian household: There has been some acceleration in the growth of high value added agricultural products such as milk, fruits and vegetables, poultry, meat and fisheries during the 1990s".*

There are no two opinions to revisit MSP policy and take some hard decision about right relative price configuration, especially in the agriculture sector wherein subsidies on fertilizer and food do not directly help the poor and various anomalies persist on user charges on inputs like power. But blaming this alone for poor performance of agriculture is not right economics, for elsewhere in the report, there is an answer in the form of a crucial statement which reads: "*the per capita availability has remained below the historic peak attained in 1991.*" i.e. - the surplus food grains do not automatically flow from higher MSP alone and certainly it is not an indication of excess supply over demand in the economy. In a land where

1/4 of population is still steeped in poverty and mal nutrition, accumulating food stocks in godowns, with all its attendant financial and real costs, including the carrying out of export at a ridiculously low international price, do not speak well of agricultural management. A judicious distribution of food for work programme would have worked out more cheaper and efficient rather than holding on to the stocks and thus incurring enormous amount of costs.

Need for Revisiting Economic reform to empower the weak and powerless: A digression

From the standpoint of lifting more than 1/4 of population above the poverty line, ensuring better living standard for the majority of the poor through increased literacy and enhanced health care, the track record of post reform India is not that pleasant to look at. The largest democracy on earth having the second largest population in the world is yet to make a sufficient homework to accelerate rate of growth in real per capita terms. It is time authorities devoted more attention to the structure of growth rather than getting obsessed with macro figure of 6 or 7 plus growth rate which does not have any real meaning to the majority of population. Thus far, the reform process has had only very little impact on improving the quality of economic and social life for the lesser privileged and vulnerable segment of the economy. This lapse and continuing indifference need further elaboration.

Media revolution, improvements in tele-communication, spread of computers, exposure to foreign brands and rising income in upper income brackets have all promoted consumer's awareness about quality and cost in the creamy layer of the society. This comparative island of economic prosperity - a kind of glass curtain economy simultaneously coexists with subsistence existence of migrant population from rural to urban areas and near poverty conditions of many small and marginal farms, a few of them committing suicide under the weight of debt burden and the collapse of agricultural prices, including lack of access to credit and irrigate facilities. In urban centres too, plant closures and lay off do take place in a subtle way and the wide ramifications of privatization process on employment front is fully realised by the organised labour. One can well imagine the plight of the unorganised.

It is ridiculous to talk about hire and fire labour policy and labour market reform of western variety when we do not have any tangible and durable social security net of the very same western standard. Retrenchment of labour, lack of jobs due to inadequate investment and too many people chasing too few jobs have made the every social fabric of the society more fragile and volatile. There is no serious attempt to tackle poverty and unemployment, and address the crucial issues of conservation of water, environment and heritage. To add insult to the injury, both the religious fundamentalists and a certain sections of the ruling class in the country in the name of exercising power and authority wage a war against the powerless thereby inflicting more economic and social injury, virtually denying thereby their very physical and economic space. Strong Macro-economic fundamentals as revealed by low and stable inflation, swelling foreign exchange reserves, and incipient current account surplus, spectacular performance of software and IT towards GDP growth do not have any analytical meaning to understand the existential dilemma of the vast majority of population which is kept outside the main stream of reform process. Who will revisit Economic Reforms, and take measures to work on this unfinished agenda of empowering the weak and poor.

The reform era was not only a witness to a drastic cut in public expenditure in areas such as education, health, sanitation, housing and food security for the poor but also saw the closure of many industrial units. Many millions of workers have been rendered unemployed. In an age and environment where globalization process relentlessly wrecks havoc on the very economic and social fabric, children are also forced to work and get caught in the web of economic and sexual exploitation of a 'greedy market economy'. Adam smith's invisible hand of competition, by furthering unemployment in the country also throws open a vast army of 'invisible work force' of children working as domestic help at various places. To these vulnerable segments, losses are more than the gains, and benefits are less than the impending danger through the globalization route. Any kind of maximization of the benefits of International Trade and Investment will hardly have a trickle down effect on those who are deprived of all kinds of basic necessities and still to cover their labour power into income earning capabilities. They can't raise their voice of dissent also as the state has become more oppressive and insensitive to the basic rights of the people to live.

However, the latest RBI report paints a rosy picture that poverty levels have been reduced considerably through the reform process. It's only a mild aberration in an otherwise objective assessment of reform era.

It should not be difficult to link the fragility of growth base with inadequate saving and investment. Gross domestic saving as percent of GDP declined from 24.4% during the period 1994-95 to 1996-97 to 23.5 of GDP in the period 1997-98 to 2001-02. And yet the Tenth Plan envisages saving at 26.8% of GDP.

Fiscal Deficit Mess: Revisiting some forgotten passages: From Jagadish Bhagwati and Dr. Singh

More than a decade after the launch of economic reform, the objective of containing fiscal deficit without tossing the economy in a recessionary spin and the consequent low growth path, remains only a distant dream.

Even the early success at moderating the deficit was mainly the result of drastic reduction in capital expenditure.

That a cut in budget deficit this way would create problems for long run growth was highlighted by Prof. Jagadish Bhagwati and T.N. Srinivasan, way back in the early 1990s, when they visited India.

To quote them "*Developmental expenditure links directly to the long term health of the economy. The reduction of developmental expenditure is likely to reduce the growth rate and therefore to come to haunt us in the shape of further pressures to resume excess spending through the budget as in the 1980s*".

> *"The cuts in (real) development expenditures by the government may well affect adversely the private investment expenditures in the economy" creating deflationary impulses in addition to those that the government had intended. Because the crucial infrastructure activities are in the public sector and private investment finds its returns dependent on the availability these infrastructure inputs (such as power), private investment has traditionally been crowded in rather than crowded out by public investment in these infrastructure sectors. Thus the government must make every effort to ensure that, despite predictable political pressures, the reductions in developmental expenditure are brutally selective, sparing areas where the infrastructure bottlenecks are currently quite severe".*

The irony of fate is that after more than a decade of launch of reform, not only fiscal deficit is at pre-1991 level but also government's capital expenditure is at ridiculously low level. This defines the existential dilemma of India's economy and act as a constraint for both stimulation of growth and alleviation of poverty in the years to come.

Dr. Manmohan's dreams during the early period of reform to lift the economy from the fiscal mess through stringent enforcement of taxation regulations and tax collections have not materialized. Further, to compensate the across the board cut in customs and tariff duties, including excise, the economy has not grown to the desired level so as to impart sufficient elasticity to revenue generation. Dr. Singh knew well that the task was not going to be easy. To quote him:

> *"Further reductions in the fiscal deficit will have to rely primarily on improved resource mobilisation. Since this will have to be achieved during a period when customs tariff will be progressively reduced, it is essential to ensure that reforms in tax policies and tax administration are implemented at a pace which ensures improvement in tax revenues, thus reconciling the government's stabilization and structural reform objectives... Through improved tax performance, the government intends to reduce the fiscal deficit to four percent of the GDP or less in 1994-95 and lower levels in subsequent years".*

It's very much obvious that Dr. Singh's awed objective of fiscal consolidation has remained at best only a wishful thinking. With declining tax-GDP ratio, and rising revenue account deficits, the economy continues to get trapped into catch 22 situation. The dismal fiscal scenario could be captured by the following:

The combined gross fiscal deficit, as a percentage of GDP rose from 7.3% in 1997-98 to 9.9% in 2001-02. The seriousness in fiscal slippages could be gauged by highlighting the fact that throughout 1990s the revenue receipts of the centre displayed a declining trend. It stood at 9.2% of GDP in 2000-01, as composed to the figure of 10.1% in the first year of the reform period 1991-92. The same is the case with gross tax to GDP ratio. From 10.1% in 1990-91 it slipped to 9% in 2000-01.

The good intentioned paradigm shift from money financed deficit to bond-financed strategy has neither helped to stimulate growth nor contain the fiscal deficit. It has only resulted in curtailment of government capital expenditure, and deepened deflationary impulses against the back drop of not healthy global economic climate.

To recapitulate this paradigm shift towards bank-fund prescription of monetary conservation and fiscal austerity, we shall move down the memory true.

In the early stages of reform period, say 1991-1995, there was a perceptible decline in FD/ GDP ratio, as it was a period of de-monetisation of fiscal deficit. Because of the self imposed monetary and fiscal discipline - an agreement signed between RBI and Finance Ministry which precluded the government from periodically issuing adhoc treasury bills to furnish a port of its deficit, there was a shift to bond-financed deficit, that too at a high interest rate. During 1997-98, FD/GDP ratio started rising and monetisation of deficit was just only 1% of GDP. With tax/ GDP ratio falling, monetary policy effort reviving in growth of money supply, and central bank not inclined to accommodate fiscal needs of the state, the much needed capital expenditure spending via Keynesian route was not forth coming. In the late 1990s and early 2000s, demonetization of deficit became a reality and the neo-liberal finance driven model, namely increasing liquidity in the system via lowering interest rate was tried in full swing replacing the Keynesian fiscal stimulus; but alas it was during that phase of soft interest rate refine weak investment incestuously was evident and growth process was eroded.

To recapitulate the fiscal situation has become only worse now and in the name of monetary and fiscal austerity, the monetisation component of fiscal deficit has become negative. This self imposed monetary discipline of doing away with money financed federal deficit, has no doubt subdued inflation rate, enabling the authorities thus to usher in softer interest rate regime and so on, but it has put a brake on the need for Keynesian spending by the State and placed a larger burden in the form of escalating interest payments. Obsession with fiscal correction has neither led to fiscal consolidation nor growth. Capital expenditure as a proportion of government expenditure is today 2 percentage points lower than what it was in 1991. This does not augur well for growth.

The financial sector is flush with funds; people who can afford to save, still save at the going low rate of interest and shy away from equities after burning their fingers rather heavily. Despite a series of fiscal concession capital market has not slumbered out of its moribund state for a longer period. RBI report draws attention to this fact of continued preference of household for bank deposits, provident and pension funds. The soft interest rate regime may have facilitated swapping states high cost debt and also marginally reducing interest payments component of federal expenditure, but it has generated negative wealth effect for household and dampened their consumption.

RBI understands the problem, but remains silent on Keynesian activism

From macro perspectives RBI deserves credit for crafting the country's monetary policy and setting a soft interest rate regime largely assisted by world wide trimming of interest rates by central bankers due to global economic sluggishness, and thus ensuring a non-inflationary growth process; it must be however reminded that there are limits to its pro-active monetary policy to stimulate growth via interest rate instrument. "The efficacy of the monetary policy in reinvigorating growth has been largely diluted due to weak sensitivity of bank lending rates to mark down in Bank rates.

While RBI is revisiting Economic Reforms, it's high time authorities also took up a course in Keynesian Open Economic macro economics. RBI report rightly concludes with Dr. Bimal Jalan quote:

> *"The historical lesson is that most of the successful cases of development are those which have managed to combine the virtues of conflicting paradigms rather than rely exclusively on a single set of preordained theoretically right policies"*

Although the fundamentally flawed logic of finance driven capitalist model as against Keynesian state activism via fiscal policy induced increase in public investment is now understood than ever before, RBI report is silent on the need for stepping up public capital expenditure via Keynesian state activism but instead argues for neo-liberal market order.

Concluding remarks

Notwithstanding the immense gains of Indian Economy from policy reforms of 1990s, the contours of growth path are bristling with fragility and volatility. This can be attributed to an all encompassing embrace of 'finance driven' model of the west and relegation of Keynesian spending via fiscal stimulus, even during the recession conditions. Obsession with fiscal correction has neither resulted in any tangible fiscal consolidation nor opened the gateway for sustained growth, as industry and manufacturing sector have not adequately compensated the vacuum left by retreat of the state.

Fiscal adjustment via demonetization of fiscal deficit eventually ended up in cut back on capital expenditure of both centre and state governments. Given the interlocking nature of investment between the state and private sector, it dampened the entrepreneurial spirit of the latter. Ultimately, it only helped to derail both growth prospects and fiscal consolidation process. To quote the report:

> *"While reduction in investment spending affected future growth prospects with consequent slow down in revenue receipts, the interest payments and public debt continued to grow, resulting in reversal of fiscal consolidation process in the latter half of the 1990s".*

The only redeeming feature is that an exuberant confidence pervades external sector; Partial capital account convertibility has been accomplished thanks to a surge in forex reserves and positive current account surplus. Rupee is reasonably stable, and inflation performance is also satisfactory, thought it has begun its upward journey in the recent weeks.

While soft interest rate regime has bottomed out, the critical constraint for growth namely inadequate investment in both private and public sectors continue to haunt. Unless Indian economy makes a serious attempt to get out of the straight jacket of neo-liberal finance driven paradigm and address itself to factors crippling investment activity, the Tenth plan target of 8% growth rate will be a "flight to utopia". With high fiscal deficit still posing a problem and inflation rate on uphill movement, albeit only slowly, easy money policy and soft interest rate bias may not be expected to stay for long. With healthy export growth and world wide weakness of dollar, rupee has tended to appreciate vis-à-vis dollar, and fall against euro. How are we going to ensure reasonable growth in a non-inflationary way will be a million dollar question?

Interestingly, a paradoxical situation is now emerging where rupee is steadily losing its purchasing power at home even while emerging as a strong currency internationally. This will be soon increasingly inconsistent with soft interest rate bias of RBI. Further, to achieve 8% target growth rate of Tenth Plan, investment rate has to jump from the current stagnated level of 24-25% of GDP to 32% and that is next to impossible in the absence of quick restoration of revenue balance.

Therefore, under the circumstances mentioned above, the Report's suggestion that high growth rate "hinges critically on improvement of the domestic saving rate, increased public saving rate, higher inflow of foreign capital as well as net terms and better delivery mechanism" and so on, cannot be just realised in a 'finance driven' model where Schumpeterian heroes are absent and FDI takes more of merger and acquisition route and speculative capital of FIIs do continual mischief.

3

Export-led Growth in India

Evidence from the VARs

*Geethanjali Natarajan**
*Pravakar Sahoo***

Introduction

Many economists [Krueger (1978), Bhagwati (1988) and Balassa (1989) etc.] advocate export promotion as a better strategy to stimulate growth than import substitution. It is argued that export promotion leads to specialization in production, resulting in productivity gains. Export-led strategy is expected to lead to a more efficient allocation of resources by shifting factors of production to the more productive export sector. Further, it is seen that rising export earnings lead to an improvement in balance of payments, lighter debt burden and support higher growth rates by increasing import capacity. Growth of exports and imports also increases access to the benefits of international trade including new ideas modern technology, competition, economies of scale and creation of domestic industries around new markets. Thus, a trade

* Research Officer, Institute for Social and Economic Change, Nagarbhavi, Bangalore-560 072.

** Research Fellow, Institute for Social and Economic Change, Nagarbhavi, Bangalore-560 072.

policy formulated to promote exports and regulate imports directly and indirectly influences economic growth. Along with exports and imports, gross investment is also seen as an essential factor for enhancing growth, as it provides the necessary inputs for expanding production of exports and demand for imports.

The proposition that international trade promotes growth of national economies has been analysed in considerable detail since the early 1970's and more so after the East Asian miracle. Until recently, in countries such as Malasia, Indonesia, Thailand, Taiwan, Philippines and South Korea which experienced consistent high growth rates for more than a decade, the process of development has been understood to be export-led i.e., no other variable has been so dynamic as a factor of economic growth as the growth of exports. However, in most of these economies, imports has been a crucial factor which contributed to increase in exports.

The literature focusing on the relationship between exports and economic growth has been extensive and largely empirical in nature. Since, the mid 1960's, the various studies-country specific, cross-country and pooled, starting with simple correlations and regressions, of late applied a wide range of time series techniques such as vector autoregressions, causality, cointegration and error correction methods. While the correlation and regression techniques are inadequate for establishing the underlying causal relationship between exports and growth, the time series methods employed in this context are also not free from limitations. The VARs consider a system of relationship, which while being flexible are general in character. The causality tests are largely confined to stationary bivariate systems. While dealing with relationships involving non-stationary variables, cointegration and error correction techniques however, are more appropriate, especially for inferring long-run causal nexus. It is pertinent here to note that the cointegration and error correction techniques proceed on the assumption that the variables concerned do not exhibit any trend breaks. This assumption is somewhat unrealistic and misleading, given the fact that the policy changes initiated under the structural adjustment programme pureed by various countries, may have caused discrete but pronounced changes in the export-growth nexus. In other words, the exogenous changes in trade regimes, deregulated environment and global integration of economies, might have resulted in trend breaks in exports as well as economic growth. Therefore, the issue of trend breaks should be properly addressed while examining the export-led growth hypothesis. In the literature, there are no studies to date in this direction. The present study makes a modest attempt to fill the gap, by testing for unit roots in the variables when the variables when exogenous as well as endogenous trend breaks occur.

In the light of the above, it is felt than an appropriate way of looking at the export-growth nexus is not by confining to bivariate relationships, but by formulating an enlarged VAR system consisting of exports, imports, growth, capital formation and trade policy as integral components. The export-growth link may then be examined within the VAR framework, accommodating for trend breaks in the components of the system. The present study, therefore, looks at this pertinent issue and attempts to reexamine the long run linkage between export performance and economic growth within the framework of VAR augmented by an error correction mechanism, by employing unit root tests, due to Perron, (1989; 1997). The remainder of the paper is planned as follows: Section-II presents a review of select studies relevant to the context, Section-III describes the data and methodology employed, Section-IV presents the empirical analysis, followed by Section-V wherein the conclusions of the studies are reported.

Review of previous work

As a background to this study, an attempts is made here to present a brief review of selected studies. It may be observed that while the early studies adopted the neo-classical production function framework, the recent ones have used the a theoretical time series techniques.

In a seminal paper, Feder (1982) provides an analytical basis for an empirical study on the relationship between exports and economic growth. The study identifies two channels by which exports influence growth. First, through positive externalities of the export sector on the non-export sector. Second through greater productivity differential in export sector as compared to the non-sector. Both the channels are tested in a neo-classical production framework using OLS regressions for a cross-country data of 31 countries including India over the period 1964-73. The empirical evidence offers support for both the channels tested, although the evidence is shown to be stronger in the first case than in the second. The study does not take into consideration 'imports' while assessing the impact of exports on growth.

Negating the general argument of dependency and world-system theory that various forms of external economic dependence have negative effects on the growth of nations, Jafee (1985) shows how export dependence, a widely used measure of international economic dependence, affects economic growth using analysis of covariance in case of less developed countries (LDC's) over the period 1960-77. Another study by Moshos (1989) brings out the effects of export expansion on economic growth in a switching regression framework. The study adopts an aggregate supply analysis in which labour and capital are construes as determinants of output. The study uses cross section data of 71 developing economies over the period 1970-1980. The results indicate existence of a critical development level below and above which the responses of output growth to its determining factors differ substantially. The evidence contradicts the view that among more advanced developing economies, the effect of export expansion on growth is stronger than among less developed economies.

Serletis (1991) investigates the relationship between export growth and GNP growth using annual Canadian data from 1970-1990. The study examines whether knowledge of past export growth promotes prediction of future GNP growth, beyond, beyond predictions that are based on past GNP growth alone. The results reveal that exports and growth are not cointegrated implying that the GNP trend is not a linear combination of export and import trends. The findings suggested that export growth and GNP growth are independent.

Following Feder (1982), Esfahani (1991) examines, among others, the inter-relationship between exports, imports and output growth in a simultaneous-equation framework. In particular, the paper examines the consequences of adding imports to the list of input requirements for output growth because of a binding foreign exchange constraint and also on account of strong correlation between exports and imports. Using the data set comprising of a sample of 31 countries including India over three time periods (1960-73, 1973-81 and 1980-86), the study mainly shows the positive impact of exports on GDP due to import-reduction rather than the Feder's type externality effect.

Rejecting both the export-led growth and growth-led export hypotheses, Dodaro (1993) suggests a reconsideration of the whole relationship between exports and economic growth in LDC's. The empirical analysis involves OLS estimations for a total of 87 LDC's including India during the period 1967-1986. Mallick (1994) estimates the causal relationship between exports and economic growth in India employing Granger, Sims and Modified Sims tests over the period 1950-51 to 1991-92. The model includes an important link variable 'imports' which enters into the production function to determine output growth, and hence the relationship between exports and economic growth. The result supports the feed back hypotheses between income and exports. Both the studies ignore testing for the stationary properties of exports and growth.

Thornton (1995) investigates the long-run relationship between real exports and GDP in Mexico during 1895-1992. The study finds a positive and significant Granger causal relationship running from exports to economic growth. Oxley (1995) using cointegration and Granger causality tests rejects the hypothesis of export-led growth in favour of reverse causality running from economic growth to exports in Portugal during the period 1865 to 1985. Henriques and Sadorsky (1996) attempt to answer the question: 'Does rapid income growth lead to rapid trade expansion, or is it the other way round? by testing three competing but not mutually exclusive hypotheses, viz., (i) export-led growth hypothesis (ii) growth-driven exports hypothesis, (iii) and feedback (between the two) hypothesis. The empirical evidence for the Canadian data supports the growth-driven hypothesis, implying that changes in GDP precede changes in exports.

In another study, Dutt and Ghosh (1996) explore the long-run relationship between exports and economic growth using cointegration framework for 26 high, low and middle income countries including four newly industrialisaed countries of Asia (NIC's) over the period 1953-1991. They conclude that exports and economic growth causality structure is economy specific and therefore attempts at generalization are inappropriate. A similar caution has been provided in Heriques and Sadorsky (1996). Using cointegration and error correction framework Kamaiah and Mohsin (1997) examine the export promotion hypothesis in Asian Countries and show mixed evidence.

Olugbenga A, Oluwole and Akorlie A (1997) find significant variation in the real output levels due to changes in exports, imports, gross investment and trade policy, in 12 Sub-Saharan African countries for the period 1965-1991 using VAR technique augmented with error correction term. Forecast error variance decomposition (FEVD) is used to separate the effects of each variable on others on its own. The study concludes that sizeable variations in real output growth in ten of the twelve countries are due to changes in trade policies and exports, with some contributions from shocks to gross investment.

Using Johansens's multiple cointegration test, the long-run relationship among real output, exports and imports for four less developed countries viz., India, Fiji, Nigeria and Papua New Guinea, is estimated by Adjaye and Charaborthy (1999). The study period is 1960-1994 in the case of India and Nigeria, 1973-1993 for Papua New Guinea and 1969-1993 for Fiji. Real output, exports and imports are found to be cointegrated in Nigeria and Fiji, and the error correction mechanism suggests that Granger causality runs from exports and imports to real output in these countries. Further, the results report that there is causality from real output to exports for Nigeria and Fiji, while in the case of India and Papua New Guinea, there is evidence of causal relationship between these variables. In addition, the study provides evidence for exports being an important source of foreign exchange for importing the much needed capital inputs for higher economic growth.

Nidugala (2000) analyses the role of exports in India's economic growth employing a modified version of Esfahani's study (1991). He tries to examine the stability of the relationship between exports and growth through switching regressions in the Indian context. An attempt is also made to test whether the monetary and fiscal factors, structure of the economy and supply shocks both domestic and external, have any significant impact on India's economic growth during the period 1960-1989. The study shows that exports play a crucial role in influencing GDP in the 1980's. However, during the period 1961-62 to 1979-80, the influence of exports is found to be weak. There is also evidence of a positive relationship between exports and growth in 1980's due to higher level of development and change in the composition of exports in favour of manufactured exports by the Indian economy. The study suffers from the same limitation as in Mallick (1994).

Sampath and Anwar (2000) also test for export-led growth hypothesis using the data of 97 countries for the period 1960-1992, using the unit root and cointegration tests. The causality between exports and GDP for those countries wherein exports and growth are related in the long run is also tested. The results indicate that in 30 countries economic growth has a positive impact on exports while in 29 countries the reserve is found.

Anorou and Ahmad (2000) show a positive relationship between openness and economic growth in select ASEAN countries for the period 1960-1997 by using Johansen's cointegration technique. The causal relationship between economic growth and openness is examined with the help of Granger causality based on vector error correction model (VECM). The study finds a long-run relationship between economic growth and openness, and shows that there is feedback causality running from both sides. The results support both the openness-driven economic growth and growth-driven openness hypotheses.

The studies reviewed above and close look at the literature reveal that some of the variables such as trade policy, imports and gross investment which have gained prominence in the 1990's have not been paid adequate attention while dealing with the issue of export-led growth hypothesis. Since 1980's many economies have resorted to the Fund-Bank sponsored Structural Adjustment Programme

(SAP) and strived towards integration of their domestic economies with the global economy to reap the benefits of international trade. This obviates the role of the trade policy in enhancing the performance of any economy. Similarly, the variables like imports, exports and gross investments have not been used together while assessing their impact on economic growth. In the Indian context, such an attempt has not been made to date to examine the dynamic interactions among these variables in the short run particularly Forecast Error Variance Decomposition (FEVD) tests, keeping in view of this observation as well as the recongitin of the need to subject to the concerned variables to trend break analysis, the present study attempts to investigate the long-run relationship and short-run interactions among exports, imports, gross investment, trade policies and economic growth during 1965-66 to 1997-98.

Methodology and data

The methodology used in this study is on the lines of Olugbengo et al (1997) and Anorou and Ahmad (2000). In addition, the study employs Perron's (1989) exogenous trend break as well as Perron's (1997) endogenous trend break unit roots tests. Accordingly, in this paper an unrestricted VAR model is employed. The components of the VAR model are chosen to be GDP, exports, imports, and gross domestic capital formation and trade policy. The VAR model is augmented by an error correction term, which is to be obtained from a cointegrating relationship.

Annual time series data for the period 1965-66 to 1997-98 (in nominal terms) are used in this study. The data are compiled from the economic survey of the government of India. Here, gross domestic capital formation is proxies by gross investment. It has been considered as an important factor promoting economic growth. To analyse the impact of the trade policies on economic growth, trade policy dummy variable is introduced in the VAR system. During the period 1965-66 to 1997-98, Indian economy was considered to be inward-oriented relying heavily on import substitution. However, the balance of payment crisis in 1991 led the Indian economy to change its trade orientation and move from being a closed economy to an open economy. To capture the impact of these trade policy changes, the trade policy dummy variable (TP) is divided in two component time periods: 1965-66 to 1991-92 and 1992-93 to 1997-98. For the 1965-66 to 1991-92 period, the trade policy dummy variables assumes a value of zero (TP = 0), and for the years 1992-93 to 1997-98 (TP = 1). The presence of both exports and trade policy variables in the same VAR system is intended to provide useful reference for discussing the causal impact of export earnings and trade orientation on growth of GDP.

The variables used in the analysis should be checked for stationary to avoid spurious results. Considering the size and power problems (Maddala and Kim, 1998) of the conventionally used unit root tests like Dickey-Fuller and Augmented Dickey-Fuller, we employ USRB (Bhargava, 1986), KPSS (1992), Perron's (1989) exogenous and Perron's (1997) endogenous structural break unit tests to examine the stationary properties of the series: exports, imports, capital formation and GDP. The unit root tests are followed by the Engle-Granger (1987) and Johansen-Juselius (1990) cointegration procedures to test for the existence of a stable long run relationship among the variables. Thereafter, the VAR augmented with error correction terms (residuals) derived from the estimated long-term cointegration relationships, are estimated to confirm the export-led growth hypothesis using the technique of forecast error variance decomposition (FEVD). The estimated VAR models with error correction term are of the following general form:

$$\Delta \, GDPt = \alpha_0 + \alpha_1 \Delta Ex_{t-i} + \beta_1 \, \Delta Im_{t-i} + \phi_1 \, \Delta ECa_{t-i} + \varphi_1 \, \Delta EC_{t-1} + \psi \, TP + \varepsilon_t$$

where Δ is the difference operator, GDP is Gross Domestic Product; Ex is exports, Im is imports, Ca is gross domestic capital formation, EC_{t-1} is the lagged error correction term,

TP is trade policy dummy variable and ε_t is white noise error term.

Empirical Analysis

The URSB (Bhargava, 1986), unit rooot test is employed for testing the stationary properties of the data. The R_1 and R_2 test statistics of the URSB test (see appendix-A.1) fail to reject the null hypothesis of a unit root for all the variables in levels. In the first difference (Δ), the R_1 and R_2 statistics are significant suggesting that the variables are integrated of order one [I (1)] i.e. stationary. Similarly, the KPSS (1992) unit root in which the null hypothesis is that a given series is stationary also confirms that the series under consideration are I (1) (see appendix-A.2). Further, the BLS (1992) unit root test and the Perron's exogenous (1989) and endogenous (1997) structural break unit root tests also reveal that the variables are non-stationary after first differencing (see appendices-A.3, A.4 and A.5). The trend breaks in the variables are also reported in the appendices-A.4 and A.5. Thus the results show that all these variables are I (1).

Since all the series are found to be I (1), testing for cointegrating relationships is a straightforward application of the Engle-Granger (1987), and Johansen-Julesius (1990) tests. The latter test (Johasen-Julesius) provides most efficient estimate of the cointegrating relationships and also identifies the number of cointegrating relationships among the non-stationary variables.

In appendix-B.2, the eigen values and the likelihood ration (LR) statistics for determining the number of cointegrating vectors (v) wherein the null hypothesis of no cointegration ($v = 0$) versus the alternative of $v \leq 1$, $v \leq 2$, $v \leq 3$, $v \leq 4$ has been tested. The results reported in appendices B.2 and B.3 reveal that the null hypothesis of no cointegration ($v = 0$) is rejected at the 5 % level of significance. But the null hypothesis that $v \leq 3$ is accepted at the 5 % level confirming that there are only three cointegrating vectors among the variables. The sharp fall in the eigen values statistics confirms this result. From, the above analysis, it may be inferred that GDP, exports, imports, gross domestic capital formation and trade policies are cointegrated with three cointegrating vectors. Further, the cointegration LR test (see appendix-B.3) based on the trace statistics also confirm the existence of three cointegrating vectors.

While the estimated cointegrating vectors show the long run equilibrium relationship among GDP, exports, imports, capital formation and trade policy, the dynamic adjustments that occur in the short run leading to stable long run relations in response to various shocks to the system remain unspecified. The dynamic relations among the series can be established in the VAR model by conducting variance decomposition (VDCs) tests of the forecast errors at different time horizons.

The results of the forecast error variance decomposition (FEVD) are reported in table-1. As noted earlier, the FEVD measures the effects of a shock in each of the variables on own as well as the rest of the variables in the system. The numbers in table-1 represent the fraction of the forecast error variance in the variables generated by innovation in each of the variable in the system as given in column-1. Considering the annual data, we have chosen eight-year forecast time horizon for the FEVDs.

The results of the exports (ΔEx) variance decompositions show that the export growth is largely explained (67 % for time horizon 2) by its own shocks. Even after eight-years of period, more than 50 % of the variance is explained by its own shocks. The results also show that import shocks have some influence (26.4 % for time period 2) in explaining the export growth. The import innovations are more significant in export forecast error variance even after eight year (33.8 %). However, gross domestic capital formation (ΔCa) and ΔGDP have no such strong influence upon the export growth. The trade policy reforms affect the export growth to some extent (3.8 % for time horizon 2) in a shorter period but it explains 10.5 % for horizon 8. Therefore, export forecast error decompositions establish the long run relationship between export and trade policy.

Coming to imports (ΔIm) variance decompositions, it is largely explained by its own shocks and shocks to exports. Shocks to capital formations and GDP account for only 1.1 % and 1.3 % in the variance of the import growth. However, export innovations account for 39 % of the forecast error variance of the import after eight years showing the long run relationship between the exports and imports. There is immediate impact of the trade policy on the imports (7.2 % for the time horizon 2) but it slows down in long period.

In the case of gross domestic capital formation (ΔCa), shocks to imports have a substantial influence (64.9 % for time horizon 2 and 40.6 % even after eight years of time horizon). This supports the view that India imports heavy capital, technology and other raw materials that are used for capital formation. The shocks to exports explain 13.6 % for period two, but it increases to 31.8 % after eight years. However, growth of gross domestic capital formation is little explained by its own shocks (16.4 % for time horizon 2) and it accounts 12.7 % after eight years. Nonetheless, GDP and trade policies (TP) have negligible impact on the gross domestic capital formation (2.3 % and 1.9 % for time horizon 2 respectively).

Turning to GDP forecast error variance decompositions, it is largely explained by the shocks to imports (71.4 % for time horizon 2). Innovations to imports explain GDP growth by more than 50 % even after eight years of period. Innovations to the exports account for 13.8 % for the time period two but it explains 29.4 % of GDP

Table 1: Forecast Error Variance Decomposition at Various Time Horizons

Variance of	*Time horizon*	*% of forecast Error Variance Explained by*				
		Δ Ex	*Δ Im*	*Δ Ca*	*Δ GDP*	*TPD*
Δ Ex	2	67.1	26.4	2.6	8.2	3.8
	4	56.4	32.3	3.2	1.1	7.0
	6	52.1	33.8	2.7	2.1	9.2
	8	50.3	33.8	2.3	4.6	10.5
Δ Im	2	31.0	59.2	1.1	1.3	7.2
	4	33.6	52.2	1.1	2.4	0.5
	6	6.6	47.0	1.1	3.2	1.9
	8	9.0	43.3	1.0	3.8	2.6
Δ Ca	2	13.9	64.9	16.4	2.3	1.9
	4	26.4	52.1	14.9	3.3	3.2
	6	29.7	48.6	13.7	3.8	4.1
	8	31.8	46.3	12.7	4.1	4.8
Δ GDP	2	3.8	71.4	5.2	2.9	6.4
	4	16.7	65.7	3.9	2.4	11.0
	6	23.5	57.3	2.9	2.9	13.1
	8	29.4	50.7	2.3	3.6	13.8
TPD	2	20.9	20.9	2.1	1.4	54.5
	4	25.5	30.1	1.6	2.2	40.4
	6	30.2	32.4	1.3	3.0	32.4
	8	34.1	33.3	1.2	3.6	27.6

growth after eighty year of horizon period. This supports the export-led growth hypothesis in the long time horizon. From, the table, it is clear that the growth of GDP is more influenced by shocks to imports, to exports and to trade policies (6.4 % for period 2 and 13.8 % for period 8). This establishes a strong relationship among exports, imports, trade policy and growth. Trade policies are more influenced by the own shocks and shocks to exports and imports.

The trade policy forecast error variance decompositions show that it is more explained by own innovations (54.5 % for period 2). Nonetheless the export and import innovations account equally 20.9 % each for period two. As the time horizon increases, shocks to exports and imports explain the trade policy variable to a considerable extent (34.1 % and 33.3 % after 8 years). This establishes a strong inter-relationship between exports and imports, and trade policy. In sum, both exports and imports influence the trade policy in the long run.

In sum, the variance decomposition tests indicate that exports growth and imports growth are endogenous to the system as they are largely explained by their own shocks. In case of trade policy also, it is endogenous but at the same it is influenced to a great extent by the shocks to exports and imports. The strong inter-relations among trade policy and exports and imports which influence the growth of GDP supports the theory of trade promotion and economic growth. The findings also support that trade policies directly and indirectly affect the growth of exports and imports and thereby influence GDP over a period of time.

Conclusion

The forecast error variance decomposition (FEVD) tests reveal that exports and imports are endogenous to the system. The results also indicate that there is a strong relationship among exports, imports and capital formation.

In fact, imports and exports have significant impact on the capital formation in both short and long runs. The relationship between imports and GDP growth has also been found to b e strong. Both imports and exports have significant effect on the GDP growth in the relatively long period. Even the FEVD statistics show a strong relationship between exports, imports and capital formation. Overall, the results of the study do not lend support to the export-led growth hypothesis, but at the same time brings out the fact that there exists a strong relationship between exports, imports, gross investment and GDP and that they are influenced by each other in the short and long run as well.

REFERENCES

1. Adjaye, J A and D chakraborthy (1999), "Export-ld Growth and Import compression: Further Time Series Evidence form LDC's", Australian Economic Papers, June, pp.164-175.
2. Anoruo, E and Y Ahmad (2000), "Openness and Economic Growth: Evidence from Selected ASEAN Countries", The Indian Economic Journal, Vol.47, No.3, pp.110-117.
3. Banerjee, A, R L Lumsdaine, J H Stock (1992), "Recursive and Sequential Test of the Unit Root and Trend Break Hypothesis: Theory and international Evidence", Journal of Business and Economics and Statistics, Vol50, pp.271-287.
4. Balassa, B (1989), "Comparative Advantage Trade Policy and Economic Development", (Harvested Wheatsheaf, Hertfordshire).
5. Bhagwati, J (1989), "Export-promoting Trade Strategy: Issues and Evidence", World Bank Research Observer, Vol.3, no.1, pp.27-57.
6. Bhargava, A (1986), "On the Theory of Testing for unit Roots in Observed Time Series", Review of Economic Studies, pp.368-384.
7. Blanchard, O and D Quah (1989), "The Dynamic Effect of Aggregate Demand and Supply disturbances", American Economic Review, Vol.79, pp.655-673.

8. Dickey, D A and W A Fuller (1979), "Distributing of the Estimators for Autoregressive Time Series with a Unit Root", Journal of American Statistical Association, vol.74, pp.427-431.

9. Dodaro, S (1993), "Exports and Growth: A reconsideration of Causality", The Journal of Developing Areas, Vol.27, pp.227-244.

10. Dutt, D S and D Ghosh (1996), "The Export growth - Economic Growth Nexus: A casualty analysis", The Journal of Developing areas, vol.30, pp.167-182.

11. Engle, R F and C W J Granger (1987), "Co-integration and Effort Correcting: Representation, Estimation and Testing ", Econometrica, vol.55, pp.251-276.

12. Esfahani, H S (1991), "Exports, Imports and Economic Growth in Semi-industrialised countries", Journal of Development Economics, Vol.35, pp.93-116.

13. Feder, G (1982), "On Exports and Economic Growth", Journal of Development Economics", vol.12, pp.59-73.

14. Henriques, I and P Sadorsky (1996), "Export-led Growth or Growth Driven Exports? The Canadian Case", The Canadian Journal of Economics, Vol.29, no.3, pp.540-555.

15. Jaffee, D (1985), "Export Dependence and Economic Growth: Reformulation and Re-specification", Social Forces, Vol.64, no.1, pp.102-118.

16. Johansen, S and K Juselious (1990), "Maximum Likelihood Estimation and Inference on Cointegration with Application to the demand for Money", Oxford Bulletin of Economic and Statistics, Vol.52, 169-210.

17. Kamiah, B and MD Mohsin (1997), "Export Promotion Hypothesis in Asian Countries: An empirical Re-examination", in D M Nachane and M J M Rao (Eds): Macroeconomic Challenges and Development Issues (Himalaya Publishing House, Mumbai).

18. Krueger, A (1978), "Foreign Trade Regimes and Economic Development: Liberalization Attempts and consequences, (Ballinger Publishing Company, Cambridge).

19. Kwiatowski, D, P C B Phillips, P Schmidt and Y Shin, (1992), "Testing the Null Hypothesis of Stationary Against

the Alternative of a Unit Root: How sure are we that economic time series have a Unit Root?", Journal of Econometrics, Vol.54, pp.159-178.

20. Maddala, G S and In-Moo Kim (1998), Unit Roots, cointegration and Structural Change", (Cambridge University press, UK)\

21. Mallick, S S (1994), "Export and Economic Growth", Journal of Indian school of political economy, vol3, no.6, pp.505-515.

22. Moshos, D (1989), " Export a Expansion, Growth and the level of Economic Development: An Empyreal analysis", Journal of Development Economics, vol30, pp.93-102.

23. Nidugala G K (2000), "Exports and Economic Growth in India: An Empirical Investigation", The Indicant Economic Journal, vol.47, no.3, pp.67-78.

24. Olugbenga A, O, O Oluwole and A N Akorlie (1997), "Trade Policy, Export Performance and Economic Growth: The Evidence from Sub-Saharan Africa", The Journal of International Trade and Economic Development, vol5, no.3, pp.341-360.

25. Oxley, L (1989), "Cointegration, Causality and Export-led Growth in Portugal: 1865 -1985", Economic letters, vol43, no.2, pp.163-166.

26. Perron, P (1989), "The Great Crash, The Oil Price Shock, and the Unit Root Hypothesis", Econometrica, vol.57, no.6, pp.1361-1401.

27. Sampath, R K and M S Anwar (2000), "Exports and economic Growth", The Indian Economic Journal, vol.47, no.3, pp.79-88.

28. Serletis, A (1992), "Export Growth and Canadian Economic Development", Journal of Development Economics, vok.38, pp.133-145.

29. Thorton, J (1995), cointegration, Causality and Export-led Growth in Mexico, 1895-1992", Economic letters, vol.50, no.3, pp.413-416.

Appendix – A.1

URSB$ Unit Root Test Statistics

Variables	*Levels*		*First Differences*			
	R1	*R2*	*R1*	*R2*	*CV(R1)*	*CV(R2)*
Ex	0.03	0.06	0.90*	1.84*	0.26	0.35
Im	0.03	0.10	0.38*	0.69*	0.26	0.35
Ca	0.03	0.06	1.34*	1.72*	0.26	0.35
GDP	0.03	0.07	0.27*	0.73*	0.26	0.35

Note: R1 and R2 which are two test statistics pf the IRSB unit root test.

* Significant at 5% level, CV refers to critical values at 5% level.

Appendix – A.2

KPSS Unit Root Test Statistics

Variables	*Levels*		*First Differences*	
	ETA(mu)	*ETA(Tau)*	*ETA(mu)*	*ETA(Tau)*
Ex	0.761	0.222	0.715*	0.195*
Im	0.777	0.226	0.577*	0.193*
Ca	0.743	0.212	0.737*	0.153*
GDP	0.899	0.206	0.724*	0.211*

Note: * refers to significant at 5% level. Here the estimated values of the ETA (mu), ETA (Tau) in the first differences is less than the values accepting the null hypothesis of no unit root in the series. KPSS procedure calculates ETA(mu) and ETA(Tau) statistics. The null hypothesis in ETA (mu) test is that the series X{t} is stationary amount a level. But in ETA (Tau) the null hypothesis is trend stationary. Critical values are obtained from KPSS (1992).

Appendix – A.3

BLS Unit Roots Test Statistics

Variables	*Levels*		*First Differences*
	Test	*ADF#*	*ADF#*
With Constant, No Time Trend			
EX	1	0.319	–14.617*
	2	0.215	–1.230*
	3	0.595	–5.087*
Im	1	0.173	–7.681*
	2	0.619	–0.609*
	3	1.045	–3.822*
Ca	1	0.395	–22.502*
	2	0.078	–1.014*
	3	0.420	–4.784*
GDP	1	0.245	–3.164*
	2	0.315	–0.385*
	3	0.932	–2.313*
With Constant and Time Trend			
EX	1	–3.484	–30.483*
	2	–0.821	–4.853*
	3	–1.499	–29.040*
Im	1	–1.939	–16.482*
	2	–0.436	–3.606*
	3	–2.450	–23.196*
Ca	1	–1.462	–43.609*
	2	–0.688	–3.932*
	3	–1.605	–30.865*
GDP	1	–0.876	–12.840*
	2	–0.049	–4.592*
	3	0.549	–31.447*

Note: * Test 1, 2 and 3 refer to BLS unit root test 1, 2 and 3

Significant at 5% level; # refers to sequential augmented Dickey-Fuller test statistics.

Critical values are obtained from BLS (1992)

Appendix – A.4

Perron's Exogenous Structural Break Test Statistics for Unit Roots

Variables	*Levels*		*First Differences*	
	t-statistics	*TB*	*t-statistics*	*TB*
Ex	2.454(–3.68)	1994	–5.318(–3.68)	1994
Im	2.822(–3.68)	1994	–5.545(–3.68)	1994
Ca	0.063(–3.68)	1994	–7.327(–3.68)	1994
GDP	2.918(–3.68)	1994	–4.845(–3.68)	1994

Note: The values inside the parenthesis refer to the critical values at 5% level, TB refers to time break. Here we have taken only model 'b' of Perron's exogenous structural break unit root test static's as the model 'a' and 'c' are reporting inconsistent result. Critical values are obtained from Perron (1989).

Appendix – A.5

Perron's Endogenous structural Break Test Statistics for Unit Roots

Variables	*Levels*			*First Differnces*	
	Models	*t-statistics*	*TB*	*t-statistics*	*TB*
Ex	IO1	–0.27	1991	–5.45**	1990
	IO2	–3.00	1987	5.75**	1985
	AO	–3.55	1988	–6.18*	1987
Im	IO1	–0.58	1978	–5.02***	1967
	IO2	–1.53	1980	–5.32***	1967
	AO	–3.95	1983	–8.41*	1981
Ca	IO1	–0.51	1994	–14.36*	1995
	IO2	–2.75	1990	–11.03*	1994
	AO	–2.97	1991	–9.21*	1985
GDP	IO1	0.92	1996	–4.93***	1993
	IO2	0.20	1990	–5.31***	1985
	AO	–3.28	1991	–4.57***	1987

Note: * significant at 1% level,

** significant at 5% level and

*** significant at 10% level

TB refers to time break critical values are obtained form Perron (1197). Perron's Endogenous tests for unit root and trend break implements several tests on breaking trend functions when the date or possible change in the intercept and the slope is not fixed a priori. The three tests implanted in this study are:

IO1: Innovational outlier with a change in the intercept

IO2: Innovational outlier with a change in the intercept and slope

AO: Additive outlier with a change in the slope only but both segments of the trend functions are joined at the time break

The method employed to choose the optimal break date is that of minimizing 't' statistics.

Appendix – B.1
Engle - Granger Cointegration Procedure

Variables	Levels URSB		First Differnces KPSS	
	R1	R2	ETA(mu)	ETA(Tau)
μ_1	0.898*	0.737*	0.244*	0.204*
μ_2	1.083*	1.086*	0.492*	0.181*
μ_3	0.829*	0.496*	0.448*	0.121*
μ_4	0.588*	0.447*	0.342*	0.185*

Note: * significant at 5% level. IN URSB the estimated values are greater than the critical values to reject the null of unit root but in KPSS the estimated values are less than the critical values to accept the null of no unit.

Appendix – B.2
Cointegration LR Tests Based on Maximum Eigen Value of the Stochastic Matrix: Exports, Imports, Capital, GDP and Trade Policy

Eigen Value	*Null*	*Alternative*	*LR Statistics*	*Critical Values*
0.981	V= 0	V=1	127.51*	37.07
0.913	V≤ 1	V=2	78.31*	31.00
0.552	V≤ 2	V=3	25.70*	24.35
0.344	V≤ 3	V=4	13.50	18.33
0.009	V≤ 4	V=5	0.29	11.54

Note: * significant at 5% level

Appendix – B.3
Cointegration LR Tests Based on Maximum Trace of the Stochastic Matrix: Exports, Imports, Capital, GDP and Trade Policy

Eigen Value	*Null*	*Alternative*	*Trace Statistics*	*Critical Values*
0.981	V=0	V≥ 1	245.33*	82.23
0.913	V≤ 1	V≥ 2	117.82*	58.93
0.552	V≤ 2	V≥ 3	39.50*	39.33
0.344	V≤ 3	V≥ 4	13.80	23.83
0.009	V≤ 4	V≥ 5	0.29	11.54

Note: * significant at 5% level.

Part—II

Monetary Policy Issues

4

A Test of Monetarist Model of Imported Inflation

A Comparison of India' case with open Economics

Kishore Kulkarni *
*Meenakshi Rishi***

Introduction

There are some salient features of monetarist approach to the balance of payment: an approach which sets itself apart from other approaches such as Alexander's Absorption approach (1951) and Keynesian elasticity approach that uses the Marshall-Lerner condition. This paper intends to (1) carry out a survey of main arguments in monetary approach to balance of payment, (2) construct a model of imported inflation with the help of monetary approach to balance of payment arguments, and (3) use the model to explain the proportion of imported inflation in some relevant countries. We selected 7 countries to have a wide regional and structural representation.

Some of the main assumptions of monetary approach involve the stability of demand for money function, law of

---

* Kishore G. Kulkarni, Ph.D., Professor of Economics, Metropolitan State College of Denver, P.O.Box 173362, Campus Box 77, Denver, CO 80217-3362, USA.

** Meenakshi Rishi, Ph.D., Associate Professor of Economics, Ohio Northern University, Ada, Ohio, USA.

one price, free trade and fixed exchange rates. It further argues that capital account changes serve as the source of disturbances on balance of payment. In this model another crucial presumption is that money supply is expressed in broader term that includes foreign reserves as its component. Hence while the absorption approach makes "changes in current account" as the main source of changes in balance of payment, the monetary approach makes changes in capital account as the main reason for changes in balance of payments of an economy. Hence capital inflows (and outflows in the reverse direction) not only dictate the behavior of balance of payments, but also are the source of augmentation of money supply and therefore creation of inflation. We think estimating these equations to search for the relevance of this approach will be an interesting exercise. We selected following countries for this estimation: India, Malaysia, Belgium, the Netherlands, Singapore and Mexico.

The present paper is organized as follows: in Section 1 we describe the main theoretical arguments of monetary approach to balance of payments, discuss the relevant studies of empirical evidence on monetary approach and construct a testable model of this approach. Section 2 uses the model for testing the relevance of monetary approach to balance of payments. We use the data of 6 countries including that of India and compare the results. Section 3 consists of summary of our arguments and conclusion of the study.

Section 1

What is the Monetary Approach?

The origins of monetary approach to balance of payments are seen in the writing of Harry Johnson (1972) of University of Chicago and Robert Mundell (1968) of Columbia University. Basically monetary approach to balance of payment extends the monetarists' feelings that the main determinant of economic changes is the amount of a broadly defined money supply in an economy. This definition of money supply includes not only the domestically originated money but also the foreign reserves held in the economy. Hence it is based on the same basic arguments as the "monetarism" that was originated in the University of Chicago in 1950s and 1960s with pioneering work of Prof. Milton Friedman.

A typical monetary approach to balance of payment can be presented with the following monetarists' arguments: Consider that the demand for money is a stable function of the economy's general price level, real GDP, interest rate and some other variables represented by an error term.

Hence a quadratic form of demand for money function is given as

$$Md = f [(P\ Y\ u)/i] \tag{1}$$

Where M_d = quantity of money demanded

P = domestic general price level

J = price elasticity of demand for money

Y = real GDP

K = income elasticity of demand for money

U = error tem

i = interest rate

F = interest elasticity of demand for money

There is an expected positive effect of P and Y on the quantity of money demanded and an expected negative effect of interest rate on it. Consider further that economy's money supply is defined in broader terms. It consists of domestically originated money supply (D) and also the foreign reserves in the economy R. The domestic money D and R are used by the banking system to create additional money supply by giving loans. Hence (D + R) represents the monetary base or high-powered money in the system. If m is the money multiplier then one can express total money supply of an economy as follows:

$$MS = m(D + R) \tag{2}$$

If interest rate is assumed to be flexible then via money market equilibrium mechanism, the quantity of money demanded will always be equal to quantity of money supplied. Hence using equation 1 and 2 above we can get the money market equilibrium when

$$(P\ Y\ u)/\ i = m(D + R) \tag{3}$$

Taking logarithms on both sides of equation (3) we can get

$$J\log P + k\log Y + \log u - F\ (\log i) = \log m + \log\ (D + R) \tag{4}$$

Differentiating equation (4) with respect to time (t) and expressing the growth rates of these variables over the period of times we can rewrite equation (4) as:

$$J(1/P)(dp/dt) + K(1/Y)(dY/dt) + (1/u)(du/dt) - F(1/i)(di/dt)$$
$$= (1/m)(dm/dt) + [D/D+R](1/D)(dD/dt) + [R/D+R](1/R)(dR/dt) \tag{5}$$

Expressing growth rates over time as "g" so that (1/P)(dP/dt) becomes gP and (1/Y)(dY/dt) becomes gY and so on, and replacing D+R by H to simplify, we can rewrite equation (5) as

$$JgP + KgY + gu - Fgi = gm + (D/H)gD + (R/H)gR \tag{6}$$

Typically the monetary approach to balance of payment treats the last term (R/H)gR as the dependent variable and expresses changes in it as dependent upon remaining variables in equation (6). Hence we can rewrite the monetary approach to balance of payment statement as follows:

$$(R/H)gR = JgP + KgY + gu - Fgi - gm - (D/H)gD \tag{7}$$

Equation (7) has become famous testable format of the monetary approach to balance of payment. It claims that changes in foreign reserves are reflections of changes in domestic economic variables such as interest rate, price level, real GDP, domestic money supply etc. More interesting for policy purposes is the effect of domestic money supply changes. A further modification and analysis in monetary terms is made as follows:

1. Notice the negative sign of the last variable in equation (7). It means that an increase in money supply of domestically originated kind, creates a negative change in foreign reserves. Hence an increase in domestic money supply would create a decline in foreign reserves of the economy. This is the popularly called offset- coefficient that became popular limitation for monetary policy effectiveness in 1970s. In this paper we test the value of this offset coefficient.

2. One can realize the changes in other domestic variables affecting balance of payment in monetarist terms. For example increase in real GDP is expected to make an increase in foreign reserves and therefore a surplus in balance of payment. This is because an increase in real GDP creates greater demand for money and if the domestic monetary policy does not satisfy this demand by increasing domestic money supply, then the financial capital flows in from outside. This generates capital inflow and therefore a surplus in balance of payment. This conclusion is exactly opposite of what elasticity approach or absorption approach will come up with. In both these approaches, an increase in real GDP increases the domestic import and creates a deficit in balance of payments. Therefore monetary approach is unique in its explanation and conclusion.

3. An increase in domestic interest rate (i), one may expect, to create surplus in balance of payment by attracting outside financial capital. But in monetary approach statement of the above an increase in interest rate will create excess supply of money in the economy as the demand for money decreases with increase in interest rate. This leads to capital outflow and hence a deficit in balance of payment. This conclusion is again in stark contrast with the absorption and elasticity approaches. In those approaches, an increase in interest rate has a negative effect on gross domestic real investment. Hence increase in interest rate reduces investment, which reduces absorption and makes balance of trade to be in surplus creating a surplus on balance of payment.

Thus for monetarist approach to balance of payment thinking, effect of interest rate change on demand for money is enormously more important than the effect of interest rate change on the real investment.

4. Few studies (such as Kulkarni (1984)) have turned equation (7) into monetarist way of explaining the importance of domestic verses foreign money supply on the domestic inflation rate. Second focus of this paper is to investigate that effect further. One can arrange equation (7) to express the growth rate of domestic price level (call inflation) to be dependent upon the remaining variables in equation (7) as follows:

$$JgP = (R/H)gR - KgY - gu + Fgi + gm + (D/H)gD \qquad (8)$$

Equation (8) justifies all the monetarist propositions of inflation formation. Therefore in monetarists' way of thinking, inflation is a monetary phenomenon as can be observed by the effect of domestic money supply growth (the last term).

What is more important for our purposes is the effect of growth rate in foreign reserves (R) on the inflation. This gives us the idea of "imported inflation" or the part of inflation that can be blamed on the foreign money supply growth. As expected, the growth of real GDP has a negative effect on price level giving us the existence of supply side (in other terms, cost-push inflation). Effect of interest rate on inflation is the so called "Fisher effect" as measured by the importance of Fgi in equation (8). Therefore to test the validity of monetarist propositions of inflation formation, testing equation (8) is also important. We carry out the econometric exercises in the next section

Section 2

Econometric Analysis and Empirical Evidence of Seven Countries

To estimate the econometric results, we converted equation (8) in a more testable form as

$$PDOT = YDOT + int\ DOT + m\ DOT + DDOT + RDOT \qquad (9)$$

Where PDOT = growth rate of prices as measured by consumer price index (CPI),

int DOT = growth rate of interest rate as measured by call money rate

YDOT = rate of growth of real GDP as measured by nominal GDP deflated by CPI,

m DOT = rate of growth of money multiplier. Money multiplier is measured as a ratio of money supply M2 and (domestic credit + total foreign reserves)

DDOT = rate of growth of domestic credit. Domestic credit is measured by Central Bank's net holdings of assets and liabilities,

RDOT = rate of growth of total foreign reserves. Foreign reserves are measured by the sum of gold holdings, foreign reserves and special drawing rights (SDRs).

Our main interest among other things is the effect of RDOT on the growth rate of prices. The estimated coefficient for this variable will measure the "imported inflation" if there is any present for that economy. Of course if the inflation is not a sever problem or if the foreign reserves do not bring a serious impact on the domestic money supply then this coefficient can be insignificant but it is the main point of monetarists' argument that it is quite possible that a part of inflation is imported from outside.

Moreover if RDOT is significant to explain the domestic inflation then the domestic monetarist policy either needs to sterilize the foreign flow of reserves by lowering the domestic part of money supply (D) or accept the depreciation of domestic currency to offset the foreign reserves inflow. If this variable is insignificant then these steps are less desirable and domestic monetary policy in this case can concentrate on the economic growth targeting.

Before running the regressions all data sets were cleaned for stationarity. We collected data of 6 countries by using the International Monetary Fund's publication of International Financial Statistics Yearbook, for 26 year sample size for all countries, ranging from year 1972 to 1997. (Except in case of India where data start from 1971). Hence before carrying out the regression we made sure that the data look robust. In most cases in order to get complete effect of independent variables, we lagged the variables on right side by one period.

Following is the list of time series, ordinary least square (OLS) results for each country:

India

$$PDOT = 13.20 + .0183\ intDOT(-1) - .688\ YDOT(-1) + .19\ MDOT(-1)$$
$$(6.07) \quad (0.568) \quad (-2.49) \quad (1.49)$$
$$+ 3.60\ DUMMY - .0978\ RDOT(-1) - .315\ DDOT$$
$$(3.60) \quad (-2.131) \quad (-1.152)$$

R-squared = .349 Standard Error of Regression 5.48. Durbin Watson statistic 2.007. Figures in the parenthesis represent t statistic for the estimated variable.

From the above results it appears that for Indian case the effect of domestic money supply on inflation is positive (not significant) and that of foreign reserves it is negative (but significant). Dummy variable is expected to represent all other variables that matter for domestic inflation determination but that is not a very significant either. One can partially rationalize these results in the Indian case by pointing out that in recent times the inflation rate has been quite moderate (less than 10%) and therefore these variables lose their ability to explain the inflation. All other indicators of regressions namely Durbin Watson statistic and standard error of regression are satisfactory which means there is an absence of autocorrelation and the model is correctly set. R square is decent, but not very impressive (.34)

Belgium

PDOT=5.505+.052intDOT(–1) –.204YDOT(–1) –.016 MDOT(–1)
(4.92) (2.86) (–.641) (–.077)
–.0086 DDOT(–1) –.0128 RDOT(–1)
(–.225) (–.295)

R-square = .318, Standard Error of Regression:= 3.01 and Durbin Watson Statistic = .64

The Belgium case is a bad news for monetary approach. Except for interest rate none of the variables have expected sign nor are they significant in explaining Belgian inflation. Only a positive effect of interest rate on domestic inflation justifies the Fisher Effect. All other relevant statistics are miserably poor: R square is low, Standard error is too high and Durbin Watson statistic is unsatisfactory being too far away from 2.0 indicating presence of autocorrelation. Thus Belgium economy shows no evidence supporting the monetarists' arguments for imported inflation.

Malaysia

$$PDOT = \underset{(-1.688)}{-2.348} \underset{(-.465)}{-.0059intDOT(-1)} + \underset{(1.745)}{.28YDOT(-1)} + \underset{(2.332)}{.291MDOT(-1)} \underset{(4.942)}{+.2254DDOT(-1)} \underset{(1.091)}{+.031RDOT(-1)}$$

R squared = .656, standard error of regression = 2.298, Durbin Watson Statistic = 1.658

There are better results for Malaysia from the perspective of monetarist model. While money multiplier (MDOT), domestic money supply and foreign reserves all have expected signs for their coefficients, domestic money supply in fact was significant in explaining inflation. This inflation therefore was indeed a monetary phenomenon! All other relevant statistics are satisfactory. However only a small portion of inflation is explained by foreign reserves hence the foreign inflows and outflows have little to say about the inflation generation domestically.

The Netherlands

$$PDOT = \underset{(.261)}{.28} + \underset{(.406)}{.00337intDOT(-1)} - \underset{(-1.085)}{.314YDOT(-1)} + \underset{(4.126)}{.663MDOT(-1)} + \underset{(4.896)}{.468DDOT(-1)} \underset{(2.984)}{+.0997RDOT(-1)}$$

R squared = .608, Standard Error of Regression = 2.114, Durbin Watson Statistic= 1.132

Just like in case of Malaysia, the Dutch inflation is nicely explained by monetary variables: both money multiplier and domestic money supply growth rate is significant and with expected positive sign to their coefficients. Thus overall inflation was explained by excessive money supply of domestic origination. R squared is satisfactory and standard error of regression is not very high. Nonetheless as in case of Malaysia, the foreign reserves flows do not make a great impact on domestic inflation, indicating that only a small part of inflation is imported from outside.

Mexico

PDOT = 3.859 + .0781intDOT(–1) – .391YDOT(–1) + .394MDOT(–1)
(.192) (.4144) (–.533) (.7605)
+ .659DDOT(–1) +.0651RDOT(–1)
(1.71) (.8101)

R squared = .4523 Standard Error of Regression = 35.974. Durbin Watson Statistic = 1.222.

Above estimation shows that just like in case of Belgium, Mexican inflation is not a monetary phenomenon. There are neither the expected signs for the important estimated coefficients nor are they very significant for explaining the inflation. The R squared is miserably low indicating low degree of relationship and standard error of regression is very high indicating questionable setting of the model. Thus monetary model is irrelevant for Mexico (and as mentioned before for Belgium).

Singapore

PDOT=2.3113+.0731intDOT(–1)+.0152YDOT(–1)+.0188MDOT(–1)
(1.192) (7.519) (.0856) (.2166)
+.0344DDOT(–1) – .0138RDOT(–1)
(1.106) (–.1838)

R-squared = .8579, Standard Error of Regression = 1.988, Durbin Watson Statistic = 1.854

In case of Singapore, the most significant coefficient is the interest rate showing the existence of Fisher effect that relates the inflation rate and interest rates in the economy. From the t-statistic values none of the other explanatory variables are important definitely not the monetary variables such as growth rate of money multiplier, domestic money supply growth rate or the growth rate of foreign reserve inflow. The R-squared is moderately high showing a good relationship, standard error of regression is reasonably low and the Durbin Watson statistic is not far away from the magic figure of 2.0. In general Singaporean case is not a great support for our monetary model. Hence the inflation is explained by other factors that the monetary factors in Singapore.

In order to confirm the results of above time series analysis, we tried another estimation. We pooled the data of all countries mentioned above and ran a cross sectional (pooled least squares) regression. The results showed no improvement, attesting to the belief that monetary model does not do a very good job of explaining inflation as a creation of foreign inflows.

Section 3

Summary and Conclusion

This paper had an objective of revising the imported inflation model of monetarism by carrying out a theoretical argument, and using the data of six countries to testify the validity of monetarists' assertion that all inflations are always and everywhere a monetary phenomenon. Another main aim was to see if international capital inflows create (or add to) inflation in the economy. Our OLS results for six countries show that with exception of two countries inflation is not a result of foreign reserve inflows. Hence the monetary model of imported inflation does not perform very well to explain the inflation generation. Therefore we join the growing camp of Rogoff (1999) that is suspicious about the explanatory capability of monetary models in modern times. While Rogoff uses the models for testing exchange determination, ours tests the inflation creation.

BIBLIOGRAPHY AND REFERENCES

1. Bilson, J.F.O., "The Monetary Approach to Exchange Rate: Some Empirical Evidence". *IMF Staff Papers*, 1978, pp. 235-242.

2. Boughton, J.M.' "The Monetary Approach to Exchange Rates: What Now Remains?", Essays in International Finance, No. 171, Princeton University Press, Princeton, NJ, October 1988.

3. Frenkel, J.A., "Exchange Rates, Prices and Money: Lessons from the 1920s", *American Economic Review*, 1980, pp. 235-242.

4. Frenkel, J.A., "A Monetary Approach to the Exchange Rate: Doctrinal Aspects and Empirical Evidence", *Scandinavian Journal of Economics*, March 1976, pp. 200-224.

5. Frenkel, J.A, "Monetary and Portfolio Balance Models of Determination of Exchange Rates" in J.A.Frenkel edited, On Exchange Rates, MIT Press, Cambridge Mass., 1993, pp. 95-116.

6. Johnson, Happy, "The Monetary Approach to the Balance of Payments", *Journal of Financial and Quantitative Analysis*, March 1972, pp. 1555-1572.

7. Kemp, Donald, "A Monetary View of the Balance of Payments", Federal Reserve Bank of St. Louis Review, April 1975, pp. 14-72.

8. Kreinin, Mordechai and Officer, Lawrence, "The Monetary Approach to the Balance of Payments: A Survey", Princeton Studies in International Finance, No. 43, University of Princeton, 1978.

9. Kulkarni, Kishore, "The Monetary Approach to the Balance of Payments and Importation of Inflation: A Further Analysis and Empirical Evidence", *Studies in Economic Analysis*, Fall 1984, pp. 11-25.

10. Macdonald R. and Taylor M.P., "The Monetary Approach to the Exchange Rate: Rational Expectations, Long-Run Equilibrium and Forecasting", *IMF Staff Papers*, March 1993, pp. 89-107.

11. Mundell, Robert, "International Economics", Macmillan Publishers, New York, 1968, Chapters 9, 11 and 15.

12. Mussa, Michael, "A Monetary Approach to the Balance of Payment Analysis", *Journal of Money, Credit and Banking*, August 1974, pp. 333-351.

13. Rogoff K.. "Monetary Models of Dollar/Yen/Euro Nominal Exchange Rtaes: Dead or Alive?", *The Economic Journal*, November 1999, pp. 655-659.

14. Salvatore, Dominick, "International Economics", John Wiley Publications, Seventh Edition, Appendix of Chapter 15, 2001.

5

Do Fiscal Deficits and Money Supply Determine Interest Rate in India?

*Hrushikesh Mallick**

*Purna Chandra Parida***

Introduction

In the recent past, the focus of most of the developing countries has been concentrated on macroeconomic policy management to maintain their economic stability and achieve higher economic growth. It may be due to the macroeconomic fluctuations of these countries characterised by economic downturns, and possibly the mismanagement of macroeconomic policies during the last few decades. The persistent distorted interest rate structure could be considered as one of the clear-cut examples of macroeconomic instability in these countries. It is evident from the economic literature that deviation of interest rate either at a higher or at a lower rate from its market determined equilibrium position is considered as one of the pertinent factors for macroeconomic instability in developing countries like India. The higher interest rate structure not

* Research Fellow, Economics Unit, Institute for Social and Economic Change (ISEC), Nagarabhavi, Bangalore-72.

** Research Fellow, RBI Endowment Unit, Institute for Social and Economic Change (ISEC), Nagarbhavi, Bangalore-72.

only presages the danger of recession, but also pushes the economy into the debt trap situation (Morley et. al, 1987). Similarly, lower rate of interest not only creates financial distortion but also disturbs the whole macro-economy by affecting the macroeconomic variables at their equilibrium growth path. Most often, it is argued that developing countries should work out policy strategies in order to bring down the higher interest rate to a minimum requirement level, which could be conducive for achieving higher economic growth (Tobin, 1965). On the other hand, it is viewed that a lower rate of interest regime discourages private sector savings as well as national savings and hence creates hindrances for the growth of an economy through the operation of various transmission channels. In India, there has been significant structural transformation of interest rates in the recent years. Following the recommendation of the Narasimham Committee Report (1991), a major structural breakthrough in interest policy was initiated in early 1990's along with the other financial sector reforms. The monetary policy strategy of the Reserve Bank of India (RBI) suggests that it strongly pursued the policies to reduce the heavily placed monetised deficit of the government of India. It is intended to leave the market to determine the rate of interest by the natural forces of demand and supply in the economy. In India, fiscal and monetary policies are two important channels through which the monetary authority and government regulate the other macroeconomic fundamentals. However, it is evident that interest rate policy follows quite independent path from other policy changes. It was kept under artificial control by the monetary authority before it left to the market determination. In the recent period, interest rate has been brought down in order to create a healthy atmosphere for investment. On the other hand, although attempt has been made by the central government to reduce the fiscal deficits but still it remains a higher level. Even the fiscal deficits has gone up during some periods. Similarly, money supply has also increased over the periods (Table 8 in appendix-1). It is very important on the part of the policy maker to know the behavior of interest rate changes along with the changes of fiscal and monetary situation in India. In this context, the present study makes an attempt to examine the influence of fiscal deficits and the money supply on interest rate under a gradual liberalised financial regime.

The rest of the study is organized into five sections. Section 2 analyses the interest rate policy scenario in India. A theoretical background of relationship among interest rates, fiscal deficits and money supply is discussed in section 3. Section 4 surveys the review of previous empirical works. Empirical results with discussion are reported in section 5 and last section concludes the study.

Interest Rates Policy in India

In India, there has been significant structural transformation of interest rates over the period. It was characterized as a regulated or what can be called as a repressed interest rate system during 1958 to 1985 (Bhole, 1999). Keeping in mind the higher level of budget deficit of the central government and the resources required to finance it, the rate of interest on treasury bill (TB) was deliberately kept at low. This was done with a view to keep the cost of government borrowing at a lower level and to help the government in the matters of internal debt management policy (Rangarajan, 1998).

The major breakthrough of interest rate policy was initiated in early 1990s with the financial sector reforms. A committee chaired by M. Narasimham was set up in 1991 to bring more transparency in the financial sector. In order to impart a greater flexibility to the banks and to make the monetary system financially stronger, the committee recommended that reserve requirements should be lowered and there should be certain changes with regard to the interest rates, which would reflect market conditions.

In order to make the government security market more vibrant, a new instrument of 364-day treasury bill was introduced in April 1992 and sold by auction, together with the withdrawal of 182-day treasury bill on April 1992. With a view to further develop the capital (security) market by moving towards a market related interest rate and offering investors a wide range of choices, the auction system was extended to the issue of 91-day treasury bill from January 1993. The auction for 91-day TB was conducted weekly and RBI participates as a non-competitive bidder. Before the introduction of auction system in 91-day TB for the improvement in liquidity position of the government security market, RBI announced conduction of auctions of Repurchase Agreements (Repos) for the Central Government dated securities from Bank's portfolio. This procedure of RBI was intended to bring changes in the liquidity position of the economy and also the rate of interest. This system was continued on regular basis till the end of February 1995, after which it had been discontinued temporarily due to low demand for Repos (RBI Annual Report, 1993).

An important step was taken both by the Government of India and the RBI in the year 1994-95 by fixing a cap on net issue of *ad-hoc* treasury bills for the year 1994-95 and proposing a complete phase out of *ad-hoc* treasury bills by the year 1997-98. This was done through a supplementary agreement by the Government of India and the RBI. This agreement recommended that the issue of *ad-hoc* TB should not exceed more than Rs. 6000 crores for the year 1994-95. Further, if its net issue exceeds Rs. 9000 crores for more than ten continuous working days, at any time during the year, the RBI will automatically reduce the level of *ad-hoc* TB by auctioning it or by selling fresh Government of India dated securities in the market.

The agreement envisaged that ceiling to be stipulated only for the year 1995-96 and 1996-97. (RBI Annual Report, 1994-95).

Facilitating the emergence of a more comprehensive yield curve, a scheme of a new category of 14-days TB on auction basis was approved on May 1997. The first auction of the bills was held on June 1997 with an implicit yield of 4.95 per cent. (RBI Bulletin 1996-97, Supplement). The Bank Rate (BR) was reactivated to serve as a reference rate as well as signalling mechanism to reflect the stance of monetary policy during 1997-98. In fact, interest rate on accommodations from RBI were linked to Bank Rate until 1997-98. Reflecting the prevailing liquidity conditions, BR was reduced in 3 steps of 1 per cent point each in April, June and October 1997 to 9 per cent per annum in Oct. 1997.

Following the reductions in BR by 1.5 per cent in April 1998, major public sector commercial banks reduced their PLR and deposit rates in April 1998. The signalling impact of changes in BR was felt on deposit and lending rates in credit market during this period. The reduction in BR in March 1999 promoted major public sector banks to reduce their deposit rates to 8-10.5 per cent. As far as lending rate for the year 1998 is concerned, it was reduced by 2 per cent and the ceiling rate on loans for the amount below Rs.25, 000 was fixed at PLR of banks.

It is important to note that the 182-day Treasury bill was reintroduced on May 1999. The issue of these securities was fixed at amount of Rs 100 crore up to August 1999 with an implicit cut off yield rate varying within the range of 9.31 and 9.97 per cent. In order to control such floating of TB with varying maturities, the RBI resorted to an active Open Market Operation (OMO) during the year 1999. This strategy was intended to neutralise large amount of private placement of Government securities and to maintain an orderly flow of liquidity in the market. Recently, RBI has brought some changes in the interest rates on small savings and provident funds to make it alignment with other market rates. The interest rates on small savings instruments were reduced with effect from January 2000 in line with the recommendation of a committee of experts on small savings (RBI Bulletin, 2000).

The above discussion on monetary policy strategy suggests that since 1990's, the RBI has taken strong policy measures to bring down the heavily placed monetised government deficits. The reason is that heavy monetisation of fiscal deficits allows little flexibility to the monetary authority in discharging its policy obligations. The higher level of monetisation neutralises the open market operations (OMO), which makes it difficult on the part of the RBI to exercise the correct policy measures in order to achieve the macroeconomic stability in the economy (Rangarajan, 1998). The accommodation of fiscal policy in the monetary policy takes away the freedom of the monetary authority to exercise the desirable policy measures. Further, an increase in government deficits through market borrowing provides a little option for the RBI to stabilize the interest rates in India. However, in the recent past, the RBI is able to reduce the monetised deficits signalling its flexibility in its policy operations. Further, in order to make a healthy environment for investment, the rate of interest in India is gradually left to the market determination. Hence, in an economic environment where a number of policy steps are being undertaken in respect of fiscal adjustments with the simultaneous monetary measures in a direction to impart gradual liberalisation in the financial market, it is worthwhile to examine the impact of fiscal deficits and money supply on interest rates in the context of India.

Theoretical Background

The theory of rate of interest determination could be dated back from Adam Smith to Keynes. According to classical school, the supply of and demand for capital under free and perfect competition determine the rate of interest. This school suggest that interest rate arises because capital is 'productive' and 'scarce' in relation to demand for it. In fact, Neo-classical school asserted that demand for and supply of loanable funds determine the rate of interest in an economy. The Keynesian theory, however, opposed to the classical *real* theory of interest rate determination. In his liquidity preference theory, Keynes argued that rate of interest is influenced by the monetary authority (Central Bank) through the variation in the money supply. The essence of Keynes' theory of liquidity preference is that the quantity of money, along with the liquidity preference determines the rate of interest. However, all these theories proved to be indeterminate for determination of interest rate when they considered separately (Hicks, 1939). Taking into account both the classical and Keynesian viewpoint a more integrated theory known as general equilibrium theory of rate of interest was developed under the IS–LM framework.

The nexus between fiscal deficits and interest rates is well documented in the form of IS-LM framework. In this framework, an increase in deficits (whether because of an increase in government expenditure or a fall in tax revenues or both) corresponds to an increase in autonomous demand or an outward shift of the IS curve, resulting rise in nominal interest rates. Further, fiscal deficit can influence rate of interest when it increases, at least part of the increase will be financed by the supply of government bonds, which will in turn depress the government securities prices and raise the yields on securities. However, the impact of fiscal deficits on rate of interest differs the way by which it is being financed. In general it is financed either through borrowing from the public (i.e., selling of bonds) or by borrowing from the central bank (i.e., monetised deficits). If it is financed through monetization, it directly leads to the increase of reserve money in the economy. Increase in reserve money leads to higher aggregate money supply and shifts the LM curve outwardly. This will lead to a greater increase in the aggregate demand, and therefore output and interest rate. But if it will be financed by market borrowing, it will lead to higher interest rate. However, increase in interest rate in the latter process would be higher than the former method of financing.

The IS-LM type of framework on interest rate and fiscal deficits is disputed by Barro (1974) and on the contrary, he supported the *Ricardian Equivalence Theorem* (RET). He claims that there is "debt-neutrality" in the economy. In other words, it makes no difference whether the deficit is financed through taxes or by bonds, the effects remain same. The mechanism runs like this: an increase of deficits is matched by expectations of higher future taxes, calling forth more current saving in order to meet the taxes in the future. The generation of additional savings, if exactly equal with the value of supply of government bonds, the nominal rate of interest would be unaffected (Dornbusch et al, 1998, pp.481-84). On the other hand, if it is financed through money creation, it enables the government to get along with lower tax revenue, which produces higher inflation in the economy. Higher inflation in turn reduces the real value of the outstanding debt, which is hold by the debt holders. If people anticipate that inflation tax is the consequence of expected money growth to finance deficits, the Ricardian equivalence theorem suggests that the deficit finance has no real effect on the interest rates.

The relationship between money supply growth and rate of interest could be explained through five distinct effects. The first one is the announcement effect. According to this effect, a positive monetary innovation (i.e., a larger than expected growth in money supply) usually leads the market to anticipate a higher growth rate of money in the future. This expected permanent higher money growth rate induces an increase in expected inflation, which pushes up interest rate upward in order to meet inflationary premium. The second effect is the Keynesian 'liquidity effect'. As the money supply increases, income and prices may slowly react to it, which would lead to a situation of excess liquidity at unchanging nominal income levels. The third effect is known as 'financial effect'. This effect states that when growth of money increases, banks find themselves saddled with excess reserves. This excess reserve cannot be immediately absorbed into the banks' portfolios, which have to be temporarily parked in short-term market securities, lowering the short-term interest rates. In fact, after some time as banks unwind their holding of securities to refurbish their loan portfolios, the effect on interest rates is reversed. There is also income effect, which affects the nominal interest rates. It has been argued that increase in money supply raises the income level. Higher the income level more is the demand for money, which ultimately reduces the real balances and pushes up the nominal interest rates. Finally, there is a Fisher or 'Price Expectations Effect' as the nominal interest rate accommodates fully a change in expected inflation.

The above theoretical perspectives suggest that both fiscal deficits and money supply influence the rate of interest directly or indirectly. On the basis of above theoretical background, the present study attempts to explore the relationship among these three macroeconomic fundamentals in the Indian context.

Empirical Review

There are only few studies have examined the long run relationship of interest rates with fiscal deficits and money supply. The existing literature in the context of developed countries concentrated exclusively the impact of budget deficits rather than fiscal deficits on interest rates. The reason may be due to the fact that developed countries used the concept of budget deficits analogously with the fiscal deficit. Nevertheless, the meaning and measurement of these two concepts are differed widely from each other in India. Indeed, very few studies examine the impact of budget deficit on interest rates (Nachane et. al., 1997). In fact, the budget deficit in India does not fully reflect the indebtedness of the government as it excludes a part of total borrowings of the government. But fiscal deficits portray the real gap arising in the government budget. Apart from considering the market borrowings fiscal deficit includes the monetized deficit, which is a major part of total borrowing, and can have significant influence on money supply and interest rates. In this context, it is imperative to study the relationship between interest rates along with money supply and fiscal deficit. This section reviews some of the existing studies to provide a background and justification for the present study.

In the empirical literature, the results are so diverse that anyone can support strongly to any particular theoretical position. For instance, Plossser (1987), Evans (1987) did not find any relationship between the budget deficit and the interest rates in context of U.S economy. On the contrary, Gupta & Moazzami (1991), Modigliani & Jappelli (1988) and other studies evidenced a significant relationship between the two across countries including the U.S.

The study by Hoelscher (1983) examines the relationship between Federal borrowing and short-term interest rates. This study uses Loanable Funds model, which specifies the rate of interest as a linear function of the expected rate of inflation, the unemployment rate as a proxy for the effects of cyclical economic activity on income and saving, the real borrowing by the Federal government, and the real purchases of securities by the central bank. The study finds that there is no significant relationship between Federal borrowing and short-term interest rates.

Further, it reports that the prime determinants of the interest rate are expected inflation, monetary factors, and economic activity.

In the context of US economy, Evans (1985) verifies the relationship between interest rates and deficits. The study uses a reduced form equation derived from the IS-LM model. The equation contains interest rate as a function of the real government expenditure, the real deficit, the real money supply, and the expected inflation rate. The results of the study indicate that there is no evidence of positive association between deficits and interest rates. Another study by Hoelscher (1986) examines the relationship between federal borrowing and long-term interest rates. It uses a similar loanable funds model as in his earlier work where the long term nominal rate of interest as a function of the expected rate of inflation, the GNP, the deficit, and the short term rate of interest. The result indicates that deficit causes higher long-term interest rate.

Considering the conventional macroeconomic theory, Evan (1987) tested the relationship between interest rate and budget deficits in the context of US economy. Using the OLS method on monthly time series data over the period from June 1908 to March 1984, it found no evidence of interest rate related to budget deficits. A study by Monadjemi (1989) examined the international evidence on the interest rate consequences of financing deficits in the context of five OECD countries. The study tested the relationship of these two variables both in the fixed and flexible exchange rate regimes. Applying OLS method, it found that interest rate maintains neutrality with changes in budget deficits and hence, it contrasts to the traditional view of large budget deficits cause higher interest rate.

Gupta and Moazzami (1991) assessed the impact of budget deficits on interest rates in the U.S. by using the

ARCH model proposed by Wickens and Breusch (1988). The result of the study suggested that budget deficits have significant and positive impact on the interest rate. Thus, the study contradicted the Ricardian equivalence proposition. Further, using both the instrumental variable estimation method and variance decomposition analysis of time series model Gupta and Moazzami (1996) examined the impact of a number of variables including budget deficit and money supply upon the interest rates in context of eleven developed countries, such as Australia, Belgium, Canada, France, Germany, Italy, Japan, Netherlands, Sweden, U.K. U.S.A., in the period from 1970:1 to 1990:4. From the overall result, they observed that deficits neither have exerted any short-term nor long-term impacts on short interest rates in Australia, Germany and the Netherlands but Canada was the only country for which deficits had a positive short-term and long-term effect on the short-run interest rates. As far as the money supply and the rates of interest were concerned, he found that money growth had a negative and significant effect on short-term interest rates in Australia, France, Germany, Japan, and Sweden but it had no influence in Belgium, Canada, Italy, the Netherlands, the U.K. and the U.S.A.

Using the IS-LM model, Saltz (1993) verifies the impact of budget deficits on both ex-post short-term and long-term real interest rates for the period from 1955 to 1985 in the context of US economy. From the regression results, the study finds that deficits do not exert any significant impact upon the ex-post short-term real interest rates. However, it reports that deficits have significant impact on the long-term real interest rates.

The study by Cebula and Belton (1993) empirically investigates the impact of government budget deficits in the United States on two short-term interest rates and three long-term interest rates. It includes net international capital flows as an additional variable in the IS-LM model. The findings of the study suggest that deficits do not affect the nominal short-term interest rates. In fact, it reports that deficits raise the long-term nominal interest rates.

In the Indian context, it is rare to find any study examined the relationship between fiscal deficits, money supply and interest rate. The reason may be due to the fact that only very recently interest rates have been left to the market. Further, the concept of fiscal deficits in India has got an importance in the recent decade. Using a co-integration technique, the study by Nachane et. al. (1997) tests the relationship between interest rates, money supply and budget deficits. It begins with certain priors: (1) that nominal interest response to money supply increases typically a small duration rise (announcement effect), followed by a fall, (liquidity effect and part of financial effect) and then an ultimate rise (financial, income and Fisher effects) and (2) Nominal interest rates respond positively to budget deficit increases. Using monthly data from April 1992 to June 2001, the study strongly supports the proposition that budgetary deficit raises interest rates. However, the result of the study may be partial because it does not consider fiscal deficits and rather uses budget deficits, which represents only one part of the total deficits.

Empirical Results and Discussion

The present study uses Johansen's Maximum Likelihood co-integration technique to examine the long run equilibrium relationship among the variables underlying the interest rate functions. Further, to know the casual relationship among the variables, the study applies Vector Autoregressive (VAR) method in terms of variance decomposition in each of the interest rate functions. The period of study covers from 1997:4 to 2001:6. The data used are monthly observations and comprise of two short-term real interest rates (91-days and 364-days real treasury bill rates), real gross fiscal deficits, and real broad money supply (M_3). Data for nominal interest rates and nominal money supply are collected from various *issues of monthly bulletins of Reserve Bank of India (RBI)* and nominal gross fiscal deficits is collected from the report of comptroller and auditor general of India (or as seen in www.nic.in).

The present study uses following standard specification of interest rate function for two different real interest rates as:

$$\text{In RIR91} = \beta_0 + \beta_1 \text{ In RFD} + \beta_2 \text{ In RMS} + \varepsilon_t \quad (1)$$

$$\text{In RIR364} = \gamma_0 + \gamma_1 \text{ In RFD} + \gamma_2 \text{ In RMS} + \varepsilon_{t1} \quad (2)$$

Where, RIR91 represents real interest rate on 91-day treasury bills, RFD indicates real gross fiscal deficits, RMS represents real broad money supply and RIR364 indicates real interest rate on 364-day treasury bills.

The study applies simple ordinary least square (OLS) method to estimate the above two equations. The results of the OLS regression are reported in Table 1. In case of RIR91 as dependent variable, the results demonstrate a good statistical fit as evidenced from its high-adjusted R^2. The coefficient of RFD is 0.465, which shows the expected sign in the context of India. It could be substantiated that

Table 1: Simple OLS Regression Results for RIR91 and RIR364 as Dependent Variables

Dependent Variables	*Constant*	*RFD*	*RMS*	R^2	*D-W*
RIR91	9.966 (1.731)	0.465 (1.082)	-1.315 (-1.280)	0.96	0.434
RIR364	22.751 (3.931)	0.213 (0.493)	–.698 (–3.580)	0.97	0.340

Note: All variables are expressed in log terms and defined in real terms. The variable RFD = real gross fiscal deficits, RMS = real money supply, RIR91 = 91-day real Treasury bill rate and RIR364 = 364-day real Treasury bill rate.

in the last few years the government of India has drastically reduced its reliance on monetised deficit and opted more in terms of market borrowings. Such a policy strategy of financing the deficit theoretically suggests that it creates market pressure on the domestic interest rate as a result with the increase in market borrowing it leads to the rise in interest rates. However, the coefficient of RFD is not statistically significant even at 10 percent level, hence; no policy suggestion could be derived from this. The coefficient of RMS also possesses expected sign (–1.315) indicating Keynesian theory holds well in the context of India. However, similar to the RFD variable, it is not statistically significant. In contrast to the case of RIR91, the results in case of RIR364 produces better outcome, where both the explanatory variables such as RFD and RMS possess the expected sign and the coefficient of RFD is statistically significant at 5 percent level. It indicates that deficit finance has strong impact on the real interest rates in India. It is evident that the results produce high-adjusted R^2 implying the interest rate in India is well explained by both the fiscal deficit and money supply variables. However, it is important to note that in both the cases there is evidence of low D-W statistics, which implies a possible spurious regression due to the probable presence of first-order autocorrelation. This may be due to the non-stationary nature of data and hence it needs unit root tests and application of co-integration technique to see whether there is any long-run equilibrium relationship among the variables.

Before applying co-integration technique and interpreting the results of co-integration, as per the usual general time series procedure, the study first examines the stationarity of all variables. In this regard, it applies three unit root tests namely, Dickey-Fuller (DF), Augumented Dickey-Fuller (ADF), and Phillips-Perron (PP) tests. The result of unit root tests is reported in Table 2 and Table 3. The results in Table 2 confirm that all variables are non-stationary (except FD) indicating that they have unit roots. However, results in Table 3 evidence that at their first difference all variables are becoming stationary rejecting the null hypothesis of unit root, that is, all series are integrated of order one i.e. [I (1)].

Table 2: Unit Root Tests

Variables	*With Levels*					
	Without Trend			*With Trend*		
	DF	*ADF*	*PP*	*DF*	*ADF*	*PP*
RFD	-8.763	-6.024(1)	-8.901(1)	-9.029	-6.358(1)	-9.248(1)
RIR91	-2.580	-2.227(1)	-2.508(2)	-2.757	-2.422(1)	-2.697(2)
RIR364	-1.847	-1.532(1)	-1.684(2)	-2.284	-1.999(1)	-2.176(2)
RMS	-0.197	-0.231(1)	-0.215(1)	-2.897	-3.503(1)	-3.176(1)

Note: All variables are in logs.

Table 3: Unit Root Tests

Variables	*With Differences*					
	Without Trend			*With Trend*		
	DF	*ADF*	*PP*	*DF*	*ADF*	*PP*
RFD	-14.313	-9.330(1)	-15.206(1)	-14.200	-9.255(1)	-15.368(1)
RIR91	-9.235	-7.158(1)	-9.405(1)	-9.268	-7.216(1)	-9.517(1)
RIR364	-9.205	-7.186(1)	-9.369(1)	-9.193	-7.199(1)	-9.435(1)
RMS	-7.041	-5.591(1)	-6.369(1)	-6.983	-5.543(1)	-9.435(1)

Note: All variables are in logs.

Confirming all variables are integrated at the same order, which is a necessary condition for the application of co-integration technique, the present study employs Johansen's maximum likelihood test to find out the long run equilibrium relationship among the variables. The result of co-integration test for interest rate function presented in the equation 1 is reported in Table 4. It is important to note that there is evidence of at least one co-integrating vector in the function. The value of trace statistics evidence that the null hypothesis of no co-integrating vector (r = 0) against the alternative hypothesis of one or more co-integrating vector (r > 0) is rejected at 5 % significance level. This is also evident in λ_{MAX} statistics, where the null hypothesis of no co-integrating vector (r = 0) against the alternative hypothesis of one co-integrating vector is rejected at 5 % significance level.

Table 4: Johansen Co-integration Results*

Null Hypothesis	*Alternative Hypothesis*		*Critical Values*	
			5%	10%
λ_{trace} test		λ_{trace} value		
r = 0	r > 0	40.338	29.68	26.79
r ≤ 1	r > 1	5.1558	15.14	13.33
r ≤ 2	r ≥ 2	0.628	3.76	2.69
λ_{MAX} test		λ_{MAX} value		
r = 0	r = 1	35.182	20.97	18.60
r =1	r = 2	4.525	14.07	12.07
r = 2	r = 3	0.628	3.76	2.69

Note: r refers to the number of co-integrating vectors.
* Based on the equation: RIR91 = f (FD, MS)

The co-integration result of interest rate function given in the equation 2 produces similar result as in the case of equation 1. The result in Table 5 shows that the value of trace statistics rejects the null hypothesis of no co-integrating vector (r = 0) against the alternative hypothesis of one or more co-integrated vector (r > 0) at 5 % significance level. The similar result is also evident from the value of λ_{MAX} statistics, where the null hypothesis of no co-integrating vector (r = 0) against the alternative hypothesis of one or more co-integrating vector is rejected at 5 % significance level. Hence, the result ensures that variables are co-integrated. That is to say, there exists long run equilibrium relationship among the variables. In general, the co-integration result suggests that variables such as real fiscal deficits, real money supply and two different interest rates considered here are related to each other in the long run.

Table 5: Johansen Co-integration Results*

Null Hypothesis	*Alternative Hypothesis*		*Critical Values*	
			5%	10%
λ_{trace} test		λ_{trace} value		
r = 0	r > 0	38.079	29.68	26.79
r ≤ 1	r > 1	2.824	15.14	13.33
r ≤ 2	r ≥2	0.108	3.76	2.69
λ_{MAX} test		λ_{MAX} value		
r = 0	r = 1	35.254	20.97	18.60
r =1	r = 2	2.176	14.07	12.07
r = 2	r = 3	0.108	3.76	2.69

Note: r refers to the number of co-integrating vectors.
* Based on the equation: RIR364 = f (FD, MS)

The above result of co-integration technique suggests that variables such as real fiscal deficits and real money supply are having long run equilibrium relationship with two real treasury bill rates. However, the dynamic adjustments that occur in the short run leading to a stable long run equilibrium relationship among the variables in response to various shocks to the system remain unspecified. This dynamic relationship among the series can be established through the variance decomposition analysis of the forecast errors at different time horizons. It is important to note that the study chooses best ordering out of different ordering of the variables. The order of the variables is real interest rate, real fiscal deficits and real money supply. It is also to note that the error variance decomposition is estimated with variables at their first difference, because all variables are found to be stationary at I (1). Further, using the Akaike Information Criteria and the Schwarz Bayesian criteria (SBC), the study determines the lag length as one.

The results of error variance decomposition for interest rate functions RIR91 and RIR364 are reported in Table 6 and Table 7 respectively. In Table 6, the error variance decomposition for 91-day real Treasury bill rate (RIR91) demonstrates that the error variance of 91-day real Treasury bill rate is largely explained by its own shocks and negligibly by money supply and real fiscal deficit variables. The result shows that in 1-step ahead time horizon, the error variance of RIR91 is fully explained by its own innovation. It could be noted that from 2-step to 24-step horizon, although the percentage of error variance of RIR91 explained by its own innovation is declining but still it is largely explained by itself. It is surprising that in a country like India, where the absolute level of fiscal deficit is at a higher level averaging around 5.2 percent of GDP does not have any influence on the rate of interest. The reasons may be due to the fact that fiscal and monetary policies in India are not effective enough as expected to be in a normal economic environment to effect the desired changes in the interest rate. Further, it is important to note that rate of interest in India is not completely left to the market. It is partially kept under control by the monetary authority, for which it is not reflecting the true equilibrium market determined interest rates. Hence, whenever change occurs in the demand and supply sides as reflected in the changes of policy variables, it might not produce desired influence on the interest rates. The true response is getting offset by the artificial pressure created on the interest rates by the monetary authority in order to help the government in the matters of its fiscal policy. Hence, it implies that the policies followed in the country, themselves are the proximate factors explaining for such underlying relationship among the variables rather than the mere magnitude of fiscal and monetary variables.

Table 6: Variance Decomposition

Period	RIR91	RFD	RMS
	Variance Decomposition of RIR91		
1	100.00	0.00	0.00
2	98.90	0.24	0.87
3	98.44	0.23	1.33
8	97.08	0.42	2.50
12	96.43	0.46	3.11
24	94.98	0.50	4.52
	Variance Decomposition of RFD		
1	1.13	98.87	0.00
2	3.24	93.41	3.35
3	3.55	92.99	3.46
8	3.55	92.94	3.51
12	3.55	92.88	3.57
24	3.57	92.71	3.72
	Variance Decomposition of RMS		
1	2.90	7.34	89.76
2	4.65	2.99	92.36
3	6.67	2.66	90.67
8	11.10	2.04	86.86
12	12.42	1.86	85.71
24	14.16	1.67	84.17

The error variance decomposition of real gross fiscal deficit (RFD) in Table 6 produces similar result as in the case of real interest rate. The result shows that it is largely explained by its own shock and less by other two variables such as the 91-day treasury bill real interest rate and real broad money supply. In 1-step ahead horizon forecast, the shocks in RFD is largely explained by its own innovation, which accounts 98.87 per cent, and while RIR91 accounts 1.13 per cent, RMS does not explain at all. In 2-step ahead time horizon forecast, RFD is also largely explained by itself by 93.41 per cent, whereas, 3.24 and 3.35 per cent by RIR91 and RMS respectively. The result also evidences that even at 24-step horizon, real fiscal deficit is more explained by its own innovation rather than by the other two variables in the system. It could be seen that at 24-ahead horizon, the RFD is explained 92.71 per cent by its own innovation, whereas it is explained merely 3.57 per cent by RIR91 and 3.72 per cent by RMS. From this result, it could be concluded that there is no causal relationship either running from real interest rate or from real money supply to the real gross fiscal deficits.

Table 7: Variance Decomposition

	Variance Decomposition of RIR364		
Period	*RIR91*	*RFD*	*RMS*
1	100.00	0.00	0.00
2	98.76	0.01	1.23
3	97.81	0.05	2.14
8	95.98	0.08	4.44
12	94.27	0.11	5.62
24	91.42	0.20	8.39
	Variance Decomposition of RFD		
1	0.04	99.96	0.00
2	1.06	95.62	3.33
3	1.13	95.39	3.48
8	1.14	95.33	3.53
12	1.14	95.28	3.5
24	1.15	95.11	3.74
	Variance Decomposition of RMS		
1	7.47	5.76	86.78
2	7.19	2.31	90.50
3	7.78	2.89	89.33
8	9.88	3.29	86.83
12	10.59	3.29	86.11
24	11.66	3.29	85.05

In contrast to the result of error variance decomposition of real interest rate and real fiscal deficits, the result of real money supply in Table 6 produces better result. Although the result evidences that real money supply is largely explained by its own innovation, however, in the long time horizon, it is significantly influenced by real interest rate along with its own influence. The result at 2-step time horizon shows that RMS is explained 92.36 per cent by its own innovation, whereas, 4.65 and 2.99 per cent by RIR91 and RFD respectively. The percentage of explanation of RMS by other two variables is dramatically changed from time horizon 2 to 24. At time horizon 24, RMS is explained 84.17 by its own innovation and 14.16 percent by RIR91 and very negligible by RFD. From the results of above three variables it could be concluded that real money supply is influenced by real interest rate in India but not in the other way around. More importantly, rate interest in India is not influenced by two core macro variables such as money supply and fiscal deficits. The reason as noticed above may be due to the fact that rate of interest is partly regulated by the monetary authority of India.

The result of VAR system containing 364-day treasury bill rate, real fiscal deficits and real money supply is reported in Table 7. Interestingly, the result shows the similar outcome as in the case of 91-day real treasury bill rate. The variance decomposition of 364-day real treasury bill rate (RIR364) demonstrates that rate of interest is largely explained (100 per cent for time horizon 1) by its own shocks. Even after 24-step time horizon, more than 91 per cent of the variance is explained by its own shocks. It implies that the influence of other two variables such as real fiscal deficits and real money supply on real rate of interest rate in India is negligible. The similar explanation would also hold here as is the case for 91-day real treasury bill rate. In case of variance decomposition of real fiscal deficits (RFD), similar result is found as in the case of real interest rate on 91-day treasury bill. The result evidences that real gross fiscal deficit is largely explained by its own shocks from time horizon 1 to 24. In 1-step time horizon, 99.96 per cent of error variance of FD is explained by its own shocks. Further, even after 24-step time horizon, more than 95 per cent of variance of fiscal deficit is explained by its own shocks. It suggests that both real rate of interest rate and real fiscal deficits are independent of each other as well as from the influence of money supply in the VAR system. However, the result of variance decomposition of real money supply looks quite different from other two variables. Similar to the case of 91-day real treasury bill rate, real money supply is not only influenced by its own shocks but also by 364-day real treasury bill rate in the long run. The result shows that at time horizon 24, the error variance of real money supply is explained 85.05 per cent by its own shocks and 11.66 per cent by real interest rate. In other words, the causality runs from the real rate of interest to real money supply in India. From this result, the study predicts that when real interest rate deviates from its artificial targeted values, in such a situation the monetary authority is probably exercising an artificial control on the money supply in order to keep the real interest rates at a desirable level to help the government in the matters of its financing programme. It could be the reason, where interest rate is indirectly influencing the money supply.

Summary and Conclusion

The present study examines the long run relationship between interest rates, fiscal deficits and money supply in the Indian context. Further, the study explores the possibility of causation among these variables by applying the error variance decomposition technique. In order to provide more reliable policy information, the study chooses two real treasury bill rates, which are 91-day and 364-day. From the co-integration result, it concludes that both the interest rates have stable long run equilibrium relationship with fiscal deficits and money supply. Further, as far as the dynamic causation among the variables is concerned, it is evidenced that none of the interest rates is influenced either by money supply or fiscal deficits. Such a result discards the validity of Keynesian theory of interest rate determination in the Indian context. Fiscal deficit, which is theoretically considered as one of the important determinants of rate of interest, found to be an insignificant factor to influence the rate of interest in India. Probably, the Ricardian theory of debt-neutrality holds good in the Indian context or it is due to the policies followed with regards to rate of interest in the economy itself, which causes such relationship among the variables. The most interesting finding to note from the study is that although the money supply does not exert influence on the rates of interest but it is influenced by the rates of interest, which supports the theoretical proposition of monetarists. According to the Monetarist when interest rate deviate from its targeted path (no matter it may be artificially targeted in India), the monetary authority controls it by varying the supply of money. Though theoretically the literature underpins the two-way causation exists between money supply and rate of interest, the present study finds one-way causation that is from rate of interest to money supply. It may be due to the artificial interest rate policy followed by the monetary authority of India.

REFERENCES

1. Barro, R. J. (1974). Are Government Bonds Net Wealth?. *Journal of Political Economy*, Vol.82, No. 4, pp. 1095-1117.
2. Bhole, L.M.(1999). Financial Institution and Markets. Tata Mcgraw-Hill Publishing Company Ltd.
3. Cebula, R.J (1988). Federal Government Budget Deficits and Interest Rates: An Empirical Analysis for the United States, 1955-1984. *Public Finance/Finance Publiques*, Vol. 43, No. 3, pp. 337-48.
4. Cebula, R.J. and W.J. Belton (1993). Government Budget Deficits and Interest Rates in the United States: Evidence for Closed and Open Systems Put into Perspective, 1985-1989. *Public Finance/Finance Publiques*, Vol.48, No. 2, pp. 188-209.

5. Dornbusch, R., S. Fischer & R. Startz (1998) "Macroeconomics" Tata Mcgraw-Hill edition, New York.
6. Evans, P. (1985). Do Large Deficits Produce High Interest Rates?. *The American Economic Review*, Vol.75, No. 1, pp. 68-87.
7. Evans, P.(1987). Interest Rates and Expected Future Budget Deficits in the United States. *Journal of Political Economy*, Vol.95, No.1, pp. 34-58.
8. Gupta, K. L. and B. Moazzami (1991). Dynamic Specification and the Long-run Effect of Budget Deficits on Interest Rates. *Public Finance/Finance Publiques*, Vol.46, N0. 2, pp. 208-21.
9. Gupta, K. L. and B. Moazzami (1996). Interest Rates and Budget deficits: A study of the Advanced Economies. *Routledge Studies in the Modern world economy*, Routledge, London.
10. Hoelscher, G. (1986). New Evidence on Deficits and Interest Rates. *Journal of Money, Credit and Banking*, Vol.18, No.1, pp. 1-17.
11. Hoelscher, G. (1993). Federal Borrowing and Short Term Interest Rates. *Southern Economic Journal,* Vol.50, No. 2, pp. 319-33.
12. Hicks, J. R. (1939). 'Value and Capital'. Oxford.
13. Monadjemi, M.S. (1989). Fiscal Deficits and Interest Rates: A Multi Country Analysis. *Australian Economic Papers*, Vol.28, No. 52-53, pp. 209-218.
14. Moreley, S. and A. Fishlow (1987). Deficits, Debt and Destabilization: The Perversity of High Interest Rates. *Journal of Development Economics*, Vol.27, No. 1&2, pp. 227-44.
15. Modigliani, F. and T. Jappelli (1988). The Determinants of interest Rates in the Italian Economy. *Review of Economic Conditions in Italy*, pp. 9-34.
16. Nachane, D. M., A.V. Karnik and N. R. Hatekar (1997). The Interest Rate Imbroglio: Monetary and Fiscal Dimensions. *Economic Political Weekly*, Vol. 32, No. 20 & 21, pp. 1167-74.
17. Narasimhan Committee Report (1991). RBI Publication.

18. Rangarajan, C. (1998). Indian Economy: Essays on Money and Finance. UBC Publishers Distribution Ltd.

19. Plosser, C.I. (1987). Further Evidence on the Relationship between Fiscal Policy and the Term Structure. *Journal of Monetary Economics,* 20, pp. 343-67.

20. Rangarajan, C. (1989). Dynamics of Interaction between Government Deficits and Domestic Debt in India. *RBI Occasional Papers*, Vol. X, No.1.

21. RBI *Monthly Reports* (Various issues). Mumbai.

22. Saltz, I.S (1993). Budget Deficits and Real Interest Rates in U.S.A.. *Indian Economic Journal*, Vol.41, No:1, pp.74-83.

23. Tobin, J. (1965). Money and Economic Growth. *Econometrica,* Vol.33, No. 4, pp. 671-84.

24. Wickens, M.R. and T.S. Breusch (1988). Dynamic Specification, the Long run, and the Specification of Transformed Regression Models. *Economic Journals,* Vol.98, No. 390, pp. 189-205.

Appendix-1

Table 8: Average of 12 months during each financial year (Rupees in Crores)

Year	*FD*	*M3*	*TB91*	*TB364*
1994-95	4808.67	478195.83	9.30	10.12
1995-96	5020.33	551286.33	12.64	12.79
1996-97	5561.08	642631.08	9.67	11.65
1997-98	7411.42	752027.58	6.81	8.33
1998-99	9445.67	875892.25	8.63	9.54
1999-00	8726.42	1055676.33	9.10	10.09
2000-01	9530.75	1222179.08	8.98	9.80

Note: Figures in the table 8 are computed from monthly bulletins of Reserve Bank of India (RBI) and the reports of comptroller and auditor general of India. FD- Fiscal deficit, M3-Broad money supply, TB91- Interest rates on 91-day treasury bills and TB364- Interest rates on 364-day treasury bills.

6

Impact of Euro on Indian Economy

*Dr. M. Ramanjaneyulu**

Introduction

A historic decision has been taken by European Union summit, which was taken place in Brussels on May 1st, 1998 for implementation of European Economic and Monetary Union with 11 countries from January 1st 1999. They are Austria, Finland, France, Belgium, Germany, Ireland, Italy, Luxembourg, Nederland, Portugal, Spain and Greece has participated in the Euro from 1st January 2001, which increases to 12 the number of Member states of the Euro zone. Electronic and non-cash transactions in the new common European Currency has been made, then the Euro conversion to notes and coins has also been taken place from January 2002 . It is a unique currency in monetary history. It has become the first international currency without backing of bullion or any national government and became the legal tender in participating countries of the European Union. It is an unprecedented experiment for a single currency across national borders of countries.

The European Union (EU) has been formed and at a conference held in Maastricht, Netherlands in 1991, the

* Reader, Dept. of Economics, Bangalore University, Bangalore-560056.

members decided to adopt a single currency to enhance economic cooperation and benefits.

This decision led to the beginning of the European Monetary Union. In 1992, a treaty was adopted forming the EMU, which includes the EU members along with other intergovernmental agencies. To become a member of EMU, certain constraints have been made with respect to meeting certain criteria, known as the convergence criteria relating to inflation, interest rates, exchange rates and fiscal position. Inflation must be less than 1.5 per cent higher than the average of the three best performing countries. Long-term interest rate should be no more than two points over this benchmark. The budget deficit should be 3 or less of GDP. The public debt should not exceed 60 per cent of GDP. There is vague criterion for the exchange rate as well.

There are three stages of Euro implementation. In phase 1, (early 1998) finalization of participating member states and European Central Bank and the establishment European Systems of Central Banks to farm a single market. In phase II beginning January 1, 1999, ECB, came out with exchange rate policy in Euro and the rates of conversion between participating currencies into single currency and Euro fixation. It became legal tender in qualifying countries, inter bank monetary capital and exchange markets, trading and payments systems are in Euro establishment of European Monetary Institute (UMI). In Phase III, starting from January 1, 2002, Euro currency notes and coins were in circulation.

The common currency was based on sound macro economic basics to push competitiveness and have a market with high liquidity, Monetary Unification, Political unity and common economic policy, Exchange and interest rate policy in the hands of European Central Bank will determine the level of employment and economic activity. Euro would have a major impact on the global economy.

All those doing business with Europe would have a significant change to adapt to Euro. Within the European Union, brokerage and transaction costs of the operating with so many currencies will be considerably reduced. The dollar Euro parity will emerge stable in course of time this would strengthen and stabilize exchange rates in the world.

Indicators of Euro-zone

Euro-zone economic growth in the third quarter increased by 0.1 per cent over the second quarter, the contribution from domestic demand was negative at minus 0.1 per cent while that from net exports was positive at 0.2 per cent. Euro-zone unemployment remained unchanged at 8.5 per cent in December 2001. Inflation has increased from 2.1 per in November 2001 to 2.5 per cent in January 2002. Industrial production in the Euro-zone has also increased by 0.8 per cent in December, as energy and consumer goods production both experienced healthy demand. Germany and

Table 1: Indicators of Euro Zone 11 Countries

Real GDP	2.21% in 1997		1.30 % in 2001Q3
Consumer Price Index	1.58 % in 1997		2.24 % in 2001Q4
Final Consumption Expenditure	2.6 % 2000Q1		0.4% 2001Q4
Unemployment rate	11.55% 2000Q1		8.40% in 2001Q3
Capital Formation to TDCF	6.6% 2000Q1		-3.2 2001Q4
Broad Money	4.18% 2000Q1		8.00% in 2001Q4
Long term interest rate	6.0 % 2000Q1		3.1 % in 2001Q4
Short term interest rate	4.05% 2000Q1		3.44% in 2001Q4
Final Govt. Consumption Expe.	3.5% 2000Q1	to	2.0% 2001Q4
Exports	12.5% 2000Q1	to	-3.6 2001Q4
Imports	10.8% 2000Q1	to	-4.3 2001Q4
Industrial Production Index (Manufacturing)	5.0% 2000Q1		3.5 % ,,

Source: Money and Finance Vol 2, Novemnber 7, Oct-Dec 2001, K.G Marg New Delhi.

Italy both experienced expansion in December, while France, experienced a decline. The German economy has contracted in the third quarter by 0.6 per cent over previous quarter, driven down by weak consumer spending and business investment. Germany's jobless rate rose sharply in October to 9.5 per cent as the number of unemployed reached 3.92 million, and further went up to 9.6 per cent of the workforce in January. Index of Business activity in Germany rose to 86.3 by January 2002.

UK Economic picture has remained relatively favorable. Real output growth declined in third quarter of 2001 to an annual rate of 2.2 per cent down from 2.3 per cent in second quarter, the 4th quarter GDP grew by 1.9 per cent.

Reflecting the imbalances within the economies, the gap between services and goods in price inflation is unusually wide at present and goods price inflation is likely as export and output price trends in manufacturing are very weak.

The spectrum of prices, taxes and social security contributions across the 12 national borders it is expected that where costs are lower and regulation softer, calling for greater uniformity through structural reforms with in the euro zone.

Indo-British Partnership Initiative

In 1993, in response to opportunities created by the bold and imaginative liberalization programme introduced in India, the British endorsed the creation of the Indo-British Partnership Initiative. Its mandate was to increase bilateral trade and investment with particular emphasis on small and medium enterprises and to promote technology and science links between the two countries. The initiative has become an important ongoing activity in promotion of bilateral relations. The European Union, as a bloc, is India's second largest trading partner. RBI study has pointed out that India's exports to and imports from the EU constituted about 20 per cent and 21.5 per cent respectively in 1995-96. However, India remains a marginal player in both the world trade and in trade with the EU. India's share in the imports from the world was about 0.40 per cent and EU's share of exports to India in its exports to the world was about 0.47 per cent in 1994. In the dominant class of exports are textiles, leather and pearls, while the promising class includes chemicals, machinery, footwear, base metals, and vehicles, miscellaneous manufactured produces, besides animal and vegetable products. In the post –liberalization period, competitiveness and world trade effects gave some boost to India's exports to the EU. There is relative price elasticity for majority of India's exports to the EU were large, the income elasticity were quite low. This perhaps, explains the sluggish growth despite the supportive stance of the rupee depreciation.

India enjoys the most favored nation status with the EU for many of its exports but the average tariff are always 5 to 10 percentage points above average. Quantitative restrictions, such as quotas, should be liberalized for Indian exports to the EU. Technical barriers in the form of product standards, certification requirements etc., greet many marine product exports to the EU.

Forex reserves will also undergo a change, with the Euro taking progressively a larger share, replacing the host of European currencies. Exporters must factor in price and income elasticity plus exchange rate risks; so they will have less to fear on account of exchange rate risks. It will lessen the cost of hedging against multiple, and volatile, exchange rates. RBI (1998) has pointed out that forward contracts cannot completely eliminate risk; so, India will gain by invoicing exports and imports in the new currency.

Invoicing in Euro should make a difference even though a lot of India's exports are exchange rate inelastic.

The advent of Euro is expected to rein in interest rates owing to the controls on government debt. Lesser degree of crowding out should lead to a fall in EU interest rates, which then should also lead to a weakening of international and Indian interest rates. On the currency-trading front, there is limited impact in India. Currency trading is also expected to disappear in most EU currencies bar sterling in India. The RBI study expects that it will affect brokers than the banks. Brokers are expected to lose up to 20 per cent of their annual income owing to the single currency, while banks lose 5 to 10 per cent. Finally, a deeper and more liquid Euro market will prompt corporate to increase external commercial borrowings exposure in Euro-dominated debt. Euro will provide more opportunities to Indian trade and industry though it could also intensify competition. Tapping of Euro markets through the equity route is disastrous for the country in the long run as compared to tapping Euro markets through debt route as the companies would be paying in the range of 25 to 30 per cent per annum to foreign investors on a discounted cash flow basis on their Indian equities on a discounted cash flow basis on their Indian equities as compared to around 8 to 9 per cent on the debt route. Indian companies have comfortably sold about $ 2 billions of their shares at prices they can only fantasize about in the domestic equity market.

Indo-British Trade

UK-India bilateral trade of goods services at £4.9 billion in 2000 has grown by 68 per cent since the India-British Partnership was formed in 1993. UK-India bilateral trade in goods in 2000 grew by 28 per cent, with UK exports to India growing by 41 per cent. UK is India's second largest trading partner after the USA and accounted for 5.7 per cent of India's total foreign trade in goods in 2000-01. The UK has also the largest share of India's markets and accounted for 8.3 per cent of India's total imports in 2000. Major items of trade in goods included non metallic minerals, gold, power generating and telecom equipment, industrial machinery (UK exports to India) and textiles and readymade garments, gems, and Jewellery, foot wear, manufacture of metal, vegetables and fruit (UK's imports from India). In respect of trade in goods, UK's exports to India has been increasing annual growth at 9.01 per cent and Indian exports to UK has also been increasing at 6.6 per cent during 1992-2000.

UK Exports to India during 2000-2001

During the period of 2000-2001 UK exports to India has been increasing positively with regard to non-metallic minerals (4.7 per cent change), Transport equipment (4.1 Per cent), Metal Ores and Scraps (71.9 per cent) , Electrical Machinery (0.1 per cent), Organic Chemicals (9.2 per cent), Textile Yarn, fabrics, made-up articles (8.1 per cent) and inorganic Chemicals (15.0 per cent) respectively. Considerable declining trend has been registered in case of Non-ferrous Metals, Power Generating Equipment, Scientific equipment, Industrial Machinery, Telecommunications, Petroleum, petroleum products and related materials, Miscellaneous Manufactured article and Iron and Steel etc. Thus, it reveals that considerable decline of imports from UK has been noticed which is more favorable balance of trade which represents more advantage to India.

UK Imports from India during 2000-2001

India's exports to UK have been increasing in various manufactured items such as cereals and cereal preparations, organic chemicals and metal manufacturers at 30.2 per cent, 22.3 per cent and 18.5 per cent respectively. Transport equipment increased by 56 per cent.

Table 2:

	UK Exposrts to India (£ million)	*2000*	*2001*	*% change*
1.	Non Matallic Minerals	741.6	776.4	4.7
2.	Non Ferrous Metals	168.1	14.0	-16.7
3.	Power Generating Equipment	114.9	98.4	-14.4
4.	Transport Equipment	64.4	87.9	4.1
5.	Scientific Equipment	79.8	56.3	-29.5
6.	General Industrial Machinery	73.6	53.8	-26.9
7.	Special Industrial Machinery	58.4	48.4	-17.2
8.	Metal Ores and Scraps	53.8	92.5	71.9
9.	Electrical Machinery	54.1	54.2	0.1
10.	Telecommunications	45.9	44.9	-2.0
11.	Petroleum, Petroleum products and Related materials	228.1	11.5	-95.0
12.	Miscellaneous Manufactured article	38.3	35.4	-7.7
13.	Organic Chemicals	27.6	30.0	9.2
14.	Textile Yarn, fabrics, made-up articles	17.6	19.0	8.1
15.	Inorganic Chemicals	16.5	19.0	15.0
16.	Iron and steel	29.7	18.6	-37.2
	Total (Other top 11 to 16 items)	**581.2**	**329.2**	**-43.4**

Source: Economic and Commercial Section British High Commission, New Delhi, October, 2001.

Non-metallic minerals, coffee, tea, cocoa, spices and manufacturers have registered a negative increase of exports. The positive trend of exports will influence positive effect on favorable Balance of Payments position and foreign exchange earnings.

Role of Indian Government on Financial Markets–Euro Issues

The role of the government in allowing companies to tap Euro-market is very crucial. From 1991 around 40 Indian companies have accessed the Euro Market. According to International Financial Corporation study on emerging capital markets, India ranks among the top 10

Table 3:

	UK Imports from India (£ million)	*2000*	*2001*	*% change*
1.	Apparel and Clothing	320.5	349.4	9.0
2.	Textile Yarn and Fabric	263.9	284.8	7.9
3.	Miscellaneous Manufactured Articles	137.8	144.5	4.9
4.	Footwear	121.2	133.7	10.3
5.	Metal Manufactures	107.3	127.1	18.5
6.	Power Generating Equipment	72.1	77.2	7.1
7.	Non Metallic Minerals	61.0	59.8	-2.0
8.	Vegetables and Fruits	50.7	51.7	1.9
9.	Organic chemicals	43.7	53.4	22.3
10.	Road Vehicles	39.7	38.7	-2.4
11.	Cereals and cereal preparations	37.1	48.3	30.2
12.	Coffee, tea, cocoa, spices and manufacturers	49.4	45.0	-8.9
13.	Fish, Crustaceans, mollusks, & aquatic Invertebrates and preparations thereof	41.8	43.9	5.0
14.	Travel goods, handbags and smaller containers	37.7	39.1	3.6
15.	Electrical machinery, apparatus and Appliances, and electrical parts.	33.8	36.9	9.2
16.	Other Transport equipment	23.1	36.1	56.0
	Other (top 11 to 16 items)	494.3	563.8	14.0

Source: Economic and Commercial Section British High Commission, New Delhi, October, 2001.

countries. The India's capital market system and procedures are quite sophisticated and well developed, compared to most of the countries in the Third World. Current account convertibility permits repayment of installments of loans and interests at the prevailing exchange rates.

Indian companies have increasingly gone for Euro-issues, either global depository receipts (GDRs) or convertible bonds. In fact, there are as many as 65 companies, both in private and public sector that have submitted proposals. GDR is a straightforward equity, a receipt is issued underlying a claim on the equity issue and the GDR gets, traded on the bourse where it is registered. Convertible bond could be a period of 5 years with the conversion to equity taking place after 18 months. Indian companies initially went in for GDRs, increasingly switch to bonds, which found a ready market.

Table 4: Indo British Trade and Investment (£ billion): 1992-2001

Trade in Goods

Year	*UK Exports to India*	*Indian Exports to UK*
1992	945	962
1993	1, 130	1, 089
1994	1, 131	1, 209
1995	1, 683	1, 436
1996	1, 707	1, 611
1997	1, 576	1, 622
1998	1, 256	1, 454
1999	1, 454	1, 482
2000	2, 056	1, 712

Source: Economic and Commercial Section British High Commission, New Delhi, October, 2001.

The government has preferred the equity for foreign investment because it does not add to the country's debt burden. Equity puts all the risk on the foreign investor. Foreign currency convertible bonds tend to technically add up to the country's external debt, till they get converted as equity. The government's modification of GDRs may explicitly encourage Euro-equity issues in preference to companies issuing foreign currency convertible bonds. Reliance Industries Ltd. has reportedly pre-paid expensive rupee and foreign exchange loans aggregating about Rs.400 crore out of cheap funds raised through the recent Euro-convertible bond issue. The savings are nearly accounting for Rs.70 crore.

From May 1992 onwards, Indian companies have been issuing Global Depository Receipts (GDRs) and Foreign Currency Convertible Bonds/ Euro Currency Bonds (FCCBs/ECBs) on the Euro market on a large scale. Up to December 1995, Indian firms raised US$5, 180 million through 64 issues of GDRs & FCCBs. During 1995-96, seven Euro issues, all in the form of GDR were made which together raised $652 million. The proceeds of Euro issues of Indian companies have been deposited in foreign branches of Indian companies or foreign banks, which are rated for short-term obligations. India also considering the profit before tax as a measure of profitability for considering Euro issue proposals as against profit after tax. To increase India's foreign exchange, Euro issue proceeds can be directly repatriated for the use of approved end uses. The ceiling of using Euro issue proceeds for working capital and general corporate restructuring has been raised from 15 per cent to 25 per cent. External commercial borrowing (ECB) was earlier possible either through floating rate note or fixed rate bonds. Companies other than those investing into infrastructural facilities like power, petroleum exploration and refining, telecommunication, ports, roads etc are required to have a three-year track record of profitability to be able to raise funds by Euro issues. Euro issues by companies to finance activities, which are predominantly with foreign equity holding inclusive of the foreign equity through Euro issues with 51 per cent, would be considered and cleared by the Department of Economic affairs. The comprehensive guidelines for Euro issues were provide greater flexibility of Indian companies to access the global market through GDR/ADR/FCCB issues. The Indian corporates have successfully launched 91 Euro issues in the international markets, raising an amount of about US $ 8332.02 million + S Fr. 172 million. Foreign Institutional Investors who register themselves as Debt Funds with Securities ad Exchange Board of India (SEBI) are permitted to make 100 per cent of their investment in Debt securities of Indian companies. Presently 100 per cent NRI investment is permissible under the RBI simplified route in areas covered by expended Annexure-III to the Industrial policy 1991.

Indo-British Investment

UK has the third largest share of 7 per cent of new investment approved since 1991, well ahead of Germany, Japan, and France. Uk has the fifth largest share of 4.5 per cent of new investments implemented since 1991, behind the Mauritius, USA, Japan and Germany. In addition, reinvestments by UK companies already existing in India are also significantly high. Since 1993, when the IBP was formed, over 1500 new India –British joint ventures have approved. In respect of investment trade in goods, UK exports to India has been increasing annual growth at 9.01 per cent and Indian exports to UK has also been increasing at 6.6 per cent during 1992-2000.

Table 5: Indo British Trade and Investment (£ billion): 1992-2000

Trade in Services

Year	*UK Exports to India*	*Indian Exports to UK*
1992	310	263
1993	358	322
1994	413	347
1995	410	367
1996	372	361
1997	551	426
1998	507	465
1999	503	591
2000	545	557

Source: Economic and Commercial Section British High Commission, New Delhi, October, 2001.

Table 6: UK Investment (Rs. million)

	Approval		*Actual*	
	UK	*UK Share of Total*	*UK*	*UK Share of Total*
1992	1176.7	3.0	760.0	11.3
1993	6227.3	7.0	2325.0	13.0
1994	12991.5	9.2	4276.0	14.4
1995	17258.6	5.4	1746.0	2.7
1996	15245.9	4.2	1809.0	2.1
1997	44907.2	8.2	4341.0	3.6
1998	32008.4	10.4	2737.1	3.1
1999	29630.5	10.4	2797.0	4.0
2000	4112.3	1.1	2985.0	3.7

Source: Economic and Commercial Section British High Commission, New Delhi, October, 2001.

Investment trade in services are also increasing the growth rate of 6.46 per cent in case of UK exports to India and 8.68 per cent in respect of Indian exports to UK. UK share of total investment approval has been increased from 3 per cent to 10.4 per cent during 1992 to 1999, but actual share of investment has been declining from 11.3 per cent to 3.7 per cent.

The greater willingness of the European Union to trade-off growth in favour of lower inflation, low economic volatility, and made certain amount of discounting of European assets. UK has exhibited greater inter-temporal stability in terms of real GDP, consumption expenditure, exports and Imports.

Conclusion

Indian Economy is predominantly agrarian one. Indian corporates entered into manufacturing activities, which were in the nature of import substitutes. Industrial sector is acquiring a degree of sophistication in its manufacturing base, which is becoming a manufacturing

Table 7: Indicators of India

Year		Real GDP %	Consumer Price Index %	Indu.Pro. Index %	S.Interest Rate %	Exchange Rate p.a	Share Price Per $	Exchange Rate per €
1998		13.2	3.3	8.0	41.3	3347.9		
1999		5.9	5.3	5.5	9.1	43.0	4136.8	49.40
2000	Q1	5.9	3.7	9.7	9.0	43.6	5440.3	44.24
	Q2	6.0	5.2	7.5	8.5	44.1	4602.1	
	Q3	5.7	4.2	4.8	9.2	43.4	4666.4	
	Q4		.3.6	5.5	9.4	46.6	3958.6	
2001	Q1	3.8	2.9	1.6	8.5	46.5	4109.3	43.71
	Q2	4.4	2.7	2.0	7.8	46.9	3514.9	
	Q3	5.3	4.8	2.0	6.7	47.3	3201.7	
	Q4		4.8	1.5	6.8	48.0	3130.7	42.72

Source: Money and Finance Vol 2, Novemnber 7, Oct-Dec 2001, K.G Marg New Delhi.

base for components for global corporations. It is evident that Indian Software companies are providing a competitive edge for their clients through cost and quality advantages, state of the art capabilities, technical trained professionals and high reliability. Large number of organizations is already gaining significant benefit from outsourcing Information Technology work to organizations in India, which is undoubtedly the leading provider of offshore IT services. India has the second largest pool of scientific manpower in the world, low manpower cost, and its democratic and legal systems provide significant advantages over the countries in attracting western business. The Indian I T industry has grown at an annual compound rate of almost 52 per cent over the last five years and exports already exceed to the worth £ 2.5 billion pounds by the year 2000.

REFERENCES

1. Economic and Commercial Section, British High Commission New Delhi, October 2001.
2. Money and Finance Quarterly Journal, vol.2, New Delhi, Novemebr, 2001.
3. Rao A.L., The challenges of European Monetary Union, The Economic Times , May 28, 1998.
4. Tandon J.K, Ero-Currency and India, Yojana, Vol.45, New Delhi, December 2001.

Part—III

Trade Policy and WTO Issues

7

Sapta and India's Trade Performance with SAARC

*Dr. Boppana Nagarjuna**
Pradeep Kumar. M and
*Vijay Kumar. V***

Introduction

Concentric 'Regional Trading Arrangements' (RTAs) had become a common feature of international life during the past decade and half. These RTAs range from preferential trading arrangements to economic union. RTAs aim to promote intra-regional trade among the members countries and there by economic co-operation and development. The SAARC[1] Preferential Trading Arrangement (SAPTA) is among such RTAs that is found in the seven South Asian Countries viz., Bangladesh, Bhutan, India, Maldives, Nepal, Pakistan and Sri Lanka.

SAPTA followed the initiative taken during the Sixth SAARC summit (Colombo. 1991) to establish a framework agreement on SAARC Preferential Trading Arrangement (SAPTA) for increasing intra-regional trade. It was finalized by the committee on economic cooperation based

* Faculty, Department of Economics, University of Hyderabad.
** And Research Students in the same department.
1 Refer to Appendix A.

on a draft prepared by Inter-Governmental Group (IGG) on Trade Liberalization. On 11th April 1993 during the Seventh SAARC Summit in Dhaka, the Foreign minister of all the SAARC member' states signed the Agreement and finally, it came into operation from 7th December 1995. The basic principle of SAPTA are as follows: (a) Overall reciprocity and mutuality of advantages; (b) Step-by-step negotiations and extension of preferential trade arrangement in stages; (c) inclusion of all types of products-raw, semi-processed and processed; and (d) special and favourable treatment to Least Developed Countries (LDCs).

SAPTA Agreement is an important landmark in the history of SAARC as it is expected to go a long way in promoting intra-regional trade and in gradually removing trade barriers presently existing among the members' countries (B.Bhattacharyya and Vijaya Katti). Now, about seven years have gone since SAPTA came into being (and seventeen years have gone since SAARC). Right from the inception of SARRC, other members of SAARC always expressed their concern regarding their unfavourable balance of trade with India (various SAARC Summit Reports). And in the Tenth and Eleventh SAARC Summits which held in Colombo (1998) and Katmandu (2002) respectively, other South Asian Countries stressed this problem as their unfavourable balance of trade with India further widened after the inception of SAPTA. A perusal of India's total volume (exports plus imports) with other South Asian Countries, which are members of the SAARC have witnessed an uneven growth over the years after the SAPTA agreement and reflects the concern expressed by other South Asian Countries. It is therefore of interest to trace the changes in India's trade performance with other South Asian Countries in the presence of uneven growth reflected by structural breaks that might have occurred over the years. Hence, the objective of the study is to examine the India's trade performance with in the framework of structural breaks in the context of major policy change (i.e., SAPTA).

To address the above mentioned issue, the present study considers the series of monthly data from 1985:1 – 2001:12[2] of India's Exports to and Imports from other SAARC countries and total volume with other SAARC countries and these series are tested for whether they have exhibited any trend breaks overtime in response to this agreement.

Of late, studies concerning investigation of structural trend break, it has been the practice to conduct unit root tests to check whether a given series has a smooth or stable growth path (i.e., stationary) or not. The absence of a unit root in the series confirms stationarity. On the contrary, the presence of a unit root indicates that the give series has become unstable or non-stationarity, showing up uneven growth. In the present context of the problem, India's total volume with the SAARC countries, that is, India's exports to and imports from the other SAARC countries has grown unevenly in response to the major policy change which had taken place in the year 1995. Therefore, the use of unit root tests in a conventional way may not be an appropriate proposition 'given the possible breaks in trend'. Hence, Perron (1989), Banerjee et al., (1992) and Perron (1997) trend break techniques have been identified and employed in the present study. Since such an attempt had not been made to the date in the Indian trade performance context, the present study assumes relevance. The rest of the paper is organized as follows; Section II explains the methodology employed in this paper; Section III discuss the empirical results of the (structural breaks, unit roots) of the study; Concluding remarks are reported in Section IV.

---

2 Since SAARC came into being in December 1985.

Methodology

In the present study, for examining the behaviour of India's trade performance with other members of SAARC after SAPTA Agreement, the study begins with an examination of the time series properties of indicator series (i.e., exports, imports and total volume series). If the indicator series is stationary, a simple comparison of means of the series before and after "agreement date" can be used to gauge the effects of the 'SAPTA Agreement'. If an indicator series is trending upward then no matter where the event date lies, the data will show that trade had subsequently rose. Such a trending series suggests the possibility of a unit root, which would make a t-test comparison of pre and post SAPTA Agreement 'means' invalid. Traditional tests for unit root, however, frequently do not reject the hypothesis of a unit root even when the series are stationary. In addition, Perron (1989) shows how standard tests of the unit root hypothesis against trend stationary alternatives cannot reject the unit root hypothesis if the true data generating mechanism is that of stationary fluctuations around a trend function that contains a one-time break. In the present case, the inability to reject the hypothesis of a unit root may instead imply the existence of a one-time break in the series at the agreement event date.

Consequently, the present study begins with testing for a unit root using Dickey-Fuller (DF), Augmented Dickey Fuller (ADF) and Phillips-Perron (PP) test, having a constant and (use of) using the significance tables provided by Dickey-Fuller (1979). Using a p-value at 0.05, it evaluates the null hypotheses of a unit root. If the null hypothesis is rejected, it uses the technique of Perron (1989) [Appendix B] to test for a trend break in the series. Finally, if there is an evidence of a unit root, and no evidence of a trend breaks in the series, test is unable to make a statistical conclusion regarding the effect of the policy or agreement event date.

The major assumption of Perron (1989) method is that the break date is to be fixed (exogenous) and chosen independently of data. This assumption has drawn much criticism in subsequent papers, based on the argument that break dates are often chosen after looking at the data [Christiano (1992), Banerjee et al., (1992), Perron (1997)]. The strategy used in all the above studies was to endogenize the choice of break date by making it data determined. Thus in contrary to exogenous fixing of the break date (which will be chosen often after looking at the data, i.e., fixing SAPTA Agreement policy date December 1995), we employ the technique developed by Banerjee et al., (1992) and Perron [(1997) see Appendix C] that allows a shift in trend at an unknown time irrespective of the policy event date.

Empirical Analysis

In the present study, the empirical investigation starts with the analysis of three indicator series (i) India's exports to SAARC countries (ii) India's imports from SAARC countries and (iii) India's trade volume with SAARC countries as provided in figures 1 to 3. Observation of these figures reveals the extent of growth in the India's foreign trade with other members of SAARC. For the entire period of the study from 1985:1 – 2001:12 the exports increased from US $ 28.96 Millions in 1985:1 to US $ 180.98 Millions in 2001:12, the average of the India's exports for the entire period is 89.57 where as the average ratio before the SAPTA agreement date (Pre-SAPTA Period) is 50.82 and after (Post-SAPTA Period) it increased to 159.09. And Figure 1 shows that the exports reached its peak in May 2001. India's imports series increased from US $ 13.24 Millions in January 1985 to US $ 37.71 Millions in 2001 December and showed a higher increase during the end period of

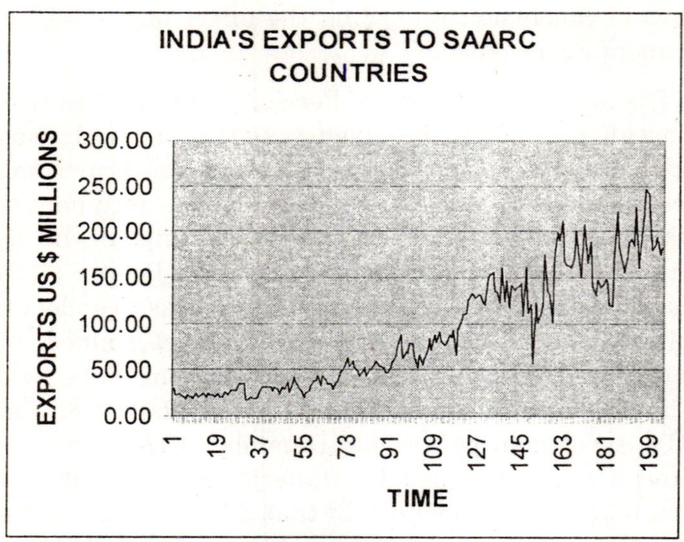
INDIA'S EXPORTS TO SAARC COUNTRIES
EXPORTS US $ MILLIONS
300.00
250.00
200.00
150.00
100.00
50.00
0.00
1
19
37
55
73
91
109
127
145
163
181
199
TIME

Fig. 1

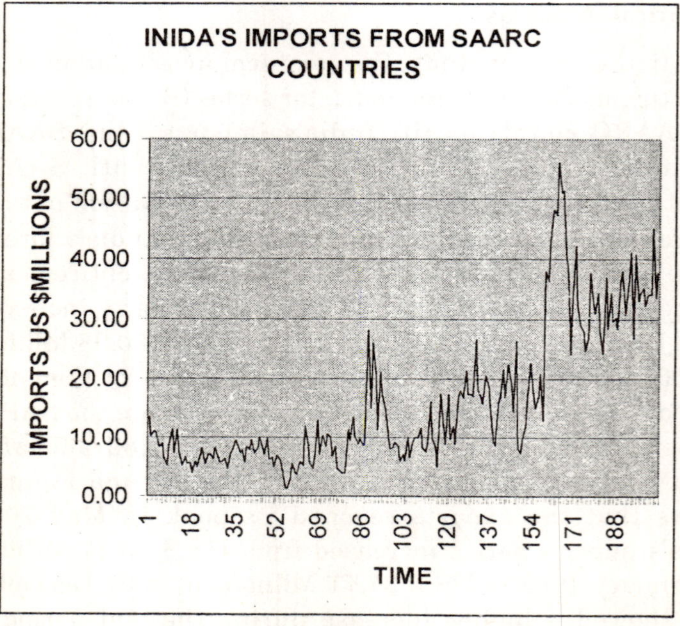
INIDA'S IMPORTS FROM SAARC COUNTRIES
IMPORTS US $MILLIONS
60.00
50.00
40.00
30.00
20.00
10.00
0.00
1
18
35
52
69
86
103
120
137
154
171
188
TIME

Fig. 2

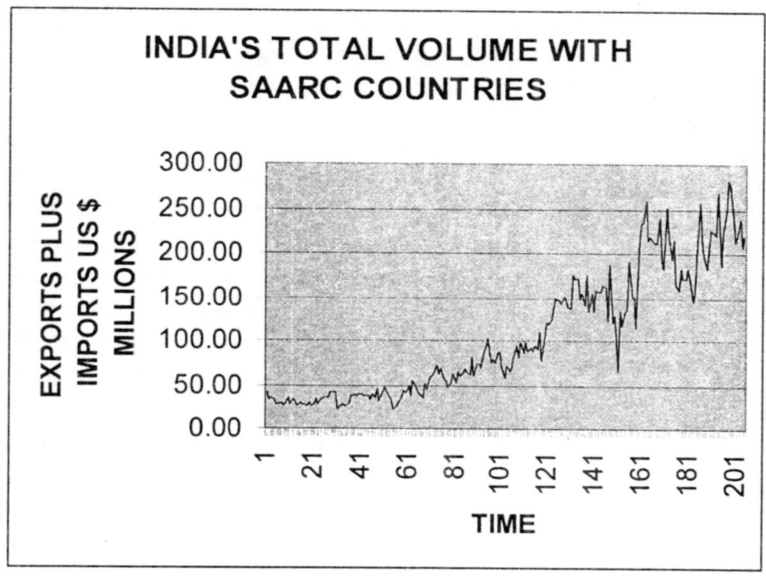

Fig. 3

1998. The average of the import series for the entire sample period is 16.10 where as it stands at 9.28 and 28.34 in Pre-SAPTA Period and Post-SAPTA Period respectively. The third series i.e., trade volume series increased over the sample period from US $ 42.20 Millions in 1985:1 to US $ 218.70 Millions in 2001:12, the average of the trade volume series of India with other SAARC countries for the entire period is 105.66 where as the average ratio before the SAPTA agreement date is 60.10 and after it increased to

Table 1: Unit Root Test statistics on India's Export Series, Import Series and Trade volume series with other SAARC countries

Series	*DF*	*ADF*	*PP*	*KPSS*
Exports	-0.857(24)	-0.856(24)	-1.57(24)	0.183(24)
Imports	-0.029(24)	-0.045(24)	-3.14(24)	0.187(24)
Trade Volume	-0.897(24)	-0.896(24)	-1.39(24)	0.202(24)

187.42. From the observation of three series it can be said that all the three series showed a steep increase in Post-SAPTA period than compared to Pre-SAPTA period.

The empirical investigation for measuring the trend break starts with the unit root test to examine the time series property of the concerned exports, imports and trade volume series. Using a P-value of 0.05 and 0.10, exports, imports and trade volume series' do not reject the null hypothesis of a unit root, hence non-stationary. Since three indicator series were found to be non-stationary, usual t-test becomes invalid and hence to detect a one time break or structural break, the Perron (1989) model [Appendix B] has been employed. The exports series doesn't display a significant change after the policy event date (defined by the significance of the dummy variables given in Table 2). The results provided in Table 2 shows that there is no significant change either in level or growth rate of series or both level and growth, which implies there is no one time break in series. These results are obtained from the coefficients of the dummy variables DTB, DTS and DT, which are not significantly different from zero.

Table 2: Perron (1989) Trend Break Test for India's Export Series

Model	*Constant*	*DMU*	*Trend*	*DTB*	*DTS*	*DT*
A	-3.16551 (-0.970)	0.9375 (0.153)	0.25310 (2.841)	16.54914 (0.988)		
B	-2.18153 (-0.633)	4.35231 (0.704)	0.27856 (3.242)		0.02757 (0.261)	
C	-2.75440 (-0.788)	-4.21029 (0.252)	0.25322 (2.835)	17.62930 (1.030)		0.03954 (0.335)

Note: Figures in Parentheses represent respective t-ratio.

It has been found from Table 3 that, there is no exogenous change in the level of the import series. At the same time, a significant improvement in the series after the agreement date permits for an exogenous change in the growth rate of the series. The results provided in table 3, exhibit one time trend break or significant improvement after the agreement date from the coefficients of the dummy variables DTS and DT, which are significantly different from zero.

Table 3: Perron (1989) Trend Break Test for India's Import Series

Model	*Constant*	*DMU*	*Trend*	*DTB*	*DTS*	*DT*
A	0.26093 (0.293)	1.63861 (1.164)	0.02553 (2.030)	-6.08609 (-1.231)		
B	1.15768 (1.152)	0.62625 (0.436)	0.02279 (1.810)		0.7282 (2.039)	
C	1.65139 (1.654)	-10.81259 (-2.027)	0.02453 (1.970)	-4.27643 (-0.878)		0.09020 (2.501)

Note: Figures in Parentheses represent respective t-ratio.

The trend break results for trade volume series are shown in Table 4. The results show that there is no significant shift in the level of the series as indicated by DTB coefficient, which is not significantly different from zero. However, one time break is observed for the growth rate of the trade volume series as it is observed form the coefficients of DTS and DT after agreement date, which are significantly different from zero.

Table 4: Perron (1989) Trend Break Test for India's Trade Volume Series

Model	*Constant*	*DMU*	*Trend*	*DTB*	*DTS*	*DT*
A	-1.54172 (-0.433)	7.43452 (1.175)	0.29864 (3.635)	7.20529 (0.375)		
B	0.00461 (0.001)	6.50311 (1.018)	0.30251 (3.689)		0.12588 (1.007)	
C	0.02047 (0.005)	-12.64373 (-0.657)	0.30604 (3.715)	11.58751 (0.592)		0.14120 (1.104)

Note: Figures in Parentheses represent respective t -ratio

The results from Banerjee et al.,[3] (1992) are reported in table 5. As evident from table 5, the Banerjee et al., (1992) sequential testing procedure for unit root and trend break hypothesis indicate that all three series exports, imports and trade volume have unit roots in their levels. And structural break has occurred in exports at October 1994, for imports on January 1998, and for trade volume series in November 1994.

Table 5: Banerjee et al., (1992) Test statistic for Unit Roots and Trend Break

Series	*ADF#*	*Break*
Exports	-1.65	118
Imports	-1.45	158
Trade Volume	-1.71	119

The results form Perron (1997) technique are reported in Table 6. For the exports series, the coefficients of dummy variables are not significantly different from zero and hence it does not report any change in the series at the endogenous break point observed in October 1994. However, in case of imports series both the coefficients of dummy variables, DU and DT are significantly different from zero, reporting January 1998 as the endogenous break point in the series. For trade volume series an endogenous break in both level and growth rate occurred in October 1994. Thus, results of these three series conclude that, though policy break date happens to be December 1995, the exports and trade volume series exhibit more dynamic profile over time much before policy event date (i.e., SAPTA agreement date), where as the import series exhibit gradual change over time in Post SAPTA period.

3 The Banerjee et al., (1992) procedure computes the Sequential Minimum Augmented Dickey – Fuller test statistics and endogenizes the break point in the time series under consideration. The degree of AR polynomial considered in this exercise is zero. 0.15 fraction at beginning and end of the total sample are not considered for the test.

Table 6: Perron (1997) Endogenous Trend Break Test for Export, Import and Trade Volume Series

Series	*Constant*	*DU*	*D(Tb)*	*Time*	*DT*
Exports	1.54238	-9.77254	-11.56249	0.56356	0.32660
	(0.35739)	(-0.66620)	(-0.69680)	(4.28605)	(2.27699)
Imports	2.67707	29.50795	-23.03712	0.08096	-0.08391
	(2.71731)	(2.98511)	(-4.57194)	(5.58744)	(-1.50237)
Trade Volume	7.54440	-28.96588	-14.87514	0.45086	0.45686
	(1.71993)	(-1.85535)	(-0.80355)	(4.77408)	(3.34741)

Note: Figures in Parentheses represent respective t -ratio

Conclusion

The main focus of this paper is to investigate the performance of India's trade after the SAPTA agreement with other South Asian Countries, which are the members of the SAARC. Using monthly data of India's Exports to, Imports from and Trade volume with other SAARC countries over the period 1985:1 – 2001:12, the study finds evidence of a structural break (trend break) around the period October 1994 for exports and trade volume series, as where for the imports series around January 1998. The findings of the study suggest that India's trade performance with the member countries of the SAARC had an early shift (trend break) before the policy event date. The evidences of the present study, on the whole, reveal the India's dynamic trade performance over time with other members of SAARC.

REFERENCES

1. Banerjee. A, RL Lumsdaine, and JH Stock (1992), "Recursive and Sequential Tests of the Unit Root and Trend-Break Hypothesis: Theory and International Evidence", *Journal of Business and Economic Statistics*, 10, pp. 271-87.
2. Bhattacharyya.B and Vijay.k, (1996) "Regional Trade Enhancement: SAPTA and Beyond", IIFT Occasional Papers, IIFT, New Delhi.

3. Debendra.k, Das., (1992): *"SAARC: Regional Co-operation and Development: Perspectives, Problems, Policies"*, (Deep & Deep Publications, New Delhi).

4. Dickey, D.A, and Fuller, W.A (1979), "Distribution of the Estimation for Autoregressive Time Series with a Unit Root", *Journal of the American statistical Association*, 74, (380), pp. 424-431

5. IMF: Direction of Trade Statistics (June, 2002), CD-ROM.

6. Joy, P.A., (1995): *"SAARC: Trade and Development"*, (Deep & Deep Publications, New Delhi).

7. Madan, D.K., (1997): *"SAARC: Origin and Development"*, (Deep & Deep Publications, New Delhi).

8. Mehrota, LL et al., (1995): *"SAARC 2000 and Beyond"*, (Omega Scientific Publishers, New Delhi).

9. Panchamukhi, V.R and Das, Ram Upendra, (1998): "SAARC Countries: A Study of India's Trade and Investment Potential", Exim Bank of India, Occasional Paper No. 65, Exim Bank of India, Bombay.

10. Panchamukhi, V.R et al., (1990): *"Economic Cooperation in the SAARC Region: Potential, Constraints and Policies"*, RIS Publications, New Delhi.

11. Perron, P. (1989), "The Great Crash, The Oil Price Shock, and the Unit Root Hypothesis", *Econometrica*, 57(6), pp. 1361-1404.

12. Perron, P. (1997), "Further Evidence on Breaking Trend Functions in Macro Economic Variables", *Journal of Econometrics,* 80, pp. 355-385.

13. Ranjit Singh et al., (2000): "Indo-SAARC Trade Scenario: Emerging Trend and Trade Off", *Indian Economic Journal*, vol.47, No.3, Jan-Mar.

14. Rajesh Mehta, (2000): "South Asian Preferential Trading Arrangement: Impact on Intra-Regional Trade", *Asia Pacific Journal of Economics and Business,* vol.4, No.1

15. SAARC Publications: *"Charter of the SAARC"*, (SAARC Secretariat, Kathmandu).

16. SAARC Publications: "SAARC Preferential Trading Arrangement Agreement", (SAARC Secretariat, Kathmandu).

17. SAARC Publications: "Regional Economic Cooperation", (SAARC Secretariat, Kathmandu).

18. Various Reports of SAARC Summits, SAARC Secretariat, Kathmandu.

19. Venkatsubblu, T., (1996): *"India's Trade with SAARC Countries",* (Discovery Publishing House, New Delhi).

Appendix A

The South Asian Association for Regional Cooperation (SAARC), comprising the seven South Asian countries Bangladesh, Bhutan, India, the Maldives, Nepal, Pakistan and Sri Lanka, came into being at the First Summit of Heads of the Governments of all the seven SAARC countries held in Dhaka (Bangladesh) on 7-8 December 1985. SAARC is a manifestation of the determination of peoples of South Asia to cooperate regionally and to work together towards finding solutions to their common economic problems in a spirit of friendship, trust and understanding based on mutual respect, equity and shared benefits. Main objectives of the SAARC are:

- To promote the welfare of the people of South Asia and to improve their quality of life.
- To accelerate economic growth in the region.
- To promote and strengthen collective self-reliance among the countries of South Asia.
- To contribute mutual trust, understanding and appreciation of one another's problems.
- To promote active collaboration and mutual assistance in the economic, social, technical and scientific field.
- To strengthen cooperation with other developing countries.
- To strengthen cooperation among themselves in international forums on matters of common interests; and
- To cooperate with international and regional organisations with similar aims and purposes.

Appendix B

Perron (1989) technique performs a unit root test of a given series in the presence of an exogenously given trend break. It considers three models, where the first allows for an exogenous change in the level of the series; the second permits an exogenous change in the growth rate of the series and the third permits both. For a given series say, these models may specified as follows:

Model A: $y_1 = C + \theta DMU_t + \alpha Trend + \beta DTB_t + U_t$

Model B: $y_1 = C + \theta DMU_t + \alpha Trend + \gamma DTS_t + U_t$

Model C: $y_1 = C + \theta^* DMU_t^* + \alpha Trend + \delta DT_t + \beta DTB_t + U_t$

where c is a constant, θ, θ^*, α, γ, δ and β are parameters, U_t's are the error terms and DTB, DMU_t, DTS_t, and DT_t are dummy variables which are defined as follows:

DTB=1 if t = TB+1 (TB is time break), 0 otherwise

DMU_t = 1 if t>TB, 0 otherwise

DTS_t = t-TB if t>TB

DT_t = t if t>TB and DMU_t^* = 1 if t>TB, DT otherwise

Presence of a trend break in the series is confirmed by the test of significance of dummy variables.

Appendix C

In contrast with Perron (1989), Perron (1997) technique conducts a unit root test of a given series when the break period is endogenously determined. It considers the following model and allows a change in both intercept and slope. The Model is given by

$$y_1 = C + \alpha_t + \beta D(Tb)_t + \gamma DU_t + \theta U_t$$

where c is constant and are parameters, is an error term, t is liner trend, Tb is endogenous time break, and, the dummy variables which are defined as follows:

DU_t = 1 if t>Tb, = t if t>Tb

$D(Tb)_t$= 1 (t=Tb+1)

Presence of trend break in the series is confirmed by the test of significance of the dummy variables.

8

Did Economic Reforms Reform the Indian Export Performance?

*T. Gopinath**

In the evolution of the Indian economy, the year 1991 has been the watershed in the wake of the wide-ranging reforms initiated in response to an unprecedented crisis, which be fell in 1990. The external sector was the focal stress point of the 1991 Balance of Payments (BOP) crisis. Perhaps for that reason, it saw the most far-reaching reforms (Acharya, 2002). This paper attempts, inter alia, to examine the impact of these reforms on the external sector, in general, with a specific focus on exports.

The scope of this paper is as follows section. Section I carries an overview of the performance of the Indian economy in the quinquennium ending 1990, which is intended to serve as a background to the presentation of reforms directly related to the external sector. Section II catalogues the performance of the external sector in the

* T.Gopinath, the ex-student of the University of Hyderabad with a Gold Medal in 1986, is currently an Assistant Adviser in the Department of Economic Analysis and Policy, Reserve Bank of India. Views expressed in this paper are those of the author and not of the Institution, he represents. Computational help rendered by Smt. M.S.Borgaonkar and Shri G.S.Jadhav of the Department are acknowledged.

post reform period and prepares the ground for a focussed analysis of the impact of reforms on exports. While Section III enumerates the methodology employed for the purpose and presents the empirical findings, Section IV makes concluding observations.

Section I

The Table 1 summaries the major macro-economic indicators during the pre-reform period of 1985-86 to 1989-90.

Table 1: Macro-Economic Indicators

Year	*GDP annual growth rate*	*Gross Fiscal Deficit as % to GDP*	*Revenue Deficit as % to GDP*	*Net Primary Deficit as % to GDP*	*Trade Deficitas % to GDP*
1985-86	4.5	7.9	2.1	3.8	-3.4
1986-87	4.3	8.5	2.5	4.2	-3.0
1987-88	3.8	7.6	2.6	3.7	-2.36
1988-89	10.5	7.3	2.5	3.2	-3.2
1989-90	6.7	7.3	2.5	3.0	-2.6
Period Average	6.0	7.7	2.4	3.6	-3.0

Source: Handbook of Statistics on Indian Economy, 2001

The real GDP during 1985-86 to 1989-90 grew at an annual average growth rate of 6.0 per cent per annum. By all standards, performance of this magnitude is commendable. However, seeds of the fiscal crisis and the debt crisis were sown during this period (Nayyar, 2002). The period under review was characterised by the build up of unsustainable deficits with gross fiscal deficit, revenue deficit, net primary deficit and trade deficit growing at an annual average growth rate of 7.7 per cent, 2.4 per cent, 3.6 per cent and 3.0 per cent of the GDP, respectively. These deficits were financed by increasing and large-scale recourse to variety of external borrowings such as commercial borrowings and NRI deposits. The degree of export bias underlying the trade regime during the pre-reform period of 1985-90 was evident from the fact that exports accounted for only 4.8 per cent of GDP, while imports constituted 7.7 per cent of GDP. Net invisibles slowed down, which averaged 1.4 per cent per annum in the first half of 1980s, to 0.8 per cent per annum in the second half. In fact external commercial borrowings and NRI deposits together constituted 2.1 per cent of GDP during the latter of the 1980s. The debt service ratio rose to a peak of 35 per cent in 1990-91. The external debt stock to GDP ratio peaked at 39 per cent at the end of 1991-92, as did the debt to exports ratio at 563 per cent. On the contrary, non-debt creating flows i.e. foreign investment flows were miniscule at 0.1 per cent of GDP. The Gulf war and the associated oil price shock tipped India's fragile external finances into a full-blown BOP crisis. Thus, the genesis of the 1991 crisis could be traced to, inter alia, the fiscal profligacy, growing dependence on external borrowings and heavily regulated trade. To address the crisis and restore the economy to good health, a wide-ranging programme of macro-economic stabilisation and structural adjustment was put in place. The salient measures undertaken focussing on the external sector included the following.

The rupee was devalued twice in July 1991 leading to 20 per cent depreciation in its value. In March 1992, the country adopted a dual exchange rate arrangement, under which 40 per cent of the current receipts was required to be surrendered to the Reserve Bank of India at the official exchange rate and this was utilised to meet the cost of essential imports. In March 1993, the dual exchange rate system was abolished and the country moved over to the unified and market determined exchange rate system. The full current account convertibility under Article VIII of the IMF was ushered-in on August 20, 1994 (Rangarajan, 2002).

A major reform of trade policy has been affected since 1991 with import licensing system being dismantled. The export bias was reduced as the exceptionally high customs tariffs were brought down from up to 355 per cent to a peak of 30 per cent and quantitative restrictions removed barring a few items under negative list.

Foreign investment friendly policy regime has been unveiled. The policy allows automatic approvals for priority industries within two weeks subject to their fulfilling certain conditions. A more favourable treatment is accorded to NRI investors, who were allowed up to 100 per cent ownership in priority industries. A Foreign Investment Promotion Board (FIPB) has been set up to consider all other proposals that do not qualify for automatic clearance. FIPB is empowered to approve up to 100 per cent foreign ownership in cases involving transfer of high technology, projects producing predominantly for exports, energy and infrastructure projects, and consultancy and trading companies.

Policies governing external commercial borrowings (ECBs) have been streamlined. Short-term debt was reduced and strict controls put in place to prevent future expansion. Medium-term borrowings were made subject to annual caps, minimum maturity requirements and end-use restrictions. The growth of NRI deposits was moderated through the rationalisation of incentives; especially controls over inflows were exercised through interest rate ceilings for different maturities of deposits and variable reserve requirements.

Accumulation of foreign exchange reserves was provided with special attention in an attempt to acquire greater insurance against external sector shocks.

Section II

On account of these and other reforms in other areas, there has been significant improvement in the performance of the external sector.

Exports, which constituted less than 5 per cent of GDP in 1980s, strengthened their performance and position consolidated by almost doubling to 8 per cent of GDP in 1990s. However, improvement in exports was more pronounced in mid-1990s (1993-94 to 1995-96) with considerable deceleration in subsequent years with negative growth posted in 1998-99, notwithstanding the recent pick up. Imports too rose, in conjunction with an up surge in industrial production, exhibiting an annual average growth rate of 9.5 per cent per annum in 1990s, though in the first four years of the post-reform period (1992-96), they grew by as much as 20.3 per annum. In the post-reform period, imports constituted 10.8 per cent of GDP. The 1990s witnessed a revival in the net invisible receipts, forming 1.6 per cent of GDP in 1990s (2.5 per cent in 1996-2000). The surge in net invisible receipts may be attributed in part to the strength of the world economy, in part to the rational incentives embodied in a market determined exchange rate system and in part to the strong growth in software exports (Acharya, 2002). As a result of the above, current account deficit remained at 1.3 per cent of GDP in the post-reform period, which is a far cry from 2.2 per cent in 1985-90.

As regards the capital account, there has been a definite transformation visibly underway with acceleration in non-debt creating flows. The growth in foreign investment flows averaged 93 per cent per annum in the 1990s. However, if the 1990s is sub-divided into an initial period (1992-96) and the subsequent period of 1996-2000, the deluge of such flows during the former becomes apparent, when they grew by, on an average basis, as much as 248 per cent per annum, which suffered significant attenuation (14.8 per cent per annum) in the subsequent period. Similar movements were observed in NRI deposits with corresponding growth rates standing at 251.4 per cent and 46.7 per cent, respectively. ECBs, on the other hand, displayed trends of contrary nature, as, in the first phase, they grew by 60 per cent as against 252.3 per cent in the later phase because of an exceptional recourse to Resurgent Indian Bonds and India Millennium Deposits, respectively. Viewed in terms of percentage to GDP, the transformation underlying the capital account could be presented as follows. Foreign investment flows, which formed a meagre 0.1 per cent of GDP in 1980s, increased their share to 1.0 per cent in 1990s, while external assistance, ECBs and NRI deposits experienced erosion in their share during the corresponding period from 0.7 per cent to 0.5 per cent (0.6 per cent in 1992-96 and 0.2 per cent in 1996-2000), 0.6 per cent to 0.5 per cent and 1.5 per cent to-0.3 per cent, respectively (Table 2 and Graph 1).

Table 2: Major BOP Indicators as Period Average Percentage Share to GDP

	1980s	*1985-90*	*1990s*	*1992-96*	*1996-00*
Exports, f.o.b.	4.7	4.8	8.0	8.3	8.5
Imports, c.i.f.	8.0	7.7	10.8	10.7	12.2
Trade Balance (A - B)	-3.2	-3.0	-2.9	-2.4	-3.7
Invisibles, net	1.4	0.8	1.6	1.2	2.5
Current Account (I + II)	-1.9	-2.2	-1.3	-1.2	-1.1
Foreign Investment	N.A.	0.1	1.0	1.2	1.2
External Assistance, net	0.6	0.7	0.5	0.6	0.2
Commercial Borrowings, net	0.4	0.6	0.5	0.2	0.7
NRI Deposits, net	0.9	1.5	-0.3	-0.3	-0.2

Source: Handbook of Statistics on Indian Economy, 2001

Notwithstanding the above, it needs, however, to be noted that improvements registered on inward foreign investment front are modest, at best, as compared to those in countries in Asia and Latin America, including China and Brazil.

Taking the constituent components of capital account together, the surplus on this account averaged 2.3 per cent

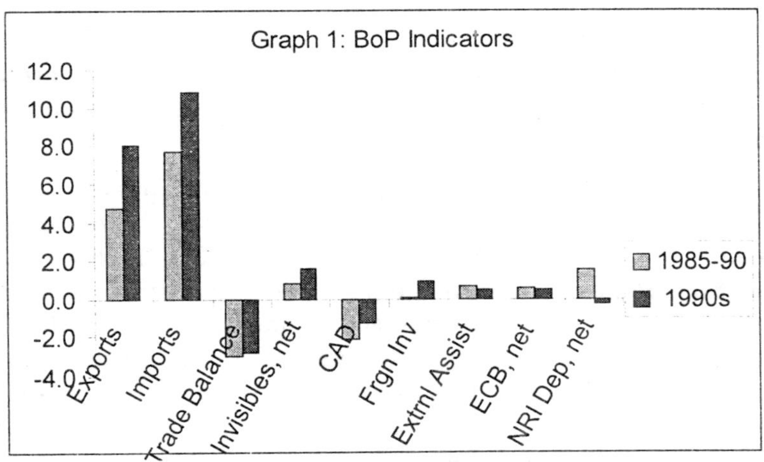

in 1990s, which has been higher than the corresponding current account deficit (save 1995-96) resulting in consistent accretion to foreign exchange reserves. Such reserves increased to US $ 37, 264 million as at the end of December 2000 from US $ 1, 205 million 10 years ago.

The culmination of all the above-mentioned changes could be seen in terms of perceptible improvements on the external debt front. The debt service ratio, which was at 35.3 per cent as at the end of March 1991, came down to 17.1 per cent 10 years hence. The external debt to GDP ratio well to 21.5 per cent from 28.7 per cent during the same period. The share of short-term debt in total external debt, on the other hand, stood at 3.4 per cent as against 10.2 per cent as on March 31, 2001.

Another note of high point in the deft management of external sector is that of exchange rate. The uneventful transition from a basket-oriented and administratively fixed system to a market determined one via an interregnum of a process of unification of dual exchange rates and the aftermath, particularly the regulation and moderation achieved in the nominal exchange rate during the turbulent periods surrounding the Asian crisis, stands testimony to this effect. The policy mix employed for the purpose included monetary policy, occasional quantitative restrictions and intervention in the foreign exchange market.

Based on the above-enumeration, it appears that there have been successful responses from the external sector to the reform initiatives (Acharya, 2002). However, as has been documented earlier, an emerging concern emanating from the external sector has been the slowdown in the performance of exports, notwithstanding the recent pick up. In this context, it needs to be noted that imparting a sustained dynamism to the export performance holds the key to the success of the on-going reforms. In the ultimate analysis, contribution of reforms would have to be measured in such a format. Against this background, an attempt is made to examine whether in the post reform period, Indian exports have been able to consolidate their hold on the global markets by increased penetration in the competitors' markets and whether foreign investment friendly FDI policies have been promoting the cause of export promotion.

Section III

In this paper, analysis of world market penetration of Indian exports is based on examining the share of select Indian exports in the total world imports of such commodities. An increase in the share signifies that Indian exports of the given commodity have been successful in penetrating its competitors' markets for the given commodity. The vice verse holds good in the case of a decline in the share. The movements in such shares are monitored on an average basis. For the purpose of capturing the impact of reforms on exports, the whole time period (1985 to 1998) is sub-divided into pre reform period (1985 to 1990) and the post reform period (1993-98) leaving the crisis ridden 1991 and 1992 aside and 1998 being the latest year for which the relevant data are available. Thus, symbolically average of x_{Ii}/M_i is calculated for respective period, where x_{Ii} is Indian exports of ith commodity and M_i is the total world imports of ith commodity.

These ratios are compiled not only for select Indian exports, but also for the Indian competitors including China, Brazil, Argentina, Thailand, Indonesia, Malaysia, Sri Lanka, Pakistan, etc. Comparison of such ratios is done across sub-periods among these countries vis-à-vis India to make a judgement on market penetration of Indian exports. The relevant data are sourced from International Trade Statistics Yearbook, various issues. Further, period average growth rates in Indian exports and world imports of select commodities are examined to make an endeavour to comment on future strategy for export promotion.

As regards examining the hypothesis of whether investment friendly FDI policies have been promoting the cause of export promotion, the following methodology is adopted. Ideally, contribution of FDI to exports needs to be studied at the balance sheet level of the recipient-exporting firm/companies. However, on account of data and time constrains, trends in exports vis-à-vis those in FDI are analysed (at broad sectoral level) to examine whether leading export commodities played host to the inward FDI during the post-reform period. The data on FDI, which are used for the exposition in Section II are not utilised in this Section for the following two reasons. Firstly, such data are not available for the pre-reform period. Secondly, they are not in conformity with the international definition of FDI, as suggested by the IMF. Instead, FDI data as available from the periodical surveys, conducted by the Reserve Bank of India on India's Foreign Liabilities and Assets, are employed as they not only confirm to the international FDI definition but also available for the pre-reform period.

The 23 commodities (at 3-digit SITC level) identified are included in Annexure 1. The share of these commodities in the total exports, on an average basis, works out to around 46 per cent. The calculated ratios for the select commodities and for the identified countries, including India, are presented in Table 3.

Table 3: Ratio/Share of Select Indian Exports to/in World Imports

SITC Code and Commodity Description		*Average Share for*		
		1985-90	*1993-98*	*1992-98*
074 Tea and Mate	Sri Lanka	16.5	15.4	15.1
	India	19.8	12.4	12.7
	China	14.9	11.4	11.8
	Indonesia	5.7	3.9	4.1
	Argentina	1.6	2.4	2.4
075 Spice	India	11.2	10.1	9.6
	Indonesia	13.1	10.1	9.9
	Brazil	8.9	2.8	2.7
	Malaysia	4.7	3.0	2.8
	Sri Lanka	2.0	2.6	2.6
	Thailand	3.3	8.1	7.9
	China	0.0	0.0	0.0
236 Cotton	India	2.6	2.4	2.2
	Pakistan	8.9	2.2	3.1
	Brazil	2.3	0.2	0.2
	China	1.8	0.6	0.9
514 Nitrogen Compounds	India	0.5	0.8	0.8
	Thailand	0.2	0.3	0.3
	Indonesia	0.2	0.6	0.5
	Brazil	1.3	0.9	0.9
	Argentina	0.2	0.2	0.2
	China	0.6	1.9	1.8
516 Other Organic Chemicals	India	0.4	1.7	1.6
	Brazil	1.4	0.9	0.9
	Argentina	0.1	0.3	0.3
	Indonesia	0.0	0.0	0.0
	Thailand	0.0	0.1	0.1
	Malaysia	0.0	0.6	0.5
	China	0.4	2.5	2.3

(Table Contd...)

Table 3: (Contd...)

SITC Code and Commodity Description		*Average Share for*		
		1985-90	*1993-98*	*1992-98*
531: Synthetic Dye	India	1.9	3.7	3.6
	Brazil	0.3	0.6	0.7
	Argentina	0.2	0.4	0.4
	Thailand	0.1	0.4	0.4
	Indonesia	0.1	0.4	0.3
	Malaysia	0.0	0.0	0.0
	China	1.0	5.0	4.7
541: Pharmaceuticals	India	0.8	0.9	0.9
	Brazil	0.4	0.2	0.2
	Malaysia	0.1	0.0	0.0
	Indonesia	0.0	0.0	0.0
	Thailand	0.1	0.2	0.1
	China	0.6	1.9	1.9
611: Leather	India	6.1	2.6	2.6
	Argentina	6.2	6.1	5.9
	Brazil	4.0	4.4	4.4
	Thailand	0.8	2.0	1.9
	Indonesia	0.7	0.1	0.1
	Pakistan	1.2	1.8	1.9
612 Leather manufactures	India	12.5	5.8	6.0
	Brazil	5.6	1.9	1.8
	Thailand	4.1	3.7	3.7
	China	0.4	7.5	7.0
625: Rubber Tyres	India	0.5	1.0	1.1
	Brazil	2.4	2.2	2.2
	Thailand	0.3	1.0	1.0
	Indonesia	0.3	0.8	0.7
	Malaysia	0.0	0.3	0.3
	China	0.6	1.9	1.8
651: Textile Yarn	India	1.3	4.3	4.0
	Pakistan	3.0	4.4	4.4
	Brazil	2.2	0.8	0.9
	Argentina	0.4	0.5	0.5
	Indonesia	0.4	2.2	2.1
	Thailand	0.8	1.6	1.5
	China	4.3	5.8	5.7
652: Cotton Fabrics, woven	India	3.5	4.4	4.4
	China	10.9	14.6	14.3
	Pakistan	3.6	5.7	5.7
	Indonesia	1.2	1.7	1.8
	Thailand	2.9	1.3	1.3
	Brazil	1.7	1.2	1.2

(Table Contd...)

Table 3: (Contd...)

SITC Code and Commodity Description		Average Share for		
		1985-90	1993-98	1992-98
653: Woven man-made Fabrics	India	0.4	1.1	1.1
	China	4.9	7.3	7.0
	Indonesia	1.6	3.6	3.8
	Pakistan	1.0	1.9	1.9
	Thailand	1.5	1.9	1.8
	Malaysia	0.5	0.9	0.8
658: Textile Articles	India	3.3	5.1	5.0
	China	15.3	18.4	18.1
	Pakistan	5.6	6.3	6.3
	Brazil	3.4	2.0	2.0
	Thailand	1.4	1.4	1.4
	Indonesia	0.4	1.3	1.4
667: Pearls	India	8.5	10.5	10.3
	China	0.5	0.8	0.8
	Thailand	2.1	2.5	2.5
	Belgium	22.0	25.4	25.1
764: Telecom Equip	India	0.0	0.0	0.0
	China	0.6	2.0	1.9
	Malaysia	1.2	3.1	3.0
	Thailand	0.3	1.2	1.2
	Indonesia	0.0	0.4	0.4
778:Electrical Machinery	India	0.2	0.2	0.2
	China	0.8	3.3	3.1
	Malaysia	0.3	0.9	0.9
	Thailand	0.5	0.9	0.8
	Indonesia	0.1	0.5	0.5
842:Men's outwear, not knit	India	0.5	0.6	0.5
	China	5.4	18.0	17.4
	Thailand	2.0	2.9	3.0
	Indonesia	1.1	2.6	2.7
	Malaysia	0.6	0.7	0.7
	Pakistan	0.7	0.9	0.9
843: Women's Outwear, not knit	India	3.7	3.6	3.6
	China	6.0	14.4	14.1
	Indonesia	1.4	2.0	2.1
	Thailand	2.5	2.0	2.1
	Sri Lanka	1.0	1.6	1.5

(Table Contd...)

Table 3: (Contd...)

SITC Code and Commodity Description		*Average Share for*		
		1985-90	*1993-98*	*1992-98*
847:Textile Clothing	India	1.9	2.0	2.0
	China	12.1	13.2	12.5
	Thailand	1.0	1.4	1.4
	Sri Lanka	0.5	1.1	1.1
	Malaysia	0.8	0.9	0.8
851: Footwear	India	0.6	0.6	0.6
	China	5.2	15.2	14.6
	Thailand	2.4	3.1	3.0
	Brazil	6.7	3.6	3.7
	Indonesia	0.6	4.0	4.0
893:Articles of plastics	India	0.1	0.4	0.3
	China	1.0	5.3	5.0
	Thailand	0.7	1.7	1.6
	Brazil	0.2	0.3	0.3
894:Toys	India	0.1	0.1	0.1
	China	6.6	13.2	12.7
	Thailand	1.0	1.4	1.5
	Malaysia	0.6	0.9	0.9

Source: Calculated from the data culled out from the International Trade Statistics, Yearbook: Various Issues

As regards the three primary commodities tea and mate (SITC code 074), spice (075) and cotton (236), India had lost its markets to its competitors. In tea and mate, India enjoyed a share of 19.8 per cent of their total world imports during the pre-reform period of 1985 to 1990. This position of pre-eminence has been eroded during the post-reform period of 1993-98, when it slide to 12.4 per cent. Its competitors such as Argentina gained an increasing market share from 1.6 per cent to 2.4 per cent in the same period. Similar picture emerges with regard to spice. During the pre-reform period, India's exports of spice accounted for 11.2 per cent of the world imports. However, in the post-reform period, they catered to 10.1 per cent of the world markets' demand for spice. Thailand and Sri Lanka had consolidated their contribution to the world imports by increasing their share to 8.1 per cent and 2.6 per cent from 3.3 per cent and 2.0 per cent, respectively. In the case of cotton too, India lost its markets. However, the deterioration in the case of Indian exports appears limited as compared to that of its competitors, notably Pakistan and Brazil.

Four commodities related to chemicals and allied products include nitrogen compounds (514), other organic chemicals (516), synthetic dye (531) and pharmaceuticals (541). Though Indian exports of these commodities improved their performance in the post reform period vis-à-vis that in the pre-reform period, significant gains were registered only in exporting synthetic dye with a very modest/negligible, at best, rise in pharmaceutical exports. Another noteworthy point in this regard has been that pick up observed in the performance of these exports from India plates into insignificance, if seen in the light of the strides that Chinese exports have made in the same period. The share of Indian exports in synthetic dye, other organic chemicals, nitrogen compounds and pharmaceuticals in their world imports rose to 3.7 per cent from 1.9 per cent, 1.7 per cent to 0.4 per cent, 0.8 per cent from 0.5 per cent and 0.9 per cent from 0.8 per cent, respectively. The corresponding ratios for China stand at 5.0 per cent from 1.0 per cent, 2.5 per cent from 0.4 per cent, 1.9 per cent from 0.6 per cent and 1.9 per cent from 0.6 per cent, respectively.

Among the 23 export commodities identified, exports of leather (611) and exports of leather manufactures (612) have lost their market share the most to their competitors. The share of Indian exports of leather manufactures in the total world imports, which was as high as 12.5 per cent in the pre-reform period, plummeted to 5.8 per cent in the post reform period. In contrast, Chinese exports of leather manufactures penetrated global markets impressively increasing their share in the world imports to 7.5 per cent from 0.4 per cent in the same period. Similarly, Indian leather exports, which accounted for 6.1 per cent of world imports in the pre-reform period lost their sheen in the global markets during the post reform period as their share plunged to 2.6 per cent. In contrast, leather exports from Pakistan and Thailand jacked up their presence with an augmentation in their share in world imports to 1.8 per cent and 2 per cent from 1.2 per cent and 0.8 per cent respectively during the same period.

Exports of rubber tyres, on the other hand, performed better enhancing their share in world imports to 1 per cent from 0.5 per cent. However, Chinese exports – which had almost similar share in world imports during the pre-reform period (0.6 per cent) – faired far better (1.9 per cent) capturing greater share in the world market than India. Indian exports of textile and textile yarn (651), cotton fabrics, woven (652), woven man-made fabrics (653) and textile articles (658) presented a better show during the post reform period as against the pre-reform period as they strengthened their presence in the overseas markets with their share in world imports edging up to 4.3 per cent from 1.3 per cent, 4.4 per cent from 3.5 per cent, 1.1 per cent from 0.4 per cent and 5.1 per cent from 3.3 per cent, respectively. However, yet again, Chinese export performance in these commodities underscores far greater consolidation of their position of preponderance during the same period. Another significant aspect of these Chinese exports has been that the consolidation of their position was on top of an already formidable presence in the world markets in the pre-reform period unlike the Indian case, where its global standing the corresponding period was modest, at best.

In contrast, Indian exports of pearls, precious and semi-precious stones (667) have cut deeper in to the competitors' markets in the post-reform period (10.5 per cent) as compared to the pre-reform period (8.5 per cent). This is on top of an impressive niche carved out in the pre-reform period.

Indian performance in terms of exports of telecom equipment (764) and electrical machinery (778) in the post-reform period has been as dismal as it had been in the pre-reform period. This observation acquires added significance in view of the fact that all its competitors did improve their hold on the world markets for these commodities. Notably, Malaysian exports of telecom equipments (from 1.2 per cent to 3.1 per cent) and Chinese exports of electrical machinery (from 0.8 per cent to 3.3 per cent) are the case in point.

Economic reforms did not appear to have helped the Indian exports of miscellaneous manufactured goods, as they failed to make any dent on the markets of their competitors. These commodities included men's outwear, not knit (842), women's outerwear, not knit (843), textile clothing (847), footwear (851), articles of plastic (893) and toys (894). In all these commodities, Indian exports displayed a lacklustre show by either maintaining their mediocre presence in the world market in both the pre and post reform period or posting a feeble mark up. These trends gather sharper focus in the light of the fact that all other competitors notably China and even Sri Lanka were able to cement their hold on the global markets.

Thus, to sum up, of the 23 commodities considered, 6 commodities (including 1 commodity i.e. women's outerwear not knit, in which fall (0.1 percentage point) was negligible) suffered decrease in their presence in the world markets during the post reform period in comparison with the pre-reform period. These included tea and mate, spice, cotton, leather, lather manufactures and women's outerwear, not knit. Thirteen (13) commodities (inclusive of pharmaceuticals, men's outerwear, not knit and textile clothing, which registered a modest/insignificant rise of 0.1 per cent during the period) exhibited increased global market penetration. These included nitrogen compounds, other organic chemicals, synthetic dye, pharmaceuticals rubber tyres, textile yarn, woven cotton fabrics, woven man-made fabrics, textile articles, pearls, men's outwear not knit, textile clothing and articles of plastics. Four commodities viz., telecom equipment, electrical machinery, footwear, toys held on to their earlier position. If commodities with negligible fall or mark up in their export performance during the post-reform period (consisting of women's outerwear not knit, pharmaceuticals, men's outerwear not knit and textile clothing) are assumed to be in the category of 'no-win-no-loss', out of the 23 commodities under review, as many as 13 suffered either erosion of or stagnation in overseas market share. These were tea and mate, spice, cotton, leather, lather manufactures, women's outerwear not knit, pharmaceuticals, men's outerwear not knit, textile clothing, telecom equipment, electrical machinery, footwear, and toys. Only 10 commodities registering clear cut gains, which included nitrogen compounds, other organic chemicals, synthetic dye, rubber tyres, textile yarn, woven cotton fabrics, woven man-made fabrics, textile articles, pearls and articles of plastics.

As explained earlier, one way to gauge the existence of potential for increasing penetration of world markets is to scrutinise the relative growth rate of Indian exports vis-à-vis the world imports. If the Indian exports grow at a higher rate than the world imports of a given commodity, it may be construed that Indian exports of that given commodity embodies the potential for enhanced penetration. The period average growth rates of select 23 India's export commodities and in their world imports are presented in Table 4.

Table 4: Period Average Growth Rates of Select Indian Exports and World Imports

	1986-90		1992-98			
	Indian Export Growth	*World Import Growth*	*Indian Export Growth*		*World Import Growth*	
516 Other Organic Chemicals*	54.4	19.8	56.5	H	6.0	H
531: Synthetic Dye*	51.3	27.0	20.3	H	3.6	H
625: Rubber Tyres*	35.2	17.7	34.1	H	6.3	H
653: Woven. Man-made Fabrics*	69.5	20.9	28.2	H	2.3	H
778:Electrical Machinery@	79.6	21.1	23.0	H	9.6	H
263 Cotton$	136.3	12.9	124.1	H	2.2	H
651: Textile Yarn*	56.1	16.6	33.1	H	4.7	H
851: Footwear@	27.8	17.6	176.3	H	3.6	H
893:Articles of plastics*	150.6	22.9	48.0	H	8.8	H
514 Nitrogen Compounds*	61.5	24.2	22.2	H	11.0	H
541: Pharmaceuticals@	152.0	22.5	62.0	H	10.9	H
074 Tea & Mate$	12.6	8.6	10.5	M	0.0	M
075 Spices$	-11.3	6.6	13.0	M	7.1	M
652: Woven cotton Fabrics*	16.7	21.1	13.8	M	1.7	M
658: Textile Articles*	17.3	19.8	16.9	M	6.2	M
667: Pearls*	19.9	19.2	13.6	M	4.5	M
842:Men's outwear not knit@	16.3	26.2	14.5	M	5.0	M
847:Textile Clothing@	46.1	18.6	17.9	M	6.0	M
894:Toys@	17.7	21.4	18.3	M	8.2	M
611: Leather$	6.7	24.1	1.8	L	6.3	L
612 Leather manufactures $	18.0	29.7	1.4	L	6.2	L
843: Women's Outwear not knit@	11.8	20.8	9.8	L	4.1	L

* Indicates increased global market penetration H: High Growth; M: Medium Growth and L: Low Growth

@ Indicates stagnant global market share

$ Indicates decreased global market penetration

High Growth signifies a period average growth rate of 20 per cent or more.

Medium Growth signifies a period average growth rate between (inclusive) 10 and 20 per cent.

Low Growth signifies a period average growth rate of less than 10 per cent.

Source: International Trade Statistics, Yearbook: Various Issues.

Of the 23 commodities, 19 fall under the category of high/medium growth in India's exports and low/medium growth (H-L, H-M and M-L) in world imports, implying that India should benefit from any future growth in world imports of these commodities, as it has the potential for increasing their presence in the overseas markets. However, of these 19 commodities, India has been able to take advantage of this potential only in the case of 10 commodities (commodities with * in Table 4) by penetrating the world markets. Thus, there is a case for focussed attention on the remaining 9 commodities (commodities with @ and $ in Table 4 within H-L, H-M and M-L categories) to capitalise on the existing potential.

With regard to 3 commodities *viz.*, leather, leather manufactures and women's outer wear not knit, both Indian exports and world imports registered low growth with former loosing their ground in the global markets during the post reform period. India, therefore, needs to build up potential for future export growth in these commodities if their world imports were to rise and India were to regain its lost position and capture the world market in the event of such a future expansion in world demand for them.

The above exposition throws up another crucial policy issue having a bearing on the need for diversification of Indian exports. As mentioned earlier, 23 commodities under review in this paper account for about 46 per cent of the total value of Indian exports. However, these commodities form only 14 per cent of the total world imports. In other words, it appears that world demand, as it evolves, has been moving away from the leading Indian exports. This observation has implications for the need for diversification of Indian exports to alien them to the emerging world demand, underscoring the requirement for greater attention to the aspect of studying the global markets for suitable signals.

As regards the role of FDI in export promotion, the following is in order. The Table 5 contains details about the period average share of outstanding FDI in the leading recipient-industries and the period average share of related exports (broad sectoral level).

Table5: Period Average Share of Select Indian Exports and Outstanding FDI

Commodity / Industry	*Export*		*FDI*	
	1986-90	*1992-97*	*1986-90*	*1992-97*
Textile Products*	2.9	2.5	4.4	3.2
Machinery & Equipment	26.8	18.6	34.2	30.7
Chemicals and related products	26.8	14.3	29.1	19.3
Metal & Metal Products#	14.0	7.6	5.3	3.9
Sub-Total	**70.6**	**43.0**	**72.9**	**57.1**

* Includes textile fabrics and waste (26) and textile yarn fabrics, etc (65).

\# Includes iron & steel (67), non-ferrous metal (68) and metal manufactures (69).

Source: International Trade Statistics, Yearbook: Various Issues for data on exports and Reserve Bank of India Bulletin: Various Issues for FDI data.

It appears that during the pre-reform period (1986-90[@]), leading FDI recipients represented leading exports. In other words, textile products; machinery and transport equipment; chemicals and related products and metal and metal products accounted for a similar share in exports and inward FDI (at about 72-73 per cent) in the pre-reform period. However, during the post reform period (1992-97[$]), while exports of these commodities suffered erosion of position of pre-eminence (from an average share of 70.6 per cent during 1986-90 to 43.0 per cent in 1992-97, as other commodities emerged as leading exports) FDI inflows

@ The FDI data are not available for 1985.

$ The FDI data are not available for 1998.

into the sectors producing these commodities continued to account for a major (though decelerated) share in the total FDI (from an average share of 72.9 per cent during 1986-90 to 57.1 per cent in 1992-97). In other words, there appears to be a wedge developing between the leading exports and the leading FDI recipients during the post-reform period. This observation tends to lend credence to the contention that efficiency-seeking FDI (export-oriented FDI) has yet to start flowing into the country in a considerable manner (Kumar, 1998). To put it differently, vast domestic market seems to be the pulling factor for inward FDI rather than the efficiency seeking considerations. In this context, it is worth noting that much of the Chinese huge export success has been due to the fact that most of the FDI went into expanding export-driven firms and the mutual reinforcement of exports and FDI (Acharya, 2003).

Section IV

Majority of external sector indicators *viz.*, current account deficit, debt and non-debt flows, foreign exchange reserves, exchange rate and external debt appear to have responded favourably to the reforms ushered in since mid 1991. However, contribution of reforms to the cause of imparting dynamism to Indian export performance remain ambiguous. Based on the analysis carried out for the identified export commodities accounting for 46 per cent of the total value, it seems that 57 per cent of them have either suffered from lose of global markets or failed to make any dent on the competitors' markets with only 43 per cent of these commodities being able to display increased world market penetration. The observed trend of most of the Indian exports of select commodities growing at a relatively faster rate than their world imports in the post reform period - implying the existence of potential for future - while ceasing to offer any comfort in the light of the above findings, emphasises the need for concerted efforts to ensure robust export performance, if world imports were to rise and if India were to capitalise on such an increase. Another point of relevance flagged in this paper is related to the need for diversification of Indian exports, as it is evident that evolving world demand has been drifting away from the leading export commodities. Finally, it appears that FDI inflows into the economy are basically large-domestic market-potential-oriented rather than export-based.

Annexure

074: Tea and Mate

075: Spice

236: Cotton

514: Nitrogen Compounds

516: Other Organic Chemicals

531: Synthetic Dye

541: Pharmaceuticals

611: Leather

612: Leather manu

625: Rubber Tyres

651: Textile Yarn

652: Cotton Fabrics, woven

653: Woven man-made Fabrics

658: Textile Articles

667: Pearls

764: Telecom Equip

778: Electrical Machinery

842: Men's outwear, not knit

843: Women's Outwear, not knit

847: Textile Clothing

851: Footwear

893: Articles of plastics

894: Toys

REFERENCES

1. Acharya, Shankar (1999): 'Managing External Economic Challenges in the Nineties: Lessons for the Future', 18th Anniversary Lecture of the Central Bank of Sri Lanka Occasional Paper No.33, September.
2. Acharya, Shankar (2002): 'Macroeconomic Management in the Nineties, ' Economic and Political Weekly, April 20.
3. Acharya, Shankar (2003): 'Half-hearted Globalisation', Economic Times, January 1
4. Kumar, Nagesh (1998): 'Liberalisation and Changing Patterns of Foreign Direct Investments: Has India's Relative Attractiveness as a Host of FDI Improved?', Economic and Political Weekly, May 30.
5. Kumar, Nagesh (2000): 'Economic Reform and Their Macro-Economic Impact', Economic and Political Weekly, March 4.
6. Nayyar Deepak (2002): 'Economic Development and Political Democracy', in The Facets of the Indian Economy, edited by Dr. Rakesh Mohan, Oxford University Press.
7. Rangarjan, C (2002): 'International Capital Flows and Exchange Rate Management: East Asian and Indian Experiences', in The Facets of the Indian Economy, edited by Dr. Rakesh Mohan, Oxford University Press.

9

International Negotiations on Transfer of Technology

*C. Niranjan Rao**

Introduction

Technological development has been identified as an important source of growth of countries. Soon after regaining their independence many developing countries[1] saw technology as the key input into the development process. They had two choices (not mutually exclusive), one to develop technology indigenously and the other to acquire technology from developed countries. As they were in a hurry to catch up they followed the latter option that of acquiring technology from developed countries. They looked at it not only as short term solution for acquiring technology for immediate production needs but also as a way of acquiring technological capability. Some of these countries introduced incentives for technology generation by domestic firms. It is interesting to note that these same countries thought that initial transfer technology would lead to long term technological capability. There are two

* Associate Professor, CESS, Hyderabad.

1 We will use the term developing countries generically, even though there are differences in the characteristics of these countries, most notably size.

ways of acquiring technology from developed countries, either through licensing or by foreign direct investment.

The regaining of independence by a large number of countries in the 1950s and later generated an euphoric atmosphere in which countries could have a choice in choosing their development paradigm. Independence restored the ability of these countries to take greater control over their development process. While the developing countries were trying to do what ever they could within their countries, they also had access to a sympathetic attitude of the international community. This international community in the form of the United Nations system helped these countries in articulating their perceived needs. The atmosphere till the 1980s was to listen to the articulations of developing countries. The situation changed in the 1980s and later to that of hardening of attitudes. The successive development decades starting in the 1960s and the 'New International Economic Order' provided the necessary background.

In the case of technology transfer this took the form of asking for a revision of the Paris Convention and negotiations of a code of conduct on transfer of technology. The basis for such moves was the necessity of development in underdeveloped countries. For example, the revision of Paris Convention was aimed at diffusion of technology through compulsory licensing rather than the effect it would have on generation of inventions, which was the most important motive as put forward by developed countries.

The experiences of developing countries have shown that patent system was hindering technological progress and licensing contracts are replete with restrictive clauses (UN [1964]; UNCTAD [1975] and UNCTAD [1982]). Developing countries have raised these issues at the United Nations and were able to convene international conferences for the revision of the Paris Convention and a code for technology transfer.[2] They both ended without any concrete results effectively in the mid-1980s. What was interesting about these negotiations was that developing countries were taking part as a group which enhanced their negotiating capabilities, unlike at GATT where they have to take part as individual countries.

The Uruguay Round of Multilateral Trade Negotiations started in 1986 with 'Trade Related Aspects of Intellectual Property Rights' (TRIPS) as a negotiating subject. This resulted in the Final Act in April 1994. Even though the developing countries have accepted the TRIPS Agreement, they do not seem to be wholly convinced that a higher level of patent protection will either generate domestic technology or result in technology transfer. The two important technology transfer related international conferences started at the initiative of developing countries have ended in failure. On the other hand the developed country initiative at GATT ended in success in a relatively short period of seven years.

How does the vastly increased power of patentees through the TRIPS Agreement going to effect technological change in developing countries and the technology gap between developed and developing countries?

Patents and Developing Countries

Many developing countries which were colonies have inherited their patent systems as a legacy of their past. Hence the patent systems they had in place at the time of independence were not chosen by them. They had no role to play in having to decide about having or not having a patent system or deciding which kind of patent system is good for them. Some countries have tried to replace the colonial patent acts with new legislation after independence

2 For a comparative analysis of these two see Delorme (1982).

and others reformed their patent laws. In the case of India it took 24 years for putting in place a new patent act, because of severe opposition from foreign interests.[3] Brazil, Colombia, Ecuador, India, Mexico, Peru, Philippines, South Korea, Sri Lanka and Thailand undertook reform of their patent laws in the 1970s (UNCTAD [1981] p.3).

If the developing countries were convinced that a patent system is at all necessary for encouraging inventions, the first thing they should have done is to experiment with a patent system which encouraged the domestic inventors (UNCTAD [1975 pp.47-48]; Balasubramanian [1987 p.AN103]; Yankey [1987 pp.62-66, 204] discuss the implications of the national treatment principle for developing countries). This could be done only if the patent system discriminated in favour of domestic inventors, (for example, by giving a longer patent term). Subramanian [1990 p.551] after discussing welfare effects of such discrimination concludes, "the possibility of the welfare superiority of discrimination could emerge in a wide range of *empirical* situations" (emphasis in original). This would have meant discriminating against foreign inventors. It is interesting to note that all developing countries followed the national treatment principle, either as members of Paris Convention or not. Countries, which were not members of the Paris Convention and hence are not obliged to give national treatment, also, followed this principle, thus foreclosing an option. It would have been interesting to see whether a higher level of protection to domestic inventors would have induced more domestic inventions. Such domestic inventions might have been more appropriate to developing countries.

Developing countries were more bothered about the dominance of foreign patents in their countries. These

---

3 Kochanek (1974) gives an account of how local and foreign business acted in concert to delay and modify a revision of the Indian patent law.

countries chose to reduce the level of protection of patents. This meant the domestic inventors also got a lesser level of patent protection. Hence, these countries chose to lessen patent protection because of the probability of misuse of foreign patents at the cost of foregoing domestic inventions.

In section 2 we are going to discuss the main issues raised at the Paris Convention revision conference. Section 3 will focus on the negotiations for a code of conduct for transfer of technology. Section 4 will review the TRIPS agreement focussing on the patents part. Section 5 contains some concluding remarks.

Diplomatic Conference for the Revision of the Paris Convention

The International Union for the Protection of Industrial Property, commonly known as Paris Convention was founded in 1883. At that time there were thirteen members, all of them except Brazil and Tunisia being developed countries. The Convention was revised six times, at Brussels (1900), Washington (1911), The Hague (1925), London (1934), Lisbon (1958) and Stockholm (1967). The 1967 revision is regarded as the most comprehensive and considerably strengthened patentees' rights. According to Patel [1974]".. Almost two-thirds of the developing-country membership is of very recent origin; these countries have acceded or succeeded to the Convention only after all its main principles were firmly established". By 1987 the developing countries constituted 63 per cent of the membership.

Even the initiative taken by Brazil on behalf of developing countries which led to the United Nations General Assembly in 1961 to ask the Economic and Social Council to study the effect of patents on developing countries and led to the publication of UN [1964] does not seem to have had any effect on the Paris Convention, which was further strengthened in 1967. By the time many developing countries regained independence and articulate their aspirations in the international fora, the international treaties have taken a rigid form.

They experienced the abuse of monopoly rights by patentees, overwhelming presence of foreign patents, which are not worked, and an international system, which puts hurdles in the way of appropriate policy responses like having a workable compulsory licensing system.

The United Nations General Assembly at it seventh special session, as part of the Second United Nations Development Decade, in 1975 recommended, "International conventions on patents...should be reviewed to meet in particular, the special needs of developing countries in order that these conventions may become more satisfactory instruments for aiding developing countries in the transfer and development of technology". By this time the Paris Convention's principles were firmly established. One wonders what the United Nations hoped to achieve by asking for a revision ostensibly to take into consideration the interests of developing countries. Contrary to the history of the Paris Convention this would have meant 'weakening' the Paris Convention.

The developing countries have been late entrants to the patent system. The working of the patent system in developing countries has been unsatisfactory. While foreign patents dominated in total patent grants there was no apparent benefits in terms of technological change. It is only working of patents, which would result in technology transfer. They saw compulsory licensing as a policy instrument to hasten this process. As many developing countries were members of the Paris convention, these countries decided to ask for a revision so that compulsory licensing can be used as an effective tool.

The work at the World Intellectual Property Organization (WIPO) for the revision started with the sixth session of the WIPO Co-ordination Committee in June 1974. Pursuant to its decision an Ad-hoc Group of Governmental Experts was set up. It adopted a declaration on the 'Objectives of the Revision of the Paris Convention'. In part it states,

> *"any revision of the Paris Convention .. should be undertaken taking into account inter alia the following objectives... (ii) to promote the actual working of inventions in each country itself; (iii) to establish the principal obligations and rights of the owners of industrial property rights; (iv) to facilitate the development of technology by developing countries and to improve the conditions for the transfer of technology from industrialised to developing countries under fair and reasonable terms; (v) to encourage inventive activity in the developing countries"* (WIPO [1979 p.7]).

Following consultations, the Director General of WIPO submitted a set of "Basic Proposals for the Revision of the Paris Convention" for consideration at the Diplomatic Conference. Between 1980 and 1984, four diplomatic conferences and seven consultative meetings were held. Although work continued in these consultative meetings the revision process has come to a halt.[4]

The most important and contentious issue for the revision was Article 5A. This article provides for compulsory licenses and forfeiture. The main features for

---

4 While the developing countries were trying to revise Paris convention's provisions on compulsory licensing, WIPO started work on patent law harmonization at the initiative of developed countries. The preparatory work on this started in 1983 and continued till 1990. The first part of the 'Diplomatic Conference for the Conclusion of a Treaty Supplementing the Paris Convention as far as patents are Concerned' (Patent Law Treaty) was held in June 1991. The substantive issues in the 'Basic Proposal' include requirement of disclosure, exclusions from patentability, rights of patent owner, term of a patent and reversal of burden of proof in the case of process patents. As of now this process is suspended because of the objection of the United States to change from 'first to invent' to 'first to file'.

the revision of this article are as follows. The right of the states to take measures to ensure working of the patents in that country (draft Article 5A(1)), the explicit recognition that import does not constitute working (draft Article 5A(2)), the provision of exclusive non-voluntary licenses if it is necessary to ensure local working (draft Article 5A(6)), and special provisions for developing countries with regard to non-voluntary licenses and forfeiture (draft Article 5A(8)).

The draft article 5A(2) is interesting. It stipulates that imports should not be regarded as working. This is to exclude the possibility of it being used to justify non-working. It is ironic that the TRIPS agreement later succeeded in including the provision that imports have to be regarded as working.

The draft Article 5A(6) stipulates exclusive compulsory licenses. The Paris Convention provides for only non-exclusive compulsory licenses, and this provision was introduced only in 1958. The reason for exclusive compulsory licenses might lie with the non-use of compulsory licensing provisions, which have been rarely used in developing countries. The main reason is that there is no strong industrial sector in these countries, which might have led to its use. If the industrial sector does not come forward with requests for compulsory licenses this provision remains unused. The failure of compulsory licensing provisions in developing countries is in fact a reflection of the failure of the industrial sector in these countries.

If a compulsory license is given to a local entrepreneur, the patentee to see to it that it does not succeed may either license the patent to others or work it himself (which has a better chance of succeeding because of availability of requisite know-how). To eliminate this possibility, and to encourage local entrepreneurs to take compulsory licenses the developing countries have asked for exclusive non-voluntary licenses.

The developed countries were not prepared to eliminate the prohibition on exclusive non-voluntary licenses. From the discussions at the diplomatic conference it was clear that what the developed countries feared was the surrendering of the right to import in case of exclusive non-voluntary licenses (Rao [1989]).

In many countries (including European countries) compulsory licensing of patents was included in their patent laws. The United States practice has resorted to compulsory licensing of patents as an anti-trust remedy. According to Neumeyer [1959] "Compulsory licensing in antitrust cases has developed in the United States as a judicial doctrine. Neither the patent law nor the antitrust laws contain any express provisions on the subject". The first judgement involving compulsory licensing of patents occurred in August 1941. Between August 1941 and April 1956 there were 94 judgements involving compulsory licensing of patents. The number of patents involved in these judgements seems to be a matter of speculation. While Scherer et al [1959] give a figure of 20, 000 patents for the period 1941-56, Hollabaugh [1960] gives the figures of 40, 000 to 50, 000 patents for the period 1941-59, Markham [1966] gives the figure of 35, 000 patents for the period 1941-57. What ever may be the real figure, they seem to be very high. The countries, which provide for compulsory licenses in their patent laws, have not granted compulsory licenses involving so many patents.

Another interesting aspect of the United States system is that while compulsory licensing applications in the countries having a compulsory licensing system in their patent laws, individuals have to apply for compulsory licenses and prove that the reasons for such an action are prevalent in the case of United States the government takes the initiative and once compulsory licenses are granted anybody is free to use them. While in other countries a compulsory license will be granted with a remuneration for the patentee or the application refused, in the case of an antitrust judgement in the United States, royalty free licensing, licensing of future patents, know-how decrees or even dedication of patents is possible. It is interesting to note that there are explicit antitrust violations, which result in compulsory licenses of patents, and non-use is not one of them. As this is a judicial doctrine the grant of compulsory licenses in antitrust judgements have declined in the United States since the early eighties.

International Code of Conduct on Transfer of Technology

Technology licensing agreements between firms from developed and developing countries constitute disembodied technology transfer.[5] It has been well known that such technology transfer agreements include restrictive clauses[6]. Both patent related and non-patent related technology transfer agreements seem to be having such restrictive clauses. But the question is whether the monopoly power given by a patent increases or decreases the incidence of restrictive clauses.

Vaitsos [1972] after studying patent license agreements says that a very high percentage of such licenses had restrictive clauses. He also indicates that patent license agreements tend to have more restrictive clauses. Greer [1973] points out that patent license agreements between a parent company and its subsidiary tend to have less restrictive clauses. This may be because

5 Vaitsos, 1972, pp.80-83 is the only one who suggests that patents and technology transfer are negatively related because patent monopoly prevents buying of technology from alternative sources.

6 A list of such restrictive practices is export restrictions, tying, field of use restrictions, unduly long duration of contracts, no-challenge clauses, restriction on adaptation etc.

of the control of the parent company on the subsidiary, which does away with the need to have explicit restrictive clauses in technology transfer agreements. Sercovich [1973] after studying technology transfer agreements in Argentina comes to the conclusion that even if the causality is unclear there is a statistical association between patent licenses and restrictive clauses. Kirim [1985] reports about the prevalence of restrictive clauses in technology transfer agreements in Turkey after abolition of product and process patents in pharmaceuticals.

Why did the developing countries ask for an 'International Code of Conduct for Transfer of Technology'? Many developing countries observed that there were restrictive clauses included in technology transfer agreements. This increases the direct and indirect costs of technology transfer. To reduce such restrictive clauses they have taken steps to prohibit such restrictive practices in licensing agreements. Some countries have adopted legislation this effect, others have issued guidelines listing what practices to avoid (see UNCTAD [1982]).

The main reason why the developing countries advocated for a code was that an international code will be more effective than domestic legislation. If there is an international code of which developed countries are also a part then the companies from developed countries will be bound to respect the code. This might have been more effective than policing the agreements at the developing country end.[7]

The United Nations General Assembly at its sixth special session in May 1974 passed the following resolution: "IV. Transfer of Technology: All efforts should be made: (a) To formulate an international code of conduct for the transfer of technology corresponding to the needs and conditions prevalent in developing countries, ...". Work at

7 The legal nature of the Code was a controversial issue.

UNCTAD started in May 1976 with the establishment of 'Inter-governmental Group of Experts on an International Code of Conduct on Transfer of Technology', which elaborated a draft code with many unresolved issues. The General Assembly of the United Nations in December 1977 decided to convene a "United Nations Conference on an International Code of Conduct on the Transfer of Technology" under the auspices of UNCTAD. Between October 1978 and June 1985 it held six sessions, without any success. The UNCTAD secretariat (UNCTAD [1995]) finally recommended that the negotiations on a Draft Code should be formally suspended.

The most important stumbling block has been including and defining restrictive practices. The developed countries always viewed these as business practices between two private parties and were reluctant to interfere. The developed countries have used anti-trust system to contain the non-competitive practices, some of which are in the Draft Code. But they were reluctant to include many, which they themselves do not view as restrictive practices. This is especially true of patent related restrictive practices. In the developed countries the governments used to view patent related restrictive business practices suspiciously, but since 1980s they have relaxed these affectivity were giving more freedom to the patent owner in the hope that this will encourage technology generation.

In fact the Draft Code (as of June 5, 1985) lists only two restrictive practices as fully agreed, viz., exclusivity arrangements and exclusive sales or representation arrangements. Restrictive practices such as grant-back provisions, challenges to validity, restrictions on research, restrictions on use of personnel, price fixing, restrictions on adaptations, tying arrangements, patent pool or cross-licensing arrangements and other arrangements, restrictions on publicity and payments and other obligations after expiration of industrial property rights figure in the Draft Code with a large body of agreed text except some crucial phrases like "unreasonably" and "unjustifiably" which are proposed by developed countries and opposed by developing countries. Restrictive practices like export restrictions and restrictions after expiration of arrangement figure in the Draft Code without any text. Other restrictive practices which figure in various proposals are restrictions on publicity, restrictions on adaptation, limitations upon use of technology already imported, obligations to use trademarks, requirements to provide equity or participate in management, does not figure in the Draft Code.

The differences of approach of developed and developing countries were in defining the restrictive practices to be avoided. The developed countries were unwilling to go beyond what is prohibited under their anti-trust laws. But what the developing countries wanted was to prohibit many restrictive practices. These different approaches were christened as 'competition test and 'development test'. Hence what the developing countries wanted was not just to follow the 'competition criteria' but to go beyond it. Correa [1988] while comparing 'competition' and 'development' tests says that while the former has history, legal precedents, extensive jurisprudence, and international recognition; the latter is disparate. But the philosophy behind the discussions on the Draft Code and indeed many other negotiations under the 'New International Economic Order' were to evolve a 'development' test. The UNCTAD (UNCTAD [1994b] p.193-194) in its assessment of the outcome of the Uruguay Round, comes to the conclusion that the TRIPS Agreement has ended the debate in favour of the 'competition' test over 'development' test. This was a major setback for developing countries in their quest for development. According to Wilner [1986] "The industrialized countries of the west sought, and largely succeeded, in grafting upon the criterion of economic development, on which the legitimacy of the practices in transfer of technology agreement was to be measured, the criterion of competition". According to Soltysinski [1988] "... it is clear that the 'development' and the 'competition' tests are practically incompatible".

In general in the United States and Europe the practices, which are considered part of patentees' rights, are restrictions as to the field of use, production quotas, quality controls, export restrictions and price fixing. Restrictive clauses which are not considered part of patentees rights are patent pools, tying, grant back, restrictions on R&D, restrictions after expiry of patents and challenging the validity of patents. But the trend in recent years in these countries is to give liberal interpretations of these provisions to expand the monopoly rights of the patentees in the hope that this will encourage more investment in R&D and hence more inventions.

Trade Related Aspects of Intellectual Property Rights

Coinciding with the slowing down of negotiations at WIPO on the Paris Convection revision and at UNCTAD on the Draft Code, the Ministerial Meeting of the General Agreement on Tariffs and Trade (GATT), at Punta-del-Este launched the Uruguay Round of Multilateral Trade Negotiations in September 1986. The Ministerial Declaration included 'Trade Related Aspects of Intellectual Property Rights' as a negotiating subject. The first two years (1987-89) marked a stalemate in the negotiations with developing countries refusing to discuss norms and standards of intellectual property rights. After the developing countries agreed to negotiate norms and standards of IPRs in April 1989, the discussion resumed. At the end of 1990, TRIPS remained the most contentious issue of the Round. It was only in 1993 that developing countries agreed to the Final Act, which was essentially the same as the draft text as at the end of 1990.

The main reason for the demand by developed countries to include TRIPS in the Uruguay Round agenda was the emergence of new technologies. Newer technologies were supposed to be easy to copy and hence difficult to appropriate. The fact that many developing countries have acquired a level of technological capability has also played a role in the ease of copying of new technologies. World wide high levels of patent protection will ensure that this does not happen (see UNCTAD [1994a]). UNCTAD [1986, p.21] enumerating the changes in the policies, laws and regulations on transfer, application and development of technology in the United States stated, ".. the international competitiveness of American industry is becoming increasingly dependent on technological innovation, and that in order to reinforce this competitiveness, it is necessary to relax antitrust rules and to strengthen intellectual property protection".

Part II, section 5 of the TRIPS agreement sets standards on patentable subject matter; duration and compulsory licensing among others. Article 2 (1) provides that the substantive provisions of the Paris conventions should be followed. Article 27 lays down that all fields of technology should be included under the patent system. Article 33 states that the duration of protection should be 20 years from the date of application; and Article 31 lays down the conditions under which a compulsory license can be given. An explicit mention that imports constitute a right of the patentee (Article 28), and non-discrimination between locally produced and imported goods (Article 27 (1)) mean that imports have to be regarded as working.

Together these amount to a very high standard of patent protection. This development negated what ever the developing countries were asking in international fora during 1970s and early 1980s. What the developing countries could not achieve in one and a half decades was achieved by developed countries in seven short years.

Article 31 deals with 'Use without the authorization of the patent holder'. This may be referring to the old compulsory licensing system. The interpretations of this article are controversial. Some say that many grounds for compulsory licenses in the old laws will be compatible with article 31 (UNCTAD [1994b]). Others say that this article defines the grounds very narrowly, hence the grounds on which compulsory licenses can be issued are not very broad (Dhar and Rao [1992]). Article 31 (c) provides for 'compulsory licenses' in anti-competitive situations. Article 40 of the TRIPS Agreement deals with control of anti-competitive practices in contractual licenses. It merely states that countries can have laws to control restrictive practices "having an adverse effect on competition in the relevant market". If this means that 'competition test' has succeeded over the 'development test', does this result in developing countries not being able to follow 'development test' in their competition policies which are applicable in their countries? How compatible is this provision to the draft code? Can a draft code doing away with 'development test' and concentrating on 'competition test' be revived?

Concluding Remarks

The initiatives taken by developing countries in international fora in the 1970s covered two issues as far as technology is concerned. The first was the revision of Paris convention with regard to compulsory licensing. The other issue was an international code of conduct on transfer of technology, to reduce the incidence of restrictive clauses in the technology transfer agreements. These initiatives did not succeed. On the other hand the TRIPS agreement considerably strengthened the rights of patentees.

What are the policy options available for developing countries in the present situation? First, they have to amend their patent laws in conformity with the TRIPS agreement. Whether they can use compulsory licensing as a policy tool within the TRIPs agreement is a moot question. The other option available will be to develop a workable anti-trust system, for use of compulsory licensing of patents as well as reduce the incidence of restrictive clauses in technology transfer agreements. The anti-trust systems, which have evolved in developed countries, may not be entirely suitable for them. The have to innovate and expand the possibilities under anti-trust systems. For example, the possibility of including non-working of patents as an anti-competitive practice.

What do these developments in international fora mean for developing countries? Does 'strengthening' of patent protection in developing countries will help these countries to build their technological capabilities? There may be two outcomes, one positive and the other negative. First the positive one, it may lead to more R&D effort by domestic private sector increasing their technological capability; it may also result in more patents being taken by foreigners which may in turn lead to technology transfer both through licensing arrangements and through direct investment. Both of these will be resulting in technological capacity building in developing countries.

Second, the negative effect. In this scenario there may not be any appreciable increase in the effort of the domestic private sectors' R&D effort. Foreign patenting may increase in effect to be used for import monopoly, with very little technology transfer. Hence, the technological capabilities of developing countries may decrease. This will result in the technology gap between developed and developing countries to widen. This will increase the technological dependency of developing countries on developed countries.

Notes

[Discussions with V V N Somayajulu, Surendra Patel, Pedro Roffe and Assad Omer were very useful.]

REFERENCES

1. Balasubramanian K [1987]: 'Pharmaceutical Patents in Developing Countries: Policy Options', *Economic and Political Weekly*, vol 22, nos 19-21, May, (pp.AN103-AN120).

2. Correa C M [1988]: 'Chapter 4 of the Draft International Code of Conduct on the transfer of technology: Alternative for Negotiations', in UNCTAD [1988], (pp.8-11).

3. Delorme J [1982]: 'The Changing Legal Framework for Technology Transfer: Some Implications', OECD, *North/South Technology Transfer The Adjustments Ahead: Analytical Studies*, OECD, Paris, (pp.88-167).

4. Dhar B and C N Rao [1992]: 'Dunkel Draft on TRIPS: Complete Denial of Developing Countries' Interests', *Economic and Political Weekly*, vol 27, no 6, February 8, (pp.275-278).

5. Greer D F [1973]: 'The Case Against Patent Systems in Less-developed Countries', *Journal of International Law and Economics*, vol 8, no 2, December, (pp.223-266).

6. Hollabaugh M A [1960]: *Compulsory Patent Licensing Under Antitrust Judgements*, Staff Report of the Sub-committee on Patents, Trademarks and Copyrights of the Committee on the Judiciary, Unites States Printing Office, Washington DC.

7. Kirim A S [1985]: 'Reconsidering Patents and Economic Development: A Case Study of the Turkish Pharmaceutical Industry', *World Development*, vol 13, no 2, February, (pp.219-236).

8. Kochanek S [1974]: *Business and Politics in India*, University of California Press, Berkeley, CA.

9. Markham J W [1966]: 'The Joint Effect of Antitrust and Patent Laws Upon Innovation', *American Economic Review*, vol 56, no 2, May, (pp.291-300).

10. Neumeyer F [1959]: *Compulsory Licensing of Patents Under Some Non-American Systems*, Study No. 19 of the Sub-committee on Patents, Trademarks and Copyrights of the Committee of the Judiciary, Unites States Printing Office, Washington DC.

11. Patel S J [1974]: 'The Patent System and the Third World', *World Development*, vol 2, no 9, September, (pp.3-14).
12. Rao C N [1989]: 'Recent Developments in International Patent System', *Economic and Political Weekly*, vol 24, nos 51-52, December 23-30, (pp.2841-2848).
13. Scherer F M; S E Herzstein Jr; A W Dreyfoos; W G. Whitney; O J Bachmann; C P Pesek; C J Scott; T G Kelly and J J Galvin [1959]: *Patents and the Corporation: A Report on Industrial Technology Under Changing Public Policy*, James J Galvin Associates, Boston, MA (2nd edition).
14. Sercovich F C [1973]: 'The Experience of Patents and Licensing Agreements in Argentina' in C M Cooper; C Freeman and F Sercovich [1973]: *The British Patent System in Relation to the International Patent Systems and Developing Countries*, Science Policy Research Unit, Brighton, (mimeo), (pp.37-84).
15. Soltysinski S J [1988]: 'Outstanding Issues in Chapter 4 and 9 of the Draft Code of Conduct on the Transfer of Technology', in UNCTAD [1988], (pp.19-28).
16. Subramanian A [1990]: 'Discrimination in International Economics of Intellectual Property Right Protection', *Economic and Political Weekly*, vol 25, no 11, March 17, (pp.549-554).
17. United Nations [1964]: *The Role of Patents in the Transfer of Technology to Developing Countries*, UN, New York, NY, (E/3861/Rev.1).
18. United Nations Conference on Trade and Development (UNCTAD) [1975]: *The Role of the Patent System in the Transfer of Technology to Developing Countries*, UN, New York, NY, (TD/B/AC.11/19).
19. UNCTAD [1981]: *Review of Recent Trends in Patents in Developing Countries*, UNCTAD, Geneva, (TD/B/C.6/AC. 5/3).
20. UNCTAD [1982]: *Control of Restrictive Practices in Transfer of Technology Transactions: Selected Principal Regulations, Policy Guidelines and Case Law at the National and Regional Levels*, UNCTAD, Geneva, (TD/B/ C.6/72).

21. UNCTAD [1985]: *Draft International Code of Conduct on the Transfer of Technology*, UNCTAD, Geneva, (TD/CODE TOT/47).

22. UNCTAD [1986]: *Policies, Laws and Regulations on Transfer, Application and Development of Technology: Periodic Report 1986*, UNCTAD, Geneva, (TD/B/C.6/133).

23. UNCTAD [1988]; *Draft International Code of Conduct on the Transfer of Technology: Report and Notes by Experts on the Outstanding Issues*, UNCTAD, Geneva, (TD/CODE TOT/52).

24. UNCTAD [1994a]: *Laws and Regulations Dealing with Transfer and Development of Technology: An Overview*, UNCTAD, Geneva, (TD/B/WG.5/10).

25. UNCTAD [1994b]: *The Outcome of the Uruguay Round: An Initial Assessment*, UNCTAD, Geneva, (UNCTAD/TDR/14-Supplement).

26. UNCTAD [1995]: *Negotiations on an International Code of Conduct on the Transfer of Technology: Report by the Secretary General of UNCTAD*, UNCTAD, Geneva, (TD/CODE TOT/66).

27. Vaitsos C V [1972]: 'Patents Revisited: Their Function in Developing Countries', *Journal of Development Studies*, vol 9, no 1, October, (pp.71-96).

28. Wilner G M [1986]: 'An International Legal Framework for the Transfer of Technology', in J R McIntyre and D S Papp (eds), *The Political Economy of International Technology Transfer*, Quorum Books, New York, NY, (pp.53-60).

29. World Intellectual Property Organization (WIPO) [1979]: *Diplomatic Conference on the Revision of the Paris Convention: Basic Proposals*, WIPO, Geneva, (PR/DC/3).

30. Yankey G S [1987]: *International Patents and Technology Transfer to Less Developed Countries: The Case of Ghana and Nigeria*, Avebury, Aldershot.

10

One Year of China's Entry to WTO

Implications for China and India

*Pradeep Agrawal**
*Pravakar Sahoo***

Introduction

The World Trade Organisation (WTO) has successfully concluded negotiations on China's terms of membership on 17th September 2001 and accepted China as its 143rd member on 11th December 2001. In this paper, we attempt to evaluate the implications of this event on China's exports, imports and inflows of foreign direct investment (FDI). We then consider the likely impact that this might have on the economy of India.

Accession to the WTO will provide China's exports with steady access to world markets, no longer dependent on yearly renewals of the most favoured nation treatment by USA and other major trading partners. This will provide greater stability to China's economy in general and exports

* Communicating author; Professor and Head, RBI Chair Unit, Institute of Economic Growth, Delhi University Enclave, Delhi-110007. E-mail: Pradeep@ieg.ernet.in. Fax: 011-766 7410. Phone: 011-766 7101.

** Faculty, RBI Chair Unit, Institute of Economic Growth, Delhi University enclave, Delhi-110007.

in particular. By making it very difficult for USA or any other member country of WTO to deny it access to their markets, the accession to WTO will reduce China's vulnerability to pressure from USA and other major trading partners on various foreign policy, human rights or other issues.

On the other hand accession to WTO will also impose obligations on China to undertake certain reforms in laws and practices relating to international trade. WTO also has associated agreement on *Trade Related Aspects of Intellectual Property Rights* (TRIPS) and may soon have another agreement on *Trade Related Investment Measures* (TRIMS), which impose additional obligations on China (as well as on all other member countries) relating to international trade, intellectual property rights and foreign investment. Thus, as a result of its accession to WTO, China will be required to further open up its markets by reducing tariff and non-tariff barriers to imports into China, eliminate certain export subsidies, eliminate dual pricing practices and give national treatment to foreign firms. This will lead to a more liberal and transparent environment for international trade and foreign investment in China.

Given the size of the Chinese market and its tremendous presence in international trade (about US $500 billion in 2001-2002), it is of considerable interest to consider the impact of China's accession to WTO on its economy – especially its exports, imports and inflows of foreign direct investment (FDI). This interest is further enhanced by the fact that these events will also have significant impact on the Indian economy, which competes with China in exports of many commodities, especially labour-intensive manufactured goods such as, textiles, garments, leather goods, light machinery etc., and in attracting inflows of foreign direct investment.

Therefore, in this paper, we attempt to evaluate the implications of China's accession to WTO for the economies of China and India. The plan for the paper is as follows, we first discuss the benefits of China's accession to WTO in terms of a steady access to world markets (Section II). Then we discuss the impact of various obligations that accession to WTO will impose on China. We consider China's obligations under WTO under two main headings: "Obligations Relating to International Trade" (Section III) and "Obligations Relating to Foreign Investment" (Section IV). The one-year experience of Chinese accession to WTO is summarised in Section-V. The obligation itself is mentioned first (in italics) and then its likely impact on exports, imports and foreign investment inflows into China are considered along with its likely impact on India. This is followed by the discussion of the overall impact of China's entry into the WTO on its exports, imports and FDI inflows (Section V). Finally, we consider the likely impact of China's entry to WTO on the Indian economy (section VI). Section VII summarises the main conclusions of the paper.

China's entry to WTO and its access to world markets

The accession to WTO would provide China's exports with a steady access to the markets of all the member countries of WTO, including USA, on a most favoured nation basis *(i.e., having to pay only the minimum tariffs that are charged on products of other member countries).* This is perhaps the most important reason why China has been eager to join the WTO. Until it joined the WTO, China's most favoured nation status in USA and many other major export markets was subject to yearly renewal. On many occasions, USA in particular, threatened not to renew the most favoured nation status of China because of certain foreign policy, or human rights grievances it had against China. Since USA accounts for about 20 percent of China's exports, any suspension of the most favoured nation treatment by USA would have created a major economic crisis in China. Thus, China always felt a certain economic vulnerability in taking its foreign policy and other decisions. The accession to WTO will largely remove this vulnerability by making it extremely difficult for USA, or any other member country of the WTO, to deny it access to its markets. Thus, China may have been willing to make some economic sacrifice, if needed, to gain greater freedom in its policy decisions.

From an economic point of view also, there was a heavy cost to the uncertainty of yearly renewal of access to the export markets as it created considerable uncertainty for China's export-oriented firms. The accession to WTO will dramatically reduce this uncertainty faced by China's export-oriented firms. This would lead to increased investment in China by both domestic and foreign firms oriented towards exports, leading to an increase in both the domestic output (GDP) and exports of China. Of course, increased investment by foreign firms means an increase in the inflows of foreign direct investment into China, which should be further helpful in enhancing export capabilities of China.

China is already in major exporter of the labour-intensive manufactured goods such as textiles, clothing, toys, leather and its manufactures, machinery, etc. (see Table 1). In fact it already accounted for nearly 34 % of world exports of labour-intensive manufactures by the year 2000. China's exports should increase further with the improved access to world markets as a result of China's entry to WTO. China's highly competitive and successful garments and textiles sector (with exports worth about $40 billion in 2001) is one of the important sectors that should see a clear benefit from WTO entry with the lifting of import quotas abroad, especially by USA and OECD countries.

China's accession to WTO could have a significant negative impact on India's exports since it also exports mainly labour-intensive manufactured goods, such as textiles and garments, leather and leather products, gems and jewellery, machinery, etc., which will face increased competition from China's exports (see Tables 2 and 1). Thus it is important to evaluate the full impact of Chinese accession to WTO on the Chinese and Indian economies. To this end, we explore in the next three sections the various implications of Chinese accession to WTO for China's exports, imports and FDI inflows. We will then evaluate the likely impact on India.

Table 1: China's Principal Exports to the World

(US $ Millions)

Commodities	*1999*	*2000*	*2001*
Electrical machinery and equipments	32, 949	24, 552	26, 951
Garments	31, 326	29, 763	30, 208
Machinery and mechanical appliances	19, 135	13, 717	16, 663
Textiles	11, 624	10, 497	10, 800
Footwear and Feathers articles	8, 678	8, 540	8, 389
Toys, games and sports articles made of plastic to the	7, 703	7, 520	7, 760
Articles of leather and articles of animal gut	5, 236	5, 583	5, 265
Plastics and articles thereof.	5, 123	4, 845	5, 161
Mineral fuels, mineral oils and products	4, 658	6, 986	5, 175
Furniture; bedding, mattresses, mattress supports etc.	5, 403	3, 804	4, 317
Optical and photographical instruments	4, 081	3, 997	4, 272
Articles of iron and steel	4, 351	3, 834	4, 190
Organics chemicals	3, 622	3, 397	3, 408

Source: India Trades, Centre For Monitoring Indian Economy (CMIE), Mumbai, 2001.

Note: Year 1999 refers to January 1999 to December 1999.

Table 2: India's Principal Exports to the World

(US $ million)

Commodities	*1997-98*	*1998-99*	*1999-2000*	*2000-01*
Gems & Jewellery	5, 351	5, 928	7, 509	7, 402
Textiles	5, 180	4, 500	5, 063	5, 725
Readymade garments	3, 880	4, 363	4, 770	5, 577
Drugs, pharmaceuticals and fine chemicals, petroleum products	1, 459	1, 486	1, 670	1, 914
Tea	1, 224	1, 459	1486	1670
Manufactures of metals	1, 024	1, 039	1226	1610
Machinery and Instruments	1, 197	1, 154	1184	1604
Marine products	1, 208	1, 038	1183	1396
Sugar	1, 129	1, 208	1038	1184
Articles of leather and articles of animal gut	886	878	825	1017
Electronic goods	760	502	681	1052
Spices	969	930	761	649
Articles of iron or steel	602	640	756	1020

Source: India Trades, Centre For Monitoring Indian Economy (CMIE), Mumbai, 2001.

China's Obligations under WTO relating to International Trade: Impact on China and India

Gradual reduction in tariffs and non-tariff barriers (over 2-6 years) and increased access to Chinese market for goods from foreign countries.

Reduction of tariffs and non-tariff barriers along with continued reduction of internal regulations and less differentiated treatment of various categories of importable commodities should increase imports into China (most of which come from developed countries). Table 3 reports reduction in China's average tariff rate over the years 1992-1997 and the corresponding increase in imports (and tariff revenues, due to increased volume of imports). As part of its commitments for accession to WTO, China is expected to reduce its weighted average tariffs from present level of about 20 percent to 8 percent over the next 2 to 6 years (see Ianchovichina *et al,* 2000). This would increase imports into China, as has been the result of falling tariff rates throughout the 1990s (see Table 3). Along with decreasing tariffs rates, reduction of import controls, removal of import licensing, increase in transparency due to extensive structural adjustments and reduction in protection measures like non-tariff barriers would make Chinese economy even more open in the future. Thus, Chinese imports should increase considerably as a result of these changes.

Table 3: Calculated Average Tariff Rates and Tariff Revenues of China

Year	*Average Tariff Rate (%)*	*Total Imports (Billion US $)*	*Total Imports (Billion Yuan)*	*Tariff Revenue (Billion Yuan)*
1992	42.5	73.82	478.4	21.28
1993	39.9	98.35	644.0	25.65
1994	36.4	111.57	1 0 96.4	27.27
1995	35.9	135.28	1 2 68.3	29.18
1996	23.0	154.13	1 2 81.4	33.98
1997	17.0	164.41	1363.0	NA

Note: Average tariff rate is a simple average of statutory tariff lines and Tariff Revenue is the actual collected revenue.

Source: *Measuring the costs of production in China*, Institute of International Economics (1998).

WTO agreement prohibits China from continuing export subsidies (on both agricultural and non-agricultural products) and subsidies to promote use of domestic inputs in place of imported ones.

China currently employs export subsidies as well as subsidies to promote the use of domestic inputs increase of imported inputs. Elimination of the export subsidies might reduce both profits and exports of affected sectors. This would also have a negative impact on inflows of export oriented FDI in the affected sectors. Elimination of subsidies on use of domestic inputs would hurt domestic producers of such inputs and may increase the imports of such inputs, but would not have much impact on China's exports or FDI inflows.

Further, China is obliged to reduce the subsidy to farm sector from more than 15 % to 8.5 %. However, since India and most other WTO member countries also have to reduce such subsidies to 10 %, the impact on exports may not be much, except in a few selected commodities where the higher rate of subsidies was particularly important. In such commodities, China's entry to WTO may create opportunities for India to expand its exports at China's expense. However, since the number of such commodities is likely to be small, the overall impact on India's exports would be minor.

To further increase its exports of agricultural commodities, India requires additional public investment (since private investment is very low in agricultural and allied sectors in India) on irrigation, power, roads, marketing and other infrastructural facilities. India also needs to attract private investment in research and development and application of more sophisticated inputs in agricultural sector. In recent years, the drastic decline in public investment on account of fiscal compression has resulted in a bottleneck in infrastructural facilities like irrigation, rural electrification, roads and marketing. Therefore, in order to access new export markets under WTO regime, the major focus should be to raise productivity by stepping up public investment, adopting cost-reducing technologies, removing restrictions on agricultural trade, and encouraging private and foreign firms in marketing and processing of agricultural products. This requires major reforms at both the central and state levels. Further, India can also extend more indirect subsidies, such as to research activities and to adoption of improved technology in its agricultural sector (which are not restricted under the WTO agreement) to make its agricultural exports more competitive. It has been claimed that use of similar indirect subsidies to agricultural sector have led to a sustained growth of agricultural exports for China.

Gradual elimination of price controls on products and services sold by domestic industries and service providers over 2-6 years.

China's current practice of price controls on many goods and services prevent imported goods of higher quality (and associated higher price) from competing in these products or services. Similarly, they prevent foreign firms who could provide products or services of a higher quality (and higher price) from competing in the domestic market. Thus, elimination of the price controls would increase imports and also inflows of FDI producing for domestic market. The elimination of price controls on inputs and services would have negative impact on domestic producers in sectors like automobiles, tobacco, food grains, wood, paper, metals and pharmaceuticals. Since most of these commodities are the principal components in India's export basket, there is scope for Indian industries to increase their exports to the Chinese market as a result of its accession to WTO. Further, China has to eliminate dual pricing of inputs (such as electricity) and other ways of differential treatment accorded to goods produced in China for domestic consumption and those produced for export purposes. This step would be likely to reduce China's exports to some extent and help the exporters of manufactured goods from other countries (including India) to increase their exports. This will also help India to increase its exports at China's expense since both China and India share similar export destinations and similar products in their export baskets (see table 1, 2, 3and 4).

Table 4: Five Major Export Destinations for China and India

China's exports		*India's exports*	
Country of destination	*Share of exports (%)*	*Country of destination*	*Share of exports (%)*
USA	20.9	USA	22.8
Hong-Kong	17.9	Hong-Kong	5.8
Japan	16.7	UK	5.3
South Korea	4.5	Japan	5.3
Germany	3.7	Saudi Arabia	4.6

Source: Country reports on China and India, Economic Intelligence Unit, Economist: Singapore, 2001.

Elimination of dual pricing of inputs (raw materials, electricity, etc.) for enterprises depending on whether they produce for domestic market or export markets (as a way to subsidise exports).

Charging lower prices for inputs from export-oriented enterprises is an important way in which China currently subsidizes exports by providing cheap raw materials, electricity, etc. Thus, its elimination is likely to have negative impact on exports, at least in some sectors where these subsidies are important to the success of the imports. In many other sectors, China has considerable cost advantage over its competitors, so that the impact may not be large. Thus the elimination of dual pricing in China following its accession to WTO would have a negative impact on China's exports. Given that China in India for competitors because of similar resource endowment, the likely impact of elimination of dual pricing on India's exports would be positive.

Increased protection of intellectual property rights under TRIPS agreement, including product patents and increased copyright protection, etc.

Increased protection of intellectual property rights under TRIPS agreement could increase prices of some products such as the newly invented pharmaceuticals, and reduce availability of pirated books, software and others products (currently China is thought to be the largest software piracy market in the world). Thereby it is expected to increase imports to some extent and increase inflows of FDI of the type for which intellectual property rights are important, such as in pharmaceutical industry and software firms. This could be useful for Indian software and pharmaceutical firms too in increasing their exports or investments in China.

Commitment to draft a transparent legislation and have an independent judicial system

China has to redraft many existing laws, draft numerous new legislations, and put into place an independent (western style) judicial system to make its economy compliant with the WTO requirements. It is said that China has to pass more than 2000 legislation's to make its economy WTO compliant. This will make the Chinese system more transparent and desirable for the foreign firms (mostly from developed countries) since this will restrict China's ability to help the domestic enterprises in partisan ways. Indian firms will also benefit in certain sectors, although the current impact will not be much as Indian investment in China so far is very small.

China's Obligations Relating to Foreign Investment and its Impact on Inflows into China and India

Foreign capital inflows, especially foreign direct investment (FDI) is becoming an increasingly important aspect of the development and globalisation process. Foreign direct and foreign portfolio investment helps the host countries by supplementing the domestic resources of capital. Foreign direct investment (FDI) also provides modern technology, improve worker and managerial skills, and can help boost exports because of the foreign firms' well-established brand names and access to the world markets (see Agrawal et al, 1995, especially chapter 3). Thus, an increasingly large number of developing countries are seeking FDI inflows. World FDI flows rose from U.S.A $ 644 billion in 1998 to $ 1.3 trillion in 2001 (World Investment Report, 2001), growing by about 26 per cent per year which is much faster than other major economic aggregates like world production, world capital formation and world trade. The global expansion of investment flows is driven by more than 60, 000 multi-national enterprises (MNEs) with over 80, 000 affiliates abroad. China has been particularly active and successful in attracting large inflows of foreign direct investment since beginning of its reforms in 1979. The volume of FDI into China and India is reported in Table 5. It is seen that the FDI inflows into India are quite low compared to China in terms of volume. The World Investment Report, 2002, provides data showing that, China has improved its position (from 61st rank in 1988-90 to 47th in 1998-2000) in FDI performance index while India is still far behind with the rank 119 in 1998-2000. A higher level of FDI in China is also reflected in higher ratios like FDI/total domestic fixed investment, FDI stock/GDP, value added by MNEs/GDP, FDI employment/ Total employment, etc. Using these ratios, UNCTAD's Transnationality Index places China (14.4 points) far above than India (2.8 points) in exposure of its economy to FDI.

Table 5: FDI inflows into China and India over the decade (US $ billion)

Year	*China*	*India*
1989-1994 (Average)	13.591	394
1995	35.849	2.144
1996	40.180	2.591
1997	44.237	3.613
1998	47.751	2.614
1999	40.319	2.154
2000	40.772	2.315

Source: World Investment Report, 2001

FDI is being looked upon favourably by many countries because it can help promote exports. In China, the exports by foreign-invested enterprises have grown rapidly and amounted to 47 percent of Chinese exports by 2000 (see Table 6) and around 50 % in 2001 (World Investment Report, 2002). Their share in China's import was more than 52 percent in 2000 (Table 6). Over all, FDI enhances the share of China in world trade by a major contribution in terms of exports and imports volume. Similarly, Table 7 reports the exports and imports by type of enterprise in 2001. The Table shows that foreign-invested enterprises export more than the state owned enterprises and others. Thus FDI has been one of the important factors contributing to the rapid growth of China's exports.

Table 6: Exports and Imports of Foreign-Invested Enterprises (US $ Billion)

Year	*Exports*	*Share in Total Exports (%)*	*Imports*	*Share in Total Imports (%)*	*Import plus Export*	*Share in Nation's Trade (%)*	*FDI Inflows ($ Billion)*
1996	61.506	40.72	75.604	54.46	137.110	47.30	41.726
1997	74.900	41.00	77.721	54.59	152.621	46.95	45.257
1998	80.962	44.06	76.717	54.70	157.679	48.68	45.462
1999	88.630	45.47	85.880	51.80	174.510	48.38	40.318
2000 (Jan-Oct)	97.125	47.35	95.180	52.29	192.306	49.67	

Source: Reproduced from Drydale and Ligang, 2000.

The FDI inflows were concentrated mostly in labour-intensive industries during the initial phase of reforms in the 1980's. But over the 1990s, foreign investors have begun participating in more capital-intensive industries as well. These include the world's leading manufactures of computers, electronics, telecommunications equipments, petrochemicals and power generating equipments. The

Table 7: Exports and Imports by Type of Enterprise, 2001 (US $ Billion)

Type of Enterprise	*Exports*	*% Change*	*Imports*	*% Change*	*Balance*
State Owned Enterprises (SOE)	44.3	-1.2	40.8	13.5	3.5
Foreign-Invested Enterprises (FIE)	51.3	19.5	49.2	14.2	2.1
Collectives	5.3	40.0	3.1	55.3	2.2
Others	1.6	99.7	2.1	162.9	-0.5
Total	**102.5**	**11.0**	**95.2**	**16.3**	**7.3**

Source: EIU Country Report on China, 2000.

prominence of FDI in high-technology industries is also manifested in China's exports - the exports of high and new-technology products by foreign firms and their affiliates increased from $ 4.5 billion in 1996 to $30 billion in 2000 (see Table 8).

Table 8: High-technology Exports from China by Ownership (US $ Billions)

Year	*Total Exports ($ Billion)*	*Foreign Firms and Affiliates*		*State Owned Enterprises*	
		Exports ($ Billion)	*Share in Total Exports (%)*	*Exports ($ Billion)*	*Share in Total Exports (%)*
1996	7.681	4.531	59	3.149	41
1997	16.310	-	-	-	-
1998	20.251	14.985	74	5.265	26
1999	24.704	18.775	76	5.928	24
2000	37.040	30.002	81	7.037	19

Source: Country Report on China, Economic Intelligent Unit, Economist, Singapore, 2000

The full extent of advantages provided by FDI depends upon the amount of exports generated, employment created, forward and backward production linkages with local firms, and contribution made to the local technological capability building. To enhance the positive aspects of FDI inflows, many countries employ some selective policy measures, such as, allowing preferential inflows of FDI in selected sectors (often those requiring higher technology or having greater export orientation), requiring foreign exchange neutrality (imports and dividend payouts in foreign exchange not to exceed exports over a period of several years), and local content requirements that aim to increase backward linkages with local firms.

The accession to WTO would provide China's exports a steady access to the world markets, including USA. This should have the effect of increasing inflows of foreign capital into China. At the same time accession to WTO would also curtail China's ability to impose many regulations and obligations on foreign firms, which would also influence inflows of foreign capital into China as well as the benefits that China derives from the foreign capital. In the rest of this section, we discuss the impact of China's entry to WTO on FDI inflows into China along with the possible impact on FDI inflows into India.

The accession to WTO would provide China's exports with a steady access to the markets of all WTO member countries, including USA, on a "most favoured nation basis".

As previously discussed in Section II, the accession to WTO would provide China's exports with steady access to the markets of all the member countries including USA on a most favoured nation basis This is perhaps the most important reason why China has been eager to join the WTO as accession to WTO will reduce uncertainty faced by China's export-oriented firms. This would lead to increased investment in China by foreign (and domestic) firms leading to an increased inflow of foreign direct investment into China, which should be also helpful in increasing China's exports.

Gradual opening up of service sectors like telecom, banking, insurance, retail and, wholesale trade, etc. to foreign investment.

China has a large domestic market. Thus, opening up of service sectors like telecom, banking, insurance, retail and wholesale trade, etc., to foreign investment could boost inflows of FDI into these sectors in a big way. Foreign firms specializing in financial and legal services such as banks, insurance companies and law firms will gain more access to the Chinese markets. Opening up the retail trade will help modernise it and may help foreign firms from developed countries to establish their own distribution channels in China in a bid to capture the vast domestic market – this would be likely to increase imports of consumer goods into China. It will have a positive impact on FDI inflows into China.

Access for most enterprises to operate and sell in all economic zones of China (with limited exceptions, such as in the case of tobacco products)

Currently, China is divided into several economic zones and firms are allowed to operate and sell their products only in the zones in which they are registered. Thus, freedom to trade throughout China will benefit foreign firms by considerably increasing their access to China's large domestic market. Thus inflows of FDI directed towards producing for China's domestic market should increase.

Changes in equity market regulations to allow foreign business houses to undertake mergers and acquisitions of domestic firms.

These regulatory changes will allow foreign equity investors to undertake acquisitions of and/or mergers with suitable Chinese firms. Thus, it would have a positive impact on foreign equity (or portfolio) investment inflows into China. The recent move of the Chinese government to disinvest in several large state-owned enterprises, and regulatory changes in the equity market would attract more foreign portfolio investment into China.

Though the cross-border mergers and acquisitions had limited success in China in terms of volume until early nineties, they have picked up since 1995 (Table 9). Thus, mergers and acquisitions are going to be another instrument for China to attract additional foreign investment. Mergers and acquisitions have also picked up in India since 1997 (Table 9). Further regulatory reforms and dis-investments in state owned enterprises might help further speed up the process in India.

Table 9: Cross-border Mergers and Acquisition in China and India

(US $ Million)

Years	*China*	*India*
1992	221	35
1993	561	96
1994	715	385
1995	403	276
1996	1906	206
1997	1856	1520
1998	798	361
1999	2395	1044
2000	2247	1219
2002	2325	1037

Source: World Investment Report, 2002

Laws relating to firms have to be published.

China currently runs much of its industrial (and other) administration with unpublished government documents. This means that the firms are often not clear about the rules and government officials are able to exercise considerable discretion, resulting in lack of accountability and in corruption. The existing system is sometimes used to give extra favours to foreign firms while avoiding public accountability. Thus, the short-run impact of a more rule-based administration could even be negative on existing foreign firms if some of the special favours are no longer available. On the other hand, many foreign and domestic firms may prefer a more transparent and rule based trading system under the aegis of the WTO framework. Such a rule-based system would minimise the possibilities of arbitrary and unfair rules being framed in future and it may be perceived to be less liable to corruption. Thus, we believe that it should have a positive influence on FDI inflows over the medium to long run.

Elimination of dual pricing of inputs for enterprises depending on whether they produce for domestic market or export markets. Currently China makes substantial use of dual pricing on raw materials, electricity, etc as a way to subsidise exports.

Charging lower prices for inputs from export-oriented enterprises is an important way in which China currently subsidizes exports by providing cheap raw materials, electricity, etc. Thus, its elimination is likely to have negative impact on exports as well as export oriented FDI inflows into China at least in some sectors where these subsidies are important to the success of the exports. Thus, the elimination of dual pricing in China following its accession to WTO would have a negative impact on FDI inflows into China. Of course, China's entry into the WTO has opened up many more areas of investment and the loss in a few sectors would be made up in other sectors, so that the overall inflows of FDI would not decline, even though the impact of elimination of dual pricing alone would be negative. Given that China and India are competitors because of similar resource endowment, the likely impact of elimination of dual pricing on FDI inflows into India would be positive (the magnitude would depend upon the FDI related policies that we pursue).

Under the proposed TRIMS agreement, foreign enterprises should be treated at par with domestic enterprises (national treatment) regarding measures falling under GATT articles III and XI. This implies requirements such as, the domestic content requirement, and the trade-balancing requirement (which links imports allowed to foreign enterprises to their export earnings) will have to be phased out over next 2-6 years.

It should be noted that the TRIMS (Trade Related Investment Measures) agreement is still being negotiated and its terms are not finalised yet. The clauses mentioned above are under negotiation and are likely to be part of the final draft. Foreign firms obviously prefer not to have mandatory domestic content requirements or exports obligations. Thus, if China removes the various TRIMS-inconsistent performance requirements on MNEs, this would increase the inflows of FDI into China. However, this will mean that the domestic industries benefiting from the local content requirement clause will suffer. There is evidence that these requirements have not been very effective and thus overall impact may not be large, except on local firms that are directly affected by it. Similarly, granting the national treatment to foreign firms will ease some of the regulations on them, and also assure them that rules and regulations affecting them cannot be changed suddenly and adversely in future—thereby reducing uncertainty that the foreign investors face. The impact of these changes on foreign direct investment inflows should be positive. However, since India, and all other WTO member countries will also have to adopt similar policies, the overall impact on FDI inflows into China or India would probably be quite small.

Overall Impact of Entry to WTO on China

In this Section, we summarise the overall impact of entry to WTO on China's imports, exports, and inflows of foreign investment in China on the basis of our analysis in Sections II, III and IV.

Imports into China will almost certainly increase considerably as the trade related obligations under WTO accession agreement would force China to open its domestic markets, reduce tariffs, reduce non-tariff barriers, including quantitative restrictions on imports (since China does not have balance of payment problems) and eliminate price controls in the domestic market. Over all, all these measures are expected to widen the export opportunities for many countries. India's exports to China may also increase a bit in selected sectors like steel, leather, agricultural products, minerals, software etc. However, the impact on India's exports would be marginal given that China currently accounts for hardly 2 percent of India's exports.

Exports from China would get influenced in two ways, and in opposite directions. One, exports would increase as a result of steady access to world markets (no longer subject to the uncertainty of being granted most favoured nation treatment by USA and other major trading partners each year) – this will reduce uncertainty faced by exporters and will encourage more firms, both domestic and foreign, to produce for exports, causing the total exports to increase. Two, WTO membership would require China to phase out export subsidies and dual pricing practices that provided inputs to exporting enterprises at a lower price over the next 2-5 years which will have a negative influence on the exports. Thus, overall impact on exports from China would depend on which of these influences is stronger. Our expectation is that the first effect will dominate in the medium to long run so that China's exports would be affected positively, at least in the medium to long run.

Note that our analysis above suggests that China's imports will increase faster than its exports. This is so because almost all influences of Chinese accession to WTO on its imports are in the direction of increasing them while the exports have both positive and negative influences.

Overall, while the exports will still grow, they will probably grow at a slower rate than the imports. Thus, the large trade surplus that China currently enjoys may decline in the future as a result of its accession to WTO.

In this context, it is worth noting that in a recent study, Ianchovichina *et al* (2000) provide some quantitative estimates of the impact of China's entry to the WTO on its exports and imports. They also estimate that as a result of China's accession to WTO, China's imports and exports will grow faster than they would have grown without accession. Furthermore, they also concur with our conclusion that the increase in imports will be larger than the increase in exports (see Table 10). Therefore, the integration of Chinese economy with the global economy will further increase in the future.

Table 10: China's Exports and Imports (as Percentage of World Economy) With and Without Accession to WTO

	In 1995	*In 2005*	
		Without Accession	*With Accession*
Exports	3.70	4.58	6.34
Imports	3.21	4.75	6.14

Source: Ianchovichina *et al*, 2000.

Finally, consider the impact of China's accession to the WTO on inflows of FDI. FDI oriented towards producing for China's domestic markets is likely to increase substantially as China opens up many additional sectors such as telecom, insurance, retail and wholesale trade, etc. There will also be additional positive effects due to elimination of price controls in the domestic markets, implementation of several TRIMS measures such as national treatment of foreign firms and improved access to the domestic markets due to elimination of economic zones and increased intellectual property rights protection.

Similarly, export oriented FDI would increase due to steady access to USA and world markets. However, such FDI would also have some negative impact due to elimination of export subsidies/ dual pricing practices, etc. It is our judgement that the first effect will dominate, leading to increases in inflows of export oriented FDI. Overall, we expect that the impact of China's entry into WTO on total (sum of export oriented and domestic market oriented) FDI inflows would be positive and substantial. However, given the already large base of FDI inflows into China, the effect may not be very large as percent of FDI inflows already coming into China.

Thus, the likely impact of China's accession to WTO is not only elimination of the uncertainty of access to USA and world export markets, but also an increase in imports, exports and FDI inflows – this implies an increase in economic activity and can be expected to lead to a higher growth rate of GDP, assuming that the exports and imports increase by somewhat comparable amounts. Technically, if the increase in imports turns out to be much larger than the increase in exports, GDP growth rate may not increase and could even decline. However, we do not expect this as China can be expected to find ways to prevent such a sharp increase in imports. Thus, entry into WTO provides China with economic benefits and at the same time, it also reduces China's vulnerability to pressures from United States and other major trading partners on foreign policy, human rights, or other issues via frequent threats of denial of access to their markets to China's exports. This explains China's eagerness to join the WTO.

Impact on India

In the last Section, we saw that China's entry into the WTO is likely to increase China's exports, imports and inflows of foreign direct investment into China. In this Section, we consider the impact of China's entry into WTO on India's exports, imports and FDI inflows.

First, consider the impact on India's exports. Both India and China have comparative advantage in the exports of labour-intensive manufactured goods due to the low costs of labour and India competes with China in the export of many such goods, e.g., textiles, garments, leather and leather products, light machinery, etc. (see Tables 1 and 2 in Section II above). Thus, India will have stiff competition from china since most of its export items are also principal commodities in the Chinese export basket (see for example, Agrawal, 2001 and Agrawal, 2003). Since the composition and direction of trade of China and India are similar (also see Tables 4 above), further integration of Chinese economy with the rest of the world would be likely to have a negative impact on India's exports. Indeed we believe that the surge in China's exports over the last 5 years may be partially responsible for the lack of significant growth in India's exports over this period. Thus, if Chinese exports increase as a result of China's accession to WTO, impact on India's exports is likely to be a reduced rate of growth.

On the other hand, an increase in China's imports would have a positive impact on India's exports. Since most of the top commodities imported by China (see Table 11) like machinery, minerals and mineral products iron and steel, organic chemicals, medical and surgical equipments, agricultural products, etc. are principal commodities in the Indian export basket (see Table 2 above). Given that china will have to lower tariffs on many of its imports and phase out many subsidies, there would be some increase in India's exports to China. However, we believe that the first influence is likely to be much stronger than the second, since India's bilateral trade with China is quite small (see Table 12) compared to its total trade. Thus, the overall impact of China entry to WTO on India's exports is likely to be negative.

Table 11: China's Principal Imports from the Rest of the World

(US $ Millions)

Commodities	*1998-99*	*1999-00*	*2000-01*
Nuclear reactors, machinery and mechanical appliances	17906	17456	17623
Electrical machinery and equipments	14634	15618	17774
Mineral fuels, mineral oils and products	6556	3649	5178
Plastics and articles thereof.	4824	4679	4948
Iron and steel.	4230	3407	3782
Aircraft, spacecraft, and parts thereof.	3763	5109	3378
Organic Chemicals	2805	2953	3899
Optic articles and medical or surgical instruments	2609	2716	3402
Vehicles and parts and accessories thereof.	2428	1815	1747

Source: India trades, CMIE, 2001.

Table 12: India's Trade with China

(Rs Crores)

Years	*Exports to China (Present Share in India's Total Exports)*	*Imports from China (present Share in India's Total Imports)*	*Total Bilateral Trade with China*	*India's Trade Balance with China*
1994-95	798.240 (0.97)	2388.01 (2.66)	3187.14	-1590.66
1995-96	1112.89 (1.05)	2716.06 (2.22)	3828.95	-1603.18
1996-97	2182.54 (1.84)	2687.03 (1.93)	4869.57	-504.49
1997-98	2668.71 (2.05)	4160.04 (2.70)	6828.75	-1491.33
1998-99	1797.05 (1.29)	4613.93 (2.59)	6410.98	-2816.88
1999-00	2334.56 (1.47)	5575.64 (2.73)	7912.21	-3241.08
2000-01	3788.32 (1.87)	6706.34 (2.96)	10494.66	-2918.02

Source: Various reports of DGCIS, Calcutta. Figures in parenthesis refer to share in total.

Next, consider the impact of China's entry to WTO on India's imports. Unlike the case of exports, the impact on India's imports from third countries is likely to be negligible since imports from third countries are unlikely to be affected much by the Chinese accession to WTO. Thus the main effect will come via the impact on Indo-Chinese trade.

Table 13 shows India's trade relation with China. It is seen that the bilateral trade between India and china is quite limited, with India's exports to china constituting about 2 percent of India's exports and India's imports from China constituting about 3 percent of India's imports in 2000-2001. Over the 1990s, there has been an increasing trend in bilateral trade deficit with China due to a more rapid growth in imports from China relative even though India's exports to China have also had a rising trend (except over 1998-99, when the East Asian crisis may have made some of the East Asian imports cheaper and therefore more attractive). The impact of China's entry to WTO on its exports to India would have both positive influences (due to increased FDI inflows into China) and negative influences (due to phasing out of various export subsidies and dual pricing practices by China). Thus, given the limited bilateral trade with China, it is unlikely that there will be a significant impact of China's entry to WTO on India's imports.

However, as we noted earlier, India's export growth would decline as a result of Chinese accession to WTO and since India often faces current account and balance of payment deficits, the slower growth of exports may also force a slower growth of imports by a roughly comparable amount. It may be interesting to note that using simulation analysis, Ianchovichina *et al* (2000) arrive at a similar conclusion (see Table 13)

Finally, let us consider the impact of China's entry into WTO on FDI inflows into India. We saw in Section IV that following its accession to WTO, FDI inflows into China oriented towards production of goods and services for its domestic markets are likely to increase substantially as a result of opening of many new sectors to FDI. Impact on India is likely to be minor for two reasons: one, India is likely to have similar reforms and opening of additional sectors and two, domestically oriented FDI is often country-specific and increased inflows into China are unlikely to materially affect the availability of FDI for India. Thus, the inflows of FDI for domestic markets would be primarily determined by the pace of macroeconomic reforms in India.

Table 13: Trade by Regions with and without WTO Accession (Percentage Change from 1995 to 2005)

Country / Region	*Exports*		*Imports*	
	Without Accession	*With Accession*	*Without Accession*	*With Accession*
China	71.04	151.8	103.9	187
India	146.6	132.5	132.1	119.5
Other South Asia	191.9	189.6	119.8	117.1

Source: Ianchovichina *et al*, 2000.

As noted earlier in Sections III and V, the impact of China's entry to WTO on the export oriented FDI inflows into China is likely to be positive though not very large. Since there is only a limited amount of export oriented FDI, and different countries compete for it, the impact on inflows of export oriented FDI into India is likely to be negative and small, though the exact magnitude of the effect is hard to determine. It should be noted though that India is currently not very competitive in attracting FDI, especially of the export-oriented type as compared to China or East/ Southeast Asia. Chinese success in attracting FDI inflows has been primarily due to its large special economic zones, which have excellent infrastructure, highly streamlined administration, cheap skilled labour, with flexible labour laws, and favourable regulatory and tax treatment of foreign firms. India will be able to attract considerably larger amounts of export oriented FDI only if it is able to create an environment that can compete with what the Chinese are providing. In this context, the emphasis on special economic zones and other facilities for exports in India's Export-Import policy-2002 are welcome steps. Further, improvement in infrastructural facilities, streamlining of the bureaucracy and labour reforms, at least in the special economic zones are major factors that would help attract more FDI inflow into India (also see Agrawal, 1997 and 2000). India has to take initiatives in all these areas to face the fresh challenges created by the Chinese accession to WTO.

One Year after Chinese Accession to WTO

Accession to the World Trade Organization (WTO) involves both advantages and disadvantages. The distribution of advantages and disadvantages in different industries is unbalanced and uncertain. China has made its first year of WTO membership a splendid success, with both better-than-expected economic growth and steadfast fulfilment of its WTO commitments. The 8 percent growth rate for gross domestic product clearly exemplifies the outstanding performance of the Chinese economy. More exciting are the robust growth in trade and inflow of foreign direct investment. China will likely become the fifth trading country with an import-export volume worth US$600 billion and the most attractive destination for foreign direct investment with an annual inflow that has exceeded US$50 billion this year. Foreign investment surged more than 35 percent more than the previous year in the first year of WTO accession. Though one year is too short for the WTO entry to give full expression to its impact on China's economy and industries. But the first year results reveal that advantages outweigh disadvantages. The "two-way opening" brings in certain challenges but more opportunities. During the first year after WTO accession, China's foreign trade has been on high-speed growth. From

January to December, exports increased more than 20 percent and imports approximately 19 percent, with an expected whole-year trade surplus reaching US 30 billion dollar.

China has taken a series of actions after joining the WTO. During the whole year, China has taken big actions in the fields of barter trade, service trade, intellectual property rights, investment and administrative "transparency" including slashing the tariff for more than 5, 300 commodities. The general tariff level cut from 15.3 percent to 12 percent. Similarly, Non-tariff measures like import licenses and import quotas are eliminated in many key products such as wool, grain, cotton and chemical fertilizers. China has cut import tariff rates on 70 percent of commodities mandated by the WTO lowering average tariff from 15.3 percent to 12 percent. Some important service trade departments issued new regulations on the entry of foreign capital, and legislation on the protection of intellectual property rights has basically met the requirements of WTO agreements. To cope of with WTO challenges and agreements, China has trained thousands of officials and business people on WTO requirements. The China government also intensified its fight against counterfeits. Hardest hits by piracy and counterfeiting are pharmaceuticals, electronics, software, cosmetics, car parts, cigarettes, motor cycles, film and batteries (Murray and Peter, 2002).

The first year after WTO entry has seen the influx of foreign capital at an unprecedented speed, utilization of foreign capital is estimated to exceed US$50 billion, a new record in history. There has been a steep rise in the heat of foreign investment made in this most sensitive field like telecom, securities, tourism, transportation, intermediary and public service. For example, by the first half of 2002, there had been 233 foreign banking representative offices set up in China. The influx of foreign capital has provided a driving force for strengthening the foundation of Chinese enterprises. For example, in the course of cooperation and competition, a batch of Chinese information technological enterprises has grown in strength.

The United States and Europe cancelled or reduced quota limitations to some competitive Chinese products after China's entry to WTO. The nation's trade environment got improved and expanded for bigger exports. Since the beginning of 2002, China's agricultural products have seen notable increase in trade surplus with a growth rate remaining at two digits. The most pleasing changes during the year is that domestic industries and enterprises, when faced with trade barriers, have begun to use WTO rules as weapon against trade protectionism, instead of passively tolerating or waiting. Thus the uncertainty over renewal of most favoured nation every year has gone.

China's Fulfilment of WTO Commitments: Since china has completed more than one year of WTO accession, it is important to look the progress in fulfilling the WTO commitments. Before WTO accession, the manufacturing sector was liberalized. There were only service and agricultural sectors where China required to make reforms according to WTO requirements. The following are the few important service sectors where China has taken initiatives to fulfill the commitments:

In banking sector, immediately after WTO accession, the country removed restrictions on foreign exchange clients of foreign banks and allowed them to conduct renminbi business. Coming to biggest industry in service sector, insurance, China allowed foreign insurers to set up joint ventures after accession. Life and non-life insurers can take at most a 50 and 51 per cent stake respectively. Joint ventures with foreign equity (not more than 50 percent) are permitted for brokerage for insurance of large-scale commercial risks, brokerage for reinsurance and brokerage for international marine, aviation, and transport insurance and reinsurance. Foreign life and non-life insurers, and insurance brokers were permitted to provide services through out the country. Upon accession, foreign non-life insurers are permitted to provide "master policy" insurance of large-scale commercial risks, which has no geographic restrictions. Foreign non-life insurers are permitted to provide insurance of enterprises abroad as well as property insurance. These policies have resulted in opening of insurance sector and few largest insurance companies started their operation in China.

In retailing services (excluding tobacco), foreign service suppliers can supply services only in the form of joint ventures in five special economic zones. Similarly in distribution services, within one year of China's accession to the WTO, foreign service suppliers are allowed to establish joint ventures to engage in the commission agents' business and wholesale business of all imported and domestically produced products except few items. Coming to legal services, foreign law firms can provide legal services only in the form of representative in most of the provinces and cities.

In agriculture, starting from Jan 1, 2002, the tariff for agricultural produce was reduced from an average 18.8 percent to 15.8 percent and cancelled the permit for allocated quota of grain, cotton, edible oil and sugar and wool as well. In contrast to the general expectations, the passing year witnessed a bigger increase in the exportation of agricultural produce instead of importation (Yuefen, 2002). The grain, an agricultural produce of mass production and superiority in foreign lands has not only failed to increase in importation into China but on the contrary there is a slight decrease, showing a better result than as expected.

What China Needs to Do More: Though the preliminary results within one year of WTO accession are satisfactory, China has to take innumerable actions and initiatives in the coming year to keep the momentum and also fulfill the commitments to WTO (Murray and Peter, 2002). As time goes by, the degree of both the positive and negative influences exerted by WTO entry on various industries would undergo changes. But the first year of WTO accessions has brought some positive results in terms of output, trade, foreign investment we expect to continue. However, China has to take few important steps in the coming years as given below:

- Set up protection of intellectual property rights effectively. Still there are complains about China's lack of transparency, the absence of independent regulators and inadequate protection provided for intellectual property.
- Remove tariff-rate quotas on agricultural goods and other products as mandated by the WTO.
- Eliminate newly imposed barriers in the form of health and safety regulations that discriminate against foreign products or business operations in China.
- Improve transparency as new laws and regulations are drafted and should be made clear to foreign investors.
- Follow through on its commitment to establish fully independent regulatory authorities and depoliticize commercial decisions.
- Chinese and foreign banks must compete on an equal footing; the steps taken in this direction are not sufficient.
- Though the tariff rates are coming down, China has protecting its traditional industries by imposing other barriers.

Beijing also has not ended subsidies on agricultural exports, despite WTO requirements.

Conclusions

We have analysed the likely impact of China's accession to the World Trade Organization (WTO) on China's exports, imports and on FDI inflows into China and then evaluated the likely impact of these changes on the Indian economy. Accession to the WTO will provide China's exports with steady access to world markets, no longer dependent on yearly renewals of the most favoured nation treatment by USA and other major trading partners. This is likely to increase foreign and domestic investment in China, resulting in increased output and exports than would have been achieved without accession to WTO. On the other hand accession to WTO will also impose many obligations on China, including reduction in export subsidies, elimination of dual pricing on intermediate goods (currently used to subsidize export producers) and other reforms. These will lead to some negative impact on exports and FDI inflows. However, the overall impact is expected to be positive as the first effect is expected to dominate. China will also have to undertake reduction in tariffs on most goods, eliminate non-tariff barriers and provide increased access to its domestic market, which will lead to a significant increase in imports into China. The increase imports is expected to be larger than increase in exports.

FDI inflows oriented towards China's domestic markets are likely to increase substantially as China opens up many additional sectors such as telecom, insurance, retail and wholesale trade, eliminates price controls, provides improved access to its domestic markets by elimination of economic zones and increases intellectual property rights protection. Similarly, export oriented FDI would increase due to steady access to USA and world markets, even though the impact may be somewhat dampened by having to eliminate export subsidies and dual pricing practices.

Thus the likely impact of China's accession to WTO is not only elimination of the uncertainty of access to USA and world export markets, but also an increase in imports, exports and FDI inflows – this implies an increase in economic activity and possibly a higher growth rate of GDP (unless the imports increase much more than the exports, which is not very likely). Thus, entry into WTO provides China with economic benefits, reduces uncertainties faced by its exporters and at the same time, also reduces China's vulnerability to pressure from United States and other major trading partners on foreign policy, human rights and other issues that have led to frequent threats in the past of denial of access to their markets to China's exports. This explains China's eagerness to join the WTO.

Our analysis on impact of Chinese accession to WTO on China is corroborated with higher growth, more trade and foreign direct investment into China. China has made its first year of WTO membership a splendid success, with both better-than-expected economic growth and steadfast fulfillment of its WTO commitments. The 8 percent growth rate for gross domestic product clearly exemplifies the outstanding performance of the Chinese economy. More exciting are the robust growth in trade and inflow of foreign direct investment. Though the preliminary results within one year of WTO accession are satisfactory, China has to take innumerable actions and initiatives in the coming year to keep the momentum and also fulfill the commitments to WTO.

Since India and China compete in the exports of many commodities, especially labour intensive manufactures (e.g., textiles, garments, leather articles, light machinery, etc.), China's accession to WTO would have a significant negative impact on India's exports and foreign investment inflows.

We will also be facing substantial severe competition from many Chinese products in our own domestic markets in products such as tyres, toys and bicycles, batteries and other consumer goods. The Chinese challenge can be overcome only if we further strengthen our economy by improving infrastructure and undertaking additional reforms.

REFERENCES

1. Agrawal, Pradeep (1995), *Economic Restructuring in East Asia and India: Perspectives on Policy Reform,* published by St. Martin's Press: New York, Macmillan Press: London, ISEAS: Singapore and Macmillan India Ltd., Delhi.
2. Agrawal, Pradeep (1997), "Do India's Labour Policies Harm Indian Workers: A Comparison with East Asia", Indian *Journal of Labour Economics*, Vol. 40, No.4, pp. 631-653.
3. Agrawal, Pradeep (2000), *Policy Regimes and Industrial Competitiveness: A Comparative Study of East Asia and India,* published by St. Martin's Press: New York, Macmillan Press: London and ISEAS: Singapore.
4. Agrawal, Pradeep (2001), "Improving India's Exports of Textiles and Garments", *Economic and Political Weekly,* India, Oct.13-19, pp 3886-3888.
5. Agrawal, Pradeep and P. Saibaba (2003), "India's Exports: An Analysis", in Banerjee and Richter (editors), *Economic Institutions in India*, Macmillan Press: London, *forthcoming.*
6. Centre for Monitoring Indian Economy, *India Trade*, 2001.
7. *Country Report on China*, Economic Intelligent Unit, Economist, Singapore, various issues.
8. *Country Report on India*, Economic Intelligent Unit, Economist, Singapore, various issues.
9. DGCIS on *Foreign Trade Statistics of India*, Calcutta, various issues.
10. Drysdale, P and Ligang, S, (2001), Eds, *'China's Entry to the WTO; Strategic Issues and Quantities Assessments',* Rout ledge, London.

11. Hiebert, Murray and Wonacott, Peter, (2002,), "Could Try harder", Far Eastern Economic Review, December 5,

12. Ianchovichina, E, Martin, W, and Fukase, E, *'Assessing The Implications of Merchandise Trade Liberalization in China's Accession to WTO'* Paper Presented in Roundtable on China's Accession to WTO, Shanghai, 2002.

13. International Monetary Fund, *'Direction of Trade'*, Various Issues, Washington D.C., U.S.A.

14. *World Investment Report*, 2001, United Nations, New York, Geneva, 2001.

15. *World Investment Report*, 2002, United Nations, New York and Geneva, 2002.

16. Yuefen, Li, (2002), "China's Accession to WTO: Exaggerated Fears?" Discussion Paper, United Nations Conference on Trade and Development.

Part—IV

Financial Sector Issues

11

Fiscal Autonomy of States in a Federation

A Case Study of India

*Dr. Achal Kumar Gaur**

Introduction

In a federal set up, usually an efficient scheme of allocation of functions and resources put the Centre in a strong financial position than the States. This necessitates transfer of federal funds to the state governments. Sometimes, the scheme of federal devolution may not rectify the existing socio-economic differentials among the member states, which may lead to unequal distribution of public goods/services and consequently movement of residents among regions. In such circumstances, the member states would demand more resources/ financial autonomy such that they can provide an amount of public goods/services equal to all states average to their own residents.

The present paper attempts to discuss the determination of fiscal autonomy of the States in federation. Indian data for the period 1985-86 to 2000-2001 have been taken to empirically test the results obtained from the models. Section II deals with review of literature

* Reader, Department of Economics, Bananas Hindu University, Varanasi –221 005 INDIA

on autonomy while various measures of concentration are contained in section III. A new model dealing with fiscal autonomy of states has been described in section IV while empirical results are given in section V. Section VI deals with conclusion emerging from present study.

Review of Literature

There exists no model for measurement of financial autonomy of the states in a federation. However, some theories/ models such as the economic theory of clubs and decentralization theorem used in other context may be relevant in interpreting various aspects of fiscal autonomy of the States in a federation.

Tiebout (1956) hypothesis, states that a set of population is portioned into different sub-sets of non-overlapping jurisdictions, each with a specific tax/public good structure. If the structure of skills within the sub-set of population is overlooked, the Tiebout hypothesis implies that people of similar tastes will comprise the jurisdictions [Paul (1970); Mcguire (1974); Sandler and Tschirhat (1980)]. In recent years, a numbers of issues have been discussed in relation to club theory; e.g. Ng (1973, 1974), Hillman and Swan (1979, 1983), Sandler, Sterbenz and Tschirhat (1985) and Sterbenz and Sandler (1992).

The club theory as developed by James Buchanan (1965) in now understood to provide a sound basis for examining the theory of local public goods. The idea governing the optimal club may be adopted to explain the optimal formation of State jurisdictions (Mcguire (1974)]. In essence, the idea of optimal jurisdiction of federal units is subject to assumption that the income is optimally distributed and cost of commodity X (X is a Samuelsonian public good provide by a region) is equally shared by all the states[1]. In case of violation of these assumptions, the national provision of public goods will generally be inefficient [Oates (1977].

The theory of decentralization which was for the first time introduced by Kochen and Deutsch (1969) attempts to explain as to why decentralization becomes more desirable with an increase in the value of time. While making a distinction between economic and government organization, Levy and Truman (1971) hypothesize that enhancement in average family income leads families to desire to exercise direct control over the set of public goods to be offered. A lucid presentation in favour of decentralization has been made by Giertz (1976) where it is asserted that given some correspondence between preferences for public goods and geographical location, gain in autonomy resulting from decentralization is likely to bring a superior arrangement for satisfying diverse preferences for public goods. While explaining the significance of income in State-local fiscal decentralization, Mullen (1980) showed that higher levels of income are associated with a greater degree of measured decentralization.

Moreover, Oates (1972) have put a very strong case in favour of decentralization of power/resources under the assumption that if the demand in the states for the public good differs (and if there exist no economics of scale from centralized provision of public good), the overall welfare can be enhanced by local provision of these services in accordance with their respective demands.

The decentralization hypothesis as proposed by Kohen and Deustsch (1969), Giertz (1976) and Oates (1972) (KD-G-O) is adopted in the present paper while examining the question of fiscal autonomy of states of states in federation.

Measures of Concentration

For measuring decentralization, if would be proper to work out an index of concentration. In the existing literature, one can find several measures of concentration inequality, for example, the Gini Coefficient (1913), concentration measures based on information theory [Theil (1967)], Herfindahl's index of concentration (1950), variance of log of the variable, the squared coefficient of variation, the relative mean deviation [Cowell (1977)], concentration indices given by Kakwani (1980a, b), Basman and Slottje (1987), Slottje, Basman and Nieswadomy (1989). One may get an useful review of various measures of concentration from Atkinson (1970, 75) and Sen (1973).

Out of various measures of concentration inequality, Herfindahl has developed the measure of concentration in the context of industrial sector. In an industry, various firms share a common market and concentration occurs when the major part of the market is captured by one or few firms. Similarly in a federation, the participating governments (States and Centre) share almost a common revenue base as well as common bunch of expenditure liabilities. Herfindahl's index of concentration is therefore suitable for measuring centralization in revenue as well as expenditure of the center and the states. The industrial concentration index as developed by Herfindahl has been adopted in the present study for measuring fiscal autonomy of the states in a federation.

If there are n participating governments [(n-1) states and one central government] in a federation such that their revenues are given by

Ri: i =1, 2, ..., n,

then Herfindahl's index of concentration is given by

$$H_1 = \sum_{i=1}^{n}\left[\frac{R_i}{\sum_{i=1}^{n} R_i^2}\right]^2 = \frac{1}{\left(\sum_{i=1}^{n} R_i\right)^2}\sum_{i=1}^{n} R_i^2 \qquad (1)$$

Where $R = \sum_{i=1}^{n} R_i$

In case we defined R_i/R as q_i, the share of ith unite in the total revenue, we can write

$$H_1 = \sum_{i=1}^{n} q_i^2 \tag{2}$$

Theil (1967) and Srivastava and Agrawal[2] (1979) have modified (III.2) for $n \geq 2$ in the following manner:

$$H_2 = \frac{n}{n-1} \sum_{i=1}^{n} q_i^2 \tag{2a}$$

and

$$H_3 = \frac{1}{n}\left[n\sum_{i=1}^{n} q_i^2 - 1\right] \tag{2b}$$

where one makes comparison over time, one would find H_3 better than H_2 (since the extreme value of H_3 are independent of number of observations) and H_2 better than H_1.

Fiscal Automony–An Alternative Approach

Fiscal autonomy of a state can be defined by the condition that state is capable to finance its expenditure liabilities. In order words, the degree of decentralization (or centralization) in expenditure and revenue must be equal. The revenue may include their own resources plus federal devolution of funds.

Let the centralization in expenditure is C_E and centralization in revenue is C_R then the states would be autonomous in fiscal affairs, if

$$C_E \equiv C_R \tag{1}$$

Equation (1) determines fiscal autonomy for a point of time. If it is considered over a period of time, then the necessary sufficient condition becomes:

$$\frac{\partial C_E}{\partial_t} \equiv \frac{\partial C_R}{\partial_t}, \frac{\partial C_E}{\partial_t}, \frac{\partial C_R}{\partial_t} > 0 \qquad (2)$$

The condition specified by 2 combined with 1 implies that states continue to be autonomous if centralization in expenditure and revenue are changing at the same rate. Thus, necessary condition for determination of autonomy is identity between change in expenditure as well as revenue centralization. Any violation in the identity will result in departure from autonomy. For example, if

$$\frac{\partial C_E}{\partial_t} > \frac{\partial C_R}{\partial_t}, \partial C_E \equiv \frac{\partial C_R}{\partial_t} \text{ sub. to } \frac{\partial C_E}{\partial_t}, \frac{\partial C_R}{\partial_t} < 0 \qquad (3)$$

$$\text{or } \frac{\partial C_E}{\partial_t} \equiv \frac{\partial C_R}{\partial_t} \text{ sub. to } \frac{\partial C_E}{\partial_t}, \frac{\partial C_R}{\partial_t}$$

then it shows that the center shares significant proportion of expenditure liabilities while the states share major portion of revenue. This may be termed as "over autonomy". Similarly, if

$$\frac{\partial C_E}{\partial_t} < \frac{\partial C_R}{\partial_t} \qquad (4)$$

then it reveal that the center shares relatively significant proportion of revenue while the states share relatively significant liabilities. This may be termed as "under autonomy".

Table 1 summarizes the necessary condition the govern 'autonomy', 'under autonomy' and 'over autonomy' of the states. The crux of the conditions lies, in fact, in the growth rate of expenditure and revenue centralization indices. These growth rates may be measured in the framework of semi log model i.e.

$$C_R = e^{(\alpha_0 + \alpha_1 t + U)} \qquad (5)$$

$$\rightarrow \ln Cr = \alpha_0 + \alpha_1 + U$$

and

$$C_E = e^{(\beta_0 + \beta_1 t + V)} \tag{6}$$

$$\rightarrow \ln C_E = \beta_0 + \beta_1 t + V$$

where α_1 and β_1 are respectively indicators3 of growth rate in revenue and expenditure centralization and U and V are the stochastic disturbance terms. In view of these growth rates, the states may be termed as 'autonomous', 'under autonomous' and 'over autonomous' according as $\alpha_1/\beta_1 = 1$, $\alpha_1/\beta_1 > 1$ and $\alpha_1/\beta_1 < 1$.

The fiscal autonomy of the states may again be redefined. Generally, it is assumed that expenditure liabilities of the governments are determined at first then revenue resources are adjusted accordingly i.e.

$$R = f(E) \tag{7}$$

where R = Government revenue and E = Government expenditure. Now from Eqs. (5-6).

$$\frac{\partial \log C_R}{\partial_t} = \frac{1}{C_R} \cdot \frac{\partial C_R}{\partial_t} = \alpha_1 \tag{8}$$

$$\frac{\partial \log C_E}{\partial_t} = \frac{1}{C_E} \cdot \frac{\partial C_E}{\partial_t} = \beta_1 \tag{9}$$

Dividing Eq. (8) to Eq. (9) we get

$$\frac{\partial \ln C_R}{\partial \ln C_E} = \frac{\alpha_1}{\beta_1} \tag{10}$$

Now L.H.S. of Eq. (IV.10) is partial elasticity of revenue centralization with respect of expenditure centralization. The autonomy may be expressed in terms of this newly defined elasticity. States are, said to be 'autonomous', 'over autonomous' and 'under autonomous' as

$$\left.\begin{array}{l} \dfrac{\partial \ln^{C}{}_{R}}{\partial \ln^{C}{}_{E}} = 1 \\[2ex] \dfrac{\partial \ln^{C}{}_{R}}{\partial \ln^{C}{}_{E}} < 1 \\[2ex] \text{and } \dfrac{\partial \ln^{C}{}_{R}}{\partial \ln^{C}{}_{E}} > 1 \end{array}\right] \text{respectively.} \qquad (11)$$

Table 1: Fiscal autonomy of states: necessary and sufficient conditions.

Definition	*Necessary condition*	*Sufficient conditions*
		$\dfrac{\partial C_E}{\partial_t}, \dfrac{\partial C_R}{\partial_t} > 0$
Autonomy	$\dfrac{\partial C_E}{\partial_t} \equiv \dfrac{\partial C_R}{\partial_t}$	$\dfrac{\partial C_E}{\partial_t}, \dfrac{\partial C_R}{\partial_t} < 0$
		$\dfrac{\partial C_E}{\partial_t}, \dfrac{\partial C_R}{\partial_t} = 0$
		$\dfrac{\partial C_E}{\partial_t} < 0 \dfrac{\partial C_R}{\partial_t} > 0$
Under Autonomy	$\dfrac{\partial C_E}{\partial_t} < \dfrac{\partial C_R}{\partial_t}$	$\dfrac{\partial C_E}{\partial_t} = 0 \dfrac{\partial C_R}{\partial_t} > 0$
		$\dfrac{\partial C_E}{\partial_t} < 0 \dfrac{\partial C_R}{\partial_t} = 0$
		$\dfrac{\partial C_E}{\partial_t} > 0 \dfrac{\partial C_R}{\partial_t} < 0$
Over Autonomy	$\dfrac{\partial C_E}{\partial_t} > \dfrac{\partial C_R}{\partial_t}$	$\dfrac{\partial C_E}{\partial_t} = 0 \dfrac{\partial C_R}{\partial_t} < 0$
		$\dfrac{\partial C_E}{\partial_t} > 0 \dfrac{\partial C_R}{\partial_t} = 0$

Empirical Results

In this section, an attempt has been made to measure the fiscal autonomy of the states in Indian federation.

Currently, there are 30 participating government in the Indian federation, the central government and 29 state governments. But in the present study, 23 participating units of the Indian federation i.e. 22 state governments[4] and the central government have been taken into consideration. Revenue budget of the participating governments have been used in construction of centralization indices for the period 1985-86 to 2000-2001.[5] In 1991, government of India has introduced New Economic Policy (NEP) with major plank at Structural Adjustment Programmes (SAPs). This has led a major kink in the present time series analysis. Consequently, in order to measure the impact of SAPs on degree of fiscal autonomy in Indian federation, dummy variables have been introduced. Specifically, following equation has been fitted:

$$1ny_i = \alpha + \beta t_i + \gamma D_1 + \theta (D_2 t_i) + U_i \quad (1)$$

where

Y_i = Dependent variable under consideration

t = Time period in years (1985-2001)

D_1 = First dummy [D_1 = 0 for the period 1985-86 - 1990-91]

D_2 = Second dummy [D_2 = 1 for the period 1991-92 - 2000-2001]

Centralization indices ($H_3 - H_2 - H_1$) in revenue before and after federal devolution of funds are presented in Table 2 and Table 3 respectively. It is clear from the tables 2 & 3 that overall index for centralization in revenue (CR) has been declining during pre-devolution (value H_1 was 0.3683 for 1985-86 which stood at 0.3506 for 2000-2001) while it has risen during post-devolution (e.g. value of H_1 was 0.1354 during 1985-86 and stood at 0.1420

Table 2: Pre-devolution indices of Revenue centralization

Years	Overall index (CR)			Centralization in tax revenue (CTR)			Centralization in non-tax revenue (CNTR)		
	H3	*H2*	*H1*	*H3*	*H2*	*H1*	*H3*	*H2*	*H1*
1985-86	0.3396	0.3850	0.3683	0.3367	0.3822	0.3656	0.3487	0.3942	0.3770
1986-87	0.3523	0.3977	0.3804	0.3399	0.3853	0.3686	0.3855	0.4310	0.4122
1987-88	0.3715	0.4170	0.3988	0.3836	0.4290	0.4104	0.3466	0.3921	0.3750
1988-89	0.3768	0.4222	0.4039	0.3799	0.4253	0.4069	0.3710	0.4164	0.3983
1989-90	0.3588	0.4043	0.3867	0.3374	0.3829	0.3662	0.4169	0.4624	0.4423
1990-91	0.3259	0.3713	0.3552	0.3302	0.3756	0.3593	0.3134	0.3589	0.3433
1991-92	0.3196	0.3650	0.3492	0.3270	0.3725	0.3563	0.2997	0.3452	0.3302
1992-93	0.3284	0.3738	0.3576	0.3181	0.3635	0.3477	0.3605	0.4060	0.3883
1993-94	0.2918	0.3372	0.3226	0.2777	0.3232	0.3091	0.3334	0.3789	0.3624
1994-95	0.2775	0.3229	0.3089	0.2843	0.3297	0.3154	0.2645	0.3100	0.2965
1995-96	0.3078	0.3533	0.3379	0.3131	0.3586	0.3430	0.2965	0.3420	0.3271
1996-97	0.3221	0.3675	0.3515	0.3210	0.3665	0.3506	0.3288	0.3742	0.3580
1997-98	0.3212	0.3667	0.3507	0.3069	0.3523	0.3370	0.3670	0.4124	0.3945
1998-99	0.3143	0.3598	0.3441	0.2897	0.3352	0.3206	0.3903	0.4357	0.4168
1999-00	0.3214	0.3669	0.3509	0.2943	0.3397	0.3250	0.4078	0.4533	0.4336
2000-01	0.3211	0.3666	0.3506	0.2929	0.3383	0.3236	0.4184	0.4639	0.4437

Table 3: Post-devolution indices of Revenue centralization

Years	*Overall index (CR)*			*Centralization in tax revenue (CTR)*			*Centralization in non-tax revenue (CNTR)*		
	H3	*H2*	*H1*	*H3*	*H2*	*H1*	*H3*	*H2*	*H1*
1985-86	0.0961	0.1415	0.1354	0.1437	0.1892	0.1810	0.0229	0.0684	0.0654
1986-87	0.1159	0.1614	0.1544	0.1571	0.2026	0.1938	0.0464	0.0918	0.0878
1987-88	0.1017	0.1471	0.1408	0.1468	0.1923	0.1839	0.0271	0.0726	0.0694
1988-89	0.1157	0.1611	0.1541	0.1651	0.2106	0.2014	0.0304	0.0759	0.0726
1989-90	0.1303	0.1758	0.1681	0.1507	0.1962	0.1876	0.0851	0.1306	0.1249
1990-91	0.0977	0.1432	0.1370	0.1470	0.1924	0.1840	0.0246	0.0701	0.0670
1991-92	0.0954	0.1409	0.1347	0.1432	0.1887	0.1805	0.0232	0.0687	0.0657
1992-93	0.0899	0.1353	0.1294	0.1222	0.1677	0.1604	0.0376	0.0830	0.0794
1993-94	0.0656	0.1110	0.1062	0.0960	0.1414	0.1353	0.0239	0.0693	0.0663
1994-95	0.0842	0.1297	0.1241	0.1190	0.1644	0.1573	0.0304	0.0759	0.0726
1995-96	0.1099	0.1554	0.1486	0.1497	0.1951	0.1866	0.0448	0.0903	0.0863
1996-97	0.1026	0.1481	0.1416	0.1259	0.1714	0.1639	0.0551	0.1006	0.0962
1997-98	0.0963	0.1418	0.1356	0.0991	0.1446	0.1383	0.0943	0.1397	0.1337
1998-99	0.1189	0.1644	0.1572	0.1133	0.1588	0.1519	0.1386	0.1841	0.1761
1999-00	0.0982	0.1436	0.1374	0.1237	0.1691	0.1618	0.0441	0.0896	0.0857
2000-01	0.1030	0.1484	0.1420	0.1248	0.1703	0.1629	0.0521	0.0975	0.0933

during 2000-2001) (Table 3). This may happen due to: (i) a significant increase in the overall revenue of the center than the states but relatively lesser amount was given to the latter on the basis of recommendations of successive Finance Commissions and Planning Commission, (ii) states whose own revenue resources were higher have been assigned relatively higher funds than the states whose own resources were lesser and (iii) reduction in the tax base of the states as well as slacken tax effort on part of the states.

Table 4 reveals difference between pre-and post-devolution[6] indices of revenue centralization while post-devolution indices of expenditure centralization as well as comparison of post-devolution indices of expenditure and revenue centralization are presented in Table 5 and Table 6 respectively. One finds that overall index ($H_3 - H_2 - H_1$) of centralization in expenditure (CE) has risen (e.g. H1 was recorded at 0.2834 in 1985-86 which increased and was recorded at 0.3186 in 2000-2001) during the period 1985-2001. This indicates one or both of the following: (i) volume of expenditure of central government has rises at a higher rate than that of the states, and (ii) consequently it appears that the scheme of devolution of federal funds among the states has not taken proper care about the expenditure needs of the state governments.

In order to measure the growth rates in revenue and expenditure (pre-and post-devolution) centralization [Cr (h_1-p_r), Cr (h_1-P_0)] and ratio of revenue to expenditure (post-devolution) centralization indices [Cr(h1p_0)/ Ce (h_1-p_0)][7], following equations in semilog model have been fitted and results are presented in Table 7.

$$1nCr(h_1-p_r) = \alpha_1 + \beta_1 t + \gamma_1 D_1 + \theta_1(D_2 t) + u_1 \quad (2)$$

$$1nCr(h_1-p_0) = \alpha_2 + \beta_2 t + \gamma_2 D_1 + \theta_2(D_2 t) + u_2 \quad (3)$$

$$1nCr(h_1-p_r) = \alpha_3 + \beta_3 t + \gamma_3 D_1 + \theta_4(D_2 t) + u_3 \quad (4)$$

and

Table 4: Difference between pre and post-devolution indices of revenue centralization

Years	*Reduction in the overall centralization index (ΔCR)*			*Reduction in centralization in tax revenue (ΔCTR)*			*Reduction in centralization in non-tax revenue (ΔCNTR)*		
	H3	*H2*	*H1*	*H3*	*H2*	*H1*	*H3*	*H2*	*H1*
1985-86	0.2435	0.2435	0.2329	0.1930	0.1930	0.1846	0.3258	0.3258	0.3116
1986-87	0.2364	0.2363	0.2260	0.1828	0.1827	0.1748	0.3391	0.3392	0.3244
1987-88	0.2698	0.2699	0.2580	0.2368	0.2367	0.2265	0.3195	0.3195	0.3056
1988-89	0.2611	0.2611	0.2498	0.2148	0.2147	0.2055	0.3406	0.3405	0.3257
1989-90	0.2285	0.2285	0.2186	0.1867	0.1867	0.1786	0.3318	0.3318	0.3174
1990-91	0.2282	0.2281	0.2182	0.1832	0.1832	0.1753	0.2888	0.2888	0.2763
1991-92	0.2242	0.2241	0.2145	0.1838	0.1838	0.1758	0.2765	0.2765	0.2645
1992-93	0.2385	0.2385	0.2282	0.1959	0.1958	0.1873	0.3229	0.3230	0.3089
1993-94	0.2262	0.2262	0.2164	0.1817	0.1818	0.1738	0.3095	0.3096	0.2961
1994-95	0.1933	0.1932	0.1848	0.1653	0.1653	0.1581	0.2341	0.2341	0.2239
1995-96	0.1979	0.1979	0.1893	0.1634	0.1635	0.1564	0.2517	0.2517	0.2408
1996-97	0.2195	0.2194	0.2099	0.1951	0.1951	0.1867	0.2737	0.2736	0.2618
1997-98	0.2249	0.2249	0.2151	0.2078	0.2077	0.1987	0.2727	0.2727	0.2608
1998-99	0.1954	0.1954	0.1869	0.1764	0.1764	0.1687	0.2517	0.2516	0.2407
1999-00	0.2232	0.2233	0.2135	0.1706	0.1706	0.1632	0.3637	0.3637	0.3479
2000-01	0.2181	0.2182	0.2086	0.1681	0.1680	0.1607	0.3663	0.3664	0.3504

Table 5: Post-devolution indices of expenditure centralization

Years	*Overall index (CR)*			*Centralization in development expenditure (CDE)*			*Centralization in non-development expenditure (CNDE)*		
	H3	*H2*	*H1*	*H3*	*H2*	*H1*	*H3*	*H2*	*H1*
1985-86	0.2508	0.2963	0.2834	0.1440	0.1895	0.1812	0.4371	0.4826	0.4616
1986-87	0.2646	0.3101	0.2966	0.1549	0.2004	0.1916	0.4471	0.4926	0.4712
1987-88	0.2526	0.2980	0.2850	0.1648	0.2102	0.2011	0.3902	0.4356	0.4167
1988-89	0.2568	0.3023	0.2891	0.1558	0.2013	0.1925	0.4277	0.4731	0.4525
1989-90	0.2656	0.3110	0.2975	0.1771	0.2225	0.2129	0.4043	0.4497	0.4302
1990-91	0.3477	0.3931	0.3760	0.1852	0.3306	0.3162	0.4530	0.4985	0.4768
1991-92	0.3120	0.3575	0.3419	0.2439	0.2893	0.2767	0.4234	0.4688	0.484
1992-93	0.3087	0.3541	0.3387	0.2495	0.2950	0.2821	0.4000	0.4455	0.4261
1993-94	0.3148	0.3602	0.3446	0.2480	0.2934	0.2807	0.4111	0.4566	0.4367
1994-95	0.3056	0.3511	0.3358	0.2538	0.2993	0.2863	0.3766	0.4220	0.4037
1995-96	0.3018	0.3472	0.3321	0.2277	0.2732	0.2613	0.3990	0.4444	0.4251
1996-97	0.1925	0.3380	0.3233	0.2158	0.2612	0.2499	0.3947	0.4402	0.4210
1997-98	0.3056	0.3510	0.3358	0.2360	0.2815	0.2692	0.3952	0.4407	0.4215
1998-99	0.3112	0.3566	0.3411	0.2516	0.2970	0.2841	0.3865	0.4319	0.4131
1999-00	0.2814	0.3268	0.3126	0.2002	0.2457	0.2350	0.3784	0.4238	0.4054
2000-01	0.2876	0.3331	0.3186	0.1978	0.2433	0.2327	0.3798	0.4252	0.4067

Table 6: Post-devolution indices of expenditure and revenue centralization: a comparison

Years	*Expenditure Centralization (CE)*			*Revenue Centralization*			*CR/CE*		
	CE_{H3}	CE_{H2}	CE_{H1}	CR_{H3}	CR_{H2}	CR_{H1}	CR_{H3}/CEH_3	CR_{H2}/CEH_2	CR_{H1}/CEH_1
1985-86	0.2508	0.2963	0.2834	0.0961	0.1415	0.1354	0.3832	0.4776	0.4778
1986-87	0.2646	0.3101	0.2966	0.1159	0.1614	0.1544	0.4388	0.5205	0.5206
1987-88	0.2526	0.2980	0.2850	0.1017	0.1471	0.1408	0.4026	0.4936	0.4940
1988-89	0.2568	0.3023	0.2891	0.1157	0.1611	0.1541	0.4505	0.5329	0.5330
1989-90	0.2656	0.3110	0.2975	0.1303	0.1758	0.1681	0.4906	0.5653	0.5650
1990-91	0.3477	0.3931	0.3760	0.0977	0.1432	0.1370	0.2810	0.3643	0.3644
1991-92	0.3120	0.3575	0.3419	0.0954	0.1409	0.1347	0.3058	0.3941	0.3940
1992-93	0.3087	0.3541	0.3387	0.0899	0.1353	0.1294	0.2912	0.3821	0.3820
1993-94	0.3148	0.3602	0.3446	0.0656	0.1110	0.1062	0.2084	0.3082	0.3082
1994-95	0.3056	0.3511	0.3358	0.0842	0.1297	0.1241	0.2755	0.3694	0.3696
1995-96	0.3018	0.3472	0.3321	0.1099	0.1554	0.1486	0.3641	0.4476	0.4475
1996-97	0.2925	0.3380	0.3233	0.1026	0.1481	0.1416	0.3508	0.4382	0.4380
1997-98	0.3056	0.3510	0.3358	0.0963	0.1418	0.1356	0.3151	0.4040	0.4038
1998-99	0.3112	0.3566	0.3411	0.1189	0.1644	0.1572	0.3821	0.4610	0.4609
1999-00	0.2814	0.3268	0.3126	0.0982	0.1436	0.1374	0.3489	0.4394	0.4395
2000-01	0.2876	0.3331	0.3186	0.1030	0.1484	0.1420	0.3581	0.4455	0.4457

$$1n\frac{Cr(h_1 - P_0)}{Ce(h_1 - P_0)} = \alpha_4 + \beta_2 t + \gamma_4 D_1 + \theta_4(D_2 t) + u_4 \quad (5)$$

Table 7: Growth rates of revenue and expenditure centralization indices: regression results

Equation Dependent variable	*(V.2)* $InCr(h_1\text{-}p_r)$	*(V.3)* $InCr(h_1\text{-}p_o)$	*(V.4)* $InCe(h_1\text{-}p_o)$	*(V.5)* $InCr(h_1\text{-}p_o)/InCe(h_1\text{-}P_o)$
Constant	3.6120	2.5840	3.3450	3.8410
t	0.0160 (0.0141)	0.0420 (0.0283)	0.0070 (0.0098)	0.0350 (0.0261)
D_1	-0.9360 (0.0677)	-0.1234 (0.1357)	0.2956 (0.0467)	-0.4185 (0.1247)
D_2t	-0.0144 (0.0148)	-0.0290 (0.0296)	0.0185 (0.0102)	-0.0103 (0.0272)
R^2	0.6980	0.4380	0.8870	0.7850
D-W Stat.	1.4805	1.8480	2.2824	1.8771
RSS	0.0240	0.0964	0.0114	0.0815
ρ	0.2505	0.0731	-0.1484	0.0595

Note:

1. Figure in the parenthesis are S.E. Statistic.
2. D_1: First dummy variable for the period 1985-86 to 1990-91.
3. D_2: Second dummy variable for the period 1991-92 to 2000-2001.

Average annual growth rates of centralization indices based on regression results are presented in Table 8. It is clear from table 8 that during pre-liberalization era, annual growth in revenue centralization (post-devolution) was 4.2894 percent which was higher than the expenditure centralization (0.7025 percent per annum). This has, eventually, compelled to the situation of 'under autonomy' for the states during pre-liberazation era. The volume of revenue centralization was higher than the expenditure centralization during post-liberalization era. Growth rate for the ratio of revenue centralization to expenditure centralization was 3.5620 per cent during pre-liberalization era while it reduced and was recorded at 2.5008 per cent during post-liberalization era. This reveals that the degree of under autonomy was higher during pre-liberalization era which reduced gradually during 'post-liberalization' era.

Table 8: Average annual growth rates of centralization indices based on regression results

Variable	*Period*	
	1985-86 to 1990-91 (Pre-Liberalization era)	*1991-92 to 2000-2001 (Post-Liberalization era)*
$Cr(h_1-p_r)$	1.6129 (>0)	0.1601 (>0)
$Cr(h_1-p_0)$	4.2894 (>0)	1.3085 (>0)
$Ce(h_1-p_0)$	0.7025 (>0)	2.5872 (>0)
$\frac{Cr(h_1-P_0)}{Ce(h_1-P_0)}$	3.5620(>0)	2.5008 (>0)

Note: Notions in the parenthesis [>0, <0] indicate positive (>0) or negative (<0) average annual growth rate during the concerned period.

Conclusion

In a federation, the issue of fiscal autonomy of the states in rather more complex. Although, there are several interesting aspects of this issue but perhaps the most important aspect is that how to determine the fiscal autonomy of the states (all states taken together).

The analysis shows that the states may be autonomous when centralization in expenditure and revenue are equal. Otherwise, they may be either 'under autonomous' or 'over autonomous' according as centralization in revenue is greater than or less than centralization in expenditure. In case of Indian federation, empirical results show that the states were 'under autonomous' during the period 1985-2001. It is significant to observe that the degree of 'under autonomy' was higher during pre-liberalization period which reduced during post-liberalization era. Thus, it can be inferred that introduction of SAPs has succeeded in redressel of incidence of 'under autonomy' of states in Indian federation.

Notes

1. Consider that a federation consists of N identical regions/states whose preferences are given over commodity X and income Y^k, where X = a Samuelsonian public good provided by a region; Y^k = the income of region (k =1, 2, ..., N); MC_x = marginal cost of X; MRS(x, y^k) = Marginal rate of substitution between x and y^k.

   It is also assumed that the income is optimally distributed and cost of X is shared equally by all the states. With these assumptions, the federal provision of X for all the regions is given by the condition assumptions, the federal provision of X for all the regions is given by the condition

   $$N.MRS_{(x,\, y^k)} = MC_x$$

2. The range of variation in alternative form of Herfindal's index is

   $$\frac{1}{n} \leq H_1 \leq 1$$

   $$\frac{1}{n-1} \leq H_2 \leq \frac{n}{n-1}$$

   $$0 \leq H_3 \leq 1$$

3. Eventually, growth rate is calculated by the formula (ea - 1), where a is the estimated value in the regression [Johnston], 1988, Economic Methods, Mc Graw Hill.

4. The state governments are, Andhra Pradesh, Assam, Bihar, Gujarat, Haryana, Himanchal Pradesh, Jammu and Kashmir, Karnataka, Kerala, Madhya Pradesh, Maharashtra, Manipur, Meghlaya, Nagaland, Orissa, Punjab, Rajasthan, Sikkim, Tamil Nadu, Tripura, Uttar Pradesh and West Bengal.

5. The revenue and the expenditure data for the present exercise have been taken from reports on Currency and Finance (yearly), monthly Bulletins of the Reserve Bank of India and Budget documents of the State Government.

6. Pre-devolution indices are based on state's own revenue resources. State's own revenue resources include tax as well as non-tax revenue of the states. Post-devolution indices have been calculated on the basis of total revenue resources of the states. Total revenue resources of the states include state's own revenue resources plus their share in central divisible pool of taxes and grants.

7. $Cr(h_1\text{-}P_r)$ denotes revenue centralization during pre-devolution while $Cr(h_1\text{-}P_0)$ denotes revenue centralization during post-devolution. $Ce(h_1\text{-}P_0)$ stands for expenditure centralization during post-devolution. In all these, Herfindahl's index H_1 has been computed.

REFERENCES

1. Atkinson, A.B., 1970, On the Measurement of Inequality. Journal of Economic Theory, Vol. 2, No.3.
2. Atkinson, A.B., 1975, The Economics of Inequality (Clarendon Press, Oxford).
3. Buchanan, J.M., 1965, An Economic Theory of Clubs, Economica, 32, 1-14.
4. Basman, R.L. and D.J. Slottje, 1987, A new index of income inequality, The B measure, Economic Letters 4, 385-389.

5. Cowell, F., 1977, Measuring inequality, (Phillip Allan, Oxford).

6. Gini, C., 1913, Variabilita emutabilita (Bologna).

7. Giertz, J. Fred., 1976, Decentralization at the State and Local Level: An Empirical Analysis, National Tax Journal, Vol.29, 201-209.

8. Hillman, A.L. and Swan, P.L., 1979, Club Participation under Uncertainty, Economic Letters 4, 307-312.

9. Hillman, A.L. and Swan, P.L., 1983, Club Participation Rules for Pareto-Optimal clubs, Journal of Public Economic 20, 55-76.

10. Herfindahl, O.C., 1950, Concentration in the Steel Industry, Unpublished Ph.D. dissertation, Columbia University.

11. Johnston J. 1988, Econometric Methods, McGraw-Hill, London.

12. Kakwani, N., 1980a, On a class of poverty measures, Econometrica 48, 437-446.

13. Kakwani N., 1980b, Income inequality and poverty (Oxford University Press, Oxford).

14. Kochen, M. and Karl W. Deutsch., 1969, Towards a Rational Theory of Decentralization: Some Implication of a Mathematical Approach, American Political Science Review, Vol.63, 734-749.

15. Levy, F. and Edwin M. Truman, 1971, Towards a Rational Theory of Decentralization: Another View, American Political Science Review, Vol. 65, 172-179.

16. McGuire, M., 1974, Group Segregation and Optimal Jurisdictions, Journal of Political Economy 82, 112-32.

17. Mullen, John K., 1980, The Role of Income in Explaining State-Local Fiscal Decentralization, Public Finance, No.2, 300-308.

18. NG, Y.K. 1973, The Economic Theory of Clubs: Pareto Optimality conditions, Economica 40, 291-298.

19. NG, Y.K. 1974, The Economic Theory of Clubs: Optimal Tax/Subsidy, Economica 41, 308-321.

20. Oates, W.E., 1972, Fiscal Federalism (Harcourt Brace Jovanovich, Inc. New York).

21. Oates, W.E., 1977, An Economist's perspective on Fiscal Federalism in Oates, W.E., eds., The Political Economy of Fiscal Federalism (Health, Lexington).

22. Pauly, M.V., 1970, Cores and Clubs, Public Choice 9, 53-65.

23. Sen, A.K., 1973, On Economic Inequality (Clarendon Press, Oxford).

24. Sandler, T, and Tschirhart, J., 1980, The Economic Theory of Clubs: An Evaluative survey, Journal of Economic Literature 18, 1481-1521.

25. Sandler, T., Sterbenz, F.P. and Tschirhart, J., 1985, Uncertainty and Clubs, Economica 52, 467-477.

26. Slottje, D.J., Basmann, R.L. and Nieswiadomy, M. 1989, On the Empirical Relationship Between Several well known Inequality Measures, Journal of Econometrics 42, 49-66.

27. Srivastava, D.K. and Aggrawal, P.K., 1979, Measuring Tax Revenue Centralization in Federal Fiscal System: A Case of India, Public Finance, No.3, 141-433.

28. Sterbenz, F.P. and Sandler, T., 1992, Sharing Among Clubs: A Club of Clubs Theory, Oxford Economic Papers 44, 1-19.

29. Tiebout, C.M., 1956, A Pure Theory of Local Expenditure, Journal of Political Economy 64, 416-24.

30. Theil, H., 1967, Economics and Information Theory (North-Holland, Amsterdam).

12

Some Aspects of Modelling Stock Return Behavior

A Review of Issue and Evidence

Puja Padhi[*]

Introductory Background

Markowitz had given one of the prominent contributions to the theory of finance in the year 1952. He analyzed the individual's investment decision under the condition of uncertainty using mean-variance analysis. Individual choose among risky investments as if they were maximizing the expected value of their utility. In mean-variance analysis maximizing the expected return for a given variance or minimizing the variance in return for a given expected return is consistent with expected utility paradigm. Which states that the individual will choose those alternatives as if he or she were maximizing expected utility. An individual preference for risky assets can be evaluated in terms of each assets expected utility. The quadratic utility function is of particular interest in financial theory because it helps to calculate the expected

* Research Scholar, Department of Economics, University of Hyderabad, Hyderabad 500 046.
The author thanks Prof B Kamaiah for comments on an earlier draft of this paper.

utility of return on risky assets as a function of the mean and variance of their probability distribution.

The evolution of efficient market is synthesized by Fama (1970). The efficient market literature had provided finance with its own research methodology, the "event study". Fama utilized three broad categories for test of market efficiency based on the "relative availability" of subsets of information underlying the tests. There are three forms of information set in the context of efficient market hypothesis. The weak form asserts that current prices fully and instantaneously reflect all information implied by historical sequence of prices. The semi-strong form asserts that the current price fully and instantaneously reflect all public information about companies including the information set on past price series. The strong form asserts that information by monopolistic access (privately held information).

The excess of expected return over risk free return is known as 'volatility'. Volatility of return is one aspect of stock return behavior. The theory of rational bubbles is an example of a model in which expectations are formed rationally and market is informationally efficient but there are large deviation between market prices and fundamental values. If the market value is greater than the fundamentals this indicate an excess volatility. The rational market hypothesis shows positive relationship between excess return and expected or *ex-ante* volatility. In almost all financial models, variance is used as a proxy for variability. The measure of variability that is based on past prices that conforms to the present variability has been conceptualized as 'volatility' in financial market. Thus volatility, as concept, can be treated as synonymous with variability in general or variance in particular. Broadly speaking there exists two broad canvases, under which stock market volatility can be modeled, *viz*, 'conditional volatility' approach and 'stochastic volatility' approach. There are various aspects, associated with volatility in stock return such as: shocks and noise trading, fads, seasonality, co movement or volatility transmission, price limit, margin trading, circuit breakers and transaction tax.

Empirical research has identified a significant amount of volatility in stock prices that cannot be easily explained by changes in fundamentals (Poterba and Summer 1988). One interpretation of the result is that asset prices respond not only to news but also to irrational demand, or "noise trading" (Black 1986). Fads interpretation of volatility test, noise trading by naïve investors plays a significant role in stock price determination explained by West (1988) and Campbell and Kyle (1986). An asymmetry reaction of conditional volatility to the arrival of news was induced both by the sign of past shocks and the size of unexpected volatility (Engle and Ng 1993). There are factors other than the sign of past shocks are responsible for the asymmetric behavior of volatilities. To examine this (Fornari and Mele 1997) proposed a model–the Volatility–switching ARCH–that captures asymmetries via the impact of past shocks on the level of volatility, rather than through the unexpected returns. Not only shocks and noise trading but also seasonality in asset behavior affects stock return. Weekend effect, January effect is some of the important factor for explaining the seasonality in stock return. The cross-sectional differences in January return of selected securities are systematically related to their returns in previous 1 to 5 years, reported by Branch (1977) and Bondt De *et al* (1987). All size–based portfolios exhibit significant January mean-reversion in the post War period explained by Jegadeesh (1991). To analyze the "week–end" for daily stock return, Jaffe and Wasterfield (1985) examined the daily stock returns for four foreign countries. Volatility transmission means, to know the role of measurable economic variable in explaining the magnitude and changes in asset price co movement. It tried to explain the "price of risk" associated with different asset prices are same or different across countries and the inter-temporal behavior of the stock price indices (King *et al* 1994). Stock exchange often employ four measures to curb stock price volatility, namely, margin, price limits, circuit breakers, transaction taxes. Price volatility has been the subject of intense debate for many decades. The purpose of price limit was to prevent stocks from excessive volatility. Margin trading was found to be an effective tool in restricting the activity of new entrants in the stock market. Circuit breakers are primarily used on a stock index. The basic purpose of the circuit breaker is to curb volatility. Transaction taxes can also be used to curb volatility. The tax is aimed at curbing the instincts of 'wild' speculators (information-less).

Many studies have been conducted abroad on issues concerning return behavior of the stock market. However no significant efforts have been made in India to examine the issues related to the return behavior of the stock market. Some of the important issues related to the return behavior such as noise trading, size and sign of shocks, week-end effect, January effect, co movement, regulatory measures, etc. This present study attempts to fill this void.

In the back drop of the above discussion, this essay presents a discussion as to how the concept of stock market volatility has been treated in the literature and the developments to model volatility. Section ii, would discuss, in brief, the return behavior of the stock market: section iii, presents factors that are responsible for creating seasonality in stock return. Section iv, tries to link changes in co-movement or volatility transmission between different stock market. In section v, the regulatory measures to curb stock price volatility has been presented. The concluding remarks is followed by the last section vi, different models of volatility.

Return Behavior of the Stock Market

The return behavior of stock market can be explained by three stylized facts such as leptokurtic, negative skewness and asymmetry return. It is a established fact that assets return tend to be leptokurtic which has been documented by Mandebort (1963), Fama(1965), Clark (1973), Nelson (1991). Fama stated that a stochastic process is thick tailed if its conditionally normal with a randomly changing conditional variance. However the relation between the conditional density and the unconditional density particularly reveals the source of observed heavy tailed. Nelson (1991) explained the tail thickness of a parameter denoted by v. When $v = 2$, it's a standard normal distribution. For $v > 2$, the distribution has thinner tail and $v < 2$, the distribution has thicker tail. In spite of this, there are some issues involved in the behavior of stock return analysis from which noise trading is one.

The average trading behavior may be characterized in two contrasting ways namely, informational trading and noise trading. Noise trading is trading that is not based on information about fundamentals. It can be said that noise traders trade for some reason unknown to analysts or model builders and hence described as noise. Information trading, in simple terms, means trading based on information about fundamentals. In the literature of financial economics, trading in stock is traditionally thought to be information trading.

Black (1986) differentiated between trading on the basis of information and on the same basis of noise. He explained that volatility tends to grow in reaction to bad news (excess return lower than expected) and to fall in response to good news (excess return higher than expected). The economic explanation given by Black was that negative (positive) excess return makes the equity value, hence the leverage ratio (debt – to - equity), of a firm increase (decrease), thus raising its risk-ness and future volatility of its asset. This phenomenon is referred to as leverage effect. He observed that a (negative) shock on the stock of a given firm raises both its leverage ratio and its riskiness. As a result of this, the volatility of a stock as a measure of the risk-ness of the firm will increase as well.

The changing risk premium hypothesis examines the influence of changing stock market volatility on the level of stock prices. This was explained by Poterba and Summer (1986). They used the daily return data on Standard and Poor (S & P) composite stock index for the period 1928-84. For explaining the impact of volatility shocks on share prices they used several different stochastic specification of volatility process. They used AR (1) process for data analysis, an AR (12) process for capturing long-run persistence and IMA (1, 3). In each case they computed the impulse response function for the level of volatility. From the elasticity of share prices with respect to volatility shocks of the model AR (1) and AR (12) it seems that volatility shocks had very small effect on share prices. The estimated results showed that changes in volatility, through their influence on investors risk premium, had a substantial effect on stock market values. Their findings suggest that shocks to stock market volatility do not persist for long period. Estimates based on both actual and *ex ante* volatilities indicate that these volatility shocks have half – lives of less than six months and in some cases as short as one month. Moreover their results suggest that substantially greater half-lives for volatility shocks can be rejected at extremely high confidence level.

The general finding that stock market volatility does not persist for long has not been supported by Pindyck (1984). His regression of excess returns on changes in volatility demonstrates that autonomous volatility changes have had an important effect on market prices. First, since changes in his volatility measure can be predicted, his regression implies that investors should be able to realize substantial profit by trading on past volatility information. Second, results are contaminated by a serious simultaneous problem. A decline in the stock market should increase volatility through leverage effect; one would expect a negative correlation between returns and volatility changes. Third, the implied relationship between volatility shocks and stock return is weak. The elasticity of share prices with respect to unanticipated volatility shocks is varying low.

Rational bubbles seemed a potential rationalization of excess volatility test. One theoretical restriction on rational bubble is that it cannot be negative. If it is negative and stock price lower than its fundamental, the possibility of an extraordinary capital gain, when bubble bursts must be compensated for by potential capital losses. West (1988) argued that excess volatility of stock prices does not strongly suggest rational bubble because he was not able to distinguish between a bubble and a noise. His tentative argument is that neither rational bubble nor traditional model of return determination can explain stock price volatility. He suggested for a non-traditional model of return determination in terms of fad for explaining volatility. In "fads" interpretation of the volatility tests, noise trading by naïve investors plays a significant role in stock price determination. In one interpretation "fads" mean that even after risk adjustment there are profitable opportunities, at least for small investors. He made another interpretation that some fraction of trading is done by naïve traders; sophisticated investor who ensures that there are extraordinary expected returns once risk is properly accounted.This does not mean that prices are driven to what ever levels in the absence of fads.

An empirical study for fads was made by Campbell and Kyle (1986). Who estimated an explicit model of trading by sophisticated investors, when a residual noise process affects stock prices? The study found that the noise accounted for over one fourth of the stock price movement in the S&P data, 1871- 1984, but did not present any evidence that this process results mainly from trading by naïve investors.

Engle and Ng (1993) analyzed a model for the response function of the future expected volatility to past-unexpected volatility known as "news impact curve". They used the volatility switching ARCH model for the estimation of the result. If the unexpected volatility (r_{t-1}) is negative, then *ceteris paribus*, negative shocks generate more volatility than positive ones. If it is reverse then positive shocks increase volatility more than negative ones. This (r_{t-1}) is able to explain the size of a shock. Small shocks are those which produce a level of volatility lower than expected; high shocks are those, which generate a level of volatility higher than expected. Rabemananjara and Zakoian (1993), suggested a switching ARCH model which might not be successful in detecting some of the nonlinear characteristics of the volatility dynamics. Following the occurrence of a shock of a certain size, the asymmetric behavior of the volatility might become reversed.

The Volatility – Switching ARCH - captures the asymmetry via reaction of the conditional variance to shocks of different sign through the sign of such shocks. Fornari and Mele (1997) proposed this model. They had shown that volatility switching density function has a fatter tails compared to the normal variant. This feature helps to capture the high number of outliers observed in empirical distribution. For empirical analysis they took six stock indices namely S&P 500 (U.S), Topix (Japan), Cacyo (France), FT- 100 (U.K), FAZ (Germany), MIB (Italy) indices. The period they had taken was 1st January 1990 to 16 October 1995. There were 1, 494 observations. They have used GJR (Glosten, Jagannathan & Runkle) and Volatility Switching (VS) model for estimation. VS model fits the pattern of the data better than GJR in all cases except Germany. The VS model out performs the GJR when re ranked the model according to the kurtosis of the residual standardized with respect to conditional standard deviation. Sign bias test (SBT), Positive sign bias test (PSBT) and negative sign bias test (NSBT) do not reveal any presence of asymmetry in the reaction of such series to the sign of the past forecast errors. The conditional variance is stationary. Volatility is time varying and persistent.

Laux and Ng (1993) provides a new and more definitive evidence on the mixture of distributions hypothesis. The essence of mixture of distributions explanation for GARCH is that price changes over discrete intervals are the sum of a random number of individual increments to price, where the random number depends on the rate of information arrival over the intervals. The data they used were prices of five actively traded currency futures traded on the Chicago Mercantile Exchange (CME). The currencies under lying these futures are British Pound, Deutsche Mark, Swiss Franc, Japanese Yen and Canadian Dollar. The time period they had taken from December 1984 to December 1986

They made a conceptual decomposition of volatility into systematic and unique sources. This decomposition is fundamental but little has been done for explaining GARCH because the process driving systematic and unsystematic volatility should be identical and the persistence of unsystematic volatility should be equal for all the assets. Second they proposed a simple measure of rate of information that is conceptually very close to the number of instances of information arrival per period – the number of price changes per period. One advantage of this measure's that it is not sensitive to the scope of the market. Increased globalization makes it vary difficulty to obtain measures of volume, but price changes occur in all the market centers in response to information arrival in any of them if arbitrage is effective. Intraday data has the significant advantage because it substantially lessens the chance that volume and volatility are simultaneously determined. Intraday returns over approximately half: hour intervals has been taken.. The return from close to open is also recorded each day. The data set includes 13,169 observations per currency. They used random walk GARCH model including systematic and unique sources volatility. They found first, univariate GARCH models involving the contemporaneous number of price changes appear to yield downward bias estimates of the coefficient on lagged volatility. Second, the predicted number of price changes does not account for some unique GARCH effects, although the factor is influential and has strong GARCH behavior.

The special properties of a filter in continuous time that characterized the dynamics of Bayesian learning about recurrent probability switches and their relation to fluctuating confidence was analyzed by David (1996). He explained how fluctuating confidence, which arise due to an updating process, is reflected in the statistical properties of interest rate and stock return process in a Cox – Ingersoll –Ross (CIR) stochastic production economy. He drew some relationship between speed of learning and the ability of the model to replicate three stylized facts; negative skew ness, excess kurtosis and predictive asymmetry. In a poison process the agents receives signal continuously from a source that jumps infrequently between two values. The source or state variables increase the drift (any return) of one industry and simultaneously decrease the drift of another industry in the economy. The agents receive the total rate of return from each industry, which consist of drift variables and some idiosyncratic noise. In models where difference in average probability of the two processes is large, the level of noise is low, and probability switches are less frequent, the agents spends a large proportion of time in states with high confidence regarding the knowledge of the probability of different assets in the economy. David calls this as "fast learning" model and one with opposite set of parameter called "slow learning" model. He showed that slow learning model generates returns that exhibit greater excess kurtosis and that fast learning generates greater negative skewness. An EGARCH model was fitted, which measures the asymmetry between return and volatility. The fast learning model generated a negative relationship between returns and volatility.

Guo H (2003) tried to explain whether stock market volatility forecasts return. For this he regressed quarterly excess returns, measured by the difference between return on S & P 500 index and the yield on three-month treasury bills, on this measure of volatility. They showed that the adjusted R^2 from this regression is 0.01, indicating that volatility accounts fcr only about 1% of the variation of the one- quarter ahead excess stock market return. He explained, in addition to risk premium, a liquidity premium is also important component of excess stock market returns. If investors have liquidity, they might be willing to hold stocks when expected return is low, even though expected volatility is high. The theory stipulates a positive relation between stock market volatility and returns after taking into account the liquidity premium. Consumption-to–wealth ratio is a proxy for liquidity premium. After taking into account the proxy for their regression, he found that past volatility explains a significant portion of excess stock returns. Both theory and empirical evidence indicate that stock market return increases when volatility rises.

From the above issues and evidences developed to study the return behavior of the stock market we found that there is a negative relationship between stock return and future changes in volatility this phenomenon referred to as leverage effect. Shocks to stock market volatility do not persist for long. Estimates based on both actual and *ex ante* volatilities indicate that these volatility shocks have half-lives less than six month and in some cases as short as one month. Knowing the sign of a volatility shock we are able to explain the size of a shock by the help of Sign Switching ARCH model. Volatility switching density function has a fatter tail compared to the normal variant. Both theory and empirical evidence indicate that stock market return increases when volatility rises.

Seasonality

There would exist seasonality in stock return if the average returns were not the same in all periods. The month-of-the-year effect would be present when returns in some month are higher than in other months. In USA and some other countries, the year-end month (December) is the tax month. Based on this fact, a number of empirical studies have found the 'year–end' effects and the January effect stock return consistent with the "tax-selling" hypothesis. But in our country the seasonality in stock return is found in the month of April.

The cross-sectional differences in January return of selected securities are systematically related to their returns in previous 1 to 5 years, reported by Branch (1977) and Bondt De *et al* (1987). There was reliable evidence that equally weighed index (EWI) exhibits mean-reversion in the sample period 1926-1988; there was little evidence of mean-reversion for the value-weighted index (VWI). It is found that the stock price mean reversion is entirely concentrated in the month of January and the estimates of long-term serial correlation outside January are indistinguishable from zero. This pattern of long-term serial correlation is found for most size-based portfolio returns. Fama and French (1988) and Kim *et al* (1988) reported the evidence of mean-reversion in stock prices is weak in the post war period.

All size–based portfolios exhibit significant January mean-reversion in the post War period explained by Jegadeesh (1991). The point estimates of the January slope coefficient were farther from zero when compared to the slope coefficient in the entire sample period 1926-1948. Mean reversions for small firm portfolio were generally more prominent than the large firm. The stock prices exhibit mean reversion in January in the post War period as well. A similar phenomenon was also observed for the EWI of stocks traded on the London Stock Exchange. They have shown it as an international phenomenon.

To analyze the "week–end" for daily stock return, Jaffe and Wasterfield (1985) examined the daily stock returns for four foreign countries. They found a so called "week-end effects" in each country. The average return on Friday is abnormally high, and the average return on Monday is abnormally low. This is so called "days-of-the week effect" or "week-end effect". They took a daily record of returns for stock market indices of Japan, Canada, Australia, the UK and the US. The specific foreign indices and time periods are Japan – the Nikkei, Dow for January 5, 1970 to April 30, 1983; Canada- the Toronto Stock exchange index from January 2, 1976 to November 30, 1983; Australia – the statex Actuaries Index from March 1, 1973 to November 30, 1982; and UK–the Finance Time Ordinary Share Index from January 2, 1950 to November 30, 1983; S & P 500 Composite Stock Index Price from 2, July 1962 to 30, December 1983. By comparing each stock market with U.S they found that the lowest mean return for both the Japanese and Australian stock market occur on Tuesday. A significant independent seasonal in the return distribution of each country after allowing for the common effects of the U.S stock market. Foreign investors confront a weekend effect in their respective stock market independent of the weekend effect in the U.S. The "time zone" theory is unable to explain the Japanese seasonal but may explain some of the Australian seasonal. They did not find any proof of either measurement error or settlement procedure cause the weekly seasonal in stock market return.

Nelson (1989) explained the stock market volatility changes in his study. He used the data from January 1928 through July 1956 of an index of 90 heavily traded stocks the "standard 90". He fitted the exponential ARCH model as an alternative to standard GARCH models in modeling and forecasting conditionally heteroskedastic process. Principal virtue of the EGARCH model is that it is capable of explaining leverage effects, which appear to be varying important for determining stock volatility. He took five factors such as (serial correlation, trading and non trading days and leverage effect, recession, financial crisis and nominal rate of interest.) for determining stock volatility. He did not have daily data on two factors such as recession, financial crisis and nominal rate of interest. This model performed quite well in episodes during which volatility rose sharply, such as the crash of 1929. In periods of sudden but short–lived volatility as occurred during Eisenhower's heart attack, the model seems to fatter tails in the conditional distribution compared to the normal or even the generalized error distribution.

McInish and Ord (1985) who report, evidence on seasonality in daily and weekly return variances. That have been documented using intraday data is that, volatility is higher when the market is open than when it is closed. They document a U-shaped pattern in return volatility during the trading days, that is, volatility is highest at the beginning and the end of the trading days. Jain and Joh (1988) show that the trading volume is different within and across days. They provide evidence of an inverted U-shape in volume across days. Monday and Friday have the lowest volume, and the most active periods are in the middle of week.

From above review we found that the stock price mean reversion is entirely concentrated in the month of January for most of the countries. But in India the seasonality in stock is found in the month of April. Mean reversions for small firm portfolio were generally more prominent than the large firm. The average return of stock market is abnormally high on Friday, and average return on Monday is abnormally low. This phenomenon is known as "week-end" effect. "Time Zone" theory is unable to explain the weekend effect. It is very difficult to find any proof of either measurement error or settlement procedure cause the weekly seasonal in stock return.

Co-movement and Volatility Transmission

It is a well-known fact that the movements in the stock prices are influenced by the flow of market information. One possible source of this information is movement in other stock markets in the world. Two stock market belonging to two different economic conditions might be related through trade and investment, so that it is possible to transmit news about fundamentals from one country to another country. Co movement explains the intertemporal behavior of the stock price indices. The contemporaneous relationship between returns and volatility across different regime is also an important factor in explaining the co movement.

King *et al* (1994) attempted to link changes in co-movements between stock markets to variation in the economic variables. The variables they had taken for the modeling were short interest rate, long interest rate, Dollar/ Yen exchange rate, industrial production, inflation (CPI weighted by GNP) in G3 countries, U.S trade account, real money supply, oil price, the Dollar/Deutschmark exchange rate and an index of real commodity prices. They assessed the role of measurable economic variables in explaining the magnitude and changes in asset price co movement and they tested whether idiosyncratic risk is priced, and whether the "price of risk" associated with each factor is common across countries. They had taken the monthly data over the period 1970-1988. The 16 countries were Australia, Belgium, Canada, Denmark, France, Germany, Italy, Japan, Netherlands, Norway, Spain, Sweden, Switzerland, U.S and U.K. Data on stock return obtained from the Morgan Stanley Capital International world indices. They have fitted the VAR model for the above variables. They had taken in total 219 observations. They fitted the equation, which included seasonal dummies. To test for serial correlation they used the standard Lagrange Multiplier–test against 12th order serial correlation. The estimated conditional covariance between U.S and U.K market was ranged from 0.25 to 0.6 for explaining the "observable" factors. The relative contribution of "observable" in the case of U.S and Japan was somewhat higher. They decompose the variance of the U.S market into three main components attributable to "observable", "unobservable" factors and idiosyncratic term. The U.S contribution of the observable to the variance is negligible. The actual change in variance was contributed by unobservable variables. The contribution of the idiosyncratic component is constant for the U.S because the components in the corresponding GARCH process were estimated to be zero. They were able to reject the null hypothesis that idiosyncratic risk is not priced and that the "price of risk" associated with the relevant factor is the same across all the countries.

The nature of international transmission of stock returns and volatility has been the focus of many studies. Becker *et al* (1990) employed opening and closing data for Tokyo stock exchange (Nikkei) and New York Stock exchange from 1985 to 1988, to study the synchronization of stock price movement. Cheung and Ng (1992) investigated the dynamic properties of stock return in Tokyo and New York, using daily close- to- close market indices from January 1985 to December 1989. GARCH types of model are used to describe the intertemporal behavior of the stock price indices. Lin *et al* (1994) examined the short-run interdependence of prices and price volatility across three major international stock markets namely; the Tokyo, London and New York with daytime and overnight return data. They used two-stage GARCH model. Rao and Nayak (1990) examined the inter-relatedness of U.S, Japan and India stock markets. Their study uses monthly stock indices of the Mumbai, New York and Tokyo exchanges, for the period January 1971 to December 1988.

The short - run linkages between NSE Nifty in India and NASDAQ composite in the U.S during 1999-2001 intra-day data was investigated by Kiran and Mukhopadhay (2002). The objective of the above study carries out a comprehensive analysis using correlations Granger Causality and GARCH model to examine the co movement and volatility transmission between U.S and India stock markets. For investigating these issues, they had taken NSE Nifty index for analyzing the India stock market as it captures the major disturbance in the Indian stock market. On the other hand NASDAQ Composite Index had been taken as a representative of the U.S stock market. They found unidirectional granger causality running from NASDAQ composite to NSE Nifty. There are three features of stock market, which are necessary for explaining the short run dynamics of stock return and volatility between NASDAQ composite and NSE Nifty. First, the exchanges do not have any overlapping trading hours and hence the case of volatility transmission can be clearly examined. Second, the economic dailies as well as official publications have been full of stories of newfound alliances between the NSE and the NASDAQ. Finally, the stock market movements of these two markets show a substantial degree of interdependence between NASDAQ Composite and NSE Nifty indices.

From the above review we found that only a small proportion of the covariance between national stock market and their time variation can be accounted for by "observable" economic variables. Major changes in the correlation between markets are driven by unobservable variables. There is a unidirectional granger causality running from NASDAQ composite to NSE Nifty. Globalization has led to national stock market moving together more closely.

Regulatory Measures to Curb Stock Price Volatility

Stock exchange often employ four measures to curb stock price volatility, namely, margin, price limits, circuit breakers, transaction taxes. Price volatility has been the subject of intense debate for many decades. The crash of October 1987 and similar large fluctuations within a short span in the U.S and else where has raised serious concern to regulators.

Margins are initial deposits that ensure that traders are well capitalized to handle their exposure to stock market. In short price are used to mitigate default risk and, thereby, systematic risk in the economy. However, margin also affects market liquidity and price efficiency. To the extent that margins impose opportunity cost, they impose a transaction cost on traders. Marginal regulation is an effective tool for reducing 'excessive' volatility of equity and derivative securities. The Brady commission and others have advocated an increase in the margin requirement on derivative securities. After the break of October 1987, margin on Futures and Options were raised from 7 and 10 % to 13 and 20 %, respectively.

A negative correlation between the level of stock prices and the level of margin credit was reported by Moore (1966). Hsieh and Miller (1990) examined the ratio of variances calculated over periods proceeding and following changes in the margin rate and find no evidence of a negative correlation between the changes in margin level and changes in volatility. Kupiee (1990) fails to find any evidence of a relation between margin restrictions and volatilities estimated using a GARCH in mean model.

An empirical investigation of the role of initial margin requirement in curbing speculative excess in the cash market was conducted by Hardouvelis (1988). The negative relation between margin requirements and volatility was checked using two measures of volatility. One annual and another monthly plus a VAR analysis. The time period they had taken was 1935-1987. The core findings is that margin requirements dampen long swings in stock prices that increase volatility at low frequencies and that originate from phenomenon such as fads, the pyramiding and depyramiding of stock prices. Margin requirement is very effective in constraining the activities of new entrants in the market.

The volatility of return of a security in a period before margin trading was compared with in a period after margin trading. Comparisons of volatilities calculated in periods of no margin activity to those calculated during margin eligibility provide no evidence of an increase in any measure of volatility. Actually, all point estimates of volatility decline once margin trading is introduced, though the statistical significance varies. He suggested that margin restrictions are not an effective policy tool for controlling volatility.

Chia–Shang James Chu *et al* (1996) explained variation in the volatility of stock returns to regime shifts in returns. They applied a Markov Switching model to stock returns and examine the variation in volatility in different return regimes. They found that a model containing six regimes with significantly different volatility across regimes best characterizes returns. They used two – stage estimation procedure to relate volatility with regime shifts in return. The time period they had taken from July 1962 to December 1993. The data was obtained from the CRSP data tape. October 1987 is an outlier accounting for a large portion of the variation in volatility. In addition, their estimates are consistent with a strong contemporaneous relationship between returns and volatility across regimes with higher volatility when returns are either above or below "normal". Furthermore, the increase in volatility is higher for negative deviations in return than for positive deviations. These observations lead us to conclude that return and volatility are related non-linearly and that the relationship is asymmetric.

Price limits are mostly used in futures contracts. Price limits constraint transactions to occur within a given range centered on the previous day's closing price. The purpose of the price limit was to prevent stocks from excessive volatility and protect the investors by limiting potential daily losses to a maximum. Regulators also see price limits as a mechanism to curb overreaction to news.

The relationship among daily stock return autocorrelation, trading volume and price limits was investigated by Chung- Hua Shen and Wang (1996). They examined whether the relationship holds true in an imperfect market like Taiwan. Twenty-four Taiwan individual stocks were taken. The time period they had taken covers November 14, 1988 to December 31, 1995. Altogether 1, 967 observations were taken. In there empirical studies they found price- limit have a stronger impact on the correlation than the trading volume. The Taiwan Stock Exchange had imposed daily limits. The purpose of the daily limit was to prevent stocks from excessive volatility and protect the investors by limiting potential daily losses to a maximum. Price limits were adjusted up or down several times according to market condition. Features of price limits as follows: the "true" price

$P^*_{i,t}$ is expected to be greater (smaller) than the closing price if the closing price (i,e the observed price $P_{i,t}$) hits the upper (lower) limit. They found the negative correlation between daily stock return and trading volume for nearly half of the stocks. The negative volume effect is contrary to the positive price limit effect. They used OLS, GARCH and (Generalized Methods of Moment) GMM to investigate the sensitivity of the estimation results. The GARCH model shows the strongest support of the volume effect and GARCH-M model is the weakest. The volume and price limits effects obtained by GMM method are both stronger than those of the OLS and GARCH methods.

Circuit breakers are primarily used on a stock index. Order-imbalance circuit breakers are triggered when markets cannot clear without significant price change. Volume-induced circuit breakers are used to mitigate system failure due to operational backlogs. Finally, price–induced circuit breakers are triggered when price changes go outside a stated range .The basic purpose of the circuit breaker is to curb volatility. Transaction taxes can also be used to curb volatility. The tax is aimed at curbing the instincts of 'wild' speculators (information-less)

Theoretically, all four regulatory measures can curtail volatility. Margin and transaction tax are better in the sense that they do not cause a market breakdown whereas price limits and circuit breakers can case trading halts.

Models for Explaining the Volatility

There are different types of models, which are helpful for explaining the stock market volatility. The most popular way to describe the time variation is the ARCH (Autoregressive Conditional Heteroskedastic) model introduced by Engle (1982) or one of its variant (GARCH, Bollerslev 1986; EGARCH, Nelson (1991)) To measure the predictive asymmetry (excess return and future changes in volatility are negatively related) an EGARCH model can be fitted. An alternative approach, which has been more popular recently, is the Stochastic Volatility model, where the variance is modeled as an unobserved component.

While analyzing inflation Engle (1982) observed that large and small forecast error appears to occur in cluster, suggesting a form of heteroscedasticity in which the variance of the forecast error depends on the size of the preceding disturbances .He suggested ARCH model as an alternative to usual time series. This model has mean zero, serially uncorrelated processes with non-constant variances conditional on the past, but constant unconditional variances. To test whether the disturbances follow an ARCH process, the Lagrange multiplier procedure was used. They tried to model this phenomenon to allow the variance to change through time in response to current development of the system. McNees (1979), suggest "the inherent uncertainty or randomness associated with different forecast periods seem to vary widely over time." He also documented that "large and small errors tend to cluster together". The ARCH class of model was originally introduced for modeling inflation uncertainty, but has subsequently found wide use in the analysis of financial time series. Many economic and financial time series exhibit volatility clustering features. This observation, together with the modern theories of price determination typically rely on some form of risk–reward relationship, underlies the very widespread application of ARCH class of time series model in economics and finance over the past decade. While evaluating the economic and financial time series temporal variation in the forecast error is an important consideration

GARCH model, which elegantly capture the volatility clustering in asset returns, was first noted by Mandelbort (1963). It was noted that: "large changes tend to be followed by large changes – and small changes by small changes". Bollerslev (1986) points out (pp 307-308) that "*Common to most applications, however, is the introduction of rather arbitrary linear declining lag structure in the conditional variance equation to take account of the long memory typically found in empirical work, since estimating a totally free lag distribution often will lead to violation of the non-negativity constraints".*

The extension of the ARCH process to the GARCH process bears much resemblance to the extension of the standard time series AR process to the general ARMA process. Autocorrelation and partial autocorrelation for the squared process may prove helpful in identifying and checking GARCH behavior in the conditional variance.

The GARCH (p, q) model conveniently captures the volatility clustering phenomenon.It does not however allow for asymmetric effects in the evolution of the volatility process. Nelson (1991) discussed some limitations is that the GARCH model has for explaining the volatility. One limitation is that changes in stock return volatility are negatively correlated with returns themselves, i, e volatility tend to rise in response to 'bad news' (returns lower than expected) and to fall in response to 'good news' (returns higher than expected). GARCH models, however, assume that only the magnitude and not the sign of unanticipated returns determines volatility.

Manieu and Schotman (1998) provide an alternative approach, known as the stochastic volatility (SV) model, where the variance is modeled as an unobserved component. It is directly connected to the type of diffusion processes used in asset–pricing theory in finance. Like ARCH models, SV can explain part of the fat–tailed ness. But given the evidence for ARCH models one would expect that time varying volatility does not fully account for the tail behavior. Part of the fat- tailed ness is attributable to time aggregation. In this paper the data used are weekly, whereas the SV model is often formulated in continuous time.

Jacquier *et.al* (1999) opines that SV class of models is more difficult to estimate than standard time–varying volatility model (ARCH). A basic univariate stochastic volatility model (SVOL) model is evolved, which is too restrictive for many economic and financial applications. The use of basic model can lead to biased volatility forecasts especially around crucial periods of high volatility. They extended the basic SVOL to allow for the leverage effect (refers to the tendency for stock prices to be negatively correlated with changes in stock volatility), through a correlation between observable and variance errors, and fat- tails in the conditional distribution. They developed a Bayesian Markov Chain Monto Carlo algorithm for this extended model. They also provided an algorithm to analyze a multivariate factor SVOL model. They found a strong evidence of non- normal conditional distributions for most series, and a leverage effect for stock returns.

Concluding Remarks

From the above review, it has been observed that there is a negative relationship between stock return and future changes in volatility. Estimates based on both actual and *ex ante* volatilities indicate that these volatility shocks have half- lives less than six month and in some cases as short as one month. Knowing the sign of a volatility shock, it may be possible to explain the size of a shock by the help of Sign Switching ARCH model. Both theory and empirical evidence indicate that stock market return increases when volatility rises. The stock prices mean reversion is entirely concentrated in the month of January for most of the countries. But in India the seasonality in stock is found in the month of April. Mean reversions for small firm portfolio are generally more prominent than the large firm. The average return of stock market is abnormally high on Friday, and average return on Monday is abnormally low. This behavior is known as Week–end effect. Only a small proportion of the covariance between national stock market and their time variation can be accounted for by "observable" economic variables. Major changes in the correlation between markets are driven by unobservable variables. Theoretically, all four regulatory measures can curtail volatility. Margin and transaction tax are better in the sense that they do not cause a market breakdown whereas price limits and circuit breakers can case trading halts.

REFERENCES

1. Anderson T.G and T.Bollerslev (1996) "ARCH and GARCH Models", Working paper, 202, Northwestern University.
2. Becker, K.G, Finnerty, J.E and Manoj Gupta (1990) "The Intertemporal Relation Between U.Sand Japanese Stock Markets", *Journal of Finance*, 45, 1297-1306.
3. Black F (1986): "Noise", *Journal of Finance*, 41, 3, 529-43.
4. Bollerslev T (1986): "Generalized Autoregressive Conditional Heteroskedastic", *Journal of Econometics*, 31, 307-327.
5. Bondt De, Werner F.M and Thaler R (1987) "Further Evidence of Investor Over Reaction and Stock Market Seasonality", *Journal of Finance*, 42, 557-81.
6. Branch Ben (1977) "A tax Loss Trading Rule". *Journal of Business*, 50, 198-207.
7. Campbell, J and Albert Kyle (1988), "Smart Money, Noise Trading and Stock Price Behavior, Unpublished Manuscript, Ptinceton.
8. Chung–Hua Shen and L. R. Wang (1996): "Daily Serial Correlation, Trading Volume and Price Limits: Evidence From Taiwan Stock Market", National Chengchi University, Working Paper.
9. Cheung and Lilian K Ng (1992), "Interrelation Between the U.S and Japanese Stock Market Indices", *JL of International Financial Markets, Institutions and Money,* 2 (2), 51-70
10. Chia-Shang James Chu, Gary J Santoni and Tung Liu(1996): "Stock market volatility & regime shifts in

returns", University of Southern Carlifornia, Working paper.

11. Clark P B (1973) "A subordinated Stochastic Process Model with Finite Variance for Speculative Prices", *Econometrica,* 41, 135-56.

12. David A (1996): "fluctuating confidence in stock markets: implications for return volatility", Division of Research and Statistics, Washington D.C.

13. Engle R F (1982): "Autoregressive conditional Heteroskedasticity with estimates of the variance of U.K Inflation", *Econometrica*, 50, 987-1008.

14. Engle R, V.NG and M. Rothschild (1990): "Asset Pricing With a Factor ARCH Covariance Structure: Empirical Estimates, *Journal of Econometrics*, 45, 213-217.

15. Engle, R F and V.Ng (1993) "Measuring and Testing the Impact of News on Volatility", *Journal of Finance,* 43, 1749-77.

16. Fabio Fornari and Mele A (1997): "Sign and volatility–switching ARCH models: Theory and applications to international stock markets", Journal *of Applied Econometrics*, 12, 49- 65.

17. Fama, E F (1965) "The Behavior of Stock Prices", *Journal of Business*, 38, 34-105.

18. Fama, E.F and K.R French(1988) "Permanent and Temporary Components of Stock Prices", *Journal of Political Economy*, 96, 246-273.

19. Guo H (2003) "Does Stock Market Volatility Forecast Return?" *The Federal Reserve Bank of ST.Louis*, Working paper.

20. Hardouvelis, Gikas A (1988) "Margin Requirements and Stock Market Volatility", *Federal Reserve Bank of New York Quaterly,* 13, 80-89.

21. Hsieh, David A and Merton H. Miller (1990) "Margin Regulation and Stock Market Variability", *Journal of Finance*, 45, 3-30.

22. Jacquier E, N .G Polson P. E. Rosi (1999) "Stochastic Volatility: Univariate and Multivariate Extensions", Working Paper, The University of Chicago.

23. Jaffe J and R Westerfield (1985): "The Weekends Effect in Common Stock Returns: The International Evidence, *Journal of Finance*, 40, 2, 433-454.

24. Jegadeesh N (1991) "Seasonality in Stock Price Mean Reversion: Evidence from U.S and U.K", *Journal of Finance*, 46, 4, 1427-1444.

25. Jain Pand G.Joh (1988) "The Independence between hourly prices and trading volume, *Journal of Financial and Quantitative Analysis,* 23, 269-284.

26. Kim, Myung, Charles R Nelson and R Startz (1988) "Mean Reversion in Stock Prices? A Reappraisal of Empirical Evidence", University of Washington, Working Paper.

27. King M, E Sentana and S. Wadhwani (1994): "Volatility and Link Between National Stock Markets", Econometrica, 62, 4, 901-933.

28. Kupiec, Paul H (1990) "Initial Margin Requirements and Stock Market Volatility: Another Look", *Journal of Financial Services Research,* 3, 287-301.

29. Kumar K. K and C. Mukhopadyay (2002): "A Case of U.S and India", Working Paper, NSE Website.

30. Laux P A and Ng L K (1993): "The sources of GARCH: Empiricial Evidence from an Intraday Returns Model Incorporating Systematic and Unique Risk", *Journal of international money and finance,* 12, 543-560.

31. Lin, Engle and Ito (1994), "Do Bulls and Bears Move Across Broders? International Transmissions of Stock Returns and Volatility", *Review of Financial Studies,* 7, 507-538.

31. Mahieu R .J and P.C Schotman (1998): "An Empirical Application of Stochastic Volatility Models", *Journal of Applied Econometrics*, 13, 333-360.

32. Mandelbort, B (1963), "The Variation of Certain Speculative Prices", *Journal of Business,* 36, 394-419.

33. McInish, T and R Wood (1992), "An Analysis of Intraday Patterns in bid/ask spreads of NYSE Stocks, *Journal of Finance,* 47, 753-764.

34. Moore, Thomas G (1966) "Stock Market Margin Requirments", *Journal of Political Economy,* 81, 328-339.

35. Markowitz H (1952) *Portfolio Selection: Efficient Diversification of Investments* (New York: Wiley, 1959), "Portfolio Selection", *Journal of Finance,* 77-91.

36. Nelson D B (1989): "Modeling Stock Market Volatility Changes", American Statistical Association, Proceddings of the Business and Economics Statistics Section, 93-98.

37. Nelson D B (1991) "Conditional Heteroskedasticity in Asset Returns: An New Approach", *Econometrica,* 59, 347-70.

38. Poterba J M and L. H Summer (1986): "The persistence of volatility and stock market Fluctuations", *American Economic Review,* 76, 5, pp 1142-1151.

39. Rabemananjara R and J.M Zakoian (1993) "Threshold ARCH Models and Assymmetries in Volatility", *Journal of Applied Econometrics,* 8, 31-49.

40. Rao, B.S.R and Umesh Naik (1990) "Inter–Relatedness of Stock Markets: Spectral Investgation of U.S.A, Japanese and Indian Markets–Note", *Artha Vignana,* 32, 3-4, 309-321.

41. Seguin P.J. (1990) "Stock volatility & margin trading", *Journal of Monetary Economics,* 26, 101-121.

42. West K. D (1988): "Bubbles, Fads and Stock Price Volatility Test: A Partial Evaluation", *Journal of Finance,* 40, 3, 639-654.

13

Interest Payment Expenditure in Sourthern States During 1990-91 to 2000-01

*M. Seenuvasan**

Introduction

Interest payment expenditure of the government comprises of interest charges on public debt and other obligations. They are interest charges on internal debt and small savings and Provident Fund, interest on loans and advances from Central Government and interest charges on reserve funds. Interest payments on internal debt consists of interest on market loans and other internal debts such as loans from LIC, Nabard (National Bank for Agriculture and Rural Development), loans from SBI and other banks, Special Securities issued to NSSF (National Small Saving Funds) and others. The expenditure incurred on the management of debt is also included under interest payments.

Interest payments incurred on Small Savings and Provident Fund includes interest paid on State Provident Fund, Incentives and Bonus to Provident Fund subscribers. Interest on trusts and Pension Fund, Interest on Insurance

* Assistant Adviser, Department of Economic Analysis and Policy Reserve Bank of India, Hyderabad-4. Ph. 23232020.
Author is thankful to Prof. B. Kamaiah, Prof. VVN. Somayajulu of Hyderabad University, and also thankful to Dr. D. Anjanayulu, ED, RBI, Mumbai.

and Pension Funds and interest on special Deposits and Accounts.

Interest payments on loans and advances from Central Government consists of interest on loans for State Plan Scheme, interest on loans for centrally sponsored plan schemes, interest on loans for non-plan schemes, interest on ways and means advances and other State loans.

A serious concern was raised about the growing interest liabilities of the governments in recent years. Increasing interest payments exacerbates the stress on revenue as a significant portion of the funds went towards interest payments leading to perennial revenue deficits. While the major rigidities on the expenditure side of the center is interest liabilities, subsidies and defense, on the state side it is interest liabilities and salary bill (Mundal and Rao, 1991). In Uttar Pradesh, bulk of the revenue expenditure is of a committed nature and the entire borrowings are used in paying interest and repayment of debts (Shankar 1998). A continuous revenue deficit leads to large interest burden and as a consequence, states are pushed towards borrowing more to meet their repayment needs (Jalan 1998). The emergence of a fiscal crisis at the state level as a consequence of expenditure outpacing revenue have been brought out in studies on state finances such as Guhan (1986) on Tamil Nadu, Jetha (1985) on Gujarat and Govinda Rao and Sen (1999) on Kerala finances. The deterioration in Kerala State finances has been caused by faster growth of interest payments and administrative expenditure. The repayment liabilities on account of borrowings, especially interest liability, are a fast growing item of expenditure for all the states (X Finance Commission). Tenth Finance Commission observed that interest payments and salaries and wages have emerged as the major components of expenditure as a direct result of the mode of financing of expenditure and the expansionary policies pursued by government. The Tenth Commission further observed that it is the burden of interest payments arising out of none too prudent use of borrowings that lies at the root of the fiscal problem. (P.5.1994). In the case of states, the rising revenue deficit has also cut into maintenance expenditure in the revenue budget. In order to accommodate the rising interest payments and the growth of wages and salaries, which have come to be regarded as committed expenditure, maintenance expenditure has been treated as a residual item. The adverse impact of increasing debt service payments on capital expenditure growth was seriously noted in recent years. (Mohan R. 2000) The implication of increasing interest burden was recognized at different levels. Gopalakrishan and Rangamannar (1996) while examinig the shortfalls in States plan outlays, pointed out that the interest burden can fuel non-plan expenditure growth that can cause a reduction in the government savings available for plan financing.

The abnormal growth in revenue expenditure cannot be attributed only a salary and pension revision, though no doubt that was an immediate cause of the actual fiscal distress felt all round. Revenue expenditure of the government at both levels is dominated by elements that are inflexible downward. Two leading items in this category are interest and subsidies (XI Commission). The XI Finance Commission further observed that among the various structural factors, which accentuated budget imbalances during the 1990s, are the rise in the interest rates. The XI Finance Commission (p.21, 2000) noted that at the current level of indebtedness, over 40 per cent of the gross revenues of the center goes into interest payments alone. In the case of the states, interest payments constituted on an average about 22 per cent of their revenue receipts (for some states over 30 per cent). Growth of interest liabilities has been a major factor in driving up revenue deficits of both center and the states in the nineties. The XI Commission recommended that governments should contain interest payments to a reasonable proportion of revenue receipts so that adequate revenues are available with the governments for providing essential public services.

The XI Finance Commission proposed a norm of 35 per cent as the desirable proportion of interest payments to revenue receipts. For the States, the proportion of interest payments to revenue receipts should be about 18 per cent. The XI Commission strongly recommended that the states endeavor to move towards this ratio keeping it as their medium term objective. (XI Commission p.21).

Though there were several studies attempted on the issues of state expenditure, there are few studies available focussing on the sensitive items of expenditure such as salaries and wages, subsidies, pension and interest payments. In recent years, state level studies have focussed on individual items of expenditure. Srivastava and Bhujanga Rao (2001) Concentrated on Subsidies. Government of India (1997) had also brought out discussion paper on subsidies. Issues on contingent Liabilities were also raised (Usha Throat and Sunando Roy 2001). Within the subsidy expenditure, issues on food subsidy was also studied closely (ERC, 2000) However, there are no specific studies available to study the trend in interest payment expenditure in southern states. Roy Allen, Kamaiah B, Govinda Rao (2000) focussed on educational expenditure of large states and also studies concentrated on Casuality between Tax revenue and expenditure of Indian States (Sham Bhat K., Nirmala V., Kamaiah B, 1991).

Objective of the Study

The objective of the present study is to analyse the trend in interest payments expenditure of Southern States during 1990-91 to 2000-01. The Study relies on published data available from State Finances studies of Reserve Bank of India published in its monthly Bulletin.

During the period from 1990-91 to 2000-01, government of Andhra Pradesh had spent about 11.58 per cent of the total expenditure on interest payments, when compared to 13.41 per cent by Karnataka, 10.25 per cent by Kerala and 8.94 per cent by Tamil Nadu. The share of interest payments expenditure in Andhra Pradesh over the years showed rising trend from 8.96 per cent in 1990-91 to 11.94 per cent in 1996-97 and again to 15.52 per cent in 2000-01. The proportion of interest payments in the total expenditure had risen from the range of 8-10 per cent in the early nineties to 12-15 per cent since 1995-96. The share of interest payments in Karnataka over the year too showed rising trend from 8.75 per cent in 1990-91 to 18.16 per cent in 2000-01 and the rise in the share was noticed substantially from 1993-94 onwards.

In contrast, the share of interest payments in Kerala had fluctuated between the maximum of 12.44 per cent in 1992-93 and the minimum of 8.49 per cent in 1993-94. The share, which was on the higher side at the beginning of nineties showed declining trend. Since 1998-99, the share of interest payments in the state again showed increasing trend. Similarly, the share of interest payments in the total expenditure of Tamil Nadu continued to be on the lower side, and its share fluctuated between the maximum of 11.91 per cent in 1999-2000 and the minimum of 5.81 per cent in 19991-92. The share of interest payments was in the range of below 10 per cent between 1990-91 and 1998-99 and thereafter-showed increasing trend to around 11 per cent.

On an average, expenditure on interest payments had accounted for 13.66 per cent of revenue expenditure in Andhra Pradesh and its share fluctuated between a minimum of 10.71 per cent in 1990-91 and a maximum of 17.19 per cent in 1999-2000 with a steady increasing trend over the years. Interest payments as a proportion of revenue expenditure in Karnataka, on an average, constituted 12.09

per cent and its share fluctuated between a minimum of 10.39 per cent in 1991-92 and a maximum of 14.31 per cent in 2000-01 and the share remained by and large the same in the range of 10-12 per cent till 1990-91 and there after showed increasing trend to the range of 13-14 per cent in the subsequent years.

Interest payment as a per cent of revenue expenditure was relatively high in Kerela constituting on average, 15.76 per cent and the share fluctuated between the maximum of 19.01 per cent in 2000-01 per cent and a minimum of 12.06 per cent in 1990-91 and the share showed increasing trend. The share of interest payments in the total revenue expenditure of Tamil Nadu government constituted, on average, 10.83 per cent with a maximum of 14.36 per cent in 2000-01 and a minimum of 6.42 per cent in 1991-92 and showed increasing trend from 8.08 per cent in 1990-91 to 14.36 per cent in 2000-01.

As a proportion of GSDP, expenditure on interest payments had accounted for an average of 1.24 per cent in Andhra Pradesh during 1993-94 to 2000-01, when compared to 1.16 per cent in Karnataka, 1.56 per cent in Kerala and 1.02 per cent in Tamil Nadu.

In absolute terms, expenditure on interest payment showed a stedy increase in all the southern states. In Andhra Pradesh, interest payment expenditure increased from Rs. 589.48 crore in 1990-91 to Rs. 3792.62 crore in 2000-01 and witnessed annual average growth rate of 20.48 per cent. In Karnataka, absolute expenditure had increased from Rs.435.6 crore in 1990-91 to Rs. 2387.55 crore in 2000-01 with a yearly rate of growth of 18.58 per cent. Interest payment expenditure in Kerala had increased from Rs. 340.64 crore in 1990-91 to Rs. 2257.60 crore in 2000-01 and showed an annual average growth rate of 21.19 per cent. In Tamil Nadu, absolute expenditure had increased from Rs. 455.54 crore in 1990-91 to Rs.3123.79 crore in

2000-01 and showed per year rate of growth of 21.43 per cent.

The expenditure on interest payments grew much faster than the revenue expenditure in all the southern states. The per year rate of growth in revenue expenditure was 15.79 per cent for Andhra Pradesh, 15.57 per cent for Karnatka, 15.59 per cent for Kerala and 15.27 per cent for Tamil Nadu. Further, expenditure on interest payments grew much faster than the state's internal debt, revenue receipts, state's own revenue and states own-tax revenue.

On an average, the magnitude of interest payments was twice the size of internal debt of Andhra Pradesh and Kerala and well over twice the size of internal debt contracted in the states of Karnataka and Tamil Nadu. Interest payment as a proportion of internal debt in Andhra Pradesh showed a declining trend in recent years with a maximum of 259.40 per cent in 1994-95 and a minimum of 74.81 per cent in 2000-01. A similar trend has been witnessed in Karnataka. Interest payments as a proportion of internal debt of Karnataka after increasing from 291.96 per cent in 1990-91 to 353.56 per cent in 1996-97 showed a declining trend there after to 104.01 per cent in 2000-01. In the states of Kerala and Tamil Nadu, the magnitude of interest payments as a proportion of internal debt remained by and large the same.

Interest payments as a proportion of revenue receipts was relatively high in Kerala followed by Andhra Pradesh, Karnataka and Tamil Nadu. On an average, interest payments as a percentage of revenue receipts constituted 18.74 per cent of revenue receipts in Kerala and its share over the years showed rising trend from 14 to 18 per cent from 1990-91 to 1997-98 to 20-25 per cent thereafter. Similarly a raising trend of a smaller magnitude was witnessed in Andhra Pradesh particularly from 1994-95 onwards. On an average, interest payments as a proportion of revenue receipts constituted 14.95 per cent in Andhra Pradesh and its share fluctuated between a maximum of 19.47 per cent in 2000-01 and a minimum of 11.02 per cent in 1990-91. Interest payments, as a proportion of revenue receipts in Karnataka was 12.80 per cent on an average and its share also showed increasing trend from 11.19 per cent in 1990-91 to 16.11 per cent in 2000-01. In Tamil Nadu, interest payments as percent of revenue receipts constituted 12.43 per cent and its share showed, increasing trend in the later years of 1990s.

Interest payment as a proportion of state's own revenue on an average constituted 26.75 per cent in Kerala, 23.30 per cent in Andhra pradesh, 17.47 per cent in Karnataka and 17.06 per cent inTamil Nadu and such as a proportion continued to be relatively on a higher side in Kerala in many years. The increase in proportion was found high since 1995-96 in A.P. and at the later years in Karnataka and Tamil Nadu. In state's own- tax revenue, interest payments in Andhra Pradesh accounted for 30.42 per cent and its share showed increasing trend. In Karnataka, interest payments as a proportion of state's own-tax revenue constituted 21.18 per cent and its share increased from 18.68 per cent in 1990-91 to 26.40 per cent in 2000-01. In Kerala, its share was 30.27 per cent against 19.44 per cent in Tamilnadu.

While interest payments as a proportion of revenue receipts and state's own-tax revenue showed an increasing trend, interest receipts by the government was less and its magnitude was not proportionate to the size of interest payments. Though the State of Andhra Pradesh witnessed relatively much improvement in interest receipts followed by Karnataka and Tamil Nadu, the magnitude of interest receipts was substantially less in Kerala. On an average interest receipts as a proportion of interest payments was on average 57.36 per cent in Andhra Pradesh, 49.18 per cent in Karnataka, 33.15 per cent in Tamil Nadu and 4.70

per cent in Kerala. However, it was noticed that the share of interest receipts in interest payments showed a declining trend in all the states. In A.P. its share declined from 91.97 per cent in 1991-92 to 38.65 per cent in 2000-01. In Karnataka, it had declined from 74.38 per cent in 1992-93 to 30.21 in 2000-01. Interest receipts as a proportion of interest payment fluctuated between the maximum of 10.86 per cent in 1995-96 and a minimum of 1.63 per cent in 2000-01.

As a result the magnitude of interest payments had become substantial in all the states. In Andhra Pradesh, interest payment expenditure on an average constituted 40.31 per cent of plan outlay followed by 32.61 per cent in Karnataka, 57.29 per cent in Kerala and 46.35 per cent in Tamil Nadu. The interest payment as a proportion of plan outlay was substantially high in almost all the states in recent years. It had fluctuated between a high of 65.69 per cent and a low of 29.92 per cent in Andhra Pradesh., between 42.11 per cent and 24.14 per cent in Karnataka, 83.54 per cent and 44.84 per cent in Kerala and 65.98 per cent and 31.45 per cent in Tamil Nadu.

In the non-development expenditure, interest payments constituted 41.72 per cent in Andhra Pradesh, 39.73 per cent in Kerala, 37.75 per cent in Karnataka and 35.07 per cent in Tamil Nadu. Actual interest payments against budgeted interest payments in the states of Kerala and Tamil Nadu over-shot in 7 out of 11 years in each of these states and such overshooting of interest payments against the budgeted figure was observed in two years each in Andhra Pradesh and Karnataka. (Tables: 1 to 8)

It is emerged from the above analysis that interest payments made by the governments showed increasing trend in all the southern states except kerala in respect of total government expenditure and revenue expenditure. Interest payments as a proportion of Revenue receipts, state's own

Table 1: Trends in Interest Payment Expenditure in Andhra Pradesh

(Rs. Crore)

Year				*As Per cent of*		
	Total Interest Payments	*Total Government expenditure*	*Total Revenue Expenditure*	*Total Government expenditure*	*Total Revenue Expenditure*	*SDP*
1990-91	589.48	6581.04	5504.78	8.96	10.71	
1991-92	694.95	7757.85	6451.56	8.96	10.77	
1992-93	829.93	8983.47	7190.17	9.24	11.54	
1993-94	1024.98	10061.64	8018.17	10.19	12.78	1.02
1994-95	1256.38	11432.35	9514.12	10.99	13.21	1.01
1995-96	1529.09	12531.43	10613.67	12.20	14.41	1.04
1996-97	1838.84	15402.26	14392.36	11.94	12.78	1.14
1997-98	2153.29	17333.36	14544.29	12.42	14.81	1.31
1998-99	2643.81	19879.67	16943.56	13.30	15.60	1.33
1999-2000	3101.05	22626.81	18037.87	13.71	17.19	1.49
2000-01	3792.62	24437.09	23070.36	15.52	16.44	1.56
AVERAGE				11.58	13.66	1.24

Source: State Finances, RBI

Table 2: Comparison of Interest Payments with major Fiscal Variables (In Percent) - AP

Year	*Interest Payments as % of Revenue Receipts*	*Interest Receipts as % of Interest Payments*	*Interest Payments as % of Plan Outlay*	*Interest Payments as % of Non-developement Expenditure*	*Internal debt as % of Interest Payments*	*Interest Payments as % of State's Own-Tax Revenue*	*Interest Payments as % of State's Own Revenue*
1990-91	11.02	77.89	34.87	38.26	45.56	22.27	17.22
1991-92	11.06	91.97	34.83	37.34	53.61	22.75	17.22
1992-93	11.74	69.63	29.92	38.30	47.87	24.49	18.58
1993-94	12.42	68.83	29.92	40.03	44.43	26.74	19.77
1994-95	14.30	61.16	31.99	39.07	38.55	29.72	21.82
1995-96	15.48	46.93	33.83	41.37	43.78	37.11	26.70
1996-97	16.43	44.82	65.69	43.71	38.26	37.67	28.26
1997-98	15.56	41.96	44.59	44.90	55.60	30.27	24.19
1998-99	18.54	43.33	39.18	46.42	73.99	33.21	26.95
1999-2000	18.45	45.79	48.75	45.58	71.59	34.42	27.08
2000-01	19.47	38.65	49.83	43.91	133.68	35.94	28.53
AVERAGE	14.95	57.36	40.31	41.72	58.81	30.42	23.30

Source: Calculated from State Finances, RBI.

Table 3: Trends in Interest Payment Expenditure in Karnataka

(Rs. Crore)

Year	Total Interest Payments	Total Government expenditure	Total Revenue Expenditure	As Per cent of		SDP
				Total Government expenditure	Total Revenue Expenditure	
1990-91	435.6	4978.74	3971.09	8.75	10.97	
1991-92	514.53	6248.24	4954.12	8.23	10.39	
1992-93	593.71	7099.96	5591.69	8.36	10.62	
1993-94	717.97	5138.24	6208.25	13.97	11.56	1.06
1994-95	871.43	5958.69	7264.52	14.62	12.00	1.07
1995-96	1047.55	6921.87	8481.18	15.13	12.35	1.06
1996-97	1208.06	7942.53	10201.08	15.21	11.84	1.10
1997-98	1393.81	9817.66	10890.21	14.20	12.80	1.22
1998-99	1616.61	10610.9	12445.61	15.24	12.99	1.19
1999-2000	2012.3	12900.37	15231.75	15.60	13.21	1.26
2000-01	2387.55	13148.64	16684.95	18.16	14.31	1.32
AVERAGE				13.41	12.09	1.16

Source: State Finances, RBI

Table 4: Comparison of Interest Payments with major Fiscal Variables (In Percent)-KARNATAKA

Year	*Interest Payments as % of Revenue Receipts*	*Interest Receipts as % of Interest Payments*	*Interest Payments as % of Plan Outlay*	*Interest Payments as % of Non-developement Expenditure*	*Internal debt as % of Interest Payments*	*Interest Payments as % of State's Own-Tax Revenue*	*Interest Payments as % of State's Own Revenue*
1990-91	11.19	54.29	26.56	36.56	34.25	18.68	15.29
1991-92	10.77	44.95	25.91	35.30	36.13	17.74	14.61
1992-93	10.95	74.38	25.93	34.01	34.11	19.17	15.22
1993-94	11.35	47.05	24.16	37.27	34.18	18.83	15.79
1994-95	12.51	46.20	29.26	37.52	22.39	20.32	16.96
1995-96	12.26	66.42	30.28	39.02	30.30	19.86	16.09
1996-97	12.55	55.84	33.54	38.74	28.28	20.94	16.99
1997-98	13.13	40.36	41.05	38.76	30.95	21.74	18.16
1998-99	14.39	41.43	38.13	38.79	53.94	23.28	19.22
1999-2000	15.59	39.84	41.79	37.31	64.35	25.98	21.51
2000-01	16.11	30.21	42.11	41.96	96.15	26.40	22.31
AVERAGE	12.80	49.18	32.61	37.75	42.28	21.18	17.47

Source: Calculated from State Finances, RBI

Table 5: Trends in Interest Payment Expenditure in Kerala

(Rs. Crore)

Year				*As Per cent of*		
	Total Interest Payments	*Total Government expenditure*	*Total Revenue Expenditure*	*Total Government expenditure*	*Total Revenue Expenditure*	*SDP*
1990-91	340.64	3376.45	2824.95	10.09	12.06	
1991-92	483.42	4005.14	3216.45	12.07	15.03	
1992-93	542.51	4362.76	3656.14	12.44	14.84	
1993-94	687.16	8089.11	4293.36	8.49	16.01	1.29
1994-95	819.67	8859.32	5066.3	9.25	16.18	1.52
1995-96	924.16	10406.09	5826.37	8.88	15.86	1.40
1996-97	1103.41	11980.52	6788.11	9.21	16.26	1.55
1997-98	1286.08	12600.49	8241.12	10.21	15.61	1.66
1998-99	1446.26	14885.58	9228.08	9.72	15.67	1.64
1999-2000	1952.27	17818.23	11565.97	10.96	16.88	1.70
2000-01	2257.6	19663.69	11877.91	11.48	19.01	1.70
AVERAGE				10.25	15.76	1.56

Source: State Finances, RBI

Table 6: Comparison of Interest Payments with major Fiscal Variables (In Percent) - KERALA

Year	*Interest Payments as % of Revenue Receipts*	*Interest Receipts as % of Interest Payments*	*Interest Payments as % of Plan Outlay*	*Interest Payments as % of Non-developement Expenditure*	*Internal debt as % of Interest Payments*	*Interest Payments as % of State's Own-Tax Revenue*	*Interest Payments as % of State's Own Revenue*
1990-91	14.18	6.29	44.84	34.10	56.84	25.41	21.99
1991-92	16.95	4.03	58.91	39.33	47.78	28.88	25.33
1992-93	16.35	4.26	60.26	40.21	54.62	28.75	25.04
1993-94	17.52	4.02	58.55	41.32	39.46	29.30	25.75
1994-95	17.57	4.61	57.89	40.90	45.98	29.28	25.65
1995-96	17.04	10.86	55.50	39.03	46.27	27.32	23.59
1996-97	17.96	5.05	52.82	41.45	46.20	28.30	25.01
1997-98	18.07	4.16	43.66	40.88	52.44	28.57	25.45
1998-99	20.09	4.91	47.14	40.16	57.87	31.11	27.77
1999-2000	24.58	1.91	67.09	38.70	48.18	37.59	34.11
2000-01	25.86	1.63	83.54	40.95	66.04	38.46	34.58
AVERAGE	18.74	4.70	57.29	39.73	51.06	30.27	26.75

Source: Calculated from State Finances, RBI

Table 7: Trends in Interest Payment Expenditure in Tamil Nadu

(Rs. Crore)

Year				*As Per cent of*		
	Total Interest Payments	*Total Government expenditure*	*Total Revenue Expenditure*	*Total Government expenditure*	*Total Revenue Expenditure*	*SDP*
1990-91	455.54	6621.23	5641.29	6.88	8.08	
1991-92	557.29	9599.68	8679.52	5.81	6.42	
1992-93	688.47	9748.4	8542.53	7.06	8.06	
1993-94	956.52	10541.2	8758	9.07	10.92	0.79
1994-95	1089.55	12459.01	9634.95	8.75	11.31	0.81
1995-96	1293.21	14300.69	10910.57	9.04	11.85	0.88
1996-97	1475.63	16264.76	13064.89	9.07	11.29	1.07
1997-98	1763.35	17745	14950.85	9.94	11.79	1.05
1998-99	2121.85	21957.45	17697.4	9.66	11.99	1.09
1999-2000	2711.47	22766.67	20727.83	11.91	13.08	1.16
2000-01	3123.79	28119.39	21752.44	11.11	14.36	1.28
AVERAGE				8.94	10.83	1.02

Source: State Finances, RBI

Table 8: Comparison of Interest Payments with major Fiscal Variables (In Percent)-TAMILNADU

Year	*Interest Payments as % of Revenue Receipts*	*Interest Receipts as % of Interest Payments*	*Interest Payments as % of Plan Outlay*	*Interest Paymenis as % of Non-developement Expenditure*	*Internal debt as % of Interest Payments*	*Interest Payments as % of State's Own-Tax Revenue*	*Interest Payments as % of State's Own Revenue*
1990-91	8.95	19.69	31.45	30.46	48.14	14.58	12.99
1991-92	8.22	138.29	31.96	31.83	47.24	14.92	11.48
1992-93	9.81	30.68	34.41	33.65	46.86	16.54	14.42
1993-94	11.86	28.78	40.31	38.21	36.65	19.92	17.37
1994-95	11.82	25.59	44.24	37.08	36.92	18.68	16.49
1995-96	12.20	26.51	47.45	36.90	36.65	18.08	16.15
1996-97	12.34	23.65	42.89	35.21	31.92	18.48	16.64
1997-98	12.98	27.58	53.65	36.83	39.57	20.30	17.98
1998-99	14.88	18.14	54.73	35.06	49.31	22.04	19.68
1999-2000	16.61	12.79	65.98	34.06	47.50	24.83	22.09
2000-01	17.05	12.92	62.83	36.51	116.89	25.43	22.32
AVERAGE	12.43	33.15	46.35	35.07	48.88	19.44	17.06

Source: Calculated from State Finances, RBI

revenue, plan outlay, non-development expenditure and state's own tax revenue showed increasing trend during the period covered in the study. Interest receipts was not sufficient to meet the increasing interest payments in all the southern states and such interest receipt was substantially low in kerala when compared to other southern states. There were incidents that actual interest payments exceeded the budgeted interest payments. The State governments should reduce the interest payments by reducing their borrowings being diverted for interest payments. Such steps should improve the expenditure on infrastructure and other essential items.

REFERENCES

1. Expenditure Reform Commission (2000); "Report on Food Subsidy. Government of India.
2. Guhan, S., "Fiscal Policy projections and performances" EPW, November 15, 1986.
3. Gopalakrishna S, Rangamannar T.S. "Shortfalls in States Plan outlays An Analysis" NIPFP, 1996.
4. Govinda Rao, M and Sen. T.K., "State Finances in Kerala selected issues", NIPFP, New Delhi, 1990.
5. Jalan, B., "State Finances Disturbing", Business Standard, December, 28, 1998.
6. Jetha, N., "A study on state finances in India: the case of Gujarat", 1995.
7. Mohan Rakesh, "Fiscal Correction for Economic Growth: Data Analysis and suggestion" EPW 2000.
8. Mundle sudipto and Govinda Rao, M (1991) "Volume and Composition of Government Subsidies in India", Economic and Political Weekly, Vol. XXVI, No.14.
9. Report of XI Finance Commission (2000-2005), Government of india, New Delhi, 2000.
10. Report of X Finance Commission (1995-2000), Government of india, New Delhi, 1994, p. 4.

11. Roy Allen, Kamaiah B, Govinda Rao "Educational Expenditure of large states" A. Normative approach" EPW (April 22, 2000).

12. Shankar, K., "Finances of U.P Government towards bankruptcy", EPW, January 17, 1998.

13. Sham Bhat K., Nirmala V., Kamaiah B. "Casuality between Tax revenue and expenditure of Indian States, Artha Vijnana (1991), V.33, N.4, 335-344.

14. Srivastava D.K., Bhujanga Rao C.: Government Subsidies in India: uses and approaches, NIPFP, 2001.

15. Throat U, Roy Sunando, "Contingent Liabilities at the state Level: Indian Experience" World Bank Conference paper, 2001 New Delhi.

14

Performance Evaluation of Mutual Funds in India

An Empirical Analysis

*Kedarnath Mukherjee**

Introduction

Infrastructure development had received lesser attention in the post-reform era in India. It was realized that without developing the infrastructure, the real globalization was not possible. But higher investment requires a well-developed capital market. During the nineties, not only the capital market gained importance, but the smaller and individual investors also enjoyed the opportunity for investing in the stocks. Such a thing became possible only through various mutual funds. Through employing professionally qualified and well experienced investment consultant and fund managers, such fund pools money and invest the same in a variety of blue chip companies, selected from a wide range of industries with the object of maximizing return on investment.

* Research Fellow, Department of Economics, University of Hyderabad, Hyderabad.
The author is thankful to Prof. B. Kamaiah and also to Boppana Nagarjuna, Department of Economics, University of Hyderabad for their valuable comments.

During the post-reform era, mutual funds have emerged as an important part of capital market in India. Unit Trust of India (UTI), Life Insurance Corporation of India (LIC), General Insurance Company (GIC), State Bank of India (SBI), Housing Development and Finance Corporation (HDFC), Canara Bank (CANBANK), Punjab National Bank (PNB), Bank of India (BOI), Indian Bank (INDBANK), Tata Group, Birla Group, Reliance Group etc., operating various schemes, are some of the important fund manager in India. Though UTI with its large network across the country is still the leader among all the mutual funds in India.

Generally, any two mutual fund schemes are not found to be alike. They are formed with a view to satisfy varied objectives of different types of investors.

On the basis of several objectives and portfolios of investment, mutual fund can be classified as- Equity Funds, Growth Funds, Income Funds, Tax-exempt Funds, Liquid Funds, Special Funds, Index-linked Funds, Leveraged Funds, Dual purpose Funds, Real-Estate Funds, Funds of Funds, Balanced Funds, Hedge Funds, Offshore Funds, New Direction Funds etc. Again, based on execution and operation, mutual funds can be classified as Closed-ended and Open-ended mutual funds.

The mutual fund market in India is estimated to be to the tune of Rs.1, 00, 000 cores (app.). Again, the overall funds managed by the Unit Trust of India (UTI) as on 30th June, 2001 was over Rs.58221crores and more than 41.80 million investors accounts are opened under 85 schemes. However, several structural and policy related factors have impeded the growth of the mutual fund industry in India. Therefore, evaluation of performance of such a means of investment in various ways has become an important issue to the researchers.

Objectives

Though there are a few attempts in the broad area of performance evaluation of mutual funds all over the world, there have been very few systematic studies in Indian scenario during the period 1997-2000. Keeping in view the importance of the issue, the present paper aims at a comprehensive evaluation of performance of mutual funds in India during that period. More specifically, the paper intends to:

1. Examine the trends and patterns of mutual funds in India;
2. Evaluate the performance of various schemes of different mutual funds by applying different ratios based on return from those funds;
3. Draw a comparison between the performances of different mutual fund schemes by considering the concerned ratios;
4. Identify the best and the worst performer in the mutual fund industry based on the above comparison.

The rest of the paper is organized into four sections. Section II contains a brief review of previous works on the performance of mutual funds. The methodologies used to measure the performance of mutual funds are described in section III. Data as well as empirical findings are recorded in section IV, while section V contains the concluding remarks.

Review of Previous Works

The prominent studies in the recent past on the performance of mutual funds in India include Barua and Varma (1991, 1994), Shome (1994), Kale and Uma (1995), Sarkar and Majumdar (1995), Yadav and Mishra (1996), Jaydev (1996, 1998), Sahadevan (1997) etc. All of these studies evaluated the performance of various mutual fund schemes by considering Sharpe Index, Treyner Index, and Jensen's Alpha. Apart from the difference in the selected schemes as well as the period of studies, almost all of the works showed a similar finding.

Barua and Varma (1991) evaluated the performance of the first closed-ended mutual fund scheme-Master share launched by the UTI between the period July 1987 and September 1990. Their findings concluded that the specific scheme was not effective for small investors. The study by Shome (1994) intended to focus on examining the performance of 17 growth schemes during the period April 1993 to March 1994. After comparing the average rate of return with the market rate on the one side, and the portfolio specific risk with the market risk on the other, the study revealed that – the average return was less than the market return, only 35 per cent of the sample schemes could beat the market return, risk of majority of the sample schemes was higher than that of the market. Kale and Uma(1995) conducted a study based on 77 mutual fund schemes to examine the degree of association between risk and return by examining the CARG yielded by different schemes. The study revealed that only the growth schemes yielded the maximum CARG (47 per cent). Sarkar and Majumdar (1995) tried to evaluate the performance of five growth schemes for the period February 1991 to August 1993 by considering Jensen's measure. Their findings did not reveal any positive significant alpha. The analysis and interpretation made by Sahadevan (1997), regarding performance of mutual funds, is one of the most exhaustive. Jaydev (1998) tried to evaluate the performance of 49 schemes. His study revealed that mutual fund schemes, generally, failed to yield any extra return.

Thus all these studies evaluated the performance of mutual funds in terms of Jensen's measure, i.e., considering the risk-adjusted return. But these studies are confounded with its own limitations. The present study evaluates the performance of Indian mutual funds in terms of return only, avoiding the limitations of measuring risk.

Methodology

There are several ways for evaluating the "performance" of different portfolios, such as measuring risk, return, risk-adjusted return associated with those portfolios. In our present study, the main emphasis is on portfolio's return, i.e., return of different mutual fund schemes in India. Under this specific method, several ratios have been applied individually in this study. Now the ratios can be summarized in the following way:

Total Return

Total return of a mutual fund scheme, during a given year, has been calculated by applying the following formula,

$$Ri = \frac{Dt + Ct + (NAVt - NAVt - 1)}{NAVt - 1}$$

Where, Ri is Total Return from ith portfolio (scheme), Dt is Net Distributed Income /Loss per unit, Ct is Capital gain Disbursement per unit, NAVt is Net Asset Value per unit at time t and NAVt-1 = Net Asset Value per unit at time (t-1).

Again, Net Distributed Income is defined as, [Investment Income – (Aggregate of Exp. + Provisions)]. NAV per unit is [(Market Value of Investment & Other Current Assets- Current Liabilities & Provisions) ÷ Fund Share Outstanding].

Expense Ratio

Trends in expenses to manage and operate mutual fund's scheme are an important indicator of their performance over a number of years. The impact of expenses can be measured in several ways by using different ratios. These are overall Expense Ratio, Expense to Net Asset Ratio (per unit), Expense to Income Ratio etc. In the present study our attempt is to analyze the overall expense ratio as well as the expense to income ratio.

Overall Expense Ratio or the Expense Ratio can be calculated in the following way:

$$\text{Expense Ratio} = \frac{\text{Total Expenses during the year}}{\text{Average Net Asset Value}} \times 100$$

where Average NAV = (Sum of the value off all net assets over the study period ÷ Number of years in that period).

Again, in order to know the impact of expenses on the earnings of various mutual fund schemes, the expense to income ratio have been taken into consideration. This ratio actually indicates how much amount has been spent out of income. It has been defined as:

$$\text{Expense to IncomeRatio} = \frac{\text{Total Expenses during the year}}{\text{Total Income during the year}} \times 100$$

Income Ratio

Though this ratio is not as significant as total return, it can be used to measure the performance of mainly income oriented equity funds and balanced portfolios, i.e., income-cum-growth schemes. It is not effective to use this ratio for those portfolios, which concentrate solely on capital appreciation, i.e., for growth oriented schemes.

Income Ratio can be calculated by the following formula–

$$\text{IncomeRatio} = \frac{\text{Net Investment Income}}{\text{Average Net Assets}} \times 100$$

where, Net Investment Income = Excess of Income over Expenditure.

Portfolio Turnover Rate

Here, the term "portfolio" does imply the combinations of various investments and deposits made by a particular mutual fund scheme. Portfolio turnover means a change in the combinations of these assets by a simultaneous purchase and sale of the same.

Portfolio turnover rate can be defined as –

$$\text{Profit turnover Rate} = \frac{\text{Lesser of Assets Purchage or Sold During the year}}{\text{Fund's Net Assets}} \times 100$$

Here, the term "Asset" implies the shares and /or bonds purchased or sold by the fund managers to change their portfolios.

If the amount of assets purchased during a year is higher than the amount of sale of assets, then the later, i.e., the sale value of assets have to be taken as the numerator of the above ratio, and vice versa.

Data and Empirical Results

To evaluate the performance of mutual funds in India, 53 schemes (Appendix- 1) of the largest mutual fund manager in India, i.e., the Unit Trust of India were selected. The selected schemes were different in nature. Some are income schemes, some are growth schemes, and the rest are income-cum-growth schemes. The schemes were selected based on convenience, i.e., only those schemes have been taken into account for which required data were available. The study covers a period of three years starting from April 1997 to March 2000. In order to analyze the evaluating techniques, applied in this study, effectively, data relating to the nature of different schemes of UTI; net distributed income as well as capital gain distributions made by different schemes; Net Asset Value (NAV) per unit; value of investment and other current assets as well as other current liabilities of those schemes; total expenses incurred as well as total income earned by different schemes; amount of assets (i.e., equities, bonds etc.) purchased or sold by these schemes etc. have been taken into consideration. The above data has been collected from Annual Reports of the Unit Trust of India (UTI) and from various websites including of UTI itself (www.unittrustofindia.com) and other organizations (e.g. www.myiris.com). It is to be noted that, some of the schemes were initiated in the market on or after 1998-99. That is why no data relating to those schemes were available prior to this period. Again, in order to make the evaluation fruitful, only those schemes, fall under the same category were considered, e.g., only the income schemes have been selected to evaluate their performance based on income ratio. It is meaningless to evaluate and compare the performance of growth schemes in the light of the above ratio, because these schemes mainly try for capital appreciation, not for current earnings.

Empirical Analysis: Total Return

In order to evaluate the performance of mutual fund in the light of "total return", we have taken a sample consist of some monthly income plans, a very few growth schemes and some income-cum-growth schemes. Table-1 shows the per unit total return of these schemes considering net distributions and change in NAVs over the study period. It is to be noted here that this approach allows for calculating returns without considering the impact of re-investment, i.e., it assumes all distributions are received at the end of the year in cash without leaving any amount for re-investment. But the published total return numbers are customarily calculated with assumption of re-investment of earnings made by the funds. That is why; there may be some difference between the calculated figures of return and the published numbers. The table confirms that the per unit total return of all the MIPs shows an increasing trend over the years. Again, there is a noticeable positive change in the return of a few growth schemes (MEP-95 and MEP-96), mainly due to high increase in the amount

Table 1: Total Return of Different Schemes of UTI

Schemes Names	*Net distributions (Dt + Ct) Amount in Rs.*			*Change in NAV (Amount in Rs.)*			*Total Return (%)*		
	97-98	*98-99*	*99-00*	*97-98*	*98-99*	*99-00*	*97-98*	*98-99*	*99-00*
MIP-97-IV	0.86	0.86	2.38	-	0.37	0.45	-	12.31	27.32
MIP-97-V	0.74	0.62	2.89	-	0.02	0.57	-	6.23	33.62
MIP-98	0.71	1.16	2.02	-	0.59	0.28	-	17.97	22.27
MIP-98-II	0.03	0.85	1.86	-	0.31	(0.29)	-	11.63	15.61
MIP-98-III	-	1.21	2.05	-	-	(0.13)	-	-	16.51
MIP-98-IV	-	0.82	2.49	-	-	0.29	-	-	24.69
MIP-98-V	-	0.38	2.00	-	-	0.76	-	-	26.21
MIP-99	-	0.09	1.58	-	-	1.12	-	-	26.76
MIP-99-II	-	-	0.98	-	-	-	-	-	-
MIP-2000	-	-	0.79	-	-	-	-	-	-
IISFUS-97-II	0.61	0.93	2.51	-	0.40	0.04	-	13.66	25.15
IISFUS-98	0.08	1.23	2.29	-	0.59	0.55	-	18.88	27.76
NRI FUND	0.04	1.14	2.07	-	0.98	0.03	-	21.33	19.23
RBUP-94	2.21	1.69	3.30	0.42	3.36	2.02	18.92	35.27	30.09
UBF-98	0.07	0.73	0.14	-	1.65	1.21	-	23.96	11.66
US-95	19.68	15.94	39.22	(0.18)	13.92	29.36	19.76	30.31	60.99
PEF-95	0.75	0.71	15.45	(3.05)	4.54	4.05	(18.47)	55.85	139.89

(Table Contd...)

Table 1: (Contd...)

Schemes Names	*Net distributions (Dt + Ct) Amount in Rs.*			*Change in NAV (Amount in Rs.)*			*Total Return (%)*		
	97-98	*98-99*	*99-00*	*97-98*	*98-99*	*99-00*	*97-98*	*98-99*	*99-00*
IISFUS-98-II	-	0.98	1.87	-	-	0.42	-	-	22.23
Grandmaster	1.46	5.28	7.27	(3.34)	1.87	(2.12)	(13.54)	(32.35)	41.50
Master Growth	1.05	0.54	13.95	-	1.41	3.84	-	12.55	104.96
RUP-II	-	1.22	2.77	0.38)	-	4.25	-	-	59.29
GUP-94	1.54	1.37	2.04	-	1.35	1.03	11.54	28.13	27.86
Master share	2.42	2.79	3.78	-	1.32	0.30	-	25.74	23.60
Master Plus	2.33	6.08	17.56	-	2.61	1.59	-	44.40	86.34
MEP-93	3.53	(2.47)	11.77	-	4.34	(1.84)	-	12.31	50.84
MEP-94	(0.76)	(3.54)	9.17	(2.36)	3.96	1.85	-	6.34	104.16
MEP-95	0.49	(3.26)	5.95	(1.64)	2.33	1.78	(16.49)	(10.36)	58.35
MEP-96	0.18	(3.04)	14.01	-	2.70	2.22	(11.60)	(3.11)	118.90
MEP-98	0.29	(2.79)	11.07	-	3.24	3.06	-	5.39	121.92
MEP-99	-	1.01	25.53	-	-	13.06	-	-	342.72
MVUP	-	1.13	18.25	-	4.34	3.68	-	54.70	152.93
GSF-Software	-	(0.01)	42.75	-	-	13.98	-	-	562.80
GSF-Service	-	(0.01)	23.06	-	-	23.21	-	-	463.16
GSF-Petro	-	(0.01)	4.55	-	-	2.72	-	-	72.77

Note: Figures in brackets represent net loss/capital loss or negative total return p.u.
Source: Annual Report, Unit Trust of India, 1997-98, 98-99, 99-00.

if distributions. The growth sector funds (GSF-software, GSF-service and GSF-petro) show a very high positive total return during 1999-2000. There is also an increase in the total return of the balanced schemes (IISFUS-97, IISFUS-98, IISFUS-98-II) during the period. Some of the schemes (NRI FUND, RBUP-94, GUP-94) show a small decline in total return during the period. Thus, solely from the point of view of TR, it cannot be denied that the performance of the GSFs is the best.

Expense Ratio and Expense to Income Ratio

The impact of overall expenses of different schemes on their net asset value as well as their total income has been shown in Table-2. The table confirms that the expense ratios of the GSFs have substantially increased from below 1 per cent during 1998-99 to above 5 per cent level just in the next year. It has been noticed that there is no considerable changes in the expense ratio of MIPs, which lies between 1.00 to 1.50 per cent during the study period. Again, the expense ratio of the income-cum-growth schemes has also not been changed considerably. Thus the performance of the income schemes is considered better than all other schemes. Again, an evaluation can also be made by considering the expense to income ratio of different schemes (as shown in Table-2). The interpretation of this ratio is such that, the higher the ratio, the larger is the total expenses incurred out of total income. The table confirms that the average expense to income ratio of most of the schemes of UTI fall within the range of 3 per cent to 10 per cent. Some of the schemes (CRTS-81, RUS-92) have the ratio below 2 per cent that may be treated as highly efficient scheme. The average ratios of the MIPs (except MIP-2000-II) fall within the range of 5 to 15 per cent. Again, the table confirms that the total expenses incurred by the schemes- CGGF-99, UBF-98, GSF-SOFT, GSF-PHARMA, GSF-SERVICE are 2.05, 1.03, 2.6, 1.48, 2.8

Table 2: Overall Expense Ratio and Expense to Income Ratio

Schemes Names	*Overall Expense Ratio (%)*			*Expense to Income Ratio (%)*		
	97-98	*98-99*	*99-00*	*97-98*	*98-99*	*99-00*
US-64	1.43	1.48	1.28	3.56	5.11	2.30
ULIP-71	0.96	1.03	1.76	2.00	1.85	10.29
CRTS-81	0.19	0.21	0.42	1.10	1.20	2.03
CGGF-86	0.44	0.38	0.62	3.23	5.27	3.15
CGGF-99	-	1.65	4.89	-	387.52	24.07
Master share Plus- 91	0.85	3.23	2.22	6.47	13.81	4.93
RUS-92	0.07	0.09	0.44	0.94	1.07	1.09
Master Growth-93	0.70	0.68	2.25	12.36	14.38	4.41
RUP-II	0.96	0.64	0.44	12.02	9.50	2.26
UBF-98	0.21	1.01	2.87	279.14	14.61	15.60
GSF-SOFTWARE	-	0.02	8.63	-	516.22	4.41
GSF-PHARMA	-	0.07	5.48	-	271.70	25.16
GSF-SERVICE	-	0.01	4.98	-	557.14	4.21
Mastershare-86	0.72	0.70	1.00	4.53	4.23	4.36

(Table Contd...)

Table 2: (Contd...)

Schemes Names	*Overall Expense Ratio (%)*			*Expense to Income Ratio (%)*		
	97-98	*98-99*	*99-00*	*97-98*	*98-99*	*99-00*
MEP-94	1.57	1.58	1.49	(0.17)	(10.01)	3.43
MEP-95	1.66	2.15	1.69	28.60	(13.40)	5.91
MIP-94-III	1.12	1.21	0.89	6.49	3.71	4.80
MIP-95	0.73	0.74	0.93	6.59	7.52	3.81
MIP-95-III	1.03	1.01	1.20	6.93	7.29	6.07
MIP-96-III	1.11	1.14	1.38	7.41	8.25	7.59
MIP-96-IV	1.11	1.10	1.28	8.15	8.10	7.50
MIP-97	1.10	1.08	1.32	0.10	16.29	3.89
MIP-97-II	1.02	1.00	1.25	8.84	12.24	4.09
MIP-97-III	1.06	1.05	1.35	11.12	8.93	5.89
MIP-97-IV	0.70	0.76	1.13	8.18	7.73	5.07
MIP-98	0.65	1.08	1.40	17.32	8.67	7.01
MIP-98-II	0.07	1.12	1.42	19.67	9.88	6.59
MIP-98-III	-	1.01	1.31	-	8.77	7.13
MIP-98-IV	-	0.78	1.31	-	8.47	5.60

(Table Contd...)

Table 2: (Contd...)

Schemes Names	*Overall Expense Ratio (%)*			*Expense to Income Ratio (%)*		
	97-98	*98-99*	*99-00*	*97-98*	*98-99*	*99-00*
MIP-98-V	-	0.60	1.34	-	14.91	7.64
MIP-99	-	0.24	1.22	-	21.85	7.99
MIP-99-II	-	-	0.94	-	-	9.14
MIP-2000	-	-	0.84	-	-	11.47
MIP-2000-II	-	-	0.10	-	-	27.21
IISFUS-97	0.48	0.43	0.89	4.16	2.88	2.94
IISFUS-97-II	0.40	0.42	0.81	6.18	3.99	3.41
IISFUS-98	0.38	0.43	1.14	30.99	3.25	4.76
IISFUS-98-II	-	0.31	0.82	-	3.25	4.35

Note: Figures in brackets indicate negative ratios

Source: Annual Reports of UTI, 1997-98, 98-99, 99-00.

times respectively more than their total income. But the higher ratio of the growth sector funds (GSFs) can be ignored initially because of their recent initiation in the mutual fund industry. The Master Equity Plans show a negative expense to income ratio during the year 1998-99, though it turned out to be a positive one in the next year.

Income Ratio

The income ratio of the sample schemes has been shown in Table-3. It can be noticed from the table that just in the year of launching, i.e., during 1998-99, the income ratio of the GSF schemes (viz. GSF-SOFT, GSF-PHARMA, GSF-SERVICE) were negative and just in the next year these schemes had become able to convert their negative ratio into a very high positive one. The performances of the two Master Equity Plans (MEP-94 and MEP-95) were also being the same. The ratio of Master share Plus-91, RUS-92, Master growth-93 have considerably increased from a lower level in 97-98 to a higher one in 99-00. The income ratio of a few MIPs has shown a decreasing trend from the year 97-98 to 98-99, though these ratios have positively changed in the year 99-00. Only the MIP-2000-II shows a figure less than 1 per cent, but it can be ignored on the ground mentioned earlier. The table also confirms that the ratio of the balanced schemes show a positive change during the period under study.

Portfolio Turnover Rate

Some of the open-ended schemes of the UTI have been taken to evaluate their performance in the light of portfolio turnover rate. Table-4 shows the year wise as well as average rate of the sample schemes. The table confirms that the portfolio turnover rate of the majority of the sample schemes lie below 50 per cent range. The scheme, having such a lower rate, has become able to keep transaction costs in a lower level. But at the same time these had to foregone

Table 3: Showing Average Net Assets and Income Ratio

Schemes Names	*Avg. Net Asset (Rs. In lakhs)*	*Income Ratio (%)*		
		1997-98	*1998-99*	*1999-2000*
US-64	1498809.87	21.49	15.12	18.25
ULIP-71	477574.76	12.46	14.45	12.20
CRTS-81	70320.26	15.87	17.31	19.23
CGGF-86	305553.27	13.14	6.90	19.00
CGGF-99	21424.85	-	(1.23)	15.42
Master share Plus- 91	89780.40	12.28	20.15	42.83
RUS-92	122755.44	7.08	8.00	40.17
Master Growth-93	43411.92	4.96	4.05	48.73
RUP-II	51895.27	7.04	6.09	19.11
UBF-98	75177.08	(0.13)	5.88	15.54
GSF-SOFTWARE	12198.75	-	(0.01)	187.04
GSF-PHARMA	4115.45	-	(0.04)	16.29
GSF-SERVICE	3994.28	-	(0.01)	113.15
Mastershare-86	107378.94	15.07	15.90	22.06
MEP-94	39371.61	(10.55)	(17.35)	50.00
MEP-95	69945.05	4.15	(18.18)	26.99
MIP-94-III	47546.29	16.10	31.51	17.57
MIP-95	55879.09	10.33	9.09	23.46
MIP-95-III	43677.36	13.81	12.82	18.50
MIP-96-III	39120.09	13.85	12.70	16.76
MIP-96-IV	85652.82	12.47	12.48	15.84
MIP-97	119895.16	10.38	5.55	32.63
MIP-97-II	161598.04	10.54	7.20	29.60
MIP-97-III	86705.52	8.47	10.67	21.65
MIP-97-IV	98255.99	7.18	9.02	21.16
MIP-98	97001.71	3.09	11.41	18.58
MIP-98-II	82964.28	0.29	10.25	20.21
MIP-98-III	140174.53	-	10.52	17.12

(Table Contd...)

Table 3: (Contd...)

Schemes Names	*Avg. Net Asset (Rs. In lakhs)*	*Income Ratio (%)*		
		1997-98	*1998-99*	*1999-2000*
MIP-98-IV	93935.57	-	8.48	22.02
MIP-98-V	86676.62	-	3.40	16.21
MIP-99	270795.61	-	0.87	14.07
MIP-99-II	131656.08	-	-	9.36
MIP-2000	136478.87	-	-	6.45
MIP-2000-II	50711.64	-	-	0.26
IISFUS-97	65814.56	11.03	14.57	28.58
IISFUS-97-II	66723.52	6.10	10.12	22.88
IISFUS-98	97033.16	0.84	12.77	22.74
IISFUS-98-II	113210.81	-	9.18	18.05

Notes: Figures in brackets shows negative ratios.

Source: Annual Report of UTI, 1997-98, 98-99, 99-00.

the opportunity of earning quicker-profits. Some of the schemes (viz. OMNI PLAN-91, MMF-97, GSF-BRAND, GSF-PHARMA, GSF-SOFT, GSF-PETRO etc.) show a noticeable high portfolio turnover rate fall between 300 per cent to 500 per cent. Such a higher rate signifies that the schemes follow an aggressive policy in the matter of security trading. In such a case, there is also a possibility, other than earning very quicker-profits, of eating up the profits by the excessive transaction costs, which is nothing but one type of inefficiency.

Concluding Remarks

In the previous section our attempt was to evaluate the performance of various sample schemes separately, based on different ratios. But, in the present section, our effort is to make a comparative study regarding the performance of those selected schemes by considering all the measures jointly. In Table-5, we have taken all the average figures of the ratios applied to evaluate the performance of the

Table 4: Portfolio Turnover Rate for Different Open-ended Schemes

Schemes Names	*Portfolio Turnover Rate (%)*			
	1997-1998	*1998-1999*	*1999-2000*	*Average*
US-64	16.75	36.07	12.61	21.81
ULIP (US)-71	15.27	13.80	12.90	13.99
CRTS-81	3.75	2.07	3.29	3.04
CGGF-86	1.74	2.11	1.30	1.72
CGGF-99	-	-	-	-
OMNI PLAN 91**	47.84	833.78	-	440.81
Master share Plus-91	-	18.25	11.87	15.06
Master growth- 93	-	-	0.78	0.78
Grand master-93	0.60	0.01	2.59	1.07
HUS-92	-	-	-	-
SCUP-93	5.53	1.53	17.05	8.04
RUP-II	0.03	0.01	-	0.02
US-95	0.29	1.05	6.87	2.74
PEF-95	0.22	0.37	0.61	0.40
MMF-97**	194.92	225.12	541.53	320.52
UBF-98	-	2.21	52.05	27.13
MIF	-	1.51	97.43	49.47
GSF Brand Equity**	-	-	431.68	431.68
GSF Pharma**	-	-	357.69	357.69
GSF Software**	-	-	458.68	458.68
GSF Petro**	-	-	504.16	504.16
MIP-GSF Service	-	-	135.22	135.22
UTI G.Sec. Fund	-	-	63.72	63.72
IAF-97	35.16	-	15.50	25.33
IT Fund	-	-	43.82	43.82
CCCF 93	0.20	1.71	0.82	0.91
RBUP-94	0.39	0.63	0.82	0.61

Note: The Schemes marked by asterisk (**) specifies high portfolio turnover rate.

Source: Annual Reports of UTI, 1997-98, 98-99, 99-00.

sample schemes of UTI. Before going to make a comparison, it is necessary to mention that – higher rate of average total return as well as average income ratio indicate good performance, while, lower figure of average expense ratio and average expense to income ratio are the indicator of good performance.

From Table-5, we have seen that both the avg. total return and avg. income ratio are highest in case of GSF-Software scheme. Thus from this point of view, the performance of this scheme should be considered to be the best. But, because of recent initiation in the market, both the avg. expense ratios as well as the avg. expense to income ratio of this scheme are too much higher than that of others. So, if consider the expense ratios, then there may be some contradiction in selecting the best performer in the mutual fund industry during the period under study. Again, though the avg. expense ratio of the scheme MIP-2000-II is the minimum, but if we set aside this scheme, the scheme RUS-92 shows a minimum avg. expense ratio (0.2 %). Thus, if we consider both the avg. expense ratio as well as avg. expense to income ratio jointly, then it can be concluded that the scheme RUS-92 is the best performer during the study period.

Now, as far as the worst performer is concerned, Table-5 reveals the fact that there is no specific mutual fund scheme that can be considered the worst as per all the measures. From the viewpoint of avg. total return and avg. income ratio, the scheme MEP-95 and MIP-2000-II respectively are the worst performers. But if we set aside the scheme MIP-2000-II on the ground of its recent initiation period, then MEP-95 is considered to be the worst based on average total return as well as average income ratio. Lastly, from the viewpoint of average expense to income ratio, the scheme MEP-94 is considered the worst.

Table 5: Table Showing Comparison between Average Ratios of Different Schemes

Scheme	*Average Total Return*	*Average Exp. Ratio*	*Avg. Exp. to Income Ratio*	*Average Income Ratio*
US-64	-	1.40	3.66 (4)	18.29 (7)
ULIP-71(US-71)	-	1.25	4.71 (9)	13.04 (21)
CRTS-81	-	0.27 (3)	1.44 ** (2)	17.47 (10)
CGGF-86	-	0.48(4)	3.88 (6)	13.01 (23)
CGGF-99	-	3.27	205.79	7.10
Master Share Plus-91	65.37 (3)	2.1	8.40 (23)	25.09 (3)
RUS-92	-	0.2** (2)	1.03* (1)	18.42 (6)
Master Growth-93	58.76 (5)	1.21	10.38	19.25 (5)
RUP-II	59.29 (4)	0.68 (9)	7.93 (19)	10.75
UBF-98	17.81 (16)	1.36	103.12	7.10
GSF-Software	562.80* (1)	4.33***	260.32	93.52* (1)
GSF-Pharma	-	2.78	148.43	8.13
GSF-Service	463.16 (2)	2.50	280.68	56.57 (2)
UTI G.SEC Fund	-	-	8.37 (21)	-
Mastershare-86	24.67 (10)	0.81 (12)	4.37 (7)	17.68 (9)
MEP-94	55.25 (6)	1.55	- 2.25***	7.37
MEP-95	10.50*** (19)	1.83	7.04 (16)	4.32
MIP-94(III)	-	1.07	5.00 (10)	21.73 (4)
MIP-95	-	0.80 (11)	5.97 (11)	14.29 (16)
MIP-95(III)	-	1.08	6.76 (12)	15.04 (14)
MIP-96(III)	-	1.21	7.75 (17)	14.44 (15)
MIP-96(IV)	-	1.16	7.92 (18)	13.60 (19)
MIP-97	-	1.17	6.76 (13)	16.19 (11)
MIP-97(II)	-	1.09	8.39 (22)	15.78 (12)
MIP-97(III)	-	1.15	8.65 (24)	13.60 (20)
MIP-97(IV)	19.82 (14)	0.86 (14)	6.99 (14)	12.66
MIP-98	20.12 (13)	1.04	11.00	11.03
MIP-98(II)	13.62 (18)	0.87 (15)	12.05	10.25

(Table Contd...)

Table 5: (Contd...)

Scheme	*Average Total Return*	*Average Exp. Ratio*	*Avg. Exp. to Income Ratio*	*Average Income Ratio*
MIP-98(III)	16.51 (17)	1.16	7.95 (20)	13.82 (17)
MIP-98(IV)	24.69 (9)	1.05	7.04 (15)	15.25 (13)
MIP-98(V)	26.21 (8)	0.97 (17)	11.28	9.81
MIP-99	26.76 (7)	0.73 (10)	14.92	7.47
MIP-99(II)	-	0.94 (16)	9.14 (25)	9.36
MIP-2000	-	0.84 (13)	11.47	6.45
MIP-2000(II)	-	0.10* (1)	27.21	0.26***
IISFUS-97	-	0.60 (7)	3.33 (3)	18.06 (8)
IISFUS-97(II)	19.41 (15)	0.54 (5)	4.53 (8)	13.03 (22)
IISFUS-98	23.32 (11)	0.65 (8)	13.00	12.12
IISFUS-98(II)	22.23 (12)	0.57 (6)	3.80 (5)	13.62 (18)

Note: Figures in Brackets indicate Rank; * = Best, ***= Worst, **= 2nd Best

Source: Different Tables of the study (Table- 1, 2, 3 & 4)

Thus, from the above analysis, it can easily be inferred that no specific mutual fund scheme can be treated as the best or the worst performer in the mutual fund industry during the period 1997-98 to 1999-2000. Again, from the overall point of view, Master share Plus-91, Master growth-93, Master share-86, MIP-95, MIP-97, MIP-97-IV, MIP-98-IV, MIP-99, IISFUS-97, IISFUS-98, IISFUS-98-II, CGGF-86, RUP-II etc. are considered to be the good performers, while the schemes CGGF-99, UBF-98, MIP-98-II, MIP-98-III, MIP-99-II etc. are not performing well.

REFERENCES

1. SEBI, Mutual Fund 2000 Report.
2. Mutual Fund in India, Marketing Strategies and Investment Practice, H. Sadhak.

3. How Mutual Funds work, Albert J. Fredman.

4. Guide to Mutual Funds and Investment portfolio, Dr. J.C.Verma.

5. Alan Pope, Successful Investing in No-Load Funds, New York:John Wiley & Sons, Inc. 1983.

6. Security and Exchange Board of India, Indian Securities Markets–Agenda for Development and Reform, September 1991.

7. Credence, Fund Research and Monitoring Agency, Mumbai.

8. Micropal, Emerging Markets Funds Moniter, November, 1995, Issues 32, London.

9. Unit Trust of India (1995), Indian Capital Market – Dynamic Growth, Mumbai.

10. UTI-ICM (1995), Mutual Funds in India – A Fact Book, Mumbai.

11. "Mutual Fund Marketing", Readings in Marketing Services Manas Publication, New Delhi.

12. Annual Report of the Unit Trust of India, 1998-99, 1999-2000, 2000-2001.

13. Kale, Sumita and S.Uma (1995), A Study on the Evaluation of the Performance of Mutual Fund in India, National Insurance Academy, Pune.

14. Shome, Sujan (1994), "A Study of the Performance of Indian Mutual Funds", Unpublished Study, Jhansi University.

15. Barman RB and Madhusoodanan TP (1993), Permanent and Temporary Components of Indian Stock Market Returns, RBI Occasional Papers, Vol. 14, No.2, pp. 81-132.

16. Barua, Samir K & Varma, Jaynath R, (1991) Mastershares: A Bonanza for Large Investors, Vikalpa, (January-March) pp.29-34.

17. Jaydev M (1996), Mutual Fund Performance: An Analysis of Monthly Returns, Finance India, Vol.X No.1 (March 1996), pp.73-84.

18. Sarkar, Jaydeep and Majumdar Sudipa, (1995), Performance Evaluation of Mutual Funds in India, Journal of Narsee Monjee Institute of Management & Research, pp. 64-78.

19. Mutual Fund Performance, Journal of Business XXXIX, Part-2 (January), pp.119-138.

20. Yadav RA and Mishra B (1996), Performance of Mutual Funds: An Empirical Analysis, MDI Management Journal, Vol. 9 No.2 (July-December), pp.117-125.

21 Reserve Bank of India, Reports on Currency and Finance, 1995-96.

22. *http://www.unittrustofindia.com*

23. *http://www.myiris.com*

Appendix I

List of Schemes Included in The Sample

Sl. No.	*Acronym*	*Name of Scheme*
1.	US-64	Unit Scheme- 1964
2.	ULIP-71(US-71)	Unit Scheme- 1971
3.	CRTS-81	Unit Scheme for Charitable & Religious Trust and Registered Societies- 1981
4	CGGF-86	Children's Gift Growth Fund- 1986
5	CGGF-99	Children's Gift Growth Fund- 1999
6	Master Share Plus-91	Master share Plus Unit Scheme- 1991
7	RUS-92	Rajlakshmi Unit Scheme- 1992
8	Master Growth-93	Master growth Unit Scheme-1993
9	RUP-II	Rajlakshmi Unit Plan (II)- 1994
10	UBF-98	UTI Bond Fund- 1998
11	GSF-Software	Growth Sector Fund- Software
12	GSF-Pharma	Growth Sector Fund- Pharma
13	GSF-Service	Growth Sector Fund- Service
14	UTI G.SEC Fund	UTI Growth Sector Fund
15	Mastershare-86	Master share Unit Scheme- 1986
16	MEP-94	Master Equity Plan- 1994
17	MEP-95	Master Equity Plan-1995
18	MIP-94(III)	Monthly Income Plan- 1994- III
19	MIP-95	Monthly Income Plan- 1995
20	MIP-95(III)	Monthly Income Plan- 1995- III
21	MIP-96(III)	Monthly Income Plan- 1996- III
22	MIP-96(IV)	Monthly Income Plan- 1996- IV
23	MIP-97	Monthly Income Plan- 1997
24	MIP-97(II)	Monthly Income Plan- 1997- II
25	MIP-97(III)	Monthly Income Plan- 1997- III
26	MIP-97(IV)	Monthly Income Plan- 1997- IV
27	MIP-98	Monthly Income Plan- 1998

(Table Contd...)

Appendix I (Contd...)

Sl. No.	*Acronym*	*Name of Scheme*
28	MIP-98(II)	Monthly Income Plan- 1998- II
29	MIP-98(III)	Monthly Income Plan- 1998- III
30	MIP-98(IV)	Monthly Income Plan- 1998- Iv
31	MIP-98(V)	Monthly Income Plan- 1998- V
32	MIP-99	Monthly Income Plan- 1999
33	MIP-99(II)	Monthly Income Plan- 1999- II
34	MIP-2000	Monthly Income Plan- 2000
35	MIP-2000(II)	Monthly Income Plan- 2000- II
36	IISFUS-97	Institutional Investor's Special Fund Unit Scheme- 1997
37	IISFUS-97(II)	Institutional Investor's Special Fund Unit Scheme- 1997- II
38	IISFUS-98	Institutional Investor's Special Fund Unit Scheme- 1998
39	IISFUS-98(II)	Institutional Investor's Special Fund Unit Scheme- 1998- II
40	OMNI Plan 91	OMNI Unit Plan- 1991
41	Grand Master 93	Grand master Unit Scheme- 1993
42	HUS 92	Housing Unit Scheme- 1992
43	SCUP 93	Senior Citizen Unit Plan- 1993
44	US 95	Unit Scheme- 1995
45	PEF 95	PEF Unit Scheme- 1995
46	MMF 97	Money Market Fund- 1997
47	MIF	Master Index Fund- 1998
48	GSF Brand Equity	Growth Sector Fund- Brand Value
49	GSF Petro	Growth Sector Fund- Petro
50	IAF 97	India Access Fund- 1997
51	IT Fund	India Information Technology Fund- 1997
52	CCCF 93	Children's College & Career Fund Unit Plan- 1993
53	RBUP 94	Retirement Benefit Plan- 1994

15

Credit Risk Measurement

Some Issues

*Manoj Kumar Barik**

A risk-less world is beyond one's imagination. Every transaction between any two parties must entail certain amount of risk. Risk is different from uncertainty in the sense that the latter is immeasurable, while the former can be captured and measurable. Risk, which arises in a financial transaction, can be measured and often eliminated altogether through different risk mitigating strategies adopted by a bank or a financial institution.

Credit risk measurement has drawn a considerable attention in recent years. This could be due to several factors, such as, one can observe that a number of bankruptcies has increased considerably in the recent past. Secondly, there has been an unprecedented growth in existing loan market and a simultaneous emergence of derivative market. Besides this, one can observe the recent banking breakdown in countries like Taiwan, Korea, Malaysia and Japan and the

* Research Scholar, Department of Economics, University of Hyderabad.
The author expresses his gratefulness to Prof. B. Kamaiah and also to Dr. B. Nagarjuna, Department of Economics, University of Hyderabad for their valuable suggestions.

sole responsible of such breakdown is the increasing and unchecked levels of bad loans.

The Basel Committee on Banking Supervision (1998) established international minimum capital standard. This, popularly known as, BIS Accord, recommended a minimum regulatory capital of 8% for banks against their exposure, which are exposed to credit risk. Again in 1996 Basel task force surveyed twenty banks of G-10 countries in order to improve the earlier accord. By this time it incorporated market risk in banks trading account in calculating capital requirement.

Since then, practitioners among themselves as well as academicians among themselves battling each other, adopting different strategy to capture credit risk, which is threatening the very existence of financial institutions, including banks. Academicians are engaged themselves in developing different models, which can be used as tools for setting criteria for granting loans, measuring risk, pricing of risky debt, setting loan reserves, and above all, setting capital requirement.

The notion of Credit Risk

In today's world, apart from traditional loan financing banks are engaged themselves in different types of activities/ transactions. They are investing on bonds, equities, letters and commitment of credit, interest rate instrument like options, swaps, futures, and other derivatives. Some times banks face delayed payment and/or non-payment of whatever it advances to its customers. In other words, the obligor fails to meet his obligations (principal and interest) as promised, in due time. This is what is termed as credit risk. It, thus, can be perceived as a chance or probability of default arising out of loan default. Various kinds of risk can a bank face in their day-to-day operation, such as, market risk, operational risk, credit risk, liquidity risk, exchange rate risk etc. Of all kinds of risk, credit risk poses a major threat to a financial institution. Hence, an active measurement and management of credit risk is an imperative need or task before a bank officer or a risk regulator.

Credit risk arises both at individual asset level as well as at portfolio level. Risk associated in a credit instrument occurs either due to default or due to changes in the value or quality of the debt instrument. Evaluation of risk of a potential borrower applying for credit is a major challenge before a bank. Any bank or financial institution needs to assess the potential client at the time of granting loans. Some decades ago, banks were using the so-called 4 C's of credit, i.e., character, capital, capacity, and collateral to grant or not to grant (Altman, 1998). However, the conventional approach for a credit risk analyst to assess the credit worthiness of borrowers is to look at letter's profiles and check their past experience with a similar profile and then use a statistical method, to accept or reject their applications.

Instead of using traditional underwriting technique, banks are now using automated underwriting technique, otherwise known as *'credit scoring'* technique. Credit scoring is a quantitative technique, which produces a score, or it is a probability default measure to gauge the future repayment performance of the borrower. The benefit of scoring is it reduces information costs and allows banker to monitor loan applications even without meeting their customers personally (W. Scott frame et al., 2001). Sometimes bank rely on vendor models, which are available in the market. Whether bank use it's own model or a model purchased from outside vendor that depends on the predictive ability of the model, i.e., how far they accurately forecast the loss distribution. It is because the final objective of credit risk models is to derive the probability density function of loss distribution. Some Vendor models are presented below in brief.

There are many facets in modeling credit risk. Since, it comes either of the two ways–default or value changes in the asset, both the modeling risk of default/probability of default and the modeling rating transition probability constitute two important ingredients in the literature of credit risk measurement. Further, there are three inputs in the measurement of default risk, such as, default rate analysis, recovery rate analysis, and default correlation analysis. The three inputs parameters are directly estimated with historical data. Default probabilities are obtained from tabulated default rates, recovery rates from loan/bond prices shortly after default, and correlations from sample correlation from changes in assets values.

The value change in debt instrument is represented by ratings, which reflects the relative credit-worthiness of an obligor (obligor may be an individual borrower, firm or a company). Rating plays a key role in the assessment of credit risk. Rating probabilities are represented through a rating transition matrix (also called rating migration matrix). Each entry in a rating transition matrix says, the probability of moving from one rating to other rating category (upgrade or downgrade or goes to default) in a given planning horizon, usually taken as one year. One of the current generation of credit risk model, that is, JP Morgan's CM is based on the rating transition probabilities. The transition probabilities may vary according to types of obligors, domicile of the obligors and the stages of business cycle (Pamela Nickell et al., 2000).

Traditional credit risk models were using bankruptcy as the single default criterion. But, recently Basel committee on banking supervision (2001a) came up with a tighter definition of default event. It defines default as follows:

- The obligor is unlikely to pay his debt obligations (principal, interest, and fees) in full;
- A credit loss due to distress restructuring, which involves forgiveness or postponement of principal, interest and fees;

- Delayed in payment of the obligor for more than ninety days; or
- The obligor has filed for bankruptcy or similar protection from creditors.

In case of India, credit risk can be seen from the perspective of non-performing loans. The surmounting non-performing assets (NPAs) could be one factor, which attributes to the occurrence of credit risk. The net NPAs raise a major concern for the solvency of a bank[1]. In other words, increasing bad loans may gradually trigger towards insolvency/bankruptcy. The NPAs of twenty-seven public sector banks shot up to Rs. 56, 608 crore in September 2001. NPAs not only reduce yields on advances but also reduce profitability of banks. Even though NPAs in gross and net term is gradually declining, the stock of NPAs has been increasing in absolute term.

Some Key Estimates

Both the estimation of *Expected Losses* as well as *Unexpected Losses* are the two key components in credit risk measurement. Expected loss corresponds to mean loss of the distribution. It is simply the amount of loss the bank would expect to experience on its credit portfolio. Unexpected loss, on the other hand, is defined as the amount by which the loss differs from the mean loss. It measures the volatility (standard deviation) of credit losses. While expected losses serve as a basis for reserve policies of an institution – the higher the expected losses, the higher the reserves required, unexpected losses play an important role in determining economic capital of banks which are engaged themselves in Risk-Adjusted Return on Capital (RAROC).

Since credit risk distribution is non-normal, highly skewed, and has a long fat tail towards right, variance is an inappropriate measure of risk. In this case quantile

[1] Report on Trend and Progress of banking in India (2000-2001).

based measures more accurately capture the risk of the portfolio. Among the quantile based risk measures, *Maximum* (percentile) *Losses, Unexpected* (percentile) *Losses* or the Credit VaR, *Expected Shortfall*, and *Expected Regret* are important. Maximum percentile losses represent the largest loss that is anticipated to occur with a given probability. Credit VaR or unexpected losses corresponds to the difference between the chosen quantile of the probability density function and the expected losses. It measures the capital required to cover unexpected losses at the chosen confidence level (99% or 99.9%). Expected shortfall, also known as tail conditional expectation or conditional VaR measures the average size of a loss given that it exceeds the Maximum loss. In other words, it measures the expected loss beyond a specified percentile of the distribution. The last one is Expected regret, which is measured with respect to a benchmark. It is calculated as the expectation of losses that exceeds some fixed threshold. Expected regret doffers from expected shortfall in that the threshold is pre-specified.

Risk measurement techniques

In the assessment of obligors the following measurement technique have been used by banks and financial institutions:

- Expert system;
- Statistical methods:
  - *(a)* Linear probability model,
  - *(b)* Logit model,
  - *(c)* Probit model,
  - *(d)* Discriminant analysis, and
  - *(e)* Neural network.

Among the statistical models, Multivariate discriminant credit scoring technique has been widely used since the seminal work of Altman (1968). The technique uses some accounting variables and produces a Z-score, which is the measuring rod to classify borrowers as defaulted and non-defaulted groups.

Recent Vendor models

Important among the vendor models are:

1. JP Morgan's Credit Metrics (CM),
2. Credit Suisse Financial Product's Credit Risk$^+$,
3. KMV model by a private firm KMV Corporation, and
4. McKinsey & Co.'s Credit Portfolio View (CPV) model.

The CM model, which is based on rating probabilities, calculates the forward distribution of changes in the value of portfolio of loan or bond. KMV model estimates the expected default frequency from observed equity prices, which proxies' value of assets. While CM model based on historical data, KMV based on actual probabilities. The actuarial model, Credit Risk$^+$ considers only default probability. It is a two state model – default and non-default state of borrowers. It first calculates the probability generating function of default and then the probability generating function of loss distribution. The fourth model, i.e., the CPV model is a macro economic causal model, where default probabilities and migration probabilities depend on macro-economic variables like GDP growth rate, unemployment rate, level of interest rate, government expenditure, saving rates and foreign exchange rate. Rating downgrades as well as defaults tend to increase in economic downturns and contrary happens when the health of the economy becomes stronger. In all the above models default rates and migration probabilities are driven by some systemic factors, which describes relevant economic conditions. The systemic factors are random in nature and assumed to be normally distributed.

Concluding remarks

Credit risk measurement is gaining importance in today's financial world. Credit risk poses a major threat to the viability and sustainability of any bank or financial institution. Since banks and financial institutions are major players in an economy, the poor performance of this sector may have a negative impact on the health of the economy. If an organ of human body gets weak or injured, the whole body cannot function properly. In the similar fashion, if banking sector does not perform well, the whole economy becomes paralyzed. If risk of default is increasing with default loans surmounting assets and if bank personnel is neglecting in controlling it, then the vary existence of the institution becomes a question mark in the years to come.

REFERENCES

1. Altman, E., Saunders, A., (1998); "Credit risk measurement: Developments over the last twenty years", *Journal of Banking and Finance*, 21, pp. 1721-1742.
2. Altman, E., and Suggitt, H., (2000); Default rates in the Syndicated bank loan market: A mortality analysis", *Journal of Banking and Finance*, 24, pp. 229-253.
3. Bucay, N., and Rosan, D., (2000); "Applying portfolio credit risk models to retail portfolio", Algo Research Quarterly, 3, (1), pp. 45-73.
4. Basel Committee on Banking Supervision, April (1999); "Credit risk modeling: Current practices and application".
5. Basel Committee on Banking Supervision (2001a); "Internal Rating-based Approach"
6. Carey, M., and Hrycay, M., (2001); "Parameterizing Credit risk models with rating data", Journal of Banking and Finance, January 25 (1), pp.

7. Carey, M., (1998); "Credit risk in private placement", Journal of Finance, 10 (10), pp.56-61.

8. CreditMetrics, (1997), Technical Document, JP Morgan.

9. Credit Suisse, (1997), "Credit Risk$^+$: A Credit Risk Management Framework", (Credit Suisse Financial Products, London).

10. Crouhy, M., Galai, D., and Mark, R., (2000); "A comparative analysis of credit risk models", Journal of Banking and Finance, 24, pp. 59-117.

11. Crouhy, M., Galai, D., and Mark, R., (2001); "Prototype of risk rating system", Journal of Banking and Finance, 25, pp. 47-95.

12. Dietsch, M., and Petey, J., (2002) "The credit risk in SME loans portfolio: Modeling issues, pricing, and capital requirements", Journal of Banking and Finance, 26, pp.303-322.

13. Gordy, M., (2000); "A comparative anatomy of credit risk models", Journal of Banking and Finance, 24, pp. 119-149.

14. Kealhofer Stephen, (1998); "Portfolio management of default risk", KMV Corporation.

15. Kiesel, R., Perraudin, W., and Taylor, A., (2001); "The structure of credit risk: Spread volatility and rating transitions, Working Paper, No. 131, May 2001, Bank of England.

16. Lopez, J. and Saidenberg, M., (2000); "Evaluating credit risk models", Journal of Banking and Finance, 24, pp.151-165.

17. Mausser, H., and Rosen, D., (1999); "Efficient risk return frontiers for credit risk", Algo Research Quarterly, 2, (4), pp. 35-48.

18. Mc Kinsey & Co. (1997); "Credit Portfolio View", Mc Kinsey & Co.

19. Moodys Investor Service, (2000); "Bank loan loss given default", Moody's special comment, November, pp.1-5.

20. Nachane, D., and Ghosh, S., (2001); "Risk-based standards, Portfolio risk and Bank capital: An

econometric study", Economic and Political Weekly, March, pp. 871-876.

21. Nickel, P., Perraudin, W., and Varotto, S., (2000); "Stability of rating transitions", Journal of Banking and Finance, 24, pp. 203-227.

22. Reddy, Y.V.(2000); "Credit rating: Changing perspectives", RBI Bulletin, May, pp.507-525.

23. Scott frame, W., Srinivasan, A., and Woosley, L. (2001); "The effect of credit scoring on small business lending", Journal of Money Credit and Banking, 33, (3), pp. 813-825.

24. Treacy, W., and Carey, M., (2000); "Credit risk rating system at large US banks", Journal of Banking and Finance, 24, pp. 167-201.

25. Wilson, T., (1998); "Portfolio credit risk", Economic Policy Review, Federal Reserve Bank of New York, October, pp. 71-82.

Part—V

Industrial Policy Issues

16

Factors contributing to Sales Turnover of Small Scale Industries in the Era of Globalisation

Empirical Evidence and Policy Implications for Karnataka State

*M. Jaya Krishna**

Introduction

Karnataka is one among the top industrialized States of India where Small Scale Industries[1] (SSI) are playing a major role in employment generation, exports and providing ancillary services to the medium and large-scale industries since few decades. Broadly speaking, the SSIs have had a special place in developmental policy with widely dispersed sectors across different geographical locations of the State. In the light of the performance of plans and programs of the State in the past, it is correct to say that it is the fastest growing state. Though it has been

* Author is working in Economics Unit of Institute for Social & Economic Change, Dr. V.K.R.V. Rao Road, Nagarabhavi PO, Bangalore 560 072.

1 A small-scale unit is defined as 'an industry in which the investment on fixed assets in plant and machinery whether held on ownership terms, on lease or on hire purchase, does not exceed Rs.100 lakhs'.

primarily agricultural state, now it is shifting towards the development of tertiary sector. It is evident from the data that primary and secondary sectors contributing to State Domestic Product was decreasing from 36.3 per cent and 25.4 per cent in 1993-94 to 28 and 25.1 per cent respectively in 2000-01. In contrast, tertiary sector is raising from 38.3 per cent to 47 per cent in the same period (GOK, 2002). However, SSIs are contributing considerably to the State's domestic product. Further, Karnataka has been a pioneer in industry and has achieved a pride of place in the global market with Information Technology related industries, Biotechnology and Research and Development Institutions which come under SSI category.

The growth of SSIs activities in Karnataka is fluctuating in 1990s. It is evident that the number of SSIs[2] registered accounts annual growth rate of 6.4 per cent between 1989–90 and 1997–98. As against, it falls to 3.2 per cent between 1998-99 and 2000-01. Correspondingly, the total investment (or employment) accounts 55.5 per cent (or 7.1 per cent) and –11.6 per cent (or –2.8 per cent) respectively (GOK, 2001 and 2002). After liberalisation, over the last few years the existence of general deceleration in industrial activity of the country as well as in Karnataka State[3]. In spite of modified comprehensive industrial policy in 2001 with a focus on harnessing resources of SSI sector

[2] Small Scale Industries are one segment among the Small Scale Enterprises (SSEs) that work under private sector. Further, SSEs includes ancillary undertakings, tiny units, export oriented units, women enterprises and small-scale service business oriented enterprises.

[3] Government of Karnataka has set up several organisations over the years to promote the development of industries, such as Visveswaraya Industrial Trade Centre, Karnataka Udyog Mitra, Karnataka State Finance Corporation, Technical Consultancy Service Organisation of Karnataka, Karnataka Council for Technology Up-gradation, Karnataka State Small Industries Development Corporation, Karnataka State Industrial Area Development Board.

to its optimality and provision for private sector participation, Karnataka registered a decline in investment to the tune of Rs.478.84 crore and employment to 73, 195 persons in 2001–02 (GOK, 2003).

Importance of the Study

In the era of liberalisation and globalization, the role of geographical and product market segmentation and government protection is getting reduced. In addition, the World Trade Organisation[4] (WTO) regulates multilateral trade agreements of its member countries; a discipline import quotas and other import restrictions and reduces import tariffs, and insists on removal of subsidies and concessions for exporting of domestic goods by 2003. This has opened up the competition from external industries (particularly after withdrawal of government protection) with the imports of quality goods from advanced countries and cheap goods from cther developing countries. In short, government policies on SSIs clearly bring out a shift from 'protection-led growth' to 'competition-led growth'. In this context, though this sector shows substantial progress in terms of its contribution to the economy, it is important to find the factors contributing to increase the competence, productivity and quality of SSIs in Karnataka and how they can cope up with today's new challenges being posed to them. Apart from policy factors there are non-policy factors, which contribute to the growth of firms. These factors are the outcome of firm's conduct, which influences the performance of firms. Further, it is essential to gauge the future scenario of SSIs and find out the policy alternatives for dealing with it.

---

4 WTO is a global international organisation dealing with the rules and regulations of trade between member nations. The core of WTO is its agreements and negotiations, which are signed and legally approved by the 145 members. The main objective behind these agreements and bnegotiations are to support producers of goods and services, intellectual property rights, exports and imports.

In addition, present study introduced year of establishment[5] and generation of the entrepreneurs6[6] for estimation. This type of estimation has been attempted scanty either for Karnataka State till date or for any other State[7]. Thus, this study may have implications for urban industries in Karnataka in particular and elsewhere in the country in general.

Objective of the Study

In the above backdrop, this paper makes an empirical analysis of the nature and magnitude of factors that contributes to sales turnover of SSIs in Bangalore rural and urban districts of Karnataka State.

Study Area

The analysis is based on both quantitative and qualitative data. The data was collected through a structured questionnaire in Bangalore rural and urban districts of Karnataka, as part of pre-testing for a large study undertaken at ISEC, Bangalore during May-June, 2002. The districts were selected because (i) sample SSIs are selected from districts, which are comparable in levels of overall development. (ii) they occupy a distinct position in terms of human development, industrialisation, infrastructure facilities and urbanisation of the State. Further, they account for 21.1 per cent of units, as well as 31.5 per cent of investment and 31.9 per cent of

---

5 This has been taken due to the birth of the WTO on January 1, 1995.

6 Generation of the entrepreneurs influences planning and strategies. For instance, first generation entrepreneurs suffered the confusion of irrational industrial policies. However, the old generations is hesitating to continue in the industry for want of a policy itself.

7 This does not mean that no studies have been done on any aspect of the SSIs in the country. This is evident, for instance, Gulati (1997) and Bhavani (2002).

employment generation in the State during 2000–01 (Krishna, 2003). In addition, qualitative data is based on field observations and discussions the author held with the small-scale entrepreneurs.

The remainder of the paper is organised as follows: Section 2 gives methodology, which highlights data and variables for estimation, model and prediction and interpretation of the study. Empirical results and their analysis were presented in Section 3. In Section 4 conclusion and policy implications are derived.

Methodology

Data and Variables for Estimation

In order to estimate factors contributing to sales turnover of the SSIs, information was collected on components of investment and expenditure, production, imports, sales and employment. Generation of the entrepreneurs was collected through informal discussion held with the entrepreneurs. A sample of 45 units was fixed arbitrarily. Over a period of two months, 38 units were canvassed using random sampling method keeping all major industrial estates and products in mind. However, only 26 entrepreneurs[8] provided all the required information. In sum, the response rate was about 76 per cent.

Variables for Estimation

From the collected information on sample units above, the following variables are listed for final estimation.

Dependent Variable

The dependent variable in all estimations is the sales turnover of all the SSIs. The main reason to take total

8 Sample units includes 7 Engineering, 2 Leather, 3 Food-processing, 2 Electronic, 3 Handicraft, 3 Garment, 2 Chemical, 2 software and 2 Electrical.

sales turnover is that the production of most of these SSIs is order based with competitive price regime and quality. There won't be a gap between production and sales. Given that SSIs are demand constraint. Hence, instead of output, sales turnover has been used as dependent variable (Hymer and Peter, 1962).

Independent Variables

The independent variables are both quantitative and qualitative. These variables are listed below:

(i) Generation of the Entrepreneurs (GE): This is a dummy-variable [=1 or 0) if the entrepreneur belongs to old generation (or first generation) entrepreneur.

(ii) Managerial Staff (M): This is actual number of managerial staff in the sample units.

(iii) Plant and Machinery (PM): This is proportion of investment on plant and machinery to total investment.

(iv) Technical up-gradation (TUG): The ratio of investment on technical up-gradation to fixed investment[9].

(v) Working Capital (WC): This is taken as per cent of working capital to total output.

(vi) Workers (W): Actual number of workers in the sample units.

(vii) Year of establishment[10] (YE): This is a dummy variable [=1 or 0] if a unit established in or before 1995 (or if established after 1994).

---

9 FI includes investment in rupee lakhs at current prices on plant and machinery; land and building, pollution control equipments, certifications, and quality control instruments.

10 The analysis made on the basis of year of establishments of the unit before 1995 or since 1995 is due to the reason that the WTO started functioning on January 1, 1995.

Model

To estimate the factors contributing to Sales Turnover (ST) of SSIs, conventional production function[11] analysis is used. However, along with the conventional variables like capital and labour, the study has taken investment on technological up-gradation of firms as an independent variable.

Accordingly, sales turnover function is written as

$$ST = f(K, L, T) \tag{1}$$

Where K = PM + WC, L = M + W and T = TUG,

The sales turnover function in equation 1 can be re-written as below.

$$ST = f(PM, WC, M, W, TUG) \tag{2}$$

Further, the study has considered qualitative variables, namely generation of the entrepreneurs and year of establishment of the unit before or since 1995 as the independent variables. Since they reflect the nature of decision making of the entrepreneurs regarding investments, marketing strategies, recruitment, certifications, quality and price of the product. Again equation 2 is modified as

$$ST = f(PM, WC, M, W, TUG, GE, YE) \tag{3}$$

In short, the above arguments can be summarized and presented as follows:

$$ST = \alpha_0 + \beta_1 PM + \beta_2 WC + \gamma_1 M + \gamma_2 W + \theta_1 TUG + \delta_1 GE + \delta_2 YE + \varepsilon \tag{4}$$

Where ε is disturbance term?

Prediction and Interpretation

The major prediction and interpretation in the estimable models are as follows. The study predicts the

11 For review on production function, see Burnside (1996)

sign of the coefficient of M, PM, TUG and W to be positive. This result may be interpreted to imply that, other things being equal, an increase in these explorative variables would have a positive effect on the sales turn over of the units. This is plausible since an increase in these variables may be contributing to higher production and /or productivity. Further, study predicts the sign of the coefficient for WC[12] to be negative. This means that, other things being equal, an increase in investment on working capital would reduce the magnitude of the production. This is presumable that as working capital increases net contribution of the units to production will come down. In regard to two dummy variables [GE and YE], the interpretation of estimated results depends on their assigned values (i.e. 1 or 0). Accordingly, the expected or mean value of the ST may be interpreted, either individually or for a combination of these dummy variables. For instance, the estimation coefficient for GE shows the extent by which the mean ST in units who belongs to old generation differs from the mean ST in units which belong to first generations. Further, if YE=1, other things being equal, we obtain the mean ST of units if the units were established before 1995.

Empirical Results

Before estimating the factors contributing to the sales turnover of entrepreneurs, some general characteristics of sample units is given in Table 1. The table reveals that majority of the units belong to manufacturing sector (61.5 per cent) and they are perennial (92.3 per cent) in nature. Interestingly, 19 units were established before 1995 and only 11 belong to first generation entrepreneurs. Further, majority of units are owned by limited companies (12 units)

12 WC is an original investment in rupee lakhs at current prices on raw material, wages, power, water, debt, taxes, rent, transport, stationary, fuel and others.

Table 1: General Characteristics of Sample SSI Units

Characteristics	*Total Units*	*Units Established after 1994*	*Units Established before 1995*	*First Generation Entrepreneurs*	*Old Generation Entrepreneurs*
1. Nature of Units:					
a. Ancillary	5 (19.2)	3 (42.8)	2 (10.5)	3 (20.0)	2 (18.2)
b. Manufacturing	16 (61.5)	3 (42.8)	13 (88.4)	8 (53.3)	8 (72.7)
c. Both	5 (19.2)	1 (14.4)	4 (21.1)	4 (26.7)	1 (09.1)
Total	26 (100)	7 (100)	19 (100)	15 (100)	11 (100)
2. Nature of Operation:					
a. Perennial	24 (92.3)	7 (100)	17 (89.2)	15 (100)	9 (81.8)
b. Seasonal	2 (07.7)	0 (0.0)	2 (07.7)	0 (0.0)	2 (18.2)
Total	26 (100)	7 (100)	19 (100)	15 (100)	11 (100)
3. Type of Ownership:					
a. Limited Company	12 (46.2)	6 (85.7)	6 (31.6)	8 (53.3)	4 (36.4)
b. Partnership	5 (19.2)	1 (14.3)	4 (21.1)	2 (13.3)	3 (27.3)
c. Proprietary	9 (34.6)	0 (0.0)	9 (47.4)	5 (33.3)	4 (36.4)
Total	26 (100)	7 (100)	19 (100)	15 (100)	11 (100)
4. Staff and Workers:	1784 (100)	399 (100)	1385 (100)	652 (100)	1132 (100)
a. Managerial staff	226 (12.7)	82 (20.5)	144 (10.4)	148 (22.7)	78 (6.9)
b. Workers	1558 (87.3)	317 (79.5)	1241 (89.6)	504 (77.3)	1054 (93.1)

Note: Figures in the parentheses are percentage to total.

Source: Survey data.

followed by proprietorship (9 units). About 87 per cent of the personnel are workers and the remaining belonging to the managerial staff. This information brings out that the first generation entrepreneurs employ more managerial staff than workers. Thereby implying that there is a demand for skilled and managerial personnel by first generation entrepreneurs.

The distinct features of the distribution of the membership or/and registration-wise status of the units are shown in Table 2. It can be seen from the table that the units established after 1994 and first generation and units established before 1995 and old generation entrepreneurs have notable similarities in the membership and registration status. Regarding the membership of units to industrial association, 96 per cent account for Karnataka Small Scale Industries Association (KASSIA) followed by Department of Industries and Commerce. It is permitted to register with SSI after few years of initial production, which is reflected in the number of registration of units established after 1994. Likewise, 88 per cent of sample units are registered under Sales Tax Act followed by Factories Act and Central Excise. As compared to units established after 1994, majority of the units is registered under Central Excise and Factories Act. However, compared to other categories of units, old generation entrepreneurs give (63.6 per cent) less importance to the Employees State Insurance Corporation (ESI) membership, which is beneficial to employees.

Table 3 presents the descriptive statistics, namely arithmetic mean, standard deviation, coefficient of variation, minimum and maximum for the quantitative variables. It clearly indicates the nature and extent of dispersion of data of the variables MSTAFF, PM, ST, TUG, WC and WORKERS. Few remarks on these results deserve special mention. First of all, the arithmetic mean and the degree on absolute dispersion or standard deviation for ST

Table 2: Membership/Registration Status of Sample SSI Units

Characteristics	*Total Units*	*Units Established after 1994*	*Units Established before 1995*	*First Generation Entrepreneurs*	*Old Generation Entrepreneurs*
1. Registration Status:					
a. Central Excise	14 (53.8)	5 (71.4)	9 (47.4)	7 (46.7)	7 (63.6)
b. Factory Act	15 (57.7)	6 (85.7)	9 (47.4)	9 (60.0)	6 (54.6)
c. Karnataka State Pollution Control Board	10 (38.5)	5 (71.4)	5 (26.3)	6 (39.9)	4 (36.4)
d. National Small Industries Corporation	3 (11.5)	0 (0.0)	3 (15.8)	1 (06.6)	2 (18.2)
e. Sales Tax	23 (88.5)	5 (71.4)	18 (94.7)	12 (80.0)	11(100)
2. Member of Industrial Association:					
a. Department of Industries and Commerce	21 (80.8)	3 (42.8)	18 (94.7)	13 (86.7)	8 (72.7)
b. Industrial Area Association	18 (69.2)	6 (85.7)	12 (63.1)	9 (60.0)	9 (81.8)
c. Industrial Product Association	15 (57.7)	4 (57.1)	11 (57.9)	8 (53.3)	7 (63.6)
d. Karnataka Small Scale Industries Association	25 (96.2)	7 (100)	18 (94.7)	14 (93.3)	11 (100)
3. Other Registrations/ Memberships:					
a. Municipality	20 (76.9)	5 (71.4)	15 (78.9)	11 (73.3)	9 (81.8)
b. Provident Fund	18 (69.2)	5 (71.4)	13 (68.4)	10 (66.7)	8 (72.7)
c. Employees State Insurance Corporation	19 (73.1)	5 (71.4)	14 (73.7)	12 (80.0)	7 (63.6)

Note and Source: Same as in Table 1.

Table 3: Descriptive Statistics: Select Measures of Central Tendency and Dispersion

Variables	*Mean*	*Standard Deviation*	*Coefficient of Variation*	*Minimum*	*Maximum*
1. MSTAFF	8.69	11.77	1.36	1.00	51.00
2. PM	94.33	161.48	1.71	0.70	790.00
3. ST	561.28	869.56	1.55	11.00	2400.00
4. TUG	13.33	25.25	1.89	0.00	100.00
5. WC	417.61	710.57	1.70	9.07	2838.37
6. WORKERS	59.82	86.35	1.44	1.00	375.00

(or MSTAFF) are the highest (or lowest). Second, in terms of relative variation or coefficients of variation, the largest (or smallest) is evident for TUG (or MSTAFF). Third, the range of observations varies widely as shown by the minimum and maximum values for different variables. Fourth, the minimum values for TUG is zero. This indicates that there was at least one sample unit, which was not spending on technology up-gradation. Fifth, WORKERS were the maximum in Beedi factory, which is labour intensive in nature.

Table 4 reveals the nature and degree of linear relationship between the quantitative variables in the estimations in terms of simple correlation coefficients. In particular, WC is having relatively high degree of positively correlated coefficients. However, relatively high (or low)

Table 4: Matrix of Simple Correlation Co-efficient

Variables	*MSTAFF*	*PM*	*ST*	*TUG*	*WC*	*Workers*
1. MSTAFF	1.00					
2. PM	0.08	1.00				
3. ST	0.20	0.42	1.00			
4. TUG	0.41	0.16	0.39	1.00		
5. WC	0.45	0.35	0.42	0.25	1.00	
6. WORKERS	0.23	0.17	0.37	-0.27	0.27	1.00

degree of linear relationship is found between WORKERS and MSTAFF (or WORKERS and TUG). In fact, the relationship is negative between TUG and WORKERS.

Since data is cross sectional, the problem of heteroscedasticity is likely to be more common. Therefore, the estimation results of multiple regression models are adjusted using heteroscedasticity-consistent covariance matrix. It is apparent that the investment on TUG and WC contributes significantly to sales turnover in all the estimations (see, Table 5). It reveals that capital is playing vital role than labour. This shows that SSIs so far are seemed to be labour intensive are not transforming into capital based. Likewise, the only other coefficient, which is significant in all the estimations except Model 1, is W. It means that the units have to upgrade technology and skill of the workers to improve both quality and productivity; otherwise they will be eliminated gradually from the market by the other competing firms. Further, units need timely working capital on par with the other significant contributing factors. The coefficients for GE, M, PM, YE as well as intercept term are statistically insignificant in all the estimations. Further, the overall explanatory power of the model is that around 48 per cent of the variation in ST, which is explained by the variables, included in the estimation. Interestingly, among insignificant variables GE contributes to sales turn over at 18 per cent level of significance. In fact, in all the estimations, the F-statistics is significant at 5% level. Of these estimations, the results in Model 3 are more plausible than the other estimations for many reasons. First, for satisfying the sign conditions for coefficients. Second, for having a large number of statistically significant coefficients. Third, for having the highest explanatory power of the model in terms of R^2 (0.4854) and lowest standard error of regression. In toto, results depict that capital, technology and skilled labour plays crucial role in increasing sales turnover of the SSIs in the era of liberalisation.

Table 5: Estimates of Sales Turnover Function–Regression Results

Dependent Variable: ST

Explanatory Variables	*Models*				
	Model 1	*Model 2*	*Model 3*	*Model 4*	*Model 5*
Constant	460.25 (1.03)	450.36 (1.03)	552.21 (1.51)	198.85 (0.40)	90.30 (0.20)
GE	-484.02 (-1.36)	-409.34 (-1.11)	-473.74 (-1.35)	-422.54 (-1.11)	
M	18.75 (1.00)		16.27 (1.05)		11.35 (0.61)
PM				328.13 (0.81)	303.13 (0.68)
TUG	14.94** (2.05)	17.84*** (2.88)	14.64* (1.90)	18.83*** (2.87)	17.86** (2.38)
WC	-2.17** (-2.35)	-1.32*** (-2.68)	-1.99*** (-2.95)	-1.27** (-2.47)	-2.03** (-2.46)
W	2.76 (1.30)	3.75** (2.34)	2.93* (1.76)	3.88** (2.33)	4.30* (1.94)
YE	140.54 (0.33)	51.84 (0.15)		127.08 (0.33)	173.32 (0.39)
R^2	0.4811	0.4648	0.4854	0.4738	0.4322
Standard Error of Regression	719.7589	715.4621	704.4800	727.8648	756.0359
F-Statistic	2.9872**	3.4736**	3.7100**	2.8509**	2.4108***
No. of Observations	26	26	26	26	26

Note: (1) Figures in the parentheses are the t-ratios.

(2) *** (*) indicate(s) that the co-efficient is significant at 1% (or 10%), and ** for 5% levels.

Conclusion and Policy Implications

The main focus of this paper is to identify the factors contributing to sales turnover of SSIs. It is estimated using 2001-02 data on sample SSIs in Bangalore districts of Karnataka. The study has used descriptive statistics and multiple regressions for analysis. The important results of the estimation are as follows. First, sales turnover of the SSIs is contributed significantly by the investment on technology, working capital and workers. Secondly, generations of the entrepreneurs are also relatively better contributors of the sales turnover of SSIs.

To rise sales turnover and compete successfully with internal or/and external industries; SSIs should use quality raw material, improve productivity, and reduce costs. To do this, the study suggests government (i) should provide good infrastructure, and technology up-gradation. (ii) invite foreign investment for better technological transfer and improve skill of the labourers. (iii) encourage old generation entrepreneurs to invest and extend marketing support for new generations entrepreneurs. (iv) encourage diversified export base, and promote role of association and non-government organisations in setting up of common facilities in technology, marketing, infrastructure and other support services through private-public partnership.

It should be emphasized that the estimation results in this study are hardly exhibitive. To generalise the results obtained, the models may have to be replicated for major product groups, in future, elsewhere in the State and the country. A study of this type is an interesting topic for future research.

REFERENCES

1. Bhavani, T.A. (2002). *Small Scale Units in the Era of Globalisation: Problems and Prospects*, Economic and Political Weekly, 37(29): 3041-3052.
2. Burnside, Craig. (1996). *Production Function Regressions, returns to scale, externalities*, Journal of Monetary Economics, 36:177-201.
3. Government of Karnataka. (GoK) (2001). Annual Report 2001-2002, Department of Industries and Commerce, Bangalore: 1-2.

4. Government of Karnataka. (GoK) (2002). Economic Survey 2001-2002, Department of Planning, Statistics and Science and Technology, Bangalore, March: 87-88 and A-20.

5. Government of Karnataka. (GoK) (2003). Economic Survey 2002-2003, Department of Planning, Statistics and Science and Technology, Bangalore, March: 193-204.

6. Government of Karnataka. (GoK) (2003). Stade Domestic Product 1993-94 to 2000-01, Directorate of Economic and Statistics, Bangalore, 11-20.

7. Gulati, M. (1997). *Restructuring and Modernisation of Small Medium Enterprise Clusters in India: A Report*, UNIDO.

8. Hymer, Stephen and Peter Pashigian. (1962). *Turnover of Firms as a Measure of Market Behaviour,* The Review of Economics and Statistics, 44(1): 82-87.

9. Krishna, M. Jaya. (2003). *Small Scale Industries in the Era of Globalisation: An Explorative Study*, ISEC Working Paper Series (In the pipeline).

17

Decomposition of TFP Growth Using Data Envelopment Analysis

A Case Study of Indian Industrial Machinery

*Mukesh Kumar**
*Partha Basu***

Introduction

With the advent of industrialization, India has been able to advance both industrially and economically at a very rapid pace, achieving a degree of self reliance in its technological know how and manufacturing processes. Industrialists, manufacturers, exporters, suppliers in India are setting up new businesses, expanding existing markets and increasing their knowledge base of industrial processes and technologies, finding cost effective and economical solutions in the form of innovative machinery, machine tools and equipment. Among the Third World countries, today India is a major exporter of heavy and light engineering goods, producing a wide range of items. The bulk of capital goods required for power projects, fertilizer,

* Faculty Member, ICFAI Business School, # 62, Nagarjuna Hills, Hyderabad–500 082.

** Professor of Economics, Department of Humanities & Social Sciences, Indian Institute of Technology, Kharagpur, West Bengal–721 302.

cement, steel and petrochemical plants and mining equipment are made in India. The country also makes construction machinery, equipment for irrigation projects, diesel engines, tractors, transport vehicles, cotton textile and sugar mill machinery. The engineering industry has shown its capacity to manufacture large-size plants and equipment for various sectors like power, fertilizer and cement. Lately, air pollution control equipment is also being made in the country. The heavy electrical industry meets the entire domestic demand.

This study makes an attempt to analyze the performance of the above two industries in terms of total factor productivity change during 1988-89 to 1997-98 by using the non-parametric method of Data Envelopment Analysis. We have taken the variable returns to scale throughout the model to decompose the Malmquist productivity index into three separate components, which was used for the first time by Ray (1997) to show the regional variation in productivity in the Indian context. Unlike the extended decomposition model by Färe et al. (1994), which assumes constant returns to scale while estimating technical change but subsequently switches to variable returns to scale to separate the scale effect, this method assumes the variable returns to scale for measuring all the components of productivity growth. The distinction among these components is quite essential for policy decision-making. For example, it may be important for decision-makers to estimate the productivity improvement achievable solely through reduction in wastefulness, without resort to new technology or larger scale of production. Estimation of productivity improvements attributable to technical change is useful in assessing the maximum benefits of introducing new technology. Likewise, measurements of productivity effects of changes in the scale of manufacturing are helpful in planning plant size (Sudit, 1995). Within the framework of the present study, the results are significantly conclusive: the technological change is found to be the major source of TFP growth in industrial machinery. However, the growth rate in TFP is depressed due to increasing inefficiencies in most of the firms under study. An investigation to the sources of TFP change and its components reveal that R & D expenditure and Import have significant impact on technological change. The demand factors have favorable impact on scale efficiency change and finally, capital utilization as well as the catching-up show the expected sign on technical efficiency change.

The paper is organized as follows: Section 2 deals with the theoretical background and describes in nutshell, how the data envelopment analysis is utilized to measure the Malmquist productivity index. The database is reported in section 3 followed by results and discussion in section 4. Section 5 presents the conclusion of the work.

The Theoretical Background

There are different approaches to productivity measurement that can be divided broadly into two groups: frontier and non-frontier.

Reference Technology

Let us consider a sample of J DMUs (Decision Making Units) from an industry producing a vector of M outputs (y) from a vector of N inputs (x).Let B denotes J x M matrix of observed outputs and A denotes the J x N matrix of observed inputs. Individual elements of M, denoted by $y^j{}_m$ measure the quantity of mth output produced by the jth DMU, while the individual elements of N, denoted by $x^j{}_n$, measure the employment level of nth input by the jth DMU, *at a particular period of time*. A production technology transforming input vector x to output vector y can be represented by the graph of technology.

$$GR\,(x, y) = ((x, y) \mid x \geq \Sigma_{j=1}\, \lambda_j\, x^j;\ y \leq \Sigma_{j=1}\, \lambda_j\, y^j;\ \lambda_j \geq 0) \qquad (1)$$

which exhibits constant returns to scale (CRS) and strong disposability of inputs and outputs. Following Afriat (1972), the assumption of CRS can be relaxed and one may allow for variable returns to scale by putting the restriction in (1): $\Sigma_{j=1}\, \lambda_j = 1$ where λ_j is an intensity variable indicating at what intensity a particular activity (firm) may be employed in production.

A Malmquist Output-Based Productivity Index

Following Shepherd (1970) and Färe (1988), the output distance function in time period t is defined as:

$$D_o^{\,t}\,(x^t, y^t) = \inf\,\{\theta \mid (x^t, y^t/\theta) \in GR^t\,\}$$

$$= [\sup\{\theta \mid (x^t, \theta\, y^t) \in GR^t\}^{-1} \qquad (2)$$

It is to be noted that $D_o^{\,t}\,(x^t, y^t) \leq 1$ if and only if $(x^t, y^t) \in GR^t$. This function is reciprocal to Farrell's (1957) output oriented measures of technical efficiency, i.e., the reciprocal of the maximum proportional expansion of the output vector, y^t, given the input vector, x^t.

To define a Malmquist productivity index, the distance functions required with respect to two different time periods are as follows:

$$D_o^{\,t}\,(x^{t+1}, y^{t+1}) = \inf\,\{\theta \mid (x^{t+1}, y^{t+1}/\theta) \in GR^t\,\} \qquad (3)$$

$$D_o^{\,t+1}\,(x^t, y^t) = \inf\,\{\theta \mid (x^t, y^t/\theta) \in GR^{t+1}\} \qquad (4)$$

The first distance function measures the *maximum* proportional change in outputs required to make (x^{t+1}, y^{t+1}) feasible in relation to the technology at time period *t*. Similarly, the second mixed-period distance function measures the maximum proportional change in outputs required to make (x^t, y^t) feasible in relation to the technology at time period *t + 1*. In both these mixed-period cases, the value of the distance function may exceed unity if the observation being evaluated is not feasible in the other period.

Caves et al. (1982) define an output-based Malmquist productivity index relative to single technology for time t as

$$M_o^{\,t} = \frac{D_c^{\,t}\left(X^{t+1}, Y^{t+1}\right)}{D_c^{\,t}\left(X^{t}, Y^{t}\right)} \tag{5}$$

and for period *t+1*,

$$M_o^{\,t+1} = \frac{D_c^{\,t+1}\left(X^{t+1}, Y^{t+1}\right)}{D_c^{\,t+1}\left(X^{t}, Y^{t}\right)} \tag{6}$$

Following Ray and Desli (1997), the productivity index in (6) and (7) can be rewritten as:

$$M_o^{\,t} = \frac{D_v\left(X^{t+1}, Y^{t+1}\right) D_c^{\,t}\left(X^{t+1}, Y^{t+1}\right) \big/ D_v^{\,t}\left(X^{t+1}, Y^{t+1}\right)}{D_v^{\,t}\left(X^{t}, Y^{t}\right) D_c^{\,t}\left(X^{t}, Y^{t}\right) \big/ D_v^{\,t}\left(X^{t}, Y^{t}\right)}$$

$$= \frac{D_v\left(X^{t+1}, Y^{t+1}\right)}{D_v^{\,t}\left(X^{t}, Y^{t}\right)} \; \frac{\mathrm{SE}^{t}\left(X^{t+1}, Y^{t+1}\right)}{\mathrm{SE}^{t}\left(X^{t}, Y^{t}\right)} \tag{7}$$

where 'v' stands for variable returns to scale and SE^t (x^t, y^t) and SE^t (x^{t+1}, y^{t+1}) represent the scale efficiency with respect to technology *t* evaluated at two different levels of inputs. Similarly,

$$M_0^{\,t+1} = \frac{D_v^{\,t+1}\left(X^{t+1}, Y^{t+1}\right)}{D_v^{\,t+1}\left(X^{t}, Y^{t}\right)} \; \frac{\mathrm{SE}^{t+1}\left(X^{t+1}, Y^{t+1}\right)}{\mathrm{SE}^{t+1}\left(X^{t}, Y^{t}\right)} \tag{8}$$

By taking the geometric mean of (7) and (8) one gets:

$$M_0^{t+1}\left(X^{t+1},Y^{t+1}X^t,Y^t\right)= \tag{9}$$

$$\left[\frac{D_v^t\left(X^{t+1},Y^{t+1}\right)D_v^{t+1}\left(X^{t+1},Y^{t+1}\right)}{D_v^t\left(X^t,Y^t\right)D_v^{t+1}\left(X^t,Y^t\right)}\right]^{1/2}$$

$$\left[\frac{\mathrm{SE}^t\left(X^{t+1},Y^{t+1}\right)\mathrm{SE}^{t+1}\left(X^{t+1},Y^{t+1}\right)}{\mathrm{SE}^t\left(X^t,Y^t\right)\mathrm{SE}^{t+1}\left(X^t,Y^t\right)}\right]^{1/2}$$

The first component of (9) can further decomposed as:

$$\left[\frac{D_v^t\left(X^t,Y^t\right)}{D_v^{t+1}\left(X^t,Y^t\right)}\frac{D_v^t\left(X^{t+1},Y^{t+1}\right)}{D_v^{t+1}\left(X^{t+1},Y^{t+1}\right)}\right]^{1/2}\frac{D_v^{t+1}\left(X^{t+1},Y^{t+1}\right)}{D_v^t\left(X^t,Y^t\right)} \tag{10}$$

where the first component of (10) is the geometric mean of two ratios, which measures the shifts in the technology calculated at x^t and x^{t+1}. The second component measures the change in relative efficiency between the years *t* and *t+1*. The second component of (9) which involves both CRS and VRS distance functions at both the time periods, measures the change in scale efficiency.

Thus,

MALM = *Technological Change x Technical Efficiency Change x Scale Efficiency Change*

In terms of the distances in Figure 1, the productivity change of firm A, which lies at point A_0 and A_1 respectively in time period t and t+1, can be described as:

$$\left[\frac{A_0X_0/T_0X_0}{A_0X_0/U_0X_0} \quad \frac{A_1X_1/T_1X_1}{A_1X_1/U_1X_1}\right]^{1/2}\left[\frac{A_1X_1/U_1X_1}{A_0X_0/T_0X_0}\right]$$

Technological Change *Technical* Efficiency Change

$$\left[\frac{\dfrac{A_1X_1/P_1X_1}{A_1X_1/T_1X_1}}{\dfrac{A_0X_0/P_0X_0}{A_0X_0/T_0X_0}} \quad \frac{\dfrac{A_1X_1/U_1X_1}{A_1X_1/U_1X_1}}{\dfrac{A_1X_1/U_1X_1}{A_1X_1/U_1X_1}}\right]^{1/2}$$

Scale Efficiency Change

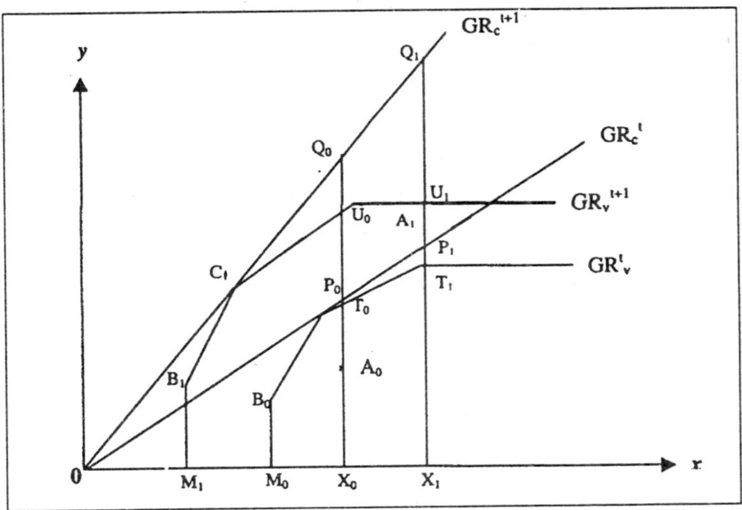

Fig. 1: Decomposition of malmquist Productivity Index.

Calculation of Distance Function: The Linear Programming Models

In order to calculate the productivity index of firm j', we require to solve the following linear programming problems: $D_v^t(x^t, y^t)$, $D_v^{t+1}(x^{t+1}, y^{t+1})$, $D_v^t(x^{t+1}, y^{t+1})$, $D_v^{t+1}(x^t, y^t)$, $D_c^t(x^t, y^t)$, $D_c^{t+1}(x^{t+1}, y^{t+1})$, $D_c^t(x^{t+1}, y^{t+1})$ and D_v^{t+1}

(x^t, y^t). The output distance function $D_c^t (x^t, y^t)$ is calculated by using the following LP problem:

$$[D_c^t (x^{j',t}, y^{j',t})]^{-1} = \text{Max } \theta^{j'}$$

$$\text{s.t.} \quad \sum_{j=1} \lambda_j X_n^{j,t} \leq X_n^{j,t}, n = 1, 2, \ldots, N$$

$$\sum_{j=1} \lambda_j y_m^{j,t} \geq \theta^{j'} y_m^{j,t}, m = 1, 2, \ldots, M$$

$$\sum_{j=1} \lambda_j = 1; \lambda_j \geq 0, j = 1, 2, \ldots, J \qquad (11)$$

The output distance function as calculated by solving the LP problem, given in (11) is the reciprocal of output-oriented Farrell's measure of technical efficiency calculated relative to technology satisfying the variable returns to scale. The CRS distance function is solved by using the above LP problem without the restriction: $\sum \lambda_j = 1$.

The mixed-period distance function, $D_v^t (x^{t+1}, y^{t+1})$ is solved by using the following LP problem:

$$[D_c^t (x^{j',t+1}, y^{j',t+1})]^{-1} = \text{Max } \theta^{j'}$$

$$\text{s.t.} \quad \sum_{j=1} \lambda_j X_n^{j,t} \leq X_n^{j,t+1}, n = 1, 2, \ldots, N$$

$$\sum_{j=1} \lambda_j y_m^{j,t} \geq \theta^{j'} y_m^{j,t+1}, m = 1, 2, \ldots, M$$

$$\sum_{j=1} \lambda_j = 1; \lambda_j \geq 0, j = 1, 2, \ldots, J \qquad (12)$$

Note that in (11), $(x^{j',t}, y^{j',t}) \in GR^t$ and therefore $D_c^t (x^{j',t}, y^{j',t}) \leq 1$. However, in (12), $(x^{j',t+1}, y^{j',t+1})$ need not to belong to GR^t and so it may take value greater than 1.

The Data

The basic data for this study has been collected from the electronic database PROWESS, provided by Centre for

Monitoring Indian Economy (CMIE), Mumbai. Company-wise information on output and inputs has been collected for the period 1988-89 to 1997-98. A single output (Gross Value Added) and two inputs – Labor and Capital are considered. Since the data on the number of employees is not available unit-wise, we have taken total wages and salaries as the proxy for the input, labor. The capital input has been taken as the gross fixed assets. All these figures given in nominal terms are converted into real values by using the suitable deflators. The data on GVA, capital and labor are deflated by the wholesale price index of industrial machinery, machinery and machine tools and consumer price index for industrial workers respectively, taken from different issues of National Account Statistics (NAS). All other information such as R & D expenditure, import, sales, etc has been taken company-wise from CMIE for the last two years of the period of study.

Results and Discussion

Efficiency Score

Since the basic components of the Malmquist index is related to measure of technical efficiency, we have reported in Table 1, the distribution of firms according to the efficiency scores. Value of unity implies that the firm is on the frontier or technically efficient and the value less than unity implies that the firm is below the frontier or technically inefficient in the associated year. As it can be seen from the table, out of 88 firms, 12 to 17 firms are technically efficient during the period of study in the case of industrial machinery. More than 80% of the firms are technically inefficient and more than 40% of the firms are having the efficiency score below 0.6.

The adoption of new technology, which is very commonly found in capital intensive industries, may sometimes result in low level of efficiency. It is so because

Table 1: Distribution of firms according to efficiency scores: Industrial Machinery

Efficiency Scores	*1988*	*1989*	*1990*	*1991*	*1992*	*1993*	*1994*	*1995*	*1996*	*1997*
0.0 - 0.3	4	5	5	6	4	5	6	7	11	16
0.3 - 0.4	19	7	6	6	12	10	8	8	11	10
0.4 - 0.5	12	13	11	19	15	13	10	16	15	14
0.5 - 0.6	14	22	15	16	19	16	12	10	10	16
0.6 - 0.7	10	9	13	8	6	8	14	15	12	11
0.7 - 0.8	10	8	11	9	9	13	9	9	9	2
0.8 - 0.9	6	6	7	6	5	5	10	4	2	0
0.9 - 1.0	1	6	7	3	2	2	2	5	4	3
1.0	12	12	13	15	15	16	17	14	14	15
Total	88	88	88	88	88	88	88	88	88	88
Average Efficiency	0.601	0.640	0.669	0.633	0.627	0.637	0.661	0.626	0.594	0.551

the question of efficiency is inextricably related to the appropriateness of the chosen technology, and more often, the fault may lie in the lack of institutional preparedness for scientific management, which is necessary for the smooth functioning of the new technology. (Ghosh and Neogi, 1993). In the case of major users of machine tools, such as in electrical, non-electrical, and 84 transport equipment, the degree of dependence on import, though declining, is still quite high. For example, in the case of electrical machinery, the percentage of imported machine as percentage of installation by user-industry in medium and large scale sector even in 1986 was as high as 43.4. The rapid diversification in manufacture of machine tools has led to an increase in the absolute number of machines installed. In the absence of a corresponding increase in employment in the major machine tools, this has led to a rise in the capital intensity. Study by Pillai and Srinivasan (1992) shows that the rate of growth of labor productivity is much lower than the increase in capital intensity in these industries, reflecting the fall in the level of efficiency.

The last rows of Table 1 gives the trends in average efficiency scores if industrial machinery as a whole during the period studied, which has been shown diagrammatically in Figure 2.

Figure 2: Trend in Technical Efficiency in Indian Food Industry

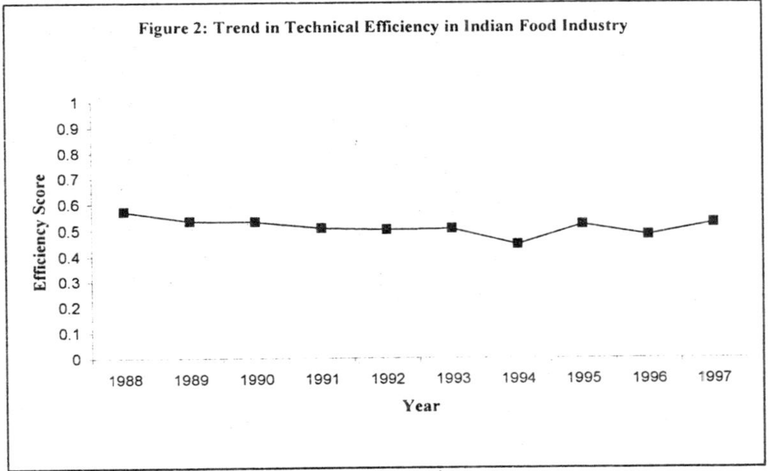

As it can be seen, the trend in technical efficiency in the case of industrial machinery is increasing till 1990-91, when the efficiency score reached the peak figure of 0.669. The efficiency trend remains almost stagnant from 1990-91 to 1994-95 and falling continuously thereafter to the score of 0.551 in 1998-99.

Next, we calculate Malmquist productivity indexes as well as the indexes for technological shift, technical efficiency change, and scale efficiency change components for each firm in our sample under the assumption of variable returns to scale throughout the model. Since this is an index based on discrete time, each company will have an index for every pair of years. This entails calculating the component distance functions using linear programming methods. We have used QSB (Quantitative System for Business) software program to solve the different linear-programming problems as mentioned in the previous section.

The value of the Malmquist index and any of its components less than 1 implies the deterioration in performance, whereas, the value greater than 1 implies improvements in the relevant performance. In order to more easily interpret these results, we have taken the natural logarithms of these indexes, which allow us to interpret these as percent changes.

Distribution of Firms: TFP Change and Its Components

Instead of presenting the disaggregated results for each firm and year, we show the distribution of firms according to different ranges of percent changes in TFP and its different components as shown in the Appendix Tables A1 to A4.

The ranges of percent changes are shown in the first column. Rest of the columns shows the number of firms associated with different range of changes in TFP in different consecutive years. The last column shows the distribution of firms in the long run, that is, during the entire period from 1988-89 to 1997-98.

As it can be seen from Table A1, the number of firms in the case of industrial machinery, which show the gain in TFP change, varies from 30 in 1997-1998 to 72 in 1990-1991 out of total sample of 88 firms. That is, 47% to 74% of the firms improve their TFP during the period of study. The industries the number of firms is comparatively much higher on the extreme range. In the long run, however, most of the firms concentrate at the lower ranges of TFP change.

Table A2 represents the distribution of firms in two industries according to technological change. As it can be observed, most of the firms achieve technological progress in the case of industrial machinery during all the years, except during 1989-1990, 1992-1993 and 1996-1997. In the long run, out of 88 firms, 84 firms improve their productivity through technological shift. However, most of the firms show the progress at the lower range of 0 to 5 percent.

As one can observe from Table A3, the number of firms showing gain in technical efficiency is higher than the number of firms showing loss in technical efficiency during all the years except 1991-1992, 1996-1997, 1997-1998. However, it does not imply that the average efficiency change is positive during these years. For example, during 1992-1993, though the number of firms showing technological regress is less than the number of firms showing technological progress, the average efficiency for the industry as whole is expected to be negative because the number of firms at the extreme negative range is much more than the number of firms at the extreme positive range. In the long run, out of 88 firms, 33 firms show gain, 48 firms suffer loss and the rest 10 show neither loss nor gain in technical efficiency.

Finally, one can observe from Table A4, the change in scale efficiency is found to be negative in the case of most of the firms in industrial machinery except during 1989-1990, 1991-1992 and 1996-1997. In the long run, out of 88 firms in the sample, 53 firms show loss and 30 firms show gain in scale efficiency. However, the rest 5 firms show no changes in scale efficiency. So, the average annual scale efficiency change is expected to be negative in the case of industrial machinery during the whole period.

Average Percentage Changes in TFP and its Components

The distribution of firms does not give the exact idea of percent changes in TFP and its components for the industry as a whole. In Table 2, we present a summary description of the average performance of all the firms together over all the consecutive time periods.

Table 2: Average change in TFP and its different components: Industrial Machinery

Year	*TFP Change Change*	*Technological Efficiency Change*	*Technical Efficiency Change*	*Scale Efficiency Change*
1988 to 1989	12.1	-0.80	7.05	5.92
1989 to 1990	13.9	8.98	6.39	-1.41
1990 to 1991	-0.90	4.59	-10.2	4.69
1991 to 1992	0.99	-2.02	1.39	1.59
1992 to 1993	0.70	3.73	-0.30	-2.63
1993 to 1994	-0.80	9.35	4.11	-14.2
1994 to 1995	-0.10	13.9	-7.80	-6.08
1995 to 1996	-9.76	-14.4	-5.23	9.89
1996 to 1997	-4.08	3.05	-8.12	0.90
1988 to 1997	1.39	2.96	-1.41	-0.20

As one can see from Table 2, the average annual growth in total factor productivity over the entire period is very low (1.4%). On an average, technological change, which is around 3% is found to be the only source of productivity growth in this industry. Except during the sub-periods, 1989-1990, 1992-1993, and 1996-1997, in all other sub-periods, the industry has experienced technological progress. The industry of machinery and machine tools of which industrial machinery is a part, is highly dependent on import of capital goods in the case of large-scale plants. However, in the case of large-scale machinery and machine tools industries, the proportion of imported machines in the total supply came down from 53.2% in 1968 to only 38% in 1985. The extent of import content varied, however, from one type of machinery to the next. In the case of major users of machine tools, such as, electrical, non-electrical and transport equipment, the degree of dependence in the inter-census period has not come down markedly. Thus the replacement of older machines is taking place at rapidly in the industry to keep it 'modern' commensurate with the requirements of the user-industries. (Pillai and Srinivasan, 1992).

The technical efficiency change, on an average is negative (-1.41%) during the period of study. On an average, the industry experiences loss in technical efficiency during all the years except during 1988-89-1989-90, 1989-90-1990-91, 1991-92-1992-93 and 1993-94-1994-95. The heavy loss in technical efficiency change is found in this industry since 1994-95 - 1995-96 onwards due to falling trend in technical efficiency since 1994-95 onwards. The scale efficiency change contributes negatively to the total factor productivity growth, particularly in the sub-period 1994-1995 and 1995-1996.

One tends to associate technical progress with advancement in science and technology and with the passage of time the production frontier is expected to shift outward making it possible to produce increasing quantities of output from any specific input bundles over time. Technical regress, on the other hand, results in an inward shift of the frontier. In other words, the same input bundle produces less and less output with the passage of time. If scientific knowledge and technical know-how is cumulative over time, a regressive shift in the production frontier seems to be impossible. The clue to this puzzle appears to lie in aggravating structural bottlenecks hindering production. Notwithstanding advancement in technical knowledge and improvement in skills, the maximum quantity of output producible from any given input bundle depends critically on the available infrastructures. Chronic and frequent shortage of power, congested transport networks, industrial disputes and prolonged political chaos disrupting day-to-day civilian life cause significant inward shift in the production frontier (Ray, 1997).

The overall trends in total factor productivity growth and its different components are shown in Figure 3.

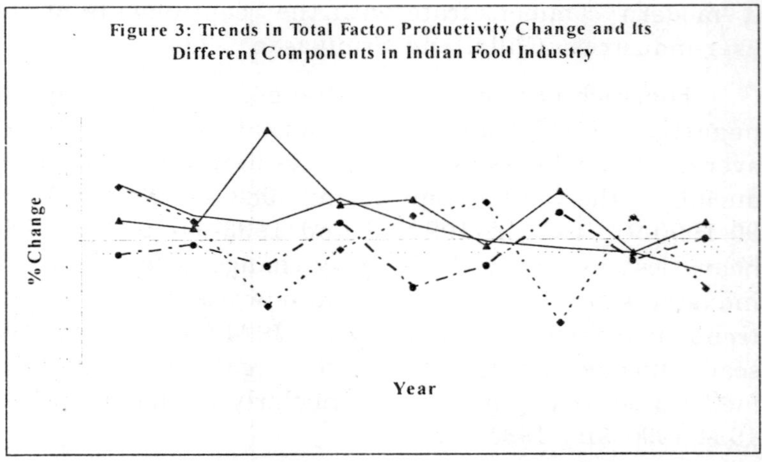

Figure 3 reveals that the trend in TFP growth in the case of industrial machinery industry is a continuously declining one and it shows a negative trend after 1993-94. All the components - technological change, technical efficiency change and scale efficiency change show zigzag trend throughout with both negative as well as positive values.

Explanation for Variations in TFP Change

It is already observed that there are wide variations of productivity growth across different firms. These variations in productivity growth are explained through technological change, efficiency change and the scale change under the variable returns to scale. Now we have at our disposal information on some economic factors–which can be used to explain the variations in productivity growth and its different components.

The dependent variables are the indexes of TFP and its components during the end period: 1997-98 which are expressed in terms of distance functions obtained as solutions to the relevant linear programming problems. On logarithmic transformation, these indexes give the rates of change in percentage. Each of these rates of change has been regressed on the logarithms of such explanatory variables as R & D expenditure, import (M), lagged technical efficiency change, advertisement expenditure, index of lagged sales growth and capital utilization. Suffice it to say that there are other important factors - internal as well as external to the industry, such as quality of technology information, rate of tariff protection, management quality, Government policy and the like (Clague, 1970; White, 1978; Patel, 1992). The non-availability of such data limits the scope of our analysis.

R & D is represented by the ratios of research and development spending to total cost (TOC). It appears to be crucial factor in favor of the innovation process. However, its effects on efficiency change may be expected as negative due to the fact that while R & D results in a positive shift of the frontier, at the same time it is the source of efficiency losses for those firms that are not able to follow this path.

Another important variable, import (M) is represented by the rate of total import (M) with respect to gross value added (M/GVA)96. Here GVA has been taken as the scaling factor as it has added advantage over gross value added because it facilitates comparison of results for different firms/industries with different material intensities. It improves comparability of data for individual establishments even with in the same industry as long as they differ with regard to the degree of vertical integration. It is expected to be a factor that improves productivity, mainly through innovation. However, like R & D, it may have negative impact on technical efficiency change, particularly in a developing country like India. The efficiency is inextricably related to the appropriateness of the chosen technology, and more often, the fault may lie in the institutional preparedness for scientific management which is necessary for the smooth functioning of the new technology (Ghosh and Neogi, 1993).

The lagged rate of growth of total sales ($SALE_{96}$/ $SALE_{95}$) is assumed to represent the exogenous growth of demand. The expansion of market can be seen as the start of cumulative process in which new products will be created and new production process will be employed. It may also result in increase in the scale of production. So, its impact is expected to be positive on all the components of productivity growth.

Like R & D, the advertisement effort is represented by the ratio of advertising expenditure to total cost $(ADVEXP/TOC)_{96}$. It is expected to boost up the level of demand and thus its possible impact on TFP change and its different components is positive.

The catching-up factor is represented by the lagged level of technical efficiency change (TEC_{96}/TEC_{95}). Productivity growth often takes place through diffusion of knowledge to more inefficient firms. In the framework of our analysis this spread effect, if it exists may be translated into a source of efficiency improvements towards the frontier by those firms which suffered a loss in efficiency during the previous interval of time. In that case catching-up factor will have a negative association with technical efficiency change in particular. But, if the more inefficient firms tend to lag behind more and more because of backlash effect, the coefficient of catching-up factor may be uncertain in relation to technical efficiency change and other components of TFP change.

Finally, the capital utilization, represented by ratio of lagged working capital to fixed capital, $(WC/FC)_{96}$ is expected to have positive impact on technical efficiency change. A mere rise in fixed capital without any concomitant rise in working capital may not lead to higher capital utilization and hence efficiency.

In Table 3, we present the results obtained by multiple regressions performed on the whole sample. The

Table 3: Elasticity Coefficients in Log-Linear Regression of TFP Index and its Components on Some Explanatory Variables

Dependent Variable / *Independent Variable*	*TFP Change*	*Technological Change*	*Technical Efficiency Change*	*Scale Efficiency Change*
Constant	-1.023 (-0.536)	0.743 (0.766)	-0.981** (-2.160)	3.180* (2.946)
R & D Exp. $(R\&D/TOC)_{96}$	0.245** (2.191)	0.314* (5.219)	-0.192 (-1.487)	-0.083 (-0.892)
Import $(M/GVA)_{96}$	0.216++ (1.862)	0.273+ (2.802)	-0.031+ (-2.463)	0.019 (0.842)
Sales Growth $(SALE_{96}/SALE_{95})$	0.186* (3.216)	0.012 (0.193)	-0.086* (-0.696)	0.128* (3.218)
Advertising Exp. $(ADVEXP/TOC)_{96}$	0.139** (1.682)	0.042 (1.012)	0.132 (1.126)	0.213* (3.457)
Capital Utilization $(WC/FC)_{96}$	0.312 (1.571)	0.046 (0.863)	0.321* (1.889)	0.069 (1.536)
Catching-up (TEF_{96}/TEF_{96})	0.186 (0.365)	--	–1.590+ (–4.672)	–0.09 (–0.981)
R^2	0.500	0.472	0.418	0.379
F	16.104	12.695	10.928	8.649
n	88	88	88	88

Note: 1. Figure in parentheses represent t-statistics

2. * and ** indicate that the coefficients are statistically significant at 1% and 5% level at one-sided tail where as, + and ++ indicate that the coefficients are statistically significant at 1% and 5% respectively at two-sides tail.

3. Years are the financial years, for example, year 1997 implies the financial year 1997-98.

4. Dependent variables are the indexes of TFP and its components during the last period: 1996-97 to 1997-98, expressed in terms of distance functions.

values of R^2 vary from 0.379 to 0.500 with F statistics ranging from 8.649 to 16.104 (significant in all the cases at 1% level). As except for import and catching-up factors, other variables are expected to have positive impact on TFP change and its components. Therefore, in general we have gone in for right-tailed test, but for the variables for import and catching-up, we have used two-tailed test since their effects may not be uniformly positive on all the dependent variables.

As expected, both R & D and import show positive and significant impact on TFP change as well as technological change. However, import shows negative and significant impact on technical efficiency change. Since the variables are in log forms, the coefficients represent the corresponding elasticity estimates. The elasticities of R & D imply that 10 % increase in R & D will results in technological progress by 3% and increase in TFP by 2.5%. Similarly, 10% increase in import results in 2.7% and 2.2% increase in technological change and TFP change respectively.

Sale's growth shows positive and significant impact on all the dependent variables except technological change. Another demand factor, advertising shows significant and positive impact on scale efficiency change. The capital utilization shows positive and significant impact on technical efficiency change. Finally, the catching-up factor shows the expected signs on technical efficiency change.

Conclusion

In this paper an attempt has been made to decompose the Malmquist productivity index into its different components, viz., technological change, technical efficiency change and the change in scale efficiency for the industry of industrial machinery in India. Further, it tries to explain the variations in TFP change and its components through some of the explanatory variables –internal to the firms.

Despite a reasonable technological change, the growth rate in TFP is found to be quite low as a result of loss in technical as well scale efficiency during the period studied. Both R & D as well as import shows significant impact on both technological change and TFP change. The demand factors show the favorable impact on scale efficiency change, where as, capital intensity as well as the catching-up factor shows the expected impact on technical efficiency change.

Technological possibilities depend on the mode of organization and various economic and institutional factors. The mode of organization, which is efficient in one country and at one time, may not be so in another country or in the same country at another point of time. Therefore, bold institutional changes are to be introduced as a part of on-going liberalization processes in order that inefficiency is substantially reduced. At the same time it is essential to spend time and money on continuous research and development for the adoption of technology to intertemporal and spatial changes in the mode of organization.

REFERENCES

1. Afrait, S. N., "Efficiency Estimation of Production Functions", *International Economic Review*, 13(3), 1972, 568-598.
2. Caves, D. W., Christensen, L. R. and Diewart, W. E., "Multilateral Comparisons of Output, Input and Productivity using Superlative Index Number", *Economic Journal*, 92(365), 1982, 73-86.
3. Clague, C., "The Determinants of Efficiency in the Manufacturing Industries in an Underdeveloped Country", *Economic Development and Cultural Change*, 18, 1970, 188-205.
4. Färe, R. Fundamentals of Production Theory, Berlin: Springer-Verlag, 1988

5. Färe, R., Grosskopf, S., Norris, M. and Zhang, Z., "Productivity Growth, Technical Progress, and Efficiency Change in Industrial Countries", *American Economic Review*, 84(1), 1994, 66-83.

6. Farrell, M. J., "The Measurement of Productivity Efficiency", *Journal of Royal Statistical Society*, 120(3), 1957, 253-281.

7. Ghosh, B and Neogi, C., "Productivity, Efficiency, and New Technology: The Case of Indian Manufacturing Industries", *The Developing Economies* 31(3), 1993, 308-328.

8. Nishimizu, M., Page, J. M. Jr., "Total Factor Productivity Growth, Technological Progress and Technical Efficiency Change: Dimension of Productivity Change in Yugoslavia, 1965-78", *The Economic Journal*, 92, 1982, 920-936.

9. Patel, I. G., "New Economic Policies: A Historical Prospective", *Economic and Political Weekly*, 27, 1992, 41-46.

10. Ray, S. C., "Regional Variation in Productivity Growth in Indian Manufacturing: A Non-parametric Analysis", *Journal of Quantitative Economics*, 13(1), 1997, 73-94.

11. Ray, S. C. and Desli, E., "Productivity Growth, Technical Progress, and Efficiency Changes in Industrialized Countries: Comment", *American Economic Review* 87(5), 1997, 1033-39.

12. Shephard, R. W. Theory of Cost and Production Functions, Princeton: Princeton University Press, 1970.

13. Sudit, E. F., "Productivity measurement in industrial operations", *European Journal of operational Research*, 85(3), 1985, 435-453.

14. White, L. J., "The Evidence of Appropriate Factor Proportions for Manufacturing in LDCs: A Survey", *Economic Development and Cultural Change*, 27, 1978.

Appendix

Table A1: Distribution of Firms: TFP Change in Industrial Machinery

TFP Change Range (%)	*1988 to 1989*	*1989 to 1990*	*1990 to 1991*	*1991 to 1992*	*1992 to 1993*	*1993 1994*	*1994 to 1995*	*1995 to 1996*	*1996 to 1997*	*1998 to 1997*
Below –15	11	3	16	16	13	12	11	14	22	1
–15 to –10	4	4	1	4	5	8	10	12	10	2
–10 to –5	5	4	15	14	6	8	11	13	16	7
–5 to 0	8	5	7	12	13	15	8	17	10	26
0	1	0	0	0	0	0	0	0	0	0
0 to 5	15	12	12	11	12	13	17	8	7	38
5 to 10	6	10	10	8	11	14	10	4	5	9
10 to 15	9	20	8	5	10	6	8	9	4	3
Above 15	29	30	19	18	18	12	13	11	14	2
+ CH	59	72	49	42	51	45	48	32	30	52
– CH	28	16	39	46	37	43	40	56	58	36
No CH	1	0	0	0	0	0	0	0	0	0
Total	**88**	**88**	**88**	**88**	**88**	**88**	**88**	**88**	**88**	**88**

Appendix

Table A2: Distribution of Firms: TFP Change in Industrial Machinery

TFP Change Range (%)	*1988 to 1989*	*1989 to 1990*	*1990 to 1991*	*1991 to 1992*	*1992 to 1993*	*1993 1994*	*1994 to 1995*	*1995 to 1996*	*1996 to 1997*	*1998 to 1997*
Below –15	1	2	0	3	0	0	0	48	0	0
–15 to –10	3	3	0	3	0	0	0	6	10	0
–10 to –5	45	3	4	30	3	0	0	4	13	0
–5 to 0	10	4	23	11	16	1	0	5	12	4
0	0	0	1	0	0	0	0	0	1	0
0 to 5	13	11	14	26	32	35	1	25	21	77
5 to 10	6	28	22	15	31	11	30	0	6	7
10 to 15	3	30	24	0	5	13	7	0	8	0
Above 15	7	7	0	0	1	28	50	0	17	0
+ CH	29	76	60	41	69	87	88	25	52	84
– CH	59	12	27	47	19	1	0	63	35	4
No CH	0	0	1	0	0	0	0	0	1	0
Total	**88**	**88**	**88**	**88**	**88**	**88**	**88**	**88**	**88**	**88**

Appendix

Table A3: Distribution of Firms: TFP Change in Industrial Machinery

TFP Change Range (%)	*1989 to 1990*	*1990 to 1991*	*1991 to 1992*	*1992 to 1993*	*1993 to 1994*	*1994 1995*	*1995 to 1996*	*1996 to 1997*	*1997 to 1998*	*1989 to 1998*
Below –15	13	7	24	18	12	10	19	27	35	2
–15 to –10	5	4	7	4	8	3	7	3	4	4
–10 to –5	3	13	12	9	9	2	12	6	12	10
–5 to 0	2	5	11	4	7	7	5	9	9	32
0	10	11	12	13	14	15	14	11	13	10
0 to 5	7	16	5	14	14	8	12	11	6	24
5 to 10	7	9	9	11	6	13	4	10	1	4
10 to 15	12	4	2	5	4	11	3	3	1	1
Above 15	29	19	6	10	14	19	12	8	7	1
+ CH	55	48	22	40	38	51	41	32	15	30
– CH	23	29	54	35	36	22	33	45	60	48
No CH	10	11	12	13	14	15	14	11	13	10
Total	**88**	**88**	**88**	**88**	**88**	**88**	**88**	**88**	**88**	**88**

Appendix

Table A4: Distribution of Firms: TFP Change in Industrial Machinery

TFP Change Range (%)	*1989 to 1990*	*1990 to 1991*	*1991 to 1992*	*1992 to 1993*	*1993 to 1994*	*1994 1995*	*1995 to 1996*	*1996 to 1997*	*1997 to 1998*	*1989 to 1998*
Below –15	4	3	5	2	5	45	17	3	6	1
–15 to –10	6	4	2	3	12	11	17	4	8	1
–10 to –5	8	21	6	12	21	10	17	2	11	2
–5 to 0	15	26	9	26	25	6	17	6	21	49
0	3	3	3	4	4	3	2	3	6	5
0 to 5	17	21	15	14	7	6	9	13	16	27
5 to 10	19	4	20	11	5	4	2	10	9	1
10 to 15	11	2	14	6	5	2	3	11	5	1
Above 15	5	4	14	10	4	1	4	36	6	1
+ CH	52	31	63	41	21	13	18	70	36	30
– CH	33	54	22	43	63	72	68	15	46	53
No CH	3	3	3	4	4	3	2	3	6	5
Total	**88**	**88**	**88**	**88**	**88**	**88**	**88**	**88**	**88**	**88**

18

Telecommunications Infrastructure and Economic Growth

An Input Output Analysis

*Ashish Dash**

The present study is an attempt to analyze the role of telecommunications on economic development through interdependence between producing sectors. Using the standard linear static Input-Output technique to assess the role of telecommunications in economic development, the study identifies three key sectors of Indian economy, which are the major users of telecommunication services, and also estimate their contribution to the National Income. In addition the key sectors are ranked in terms of six different types of linkages and compared with the overall degree of interdependence of the Indian economy.

Telecommunication is one of the important infrastructures of the economy. It serves a variety of economic wants by providing access to markets previously barred physically by distance and costs, generating economic savings and increased productivity for household, farms and government through substitution of telephone

* Doctoral fellow (Economics), Institute for Social and Economic Change, Nagarbhavi, Bangalore-72.
The author is extremely grateful to Prof. M.R. Narayana for his valuable comments.

usage for more expensive form of communication such as travel; improving market efficiency and competitiveness for business and firms through better information flow on prices, products, and attributes; and increasing business efficiency and profitability in the areas of client/customer relations, ordering, stock control, improved distribution channels, and the like (Kayani and Dymond, 1997). With the process of globalisation and liberalization, information as a prerequisite for production process is gaining importance. Improved communication is vital for productivity in economic activities such as constructions, transport, trade and commerce to mention a few. Being the backbone of information economy, telecommunication reduces transaction costs. Norton (1992) found that the links between transaction costs, telecommunication and economic growth comes from two facts. First, there is a lack of readily available information in developing countries. This results in inability to make and implement decisions. The presence of a well-developed telecommunication infrastructure is a necessary condition to overcome this difficulty. Second, is the existence of an inverse relationship between the transaction cost and output rate. Output rate increases with the fall in transaction cost and telecommunication infrastructure helps in reducing transaction cost.

There are very few empirical studies estimating impact of telecommunication on national income. Literature has focused on two way relationship between telecommunication and economic growth. The increase in economic growth may depend on the telecommunication infrastructure and services. On the other hand the increase in the telecommunication services may be attributed to increase in economic growth.

For instance, using the data of 47 countries for the period 1957-1977, Norton (1992) estimated the effects of the average stock of telephones between 1957-1977 on the mean annual growth rate of domestic/national product after controlling for the stock of telephone in 1957 (telephone population in 1957) and a number of macro economic variables along with the average telephone population for the period of study. He found that average stock generates powerful diagnostics. By examining the performance of telephone stock of 1957 and average telephone population he concluded that the relationship between telecommunication and rate of growth of GDP is not clearly due to reverse causality and, hence, the existence of telephone stock reduces the transaction cost as output rises " when the infrastructure is present". This interpretation makes sense as the coefficient for the initial stock of telecommunication as well as the average telephone population turns out to be positive and significant. This implies that countries with larger initial stock of telecommunication have grown faster than the countries with low initial stock of telecommunication capital. The presence of important telecommunication variable makes the negative value of income per capita stronger and more robust supporting the convergence hypothesis. The negative value is expected for the coefficient of income per capita because countries with a lower output capita should grow faster as a result of technology diffusion to less developed countries.

Roller and Waverman (2001) used cross-country panel data to examine the impact of telecommunication on economic growth. Their fixed effect model[1] under a simultaneous equation framework endogenizes the telecommunication sector by specifying a micro model of demand and supply and jointly estimating with the macro production equation. Their data set consists of both economic variables relating to countries characteristics and characteristics relating to telecommunication development. Given that the OECD has grown at around 1.96 percent,

1 21 OECD countries over 20 years (1970-1990).

the fixed effect model of Roller and Waverman (2001) shows that one-third (0.59 per cent) of the growth can be attributed to the telecommunication investment. According to their estimate allowing for fixed effect, the tele density elasticity is found to be 0.045. A Telecom Penetration (TP) above 40 percent has significant growth impact. Such a rate of TP corresponds to Universal Service with roughly 2 to 2.5 people per household. The critical mass corresponds to 40 percent TP rate. Such a TP rate exists in most of the OECD countries. Those countries that are above the critical mass would have a higher growth rate where as others would grow much slower. Hence convergence in telecommunication infrastructure would offset the divergence in economic performance.

Roller and Waverman (2001) study employs macro economic variables like GDP, GDP deflator, capital stock, population, CPI, Gross Domestic Investment, government deficit (or surplus), geographic area, population density, labour force, unemployment rate, and the percentage of school age children in primary and secondary school and variables relating to telecommunication such as mainlines, residential mainlines, waiting list for mainlines, national and international trunk traffic, income from telephone services, the number of data terminals circuits end connected to automatic switching exchanges, machines equipped for direct dialing and investment in telecommunication in their analysis. The endogenous variable comprises of demand side variable such as telecom penetration i.e. mainline per capita (the proxy for stock of telecommunication infrastructure) and supply side variables, such as, price of telephone service - the proxy for which is the telephone revenue per mainline and investment in telecom infrastructure. On the other hand, the exogenous variables are non-residential capital stock net to telecom, Human capital stock, GDP etc.

The variables such as GDP, the investment in telecommunication infrastructure and the non-residential capital stock net of telecommunication capital might be non-stationary in nature. Applying a framework and a specification as close as possible to that of Roller and Waverman (2001), Torero et al (2002) estimated a similar four-equation model with first difference of the variables in order to correct for the unit root problem. They found that a 1 per cent increase in the TP results in a 0.03 per cent increase in the economic output for the 95 countries. With the primary aim of examining whether the idea of critical mass is valid for a large sample of nations, they assembled a data set that includes data on 113 countries over the time period 1980-2000.They found that for poor countries, where a critical mass of telecommunication does not exist (with the mean TP rate of 0.58 per cent), a marginal increase in the TP rate would not initiate economic growth. For high middle-income countries for TP level of 5 to 11 percent, telecommunications infrastructure has a positive and statically significant impact on aggregate output. For the 20 countries in this group, they found that 1 per cent increase in the TP would result in a 0.064 per cent increase in the GDP. On the other hand, for the 26 countries in the group of OECD and other high-income countries a one per cent increase in TP would result in only .015 per cent increase in GDP. These countries have a TP rate of about 40 per cent. Hence they conclude that for this group of countries the growth effect is muted.

One can think of various alternative methods to evaluate the impact of telecommunication services on economic Growth. These methods can be broadly classified under "Macro-Economic Approach" and "General Equilibrium Framework". All the existing studies discussed above focus on the macroeconomic approach by describing how the country specific growth variables (for e.g. growth rate of GDP) influence or is influenced by sector specific telecom variables (for instance growth rate of direct exchange lines). These studies, examines whether convergence in telecommunication infrastructure would offset divergence in economic performance. To our knowledge, a general equilibrium approach to estimate the impact of telecommunication on economic growth is yet to be attempted in India. To attempt the same, a simple linear static open Input-Output Model has been applied in the context of present research, as an empirical manifestation of general equilibrium analysis.

Inter-industry analysis under the IO framework provides solution for a range of empirical problems. For instance the increase in demand for a specific sector will have quite a different effect on specific sector of an economy from an increase in demand for some other sector, but these differences are not distinguished in an aggregate analysis. Moreover, the increase in the demand for a specific sector will generate inter industry demand for a "bundle of output of other industry and its own output" which might be altogether different from the bundle of input required as a result of increase in the demand for some other industry. By using the IO framework one can study the impact of the change in the final demand of a particular sector's output, on the level of Gross Value of Output[2] (GVO), the final demand of the rest of the sector remaining same. Moreover the IO analysis provides an opportunity to compute various types of linkages that exists among industries and hence provides a guideline for investment decisions to allocate limited fund among the competing sectors in an underdeveloped economy in particular pursuing unbalanced growth strategy.

This paper is organised as follows. Section II outlines the basic model along with the technique to compute

---

2 GVO is the sum of sum of gross value added and the total input at purchase price due to. Hence one can compare between different levels of output.

various types of linkages and coefficient of interdependence; The database and its limitation are discussed in section III; Section IV specifies the computational methodology to study the impact of exogenous changes in final demand to a particular sector, on the rest of the sectors including the sector itself and on the total volume of output; Section V discusses the numerical findings of the basic model as well as the results obtained from the simulation introduced through the exogenous changes in the final demand; Section V concludes.

Basic Model

Input-output table is a systematic description of the interdependence (through the flow of goods and services) among different branches of the economy in industry form. The row corresponding to the sector gives the use pattern of the total supply of the sector, while the column gives the details of the input absorbed by the sector.

The input-output model provides a link between the final demands and the output levels of different sectors. It is a set of simultaneous linear equations in which the equilibrium level of production of different sectors are unknown and can be determined on the basis of the information contained in the input coefficients and final demand for different sectors. The input output model is based on the following assumptions.

1. Each sector produces a single homogeneous output with a single structure of input. No two products are produced jointly. If at all there is such a case then it is assumed that they (products) are produced in fixed proportion. This is essential because the input coefficient for a single commodity may remain stable if there is no change in technology. However, corresponding coefficient of an aggregated sector may not be stable even without the change in technology. The

cause of instability may also be the change in proportion of output of different constituents of the sector as the input coefficients of the sectors are the weighted average of the corresponding coefficients of the constituents, the weights being their value of output.

2. The quantity of each input used by any sector is a constant proportion only of the level of output of that sector.

3. The output X_i should not be less than the direct and indirect requirements of the output of this sector for producing X_i.

Structure of the Model

The supply of and demand for output of the ith sector is equal to:

$$X_i = \sum_j X_{ij} + F_i \qquad (1)$$

Where i = 1, 2, 3, 4.......n

Here

$\sum_j X_{ij}$ is the total intermediate demand for the output of sector

F_i is the sum of the output consumed by the component of final demand

X_i is the observed output vector.

These equations mean that the output of any sector is equal to the total of the output consumed by different sectors (including the sector itself) and the final demand

On the basis of the proportionality assumptions.

$$X_{ij} = a_{ij} X_j$$

$$\Rightarrow a_{ij} = \left(\frac{X_{ij}}{X_j} \right)$$

where a_{ij}'s are known as the structural or technical coefficients

Hence the above balance equation (1) can be written as

$$X_i = \sum_j a_{ij} X_j + F_i$$

In matrix form, the set of linear equation can be represented as follows

$$(I–A)X= F \quad (2)$$

Where, A is the technical coefficient matrix.

I is the identity matrix (n×n)

F is the final demand vector (n×1)

X is the transaction matrix (n×n)

Pre-multiplying $(I–A)^{-1}$ on both the side of equation (2), we can determine the equilibrium level of output as follows:

$$X = [I–A]^{-1} F \quad (3)$$

where, the elements of $(I–A)^{-1}$ matrix say r_{ij} are the output of sector i required directly or indirectly for producing one unit of output of sector j.

Backward Linkages, Forward Linkages and Coefficients of Interdependence

The column sum of the Leontief "input inverse" (intermediate inputs as a share of total input including value added) provides a measure of backward linkages. However its row sum cannot provide the measure for forward linkages. Jones approach solves the problem by providing a meaningful symmetrical measure of forward linkage, which can be derived from the row sum of the "output inverse" matrix (i.e. intermediate sales as a share of total sales including final demand) (Jones, 1976). If we define the following

1. $F_f \equiv$ *International input flow matrix (n×n).*
2. $X \equiv$ *Total output flow vactor (n×1).*
3. $|X| \equiv$ *Diagonal matix (n×n) whose digonal elements are those of the X vector.*
4. $I \equiv$ *Identity matrix (n×n).*
5. $1 \equiv$ *unity matrix (n×1).*
6. $A \equiv F_f\ |X|^{-1}$*(input coefficient matrix).*
7. $B \equiv$ *(Output coefficient matrix).*
8. $Z \equiv (I-A)^{-1}$ *(input inverse or leontief inverse).*
9. $W \equiv (I-B)^{-1}$ *(output inverse).*

With the above definitions, we can compute the six different types of linkages equation 5 to 10 and also the coefficient of interdependence using equation 11.

$$L^*F \equiv B1 \quad (4)$$

$$L^*B \equiv 1'A \quad (5)$$

$$LF \equiv W1 \quad (6)$$

$$LB \equiv 1'Z \quad (7)$$

$$FL(I) = LF - L^*F \quad (8)$$

$$LB(I) = LB - L^*B \quad (9)$$

$$\text{The coefficient of interdependence} = X'LF \div x'1 \quad (10)$$

Where

L*F = Direct Forward Linkages

L*B = Direct Backward Linkages

LF= Direct and Indirect Forward Linkage vector

LB = Direct and Indirect Backward Linkage vector

LF(I) = Indirect Forward Linkage

LB(I) = Indirect Backward Linkage

The output-weighted average of either backward or forward linkages (e.g. $X'L_f \div X'1$) is a scalar value and is called "coefficients of interdependence". The coefficient of interdependence provides a standard for separating high and low linkages industry (Jones, 1976).

Database and its Limitations

To capture the effect of communication (telecom) sector on the economy, the *commodity×commodity* matrix has been taken from 1993-94 input-output table[3] of India prepared by Central Statistical Organisation (CSO). Here the communication sector comprises of services rendered by public and private communication organisations/

---

3 The input output table provided by CSO contain three different types of matrix The basic input-output table is a *commodity× industry* table, recording the flow of the inputs of commodities into industries. Most of these inputs are required to produce the characteristic product of the industry but some are required to produce its subsidiary products. While determining the entries in the rows, a by?product of an industry is transferred to the sector (commodity row) whose principal product is the same as the by?product under reference. The columns, however, show the total of principal products and by?products of each industry. In a *commodity×commodity* table both rows and columns represent the commodity group sectors. If the secondary products of an industry-group along with its inputs are transferred to the industry group where they are the principal product, the resulting table is a commodity x commodity input-output table. On the other hand, in an *industry× industry* table, both rows and columns represent industry group sectors comprising of a mix of different commodity groups. The row of a sector in this table gives the supply of all primary products and secondary products (as a mix) produced by the corresponding industry group for different intermediate and final uses.

enterprises. The activities of Department of Posts relating to Post Office Saving Bank & Postal Life Insurance are excluded from communication, as the same are included in banking & insurance sectors, respectively. Similarly the activities of the Department of Telecommunication relating to telecommunication factories and administrative services are excluded from communication sector and merged in the concerned sectors. Since there is no independent sector for telecommunication in the Input Output table provided by CSO, its next best alternative i.e. communication sector has been taken for the analysis purpose.

The *115×115* matrix has been reduced to 14×14 matrix, where the first 13 sectors are Trade, other transport services, construction, banking, miscellaneous manufacturing, Electricity, other services, other non-electrical machinery, Electronic equipments (incl TV), insurance, Communication, Miscellaneous metal products and Non-Ferrous basic metal (all these sectors independently uses more than one per cent of total communication output as input in there production process). The 14th sector includes all other sectors.

Computational Methodology

1. Lets denote the equilibrium level of output as X*. A simulation analysis has been done to see the impact of 10 per cent change in the final demand of each of these sectors on total output, the final demand for other sector remaining constant in order to evaluate how telecommunications influence economic growth[4].

$$\dot{X}_i = [I - A]^{-1} \times \tilde{F}$$

Where = $\tilde{F} = F + \dfrac{(F \times 10)}{100}$

4 National income is defined as the sum of gross total output of all the 14 sectors.

2. Maximum of gross total output obtained from the above 14 "equilibrium output vectors" can be represented as:

$$\hat{\hat{X}} = \max\ \{\hat{x}_1, \hat{x}_2, \hat{x}_3, \hat{x}_4, \hat{x}_5, \hat{x}_6, \hat{x}_7, \hat{x}_8, \hat{x}_9, \hat{x}_{10}, \hat{x}_{11}, \hat{x}_{12}, \hat{x}_{13}\} \quad (11)$$

$\hat{x}_j = \sum_{j=1}^{14} \dot{X}_i$ where, final demand for the jth sector has increased by ten percent the final demand of other sector remaining same.

Since the 14th sector consists of rest of the sectors, which is the sum of 102 sectors, it has been dropped for all the comparison purpose.

Numerical Findings and Discussions

1. The major sectors in terms of contribution to the total volume of output are Construction, other transport services and Trade sectors (See table 1).

2. Telecommunication (communication) sector is found to be a sector with low backward and high forward linkage. A rank correlation has been calculated between forward linkages (LF) and backward linkages (LB) of the 14 sectors. The Spearman rank correlation coefficient between LF and LB is found to be 0.81 in the 14×14 "commodity × commodity" matrix.

3. The "coefficient of interdependence" computed from the 14 × 14 "commodity × commodity" matrix is equal to 1.80 (from equation 11).

4. $\hat{\hat{X}}$ will be achieved (from equation 12) when the final demand for construction sector is increased by ten per cent, the final demand for other sector remaining constant (See table-8).

5. If one would rank the sectors in terms of maximum percentage increase in national income

Table 1: Constribution of ith sector to total volume of Outpur

Sectors	*i^{th} sector's contribution to the total volume of output (in Rs. Lakh)*
Trade	14425512.71 (9.62)
Other transport services	9929571.98 (6.62)
Construction	10733022.48 (7.15)
Banking	4260318.735 (2.84)
Miscellaneous manufacturing	1994711.925 (1.33)
Electricity	5127578.097 (3.42)
Other services	5368348.14 (3.58)
Other non-electrical machinery	1308683.566 (0.87)
Electronic equipments (incl.TV)	631011.4263 (0.42)
Insurance	673326.6747 (0.45)
Communication	1130656.753 (0.75)
Miscellaneous metal products	1433154.722 (0.96)
Non-ferrous basic metals	1140792.27 (0.76)
Rest of the sector	91854681.86 (61.23)

Source: Computed by the author.
Figures in the parenthesis are percentage contribution of ith sector to the total volume of Output.

as a result of ten per cent increase in the final demand of that sector alone, construction, trade and other transport services sector occupy first three ranks respectively (see table-8). These are the sectors, which use 29.4 per cent of the total communication output in their production process (see appendix-1).

6. If one evaluates the contribution of these industries in terms of value added at factor cost, communication sector occupies the 7th rank (see table-2). Here too trade construction and other transport sector occupies the first three ranks respectively. Thus, communication serves as a basic input for those sectors, the increment in

whose final demand is leading the economy to the maximum percentage increase in national income as well as gross value added.

Table 2: Contribution of ith sector in terms of Value Added

Sectors	i^{th} sector's contribution in terms of Value added (in Rs. Lakh)
Trade	10703514.37 (1)
Construction	4084052.88 (2)
Other transport services	3831393.30 (3)
Banking	3625574.87 (4)
Other services	
2687959.97 (5)	
Electricity	1672850.08 (6)
Communication	942000.38 (7)
Miscellaneous manufacturing	780579.60 (8)
Insurance	540932.69 (9)
Other non-electrical machinery	490197.00 (10)
Miscellaneous metal products	392495.55 (11)
Electronic equipments (incl.TV)	186775.98 (12)
Non-ferrous basic metals	170420.06 (13)
Rest of the sector	49930753.34

Source: Computed by the author.
Figures in the parenthesis are rank

7. For ten percent increase in final demand of construction sector, 0.97 per cent increase in the communication output is required to fulfill the direct and indirect requirements of inputs for construction sectors (see table-9).

Limitations of the Study

John's output coefficient matrix violates the assumptions of constancy of input coefficients in the basic leontif model. In fact this model is used to derive the

Table 3: Estimation results of various types of forward and backward linkages

Sectors	*Direct Backward Linkage*	*Direct and Indirect Backward Linkage*	*Indirect Backward Linkage*	*Direct Forward Linkage*	*Direct and Indirect Forward Linkage*	*Indirect Forward Linkage*
Trade	0.25	1.43	1.18	0.45	1.78	1.34
Other transport services	0.52	1.93	1.41	0.50	1.87	1.37
Construction	0.59	2.03	1.44	0.13	1.24	1.10
Banking	0.15	1.22	1.07	0.78	2.44	1.66
Miscellaneous manufacturing	0.59	2.11	1.53	0.51	1.95	1.44
Electricity	0.64	2.23	1.59	0.91	2.88	1.98
Other services	0.46	1.83	1.37	0.46	1.82	1.37
Other non-electrical machinery	0.62	2.15	1.53	0.30	1.54	1.24
Electronic equipments (incl.TV)	0.67	2.21	1.54	0.08	1.13	1.05
Insurance	0.19	1.31	1.12	0.95	2.77	1.81
Communication	0.16	1.29	1.13	0.65	2.22	1.57
Miscellaneous metal products	0.68	2.30	1.62	0.45	1.78	1.32
Non-ferrous basic metals	0.71	2.43	1.72	1.14	3.38	2.24
Rest of the sector	0.45	1.80	1.35	0.42	1.74	1.32

Source: Computed by the author using equation 5 to equation 8.

Table 4: Rank of various sectors in terms of direct plus indirect forward linkage

Sectors	*Direct plus Indirect forward linkage*	*Ranks*
Non-ferrous basic metals	3.38	1
Electricity	2.88	2
Insurance	2.77	3
Banking	2.44	4
Communication	2.22	5
Miscellaneous manufacturing	1.95	6
Other transport services	1.87	7
Other services	1.82	8
Trade	1.78	9
Miscellaneous metal products	1.78	10
Rest of the sector	1.74	
Other non-electrical machinery	1.54	11
Construction	1.24	12
Electronic equipments(incl.TV)	1.13	13

Source: computed by the author.

backward linkage. Consequently the forward and backward linkages cannot be added to arrive at a measure of total linkage. Moreover the above six linkages give a measure of potential linkage of a given sector (Riedel, 1976) rather than the actual linkage. The limitations above underline the potential of the study for further extension of computation of total linkage along with forward and backward linkages, which does not violates the assumptions of constancy of input coefficients in Leontieff model. Preliminary ways of extensions are provided in Cella (1984).

Concluding Remarks

Though the results of this study are not comparable with the earlier studies based on "macroeconomic-

Table 5: Rank of various sector in terms of direct plus indirect backward linkage

Sectors	*Direct plus indirect backward linkage*	*Rank*
Non-ferrous basic metals	2.43	1
Miscellaneous metal products	2.30	2
Electricity	2.23	3
Electronic equipments(incl.TV)	2.21	4
Other non-electrical machinery	2.15	5
Miscellaneous manufacturing	2.11	6
Construction	2.03	7
Other transport services	1.93	8
Other services	1.83	9
Rest of the sector	1.80	
Trade	1.43	10
Insurance	1.31	11
Communication	1.29	12
Banking	1.22	13

Source: computed by the author.

Table 6: Degree of interdependence of Indian Economy

Coefficient of interdependence	1.80

Source: computed by the author.

Table 7: Rank correlation between direct plus indirect forward linkage and direct plus indirect backward linkage

Rank correlation	0.81

Source: computed by the author.

approach", the results do indicates that investment in telecommunication has a positive impact on national economic growth. Although the magnitude of the impact of telecommunications sector on economic growth is smaller

Table 8: Contribution of ith sector to GNP as a result of 10 per cent increase in the final demand of the ith sector

Rank	*Sectors*	$\hat{X}_j$ *(in Rs. Lakh)*	*Percentage increase over equilibrium level of output*
1	Construction	151903134.9	1.261
2	Trade	151147169.2	0.757
3	Other transport services	150967584.9	0.637
4	Other services	150546411	0.357
5	Miscellaneous manufacturing	150218572.5	0.138
6	Other non-electrical machinery	150207820.7	0.131
7	Banking	150191684.4	0.120
8	Miscellaneous metal products	150138989.4	0.085
9	Electricity	150125003.5	0.076
10	Electronic equipments(incl.TV)	150116197	0.070
11	Communication	150061831.6	0.034
12	Non-ferrous basic metals	150050383.3	0.026
13	Insurance	150015425.1	0.003

Source: Computed by the author.

than most other sectors government needs to assure proper investment in the sector. Neglecting telecommunication sector may obstruct the growth of big industries such as construction and trade: the major contributor to national income. Moreover the nature of telecommunication services is such that each subscriber's welfare rises with the number of other people who have the access to the network and with whom communication can therefore be made. This feature means that the benefit of telecommunications investment increases exponentially as expansion permits new participants to join the system. Hence as tele-density increases one can expect proportionately more use of telecommunication infrastructure in various sectors of the economy and hence a higher linkages.

Table 9: Additional requirement of output as a percentage of total output due to 10 per cent increase in the final demand for the following sectors independently

Sectors	*Corresponding additional requirement of telecommunication output as a percentage of equilibrium output.*
Construction	0.97
Trade	0.89
Other transport services	0.77
Other services	0.25
Miscellaneous manufacturing	0.18
Other non-electrical machinery	0.19
Banking	0.11
Miscellaneous metal products	0.21
Electricity	0.11
Electronic equipments(incl.TV)	0.04
Communication	3.50
Non-ferrous basic metals	0.03
Insurance	0.01

Source: Computed by the author.

REFERENCES

1. Cella G (1984), "The Input-Output Measurement of Inter industry Linkages", *Oxford bulletin of Economics and Statistics,* 46, No 1.73-84.
2. Government of India (2000). "Input Output Transaction Table 1993-94" Central Statistical Organisation, Ministry of Statistics and Programme implementation, New Delhi
3. Hirschman A.O.(1958) "The *Strategy of Economic Development*", Yale University Press.
4. Jones L. P. (1976), "The Measurement of Hirschmanian Linkages", Quarterly Journal of Economics. 90(2), 323-333.
5. Kayani, R. and Dymond, A. (1997), "Options for Rural Telecommunication Development" World Bank technical paper., No.359.

6. Norton S. W. (1992), "Transaction Cost, Telecommunication, and the Microeconomics of Macroeconomic Growth", *Economic Development and Cultural Change*, October 1992, 41(1), 175-96.

7. Riedel J. (1976), "A Balanced-Growth Version of The Linkage Hypothesis: A Comment", Quarterly Journal of Economics., 90(2), 319-322.

8. Roller, H.L. and Waverman L. (2001), "Telecommunications Infrastructure and Economic Development: A Simultaneous Approach", *The American Economic Review*, 91, No. 4, 909-923.

9. Torero M. Chowhury S. and Bedi S. A. "Telecommunication Infrastructure and Economic Growth a Cross Country Analysis", International Seminar on ICT and development, Bangalore, 9-11, Dec 2002.

Appendix-1

Sectors	*Output of communication service used as input in other sectors (Rs. Lakh.)*	*Rank*
Trade	142465 (12.60)	1
Other transport services	120900 (10.69)	2
Construction	69094 (6.11)	3
Banking	49593 (4.68)	4
Miscellaneous manufacturing	28872 (2.55)	5
Electricity	26684 (2.36)	6
Other services	23691 (2.09)	7
Other non-electrical machinery	22143 (1.95)	8
Electronic equipments(incl.TV)	21069 (1.86)	9
Insurance	19757 (1.74)	10
Communication	13920 (1.23)	11
Miscellaneous metal products	13183 (1.16)	12
Non-ferrous basic metals	11762 (1.04)	13
Rest of the sectors	176923 (15.65)	

Source: Computed by the author.

Figures in the parenthesis are in percentage term.

Part—VI

Privatization and Foreign Investment Issues

19

Public Sector Reforms, Disinvestment and Privatization in India

*Boppana Nagarjuna**
*V.V.M. Satish Reddy***

The concept 'public sector reform' or 'restructuring' is used more or less as synonyms. However, a World Bank report[1] prefers to distinguish between the two. Reform refers simply to an improvement in the existing system whereas restructuring implies changing of the entire system including inter-related areas. Both these concepts aim at maximizing efficiency by the application of science and reason or logic to the process of production, pricing, marketing and organizing of Public Sector Enterprises (PSEs).

In India the term 'public sector reforms' is synonymous with public enterprise reforms, which include 'Attempts to improve performance', 'Privatization' and 'Liquidation'. Attempts to improve performance while retaining public ownership include: restructuring of existing financial,

* Faculty, Department of Economics, University of Hyderabad, Hyderabad.

** Research Student, Department of Economics, University of Hyderabad, Hyderabad.

1 World Bank Report (study) on reform of Public Sector mangement, September, 1991.

technical and organization structures; clarifying enterprise objectives and goals; streamlining the relationship between the Government and the managers of the public enterprises so as to bring in the required levels of managerial autonomy and accountability, imposing financial discipline, creating a market and thereby competition, and improving the performance monitoring systems.

Overview of public sector reforms in India

1. Greater operational autonomy and delegation of powers granted to profit making PSEs in terms of
   - Incurring capital expenditure and Establishing joint ventures and subsidiaries for strategic alliances.
   - Restructuring and implementation of schemes for HRD subject to meeting the eligibility criteria and guidelines.
2. Induction of professionals on the Boards of PSEs.
3. PSEs brought within the ambit of Sick Industrial Companies Act (SICA), 1985 and BIFR.
4. Concept of Navaratnas and Miniratnas.
5. Disinvestment of PSEs.

Restructuring/Rehabilitation attempts of sick PSUs in India

In India, the Government had made several attempts from time to time for the Restructuring and Rehabilitation of various sick Public Sector Undertakings (PSUs); these are summarized in the table 1.

The revival packages include a combination of some or all of the following:

1. Conversion of cash losses to interest free loans or equity
2. Moratorium on payment of all loans

Table 1: Illustrations of some PSEs where Restructuring/Rehabilitation has been undertaken

(Amounts in Crores of Rupees)

Sl. No.	PSE	No. of rehabilitation/ restructuring attempts made for revival	Approx. amount of waiver/ fresh funds infused*	Paid up capital	Net Worth (31.3.99)	P&L A/C accumulated losses (31.3.99)
1.	Bharat Refractories Ltd.	Two revival packages approved (July 1996 and Jan 1999)	61.64	103.90	-28.79	131.57
2.	Heavy Engineering Corp.	Six attempts (1972, 1975, 1981, 1989, 1997, 1999)	N/A	437.88	-638.40	-1095.35
3.	Hindustan Cables Ltd.	January 1999	122.60	408.29	-57.02	-520.43
4.	Hindustan Shipyard	Two attempts since 1995	470.90	96.81	-988.19	-1085.10
5.	Hindustan Steel Works Constr. Ltd.	1997-99	975.17	20	-1363.26	-1383.28
6.	IDPL	1994, 1996, 1997	328.92	116.88	-872.06	-1201.55
7.	Instrumentations Ltd.	Referred to BIFR in 1993	17	24.05	-7.15	-72.94
8.	Jessop & Co	Two attempts (1986, 1997)		40	-170.73	-258.48
9.	Mining and Allied Machinery Corporation	Several attempts (1973, 76, 80, 86)	134.0	39.19	-881.39	-897.72
10.	Rashtriya Ispat Nigam Ltd.	Two attempts; Capital restru-cturing (July 1993 & May 1998)	N/A	6493.85	3751.69	-4053.83

Source: Presentation on Disinvestment, Indian Embassy, Belgium, May 2001.

* Indicates only one part of rehabilitation packages, which included many other concessions as shown.

3. Interest holiday on outstanding government loans
4. Write off of outstanding non-plan loans
5. Write off of interest on Government loans
6. Conversion of dues towards tax and interest into soft loans
7. Waiver of bank interest and dues
8. Conversion of outstanding cash credit into working capital term loan
9. Concession on existing power tariff (by State Government)
10. Release of fresh loans
11. Conversion of loans into equity etc.

As mentioned earlier, in India public sector reforms are synonymous with public enterprise reforms, which include 'Attempts to improve performance', 'Privatization' and 'Liquidation'.

Privatization

Although there are several definitions of Privatization which differ greatly, privatization can be defined in terms of the transfer of three kinds of rights from the State to the private sector: ownership rights, operating rights and development rights Depending on the form of privatization chosen, the private sector may acquire any one of these rights or a combination of them.

Corporatization, depending on the terms involved, may relieve the State of both the operating rights and financial risk. An operating concession transfers both operating and development rights, and consequently any financial or investment risk to the private sector operator in build-own-transfer schemes, the State transfers development and operating rights (until the asset reverts to the State), including investment and financial risks, to the private sector. Leases are sometimes also designed to transfer both operating and development rights, resulting in enhancement of the existing assets. Build-own-operate schemes entail transfer of ownership, operating and developing rights to the private sector. On the other hand, built-transfer schemes give the private sector only development rights.

Privatization could, therefore be defined as the transfer of ownership, operating and/ development rights from the public to the private sector; and the application of private sector objectives and disciplines in the operation and management of public enterprises, combined in most cases with the transfer of commercial and financial risks to their management.

Privatization is to be understood not merely in the structured sense of who owns an enterprise, but in the substantive sense of how far the operations of an enterprise are brought within the discipline of market forces through measures such as liberalization and deregulation. Privatization encompasses a broad spectrum of possibilities, between denationalization at one end and market discipline at the other. Broadly, it may consist of Divestiture and Non-divestiture options.

Non-divestiture options

Non-divestiture options could be viewed as an intermediate step towards ultimate sale of the enterprise by demonstrating the commercial viability of the public enterprises to be sold. They could even be important measures in themselves and could even be considered as alternatives to divestiture. Non-divestiture options range from 'Corporatization' to 'Management controls' and involve removal of subsidies, as well as exposure of the public enterprise to private sector discipline and competition. The main types of non-divestiture options could be:

- Organizational, financial and operational restructuring, together with commercialization and corporatization;
- Privatization of management (management contracts, leases or concessions);
- Contracting out; and
- Joint ventures between public and private enterprises.

Restructuring

Restructuring means making changes in the public enterprises allowing it to operate more efficiently and/or rendering it more attractive to potential investors before divestiture takes place. Thus the purpose of restructuring is to enhance the value of the public enterprise.

Broadly, there are three kinds of restructuring

1. *Organizational and labour restructuring:* This type involves reorganization of the public enterprise into more rational or smaller units and any necessary labour shedding. Organizational restructuring is to put the public enterprise on a sound financial and commercial footing, and to increase the net worth of sales value of the public enterprise.
2. *Financial restructuring:* Financial restructuring involves writing off excessive debts of the public enterprise. It allows an enterprise saddled with accumulated losses to "clean up" its balance sheet. If divestiture is contemplated, financial restructuring prior to sale can put a public enterprise on a sound financial footing, thus enhancing its sales value.
3. *Operational restructuring:* This type of restructuring involves infusion of new investment

or technology into the public enterprise. Thus it involves new investment in order to upgrade the enterprise's physical capacity or technology.

Commercialization

Commercialization is the introduction of commercial principles and objectives into the management and operations of a public enterprise. This may involve removal of subsidies, and exposure of the public enterprise to market disciplines in addition to hard budget constraint.

Corporatization

Corporatization goes further than commercialization because it deals with the transformation of a public enterprise into a corporation or some other business organization determined by relevant laws.

Privatization of management

Its aim is to increase the efficiency of a public enterprise through introduction of private sector disciplines and management techniques. Some of the methods of privatizing management are granting a management contract, a lease or an operating concession to a private sector operator.

Management contracts

Management contract is an agreement by which a public entity contracts with a private firm or individual for the operation of a public enterprise. Here, only operating rights (not ownership rights) are transferred to the private operator. It is different from a lease in that the managing operator is paid a fee and is usually not entitled to a share of the profits. The public entity continues to make financial provisions for operating costs and investments. Management contracts are used especially where the Government hopes to revitalize a loss-making public enterprise by introducing private sector management methods.

Joint ventures

A private enterprise owns a part of equity in PSUs and the Government owns the balance. The joint venture model is considered to be transitional arrangement, leading to eventual total disinvestment.

Leasing

The assets, particularly, the idle and underutilized ones, are leased out to private sector. Ownership continues to be with PSUs.

Contracting-out

Certain stages of production in PSUs may be contracted out to the private sector though the final product is still manufactured by the PSUs. With competitive bidding, the production cost of final output can be brought down.

Divestiture options

Divestiture options involve the transfer of ownership rights from the public to the private sector. Divestiture options may be preceded by non-divestiture privatization techniques, which are usually aimed at improving the financial and operational position of the public enterprise, thus increasing its potential value.

Forms of Divestiture

Divestiture could take one of the following forms:

1. Public flotation on the stock exchange, either by fixed price or by tender offer with a minimum price,
2. A management/employee buy-out,
3. Placing with a group of "strategic" investors or joint venture partners,

4. A trade sale in which a company is sold to a single person or consortium,
5. Public auctions (usually for small or medium enterprises),
6. Mass or voucher privatization, and
7. Liquidation, followed by sale of assets (usually for PEs which are not viable).

Divestiture could take place in one of the many ways depending upon the objectives of privatization.

Privatization has been known to have numerous nomenclatures. In India and Pakistan, privatization is called 'disinvestment'. Privatization involves disinvestment of Government share below 51 percent with consequent change of the management of the enterprise from Government control to new management of the strategic partner or to a professionally managed Board of Directors, as decided by the shareholders of the company.

Disinvestment

It involves Government selling whole or part of its equity in PSUs to private enterprises and/or the investing public.

Disinvestment means divesting (selling) a portion of Government equity in a public enterprise to retail investors, mutual funds, foreign institutional investors (FIIs), employees of the unit etc to raise funds. It does not involve transfer of management. In other words Disinvestment refers to the sale or closure by a firm of part of its business. In, India, with the onset of the era of liberalization and globalization, the Government came to realize that the public sector units were being plagued by financial crisis and mismanagement and were no longer in a position to take the economy to commanding heights. Disinvestments offered a viable solution to provide strength to these sick PSUs. Today profit making PSUs are also targeted for disinvestment.

Background

The policy of the Government on disinvestment has evolved over a period. Its beginning could be traced to 1991-92 when in a bid to broad base equity, improve management, enhance availability of resources for public sector enterprises and yield resources for the exchequer, it was decided to divest up to 20 percent of the Government equity in selected PSUs in favour of public sector institutional investment. This whole exercise was expected to yield Rs. 2500 crores to the exchequer.

Choice of PSEs for Disinvestment

PSEs were chosen for divestment on the basis of likelihood of raising maximum revenue through the public offering, since one of the main goals and stated reasons for divestment was to raise revenue for the Government. Thus the companies where the Government has divested a stake have been generally large profitable companies.

Disinvestment policy of the Government of India:

The Initial Phase: The policy of the Government on disinvestment has evolved over a period and it can be briefly stated in the form of following policy statements made in the chronological order:

Interim Budget 1991-92[2]

The policy, as enunciated by the Chandrashekhar Government, was to divest up to 20 percent of the Government equity in selected PSEs in favour of public sector institutional investors. The objective of the policy was stated to be to broad-base equity, improve management, and enhance availability of resources for these PSEs and yield resources for the exchequer.

2 Interim Budget 1991-92. Government of India, 1991.

Statement on Industrial policy statement, 1991[3]

The industrial policy of 24th July 1991 stated that the Government would divest part of its holdings in selected PSEs, but did not place any cap on the extent of disinvestment. Nor did it restrict disinvestment in favour of any particular class of investors. The objective for disinvestment was stated to be to provide further market discipline to the performance of public enterprise.

Budget: 1991-92[4]

In this pronouncement, the cap of 20 percent for disinvestment was reinstated and the eligible investor's universe was again modified to consist of mutual funds and investment institutions in public sector and the workers in these firms. The objectives too were modified, the modified objectives being: "to raise more resources, encourage wider public participation and promote greater accountability".

Rangarajan committee report[5]

The Rangarajan committee recommendations emphasized the need for substantial disinvestment. It stated that the percentage of equity to be divested could be up to 49 percent for industries explicitly reserved for the public sector. It recommended that in exceptional cases, such as the enterprises, which had a dominant market-share or where separate identity had to be maintained for strategic reasons, the target public ownership levels could be up to 26 percent, that is, disinvestment could take place to the extent of 74 percent. In all other cases, it recommended 100 percent divestment of Government

---

3 Statement on Indusrial Policy, 24th July, 1991, Ministry of Industry, Government of India.

4 Budget Paper 1991-92, Government of India.

5 Rangarajan Committee Report on the disinvestment of shares in PSEs. Government of India. April 1993.

stake. Holding of 51 percent or more equity by the Government was recommended only for 6 schedule industries, namely:

1. Coal and lignite
2. Mineral oils
3. Arms, ammunition and defence equipment
4. Atomic energy
5. Radioactive minerals and
6. Railway transport

The Common Minimum Programme (CMP)[6]

The highlights of the policy formulated by the United Front Government were, as follows:

- To set up a Disinvestment Commission for advising on the disinvestment related matters.
- To take and implement decisions to disinvest in a transparent manner;
- Job security, opportunities for retraining and redeployment to be assured.

No disinvestment objective was, however, mentioned in the policy statement.

Disinvestment Commission Recommendations: Feb 1997-Oct 1999[7]

Pursuant to the above policy of the United Front Government, a Disinvestment commission was formed in 1996. It made recommendations on 58 PSEs. The recommendations indicated a shift from public offerings to strategic/trade sales, with transfer of management, as the following table shows:

6 The common Minimum Programme (CMP). United Front Governemnt. 1996.

7 Disinvestment Commission Reports I. XII. Government of India.

Table 2: Mode of Disinvestment recommended and Number of PSEs

Mode of Disinvestment recommended	*Number of PSEs*
A. Involving change in ownership/Management	
1. Strategic sale	29
2. Trade sale	08
B. Involving no change in Ownership/Management	05
C. No change	
1. Disinvestment deferred	11
2. No Disinvestment	01
D. Closure/Sale of assets	04
GRAND TOTAL	58

The Second phase

Budget: 1998-99[8]

In its first budgetary pronouncement, the new Government decided to bring down Government shareholding in the PSUs to 26 percent in the generality of cases, thus facilitating ownership changes, as was recommended by the Disinvestment Commission (DC). It however, stated that the Government would retain majority holdings in PSEs involving strategic considerations and that the interests of the workers would be protected in all cases.

Budget: 1999-2000[9]

The policy for 1999-2000, as enunciated by the Government was to strengthen strategic PSUs, privatize non-strategic PSUS through gradual disinvestment or strategic sale and devise viable rehabilitation strategies for weak units. A highlight of the policy was that the expression 'Privatization' was used for the first time.

---

8 Budget Paper 1998-99. Government of India.

9 Budget Paper 1999-2000. Government of India.

Strategic and Non-Strategic classification

On 16th March 1999, the Government classified the public sector enterprises into strategic and non-strategic areas for the purpose of disinvestment. It was decided that the strategic public sector enterprises would be those in the areas of:

- Arms and ammunition and the allied items of defence equipment, defence aircrafts and warships;
- Atomic energy (except in the areas related to the generation of nuclear power and the application of radiation and radio-isotopes to agriculture, medicine and non-strategic industries);
- Railway transport

All other PSEs were to be considered non-strategic. For the non-strategic public sector enterprises, it was decided that the reduction of the Government stake to 26 percent would not be automatic and the manner and pace of doing so would be worked out on a case-to-case basis. A decision in regard to the percentage of disinvestment i.e. Government stake going down to less than 51 percent or to 26 percent, would be taken on the following considerations:

- Whether the industrial sector requires the presence of the public sector as a countervailing force to prevent concentration of power in private hands, and
- Whether the industrial sector requires a proper regulatory mechanism to protect the consumer interests before public sector enterprises are privatized.

Budget: 2000-01[10]

The highlights of the policy for the year 2000-01 were that for the first time the Government made the statement

[10] Budget Paper 2000-01. Government of India.

that it was prepared to reduce its stake in non-strategic PSEs even below 26 percent if necessary, that there would be increasing emphasis on strategic sales and that the entire proceeds from disinvestment would be deployed in social sectors, restructuring of PSEs and retirement of public debt. The main elements of the policy were reiterated as follows:

- To restructure and revive potentially viable PSEs;
- To close down PSEs which cannot be revived;
- To bring down Government equity in all non-strategic PSEs to 26 percent or lower, if necessary;
- To fully protect the interests of workers;
- To put in place mechanisms to raise resources from the market against the security of PSEs assets for providing an adequate safety net to workers and employees;
- To establish a systematic policy approach to disinvestment and privatization and to give a fresh impetus to this programme, by setting up a new Department of Disinvestment;
- To emphasize increasingly on strategic sales of identified PSEs;
- To use the entire receipt from the disinvestment and privatization for meeting expenditure in social sectors, restructuring of PSEs and retiring public debt.

***Budget: 2001-02*[11]**

The Budget speech of the Finance Minister stated the objectives of Disinvestment as follows:

11 Budget Paper 2001-2002. Government of India.

To use the proceeds for providing

- Restructuring assistance to PSUs
- Safety net to workers
- Reduction of debt burden
- Additional budgetary support for the plan, primarily in the social and infrastructure sector (contingent upon realization of the anticipated receipt).

Budget: 2002-2003 [12]

The Budget 2002-03 outlines the following:

- The target for disinvestment for the year as Rs.12000 crores.
- It expects to complete disinvestments in another 6 companies and the remaining hotels in HCI and ITDC.

The need for Disinvestment/Privatization[13]

1. The cornerstone of the case for privatization is the concept that private ownership leads to better use of resources and their more efficient allocation. Through out the world, the preference for market economy received a boost after it was realized that the State could no longer meet the growing demands of the economy and the State shareholding inevitably had to come down. The 'State in business' argument thus lost out and also the presumption that direct and comprehensive control over the economic life of citizens from the Central government can deliver results better than those of a more liberal system that directly responds according to the market driven forces.

---

[12] Budget Paper 2002-2003. Government of India.
[13] Ministry of Disinvestment. Government of India.

2. Another reason for adoption of privatization policies around the globe has been the inability of the Governments to raise high taxes, pursue deficit/inflationary financing and the development of money markets and private entrepreneurship.

Further, technology and W.T.O. commitments have made the world a global village and unless industries, including public industries do not quickly restructure, they would not be able to survive. Public enterprises, because of the nature of their ownership, can restructure slowly and hence the logic of privatization gets stronger. Besides, techniques are now available to control public monopolies like Power and Telecom, where consumer interests can be better protected by regulation/competition, and investment of public money to ensure protection of consumer interests is no longer a convincing argument.

The objectives of the disinvestment programme vary from improving efficiency of the Public Sector Enterprises to transformation of the society.

Rationale for Disinvestment[14]

Because of the current revenue expenditure on items such as interest payments, wages and salaries of Government employee and subsidiaries, the Government is left with hardly any surplus for capital expenditure on social and physical infrastructure. Whereas the Government should be spending on basic education, primary health and family welfare, huge amounts of resources are blocked in several non-strategic sectors such as hotels, trading companies, consultancy companies, textile companies, chemical and pharmaceuticals companies, consumer goods companies etc. Not only this - the continued existence of the PSEs is forcing the Government to commit further resources for the sustenance

---

14 Ibid.

of many non-viable PSEs. The Government continues to expose the taxpayers' money to risk, which it can readily avoid. To top it all, there is a huge amount of debt overhang, which needs to be serviced and reduced before money is available to invest in infrastructure. This makes disinvestment of the Government stake in the PSEs absolutely imperative.

The primary objectives for privatizing the PSEs are, therefore, as follows:

- Releasing the large amount of public resources locked up in non-strategic PSEs, for redeployment in areas that are much higher on the social priority, such as basic health, family welfare, primary education and social and essential infrastructure;
- Stemming further outflow of these scarce public resources for sustaining the unviable non-strategic PSEs;
- Reducing the public debt that is threatening to assume unmanageable proportions;
- Transferring the commercial risk, to which the taxpayers' money locked up in the public sector is exposed, to the private sector wherever the private sector is willing and able to step in - the money that is deployed in the PSEs is really public money and is exposed to an entirely avoidable and needless risk, in most cases;
- Releasing other tangible and intangible resources, such as, large manpower currently locked up in managing the PSEs, and their time and energy, for redeployment in high priority social sectors that are short of such resources;

The other benefits expected to be derived from privatization are:

- Disinvestment would expose the privatized companies to market discipline, thereby forcing them to become more efficient and survive on their own financial and economic strength or cease. They would be able to respond to the market forces much faster and cater to their business needs in a more professional manner. It would also facilitate in freeing the PSEs from Government control and introduction of corporate governance in the privatized companies.
- Disinvestment would result in wider distribution of wealth through offering of shares of privatized companies to small investors and employees.
- Disinvestment would have a beneficial effect on the capital market; the increase in floating stock would give the market more depth and liquidity, give investors easier exit options, help in establishing more accurate benchmarks or valuation and pricing, and facilitate raising of funds by the privatized companies for their projects or expansion, in future.
- Opening up the public sector to appropriate private investment would increase economic activity and have an overall beneficial effect on the economy, employment and tax revenues in the medium to long term.
- In many areas, e.g., the telecom sector, the end of public sector monopoly would bring relief to consumers by way of more choices, and cheaper and better quality of products and services - as has already started happening.

Disinvestment *Process in India*

The disinvestment process comprises two major elements viz., (a) Formulation of decision model for selecting the portfolio of PEs for disinvestment, and (b) setting up a committee to select appropriate techniques of share valuation for enterprises proposed to be disinvested.

1. Formulation of a decision model: Developing a pragmatic model for deciding the portfolio of PEs whose shareholdings have to be disinvested is the most critical component of the disinvestment process. The literature on PEs shows as to how such model could not be formulated nor does the practice offer any guiding principles. The model could therefore, take into account a host of factors viz., financial success, marketing structure, social obligations, classification of PEs into certain cognate groups, etc.

2. Share valuation of PEs: The Department of Disinvestment, Government of India sets up a reserve price based on a complex valuation procedure. When the government calls for bids for a portion of its stake in a Public Sector Undertaking (PSU), it is essentially conducting an auction. As with any auction, the seller (in this case the Government) sets a price below which he (it) is unwilling to sell. The highest bid above this price becomes the price at which the auction is then concluded. This price below which the Government is unwilling to sell its stake is referred to as the reserve price.

Based on the recommendations of the erstwhile Disinvestment Commission and taking into account the comments of a Parliamentary Standing Committee on the subject, the Department of Disinvestment has set out certain guidelines for the valuers to use in the valuation of PSUs. As per the guidelines, four methods of valuing companies are to be used in arriving the reserve price of a PSU. These are:

(a) Discounted Cash Flow (DCF) Method.

(b) Balance Sheet Method.

(c) Transaction Multiple Method.

(d) Asset Valuation Method

While the first three are business valuation methodologies generally used for valuation of a going concern, the last methodology would be relevant only for valuation of assets in case of liquidation of a company. Let us now have a brief discussion of these methods:

(a) *Discounted Cash Flow (DCF) method*[15]

The Discounted Cash Flow (DCF) methodology expresses the present value of a business as a function of its future cash earnings capacity. This methodology works on the premise that the value of a business is measured in terms of future cash flow streams, discounted to the present time at an appropriate discount rate.

This method is used to determine the present value of a business on a going concern assumption. It recognizes that money has a time value by discounting future cash flows at an appropriate discount factor. The DCF methodology depends on the projection of the future cash flows and the selection of an appropriate discount factor.

(b) *Balance Sheet method*[16]

The Balance sheet or the Net Asset Value (NAV) methodology values a business on the basis of the value of its underlying assets. This is relevant where the value of the business is fairly represented by its underlying assets. The NAV method is normally used to determine the minimum price a seller would be willing to accept and, thus serves to establish the floor for the value of the business. This method is pertinent where:

---

15 Ministry of Disinvestment. Government of India.

16 Ibid.

- The value of intangibles is not significant;
- The business has been recently set up.

This method takes into account the net value of the assets of a business or the capital employed as represented in the financial statements. Hence, this method takes into account the amount that is historically spent and earned from the business. This method does not, however, consider the earnings potential of the assets and is, therefore, seldom used for valuing a going concern. The above method is not considered appropriate, particularly in the following cases:

- When the financial statement sheets do not reflect the true value of assets, being either too high on account of possible losses not reflected in the balance sheet or too low because of initial losses which may not continue in future;
- Where intangibles such as brand, goodwill, marketing infrastructure, and product development capabilities, etc., form a major part of the value of the company;
- Where due to the changes in industry, market or business environment, the assets of the company have become redundant and their ability to create net positive cash flows in future is limited.

(c) Market multiple methods[17]

This method takes into account the traded or transaction value of comparable companies in the industry and benchmarks it against certain parameters, like earnings, sales, etc. Two of such commonly used parameters are:

- Earnings before Interest, Taxes, Depreciation & Amortizations (EBITDA).

---

[17] Ibid.

- Sales

Although the Market Multiples method captures most value elements of a business, it is based on the past/current transaction or traded values and does not reflect the possible changes in future of the trend of cash flows being generated by a business, neither takes into account the time value of money adequately. At the same time it is a reflection of the current view of the market and hence is considered as a useful rule of thumb, providing reasonableness checks to valuations arrived at from other approaches. Accordingly, one may have to review a series of comparable transactions to determine a range of appropriate capitalization factors to value a company as per this methodology.

(d) Asset Valuation Method[18]

The asset valuation methodology essentially estimates the cost of replacing the tangible assets of the business. The replacement cost takes into account the market value of various assets or the expenditure required to create the infrastructure exactly similar to that of a company being valued. Since the replacement methodology assumes the value of business as if we were setting a new business, this methodology may not be relevant in a going concern. Instead it will be more realistic if asset valuation is done on the basis of the new book value of the assets. The asset valuation is a good indicator of the entry barrier that exists in a business. Alternatively, this methodology can also assume the amount which can be realized by liquidating the business by selling off all the tangible assets of a company and paying off the liabilities.

The asset valuation methodology is useful in case of liquidation/closure of the business. In this case certain adjustments may have to be made to the equity value

---

18 Ibid.

arrived at by this method including settlement of all borrowings on the company's balance sheet on the date of valuation and settlement of employee dues. These adjustments should include all the process related cost involved in closure and liquidation.

Although the aforesaid valuation methodologies being followed are broadly based on the discussion papers of the Disinvestment Commission and the best market practices, it is necessary to standardize the valuation methodology for all PSU disinvestments so that there are no variations from case to case. Therefore, all the four methodologies for valuation should be followed for all PSU disinvestments,

Progress of Disinvestment in India

Beginning from the 1991-92 round of disinvestment, Government has sold its equity in 48 central PSUs up to November 2002. In the process, a total amount of Rs. 30, 917 crores has been realized. The details of the CPSUs, where disinvestment has taken place, amounts realized as a result of disinvestment and the methodology adopted for disinvestment has been given in Tables 3, 4, and 8.

Other than Modern Food Industries (India) limited, only minority stakes in different PSEs were sold before the year 2000. The Government has since modified its policy to emphasize on strategic sales. The disadvantages of sale of minority stakes by the Government have been found to be as follows:

- Lower realizations because the management control is not transferred. Moreover, it signals lack of commitment to efficient governance of PSEs.
- With the limited holding remaining with the Government after minority sales, only small stakes can be offered to the strategic partner, if it is decided to go for a strategic sale subsequently. This depresses the possibility of

Table 3: PSU-wise details of shares divested from April 1991 to March 1999

Sl. No.	Name of the PSE	Total Shares (in lakhs)	Shares divested (in lakhs)	% shares divested	% age of Government holding as on 31.3.1999	Amount realized excluding 1991-92 (Rs. in Crores)@
1	Andrew Yule@	130.7	12.55	9.60	62.84**	0.00
2	Bharat Earthmovers Ltd.	340.8	133.56	39.19*	60.81	48.27
3	Bharat Electronics Ltd.	800.0	193.12	24.14	75.86	47.17
4	Bharat Heavy Electricals Ltd.	2447.6	790.09	32.28	67.72	309.55
5	Bharat Petroleum Corp. Ltd.	1500.0	507.00	33.80	66.20	331.18
6	Bongaigaon Refineries Ltd.	1998.2	510.34	25.54	74.46	45.40
7	CMC Ltd.@	151.5	25.29	16.69	83.31	0.00
8	Cochin Refineries Ltd (Kochi Refineries Ltd.)@	689.3	42.19	6.12	55.04**	0.00
9	Container Corp. of India Ltd	649.9	240.46	36.92*	63.08	335.48
10	Dredging Corp. of India Ltd.@	280.0	4.03	1.44	98.56	0.00
11	Engineers India Ltd.	189.9	11.36	5.98	94.02	67.63
12	Fert. & Chem.(Travancore) Ltd.	3547.7	60.31	1.70	97.38**	1.30
13	Gas Authority of India Ltd.	8456.5	2789.80	32.66*	67.34	1802.12
14	HMT Ltd.	841.5	71.02	8.44	91.56	23.38
15	Hindustan Cables Ltd.@	1608.9	16.73	1.04	98.96	0.00

(Table Contd...)

Table 3: (Contd...)

Sl. No.	Name of the PSE	Total Shares (in lakhs)	Shares divested (in lakhs)	% shares divested	% age of Government holding as on 31.3.1999	Amount realized excluding 1991-92 (Rs. in Crores)@
16	Hindustan Copper Ltd.	3382.0	41.94	1.24	98.76	8.07
17	Hindustan Organic Chemical Ltd.2	672.6	278.39	41.39*	58.61	0.00
18	Hindustan Petroleum Corp. Ltd.	2085.5	1020.64	48.94*	51.06	894.96
19	Hindustan Photo films Mfg Co. Ltd.@	1944.4	191.91	9.87	90.13	0.00
20	Hindustan Zinc Ltd.	4225.3	1017.45	24.08	75.92	81.55
21	Indian Oil Corp. Ltd.	3892.7	729.49	18.74	81.14**	2298.65
22	Indian Petrochemicals Corp. Ltd.@	2490.2	997.33	40.05*	59.95	0.00
23	IRCON International Ltd.@	49.5	0.13	0.27	99.73	0.00
24	Indian Telephone Industries Ltd.	880.0	202.22	22.98	76.67**	15.63
25	Indian Tourism & Development Corp.	627.4	62.93	10.03	89.97	51.99
26	Kudremukh Iron Ore Co. Ltd.	6345.1	63.45	1.00	99.00	11.40
27	Madras Refineries Ltd.@	1436.1	242.99	16.92	53.80**	0.00
28	Mahanagar Telephone Nigam Ltd.	6000.0	2628.00	43.80*	56.20	2360.07
29	Minerals & Metals Trading Corp. Ltd.@	500.0	3.35	0.67	99.33	0.00

(Table Contd...)

Table 3: (Contd...)

Sl. No.	Name of the PSE	Total Shares (in lakhs)	Shares divested (in lakhs)	% shares divested	% age of Government holding as on 31.3.1999	Amount realized excluding 1991-92 (Rs. in Crores)@
30	National Aluminium Co. Ltd.	12886.2	1655.88	12.85	87.15	244.30
31	National Fertilizers Ltd.	4905.8	115.29	2.35	97.65	1.00
32	National Mineral Development Corp. Ltd.	1282.0	20.77	1.62	96.36**	17.88
33	Neyveli Lignite Corp. Ltd.	17967.8	1079.86	6.01	93.99	70.43
34	Oil & Natural Gas Corp.	13959.2	2286.52	16.38	83.62	3746.67
35	Rashtriya Chemicals & Fertilizers Ltd.	5516.9	413.77	7.50	92.50	30.36
36	Shipping Corporation of India Ltd.	2823.0	561.21	19.88	80.12	28.08
37	State Trading Corp.	175.6	15.75	8.97	91.03	2.25
38	Steel Authority of India Ltd.	41304.0	5856.91	14.18*	85.82	736.06
39	VSNL	921.7	433.20	47.00*	53.00	1239.53
	1991-92@					3038.00
	Reconciliation difference					644.29
	Total	**159905.5**	**25327.22**	**15.84**		**18532.55**

Source: Ministry of Disinvestment, GOI.

@PSE-wise amounts realized fro 1991-92 are not available since the shares were sold in bundles in that year.

* Including dilution of Government shareholding by public issues/GDR issues.

** The Balance equity is held by state governments/other collaborators.

Table 4: Strategic Disinvestment beginning 1999-2000

Sr. No.	Name	GOI Equity sold (in million)	Realization (Rs. in crores)	Govt. borrows @ 10%; Interest on realization annually	Dividend recd by Govt. on equity sold average of last 8 years up to 2000
1a.	MFIL	9.63	105	10.5	0.48
1b.	MFIL – Phase II	3.38	44**	4.4	0.17
2.	BALCO	112.52	826.5*	82.65	5.69
3.	CMC	7.73	152	15.2	0.8
4.	HTL	11.1	55	5.5	0.29
5.	LJMC	0.77	2.53	0.25	Nil
	ITDC-19 HOTELS				
6.	Agra	1.70	3.61	0.36	NIL ## (Annual Loss 1.51)
7.	Bodhgaya	0.44	1.81	0.18	NIL ## (AL 0.30)
8.	Hassan	0.21	2.27	0.23	NIL ## (AL 0.63)
9.	Mamallapuram	0.83	6.13	0.61	NIL ## (AL 0.51)
10.	Madurai	0.71	4.97	0.50	NIL ## (AL 0.89)
11.	Bangalore	0.96	39.41(up-front fee); (4.11 – MGAP)	6.00 *	NIL ## (AL 1.78)
12.	Qutab	0.83	34.46	3.85 *	NIL ## (AL 0.2)

(Table Contd...)

Table 4: (Contd...)

Sr. No.	*Name*	*GOI Equity sold (in million)*	*Realization (Rs. in crores)*	*Govt. borrows @ 10%; Interest on realization annually*	*Dividend recd by Govt. on equity sold average of last 8 years up to 2000*
13.	Lodhi	0.96	71.93	8.68 *	NIL ## (AL 2.0)
14.	LVPH, Udaipur	0.55	6.77	0.68	NIL ## (AL 1.0)
15.	Manali	0.63	3.65	0.37	NIL ## (AL 0.3)
16.	Kovalam	1.85	40.39	4.04	NIL ## (AL 1.9)
17.	Aurangabad	1.16	16.50	1.65	NIL ## (AL 1.1)
18.	Airport Kolkata	0.66	19.39	1.94 *	NIL ## (AL 2.6)
19.	Khajuraho	0.97	2.19	0.22	NIL ## (AL 0.80)
20.	Varanasi	1.74	8.38	0.84	NIL ## (AL 1.9)
21.	Kanishka	1.90	92.37	10.97 *	NIL ## (AL 7.6)
22.	Indraprastha (AYN)	0.80	43.39	5.18 *	NIL ## (AL 3.4)
23.	Chandigarh project	7.00	17.27	2.03 *	Incomplete project
24.	Ranjit	3.20	29.20	2.92	NIL ## (AL 3.2)
	Sub-total	**27.10**	**444.09**	**51.25**	**NIL ## (AL 31.6)**
	HCI-3 HOTELS				

(Table Contd...)

Table 4: (Contd...)

Sr. No.	*Name*	*GOI Equity sold (in million)*	*Realization (Rs. in crores)*	*Govt. borrows @ 10%; Interest on realization annually*	*Dividend recd by Govt. on equity sold average of last 8 years up to 2000*
25.	Juhu, Bombay	8.95	153	15.3	NIL ## (AL 1.56)
26.	Rajgir	1.72	6.51	0.65	NIL ## (Profit 0.32)
27.	Airport, Mumbai	4.0	83	9.96 *	NIL ## (AL 3.24)
	Sub-total	**14.67**	**242.51**	**25.91 ***	**NIL ## (AL 4.48)**
28.	IBP	7.44	1153.68	115.36	1.84
29.	VSNL	71.25	3689^	368.9	10.4
30.	STC	—	40	4	—
31.	MMTC	—	60	6	—
32.	PPL	320.16	151.70	15.17	(-) 71#
33.	JESSOP	68.13	18.18 **	1.82	(-) 55#

(Table Contd...)

Table 4: (Contd...)

Sr. No.	Name	GOI Equity sold (in million)	Realization (Rs. in crores)	Govt. borrows @ 10%; Interest on realization annually	Dividend recd by Govt. on equity sold average of last 8 years up to 2000
34.	Hindustan Zinc Ltd.	109.85	445	44.5	3.5
35.	Maruti Udyog	66.00	2424 ^^ **	242.4	13
36.	IPCL	64.5	1490.84	149	16.24
	Grand Total	**894.23**	**11344.03**	**1142.79**	**- 73.59**

Source: Ministry of Disinvestment, GOI.

• Including NPV of future earnings on MGAP & lease rentals

** expected

Loss making for latest years

^ including dividend & dividend. Tax

^^ Minimum amount to be received over 3 tranches; could go up to Rs. 3158 cr.

Restructuring/Conversion of Loan into equity & waiver of interest - hence a loss. Companies at Sr. No. 5, 23, 25, 26, 27 & 33 are subsidiaries.

Sale at 33 to be approved by Government/BIFR

• Includes proceeds from the sale of 51% equity (amounting to Rs. 551.50 crores), Rs. 244 cr. from the capital restructuring of BALCO, and another Rs. 31 cr. as tax on this amount, prior to disinvestment.

higher realizations from the strategic partner, especially since the latter has to offer the same price to other shareholders also through an open offer.

- The minority sales also give the impression that the main objective of the Government is to obtain funds for reducing its fiscal deficit, and not to improve performance or governance.

Strategic sale

It can be also called strategic disinvestment or privatization and means the sale of a portion or whole of Government equity along with transfer of management control.

Because of the above disadvantages of minority sales the Government of India, decided to adopt the policy of strategic sale or strategic disinvestment from the year 1999-2000 onwards.

The list of PSUs that have been privatized is given in Table 4 & 6 Till November 2002, about 14 PSUs have been privatized.

The Government has received Rs. 11344.03/- crores from these sales during the period 1999-2000 to November 2002. Some sales also lead to annual revenue. The Government of India's borrowing rate is of the order of 10%. Hence, this realization would lead to a benefit of Rs. 1142 crores to the country every year in perpetuity. As against this benefit, the dividends received by Government on its equity, which has been sold, averaged Rs. 52.41 crores during the last eight years. However, PPL and Jessop led to an average annual outgo of Rs. 126 crores as shown in the Table 4. Thus, the Government lost Rs. 73.59 crores ever year due to its majority equity presence in these companies. The sales of part of equity in 16 companies would bring an annual real benefit to the economy to the tune of Rs.1140 + 73 = Rs. 1213 crores. There can be no justification for maintaining public sector character in these industries, if the taxpayer has to lose more than Rs. 1213 crores every year by non-privatization.

There is often an argument that the Government should not sell profit-making companies. BALCO was a profit making company, which earned the Government an average dividend (over eight years) of Rs. 5.69 crores every year on the equity sold. As shown in Table 4, the Government would now get Rs. 82.65 crores every year. CMC was a very well managed and profitable company, yet the average dividend was only 0.80 crores. The Government's benefit now is Rs. 15.2 crores annually. Similarly, Maruti Udyog Ltd. gave average returns to the tune of Rs. 13 crores annually to the Govt. and IPCL gave Rs. 16.24 crores on equity sold against Rs. 242 crores and 149 crores respectively which can be expected now. There can possibly be no justification of maintaining public sector character in such companies. The argument can be multiplied in each sale implemented so far.

Before the year 2000, the Government had primarily sold minority shares in public sector companies. The price realized through the sale of shares, even in blue chip companies like IOC, BPCL, HPCL, GAIL & VSNL was low as the Table 7 showing Price to Earning Ratios would indicate. On the other hand, the prices realized through strategic disinvestment have been very high.

Trends in Privatization

PSEs were chosen for divestment on the basis of likelihood of raising maximum revenue through the public offering, since one of the main goals and stated reasons for divestment was to raise revenue for the Government. Thus the companies where the Government has divested a stake have been generally large profitable companies.

Table 6: Privatized PSUs, Month and Buyer

Company	*Month*	*Buyer*
CMC	Sept-01	Tata Sons
HTL Limited	Oct-01	Himachal Futuristic Communications Limited (HFCL)
ITDC:		
1.Hotel Agra Ashok	Feb-02	Mohan Singh
2.Hotel Madurai Ashok	Jan-02	Sangu Chakra Hotels Pvt Ltd.
3. Hotel Bodhgaya Ashok	Nov-01	Lotus Trans Travel Pvt. Ltd.
4. Hotel Hassan Ashok	Nov-01	Malnad Hotels and Resorts Pvt. Ltd.
5. TABR, Mamallapuram	Feb-02	G.R Thanga Maligai Ltd.
6. Hotel Ashok Bangalore	Nov-01	Bharat Hotels Ltd.
7. Qutab Hotel, New Delhi	Feb-02	Sushil Gupta & consortium
8. Lodhi Hotel, New Delhi	Feb-02	Silverlink Holdings Ltd.
9. LVPH, Udaipur	Feb-02	Bharat Hotels Ltd.
10.Hotel Manali Ashok	May-02	Auto Impex Ltd.
11. KABR, Kovalam	May-02	M Far Hotels Ltd.
12. Hotel Aurangabad Ashok	May-02	Lok Sangam Hotels & Resorts Pvt. Ltd.
13. Hotel Airport Ashok, Kolkata	May-02	Bright Enterprises Pvt. Ltd.
14. Hotel Khajuraho Ashok	Aug-02	Bharat Hotels Ltd.
15. Hotel Varanasi Ashok	Aug-02	Ram Nath Hotels Pvt. Ltd.
16. Hotel Project at Chandigarh	Oct-02	Taj GVK Hotels & Resorts Limited
17. Hotel Kanishka, New Delhi.	Oct-02	Nehru Place Hotels Limited
18. Hotel Indraprastha, New Delhi	Oct-02	Moral Trading & Investment Ltd.
19. Hotel Ranjit	Oct-02	Unison Hotels Ltd. & Formax Commercial Pvt. Ltd.
VSNL	Feb-02	Tata Group
IBP	Feb-02	IOC
Paradeep phosphates Ltd.	Feb-02	Zuari Maroc Phosphates
Jessop & Co.	Feb-02	Ruia Kotex

(Table Contd...)

Table 6: (Contd...)

Company	*Month*	*Buyer*
Hindustan Zinc Ltd.	Feb-02	Sterlite Industries
HCI-3 HOTELS		
1. Hotel Juhu, Mumbai	Oct-01	Tulip Hospitality
2. Hotel Rajgir	Oct-01	Inpec Travels
3. Hotel Airport, Mumbai	Oct-01	A.L Batra hospitality Services
IPCL	May-02	Reliance Industries
Maruti Udyog Ltd.	May-02	Suzuki Motor Corp.
LJMC	Jun-2000	Murlidhar Ratanlal Exports Ltd.
Modern Food Industries Ltd.	Jan-2000	Hindustan Lever Ltd.
BALCO	Mar-01	Sterlite Industries

Source: Ministry of Disinvestment, GOI.

On the other hand, it has been observed more often than not that while large, Profit making PSUs are attracting potential buyers and are being sold off easily, their loss making and less profit-making (occasionally profit-making) counterparts (PSUs) are not able to attract the potential buyers, hence generally finding no takers.

PSUs which could not be privatized

The table 5 shows the PSUs returned (those, which were offered for disinvestment by the Ministry of Disinvestment, but were returned back for the want of buyers).

Table 5: PSUs which could not be privatized

S.No.	*Name of Public Sector Enterprise*
1	Bharat Breaks & Valves Limited (BBVL)
2	Bharat Pumps & Compressors Ltd. (BPCL)
3	Hindustan Insecticides Ltd. (HIL)
4	National Industrial Development Corporation (NIDC)
5	Praga Tools Ltd.
6	Scooters India Ltd. (SIL)

Source: Ministry of Disinvestment, GOI.

Conclusion

As already mentioned, it is the large, profit-making PSUs, which are the most favourite candidates for disinvestment for the Government and the most attractive for the potential buyers, but there are few or generally no takers for the loss making ones. If the same trend continues then the Government will be left with less profitable PSUs.

Table 7: Price to Earning Ratios

Sale of Shares Vs. Strategic Disinvestment

	Sale of Shares 1991-99		*Strategic Disinvestment 2000-2002*	
1.	IOC	4.9	BALCO	19
2.	BPCL	5.7	CMC	12
3.	HPCL	5.9	HTL	37
4.	GAIL	4.4	MFIL	very high as earning per share was negative.
5.	VSNL	6.0 (in monopoly days)	LJMC	- do-
6.			PPL	- do-
7.			JESSOP	- do-
8.			IBP	63
9			VSNL	11 (inclusive of income from dividend etc.) (after the end of monopoly)
10.			HZL	26
11.			MARUTI	89
12.			IPCL	58

Source: Ministry of Disinvestment, GOI.

Moreover, the Indian disinvestment programme suffers a great deal from a wide divergence between Targets and Actual receipts from disinvestment (refer Table 8 & 9). With an exception of some years, the actual receipts from

Table 8: Actual Disinvestment from April 1991 onwards and Methodologies Adopted

Year	*No. of Companies in which equity sold*	*Target receipt for the year (Rs In Crore)*	*Actual receipts (Rs In Crore)*	*Methodology*
1991-92	47 (31 in one tranche and 16 in other)	2500	3038	Minority shares sold by auction method in bundles of "very good", "good", and "average" companies.
1992-93	35 (in 3 tranches)	2500	1913	Bundling of shares abandoned. Shares sold separately for each company by auction method.
1993-94	—	3500	Nil	Equity of 7 companies sold by open auction but proceeds received in 94-95.
1994-95	13	4000	4843	Sale through auction method, in which NRIs and other persons legally permitted to buy, hold or sell equity, allowed to participate.
1995-96	5	7000	362	Equities of 4 companies auctioned and Government piggy backed in the IDBI fixed price offering for the fifth company.
1996-97	1	5000	380	GDR (VSNL) in international market.
1997-98	1	4800	902	GDR (MTNL) in international market.

(Table Contd...)

Table 8: (Contd...)

Year	*No. of Companies in which equity sold*	*Target receipt for the year (Rs In Crore)*	*Actual receipts (Rs In Crore)*	*Methodology*
1998-99	5	5000	5371	GDR (VSNL)/Domestic offerings with the participation of FIIs (CONCOR, GAIL). Cross purchase by 3 Oil sector companies i.e. GAIL, ONGC & Indian Oil Corporation
1999-00	2	10000	1829	GDR—GAIL VSNL-domestic issue, BALCO restructuring, MFIL's strategic sale and others
2000-01	4	10000	1870	Strategic sale of BALCO, LJMC; Takeover - KRL (CRL), CPCL (MRL), BRPL
2001-02	10	12, 000	5632 #	Strategic sale of CMC – 51%, HTL –74%, VSNL – 25%, IBP – 33.58%, PPL— 74%, and sale by other modes: ITDC & HCI; surplus reserves: STC and MMTC
2002-03	6	12, 000	4777 #	Strategic sale of JESSOP-72%, HZL – 26%, MFIL-26%, IPCL – 25% and other modes: HCI, Maruti
Total	**48 ***	**78, 300**	**30917#**	

Source: Ministry of Disinvestment, GOI.

* Total number of companies in which disinvestment has taken place so far.

\# Figures (inclusive of amount expected to be realized, control premium, dividend/dividend tax and transfer of surplus cash reserves prior to disinvestment etc.)

Disinvestment were far less than the targeted levels, thus leading to a wide divergence. Unless this is narrowed down, the Indian disinvestment programme is not likely to taste success and the very objectives of Disinvestment may not be fulfilled. This divergence between targets and actual receipts from disinvestment is shown in the figure 1.

Table 9: Targets and Actual receipts from the Disinvestment Programme

Year	*Target receipt for the year (Rs in Crores)*	*Actual receipts (Rs. in Crores)*	*Divergence (Rs. in Crores)*
1991-92	2500	3038	+538
1992-93	2500	1913	-587
1993-94	3500	Nil	-3500
1994-95	4000	4843	+843
1995-96	7000	362	-6, 638
1996-97	5000	380	-4, 620
1997-98	4800	902	-3, 898
1998-99	5000	5371	+371
1999-00	10000	1829	-8, 171
2000-01	10000	1870	-8, 130
2001-02	12, 000	5632 #	-6, 368
2002-03ψ	12, 000	4777 #	-7, 223
Total	**78, 300**	**30917#**	**-47383**

Source: Ministry of Disinvestment, GOI.

\# Figures (inclusive of amount expected to be realized, control premium, dividend/dividend tax and transfer of surplus cash reserves prior to disinvestment etc.)

ψ Till November 2002.

REFERENCES

1. Arun, T.G and Nixon, F.I (2000): "The Disinvestment of Public Sector Enterprises: The Indian Experience", Oxford Development Studies, vol.28, No.1, 2000.

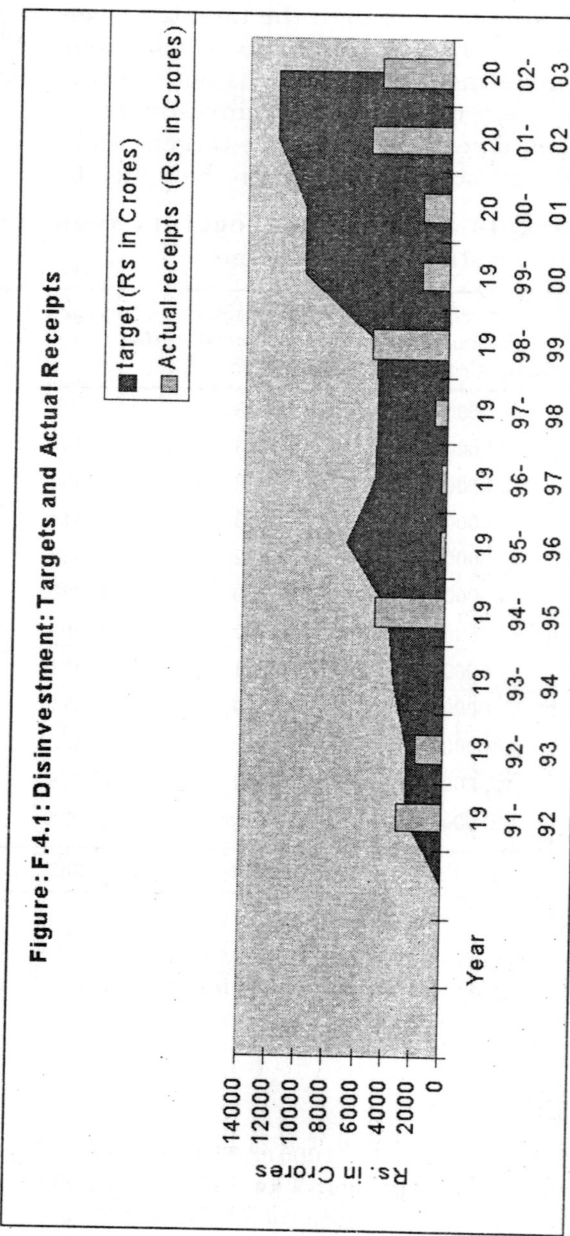

Fig. 1 Disinvestment: Targets and Actual Receipts

2. Budget Papers (various years), Ministry of Finance, Government of India.
3. Dhameja, N & Sastry, K.S (1998): *'Privatization: Theory and Practice'*, Wheeler Publishing, New Delhi.
4. Disinvestment Commission Reports I-XII, Government of India.
5. Ganesh, G: *'Privatization Experience around the world'*, Mittal Publication, 1997.
6. Gouri, Geeta: "Public Enterprise Restructuring", in *'Privatization and Public Enterprise: The Asia Pacific Experience.* (ed.), Geeta Gouri, Oxford & IBH, 1991.
7. Government of India: *Public Enterprises Survey*, 2000-01 (New Delhi, Department of Public Enterprises, Ministry of Industry).
8. Government of India (1991-2002): *Economic Survey,* 1991-92 to 2001-02 (New Delhi, Ministry of Finance).
9. Rangarajan Committee Report: *Report of the Committee on Disinvestment of Government shareholding in Public Sector Enterprises*, Government of India, April 1993.
10. Statement on Industrial Policy, Ministry of Industry, Government of India, July 1991.
11. World Bank Report (study) on Reform of Public Sector Management, September 1991.

20

FDI and Export competitiveness in India

*Pravakar Sahoo**

The wave of globalisation and liberalisation sweeping across the world has highlighted the role of exports in boosting the economic growth of countries. Another important factor for growth in recent years has been Foreign Direct Investment (FDI) which enhances the export competitiveness (Heplman *et al*, 2003; Mary *et al*, 2002; Young, 1995 and Atiken *et al*, 1997) FDI is undoubtedly the good side of globalisation which is reflected by unparalleled expansion of international capital in recent decades. FDI in India as in most part of the world is seen as a means to supplement domestic investment for achieving a higher level of economic growth and development. The total FDI in 2001-2002 is US $ 4.06 billion and FDI inflows into India are expected to touch US$ 8 billion in the next couple of years. Infact, lately one can also see a link between FDI and technology exports enhancing the export competitiveness of a country. A considerable body of research by UNCTAD, ESCAP and World Bank shows that the late industrialising countries (for example Japan and subsequently S. Korea) acquired technology from abroad instead of 're-inventing the wheel' in each case, thereby

* Faculty, RBI Endowment Unit, Institute of Economic Growth (IEG), North Campus, Delhi University Enclave, Delhi-110007.

saving time and resources. FDI is the cheapest and most effective way of obtaining latest technology from abroad instead of direct purchasing of capital goods or licensing. It is essential that proper bargaining takes place between the host country and foreign investor with regard to conditions of investment including local content, the transfer of R &D activities as part of FDI, and the technology to be transferred.

To upgrade the primary and labour intensive exports into higher value-added items, developing countries move into new, more advanced inputs and technology. These countries can attain these objectives by improving and deepening the capabilities of domestic enterprises; by tapping into Transnational Corporation (TNC) networks ad conduits of trade or by attracting FDI into export activities. Considering the beneficial effects such as creation of new employment, transfer of technology & strengthening of domestic capabilities and enhancement of marketing expertise, FDI is encouraged in these countries as TNCs bring technology, which helps the host country to improve its export competitiveness and economic growth. In recent years, export promotion is the key reason for the government's desire to attract FDI. The government uses FDI to channelise capital and upto date technology into industries that have the potential to compete internationally. This has been reflected through an unparalleled expansion of international capital in recent decades. The World FDI flows rose from $ 644 billion in 1998 to $ 1.3 trillion in 2001 growing annually at 18 per cent, faster than other economic aggregates like world production, capital formation and trade. The global expansion of investment flows is driven by more than 60, 000 TNCs with over 80, 000 affiliates abroad (Mathur, 2002). The experience of China, Singapore and other East Asian countries support FDI-led export growth theory and show that international competitiveness and export capabilities are closely linked to R&D, innovation capabilities of FDI and technology exports in a country.

There have been a large number of studies in the recent years that technical and technology export capabilities and performance are increasingly important factors in enhancing the international competitiveness of a nation and of an enterprise in the emerging knowledge driven economy (Heplman *et al*, 2003; Young, 1995 and Atiken *et al*, 1997). Some of the other factors usually considered for international competitiveness include investments or capital, market size, population, GDP, per capita income, labour costs, domestic demand and exports etc. The World Investment Report (WIR), 2002 rightly points out that export composition has shifted from primary products to high technology manufacturing products and the importance of new developed technology through FDI has become an essential element in government policies of many developing countries (see table-1 and table-2). Table-1 indicates that the share of manufactures in total exports of South Asian and East Asian countries is generally about 90 per cent except Sri Lanka and Thailand. Further, manufactured exports of South Korea, China and Taiwan etc. are more of high value added or more technology intensive nature than that of India. Table–2 reports comparative details of the intensity of technology exports of various other developing countries. The annual studies being done by IIFT with the support of DSIR, about technology intensive exports of India for the years 1994-95 to 1999-2000, estimated at Rs. 26, 734 crores during 1999-2000, having a share of 16.75% in total exports, and registered an increase of 31.92% over the previous year. Technology intensive exports may be treated differently than high tech exports. Exports of construction contracts during 1999-2000 registered the highest growth of 79.30 per cent

This explains the importance, which the MNCs and TNCs have in increasing the export share of several

Table 1: Share of Manufactures in Total Exports of Select Countries of Asian Region

Country	*1990*	*1997*	*1999*
		SOUTH ASIA	
Bangladesh	77	87.5[a]	92
India	72	74.0[a]	81
Nepal	83	89.4	97
Pakistan	76	86.1	90
Sri Lanka	53	70.2[b]	77
		EAST ASIA	
China	73	86.7	90
Hong Kong	96	95.6	96
Indonesia	36	55.4	56
Korea	93	88.1	93
Malaysia	55	78.5	82
Philippines	68	87.6	90
Singapore	73	86.9[c]	87
Taiwan	93	94.3[c]	96[c]
Thailand	61	73.3	75

Note: [a]1996, [b]1994, [c]1998

Source: International Trade Centre & Export Performance: Increasing Competitiveness through new sources of productivity growth (occasional paper 18, 2001), by Prof. B. Bhattacharyya, Dean, IIFT, New Delhi.

developing countries, particularly shifting the export composition from primary and labour intensive products to high technology manufacturing products (Heplman *et al*, 2003; Mary *et al*, 2002; Young, 1995 and Atiken *et al*, 1997). One of the primary objectives of attracting FDI in India is to enhance the international competitiveness of industries and thereby exports, besides bringing long term additional capital for economic growth.

However, after one decade of economic reforms and government initiatives to attract FDI, there has not been

Table 2: Technology Intensive Manufacture Exports

(Value in US$ million, growth in % p.a.)

Group of Products	*Value 1999*	*Growth 95-99*	*Share in exports*
China	57, 629	17	30
Hong kong	6, 719	-10	30
India	4, 724	8	14
Korea	65, 059	5	46
Malaysia	49, 300	9	58
Philippines	24, 450	29	71
Singapore	82, 677	1	72
Taiwan	69, 711	8	58
Thailand	23, 766	6	41

Source: International Trade Centre UNCTAD/WTO

any substantial gain in FDI towards export promotion. This forces to look at the experience of China and Singapore where FDI has contributed in a big manner in improving their export competitiveness and volume of exports, particularly the technology-intensive exports.

China:-Technology-intensive exports in China constitute around 30 % of the total exports and it has been growing at the annual rate of 17 % (1995-1999), which is highest among different kinds of exports (International Trade Centre, WTO). In recent years, China is exporting more than 300 technical products in the field of electronics, information, aerospace, optics, digital or computer programmed machinery, space and ocean engineering technologies. Some of these commodities are principal exports in the Chinese export basket contributing substantially to its total exports. In 1986, Foreign Investment Enterprises (FIE's, China's definition of firms with foreign investment) exported just over 2 % of the total exports (US $ 500 million of US 30 billion dollar). However, the share of FIE's in total exports has increased to around 50 % in 2002, thereby reflecting the close link between foreign investment and Exports. China is the third largest producer of computer and peripheral products and largest manufacturer of many consumer durables such as colour television, washing machines and refrigerators, revealing the role of foreign investment and technology-intensive manufacturing products. More than half of China's major electronics, telecommunication equipment and engendering firms are foreign invested firms. Armed with foreign technology and foreign capital, the electronics industry alone is exporting more than 10 per cent of the total exports. High volume of FDI along with continued economic reforms, China has been able to import updated technical know-how to develop a wide range of high tech products and enterprises, matching international standards and competitiveness. The most important aspect is that, China has been able to attract huge FDI by pumping large investment into its R&D sector. As a result its export competitiveness has improved substantially over the years and its domestic industry is also established in the international market due to appropriate policies of the Chinese government. China undoubtedly is a classic example of high exports with high technology exports due to huge FDI inflow.

On an average, about 70 % of FDI inflows into China are in the form of equipment and technology. Of the different forms of FDI, namely, equity, wholly owned subsidiaries and contractual joint ventures, there is a maximum contribution of 15 % that technology and industrial property rights can form as part of the capital structure of a joint venture company. This form of FDI is considered to be the most effective channel for the acquisition of advanced technology and management. To sum up, China has been successful in attracting huge FDI along with developed technology due to conducive government policies such as: (i) MNCs and TNCs bringing advanced technology and capital are exempt from both business and income tax, and (ii) technology related equipments, components and spares brought into China for ungradation of joint ventures or for foreign invested research and development centers are exempt from import duty. Moreover, the simplified labour laws with conducive government policies for FDI firms make China as one of the most suitable platforms for manufacturing for foreign firms. This is clearly reflected in recent years where many of the big MNCs and TNCs have shifted their manufacturing units to China, for example, Japanese electronics and telecommunication industries.

*Singapore:-*Singapore is another example of FDI supporting the national export effort which has successfully transformed its export composition towards technology and knowledge-based industries. The annual average inflow of FDI into Singapore amounted to about US $ 8 billion from 1995 to 1998. Exports are dominated by electronic products (60 %), chemicals and chemical products (8 %), petroleum products and machinery respectively. Each of these four leading export industries (i.e. electronics, chemicals, petroleum products and machinery) has also been the recipient of the largest amounts of FDI. The share of foreign investment is extremely high in these leading export sectors; for example the share of foreign equity is 86 % in electronics and 87 % in chemicals. Also, it is very interesting to note that foreign subsidiaries have a much higher export orientation than the domestic firms in Singapore. In 1997, the export-to-sales ratio was as high as 70 % for wholly owned foreign subsidiaries. Thus the success of Singapore and also East Asian in boosting its export shows the close link between FDI and Exports (ESCAP, 2001).

Both Singapore and China have successfully directed foreign investment in high technology exports through different industrial policies like, directing FDI into high value added activities, emphasising MNCs and TNCs to increase R & D expenditure, allowing public sector for FDI, pushing FDI into specialised high technology export market. As a result there has been a dramatic increase in the share of local companies in the total industrial investment, output and also in total exports of the country. Overall, China, Singapore and also East Asian countries followed three broad policies to give a boost to high value-added export industry such as (i) open door policies on FDI without any substantial government intervention, particularly in export oriented industries; (ii) allowed participation of TNCs in manufacturing but intervened selectively to guide investors in directions towards technological activity considered to be desirable for industrial upgrading, and (iii) allowed collaborative arrangements with set of policies to deepen the manufacturing sector, promote local linkages and increase local innovative capabilities

Foreign Direct Investment and Export Competitiveness in India: India could be an attractive destination for FDI which will boost technology exports in the country for following reasons, (1) huge and growing consumer market, (2) easy access to markets of east and south-east countries, (3) availability of skilled manpower and professional managers at competitive cost, (4) strong and mature private sector accounting for 75 per cent of the GDP, (5) abundance of natural resources and (6) agricultural self-sufficiency and developed banking system with network of 61, 000 branches all over the country.

The FDI-led technological promotion would benefit domestic industries as well as the Indian consumers by providing opportunities for technological upgradation, access to global managerial skills and practices, optimum utilization of human and natural resources, making Indian industries internationally competitive. Moreover, the global linkages of TNCs and MNCs can facilitate their access to foreign markets creating new export markets, providing forward and backward linkages, and access to international quality goods and services. In this context, some favouable policies have taken place to attract FDI into export-oriented and high value-added sectors like: (1) access to the automatic route for FDI (except for a small negative list), (2) access to telecom services (74 per cent), insurance sector (26 per cent) and banking sector, (3) permission for foreign technology collaborations through the automatic route and creation of 100 per cent export oriented units/ export processing zones/special economic zones, electronic hardware technology park and software technology park schemes and (4) facilitation for FDI proposals through Foreign Investment Promotion Board (FIPB), Foreign Investment Implementation Authority (FIIA), Foreign Investment Promotion Council (FIPC), and Secretariat for Industrial Assistance (SIA, December, 2001)

In India, Foreign Technical Agreements (FTA's) were at their peak in early nineties but have declined since then, FTA's numbered 660 in 1997 and 247 in 2001. Infact there is a steep decline in FTA's as a percentage of total FDI approvals establishing the fact that in the case of India, at present, FTA'S and FDI do not go hand in hand (see table-3 and table-4). However, since technical collaboration is part of the foreign investment now, it is difficult to get the clear picture whether technical transfers take place at the same speed along with foreign investment. Moreover, FDI approvals have consistently risen since 1991, the actual inflow (around 20 to 25 % of approvals) of FDI has been far below the actual amount approved. But this cannot negate the fact that there is a vast scope for increasing actual FDI in the country along with FTA's as the recent budget 2002-03 and the EXIM policy 2002-07 has provided many sops to increase technology related exports. For instance, the software industry in India is a good example of technology intensive exports from India as nearly 19 % of total softerware exports are contributed by 79 foreign subsidiaries. However, despite the entry of several major IT MNE's into the country and the belting up of subsidiaries and joint ventures for software development, FDI inflow has not been substantial (Totaling US$ 115 million by 1999).

Table 3: Approvals of FDI in India and Foreign Technical Agreements: 1991-2001

Years	*1991-95 (Ave)*	*1996*	*1997*	*1998*	*1999*	*2000*	*2001*
Number of FTAs approved	791	744	660	595	498	418	247
Number of FDI proposals approved	837	1559	1665	1191	1726	1726	1590
Amount Approved in (Rs.crore)	11908	36147	54891	30814	28367	37039	23266
Actual inflow of FDI (Rs. Crore)	2584	10389	16425	13340	16868	19342	16127

Source: Economic Survey 2001-02 (Jan-October)

Table 4: Foreign Investment as a percentage of GDP

Year	*Foreign Investment as a % of GDP*	*Foreign Direct Investment as a % of GDP*
1990-91	0.03	0.03
1994-95	1.6	-
1995-96	1.4	-
1996-97	1.6	-
1997-98	1.3	-
1998-99	0.6	0.6
1999-00	1.1	0.5
2000-01	1.1	0.4

Source: India Development Report, 2002 and Economic survey: 2001-02

The increasing rate of FDI is a positive reflection of global interest in India and the ease of entry into the country. Though, USA has traditionally been the largest foreign investor (accounting nearly 20% of total FDI inflow), other leading investor countries have been Mauritius, UK, South Korea, Japan, Germany, Australia, Malaysia, France and Netherlands. The inflow from Mauritius has been substantial in recent years since investment is being routed through Mauritius. The small island managed to double its per capita income (with unemployment rate less than 2 %) in last two decades by giving special tax incentives along with creation of special export processing zones. This only further proves the fact that FDI is an important pre-requisite for increased economic growth.

In order to attain an annual foreign investment inflow of US $ 7.5 billion per year and 8 per cent economic growth in the Tenth Five-Year Plan, a high power committee under Planning Commission member Shri N.K. Singh has favoured (FDI Report, 2002) enhancing FDI limits in telecom, insurance, civil aviation, non-retail trading, banking, plantations (other than tea, real estate) and others. The Committee has made some other major recommendations. These are (i) giving national treatment to foreign firms (ii) making foreign investment in most sectors automatic by removing controls from FIPB and FIIA (iii) allow up to 49 per cent investment in insurance and airlines (including FDI by foreign airlines) and (iv) permit up to 100 per cent FDI in petroleum refining, oil marketing, diamond mining, petroleum exploration, coal washery, airports, banking and investing companies, radio paging, advertising and trade, putting all proposals (except plantation and housing with only 49 per cent) on automatic route.

The opening up of capital-intensive infrastructure industries such as power, telecom and oil has boosted FDI in some of these sectors in India. Infact, most of the commodities in the top 10 exports of India also happen to be the major recipients of FDI (accounting around 30 % of total FDI inflows). Some of the top exports of India such as engineering; electronics, electrical equipment, pharmaceuticals and chemicals are also the sectors that are attracting a fair amount of FDI. For instance, nearly 12% of the total FDI in the country is in the electronics sector and nearly 4% of the total FDI is going into the pharmaceutical industry. Though FDI has been increasing over the years, foreign investment as a percentage of GDP has remained low over the last decade. Foreign investment as a percentage of GDP was 1.1 percent in 2000-01 and FDI constituted just 0.4% of GDP.

There is a vast scope to increase technology related FDI inflow and technology exports in the country because manufacturing exports have been increasing since the reforms were launched in 1991 and it is in manufacturing that technology is used maximum enhancing the link between FDI and technology exports and thereby export competitiveness. The following table-5 shows total exports of India along with exports of manufactures. Nearly 77 percent of our total exports are manufactures. This enhances the scope for increasing use of technology exports in manufacturing and thereby enhancing export competitiveness of our economy. The export basket of India reveals that there is a scope to increase FDI in textiles, leather, gems and jewellery, machinery and metallic

Table 5: The share of Manufacturing Exports in Total exports

Year	*Total exports (US$ million)*	*Exports of Manufactures (US$ million)*
1980	8501	5105 (60.05)
1990	18477	12996 (70.34)
1999	37542	29714 (79.15)
2000	44894	34511 (76.88)

Note: The figures in parent thesis refer to the share of Manufactures in total

Source: www.worldbank.org

manufactures including steel. Furthermore, oil marketing, food processing, auto and auto components, airports, financial services and real estate are new FDI attractive sectors. India is a preferred destination for sectors requiring skilled labour and steps are being taken by the government to enhance FDI to US $ 10 billion in the next couple of years through FDI and disinvestment policy.

The total FDI in 2001-2002 is US $ 4.06 billion and FDI inflows into India are expected to touch US $ 8 billion in the next couple of years. The Global Competitiveness Report, 2000, ranks India at number one position in terms of liberal regime for the import of foreign technology (Annual Report, DIPP, 2002). The recent budget 2002-03 and the EXIM policy (2002-07) have also provided many sops to increase technology related FDI and exports in some sectors such as automobiles and auto components. As a result of all pro-FDI policies of the government, FDI approvals have been high in high value added industries like telecom (20 per cent), power (16 per cent), oil refinery (12 per cent), electrical equipments (10 per cent), transport (7 per cent) and services (6 per cent) (Annual Report, DIPP, 2002). However, the actual trend (2000-01) shows that, the maximum FDI inflows are in the electrical equipments (22 per cent), services (37.7 per cent) and computers (12.7 per cent).

Government has taken a number of measures to liberalise FDI policy, including allowing upto 100 per cent FDI in airports, courier services, real estate, banking and development of integrated townships including housing. Despite the industrial slowdown, the manufacturing sector performed well which is reflected in the sectors rising share of exports. The exports of manufactures that had been growing at the rate of 46 per cent in 1995-96 increased to 53.96 per cent in 2000-01. However, technology exports as a percentage of total exports continued to be less. In the year 1999 according to the World Development Report

2001, high technology exports comprised 35% of manufactured exports in USA, 32 % in Korea, 17 % in China and only 6 % in India. This shows that there is a fast potential for increasing technology exports from India. Increase in manufactured exports should be complemented by increased in technology exports. Only then can India take rapid strides in enhancing its exports through technology exports and attracting FDI in areas where high technology is used. The role of FDI in enhancing technology intensive exports of India and thereby improving its export competitiveness need hardly be emphasised.

Conclusion

The principal exports of India such as engineering, electronics, electrical equipment, pharmaceuticals and chemicals are also the sectors that are attracting a fair amount of FDI. This could partially establish the fact that there is a link between FDI and exports in India, though it is difficult to say whether FDI is causing increased exports of certain products or that increase in exports of certain items is attracting investment in these sectors. However it is a fact that TNCs played an important role in exports of electronics, automotive and apparel industries in recent years across the countries (WIR, 2002). In India also, services, electronics, electrical components and computers constitute 72 % of FDI inflows under the government (SIA and FIPB) and RBI route. Thus, there is an upward move in FDI flow in these capital intensive and high technology sectors that would contribute to exports. Nearly 77 % of our total exports are manufactured products where technology can play major role in improving market share in the years ahead. Therefore, the importance should be given to FDI bringing home the technology or investing in R & D activities. This would enhance the scope for increasing technology exports, inturn, enhancing export competitiveness of our economy. The export basket of India reveals that there is a scope to increase FDI in textiles sector, leather, gems and Jewellery, machinery and metallic manufactures including steel. However, India's share is around 1.5 per cent and 0.5 per cent of the total FDI and FI inflows to developing countries respectively. Thus there is an immense potential to increase our technology intensive and technology related manufacturing by attracting more FDI to enhance export competitiveness. In this context, the policy makers should take a note of the success stories of China and Singapore on FDI policy and technology exports and should stop politicking over policies, and further economic reforms with more rigor.

REFERENCES

1. Atiken, B., Gordon, H., and Ann, H., (1997), "Spillovers, Foreign Direct Investment, export behaviour", *Journal of International Economics*, Vol.43, No.-1, pp. 103-132.
2. Department of Industrial Policy and Promotion (2002), *Annual Report-2002*, Government of India.
3. ESCAP, (2001), *'Export competitiveness and Sustained Economic Recovery'*, UN publications, New York, .
4. Helpman, E., Melitz, M., and Yeaple, S (2003), "Exports VS FDI", *NBER Working Paper No-9439*, NBER.
5. Mary, H., Larossi, G., and Sokoloft, K, (2002) "Exports of manufacturing Products in East Asia: A Comparative Analysis with the Firm Level data", *World Bank Working Paper*, 2002.
6. Mathur, Vibha, (2002) *'Trade liberalization and Foreign Investment in India: 1991-2001'*, New Century publications, New Delhi, 2002.
7. Planning Commission, (2002)*'Foreign Investment in India'*, Government of India, September 2002.
8. United Nations, *'World Investment Report: 2001 and 2002'*, New York.
9. Young, A, (1995), "The Tyaranny of numbers Confronting the Statistical realities of the East Asian growth Experience", *Quarterly Journal of Economics*, Vol.110, no.2, pp. 641-680.

21

Private Foreign Investment in Liberalized India

An Investigation for Determinants

*M. Jaya Krishna**
*J. Venugopal**

Introduction

Private Foreign Investment (PFI) gained momentum as a result of internal and external financial deregulation in both industrial and developing countries. The cross-border investment depends mainly on the bilateral and multilateral agreements among the nations. In recent past, close integration of national economies, driven by worldwide competitive pressure, economic liberalization, and opening up of new areas to investment have resulted in policy duplication among the countries especially in developing countries. These countries are tuning their policies by imitating advanced nations. In addition, one can observe these changes of developing countries in changing their regimes from import substitution in the 1950s and 1960s to natural resource-led development in the 1970s.

* Dr. M. Jaya Krishna is working in Economics Unit and Shri J. Venugopal is Research Fellow respectively of the Institute for Social and Economic Change, Dr. V.K.R.V. Rao Road, Nagarabhavi, Bangalore 560 072, INDIA.

Further, there has been a move towards structural adjustment and transition to market economies in the 1980s and an increasing role for the private sector in the 1990s.

The need for foreign capital to supplement domestic resources was felt by the developing economies, in view of growing mismatch between their capital requirements and saving capacity. Further, many developing countries view foreign capital as a key element in their development strategy against the other forms of foreign financing, as it aids in upgrading technology in hi-technology concentrated industries. Foreign capital generates employment in the host country when a foreign multinational enterprise directly employs a number of host country citizens. It is argued that PFI would play an important role in the future as a source of capital, managerial expertise, and technology for both the developing economies and economies in transition. The direct and indirect benefits from appropriate PFI are substantially greater than normally assumed, but host countries have problems in realising these flows.

In recent times, PFI flows have continued to expand despite the recession in global trade. Although investments in the developing economies have increased, much of this capital (viz. portfolio capital and trade related lending) has a high degree of volatility. It is subject to massive inflows or outflows resulting from speculative attacks. It has been estimated that the growth rate of global PFI flows during 1960 to 1990 exceeded 10% over that of the growth of global Gross Domestic Product (GDP) resulting in a significant increase in the ratio of PFI to GDP (UNCTC, 1988; UNCTAD, 1993). In the 1990's, PFI has been the single largest source of external finance for developing countries. However, total global PFI accounted for about half of all private capital and 40% of total global flows to developing countries in 1998. Further PFI flows to Asia accounted for 28% of the total. Further, India's share was only 2.27% among South, East and South East Asian countries (UNCTAD, 1998).

India, like many developing countries, has sought capital and technology from developed countries. For more than three decades after independence, India has adopted an approach of self-reliance, protection of national industry and entrepreneurs, import of selective technology and export promotion (Goyal, 1979; Kidron, 1965). Keeping in view the changing pattern of investment in the world, Structural Adjustment Programme (SAP) reflects a major effort to attract PFI for the country, since the adoption of new economic policies in July 1991. [The SAP involves opening up of the economy, it more competitive, getting the Government out of the huge morass of regulations, second generation reforms empowering the States to take more responsibility for economic management. This is believed to have created a conducive atmosphere for competition among them for PFI.]

In India, the role of PFI has grown dramatically over the course of the 1990s, from Rs.326 crores in 1991-92 rose to 21, 773 crores in 1996-97 and again to Rs.28, 275 crores in 2001-02. Likewise, DFI was Rs.316 crores, Rs.10, 015 crores, Rs.18, 658 crores whereas FPI was Rs.10 crores, Rs.11, 758 crores, Rs.9, 617 crores respectively. Further, FII contributes about 80% of the FPI. However, compared to the growth of PFI, DFI and FPI have been quite uneven. The PFI flows were estimated to have an average annual growth of 7.79 whereas DFI recorded a meager of growth rate of 5.3 during the same period. However, FPI scored an average annual growth of 87.3. The high growth is attributed to major policy changes in the new regime to permit higher equity share to foreign investors in high technology and export oriented enterprises and contraction in the products reserved for public sector, notably transport, power and telecommunications.

Many international investors have been coming to India, especially due to superior conditions regarding the rule of law, democracy and the widely spoken English language, availability of skilled labour which are major attracting factors in India, when compared to its neighbors. Further, India provides the second largest market in the world after China. It has not been able to attract substantial volume of PFI when compared to other Asian countries. To understand this, one should know the areas in which foreign investment will flow and minimal acceptable terms on which the foreign investors will be likely to come to the host country. Thus, the present study attempts to analyse the empirical determinants[1] influencing the inflows at present with a view to understanding of the prospects for the magnitude of PFI flows in future, which is a major challenge.

The rest of the paper is organized as follows: Section 2 presents a review of existing studies relevant to the context. Section 3 looks at the sources of data and the variables considered for the study. Section 4 deals with the methodology employed in the paper. While, section 5 presents the empirical results. The last section draws certain conclusions and offers policy suggestions.

A Review of Related Literature

With the increase in foreign investment flows, theoretical and empirical models have evolved to explain and interpret the observed flows of investment funds throughout the world. Many theories[2] have attempted to explain the determinants of foreign investment flows to host countries. As a background to this study, an attempt is made here to present a brief review of selected studies which have a direct relevance to the present study.

A pioneering study by Dunning (1973) identifies the determinants of foreign investment under three categories.

First, market factors such as the size and growth of host country; second, cost factors like the availability of labour or low labour costs; and finally, the investment climate as measured by foreign debt or the balance of payments situation. In an extensive work, Root and Ahmed (1979) empirically describe both demand and supply side determinants by using multiple discriminate analysis across 56 developing countries from 1966 to 1970. The study includes 38 variables to which foreign investment across various countries and identified per capita GDP, economic growth, urbanization, commerce, transport and communication as the most significant demand side variables.

Negating the various determinants of FDI, Lucas (1993) used a simple model for finding determinants of foreign investment by multiple product monopolists for selected East and Southeast Asian countries over the period 1960 to 1987 using log linear OLS and pooled time series data. The empirical evidence reveals that inflows are less elastic with respect to cost of capital than to wages. Further, it is more elastic with aggregate demand in export markets than domestic demand. The results indicate that higher employment costs make production in the host country less attractive than elsewhere, and may also result in substitution of capital for labour. The study concludes that political risk influences the investor's decision to invest.

Using a traditional gravity model, Hufbauer et.al. (1994) analyse important factors that determine for countries like America, Japan and Germany's for the years 1980, 1985 and 1990. The study finds that regionalism plays a significant and consistent role in the investment of stock placements in America and Japan. It says that the size and openness of partner economies are important determinants of the distribution of investment stocks. The findings suggest that firms tend to invest wherever their capital can yield highest return. However, Shamsuddin (1994) explores the economic determinants of PFI by using a single equation econometric model for 36 Less Developed Countries for 1983. Further, the study reports market size of the host country as an important factor in attracting foreign investment than wage cost, per capita debt, energy availability and volatility of price. Besides, the study lists higher wage rate, poor investment climate and economic instability in the host countries contributing to reduced inflows.

Yet another study by Chatterjee and Prajuntaborai (1995) empirically investigates the determinants of foreign investment in Thailand over the period 1978 to 1990 using multiple regression technique. The study finds that market size, home wages and urbanization are significant variables to influence foreign investment inflows to Thailand. Jun and Singh (1996) analyses various determinants of foreign investment in 31 developing countries using 1970-1993 data. The study finds qualitative index of political risk, taxes, industrial disputes and exports are significant. However, export orientation ranks as the strongest exploratory variable attracting investment flows. In the context of India, Gopinath (1997) analyses the factors influencing foreign investment in India over the period 1980-81 to 1994-95 using OLS. The study finds a composite indicator comprising of gross fiscal deficit and debt service ratio being equally important in attracting foreign investment inflows. Both the studies, however, do not test for the stationary property of the variables.

A study by Christian (1998) provides evidence on the determinants of foreign investment from MNCs across 21 host countries over the period 1980 to 1993 using pool time series cross sectional data. The study examines tax variation of countries, GDP and the role of wages in attracting foreign investment inflows. There is an evidence of a positive relationship between investment and export credit for Latin American countries. Further, it suggests the use of a regional policy instrument to rise inflows in South-East Asia.

Recently, Nishat and Aqeel (1998) attempt to identify the determinants of foreign investment in Pakistan over the period 1961 to 1994. Using OLS, the study estimates the macro level determinants using economic, social and political parameters. It is evident that political stability, law and order situation, level of technical labour force and mineral resource exploitation etc. attract foreign investment. The study supports the existing liberal policies in successfully attracting foreign investment in Pakistan. The study suffers from the same limitation as in Gopinath (1997). Where as, Anwar (1999) puts forth analytically interesting determinants like size of the market, openness and political stability, privatization and incentives for foreign investment in host countries.

Around the same time, World Investment Report (UNCTAD, 1998) presents an explanation of the inward foreign investment stocks in 142 countries at intervals between 1980 and 1995. The study shows that market size and institutional factors like political stability and location have some influence among the developing countries. In contrast, it is seen that institutional factors do not influence foreign investment for world economy as a whole. Further, the results report that there is less variation across countries in the recent years.

Yang et.al. (2000) carried out an econometric analysis of the determinants of foreign investment flows into Australia using quarterly data from 1985-1994. The study tests variable stationarity using unit root tests. The results reveal that interest rate, wages, openness and industrial disputes as important determinants of investment flows into

Australia. The estimated model performed well in terms of within sample variability. Howard & Banik (2001) studied determinant of attracting private foreign investment in to Caribbean during 1973-1997 using regression. The study found openness as the important determinant. The study does not consider other variables like infrastructure, skilled labour and market size for the analysis.

A close look at the studies reviewed above reveals that though there are substantial studies explaining the determinants of foreign direct investment but the studies which explains the determinants of PFI inflows especially in the post-reform period are scanty. The present study differs from the existing literature in the following ways. First, in view of the fact that there are no studies are explaining of post-reform determinants of PFI in India or else where, the present study mainly focuses on post-reform period. Second, instead of using the conventional unit root tests such as Dickey-Fuller (DF) and Augmented Dickey-Fuller (ADF), the study employs certain other tests namely Phillips-Peron (PP) and Kwiatkowski, Phillips, Schmidt and Shin (KPSS) to examine the stationary properties of the series to avoid spurious results. Hence, this empirical work is expected to contribute for developing a better understanding of the determinants of PFI in India. The study makes attempt to suggest a suitable combination of variables which could explain the determinants of PFI either through DFI or FPI. This would help for future policy research for developing countries in general and India in particular.

Sources of Data and the Variables Considered

The present study has used quarterly time-series data for the variables in nominal terms over the period September 1991 to June 2001. The dependent variables are PFI, FDI and FPI. This data has been compiled from various issues of the Reports of Currency & Finance published by the

Reserve Bank of India (RBI). In case of explanatory variables, corporate tax (CTAX) and infrastructure (INFRA), exports, imports and Gross Domestic Product (GDP) figures have been collected from various issues of Monthly Abstract of Statistics published by the Central Statistical Organisation of Ministry of Planning & Program Implementation, Government of India. Infrastructure is proxied by the ratio of taxes on income and profits of electricity, gas, water supply, trade, hotels, transport, communication, restaurants and storage to GDP. Openness (OPEN) of the economy is the ratio of imports and exports as a percentage to GDP. The source for number of man days lost on account of labour disputes (MDLOST) is from various issues of the monthly Indian Labour Journal published by the Ministry of Labour, Government of India. Major commercial banks average Call Money Rate (CMR) various of and Bombay stock exchange (BSE) is collected from various issues of the Monthly Bulletin published by the RBI. The stock of science and engineering personnel (SE) are from various Science & Technology Pocketbook published by Department of Science and Technology, Government of India. Exchange rate of the rupee vis-a-vis the special drawing rights (ERATE) have been collected from various issues of the International Financial Statistics of International Monetary Fund. Likewise, outright total Treasure Bills (TBILL), Foreign Institutional Investment (FII), Index of Industrial Production (IIP) is from the Handbook of Indian Economy published by RBI. London Inter Bank Offered Rate[3] (LIBOR) is collected from British Banks Association.

Methodology

In the light of the existing empirical studies, the following models have been estimated with alternative combinations of explanatory variables to identify the determinants of foreign investment inflows to India with the help of multiple regression as specified below:

The model

Private Foreign Investment

$$PFI_t = \beta_0 + \beta_1 BSE_t + \beta_2 CMR_t + \beta_3 CTAX_{(t-1)} + \beta_4 ERATE_t + \beta_5 FII_{(t-1)} + \beta_6 IIP_{(t-1)} + \beta_7 INFRA_{(t-1)} + \beta_8 LIBOR_t + \beta_9 MDLOST_{(t-1)} + \beta_{10} OPEN_{(t-1)} + \beta_{11} SE_{(t-1)} + \varepsilon_t \quad (1)$$

Foreign Direct Investment

$$FDI_t = \beta_0 + \beta_1 BSE_t + \beta_2 CTAX_{(t-1)} + \beta_3 ERATE_t + \beta_4 IIP_{(t-1)} + \beta_5 INFRA_{(t-1)} + \beta_6 LIBOR_t + \beta_7 MDLOST_{(t-1)} + \beta_8 OPEN_{(t-1)} + \beta_9 SE_{(t-1)} + \varepsilon_t \quad (2)$$

Foreign Portfolio Investment

$$FPI_t = \beta_0 + \beta_1 BSE_t + \beta_2 CMR_t + \beta_3 ERATE_t + \beta_4 FII_{(t-1)} + \beta_5 IIP_{(t-1)} + \beta_6 INFRA_{(t-1)} + \beta_7 LIBOR_{(t-1)} + \beta_8 OPEN_{(t-1)} + \beta_9 TBILL_{(t-1)} + \varepsilon_t \quad (3)$$

where t-1 shows the lag of one quarter and ε_t white noise term.

The literature in the recent past has had explosion of unit root tests for testing the stationarity of time series. Unit root tests are generally employed to establish the order of integration. Keeping in mind the problems of size distortion and low power (Maddala and Kim, 1998) of the conventionally used unit root tests like DF and ADF, this study includes PP (1988) and KPSS (1992) tests also to examine the stationary properties of all the series. If a unit root is present at levels, the variables are tested at first difference. Both the tests find variables such as CTAX, FII, IIP, INFRA, MDLOST, OPEN, SE, are non stationary at levels. Given the nature of the variables and the relatively short span of data, tests for a unit root in the first difference (Δ) of all the variables is carried out. It is found that, first difference I(1) form is sufficient to induce stationary in all the variables.

Predictions

As economic theory presumes, along with the current state of the economy, the past economic stability of a nation is obviously an important factor. The adaptive expectations model of foreign capital flows states that if an economy has done well in the past, then investors should have more confidence that it will have economic success in the future as well. The basic purpose of the model is to test whether PFI and openness during the previous quarters (OPEN) of the economy is positively related. Greater openness of the economy encourages both PFI and trade flows implying positive correlation between them, other things remaining the same. BSE ERATE and past FII reflect political stability and strength of external payment positions in the host country and also sentiments of the investors. They are positively related to the investment flows. In contrast, CTAX in the previous quarter is presumed to have an inverse relationship with foreign investment. This is because investors will be considering the ratio of taxes, which acts as a check on the profits. Likewise, if CMR increases, foreign investment will right to increase due to lower domestic investment in the host countries, which encourages foreign investors. TBILL in the previous quarter is expected to be having positive relationship due to the confidence through guarantee issued by host government for the investors. In the case of MDLOST in the last quarter, higher labour disputes are less attractive and discourage foreign capital. They will also result in substitution of capital for labour. Higher stock of diploma, engineering and science graduates during last quarters (SE) reveals the higher rate of unemployment. These results in considerable fall in wages. Therefore, attempts to increase skilled personnel increases unemployment and reduces wages, thereby attracting private foreign investors. This variable has been proxied as availability of cheap skilled and semi skilled labour.

A highly educated labor force with low wages is preferred by MNCs.

Better INFRA in the past in an economy is more attractive to foreign investors. Foreign investment is negatively related to LIBOR which reflects the fact that higher interest rate in the home country discourages investors to go abroad. Direct and positive relationship is presumed between the investment inflows and IIP in the previous quarter, which in turn measures the productivity, performance and industrial growth in the recipient country.

In short, above arguments can be summarized and presented as follows:

$$PFIt = f\,[\overset{(+)}{BSE_t}, \overset{(+)}{CMR_t}, \overset{(-)}{CTAX_{(t-1)}}, \overset{(+)}{ERATEt}, \overset{(+)}{FII_{(t-1)}}, \overset{(+)}{IIP_{(t-1)}},$$

$$\overset{(+)}{INFRA_{(t-1)}}, \overset{(-)}{LIBOR_t}, \overset{(-)}{MDLOST_{(t-1)}}, \overset{(+)}{OPEN_{(t-1)}}, \overset{(+)}{SE_{(t-1)}}]$$

$$DFIt = f\,[\overset{(+)}{BSE_t}, \overset{(-)}{CTAX_{(t-1)}}, \overset{(+)}{ERATE_t}, \overset{(+)}{IIP_{(t-1)}}, \overset{(+)}{INFRA_{(t-1)}},$$

$$\overset{(-)}{LIBOR_t}, \overset{(-)}{MDLOST_{(t-1)}}, \overset{(+)}{OPEN_{(t-1)}}, \overset{(+)}{SE_{(t-1)}}]$$

$$FPIt = f\,[\overset{(+)}{BSE_t}, \overset{(+)}{CMR_t}, \overset{(+)}{ERATE_t}, \overset{(+)}{FII_{(t-1)}}, \overset{(+)}{IIP_{(t-1)}},$$

$$\overset{(-)}{INFRA_{(t-1)}}, \overset{(-)}{LIBOR_t}, \overset{(+)}{OPEN_{(t-1)}}, \overset{(+)}{TBILL_{(t-1)}}]$$

Empirical Results

The PP unit root test is employed for testing the stationary properties of the series after seasonal adjustment of the series. This test fails to reject the H0 of a unit root for a few variables at levels (Table 1). In the first difference, statistics [I(1)] are significant suggesting that the variables are stationary. Similarly, the KPSS unit root in which the null hypothesis is that a given series is stationary also confirms that the series under consideration after first difference. The results in table 1 show that all these variables are I(1).

In the case of PFI, the estimation results of equation 1 in table 2 shows that all the variables are significant but the coefficients do not show the predicted sign for infrastructure and openness. The negative sign of INFRA may strength the arguments that existing infrastructure is the main bottleneck for inflows of foreign capital in post reform India. Likewise, in contrast to the more common argument that PFI bears a positive relationship with openness thereby implying a situation where PFI goes up when the degree of openness also goes up, the results show an inverse relationship between OPEN and PFI. In this context, institutional reforms has to be implemented and bottlenecks have to be removed (f.g. weak protection for property rights). Such a relationship may propose that inflows are a substitute for trade so that a fall in trade flows may be associated with a rise in inflows.

In contrast, political stability and strength of external payment position variables BSE, and FII are contributing significantly in attracting foreign investment in all the models at below or 5% level. Sentiments of the investors play a vital role in share price and FII. ERATE and PFI are presumed to have positive relationship. It may be due to a decrease in exchange rate, which reflects the strength of external payment position, leads to an increase in foreign investment. This can be attributed to lower cost of investment and production in the recipient countries due to depreciation, thereby leading to increase in PFI. Further, ERATE also argues the above reasons but it is significant at 10% level or even insignificant in model 3. Interestingly, CMR, CTAX, MDLOST and OPEN are found insignificant.

Table 1: Results from the Unit Root Tests

Variable	*Selected Lag Length*	*Test-Statistics*		
		DF	*PP*	*KPSS*
BSE	0	-3.1713**	-3.4707**	0.0415
CMR	0	-3.8775**	-3.8774**	0.0267
CTAX	1	-3.4602**	-3.0890*	0.0862
DFI	0	-3.4834**	-3.4830**	0.0788
ERATE	0	-3.7717**	-3.9570**	0.0949
FII	1	-3.9070**	-3.9070**	0.0777
FPI	0	-3.4740**	-3.4740**	0.0327
IIP	1	-6.9882***	-6.9890***	0.0741
INFRA	1	-3.7542**	-4.9822***	0.0741
LIBOR	0	-4.0797***	-3.7977**	0.0456
MDLOST	1	-6.2811***	-6.2811***	0.0758
OPEN	1	-4.0366**	-4.0352**	0.0455
PFI	0	-3.7111**	-3.7111**	0.0423
SE	1	-4.9685***	-4.9680***	0.0924
TBILL	0	-4.5803***	-4.5800***	0.0823

Note:

1. ***, ** and * refers to significant at 1%, 5% and 10% level respectively.
2. In DW and PP tests, the estimated values are greater than the critical values to reject the null of unit root but KPSS the estimated value are less than the critical values to accept the null of no unit root in the series.
3. DW stands for Dickey-Fuller, PP for Phillips-Perron and KPSS for Kwiatkowski, Phillips, Schmidt and Shin tests.
4. Critical values are obtained from PP (1988) and KPSS (1992) tests.

This depicts that foreign investors do not give much importance for call money rates, corporation tax, man days lost due to labour problems and openness compared to other determinants. However, stock of skilled personnel is significant at 10% level. It is natural that skilled labours

Table 2: Determinants of Private Foreign Investment flows in Liberalised India

Dependent Variable: PFI

Explanatory variables	*Regressions*				
	Model 1	*Model 2*	*Model 3*	*Model 4*	*Model 5*
BSE	0.564(1.972)**	0.520(1.757)*	0.571(1.828)*	0.508(1.669)*	0.565(2.038)**
CMR	89.529(1.112)			18.568(0.254)	104.840(1.500)
CTAX(t-1)	-0.177(-1.124)	-0.137(-0.870)	-0.104(-0.615)	-0.137(-0.855)	-0.185(-1.226)
ERATE	874.271(2.714)***		109.978(0.572)		862.162(2.903)***
FII(t-1)	1.837(1.792)*	2.036(2.127)**	1.742(1.588)	2.009(2.055)**	1.952(2.059)**
IIP(t-1)	20.470(0.390)	71.032(2.324)**	92.750(1.894)*	70.532(2.268)**	
INFRA(t-1)	-117.572(-2.202)**	-111.822(-2.114)**	-115.339(-2.143)**	-105.886(-1.807)*	-119.579(-2.340)**
LIBOR	-1497.695(-3.014)***	-737.082(-1.843)*	-852.375(-1.886)*	-692.500(-1.655)*	-1485.292(-3.126)***
MDLOST(t-1)	-0.001(-0.008)	-0.001(-1.132)	-0.001(-1.161)	-0.001(-0.966)	
OPEN(t-1)	-114.347(-0.597)	-244.157(-1.234)	-218.231(-1.064)	-249.792(-1.236)	-93.177(-0.521)
SE(t-1)	6.637(2.797)***				7.039(3.624)***
Constant	675.221(0.145)	4731.352(1.263)	5933.167(1.369)	4697.709(1.234)	1747.109(0.465)
$\overline{R}^2$	0.6059	0.5372	0.5269	0.5228	0.6298
DW	1.8940	1.4775	1.5033	1.4600	1.9247
SEE	1531.8354	1660.0007	1678.3291	1685.6327	1484.7949
F-Statistic	6.4513	6.6591	5.8269	5.7477	8.3705

Notes:
1. Figures in the parentheses are t-ratios.
2. ***, ** and * dencte that coefficients are significant at 1%, 5% and 10% levels respectively.
3. SEE stands for Standard Error of Estimate and DW for Durbin-Watson Statistic

are available at lower wages compared to other recipient countries, investors will attract towards the country where cheap and skilled labour is available. Index of industrial production is significant in all the models except model 1. As presumed IIP indicates the industrial growth of the country, it depicts that higher growth of the country will be attracting more and more foreign investment.

In-to-to, all combinations are found to be significant. However, equations 5 is chosen as a robust combination due to the reason that it satisfy all the qualitative criteria such as high ¯2, significant coefficients, highly significant F statistics and low SEE. In addition, DW also supports that there is no auto correlation. Furthermore, alternative models explain around 60 per cent of variation in determining PFI in post-reform India.

In the case of DFI, the estimation results of equation 2 in table 3 reveals that all the variables are not significant except BSE in different specifications. As earlier, the coefficients do not show the predicted sign for infrastructure and openness. In contrast, CTAX and OPEN is in not significant in attracting the DFI. Foreign investors tend to observe behavior of the variables like CTAX, IIP, INFRA, MDLOST, OPEN, SE in the previous quarters in turn they will decide to invest. Other variables are representing the current political stability and sentiments of the investors. BSE is playing a vital role at 1 per cent level of significance in all the models. IIP (MDLOST) is significant at 10 per cent (1 per cent) level in all the models except model 1 where it is insignificant.

In the model 1, the entire variables are insignificant except BSE. Sentiments of the investors are positive, which will be drawing more DFI. Model 2 dropped ERATE, OPEN and SE from the model 1 and found that all the variable are significant with highest ¯2 The remaining alternative models are not significant compared to model 2. The validity

Table 3: Determinants of Direct Foreign Investment flows in Liberalised India

Dependent Variable: DFI

Explanatory variables	*Regressions*				
	Model 1	*Model 2*	*Model 3*	*Model 4*	*Model 5*
BSE	0.183(1.924)*	0.178(1.933)*	0.176(1.871)*	0.175(1.852)*	0.187(1.996)**
CTAX(t-1)	-0.047(-0.857)	-0.054(-1.045)	-0.055(-1.027)	-0.055(-1.040)	-0.050(-0.923)
ERATE	139.745(1.346)		8.321(0.148)		155.219(1.645)*
IIP(t-1)	18.486(1.060)	28.231(3.573)***	30.176(1.964)**	27.133(2.920)***	
INFRA(t-1)	-22.612(-1.282)	-27.794(-1.666)*	-27.901(-1.646)*	-26.791(-1.534)	-24.402(-1.415)
LIBOR	-160.117(-1.017)	-256.485(-2.113)**	-244.377(-1.654)*	-253.072(-2.040)**	-216.211(-1.494)
MDLOST(t-1)	-0.001(-0.984)	-0.001(-1.907)*	-0.001(-1.878)*	-0.001(-1.886)*	
OPEN(t-1)	-26.473(-0.435)			-14.162(-0.234)	-41.874(-0.738)
SE(t-1)	1.084(1.498)				1.511(2.446)**
Constant	-2335.020(-1.484)	-1275.4336(-1.263)	-1164.5030(-0.9183)	-1430.664(-1.172)	-3056.974(-2.238)**
$\overline{R}^2$	0.7560	0.7610	0.7537	0.7540	0.7606
DW	1.9472	1.7602	1.7904	1.7866	1.8926
SEE	551.1407	545.4633	553.7298	553.4486	545.9906
F-Statistic	14.4275	21.6987	18.0509	18.0839	18.6967

Notes: same as in table 2.

of the predictions and justification presented in the previous paragraphs keeps valid here for DFI also. In short, all combinations are found to be significant where in equation 2 is chosen as a robust combination due to the reason that it satisfies all the qualitative criteria such as high ¯2 significant coefficients, highly significant F statistics and low SEE. In addition, DW also supports that there is no serial correlation. Furthermore, alternative models explain around 76 per cent of variation in determining DFI in post-reform India.

Finally, turning to FPI, the results (see table 4) find BSE, INFRA and LIBOR are influencing the investors to invest in post-reform India. In contrast, CMR and OPEN are having insignificant relationship with FPI inflows. FPI is basically for short span of time. They may go back at any moment. It depends on political situation and sentiments of the recipient countries. The signs are as predicted except OPEN and INFRA. Indeed, TBILL is significant at 1 per cent level except in model 4. To sum up, as observed in the above tables, all combinations are found to be significant where as equations 2 is chosen as a robust combination. It satisfies all the qualitative criteria such as high ¯2 significant coefficients, significant F statistics and low SEE. Further, alternative models explain around 43 per cent of variation in determining DFI in post-reform India.

Concluding Observations

The main focus of this paper is to identify various determinants of private foreign investment, foreign direct investment and foreign portfolio investment inflows in post reform India, using quarterly data of the variables over the period September 1991 to June 2001. Index of share prices, exchange rate, foreign institutional investment, infrastructure, London Inter Bank Offered Rate and stock of science and engineering personnel's are found to be the

Table 4: Determinants of Foreign Portfolio Investment flows in Liberalised India

Dependent Variable: DFI

Explanatory variables	*Regressions*				
	Model 1	*Model 2*	*Model 3*	*Model 4*	*Model 5*
BSE	0.658(2.270)**	0.662(2.324)**	0.646(2.213)**	0.770(2.521)***	
CMR	12.304(0.195)		8.024(0.131)	77.431(1.279)	21.787(0.324)
ERATE	-331.019(-1.812)*	-324.098(-1.837)*	-168.418(-1.326)	-266.905(-1.383)	-293.374(-1.514)
FII(t-1)	0.929(0.954)	0.956(1.001)	1.185(1.235)	1.125(1.083)	1.626(1.652)*
IIP(t-1)	52.334(1.229)	50.164(1.240)		64.362(1.425)	49.164(1.085)
INFRA(t-1)	-128.363(-2.325)**	-133.127(-2.733)***	-136.604(-2.473)***		-149.214(-2.574)***
LIBOR	-910.036(-2.361)**	-922.179(-2.463)***	-694.083(-2.007)**	-857.368(-2.085)**	-668.062(-1.694)*
OPEN(t-1)	-71.943(-0.373)	-68.734(-0.364)	-17.372(-0.092)	-79.222(-0.385)	-146.213(-0.723)
TBILL(t-1)	0.018(1.744)*	0.018(1.788)*	0.020(1.886)*	0.010(0.924)	0.025(2.318)**
Constant	12955.371(2.998)***	12947.803(3.044)***	11368.917(2.735)***	5927.533(1.796)*	15564.136(3.509)***
$\overline{R}^2$	0.4073	0.4257	0.3976	0.3231	0.3280
DW	1.5557	1.5781	1.5844	1.2686	1.5691
SEE	1496.7380	1473.3293	1509.0129	1599.5982	1593.8397
F-Statistic	3.9785	4.6143	4.2175	3.3269	3.3791

Notes: same as in table 2.

superior and formed a robust combination for attracting more private foreign investment during the reference period. Similarly, share prices, index of industrial production, infrastructure, London Inter Bank Offered Rate and man days lost are found to be the superior combination for influencing direct foreign investors. Lastly, share prices, exchange rate, infrastructure, London Inters Bank Offered Rate and treasury bills are found to be the important determinants of foreign portfolio investment during the reform period in India.

Therefore, in conclusion it can be said that some of the reform policies of the government with regard to foreign investment have been successful in attracting private foreign investment inflows to India. However, it could be inferred from the results of this study that foreign investment would flow only if the investment policies are considered investor-friendly. More than one factor would be responsible in creating an investor-friendly environment. Thus, the paper offers inputs to policy makers in attracting foreign investment on sustainable basis. Further, the study suggests that the government needs to concentrate on specific policies as the findings indicate to attract more private foreign investment in future either in the form of direct or portfolio investment. The study recommends to strengthen the existing infrastructure and amendment of the existing labour laws in turn will attract more investment. The study also recommends the strengthening of market institutions and implementation of transparent regulations will increase inflow of foreign capital in high technology industries. This would call for some hard reform measures.

REFERENCES

1. Aggarwal, R (1977). Theories of Foreign Direct Investment: A Summary of Recent Research and a Proposed Unifying Paradigm, *Economic Affairs*, 22:31-44.

2. Anwar, Syed Aziz (1999). Reassessing Determinants of FDI in Some Emerging Economics, *Foreign Trade Review*, XXXIV (2): 1-12.

3. Bain, J. (1956). *Barriers to Competition*, Mass: Harvard University Press, Cambridge.

4. Chatterjee, Srikanta and Yutin Prajuntaborial (1995). The Eastern Promise? On the Determinants of Foreign Investment in Thailand 1979-90, *Indian Journal of Quantitative Economics*, 10(1): 111-123.

5. Christian, Chung Yuan (1998). The effects of International Competition of Fiscal Incentives on Foreign Direct Investment, *Economia Internazionale*, 51(4): 497-516.

6. Dunning, John H (1973). The Determinants of International Production, *Oxford Economic Papers*, N.S.25:289-336.

7. Gopinath, T (1997). Foreign Investment in India: Policy Issues, Trends and Prospects, *Reserve Bank of India Occasional papers*, 18(2&3):453-470.

8. Goyal, S.K (1979). *Role of Transnational Corporation in India's Exports*, Indian Institute of Foreign Trade, New Delhi.

9. Grubel, Herbert G (1982). The Theory of International Capital Movements. In Johns Black and John H Dunning (eds.) *International Capital Movements*, International Economic Study Group, Macmillan Publishers.

10. Hennart, J.F (1982). *A Theory of the Multinational Enterprise*, University of Michigan Press, Michigan.

11. Howard and Banik (2001). Private Capital Inflows to the Caribbean, *Economic and Political Weekly*, July 21: 2773:78.

12. Hufbauer, G., D.Lakdawalla, and A.Malini (1994). Determinants of Direct Foreign Investment and Its Connection to Trade, *UNCTAD Review*, 39-51.

13. Hymer, S.H (1960). *The International Operations of National Firms: A study of Direct Investment*, MIT Press, Cambridge.

14. International Monetary Fund (IMF) (1993). *Balance of Payments Manual*, 5th Ed.

15. Jun, Kwang W and Harinder Singh (1996). The determinants of foreign direct investment in developing countries, *Transnational Corporations*, 5(2), August: 67-101.

16. Kidron, M (1965). *Foreign Investment in India*, Oxford University Press, New Delhi.

17. Kindleberger, Charles P (1969). *American Business Abroad*, Yale University Press, New Haven, CT.

18. Krishna, M Jaya (2001). PFI in post-reform India: A search for proximate determinants, *ISEC Working Paper*, No.87: 1-19.

19. Kwiatowski, D, P.C.B.Phillips, P.Schmidt and Y.Shin (1992). Testing the Null Hypothesis of Stationarity against the alternative of a Unit Root: How sure are we that economic time series have a Unit Root?. *Journal of Econometrics*, 54:159-178.

20. Lucas, Robert B (1993). On the Determinants of Direct Foreign Investment: Evidence from East and Southeast Asia, *World Development*, 21(3):391-406.

21. Maddala, G.S. and In-Moo Kim (1998). *Unit Roots, Co-integration and Structural Change*, Cambridge University Press, Cambridge.

22. Nishat, Mohammed. and Anjum Aqeel (1998). The Empirical Determinants of Direct Foreign Investment in Pakistan, *Saving and Development*, XXII(4):471-479.

23. Phillips, P.C.B and P.Perron (1988). Testing for a Unit Root in Time Series Regressions, *Biometrika, 75:335-346*.

24. Root, F. and R. Ahmed (1979). Empirical Determinants of Manufacturing Direct Investment in LDCs, *Economic Development and Cultural Change*, 27(4): 751-767.

25. Shamsuddin, Abul F.M. (1994). Economic Determinants of FDI in Less Developed Countries, *The Pakistan Development Review*, 33(1):41-51.

26. United Nations Conference on Trade and Development (UNCTAD) (1993). *World Investment Report: Transnational Corporations and Integrated International Production*, United Nations, New York.

27. United Nations Conference on Trade and Development (UNCTAD) (1998). *World Investment Report: Trends and Determinants*, United Nations, New York.

28. United Nations Conference on Transnational Corporations (UNCTC) (1988). *Transnational Corporations in World Development: Trends and Prospects,* United Nations, New York.

29. Vernon, Raymond (1966). International Trade and International Investment in the Product Cycle, *Quarterly Journal of Economics*, 83(1):190-207.

30. Yang, Jeannie Yih Yun, N Groenewold and M Tcha (2000). 'The Determinants of Foreign Direct Investment in Australia', *The Economic Record*, 76(232):45–54.

Part—VII

Educational Economics Issues

22

Economics of Schooling in India

An Empirical Analysis

*J. Srinivasan**

Introduction

Economics of Education has started developing in India, soon after the pioneer attempt, the one made by A. M. Nallagounden and subsequently by P.R Panchamukhi, in the mid-sixites and late sixties respectively. There are numerous number of studies have been carried out on Economics of Education both in India and abroad countries. In a comprehensive survey article, Heyneman (1995) has advocated for new innovation in educational economics employing new techniques to respond to new questions, relevant to new theories and new practice.

In this paper, an attempt has been made to analyse various deciding factors of demand for schooling at the secondary and higher-secondary levels in the state of Tamil Nadu. Though, there are quite a few studies available in India. (Arumugam, 1984; Duraisamy, 1988, 2001; Thangam, 1989) but none of these studies have treated, the average amount spent on schooling as a dependent variable. Therefore, this pare would be considered as a peculiar one as it differs from other studies as mentioned above.

* Vivekananda College, Chennai.

The terms, "Economics of Education" and Economics of schooling may be treated as similar in this paper, though, they are originally not so. (This is only for our convenient in understanding).

In the process of analysis, care has been taken, to locate the distinguishing factors of demand for schooling in the context of rural and urban areas. Moreover, the regression analysis has been done, both for males and females separately.

In this paper, an attempt has been made (i) to estimate the demand for schooling particularly at the secondary level i.e., (14-15) age group and at the higher secondary level i.e., (16-17) age group. (ii) To find out the different demand for schooling, of the above said levels in both rural and urban Tamil Nadu.

There are some important studies available on this research problem in India. In this context, an attempt has been to present a thematic review of these studies. In his study, Kumar (1980) has tried to find out (i) the socio-economic background of high school students (ii) the relationship and effect if any of the socio-economic factors on the demand for higher education and the educational level sought and (iii) the factors other than social and economic which had a bearing on effective educational demand. His study was related to Allahabad City. He has found that more than 84 percent of students demanded higher education. Further, he has observed that the proportion of girls demanding higher education was more than that of boys. Studies made by Arumugam (1984) and Duraisamy (1988, 2001) have identified that the economic status of the family as measured by family income, size of land holdings etc., was the most important variable related with the schooling of children.

Andhra Pradesh is one of the low literacy states in India, having the 25th rank among the 31 states and union territories. Literacy rates are low among all population subgroups in Andhra Pradesh as compared to the Nation as a whole.

In Karnataka, literacy rate is 56 percent for the state as a whole –67 percent among males and 44 percent among females. There are large inter-district variations, ranging from 76 percent in Bangalore and Dakshina Kannada to 44 percent in Raichur. The difference between male and female literacy at the state level is more than 22 percent. In the context of urban areas, literacy rate for the state as a whole stands at 74 percent. (82 percent among the males and 66 percent among the females). The patterns for literacy rate are quite similar to those for enrolment and drop-out rates.

Tamil Nadu: The overall literacy rate (1991 census) in the state is 62.7 percent female rural literacy is as low as 42.6 percent.

The enrolment rate in the districts of Tamil Nadu varies from 85.5. in Chennai (Madras) to 119.7 in Kanyakumari. The number of students reported to be enrolled is generally higher for various reasons than the number of children actually attending classes. One important variable that determines the level of enrolment seems to be current level of literacy in the district. The rakings of the districts according to enrolment rates of boys and girls show only marginal differences.

The average teacher-pupil ratio in Tamil Nadu is 1:46.2. The lowest ratios were found in Kanyakumari (38.8), Ramanatha puram (39.1), Chidambaranar and Tirunelveli (40.7). the districts reporting high ratios were Pudukottai (53.2), Coimbatore (52.8) and Dharmapuri (52.4). In eight districts the rates is higher than the state average which reveals that schools in these districts are over burdened affecting the quality of education.[1]

---

1 This section is based upon the South India: Human Development Report (2002), Analysis is based upon secondary level data.

Table1: Gross Enrollment Rates of Boys and girls by schooling levels in India, 1950-51 to 1990-91

Year	*Primary Classes (I-V)*		*Middle Classes (VI-VIII)*		*Secondary Classes (IX-X)*	
	Boys	*Girls*	*Boys*	*Girls*	*Boys*	*Girls*
1950-51	60.6	24.8	20.6	4.6	8.7	1.5
1960-61	82.6	41.4	33.2	11.3	16.7	4.1
1970-71	92.6	59.1	46.5	20.8	27.1	10.2
1980-81	95.8	64.1	54.3	28.8	23.1	11.1
1990-91	115.3	86.0	73.4	46.1	29.8	14.4

Note: Percent of enrollment exceeds 100 due to repetition by some children.

Source: Education in India (various volumes) Ministry of Human Resources Development (M.H.R.D), Government of India.

The gross enrollment rates in the case of boys and girls in India according to different school levels for the period between 1950-51 and 1990-91 are given in Table. 1.

The plan of this paper is as follows: Section-2 explains the concept of demand for schooling with reference to socio-economic perspective; Section-3 provides a theoretical framework; Section-4 presents the empirical analysis; Section-5 reports the findings based on the econometric results and Section-6 gives summary and major conclusions of the study.

The Concept of Demand for Schooling: A Socio-Economic Perspective

In demand analysis, we investigate the choices that individuals make between the goods and services that are available to them in the market at a given price level, (Simmons, 1974). The term demand refers to the quantity or the amount of a particular commodity purchased at a given price level. The term "demand" is associated with the price of the commodity in question.

The quantity demanded in the context of education has been explained in the following manner:

(i) The number of years of education an individual has acquired. This can be measured in terms of number of years of schooling.

(ii) Whether the child is enrolled in the school or not. This aspect is known as the enrolment index. A variant of this measure is the enrollment ration, where it is measured as the percentage of children enrolled.

(iii) School expenditure on children is calculated as the expenditure on education such as school fees, transportation cost etc.,

As far as price of schooling is concerned there are two kinds of price.

(1) Supply price and (2) Demand price

The supply price is the price at which the supply of education can be offered to the public which includes Government and Non-Government outlays on educational institutions. The demand price is the price at which the consumers are willing to obtain education. If supply price and demand price converge, in this case, it is named as the equilibrium price.

The demand price is the costs of education borne by the households. The total costs of education comprise of the direct costs and indirect costs. Direct costs are further sub-divided into two components. Viz., Expenditure on books, uniforms, papers, pen, pencil etc., and expenditure on school fees, examination fees etc., the other expenses block also includes three more components like travel cost, boarding and lodging (for students who are staying outside home).

The opportunity cost of education of children or the earnings foregone by the students is the indirect cost of education. This cost is the amount of earnings foregone by the students while they are at school. Sheehan (1973) in his book on "Economics of Education" has said that there are two kinds of costs of education (measured by the expenses on fees, books and other items) as well as the indirect costs of education (the earnings foregone amount) which are a real cost to him.

There are some empirical evidence on the costs of education in India. Psacharopoulos and Woodhall (1985) found that many poor parents in India do not send their children to school mainly because they cannot afford to pay direct costs of education. While analyzing the private costs of education in Baroda City of Gujarat State, Shah (1968) has shown that the non tuition costs (e.g. costs of education other than fees) incurred by the students are more significant than the fees. In a pioneer study, Panchamukhi (1967) observed that for the Indian context there is a complementary effect operating between public and private education expenditures. In this study on cost and demand relationship for secondary education in Coimbatore district of Tamil Nadu State Arumugam (1984) identified that the cost factors are important in deciding the demand for education.

In their survey, Kothari and Panchamukhi (1975) have opined that the indirect cost of education can be captured in terms of the foregone work opportunity of the individuals. There are rate of return studies in India which have estimated the foregone earrings on the basis of age-earnings Profiles based upon various surveys. The most important one made by Nalla Gounden in 1965 subsequently the work has been published in an international journal in 1967.

So on this basis of the above discussion; we would like to conclude that especially in a country like India, the cost factors are playing a crucial role in deciding the educational attainment of school going children. Hence, while analyzing the demand aspect of education, cost factors ought to be taken into consideration.

Thus, on the whole demand for education can be considered as a functional relationship in which price of education, family income and socio-economic factors as its elements. We can expect a negative price effect and a positive income effect. On the average, there is some tendency that as the family income goes up, Households will also spend more on education of their children.

The following section presents a theoretical framework in order to analyze the demand for schooling.

Demand for Schooling: A Theoretical Framework

The theoretical model is purely based upon the new household economics framework. This new framework is the same as the neo-Classical framework where we want to maximize the household utility function subject to both the income constraint and the time constraint. The household utility function consists of commodities like education (i.e. human capital per child), number of children and other Hicksian composite consumption commodities.

Some of the pioneer studies which have used this model are Becker (1965; 1976), Michael (1974), Willis (1973), Grossman (1972). They have attempted for time allocation, efficiency in production, fertility behavior and demand for health respectively. For the Indian context, studies made by Rosenzweig and Evenson (1977), Duraisamy (1984), Arumugam (1984), Srinivasan (1987) have employed this model. While the first two studies related to Rural India, the latter two studies connected to Urban India.

Instead of directly fitting some ad hoc demand function, we develop a household model which provides a framework or language to investigate the demand for schooling. By demand, we mean enrollment in schools after completing a stage, continuity of schooling is also considered as an element of demand.

The Model

Unlike the traditional Utility function, this new home economics utility function has elements like dinner, number of children, health care, going to music performance etc., These commodities are not purchased from market rather they are produced at home. For the production of these commodities, the inputs viz., goods and services are produced from the market.

The household's utility function takes the following form with the given commodities as its elements.

$$U= U(Z_{e,} Z_n, Z_s) \quad (1)$$

Where U is the utility function, assumed to be twice continuously differentiable and strictly concave, $Z_{e\,=}$ amount of human capital per child, Z_n = number of children and Z_s = other Hicksian composite consumption commodities.

Each of these arguments of the utility function is assumed to be produced by the household through the combination of market purchased goods ($X_{i,}$ i =e, n, s) and the time inputs of some or all the members ($T_{ij,}$ j = h, w, c where h is the husband, w is the wife and c is the child) according to linear homogenous production function with the given level of technology.

$$Z_i = f(X_{i,} T_{i\,j,} E), I = n, e, s \quad (2)$$

Where E is a vector of environmental variables like health, age, education of the parents etc., which is assumed to effect the efficiency of the production process.

In developing countries like India, the economic contribution of children may be an important component of family income. Thus the family income is the sum of market labour income of parents as well as children and unearned income (V) from non-labour sources. The household labour income is equal to the time each member devotes to the market times their respective wage rates (w_i). The household income used in the production of n, e and s. The budget constraint is

$$V + w_0 T_{wh} + w_1 T_{ww} + w_2 T_{we} Z_n = PeXeZ_n + P_s X_s + P_n X_n \qquad (3)$$

Where Pi is price of market goods used in the production of the ith commodity (i = n, e, s) where T_{wh} = time of the husband spent at work.

T_{ww} = time of the wife spent at work

T_{wc} = time of the children spent at work, per child.

W_i = (i =0, 1, 2) is the wage rate of husband, wife and children.

The time constraints are

$$T_c = T_{ec} + T_{wc} + T_{sc} \qquad (4)$$

$$T_w = T_{nw} + T_{sw} + T_{ww} \qquad (5)$$

$$T_h = T_{hw} \qquad (6)$$

Where T_c = total time available per child.

T_w = total time of the wife.

T_h = total time of the husband.

Income and time constraints can be collapsed with one single constraint. Thus the resource constraint can be written as

$$w_0 T_h + w_1 T_w + w_2 T_c Z_n + V = Z_n Z_e (P_e X_e + w_2 T_{ec}) + Z_n (P_n X_n + w_1 T_{nw}) + Z_a (P_s X_s + w_2 T_{sc} Z_n + w_1 T_{sw}) \qquad (7)$$

we can form the Lagrangian function as utility function plus the Lagrangian multiplier times the resource constraints.

$$L = U(Z_{e,} Z_{n,} Z_s) + \lambda [Zn\ Z_e (P_e X_e + w_2 T_{ec}) + Z_n (P_n X_n + w_1 T_{nw}) + Z_s (P_s X_s + w_2 T_{sc} Z_n + w_1 T_{sw}) - V - w_2 T_c Z_n - w_1 T_w - w_0 T_h] \quad (8)$$

Maximizing the utility function (1) subject to the resource constraint (8) gives the following:

One very important assumption is that there is no joint ness in the production.

Partially differentiating "L" with respect to Zn, Ze, Zs and λ we obtain the first order conditions for an interior equilibrium.

$$\frac{\partial L}{\partial Z_n} = (Z_e P_e X_e + P_n X_n + w_1 - T_{nw} w_2 T_{wc}) \quad (9)$$

$$\frac{\partial L}{\partial Z_e} = (P_e X_e + w_2 T_{sc} Z_{n+} w_1 T_{sw}) \quad (10)$$

$$\frac{\partial L}{\partial Z_s} = (P_s X_s + w_2 T_{sc} Z_{n+} w_1 T_{sw}) \quad (11)$$

$$\frac{\partial L}{\partial \lambda} = [Z_n Z_e (P_e X_e + W_2 T_{ec}) + Z_n (P_n X_n + w_1 T_{nw}) + Z_s (P_s X_s + W_2 T_{sc} Z_n + w_1 T_{sw}) - V - Z_n w_2 T_c - w_1 T_s - w_0 T_h] = 0 \quad (12)$$

where λ is the marginal utility of money income. Let πi be the corresponding shadow prices of the Zi commodities. Then the shadow prices can be given as

$$\pi_n = Z_e P_e X_e + P_n X_n + w_1 Y_{nm} - w_2 T_{wc} \quad (13)$$

$$\pi_e = Z_n (P_e X_e + w_2 T_{ec}) \quad (14)$$

$$\pi_s = P_s X_s + w_2 T_{sc} Z_n + w_1 T_{sw} \quad (15)$$

Thus the shadow prices are explicit function of goods prices, opportunity costs of time and the household production technology.

We can express the first order maximization conditions in terms of shadow prices

$$\frac{\partial L}{\partial Z_n} = \lambda \pi_n \qquad (16)$$

$$\frac{\partial L}{\partial Z_e} = \lambda \pi_e \qquad (17)$$

$$\frac{\partial L}{\partial Z_s} = \lambda \pi_s \qquad (18)$$

$$\frac{\partial L}{\partial \lambda} = \pi_n Z_n + \pi_e Z_e + \pi_s Z_s = 1 \qquad (19)$$

Where I is the full income of the family. The quantities of Z_n, Z_e and Z_s are demanded as a function of the parameters. πi and I can be derived by solving the equation (16) through (19) simultaneously. Then the solutions in implicit form give the following demand functions.

$$Z_i^* = Z_i (\pi_n, \pi_e, \pi_s, I) \qquad (20)$$

The above demand functions are homogeneous of degree zero in iand I satisfy the Slutsky sign and symmetry conditions. In equilibrium the consumption pattern for the family is given by

$$\frac{\partial L / \partial Z_i}{\partial L / \partial Z_j} = \frac{\pi_i}{\pi_j} \quad \text{Where i, j = n, e, s} \qquad (21)$$

i.e. ration of marginal product = ratio of marginal cost.

In order to avoid the estimation problem, we derived a demand function for education, and which is a function of goods prices, wage rates and non-labour income. Accordingly, demand function for the education can be estimated as

$$Z_i^* = Z_i (P_i, w_0, w_1, w_2, V, \delta, \beta, E) \qquad (22)$$

when I = n, e, s

where the consumption of commodity 'i' is a function of (a) the prices of market goods, Pi (b) wage rates of husband, wife and children w_0, w_1, w_2 (c) Non labour income V(d) parameter of the household technology, δ (e) parameter of the production technology, β and (f) environmental variables E.

In the next section, we verify this theoretical model empirically with the help of the primary level data.

Empirical Analysis

The data, empirical model and variables

The data used in this study is drawn from a primary survey of both rural and urban households in the State of Tamil Nadu, and refers to the year 1989-90. the data collection procedure has been used the simple stratified random sampling method, for collection the information from the required number of households.

Data have been gathered from 300 households in Madras city (i.e., urban sample) and 300 households in six villages from Dharmapuri and Tirunelveli Districts (i.e., rural sample). Altogether, there were 600 households for primary level survey. District interview method was followed to collect the data. In the interview schedule, there were questions pertaining to socio-economic and demographic characteristics of the individuals and family.

There are two methods to estimate the demand for education and these can be explained as follows:

Let "Y" be the dependent variable which represents the enrolment decision of school going children.

Y = 1, if the child is going to school

= 0, if the child is not going to school.

Now, consider the following econometric equation: $Y = \alpha_i + \beta_i X_i + U_i$, i = 1 to n.

Where α_i denotes the intercept term, "β_i" are the coefficients of the independent variables (for e.g. economic and sociological variables) and "U_i" is the random disturbance term. One important handicap with this model is that U_i term is to following the normal distribution. Rather, it follows a distribution with zero mean and non-constant variance, σ_i^2.

Therefore, we will end up with the hetroscadasticity problem while estimating the equation. Even if we try to apply the Ordinary Least Squares (OLS) technique to estimate the equation the resultant parametric estimates would be unbiased but in-efficient.

In this paper, we have treated the Average amount spend on Education (TEE) as the dependent variable (Y). This variable has been regressed on independent variables (X_i's) like parent's educational level, age, community, facilities available at home, family income, and size of the agricultural land holdings.

Method -II

When the dependent variable is dichotomous in nature, the suitable econometric tools for estimation will be the Probit/Logit methods.

Probit model[2] maybe defined as given below:

$$F^{-1}(P_i) = \frac{-\mu + 1}{\sigma} \frac{X_i + U_i}{\sigma}$$

Where $U_i = E_i \frac{dF / P_i}{dP_i} = i$, $\quad i$ = 1ton

P_i = 1 where a child is going to school = 0 otherwise i.e., P_i is the probability of an individual who belongs to a dependent category.

White the Logit model takes the following form

$$L_i = \text{Log}\left[\frac{P_i}{1P_i}\right] = \beta_1 + \beta_2 X_i + U_i, \ i = 1ton$$

In order to estimate this model, apart form the values of X_i (the independent variables such as sociological, economic variables) we are in need of the values for Logit "L_i". We can estimate this model by employing the Maximum Likelihood Estimation (MLE) technique. However, due to some reasons, this paper could not apply methods viz., the probit/Logit.

The detailed definition of variable and their means and Standard Deviations are given in Table.2

Empricial Results: A Discussion

(14-15) Age Group; Secondary Level Education

Rural Sample (For total only)

We have only given the selected regression equations, though we have tried for three alternative specifications. Accordingly, our discussion is based upon the second specification. Male head of the families, who have secondary, P.U.C are spending comparatively more on average amount on educating as compared to male head of the families who had no schooling, U.G, or P.G. This variable (SECO) is significant at 10% level. Monthly consumption expenditure has significant positive influence over the average amount spent on their children's educating. This indicates that, education is also one of the priority items in their family budget expenditures. The value of R^2 is 0.14. In the third specification, the results are the same. The total number of school going children (NOS) has a negative significant effect on the average amount spent on education of their children. More the number of school going children in the family, less will be the average amount spent on education. This means that, the share of expenditure on each child's education becomes negligible figure, if the family is happened to be a large one.

Table 2: Means and Standard Deviations for the Variables

Variable	Meaning	Rural Sample		Urban Sample		Total	
		Mean	S.D	Mean	S.D	Mean	S.D
Male	It is a dummy variable =1 if the gender of the child is male, or "0" otherwise	0.95	0.22	0.89	0.31	0.92	0.27
PRIM	It is a dummy variable =1 if the Husbands education level is primary, elementary or "0" otherwise	0.33	0.47	0.23	0.42	0.28	0.45
SECO	It is a dummy variable = 1 if the Husbands education level is secondary, P.U.C, or "0" otherwise	0.26	0.44	0.46	0.50	0.36	0.48
WPRI	It is a dummy variable = 1 if the wife's education level is primary, elementary or "0" otherwise	0.33	0.47	0.36	0.48	0.34	0.48
WSEC	It is a dummy variable = 1 if the Wife's education level is secondary, P.U.C, or "0" otherwise	0.17	0.38	0.41	0.49	0.29	0.45
HAGE	Husband's age (in years)	43.38	13.29	45.26	11.65	44.27	12.52
WAGE	Wife's Age (in years)	38.82	6.69	38.49	5.93	39.11	6.30
L_n(fin)	Logarithm of family income	9.06	0.77	9.73	0.71	9.40	0.81
B.C	It is a dummy variable = 1 if the family belongs to Backward Class Community, or "0" otherwise	0.42	0.58	0.63	0.48	0.73	0.44
SC/ST	It is a dummy variable = 1 if the family belongs to Scheduled Castes/Scheduled Tribes, or "0" otherwise	0.23	0.41	0.10	030	0.10	0.30

(Table Contd...)

Table 2: (Contd...)

Variable	Meaning	Rural Sample		Urban Sample		Total	
		Mean	S.D	Mean	S.D	Mean	S.D
NOS	Total number of school going children in the family	2.31	1.16	2.21	1.01	2.25	1.08
FACM	It is a dummy variable = 1 if the facilities available, or "0" otherwise	0.79	0.41	0.87	0.33	0.83	0.38
MCON	Monthly consumption Expenditure (in Rs)	412.06	315.49	1055.76	640.51	731.61	598.38
SUJOO	It is a dummy variable = 1 if the parental support is very high, or "0" otherwise	0.61	0.49	0.73	0.44	0.67	0.47
SKILL	It is a dummy variable = 1 if the husband's occupation is an excutive, clerical, Administration Technical, Professional skilled labour, school teachers college/ University teachers, agricultural workers	0.12	0.39	0.59	0.49	0.48	0.50
ARM	It is a dummy variable = 1 if the parental attitude regarding schooling is favorable, or "0" otherwise	0.94	0.23	0.94	0.23	0.94	0.23
HINDU	It is a dummy variable = 1 if the religion of the family is "HINDU", or "0" otherwise	0.87	0.34	0.90	0.30	0.89	0.32
Land	Size of the agricultural land holding (in acres)	0.76	2.23	-	-	-	-

(14-15) Age Group: Secondary Schooling

Rural sample (for boys)

In the first specification, none of the variable is significant. The value of R^2 is too low. Hence, we are adopting the second specification for our explanation. In this equation, the monthly, consumption expenditure (MCON) has a significant positive impact upon the average amount spent on their son's education. This variable is significant at 1 percent level. This shows that parents are attaching a greater value to their son's education, as good as the consumption expenditure. 14 percent variations in the average amount spent on schooling is explained by the socio-economic variables. In the third specification, we have introduced one new explanatory variable, namely agricultural land holdings (LAND) and it has an insignificant positive effect on the average amount spent on their children's education. This in our rural sample, as there are not more numbers of large-size farmers, we have ended up with this result.

(14-15) Age Group; Secondary Schooling

Rural sample (For Girls)

We found that male head of the family who have secondary, P.U.C education are spending relatively more on their daughter's schooling as compared to male head of the families who had no schooling or U.G or P.G. This has happened because our rural sample constituted only a meager percentage of degree holders (U.G) and Post-Graduates. This variable is statistically significant at 1 percent level. This is because, male head of the families with secondary level education, wanted to educate their daughters at least up to the secondary schooling level. Wife's ages (WAGE) has a positive association on the average amount spent on their girl's schooling. This variable is significant at 10percent level. This tries to

Table 3: Least Squares Estimates of Tee Equations for (14-15) and (16-17) Age Groups: Rural Sample, Tamilnadu

Independent variables	*(14-15) Age Group*			*(16-17) Age group*		
	Boys	*Girls*	*Total*	*Boys*	*Girls*	*Total*
Male	-	-	-56.1885(0.38)	-	-	111.6119 (0.64)
PRIM	53.1240 (1.04)	157.3518 (1.99)	143.8158 (1.90)	-97.2746 (1.09)	-145.1943 (1.54)	-93.4433 (1.07)
SECO	156.3396 (2.81)	155.0974 (1.74)	155.1519 (1.81)	22.6561 (0.23)	-0.5523 (0.01)	13.4898 (0.14)
WPRI	-4.8523 (0.10)	60.4332 (0.38)	34.5203 (0.46)	5.9940 (0.07)	20.2359 (0.21)	5.00006 (0.06)
WSEC	4.2196 (0.07)	97.7908 (1.08)	81.8129 (0.93)	146.1881 (1.15)	188.1693 (1.38)	139.6397 (1.14)
HAGE	-1.9733 (0.96)	-2.4982 (0.80)	-2.6337 (0.87)	1.9378 (0.73)	1.9890 (0.72)	1.9161 (0.74)
WAGE	5.6411 (1.47)	4.2325 (0.71)	3.8534 (0.69)	10.5075 (1.84)	9.4141 (1.55)	10.3548 (1.91)
B.C	-46.1519 (0.53)	36.1228 (0.24)	36.4889 (0.27)	86.8899 (0.66)	114.7830 (0.83)	69.9381 (0.57)
SC/ST	30.5884 (0.29)	38.3516 (0.21)	81.1443 (0.49)	48.8201 (0.28)	78.9151 (0.43)	31.3092 (0.18)
NOS	-95.5606 (5.19)	-105.7775 (3.66)	-115.3806 (4.20)	-117.6979 (4.05)	-126.9654 (4.09)	116.910 (4.20)
FACM	-52.5433 (1.00)	-35.9187 (0.43)	-10.5251 (0.13)	-65.7396 (0.77)	-57.3200 (0.64)	63.7958 (0.78)
Ln(FIN)	78.5119 (1.52)	-2.5735 (0.03)	32.3179 (0.43)	-0.4954 (0.01)	9.8656 (0.12)	0.9440 (0.01)
MCON	0.3153 (2.85)	0.4202 (2.39)	0.3561 (1.13)	0.2345 (1.29)	0.2082 (1.12)	0.2203 (1.23)

(Table Contd...)

Table 3: (Contd...)

Independent variables	*(14-15) Age Group*			*(16-17) Age group*		
	Boys	*Girls*	*Total*	*Boys*	*Girls*	*Total*
SKILL	-127.1663 (2.28)	-65.4872 (2.39)	-86.3754 (0.10)	22.9928 (0.24)	59.9017 (0.59)	18.0426 (0.19)
ARM	-19.1275 (0.16)	40.7998 (0.21)	22.4408 (0.12)	56.9772 (0.36)	41.3359 (0.59)	65.9753 (0.42)
HINDU	-96.2274 (0.55)	-53.4077 (0.52)	-54.9929 (0.55)	-64.1481 (0.61)	-74.2581 (0.64)	60.0718 (0.58)
SUOO	27.5905 (0.55)	2.8778 (0.04)	13.6495 (0.19)	104.6698 (1.24)	126.2671 (1.34)	98.6194 (1.19)
R^2	0.39	0.17	1.90	0.30	0.33	0.30
F-VALUE	4.98	1.84	1.90	2.85	2.81	2.78
N	143	158	166	124	112	129

Note: TEE can be defined as follows:

(i) TEE = Average amount spent on education:

$$= \frac{\text{Total Expenditure on Education}}{\text{Family Income}}$$

(Note that, the same cane might be interpreted as the share of family income which goes as expenditure on children's schooling).

(ii) Only selected specifications are given for each category.

(iii) "t" values are given in parentheses.

indicate that more aged mother's are viewing schooling with due respect, as compared to less aged mothers. To cite an illustration in this context, normally grand mothers are more worried about their grand daughter's schooling. Monthly consumption expenditure (MCON) has a significant positive effect on the average amount spent on their daughter's schooling.

This variable is significant at 1 percent level. Male head of the families with "SKILLED" occupations are spending comparetatively less on average amount in the case of schooling, with reference to male head of the families with "LABOUR" occupation category under estimates the economic value of schooling. (refer Table.3)

(16-17) Age Group; Higher-Secondary Schooling

Rural Sample (For Total Only)

According to the given results (refer Table.3) wife's ages (WAGE) has a positive significant effect on the average amount spent on their children's Education. This is nothing but, more aged mothers are more smart in sending their children to school, a s compared to less aged mothers. This variable is significant at 5 percent level. Monthly consumption expenditure (MCON) has a significant positive effect on the average amount spent on their children's schooling. This variable is significant at 5 percent level. Therefore, parents are not keeping education as the last position in designing their family budget. The value of R^2 is 0.24.

(16-17) Age Group; Higher-Secondary Schooling

Rural Sample (For Boys)

As per the results, wife's ages (WAGE) variable has a significant positive effect on the average amount spent on education. This variable is significant at the 5 percent level.

Table 4: Least Squares Estimates of Tee Equations for (14-15) and (16-17) Age Groups: Urban Sample, Tamilnadu

Independent variables	(14-15) Age Group			(16-17) Age group		
	Boys	*Girls*	*Total*	*Boys*	*Girls*	*Total*
Male	-	-	-171.7714 (0.38)	-	-	143.9503 (0.64)
PRIM	-93.3321 (0.59)	-183.2861 (0.92)	-158.9530 (1.05)	-114.5085 (0.65)	-117.3443 (0.05)	-129.1541 (0.81)
SECO	-32.0658 (0.26)	-109.1405 (0.71)	-100.2969 (0.84)	-71.0.21 (0.47)	-44.9531 (0.93)	-85.8458 (0.61)
WPRI	70.2841 (0.50)	-39.5385 (0.24)	0.2515 (0.00)	-111.3399 (0.74)	-98.9457 (0.63)	-109.7473 (0.78)
WSEC	270.8509 (2.02)	167.9665 (1.10)	166.4610 (1.34)	83.61581 (0.55)	145.3089 (0.94)	91.5761 (0.65)
HAGE	-3.9959 (0.75)	-2.2262 (0.36)	-1.5536 (0.31)	-0.3800 (0.07)	0.6255 (0.11)	0.4351 (0.08)
WAGE	-4.5768 (0.44)	-7.8209 (0.64)	-8.3181 (0.85)	-12.1819 (1.04)	-4.2017 (0.36)	-10.8528
B.C	-38.9019 (0.36)	-74.8150 (0.57)	-80.0264 (0.77)	14.9970 (0.11)	60.45050 (0.45)	27.0262 (0.22)
SC/ST	-160.9471 (0.95)	-120.3508 (0.59)	-210.6236 (1.33)	-186.7447 (0.81)	-125.1317 (0.54)	- 91.2485 (0.87)
NOS	-183.9471 (3.73)	-206.9097 (3.51)	-203.6294 (4.29)	-250.8573 (4.50)	-153.8453 (2.47)	-245.7630 (4.61)
FACM	-77.2757 (0.48)	-34.6230 (0.17)	-52.2045 (0.34)	-6.9457 (0.04)	-122.2503 (0.74)	-47.0603 (0.31)
Ln(FIN)	118.2645 (1.08)	156.1294 (1.24)	159.7751 (1.55)	10.9242 (0.09)	8.02341 (0.24)	9.6195 (0.31)
MCON	-0.0438 (0.36)	-0.0464 (0.34	-0.0713 (0.66)	0.0375 (2.62)	0.2800 (2.35)	0.2761 (2.61)

(Table Contd...)

Table 4: (Contd...)

Independent variables	*(14-15) Age Group*			*(16-17) Age group*		
	Boys	*Girls*	*Total*	*Boys*	*Girls*	*Total*
SKILL	-69.1034 (0.67)	-62.8970 (0.52)	-42.6679 (0.43)	2.98688 (0.03)	-13.6473 (0.11)	-5.2786 (0.05)
ARM	56.5718 (0.23)	8.87438 (0.0.)	81.4379 (0.34)	-60.7990 (0.24)	-70.0085 (0.28)	-37.0037 (0.16)
HINDU	165.4805 (0.92)	201.9816 (1.07)	183.7414 (1.13)	160.1635 (0.76)	-70.0085 (0.28)	120.5132 (0.65)
SUOO	52.8378 (0.43)	78.8685 (0.52)	46.9925 (0.38)	85.05828 (0.65	159.7469 (0.85)	100.1287 (0.80)
R^2	0.17	0.18	0.37	0.26	0.33	0.26
F-VALUE	1.63	1.47	12.62	2.71	1.92	2.77
N	145	131	163	144	126	155

Note: TEE can be defined as follows:

(i) TEE = Average amount spent on education:

$$= \frac{\text{Total Expenditure on Education}}{\text{Family Income}}$$

(Note that, the same cane might be interpreted as the share of family income which goes as expenditure on children's schooling).

(ii) Only selected specifications are given for each category.

(iii) "t" values are given in parentheses.

Monthly Consumption expenditure (MCON) has a positive significant effect on the average amount spent on education of their sons and their overall explanatory power is 23 percent.

(16-17) Age Group; Higher-Secondary Schooling

Rural Sample (For Girls)

In this case, wife's ages (WAGE) variable has a significant positive effect on the average amount spent on education. This variable is significant at the 10 percent level. More aged mothers feel education is quite useful to other daughters. Monthly Consumption expenditure (MCON) has a positive significant influence over the average amount spent on education of their children. This variable is significant at 5 percent level, 27 percent variation in the average amount spent on education is explained by the explanatory variables.

An Overview

The average amount spent on children's education, in the case of rural sample is monthly governed by factors like mother's education and monthly consumption expenditure. Caste factor plays an important role in the average amount spent on boy's education. Among girls, religious factor significantly affects the average amount spent on schooling. Our results reveal that Hindu households are spending much more less on average amount in the case of their daughter's schooling as compared to Muslim and Christian households. This is a quite contradictory results the main reason is that our date set did not contain more number of Muslims and Christians. Therefore, this finding should not be generalized under any circumstances. The effect of Monthly consumption expenditure on children's schooling could be interpreted as the income effect.

(14-15) Age Group: Secondary Level Education

Urban Sample (For Total Only)

We have tried out for two specifications in both of the specifications none of the variable is statistically significant.

(14-15) Age Group: Secondary Level Education

Urban Sample (For Boys)

In this case also, we have experienced the same thing.

(14-15) Age Group: Secondary Level Education

Urban Sample (For Girls)

As before we have shown the similar results.

(16-17) Age Group: Higher Secondary Level Education

Urban Sample (For Total Only)

In the first specification, only one variable namely wife's age (WAGE) is statically significant and its sign is positive Hence, more aged mothers are in favor or their children's schooling, as compared to less aged mothers.

The value of R^2 is 0.17. In the second specification, none of the variable is statistically significant.

(16-17) Age Group: Higher Secondary Level Education

Urban Sample (For Boys)

In the first specification, only one variable namely wife's age (WAGE) is statically significant.

(16-17) Age Group: Higher Secondary Level Education

Urban Sample (For Girls)

In the first specification none of the factor is statistically significant. We have picked up the second specification for our main interpretation. It is noted that, wife's age (WAGE) variable has a significant positive influence over the average amount spent on their children's education.

This variable is statically significant at 10 percent level. Monthly consumption expenditure (MCON) variable has a significant positive impact upon the average amount spent on their children's education. It seems that, monthly consumption expenditure is normally decided by the family income and hence its effect on the average amount spent on education is positive.

An Overview

For the urban sample, the average amount spent on children's education is decided by the factors such as mother's age (WAGE) and monthly consumption expenditure. Mother's age influences the average amount spend on their daughter's education. If we want to raise the level of average amount spent on children's education, the economic status of the family should be increased.

Table. 5: Estimated Monthly Average Amount Spent on Education by level of school, by sex, Rural House holds, Tamil Nadu, 1989-90.

Level of Schooling	*Male Rs.Ps.*	*Female Rs.Ps*
1. School Education (All Stage)	8.01	7.45
2. Secondary and Higher Secondary	8.27	7.69
3. Secondary Level	7.97	7.01
4. Higher Secondary Level	8.18	8.37

Source: Survey Data, Srinivasan (1991) For Urban Sample, We are unable to profile the same due to some reason.

We have given in the table 5 the estimated values of monthly average amount spent on education according to the level, sex. For the first 3 cases namely school education (all state), secondary and higher-secondary level, secondary level, the monthly, average amount spent on for boys is more than that of girls', this underscores the fact that, women's is how far neglected in rural areas, as compared to urban areas.

If we consider the higher secondary school level, parents are spending more on their daughters as compared to their sons. This is only a rare case and it cannot be generalized under any circumstances.

Schooling Participation Rates: A Rural-Urban Comparison

In rural areas, the average amount spent on their children's education is often determined by factors such as mother's age, monthly consumption Expenditure and number of school going children in the family. Boy's education is crucially determined by the caste variable. Among girls, religious group significantly affects the average amount spent on education.

On the contrary, in urban areas the average amount spent on children's education., is mostly decided by the factors such as mother's age and monthly consumption expenditures. In this case, the number of school going children in the family does not seem to be affected much the schooling of children.

Schooling Participation Rates: Secondary Level Vs Higher Secondary Level

In the case of secondary level, father's education level, mother's age, occupation of the head of the family, the total number of school going children in the family (for rural sample alone) and monthly consumption expenditure are the deciding factors of schooling. Whereas, for the urban context, none of these variable is responsible for the behavior of schooling expenditure on their children.

Now, in the case of higher secondary level, mother's age, monthly consumption expenditures are responsible for the pattern of trend in the expenditure on schooling but in the case of urban areas, only mother's age ascertains the schooling expenditures on higher secondary level.

Summary and Conclusions

In this paper, an attempt has been made to locate the various determinants of demand for shielding in rural, urban areas separately and also between different levels of school education namely Secondary and Higher Secondary levels. Some of the striking conclusions that have been merged form this study are as follows.

1. In both rural and urban areas, the average amount spend on schooling is mostly decided by the socio-economic factors such as mother's age, caste, monthly consumption expenditure and number of schoolinging children in the mainly (except in urban areas)

2. The most important determinant of demand for schooling is found to be the monthly consumption expenditures and that again depends only upon family income

3. Mother's age effect on children's schoolings is more decisive and concrete than father's age factor.

4. The deciding factors in case of rural and urban areas in explaining the demand for schooling are also different

Hence, we have empirically tested out theoretical model in explaning the economic schooling. The results support the theoretical predictors of the framework. As no plenty of studies that are available on this problem in Tamil Nadu as well as in India, therefore researchers more seriously think and do some crucial research work to fill this gap in the understanding of our knowledge.

The findings of this study support the results of earlier attempts made by Arumugam (1984); Duraisamy (1988, 2001).

REFERENCES

1. Arumugam, P. (1984) "Cost and demand for Secondary Education in Tamil Nadu, Unpublished Ph.D., Thesis, Department of Econometrics, University of Madras.
2. Becker, G.S. (1965) "A Theory of Allocation of Time, Economic Journal, September, No.299, Vol.LXXV, pp. 493-517.
3. Becker, G.S (1976), "The Economic Approach to Human Behavior", The university of Chicago Press.
4. Duraisamy, (1988), "An Econometric Analysis of Fertility, Child Schooling and Labour Force Participation of Women in Rural Indian Households", Journal of Quantitative Economics, 4(2), pp. 293-316.
5. Duraisamy, (2001), "Intra-Family Allocation of Resources to Schooling of Boys and Girls in India", Journal of Quantitative economics 17(1), pp. 70-83.
6. Grossman, M. (1972), "The Demand for Health: A Theoretical and Empirical investigation, Occasional paper-119, NBER, New York.
7. Heyneman, S.P. (1995), "Economics of Education: Disappointments and Potent ional in Prospects", No.4
8. Johnston, (1985), "Econometric Methods", Mc Graw Hill 3rd Edition.
9. Kothari, V.N and P.R Panchamukhi (1975), "A survey of Research in Economic of Education in India", ICSSR, August, New Delhi.
10. Micheal, R.T. (1974), "The Effect of Education of Efficiency in Consumption in T.W.Schultz(ed) Economics of the Family; Marriage, Children and Human Capital", University of Chicago
11. Nalla Gounden, A.M. (1965), "Education and Development study of Human Capital Formation and its Role in Economic Development in India", Unpublished Ph.D Thesis, Kurkshetra University.

12. Panchamukhi, P.R. (1967), "Measurement of the Effects of Public Expenditures", Unpublished Ph.D Thesis, University of Bombay.

13. P. Sacharopoulos G and Woodhall M (1985), "Education for Development: A world bank Publication", OUP.

14. Rosenzweig, M.R and Evenson (1944), "Fertility, Schooling and the economic Contribution of Children in Rural India: An Econometric analysis", Econometrica, Vol.45, No.5, July, pp. 1065-1079.

15. Srinivasan, J. (1987), "Educational Opportunities: An Economic Analysis", Unpublished M.Phil Thesis, Department of Econometrics, University of Madras.

16. Srinivasan, J. (1991), "Demand for Education:A Socio-economic Analysis", An unpublished Ph.D thesis, University of Pune.

17. Srinivasan, J. (2003), "Demand for Education in India: A Socio-Economic Analysis", Essay in honour of Prof P.R. Panchamukhi, edited by M.J. Manohar Rao, Himalaya Publishing House.

18. South India, "Human Development Report (2002).

19. Shah, K.R. (1968), "Outlay on Education and its Financing in India 1950-51 to 1960-61, Unpublished Ph.D Thesis, M.S University, Baroda.

20. Sheehan, J. (1973), "The Economics of Education", George Allen & Unwin Limited, London.

21. Wills, R.J. (1973), "Economic Theory of Fertility Behavior, Journal of Political Economy, May/April.

23

Information Technology Education and Training in the era of Economic Reforms

Implication of Accessibility

*Nagaraju Gundemeda**
*E. Haribabu***

Introduction

Historically human beings, as toolmakers, transformed the techniques of production and gained control over nature by deploying tools. Social Scientists in the recent past have recognized the need to understand the socio-economic and cultural context, which influences the development of technologies at different levels and different points of time and its impact on society. Information Technology (IT) is going to have far reaching implications for production, services and culture.

However, for a country to develop IT, human resources in terms of quality and quantity are prerequisites. In order to build human resources in IT, institutes that impart education have to be established in adequate numbers. The

* Nagaraju Gundemeda is a Research Scholar at Department of Sociology, University of Hyderabad.

** E Haribabu is Professor at Department of Sociology, University of Hyderabad.

demand for IT professionals has generated flow of trained IT personnel across countries and continents. Due to monetary benefits and a number of perks associated with IT jobs, members of diverse social groups have begun to attach a great deal of prestige to IT education. It is the private sector, which has taken the lead in IT industry especially the software industry, IT education and training. This has to be understood in the context of economic reforms initiated by the Government of India.

The decade of 1990's witnessed various changes taking place through out the world. Although the move towards privatization, initiation of policies pertaining to economic reforms had their origin in the 1980's it is only in the wake of the globalization process this acquired new momentum. The economic reforms initiated in the early 1990's in India are considered as a landmark change. This brought about significant changes in various sectors both at the structural and functional level. IT industry is one of the sectors that was greatly affected by these changes. We attempt to look into the implications of economic reforms in shaping IT education industry and their implications for accessibility to various social groups.

Economic Reforms in India

The Nehruvian model of mixed economy transformed Indian economy that was devastated by 200 years of colonial rule. Response to the severe crisis in balance of payments in 1990's led to initiation of economic reforms by the then Prime Minister P.V. Narasimha Rao and his Finance Minister Manmohan Singh. Ahluwalia (1999) claims that rethinking over the economic policies adopted by then governments started in 1980's but agenda of reforms materialized in 1990 only.

These economic reforms are considered as landmark in the development of national economy as they lifted state controls. Major emphasis was laid down on private investments, opening the economy to foreign investments, reforms in the financial sector, structural adjustment policies and integrating the national economy into the world economy. According to Teltumbde (1996) the crux of these economic reform programmes is to depend more on global market forces, steadily lifting the controls, limiting the role of state, and shift towards private sector based economy instead of public sector evolved under Jawaharlal Nehru's vision.

Economic reforms had implications for diverse sectors including educational sector. As a part of the structural adjustment policy, the reforms work in the form of decontrol of industries, aggressive privatization of government-owned entities and structural changes. Varshney (1999) raised a set of questions on the process of economic reforms; firstly, how many people are affected by these economic policies? Secondly, how organised they are, and Thirdly, whether the affect is direct, obvious, and short run, or indirect, subtle and long run. According to the author, there is a corresponding relation between the economic reforms and its impact on diverse sectors and various social groups. The more the coverage of the economic policy, the more the people that get affected.

Objectives of the paper

With the above backdrop the present paper aims to address the following questions:

1. How IT education expanded in the era of economic reforms?
2. Which sections of the society have been gaining access to IT education? How could they gain access? and
3. What does economic reforms mean for the rural and underprivileged sections?

Before going to address the above questions it is quite important to understand the social, economic and historical context of IT and consequently IT education across the regions over a period of time particularly from the 1980's.

Growth of IT Industry in India

Information Technology is a very broad concept with applications in sciences, engineering, education, economy, polity and service sectors. It deals with using information, computing, and communication. It affects virtually all the institutions and organizations of simple to complex nature. The growth of IT industry could be understood in the context of liberalization of Indian economy during 1990s. The basic philosophy of reforms is integrating the Indian economy into the world market forces and to strengthen the domestic economy with private sector initiatives. IT industry is one of the most successful industries in India. The potential of IT sector, especially the software industry can be understood by looking at its contributions to the national economic growth and in accommodating large chunk of human resources. It is commendable when compared with the any other industries.

The following table provides the growth of Indian Software exports over the last two decades.

Table No.1 shows the profile of Indian software exports and its growth rate. It indicates that since 1980 software Industry, particularly the exports registered a significant growth rate. The latest statistics (2001-02) show negative growth from the year 1999-2000. The impact of slowdown in IT industry is evident from the slip in the growth rate.

Table No.2 shows the status in terms of the growth of software exports in crores of Rupees. Although software exports registered a significant growth with 45% in 1999-2000, and 64% in the year 2000-2001, the consequent years experienced a declining trend with 21% and 22% in 2001-2002 and 22% respectively. The IT enabled (IT-E) services segment show impressive growth rate though it showed

Table 1: Indian Software Export Figures

Year	*Software Exports (US$m)*	*Export growth (%)*
1980	4.0	—
1981	6.8	70%
1982	13.5	99%
1983	18.2	35%
1984	25.3	39%
1985	27.7	9%
1986	38.9	40%
1987	54.1	39%
1988/89 (Apr-Mar)	69.7	(29%)
1989/90	105.4	51%
1990/91	131.2	24%
1991/92	173.9	33%
1992/93	219.8	26%
1993/94	314.0	43%
1994/95	480.9	53%
1995/96	668.0	39%
1996/97	997.0	49%
1997/98	1650	65%
1998/99	2180	32%
1999/2000	3600	65%
2000/01	5100	42%
2001/02	7300	43%

Source: Richard Heeks (2002).

Table 2: Software Export Growth Rs (in crores)

Item	*1999-2000*	*%*	*2000-2001*	*%*	*2001-2002*	*%*	*2002-2003*	*%*
SW exports	14, 750	45	24, 250	64	29, 400	21	35, 800	22
ITe Services	2400	85	4100	71	7, 100	73	11, 700	65
Total	**17, 150**	**50**	**28, 350**	**65**	**36, 500**	**29**	**47, 500**	**30**

Source: Data Quest (2002).

negative growth rate in the year 2002-2003 when compared with the previous year (2001-2002). From Table no.2 we conclude that the IT-E services sector has been playing a vital role in the growth of IT industry in India due to its strength in human resources in the country.

Table no.3 provides the overall Industry segmentation in Rupees both in Software Exports segment as well as in domestic sector. Since we have shown the growth of software exports in table no.2 now we concentrate on the growth rate in domestic sector. Starting with 23% in 1991-92 it was registered a significant growth rate of 44% till 1994-1995. Although it registered relatively lesser growth upto the year 2000 but once again one could see increase in growth rate (65%) in the 2001. Overall, industry growth slipped from 65% in 2001 to a meager 14% in 2002. It was mainly because of the contrasting growth of 73% in IT e Services and software growth of 19%. It is evident that the year 2001-02 was bad year for domestic industry.

Table 3: Overall Industry Segmentation (RS in crores)

Year	*SW Exports*	*Domestic (D)*	*Growth rate % (D)*
1991-92	676	2041	23
1992-93	931	2524	27
1993-94	1405	3356	38
1994-95	1882	4956	44
1995-96	2681	7032	42
1996-97	4847	8587	38
1997-98	7180	10, 835	34
1998-99	10, 752	13, 204	33
1999-2000	16, 050	17, 002	38
2000-2001	29, 896	24, 670	65
2001-2002	37, 846	24, 288	14

Source: Data Quest (2002).

What one could draw from table No.3 is that the domestic players have been playing a crucial role in the sustenance and the growth of IT industry in India. The role of IT industry in the growth of national economy seems to be remarkable. Table no.4 provides the sectoral contribution of growth percentage in domestic IT industry.

While talking about the role of IT in the growth and development of economy Helmut (1988) emphasized on the contradictory nature of IT. According to the author IT works positively for developed nations and makes the developing countries as dependent nations in relation to the former. According to him IT is considered to be the threat because its spread may lead to technological re-colonization or over-dependence on the developed nations (*Ibid*). The above observations are perhaps right in case of the Indian IT industry, which in its operation, and market demand tend to depend on the national economies of developed countries.

Table 4: Trends in Domestic Sectoral Spending

Year	*Government %*	*Public Sector %*	*Private Sector %*
1998-1999	19.4	14.4	66.2
1999-2000	14.2	16.5	69.3
2000-2001	15.1	18.9	66
2001-2002	12.0	15.0	73

Source: Data Quest (2002)

The Indian IT software industry and services accounts for almost 2% of India's GDP. The government of India has been consistently supporting the IT industry by removing the bottlenecks in the path of its development. As part of policy measures, each ministry was asked to allocate 2-3 % of their respective budgets to the promotion of IT. The Government of India initiated programmes such as E- governance; E- economy, E-Health, and E-learning and policies such as Information Technology for all are some of major steps for promoting IT. (India, 2002). Table no.4

indicates that the main engine behind the growth of IT industry is the private sector. The proportional representation of private sector in IT industry is accelerating year by year. On the whole the private sector remains a dominant player in IT industry.

Demand for IT Professionals: Projections

It is very clear from job advertisements particularly from early 1980's that one's chances of getting employed are enhanced by the possession of qualifications in micro-electronics, computing, systems analysis, telecommunications, fiber optics, and so on According to Webster (1989), advent of IT in the late 70's education systems of Western countries and America witnessed a gradual transition towards IT oriented streams. IT courses got institutional support because of its market reputation, as a result of which number of seats in these streams raised significantly.

The rise of information society in the West is fundamentally driven by the wider application of IT in all the spheres of life. Still most of the developed countries have shortage of IT professionals. So they are on the look out for IT professionals from out side to fill in the vacuum.

IT Professionals Required by Advanced Countries

According to the IT industry estimates, US apart from its present ten million IT workforce need to fill 1.6 million new jobs in the next few years. In Europe there is a shortage of over 2,00,000 IT professionals, Japan needs nearly one million new jobs, Germany is looking for 20,000 IT specialists and Italy is seeking 15,000 additional manpower. All these countries are looking towards India to fill the gap (Verma, 2001).

IT Professionals Required by India

Although India is one of the major sources of human resources for software production and promotion the existing human resources is not sufficient to meet the requirements of India by 2008 if the present trend of growth continues in IT education. Globally, India is considered as a major source of software providers and developers next only to United States.

Even in United States, Indians form a large and highly respected section of the software development community. There are multiple reasons in making India the most preferred center for software development; firstly, well structured secondary and university education, secondly, English language skills, thirdly, government support for the IT industry (e.g. preference in power supply at subsidized rates, tax incentives etc, pro-active legal framework) and fourthly, protection of contractual rights. The above factors pave a way to the Indian software professionals to enter into the global software industry.

A large number of IT professionals are trained in Indian have been migrating to USA, Europe, and some of the Asian countries like Singapore, Thailand and Malaysia to render their services in their expert domain. The push factors for the migration of IT workers are limited employment opportunities, under employment, low salaries and lack of infrastructure. The pull factors are high salaries, social recognition, rich lifestyles and good employment in the countries of destination. Due to high esteem and social prestige in addition to the monetary benefits and number of perks associated with the IT jobs, members of diverse social groups have begun to attach a great deal of importance to IT education.

Table No.5 shows that, the total demand for IT professionals is expected to grow by three fold, from 4,16,000 in 2001-02, to 11,76,240 by 2004-05, but the supply rate is not corresponding to that of the demand, it would be only double from 4,28,000 to 8,75,000 during the corresponding period and this results in a shortage of 3,01,240 IT professionals.

Table 5: India IT Labour Supply: Software*

Name	*2001-02*	*2002-03*	*2003-04*	*2004-05*
Existing Work Force	3, 60, 000	4, 28, 636	5, 42, 494	6, 75, 252
New IT Labour	1, 32, 986	1, 58, 099	1, 72, 977	192194
Effective no of IT Professionals returning to India**	-64350	-44241	40219	7800
No of IT Professionals	4, 28, 636	5, 42, 494	6, 75, 252	8, 75, 246

** Based on the number of IT professionals leaving the country and the number of those returning to India.

* Excludes IT Enabled Service (ITe) Professionals.

Source: Nasscom, Extrapolation and analysis by Data quest (2002).

IT Education and Training

The foregoing account presents the far-reaching implications of IT for diverse fields. With the above background, we present how IT education expanded in the era of economic reforms in addition to the importance attached to the IT education by different social groups.

According to Ganesh Natarajan (2002), the phenomenal growth of IT industry across the globe and in India led to massive demand for IT training. The college going youngsters were the first who attached lot of significance to IT education and training across the country. It also led to significant changes in educational priorities. Table No.6 provides the growth of IT education and training industry over the last 7 years.

The percentage of IT training in the overall IT segmentation in the year 2001-02 was 2% (Rs 1467 crores). It is very less when compared to the year 1998-99. The above table shows that the average of growth rate of IT education is more than 35%. Although there is consistency in the growth, due to the slowdown in the global as well as in domestic IT industry, IT education segment has been

Table 6: Status of IT Training Industry

Year	*Revenue*	*Growth (%)*
1995-96	458	38
1996-97	662	44
1997-98	912	38
1998-99	1333	46
1999-00	1753	31
2000-01	2594	48
2001-02	1575	-39

Data Quest (2002)

severely affected by these developments. As a result it registered a negative growth rate.

Pillai (2000) claims that the process of economic reforms strengthened the growth of IT industry and the IT education sector to train human resources. This can be seen in the proliferation of IT related courses in colleges and mushrooming growth of computer engineering in engineering colleges.

The evolution and development of IT education in India and Andhra Pradesh are largely in response to the social demand where diverse sections of the society have come to attach a great deal of significance to IT professional jobs which consequently has boosted the growth of IT education and training industry in different parts of the country. Here a systematic analysis has been made to understand the socio-economic background of the students from different social groups who are enrolled in the private IT education institutes. The analysis here is based on the empirical study conducted in IT education centres in Andhra Pradesh.

IT Education: Formal Sector

In India, there has been consistent encouragement to run three-year MCA programs, four year B.Tech and

M.Tech, in government and private colleges. Private sector has taken the lead in promoting and imparting IT education and training at various levels to meet the requirements of diverse categories of students. Almost all universities started/ expanded degree level programmes in IT to meet the growing demand for software professionals.

The Government has been offering affiliations to specialized privately run institutes that focus exclusively on IT degree programmes (S.N.Maheswari, 2000). Figures indicate that 500 out of 700 engineering colleges offer B.Tech. Programmes in electronics, computer science and engineering, and 300 universities/colleges, offer BCA/BIT, three/four year programmes. It should be noticed that the formal sector, at degree level trains 75,000 graduates every year.

Non-formal Sector

Private IT training institutes spread all over the country play a critical role. The non-formal sector, particularly institutes such as NIIT, Aptech and DOEACC scheme provide not only short-term, skill-oriented programmes, but also provide opportunities to university students, who could not get admitted to degree programmes in IT, to pick up IT expertise while being enrolled in a non-IT degree courses.

The non-formal sector has over 5000 training institutions and is rapidly increased at the rate of around 20% per annum during 1990s. The total income being generated by this sector currently is around RS 1,200 crores. The IT- enabled services are likely to provide one million jobs over the next eight years as projected by the NASSCOM-McKinsey (NM-1) study. According to the estimates the private initiatives in providing training in the areas of call centres, medical transcription and back office operation are likely to grow explosively to take full advantage of the emerging opportunities. (S.N.Maheswari, 2000).

The phenomenal growth of non-formal sector has two dimensions; one the limitation within the formal sector, two, the market demand and periodical shift in approaches of the non-formal sector in relation to changing market demands. The World Bank report (2000) pointed out that the education system is facing new challenges posed by globalization of the economy, modernization of industry and the moves towards knowledge based society. Some of the major problems faced by the higher education of India are as follows.

Firstly, the impact of globalization of economy: extensive liberalization of Indian economy led to an integration of Indian economy into the world economy. It resulted in high international mobility of the workforce, and drastic transformation of the society into a knowledge-based society and this has posed new challenges to the higher education system. The employment potential for professional graduates significantly widened from mere state and national level to international market places. Most institutions have failed to meet these new challenges.

Secondly, over-centralization and lack of autonomy and accountability of institutions resulted in malpractice in examinations, outdated curricula, and poor infrastructure etc.

Thirdly, the large wastage of the scarce resources in the form of dropout and failure rates which are as high as 40%, and an over supply of graduates from traditional disciplines have led to huge unemployment and under employment.

Fourthly, the mismatch between student demand and market requirements and institutional output and training modalities.

Fifthly, the high demand for admission for professional streams has resulted in the creation of admission capacity in many areas far beyond the needs of the economy. On the one hand there is over-supply of engineering graduates in specific disciplines like mechanical engineering and electronics, on the other there is shortage of manpower in disciplines like IT related courses. This reflects both unscientific planning of programs and the poor quality of training in most of the colleges.

Sixthly, despite of the phenomenal expansion of higher education in the country since independence, only 6% of the relevant age group of 18-23 years is enrolled for higher education due to the limited capacity. (Share of the science and technology education account for less than 2%). This limits the access particularly to the professional courses, a trend which has led to mushrooming of thousands of private institutions. Seventhly, there is wide disparity between regions in India in the development of IT educational institutes due to the socio-economic and historical background.

The above-mentioned factors are responsible for the leading role of private sector in IT education. The limitations and structural and functional problems of the public sector is the base on which the private players thrive. The predominant role of private sector in imparting IT education has larger implications for the questions of equality of opportunities. These questions are more relevant and important in India, which is hierarchically organised society. Access to educational opportunities tends to vary across social groups (caste, class) in the stratified social order.

IT Education and Training: Andhra Pradesh

Andhra Pradesh in one of the major sources of human resource in India. Different social groups in Andhra Pradesh have attached lot of significance to the IT professional jobs. It has resulted in the spread of IT education and training across the state, particularly in towns and cities. There has been increasing social demand for IT education.

The government of Andhra Pradesh has quickly recognized the potential of IT to boost the state economy and its applicability in shaping the state towards E-Governance. IT courses have been opened in a number of government colleges as well as privately managed colleges. The number of engineering colleges increased from 32 in 1995 to 225 by 2002. Most of the IT training institutions and colleges are private funded and managed. Bachelors in Computer Application (BCA) has been introduced in 414 colleges and MCA course is introduced in 116 colleges. Together these institutions produce about 10,000 IT/ software graduates, about 5000 MCAs and over 16,000 BCA s per year.

According to Data Quest, a computer magazine, 23% of the total software engineers in India are from Andhra Pradesh. Another major initiative of the state is the move towards ushering in electronic governance. The primary motive of these efforts is to leverage the power of information and communication technology to enable Government function effectively (Chowdary, 2000).

Table No.7 demonstrates the skewed distribution of IT education centres in Andhra Pradesh. The concentration pattern reveal that major cities, such as Hyderabad, attract maximum number of IT training centres compared to any other cities in the state. A significant proportion of IT education centre concentrated in coastal region of Andhra Pradesh, which is more developed than Telangana and Rayalaseema regions. Even the Mandals, which are considered to be the centres of agrarian activities and connected by the villages, are cut out of the IT education. The above trend depicts that the major destination of IT education centres is capital cities followed by well-developed commercial towns. As a result access to IT education is limited for rural areas aspirants.

Table 7: Distribution of IT Education Centres at Regional Level

Name of the Region	*Frequency of Centres*	*Percentage*
Coastal Andhra	38	17
Telangana	18	08
Hyderabad	145	64
Rayalaseema	21	10
Total	**222**	**100**

Source: Data Quest (2001)

To examine the relation between the socio-economic background and the degree of access to IT education, the following indicators such as caste, class, gender and rural and urban background have been taken into consideration.

Caste Affiliation and Opportunities of IT Education

Data was collected from 16 IT education centres in four cities of Andhra Pradesh namely Hyderabad, Vijayawada, Tirupathi and Warangal. Sociologists regard caste as an ascribed entity. Social stratification system and the educational system are not independent entities. They are interrelated. The representation of different caste groups seems to depend upon their position in the caste hierarchy. These positions determine the degree of power and status wielded by the particular groups.

Categorization was done on the basis of the respondent's affiliation to a particular caste group.

(i) UC (Upper castes) includes the respondents belonging to the upper castes namely Brahmin, Vaishya (Komati), Khsatriya, Kamma, Reddy, Kapu, and Velama etc.

(ii) Other backward castes (OBC) consist of Golla, Gouda, Chakali, Mangali, Mudiraju, Kammari, and Kummari etc.

(iii) Mala, Madiga etc., castes fall under the SC category. Lambada, Yerukala, and Koya etc fall under the ST category.

Table No.8 reveals that 58% of the students belonged to the upper castes, 32% belonged to backward communities, 9% belonged to Dalit communities, and 1% of belonged to the Scheduled tribes. ST's representation is insignificant compared to the other caste groups. The proportion of the upper castes is almost double that of the other backward castes and five times higher than the representation of scheduled castes in the IT education enrollment. The reforms in major sectors tend to have uneven impact on diverse social groups who's socio-economic and cultural background vary significantly from each other.

Table 8: Caste Affiliation and Opportunities for IT Education

Caste	*Frequency*	*Percentage*
UC	131	58
OBC	72	32
SC	21	9
ST	01	1
Total	**225**	**100**

The above table clearly demonstrates that the upper caste students outnumber the Dalit and other backward caste students. The reasons could be attributed to the control and access to means of production and services. The economic position seems to have a rough correlation with social position in the stratification system, higher the caste, higher the economic position. The economic reforms seem to have perpetuated the existing inequalities leading to greater marginalization of the socially backward and poorer sections.

Since the IT education is predominantly controlled by the private sector, and due to lack of any government provision like reservations, only the affluent sections of the society are taking advantage of IT education. From the above table we can conclude that the students belonging to upper castes have better access to IT educational opportunities when compared to backward castes, scheduled castes and scheduled tribes.

Sex disparities in educational opportunities tend to be greater in developing countries, and India is not an exception to it. National statistics show the low percentage of women in education at different levels. The 1960-70s green revolution in agriculture sector, steady growth of Industrial sector and economic liberalization has led to significant growth of women in both education and employment sectors.

Table 9: Gender Profile of Students

Gender	*Frequency*	*Percentage*
Male	144	64
Female	81	36
Total	**225**	**100**

IT education attracted a significant number of women due to its unique characteristics such as, in-house of jobs nature, decent salaries, less physical strain, and perks. Table No.9 displays gender composition of the respondents. Sixty-four percentage of respondents were male and 36 percent were women. Trends exhibit that the presence of women in IT education is significant though the strength of male students is 3 times greater then that of female students.

One finds a correlation between proportion of women employed in IT industry and the percentage of women in IT education. The trends also point to the fact that numerical strength of women in IT education is high when compared to other educational fields and sectors of employment. The concept of career women also gave immense importance to the significant growth of women in IT education. The philosophy of liberalization also significantly changed the occupational structure, a move from public sector jobs to private sector jobs. The strategic changes in economic reforms and consequent generation of employment opportunities in private sector paved the way for women to enter IT education to seek diverse kinds of jobs.

The ongoing developments in IT industry have had far-reaching implications, particularly for women IT aspirants. Studies showed that nearly 30% of the IT companies employed women IT professionals in core and auxiliary service of IT industry. (Data Quest, 2001). This trend gives an impression that women's participation in IT education is growing day by day. However, still the proportion of women in IT education is less when compared to that of men. The causes for lesser representation of women could be attributed to the socio economic and cultural factors.

Although women constitutes half the population, due to continuous discrimination and dependence on males in one way or other led to the lower percentage in IT education when compared to the men. The other reason for the lower proportion of rural women in IT education is due to a lack of IT training centres in rural areas. Even though parents have the potential to afford education, age-old traditions work as constrains on women's mobility. In our study we came to know that only one Dalit woman is pursuing IT education from rural background.

According to Indira and Nagaraju (1997) access to educational opportunities is determined by the gender of particular individual. Although the expansion of the number of women in education system is evident, the severe social, economic and cultural constraints act against the utilization of educational opportunities by all women.

Further Indira and Nagaraju notes that while women generally experience some sufferings, the disadvantaged sections among women like rural women, women of scheduled castes and tribes and women from orthodox and conservative families bear severe discrimination.

Access to IT Education: Rural–Urban Contrast

Rural and urban disparities in educational opportunities tend to be greater in India and Andhra Pradesh is no exception to this. Table No.10 indicates the representation of students from rural and urban areas enrolled in the IT education centers included in the study.

Table 10: Place of Residence: Profile of Respondents

Place	*Frequency*	*Percentage*
Rural	76	33.8
Urban	149	66.2
Total	**225**	**100**

Table No.10 reveals that 34% of the respondents hail from rural areas where as 66% of the respondents had an urban background. Although demographically the proportion of rural population is nearly four times greater than urbanites, the study suggests that the urbanite has greater access to IT education compared to their rural counterparts. The advantages of the urbanites are becoming a barrier for rural students. Latently, this has the effect of insulating educational facilities from the latter.

Although the impact of economic reforms brought about changes at structural level or macro level; i.e. structural adjustment reforms, private initiative in education, service sector, and industries of various kinds, these reforms tend to be limited to particular sectors at specific level. The reforms at the micro level tend to uneven impact.

The reasons for less proportion of rural students, concentration in IT education are: lack of purchasing power among the rural masses, lack of proper awareness about the education and particularly IT education, and unwillingness of the market forces to invest in rural setup.

·The flow of finance, modern means of communications, concentration of educational centres give a decisive edge to urban dwellers over their rural counter parts, which only tightens the difficulty they already face arising from their migration to the cities to pursue education (Jayaram1990).

Educational qualifications of the father and Access to IT education opportunities:

The study categorizes the educational qualifications of their fathers into five broad categories. The categories are as follows:

Table 11: Educational Qualifications of Respondents Fathers

Education of the fathers	*Frequency*	*Percentage*
Primary	08	3.6
Secondary	26	11.6
Graduation	108	48.0
PG	62	27.6
Above PG	08	5.8
Total	**225**	**100**

(*a*) Primary education,

(*b*) Secondary education,

(*c*) Graduation and below,

(*d*) Post-graduation

(*e*) Post-graduation and above.

Table No.11 shows that the representation of fathers who had just primary education is very less in number

(3.6%), 11.6% have secondary education, nearly half (48%) are graduates, 27.6% are postgraduates, and 5.8% had more than PG qualification.

The trend gives an impression that students whose fathers were graduates and postgraduates have better chances of acquiring IT education than the students whose fathers have only primary and secondary school education. Based on the above data, we may conclude that education of the father significantly determines the student's access to IT educational opportunities.

Students whose fathers educational qualifications were post graduation constitute nearly 30%. It shows that highly qualified parents attach a lot of significance to IT education to enhance their standard of life and achieve upward mobility. Educated sections of all were the first to embrace new professional streams. Since IT professionals provide a testimony to economic benefits and social prestige, IT education acquired tremendous importance among all the social groups in general and particularly among the educated sections in all social groups.

Table No.12 displays that father's income in cases of 28% of the respondents is less than 5000 rupees per month. 35% fall in the category of 5000-10,000 rupees per month, 24% in 10,000-15,000 rupees per month, and nearly 7% fall into the income group of 1rupess 5,000-20,000 per month. Students coming from household with more than 20,000 income accounts for 6%. The above-mentioned data reveals that majority of the IT education aspirants belong the category households with less than rupees 10,000 per month. They are salary holders working as class II, class III employees in public and private sectors.

It was observed that students from lower income groups experienced cumulative difficulties at various levels. The admission involves, significant amount of money. Later on money required for test fee, course material, and

Table 12: Income Levels of Father and IT Education Opportunities

Income group	*Frequency*	*Percentage*
Less than 5000	64	28
5001-10, 000	78	35
10, 001-15, 000	53	24
15, 001-20, 000	16	07
20, 001+	15	06
Total	**225**	**100**

stationary to name a few of these is difficult to come by. According to the study nearly 60% of the respondents chose to pay fees on installment basis. The number of respondents who paid the entire fee at the time of admission was only 40%. One-woman respondent, who was the daughter of a government civil engineer, felt that the fees charged by the IT education and training centre was beyond the capacity limit of even the middle classes. Discussion on these issues with students led us to conclude that income plays a crucial role in gaining access to IT education among diverse social groups.

According to Sachidanada (1997), the high-income groups have better educational access than the middle and lower income groups. Preferential access to students on the basis of paying capacity at the private educational institutions becomes a potent factor in continuation of differences.

The above trend gives a picture that the IT education is including particular salaried groups at the same excluding the other groups whose income is less than that of salaried groups. Disparities lead to differential access to social groups based on their positions in the class structure.

The present study operationalised the concept of class on the basis of the perceptions of the respondents.

Table 13: Class and IT Education Opportunities

Class perception	*Frequency*	*Percentage*
Higher class	11	4.9
Middle class	199	88.4
Lower class	15	6.7
Total	**225**	**100**

Table No.13 clearly indicates that the middle classes representation is the largest compared to other classes both higher and lower classes. The main reason for the largest number of the students of middle classes in IT education centers has to be understood within the framework of aspirations and motivations to achieve upward mobility in society. The structural changes in agrarian and industrial sector in Andhra Pradesh led to the attribution of new values to the educational streams particularly in the case of professional streams. The middle classes seemed to have attached a great deal of importance to IT Industry, and its allied services. There are multiple factors responsible for this trend; one, IT professionals are best paid since the 1990's. The high salaries paid by the software companies literally lured the parents, cutting across the class, and caste, but the middle classes are the main vanguard of IT education.

Secondly, possibility of employment outside India particularly America and Europe motivate the students to take part in IT education. Basically working abroad enhances the parents' prestige among their relatives, castes groups, and village as a whole. The social elite has continued to leverage the benefits of private education through out the 20th century and the same trend is continuing even today. The demand to equip their offspring with academic credentials has been gaining momentum (Brown 1997).

Conclusion

The initiation of economic reforms was in response to the severe crisis brought about by balance of payments in 1990's. The reforms integrated the Indian economy with the world economy at macro level simultaneously opening up the space to private players. Growth of IT industry and consequently IT education was primarily in response to the economic reforms. Critical examination of economic reforms reveals that reforms unleashed larger implications for different regions and diverse social groups. Although private sector has been playing a critical role in imparting IT education and training by training 0.5 million students per year, but the organization of IT education centres across country shows a skewed distribution. It is limited to the urban centres and developed regions and rural areas are totally excluded.

One could find the relation between the role of private sector in IT industry and its impact on diverse sections of the society. Data shows that gender inequalities in education is continuing in the era of economic reforms in different forms, although at one level it mapped the urban women, on the other hand rural women were marginalized from IT education. The socio-economic background of the students also indicates that only the upper castes and other backward caste students got access to IT education while the Dalits and tribals are marginalized from the IT education opportunities. The impact of reforms at micro level tends to be uneven on different groups. Some groups tends get included and gain from reforms while many others get excluded. The study argues that the state should intervene in providing and promoting IT education in rural areas and include the so-called excluded social communities such as Dalits, tribes and rural women in IT education.

REFERENCES

1. Ahluwalia, KS (1999), 'India's Economic Reforms: An Appraisal' in India in the Era of Economic Reforms (ed)

Saches, D. Jeffrey, Varshney, Ashutosh, Bajpai Nirupam, Oxford, Oxford University Press.

2. Brown Philip (1997), *'The Third Wave': Education and the ideology of parentocracy* in Halsey, A.H et al (ed) Education, Culture, Economy and Society, Oxford: Oxford University Publications.

3. Chowdary T.H. (2000), "IT in the services of Government and people of Andhra Pradesh", Pravasandhrula pratyeka sanchika, Telugu Academy: Hyderabad.

4. Data Quest (2002), Year of Survival, vol.XX.13.

5. Hellmut, Schutte (ed) (1988), Strategic issues in IT International implications for decision-makers. Pergamon InfoTech LTD, England.

6. Heeks Richard (2002), India's Software Industry, http://idpm.man.ac.uk/isiexpt.htm

7. Indira, R and Nagaraju, R (1997), *Gender as a source of Inequality in Education* in Sinha, R.P. (ed) Inequality in Indian Education, Vikas Publishing House pvt ltd.

8. Jayaram, N. (1990), Sociology of Education in India. New Delhi. Rawat Publications.

9. Maheswari.S.N. (2000), "IT Education in India-Incorporation of quality" the journal of Public Administration, July-sep 2000. Vol.xlvi-No.3.

10. Parth, Shubhendu (2002). The HR Time Bomb, Data Quest, May First Issue.

11. Pillai Gopinath (2000), "Higher education in the 21st century". Social Action, pp.390-403. Oct-Dec. vol.50. No.4.

12. Sachchidannada (1997), *Social Stratification and Educational Inequalities* in Indian Education, New Delhi, Vikas Publishing House pvt ltd.

13. Stonier, Tom (1983) The wealth of Information: A profile of the Post-Industrial Economy, Norwood, New Jersey: Ablex.

14. Teltumbde, Anand (1996), 'Impact of New Economic Reforms in India' A Paper Presented in the Seminar on 'Economic Reforms and Dalits in India' Organised by the University of Oxford, Oxford, UK, on November 8, 1996. http://www.foil.org/inspiration/ambedkar/ecoreforms.html

15. Varma Yograj Rani Sarita and (2001). Reality? Not anymore! Data Quest, May first issue.

16. Varshney Ashutosh (1999), 'Mass Politics or Elite Politics? India's Economic Reforms in Comparative Perspective' in India in the Era of Economic Reforms (ed) Saches, D. Jeffrey, Varshney, Ashutosh, Bajpai Nirupam, Oxford, Oxford University Press.

17. Webster, Frank and Robins, Kevin (1989) IT: A Luddite Analysis, Norwood, NJ: Ablex.

18. World bank document "Scientific and Technical manpower development in India", (2000). www.worldbank.org/education/tertiary/stmdreport3a.htm

Part—VIII

Agriculture, Forestry, Tourism and other Issues

24

An Empirical Validity of Complementarity between Public and Private Investment in the Indian Agricultural Sector

K. Sham Bhat[a]
Tripura Sundari.C.U.[b]
I.Mohamudha Begum[c]

Agriculture has been the prime mover of rural India and its growth depends on four major factors. They are: (i) high quality of input should be available as and when required, (ii) Update technology which should be available for use on farm at affordable costs (iii) availability of infrastructure, such as power, irrigation, input supply systems, markets, processing, storage and transport facilities etc., and (iv) the remunerative price for the producers. All these four factors would determine the growth of agriculture, which in turn depends on availability of finance. Finance in agriculture would seek to support either production operations or investments in productive assets and infrastructure.

[a] Professor and Head, Department of Economics, Pondicherry University, Pondicherry–14.

[b] Ph.D., Scholar, Department of Economics, Pondicherry University, Pondicherry–14.

[c] M.Phil. Scholar, Department of Economics, Pondicherry University, Pondicherry–14.

Modern agriculture capital includes all those forms of capital, which are made in the industrial sector under factory conditions; it includes all types of machinery from irrigation pumps to tractors, from sprayers to combine harvesters, as well as various inputs into current production such as chemical fertilizers, pesticides and herbicides. Traditional agricultural capital, by contrast is produced largely if not entirely by labour alone within the agricultural sector. The obvious type of traditional capital is land itself. The theme that 'land is man-made' (Simon, 1997) and that 'the soil of today, owes as much to nurture as to nature'(Lakdawala, 1946) has been stressed by many writers. Boserup (1981) lists a number of labour investment activities associated with land, such as clearing, leveling, terracing, building, irrigating and draining.

A second form of investment in Indian traditional agriculture is livestock. In this context, Raj (1969) has pointed out that cattle can be considered as investment good in the sense that, they produce a number of goods and services (milk, manure, traction and young cattle) over an extended period of time. Moreover, farmers in many parts of the world put in considerable labour building structures and farm implements. And finally, considerable labour is used to prepare circulating capital in the form of seeds and manures.

The role of investment as the prime mover of economic growth is prominently recognized. The low level of economic development in less developed countries is attributable to the meager stock of capital per head of population and the low rate of capital formation. Capital formation or investment in agriculture is pre-requisite for the growth of agriculture and is vital for sustained economic growth of the sector in order to meet the increasing demands. The sustained economic growth of agriculture in a region largely depends upon the level of investment on fixed assets of farm and the rate of capital formation. The influence of investment and capital formation on farm economy is reflected through growth stimulating effects of agricultural development in terms of increased farm income, saving and increased demand of market inputs such as farm machinery, fertilizers, and pesticides and so on. The technological changes evolved in agricultural production during the recent past generated growth awareness among the farm people to modernize their farming by means of higher investment. During the last few decades, the structure of Indian economy has undergone significant changes with the share of agricultural sector in net domestic product declining over the years especially during the eighties, due to relatively lower investment in agriculture (Mallick, 1993).

The capital formation has picked up remarkable momentum only in those areas where conditions are existing for transforming the subsistence production system into a commercial one. It is mainly due to the fact that capital formation is a function of productivity, which in turn, is a function of capital investment and an increase in capital investment leads to higher productivity in agriculture. Therefore, the capital formation is positively correlated with the productivity potential of a particular area. The areas which have lower productivity potential and are poorly equipped with the agricultural production infrastructure have been decelerating in agricultural investment and lagging behind in capital formation.

Capital formation in agriculture comes from public and private investment. Public investments in Indian agriculture enlarge the productive base of agriculture. Public sector investment has played a crucial role in the development of Indian agriculture, more so since the independence of the country in 1947. This development effort has been motivated by one single most objective, namely, food security. For a large nation like ours we cannot escape from expansion in domestic production of food grains commensurate with its growth demand due to rising population and income effects. This objective has been achieved through:- (i) Government price support for important grain crops, (ii) subsidization of key farm inputs like chemical fertilizers and electricity for irrigation pump sets, (iii) Institutional credit support from co-operative and commercial banks of the public sector to meet working and fixed capital needs of farmers, and (iv) a host of other agricultural support measures such as productive base of the farm sector has sought to be enlarged through direct public investments in irrigation schemes, soil and water conservation works, land reclamation, construction of regulated market structures for farm produce, research in farm technologies, etc. In short, the Government departments of irrigation and agriculture tried to enhance capital formation in Indian agriculture.

There is a school of thought, which considers public investments to be essential for inducing private investment in agriculture and it is known as complementarity of public and private investment hypothesis. According to this hypothesis, Public investment in agriculture typically creates infrastructure necessary for agricultural operations to thrive. For example, if a major or medium irrigation project is commissioned, a vast command area would switch from dry land farming to irrigated farming. This would lead to diversification and use of technology. This shift requires the farmer to make additional investment in order to exploit the full potential of the infrastructure made available. Similarly, a milk route combined with processing facility, would lead to an increase in number of milch animals maintained by the local community. The private investment in these cases complements public investments. In fact, public investment must induce the private enterprise to invest, so that the opportunities for incomes and growth are fully tapped.

The second proposition is that of the confidence of the private enterprise in the local area where public investment flow not only creates physical assets and infrastructure, but also provides income to the people and improves their risk taking ability, which is necessary for enterprise development. Thirdly, such increase in incomes also generates additional demand for a variety of produce, which makes it remunerative for the farmer to produce different varieties on account of higher demand. In turn, this leads to further investment. In sum, investments generate demand and increased production. Given the market for the increased production, income levels also increase, which in turn, make available investible resources in the hands of people. This cycle of public investments leading to private investments and incomes and demand for goods and services, which create a need for further investments, is the essence of the theory of complementarity.

Another side of the argument is that Private investments in agriculture would depend on two key factors: (i) the return on investment and (ii) the availability of investible resources, especially institutional credit. It had been a recurrent theme of many academicians that the terms of trade in agriculture are adverse. Agriculture suffers from implicit taxation on account of the protection given to the industrial sector. There is a widespread feeling, not without justification that farmers do not realize remunerative prices even in spite of advances made in production and productivity on account of movement controls, centralized procurement and low support prices. The low profitability in Indian agriculture adversely affects the farmer's ability and willingness to make further investments in agriculture. Hence, complementarity between Public and Private investment is refutable.

In this context, an empirical investigation of complementarity hypothesis is highly relevant in Indian context due to the following reasons: (i) Indian economy is in the process of Globalization and it is looking for extending it to agricultural sector (ii) acceptance of complementarity between public and private investment trends to rejection of economic reforms in Agricultural sector. A number of studies have attempted to analyze the various dimension of capital formation in agriculture. Some of the important issues brought out by those studies include (i) declining trend in public capital formation in Indian agriculture over time (Rath 1989 and Rao, 1994), (ii) complementarity between public and private investment (Krishnamurty, 1985; Bhattacharya and Rao, 1986; Shetty, 1990 and Rao, 1994). Some scholars argue that the complementarity between public and private capital formation will adversely affect the gross capital formation in agriculture (Kumar, 1992). Recently, Mishra and Ramesh Chand (1995) have questioned the validity of complementarity hypothesis. On the other hand, one of the recent studies has shown that the discussions in terms of complementarity between public and private capital formation is irrelevant and hence public investment may not crowd-in private investment and vice versa. (Mishra, 1995).

Karmakar.K.G. (1988) examined the growth trends in capital formation in agriculture, in both public and private sector, and also discussed the impact of economic reforms on investments in agriculture. He opined that public and private investments are complementarity, rather than substitutes, and thus falling investment is affecting private capital formation in agriculture.

Mishra S.N. and Ramesh Chand. (1995) have attempted to provide an explanation of the behavior of public and private capital formation in agriculture during the post-green revolution period and also examined the efficiency of capital use in agriculture. The study has taken issue with claims and contentions in particular with the hypothesis of complementarity. Fitting a regression equation between private & public formation series and finding high positive elasticity of the farmer with respect to the latter and thereby claiming high complementarity between the two is not correct. This is due to the fact that it shows only the impact of public investment on private investment.

Jairath. M.S. and Brijesh Purohit.C. (1996) estimated the trends in capital formation, private and public and its composition in agriculture and also examined the efficiency of capital use in agriculture. The study mainly draws information from various official documents. Appropriate statistical techniques have been used to estimate the trends in capital formation. Depending upon the availability of data, time series analysis has been adopted for the period 1980-81 to 1991-92. It is observed that gross fixed capital formation in agriculture which was steadily raising during the period 1980-81 to 1980-87 became subdued during 1987-88 and there after it fell sharply to the level of about Rs.12, 000 Crores and again picked up marginally after 1990-91. The composition in the agriculture sectors revealed that the share of public and private capital formation accounted for nearly 42 per cent and 58 per cent respectively during 1981-82. The high degree of complementarity between public and private investment suggested that there is an urgent need to enhance public investment in agriculture sector, which in turn will influence private capital investment in the agricultural sector. The marginal efficiency of capital increased from 0.74 to 1.02. This indicates that public capital formation and its efficiency in agriculture declined during the decade.

Janaiah (1996) examined the trends in capital formation, capital productivity, resource flow, gross value of output and incremental capital output ratio in Indian agriculture and to test the complementary relationship between capital formation and output. The analysis is based on data covering the period 1960-61 to 1994-95. The compound growth rates were computed with the help of an exponential function. The relationship between the flow of capital and output level was analyzed by using semi-log model. The sources of growth in agricultural output were estimated by decomposition analysis. The results showed that the ratio of capital formation in public sector to private sector is widening over the period (1965-66 to 1994-95). However, gross capital formation increased in real terms, i.e. from Rs.2, 306 crores in 1965-66 to Rs.4, 895 crores in 1994-95. The Study observed that the gross capital formation has increased at the declining rate. But at the same time, gross output value in the agricultural sector has increased significantly from 1.21 per cent during 1960-61 to 1970-71 to 3.57 per cent during 1981-82 to 1994-95. The growth in capital productivity showed a negative trend except in the 1980's, implying diminishing rate of marginal returns on investment. The positive growth in capital productivity during the 1980's and the early 1990's may be partially attributed to increased output and decline in investment in agriculture. Furthermore, it was also observed that the capital formation during current year has positively and significantly associated with output level in the previous year and vice versa. This implied that the agriculture growth could be accelerated only by pumping more investment to the core sector. Hence, the study concluded that, the existence of complementarity relationship between investment flow and output level is a warning signal to increase more investment in agriculture, on the one hand and to generate more agricultural output by using present resources efficiently and judiciously, on the other.

Ramesh Chand. (2001) examined the emerging trends and issues in public and private investments in Indian agriculture across Indian states. Regression analysis was employed and the study showed that there is wide spread decline of public investment across the states. The lack of complementarity between private and public investments stands out prominently even when the public investment is broadened to include all investments relevant to agriculture. Terms of trade for agriculture and flow of institutional credit are found to be the strong determinants of private investments in agriculture. The impact of public investment on private investment would vary depending upon the type of public in different regional settings. All kinds of public investment may not lead to private investment. Some of the private investment in Indian agriculture may be induced by public investment and some may be autonomised. The importance and role of public investment to create infrastructure and to promote long-term agricultural growth should not be undermined by lack of complementarity between public and private investments. Thus, the study concluded that, however, public investment would be effective in playing the role only if it serves the purpose for which it is created.

The earlier studies are having the following limitation: (i) most of the studies examined the validity of complementarity hypothesis between private and public investment in agriculture, with the help of regression analysis. Regression analysis explains the effect of one variable on another but not the complementarily between the two. (ii) secondly, verifying the complementarity between two series is not correct without identifying the stationery of the data series. This is due to the fact that common attraction between the two series requires stationarity of the series. (iii) Public investment in agriculture is at peak in the year 1980-81. Later, it started to decline. This might have a significant impact in obtaining the results.

On the above background, the present article investigates the complementarity between private and public investment in Indian agricultural sector. The rest of the papers are as follows:- after the brief introduction, section II presents the methodology of the study. Empirical results and discussions were presented in section III. Finally, concluding remarks were presented in section IV.

Section II: Methodology

Simple ratios and percentage methods were employed to examine the trend and pattern of investment in Indian Agricultural sector. Further, Dickey-Fuller test (1979) was employed to examine the stationarity of the data series, which is the pre condition for testing the complementarity between two series. The necessary equation estimated for examining the stationarity of the data series is given below.

$$Y_t = a_0 + a_1 y_{t-1} + a_2 T + a_3 D + U_i$$

Where,

Y_t = Public/Private investment

T = trend

D = dummy variable representing "0" for the year 1960 to 1980 and "1" for 1980-2000 and U_i random error term.

The above equations are estimated both at Zero, First and Second order level. Once the stationarity is established, then the present paper attempts to employ co-integration technique to verify the complementarity between private investment and pubic investment in the Indian agricultural sector. The necessary information's were collected from various issues of National Account Statistics and Economic Survey of India for the year 1960-61 to 2000-2001. The private and public investment data series were considered at 1980-81 prices for the analysis.

Section III: Empirical Results and Discussion

Dickey-Fuller test, Co-integration technique were employed to examine the complementarity between private investment and pubic investment in the Indian agricultural sector. Before entering to this issue, let us examine the role of agricultural sector in terms of income generation and investment. Table 1 reveals the trend of income generated in the agricultural sector. In absolute terms, the income originated in the agricultural sector has increased from Rs.9, 547 crores in 1950-51 to Rs.19, 78, 042 crores in 2000-2001. However, during the same year its share in terms of Gross domestic product has declined from 52.4 per cent to 25.3 per cent. This is a reflection of higher levels of growth rate of secondary and tertiary sector compared to agricultural sector.

Table 1: Trend of Income from agricultural sector (Rs. Crores)

Year	*Gross Domestic Product In Agriculture*	*Total Gross Domestic Product*	*Percentage of Gross Domestic Product in Agriculture to Total Gross Domestic Product*
1950-51	5009	9547	52.4
1955-56	4579	10332	44.3
1960-61	6990	16220	43.0
1965-66	10600	25586	41.4
1970-71	17937	42222	42.4
1975-76	28839	75709	38.0
1980-81	46649	130176	35.8
1985-86	77224	249547	30.9
1990-91	148001	510954	28.9
1995-96	276852	107321	25.7
2000-2001	500532	1978042	25.3

Source: National Account Statistics, A handbook Of Statistics on Indian Economy.

The result of trend of Capital Formation in Indian agriculture is presented in table 2. The total capital formation in Indian agricultural sector at 1980-81 prices has increased four times during the study period i.e from Rs. 1, 668 crores in 1960-61 to Rs. 7, 232 crores in 2000-

2001. When we split the total capital formation into public and private capital the growth of private capital formation out way the public capital formation in agricultural sector.

Table 2: Trend of Capital Formation in Agriculture

(Rs. Crores)

Year	*Public Capital*	*Private Capital*	*Total Capital*	*Percentage of Public Capital to Total Capital*	*Percentage of Private Capital to Total Capital*
1960-61	589	1079	1668	35.31	64.69
1965-66	763	1515	2278	33.49	66.51
1970-71	750	2133	2883	26.01	73.99
1975-76	1088	2359	3447	31.56	68.44
1980-81	1787	3410	5197	34.39	65.61
1985-86	1765	2880	4645	38.00	62.00
1990-91	1368	3498	4866	28.11	71.89
1995-96	1208	5693	6901	17.50	82.50
2000-2001	1332	5900	7232	18.42	81.58

Source: Economic Survey and National Account Statistics.

Besides, it is interesting to note that the share of public capital formation to total capital formation in Indian agricultural sector has remained more or less 31-38 per cent during 1960-61 to 1985-86 except in the year 1970-71, then its share has declined drastically over the years. Hence, it can be concluded that the dominance of private capital formation in agricultural sector has increased over the years compared to public capital formation in Indian agricultural sector.

Table 3 reveals the results of Dickey-Fuller test pertaining to public and private investment in agricultural sector. The test has been conducted by introducing trend and dummy variable. Since 1981-82, there is a drastic reduction of capital formation in Indian agriculture at 1980-81 prices, we introduced dummy variable to capture its impact in the estimated equation to verify the

Table 3: Results of Dickey-Fuller test

Variables	*Order*	*Constant*	Y_{t-1}/x_{t-1}	*Dummy*	*Trend*	R^2	R^2	*F*
$Y_t = f(Y_{t-1})$	0	0.187 (2.02)**	0.942 (31.12)*	-	-	0.962	0.961	968.159*
$Y_t=f(Y_{t-1}, T)$	0	0.117 (0.935)	0.968 (22.14)*	-	-4.98E-04 (0.84)	0.963	0.961	480.779*
$Y_t=f(Y_{t-1}, D)$	0	-7.97E-02 (0.59)	1.035 (22.63)*	-3.72E-02 (2.06)*	-	0.968	0.966	560.97*
$Y_t=f(Y_{t-1}, D, T)$	0	-6.94E-02 (0.52)	1.028 (22.49)*	-5.47E-02 (2.77)*	9.657E-04 (1.275)	0.969	0.967	380.86*
$\Delta Y_t = f(\Delta Y_{t-1})$	1	4.7E-03 (1.02)	0.508 (3.54)*	-	-	0.26	0.24	12.53*
$\Delta Y_t=f(\text{Ä}Y_{t-1}, T)$	1	1.522E-02 (1.385)*	0.46 (3.07)*	-	-4.44E-04 (1.05)	0.28	0.24	6.83*
$\Delta Y_t=f(\Delta Y_{t-1}, D)$	1	1.55E-02 (2.19)**	0.42 (2.85)*	-1.77E-02 (1.95)	-	0.331	0.29	8.66*
$\Delta Y_t=f(\Delta Y_{t-1}, D, T)$	1	5.50E-03 (0.47)	0.422 (2.89)*	-3.32E-02 (1.94)	8.19E-04 (1.07)	0.35	0.296	6.17*
$\Delta 2Y_t = f(\Delta 2Y_{t-1})$	2	-6.59E-05 (0.013)	-0.10 (0.60)	-	-	0.01	-0.02	0.36
$\Delta 2Y_t=f(\Delta 2Y_{t-1}, T)$	2	-1.62E-03 (0.13)	-0.10 (0.598)	-	6.75E-05 (0.14)	0.01	-0.047	0.185
$\Delta 2Y_t=f(\Delta 2Y_{t-1}, D)$	2	3.39E-03 (0.42)	-0.109 (0.64)	-6.07E-03 (0.57)	-	0.02	-0.04	0.339
$\Delta 2Y_t=f(\Delta 2Y_{t-1}, D, T)$	2	-1.19E-02 (0.82)	-0.155 (0.89)	-2.91E-02 (1.38)	1.23E-03 (1.26)	0.065	-0.02	0.76

(Table Contd...)

Table 3: (Contd...)

Variables	*Order*	*Constant*	Y_{t-1}/x_{t-1}	*Dummy*	*Trend*	R^2	R^2	$FX_t = f(X_{t-1})$
0	0.128 (1.53)	0.968 (39.77)*	-	-	0.98	0.976	1581.72*	
$X_t=f(X_{t-1}, T)$	0	0.471 (1.965)**	0.855 (11.005)*	-	2.075E-03 (1.52)	0.978	0.977	819.53*
$X_t=f(X_{t-1}, D)$	0	4.70E-02 (0.38)	0.99 (26.35)*	-1.36E-02 (0.89)	-	9.77	0.976	786.97*
$X_t=f(X_{t-1}, D, T)$	0	0.741 (3.18)*	0.76 (9.99)*	-5.85E-02 (3.09)*	5.817E-03 (3.37)	0.98	0.981	675.36*
$\Delta X_t = f(\Delta X_{t-1})$	1	1.66E-02 (2.73)*	0.142 (0.87)	-	-	0.02	-0.007	0.75
$\Delta X_t=f(\Delta X_{t-1}, T)$	1	2.59E-02 (2.04)**	0.129 (0.776)	-	-4E-04 (0.84)	0.040	-0.015	0.72
$\Delta X_t=f(\Delta X_{t-1}, D)$	1	2.73E-02 (3.06)*	7.69E-02 (0.46)	1.7E-02 (1.61)	-	0.088	0.036	1.687
$\Delta X_t=f(\Delta X_{t-1}, D, T)$	1	1.62E-02 (1.197)	3.48E-02 (0.21)	-3.71E-02 (1.75)	1.02E-03 (1.09)	0.119	0.041	1.527
$\Delta 2X_t = f(\Delta 2X_{t-1})$	2	-1.32E-03 (0.22)	-0.50 (3.47)*	-	-	0.26	0.24	12.07*
$\Delta 2X_t=f(\Delta 2X_{t-1}, T)$	2	-7.11E-05 (-0.005)	-0.498 (3.42)*	-	-5.45E-05 (0.096)	0.26	0.21	5.87*
$\Delta 2X_t=f(\Delta 2X_{t-1}, D)$	2	4.76E-04 (0.05)	-0.50 (3.44)*	-3.17E-03 (0.26)	-	0.26	0.214	5.91
$\Delta 2X_t=f(\Delta 2X_{t-1}, D, T)$	2	-2.91E-03 (0.17)	0.50 (3.39)*	-8.19E-03 (0.34)	2.71E-04 (0.24)	0.26	0.19	3.85

Y = Public; X = Private

stationarity in public and private capital formation in Indian agriculture. We formulated the null hypothesis that "β" coefficient is not negative against the alternative hypothesis, that it is negative. The experiment of Dickey-fuller test was conducted at zero, one and second order level. The test results of "β" coefficient of public and private investment in table 3 are not negative and statistically significant at the identical order. Hence, it can be concluded that both private and public investment data series in the Indian agricultural sector are not stationary at the order selected for our study. Hence, existence of co-integration between private and public investment in Indian agricultural sector is completely ruled out, which implies that there is no complementarity between private and public investment in Indian agricultural sector.

Section IV: Concluding Remarks

Dickey-Fuller test is employed to examine the complementarity between private and public investment in Indian agriculture. The necessary information's were collected from various issues of National Account Statistics and Economic Survey of India for the year 1960-61 to 2000-2001. Besides, the public and private investment data series considered for the study are at 1980-81 prices.

The analysis reveals the non- existence of complementarity between private and public investment in Indian agriculture. The possible reasons for non-existence of complementarity between private and public investment in Indian agricultural sector are (i) private sector capital formation in Indian agriculture may be mainly influenced by autonomous than public investment. (ii) The efficiency of public investment in Indian agricultural sector is highly questionable which may be acting as disincentive for private capital formation in Indian agriculture sector (iii) generally, private investment in agriculture will mainly depend upon return on investment and availability of investible resources, especially institutional credits. However, the terms of trade between agriculture and industries are adverse. Besides, farmers do not realize remunerative prices even in spite of advances made in production and productivity on account of movement controls, centralized procurement and low support prices. This affects the farmer's ability and willingness to make further investments in agriculture.

Hence, the present study calls for the following policy options: (i) the government should allow the market forces to operate across Indian states, without putting restrictions such as movement controls and centralized procurement, (ii) the support prices fixed by the government, should take into account the actual cost and normal profit of farmers in agricultural sector and (ii) the efficiency of public investment should be mounted up by concentrating on infrastructural side and as far as possible populistic measures: such as subsidizing agricultural inputs, institutional credits should be reduced in a phased manner.

REFERENCE

1. Bhattacharya, Rao (1986), "Agriculture-Industry Interaction: Issues of Relative Prices and Growth in the context of public Investment", Presented in the Eighth World Economic Conference, New Delhi, December 1-5.
2. Boserup, E.(1981), Population and Technology (Basil Blackwell, Oxford), p.45.
3. Dickey, D.A and W.A.Fuller (1979), "Distribution of the estimators for Autoregressive time series with unit root", *Journal of the American Statistical Association*, Vol.74, PP.427-431.
4. Jairath. M.S. and Brijesh Purohit.C. (1996), "Trends and Capital Formation in Indian Agriculture a case of Arid India", *Indian Journal of Agriculture Economics*, No.4, Oct-Dec, pp.587-596.
5. Janaiah (1996), "Flow of Investment and Transformation of Indian Agriculture holds Complementarity relationship",

Indian Journal of Agriculture Economics, Vol.51, No.4, Oct-Dec, pp.613-615.

6. Karmakar.K.G. (1988), "Capital Formation In Agriculture and Role of Institutional Credit", *Journal of Rural Development*, Vol.17, No.1, pp. 37-52.

7. Krishnamurty, K.(1985), "Inflation and Growth: A Model for India", in K. Krishnamurty and V.N.Pandit (Eds.) (1985), *Macro Modelling of Indian Economy: Studies in Inflation and Growth*, Hindustan Publishing Corporation, Delhi.

8. Kumar, A.Ganesh (1992), "Falling Agricultural Investment and Its Consequences", *Economic and Political Weekly*, Vol.27, No.42, October 17.

9. Lakdawala, D.T. (1946), Justice in Taxation in India (popular book Depot, Bombay), p.127.

10. Mallick, S.K.(1993), "Capital Formation in Indian Agriculture- Recent trends", *Indian Journal of Agriculture Economics*, Vol.48, No.4, Oct-Dec, pp.667-676.

11. Mishra S.N. and Ramesh Chand. (1995), "Public and Private Capital Formation in Indian Agriculture-Comments on Complementarity hypothesis and others", *Economic and Political Weekly*, Vol.30, No.25, pp A-64 to A-79.

12. Nilakantha Rath, (1989), "Agricultural growth and Investment in India", *Journal of Indian School of Political Economy*, Vol.1, No.1, Jan-Jun, pp.64-75.

13. Raj, K.N.(1969), "Investment in Livestock in Agrarian Economics", *Indian Economic Review*, Vol.IV (1) New Series, p.2.

14. Ramesh Chand(2001), "Emerging trends and issues in Public and Private investments in Indian Agricukture: An state wise analysis", *Indian Journal of Agriculture Economics* Vol.56, No.2, April to June, pp.161-182.

15. Rao, (1994), "Agricultural Growth, Rural poverty and Environmental Degradation in India", Oxford University press, New Delhi.

16. Shetty, S.L.(1990), "Investment in Indian Agriculture: Brief Review of Recent Trends", *Economic and Political Weekly*, Vol.25, No.7 and 8, February 17-24.

17. Simon, J.L.(1977), "The Economics of Population Growth"(Princeton University Press, Princeton), p.238.

25

Decadal Performance of Foodgrains Productivity in West Bengal

An Inter-District Analysis

Kakali Majumdar *
Partha Basu **

Introduction

West Bengal, a leading state of Eastern India is predominantly a food grains producing state. The area under food grains constitutes more than 85% [Chatterjee and Roy, 1998] of the gross cropped area of the state. Unfortunately for many years the growth of food grains in this state remained low. Up to 1980 we had agrarian impasse. Green Revolution which was found during 1964-65 at all India level, was basically concentrated in the North-Western states like Punjab, Haryana, Uttar Pradesh etc and was confined mainly to wheat. Of course even in the rice producing Eastern state of West Bengal a significant positive trend break was found during mid 60s

* Research Scholar of Economics, Department of Humanities and Social Sciences, Indian Institute of Technology, Kharagpur, West Bengal–721302.

** Professor of Economics, Department of Humanities and Social Sciences, Indian Institute of Technology, Kharagpur, West Bengal–721302.

[Boyce, 1987] as a result of the adoption of new agricultural technology but it was relatively mild and short lasting. During 1970s the average growth rate of food grains was only .5 percent per annum [Sen and Sengupta, 1995]. After a long period of stagnation during 1980s West Bengal witnessed a remarkable growth rate in food grains output. But this growth was not sustained for a long time. Once again a sharp fall was noticed during the next decade.

Decomposition theories say growth in agricultural output is the net result of the growth in area and productivity and these are the two basic factors through which the ups and downs of agricultural output growth can be explained. Productivity can again be subdivided into yield growth and cropping pattern change. While the first one measures the impact of change in output per unit of area the last one measures the shift of acreage from low valued crop to high valued crop. However since the scope of bringing more area under cultivation is limited, emphasis has been laid mainly on increasing productivity of different crops by using different reform practices during different times. In this connection the present paper is an attempt to make an idea about the nature and extent of productivity (valued at constant price) growth of food grains in West Bengal over the period 1970-71 to 1999-2000.

The objectives of this paper are as follows:

(i) To estimate the growth rate of value food grains productivity (VFP) from the best fitted functional form at the state and district level during the period under study.

(ii) To find out if there is a significant change in the slope of the best fitted functional form.

(iii) To measure the contribution of VFP growth to the VFO (value food grains output) growth at the state level.

The main sources of data for this paper are the Government of West Bengal's Economic Review and Statistical Abstract for different years.

Here the study is done for the period 1970-71 to 1999-2000 because the agricultural reform programs in West Bengal were started during 1970s and at the time of data collection for this study the availability was up to 1999-2000.

The paper is arranged as follows. An overview of literature is in the section II. The method of analysis is discussed in the Section III. Results and discussions of this study are in section IV. The last Section i.e. Section V summarises the findings and implications of this paper.

Overview of Literature

Different authors have used various functional forms for studying the pattern and rate of growth of total agricultural productivity or a part there of at all India, state and some times even at the district levels. Among the diverse form, exponential function has been the most common one. So much so that there is the only functional form used by authors like Narain (1977), Sau (1983), Chatterjee and Roy (1998) in their studies relating to productivity growth of agriculture. Both exponential and log quadratic forms have been used by Srinivasan (1979), Boyce (1987), Saha and Swaminathan (1994). The last study has used adjustment for rainfall in the context of exponential function. Linear form was used by Patel (1966), Basu (1998) etc. Gompertz curve, along with exponential form, was introduced for the growth analysis of Indian agriculture and/or industry for the first time by Rudra (1970). This was followed up by Dey (1977), Chattapadhyay and Bhattacharya (1986). Chattapadhyay and Bhattacharya (1986) included the logistic curve " to check whether the trend growth as obtained in the gompertz fit remained largely valid even after the introduction of the logistic curve". Thus over the years variety and complexity of the alternative functional forms has substantially increased in this type of analysis. In terms of frequency of use linear form is second only to exponential function.

Methodological Issues

Many of the authors who considered alternative functional forms for analysis of the agricultural growth used one or more criteria either to explicitly select the best form or at least to describe comparability performances in terms of those norms. Simplest among them is the criterion of R or R^2 used by Sau (1983), Vani and Vyasula (1996) etc. However R^2 can describe the goodness of fit of a statistical relation only when the disturbance term is random, nonautocorrelated and homoscedastic. Among the different violations of these assumptions the problem of autocorrelation is the most common and serious one in the time series data on agricultural production. For this reason Chatterjee and Roy (1998), among others, reported the values of DW statistic along with R^2 in this context. However in the case of the latter study because of the introduction of single and multiple kinks, degrees of freedom differ from function to function. In all such cases along with DW adjusted coefficient of determination (‘$\overline{R}^2$) should be reported and compared as done by Srinivasan (1979), Basu (1984), Saha and Swaminathan (1994). Authors like Dey(1977), Chattopadhyay and Bhattacharya(1986) etc. used D statistic to measure, for the same purpose, the proportion of variation in Y unexplained by the proposed relationship. However little bit of inaccuracy is involved in the use of either D or R2 even in the sense to compare the goodness of fit of a function involving Y and X (and some times other power of these variable) and one involving logarithmic or reciprocal transformations of either Y or X or both. To meet this theoretical objection authors like Chattapadhyay and

Bhattacharya(1986), made use of C statistic in those cases where such complications are involved and at the same time difference in '$\overline{R}^2$ is small. This innovative measures gives, like DW statistic an idea of not only the degree of autocorrelation in the model but also the extent of fluctuation of the dots of the scatter diagram around the trend line.It is rough and ready, since, unlike DW, it is based on only the signs and not the magnitude of the residuals. But for the same reason it can be used to compare the proximity of the dots of the scatter diagram to the trend for alternative functional form involving y, log y, 1/y, log 1/y etc.

Though sub-period wise analysis has come on the limelight in the recent years yet it may be traced back to Dey (1977), Srinivasan (1979), Chattapadhyay and Bhattacharya (1986). Among them Chattapadhyay and Bhattacharya (1986) did separate estimate for separate sub-periods. However, Dey (1977) and Srinivasan (1979) carried out the sub-period analysis jointly by introducing time dummy to derive the advantage of degree of freedom. But it was Boyce(1987) who for the first time introduced Kinked exponential model for the analysis of agricultural growth not only in West Bengal but, to the best of our knowledge even in the Indian context. Kink was introduced to measure the growth rates and test the trend breaks between the two sub-periods. Boyce's study was quickly followed up by Saha and Swaminathan(1994), Chatterjee and Roy(1998) etc. Chatterjee and Roy(1998) used both single and double kink in the exponential model.

Method of Analysis

Concept of VFP and VFO

$$VFP = \frac{VFO}{A} \qquad VFO = \Sigma W_i Q_{it}$$

Where VFP = value food grains productivity

VFO = value food grains output

W_i = constant price weight of the i th crop.

Q_{it} = physical output of the i th crop at time period t

A_t = area under food grains at time period t, which is nothing but the area total of the individual food crops.

Average farm harvest price of the three normal year (1987, 1988, 1989) has been taken here as constant price weight. Aus rice, Aman rice, boro rice, wheat, barley, gram and other pulses are considered in the food grains item. As the harvest price for the other pulses are not directly available, an estimate on the basis of price ratio to similar crops has been made for the present analysis.

The present study makes an attempt to include in the trend selection procedure the kink models in *linear, exponential, log quadratic and parabola function along with their simple forms*. From the scatter diagram we found there is a possibility of getting two abrupt changes in the growth profile in almost all the district and also in West Bengal as a whole during the period 1983-84 and 1991-92. Because of that we have introduced kink in the two years in the above mentioned forms. For these models the following equations have been derived by the present authors:

Double Kink Linear →

$$Y_t=a_1+b_1D_1t+b_2(D_2t+D_3K_2)+b_3(D_3t-D_3K_2)+ u_t \quad (1)$$

Double Kink Exponential →

$$Ln\, Y_t = a_1 + b_1D_1t + b_2(D_2t + D_3K_2) + b_3(D_3t - D_3K_2) + u_t \quad (2)$$

Double Kink Parabola →

$$Y_t = a_1 + b_1D_1t + b_2(D_2t + D_3K_2) + b_3(D_3t - D_3K_2)+ c_1D_1t_2 + c_2(D_2\, t_2 + K_2^2\, D_3) + c_3(D_3t_2 - K_2^2D_3) + u_t \quad (3)$$

Double Kink Log Quadratic →

$$\text{Ln } Y_t = a_1 + b_1D_1t + b_2(D_2t + D_3K_2) + b_3(D_3t - D_3K_2) + c_1D_1t^2 + c_2(D_2\,t^2 + K_2{}^2\,D_3) + c_3(D_3t^2 - K_2{}^2D_3) + u_t \quad (4)$$

where Y_t is the VFP, a_i, b_i, c_i are the parameters estimated on the basis of observed data, t is the time period, D_js are the dummy variables which takes the value 1 in the jth sub-period and 0 otherwise. Here the sub-periods are 1970-71 to 1982-83, 1983-84 to 1990-91 and 1991-92 to 1999-2000. ut is the disturbance term. i, j = 1, 2, 3.K_1 and K_2 are the two break points.

Kink linear trend implies sharp change in the absolute rate of growth or slope on arithmetic scale. Kink exponential trend implies sharp change in the relative rate of growth or slope on semi log scale. Kink in parabolic form implies a jump in the rate of change of rate of absolute growth. Kink log quadratic trend indicates sharp change in the rate of acceleration and deceleration.

Method of selecting trend equation

However there is no full proof method of selecting a best fitted model from different functional forms. In the preset study the above mentioned functional forms have been divided in to two groups depending on the form of the dependent variable and the structure of the functions. Group I includes simple as well as double kink forms of both linear and parabolic equations. Group II covers simple as well as double kink forms of both exponential and log quadratic equations. From these two groups the following models have been dropped at the outset.

1. Auto correlated models
2. Simple models with non-significant coefficient of the quadratic term, if any.
3. Double kink models without any significant evidence of trend break at either kink and non

significant coefficient of the quadratic term, if any in such models, in all the three sub-periods.

There after for each of these two groups the model(or models in case of tie) with highest '$\overline{R}^2$ has been selected at the group level. While choosing between the models selected from groups I and II, if the difference in '$\overline{R}^2$ is substantial the form with highest '$\overline{R}^2$ has been chosen. Since '$\overline{R}^2$ between different groups is not strictly comparable because of the different forms of the dependent variable in case of small gap in '$\overline{R}^2$ the model with lower value of C statistic (Chattapadhyay and Bhattacharya, 1986) has been given preference.

Estimation of growth rates

If we have Linear trend then average growth rate(G_t) of a period is given by G_t = (b/'$\overline{Y}_t$)×100. In case of exponential trend the growth rate is G_t = b×100. For log quadratic trend G_t = (b + 2c$\overline{t}$.) ×100 If the trend equation is of the parabolic form then Gt = [(b+2c$\overline{t}$)/$\overline{Y}$]×100, where $\overline{Y}_t$ and $\overline{t}$ are respectively the harmonic mean VFP and time of a period. b, c are the parameters of the estimated equation.

Test of trend breaks

It has been already mentioned that there is a possibility of the coming up of two sharp changes, better to say two trend breaks, in growth rate of food grains productivity in West Bengal both at state and district level, one is in the year 1983-84 another one is in 1991-92. The first expected break is positive one and the second one is negative. To test the level of significance of the trend breaks the following equations, which are nothing but the modified forms of equation 1, 2, 3, 4, have been used.

For Kink Linear: $Y_t = a_1 + b_1t + b^* t (D_2 + D_3) + b^{**}$

$(D_3t - {}^8D_3)$ (5)

For Kink Exponential: $\ln Y_t = a_1 + b_1 t + b^* t (D_2 + D_3) + b^{**} (D_3 t - 8D_3)$ (6)

For Kink Parabolic: $Y_t = a_1 + b_1 t + b^* t (D_2 + D_3) + b^{**} (D_3 t - 8D_3) + c_1 t^2 + c^* t^2 (D_2 + D_3) + c^{**} (D_3 t^2 - k_2^2 D_3) + u_t$. (7)

For Kink Log Quadratic:

$\ln Y_t = a_1 + b_1 t + b^* t (D_2 + D_3) + b^{**} (D_3 t - 8D_3) + c_1 t^2 + c^* t^2 (D_2 + D_3) + c^{**}(D_3 t^2 - k_2^2 D_3) + u_t$ (8)

Here b^*, b^{**}, c^*, c^{**} are indicating the differences between b_1 & b_2, b_2 & b_3, c_1 & c_2, c_2 & c_3 of equation 1, 2, 3, 4 respectively.

For Kink Linear and Kink Exponential Models the null hypotheses H_{01}: b = 0 and H_{02}: c = 0 have been tested against two-sided alternatives.

For Kink Parabolic and Kink Log Quadratic Models the null hypotheses H_{03}: x = 0 and H_{04}: y = 0 have been tested against two-sided alternatives.

Results and Discussions

Selected Trend Equations

Double kink linear model as compared to other models is giving good fit in West Bengal during the chosen time period. And out of it's 15 districts, in 10 districts this model is best fitted model. These 10 districts are Bardwan, Bankura, Midnapore, Hooghly, 24-Pargana, Nadia, Murshidabad, West Dinajpur, Jalpaiguri and Cooch Behar. In the districts of Howrah and Malda double kink parabola model is giving good fit. Double kink exponential model is giving good fit in the district of Birbhum.In the district of Darjeeling and Purulia, none of the trend equations is giving good fit. For these two cases we have just taken the equation with highest $\overline{R}^2$ ignoring all the above mention procedures and found for both the cases in DKP model the $\overline{R}^2$ is highest.

Table 1: Selected trend equations of the districts and their respective $\overline{R}^2$, DW (at 1% level)

District / State	*Chosen Trend Equation*	$\overline{R}^2$	*DW(1%)*
West Bengal	DKL	.93	2.06
Burdwan	DKL	.91	1.96
Birbhum	DKE	.78	1.46
Bankura	DKL	.88	2.06
Midnapore	DKL	.86	2.12
Howrah	DKP	.78	2.61
Hooghly	DKL	.86	2.48
24 Pargana	DKL	.80	2.17
Nadia	DKL	.95	1.52
Murshidabad	DKL	.86	1.85
West Dinajpur	DKL	.92	1.97
Malda	DKP	.93	2.23
Jalpaiguri	DKL	.42	2.19
Darjeeling	DKP	.28	1.63
Cooch Behar	DKL	.76	1.67
Purulia	DKP	.56	1.69

Growth rates

The calculated state level sub-periods linear growth rates of food grains productivity are respectively 1.06, 5.2 and 1.4. Among the10 districts, where double kink linear model is giving best fit, during sub-period I maximum growth rate is found in the district of Nadia, 3.6 and that of minimum is in Jalpalguri, -1.86. In sub-period II the respective figures are 6.46 and 3.8 in the districts of Murshidabad and Cooch Behar respectively.During sub-period III maximum growth rate is found in West Dinajpur and minimum is in Nadia. The figures are respectively 1.97 and .45. In double kink parabolic cases maximum growth rate for the sub-period I is 2.9 and minimum is -.49. In the sub-period II the maximum growth rate growth rate is 4.7 and minimum is .36. In sub-period III the maximum and minimum growth rates are 5.07and -2.09 respectively. In Birbhum district, only where the double kink exponential model is giving best fit the three sub-periods growth rates are respectively .7, 5, 1.6.

Table 2: Sub-period-wise Growth Rates of West Bengal and the districts

District / State	*Sub-Period I*	*Sub-Period II*	*Sub-Period III*	*Whole Period*
	Trend Equation- Double Kink Linear			
West Bengal	1.06	5.2	1.4	2.7
Burdwan	1.53	5	1.21	2.8
Bankura	.68	5.7	1.83	3.19
Midnapore	.74	6.06	.49	2.9
Hooghly	.79	4.2	.81	2.2
24 Pargana	1.42	5.3	.51	2.5
Nadia	3.6 •	6.04	.45 *	3.2
Murshidabad	.46	6.46•	1.64	3.05
West Dinajpur	-1.28	6.25	1.97•	3.4
Jalpaiguri	-1.86 *	4.16	.60	.96
Cooch Behar	-.04	3.8 *	.58	1.65
	Trend Equation- Double Kink Exponential			
Birbhum	.7	5	1.6	1.7
	Trend Equation- Double Kink Parabola			
Howrah	.69	4.7•	1.06	2.7
Malda	2.9•	3.17	3.39	2.4
Darjeeling	-.49 *	.36 *	-2.09*	.2
Purulia	-.05	3.05	5.07•	2.2

• → Maximum Growth Rate *→ Minimum Growth Rate

To measure the contribution of the of VFP to VFO, the appropriate model for VFO and form that the growth rates of it has been calculated at the state level following the same above mentioned procedures. Like VFP in case of VFO also the double kink linear model is selected as the appropriate model for the state and the growth rates calculated accordingly for the three sub-periods are .54, 5.86 and 1.96 percent per annum respectively. It is already mentioned that the respective figures for VFP are 1.06, 5.2 and 1.4. In the first sub-period the growth rate of VFO is less than the growth rate of VFO. This happens because of the negative area growth rate of that period. However during second sub period, 89% and during third sub-period 71% of the VFO growth rate is being explained by the growth rate of VFP. The contribution of area during this two sub-periods are respectively 11% and 29%.

Table 3: Growth rates of VFO, VFP and Area in West Bengal

Growth Rate	*Sub-periodI*	*Sub-periodII*	*Sub-periodIII*
VFO	.54	5.86	1.96
VFP	1.06	5.2 (89)	1.4 (71)
Area	-.52	.66 (11)	.56 (29)

Figures in the parentheses are the % contribution of the item to VFO

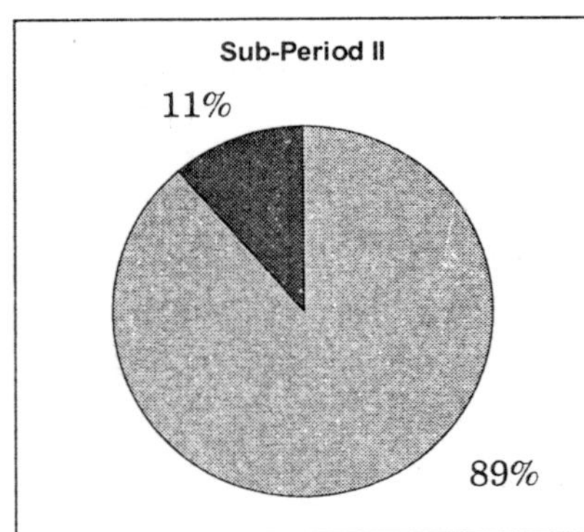

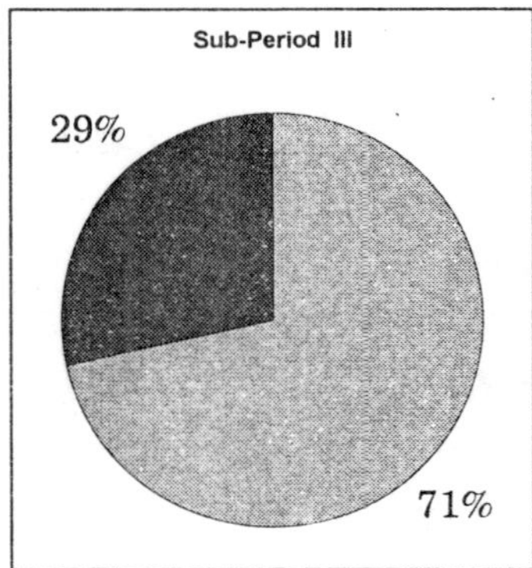

Fig. 1: % contribution of VFP and Area to VFO in West Bengal

The kink models are generally used to measure the sub-period growth trend. Long term growth trend has to be seen without introducing kink i.e. from the simple models. In this present study among the simple forms, parabola model is giving good fit in maximum cases.

In West Bengal the whole period(1970-71 to 1999-2000) parabolic growth gate is 2.7 percent per annum. Among the districts maximum growth rate is found in the district of Bankura, 3.19, and minimum is in Jalpaiguri district, only .96.

Trend breaks

In double kink linear cases, including West Bengal, the state as a whole and in the district of Bardwan, Bankura, Midnapore, Hooghly, 24-Pargana, Nadia, Murshidabad, West Dinajpur and Cooch Behar both the trend breaks are found statistically significant. That means a sharp increase in the absolute rate of growth during

Table 4: Results of Trend Break DKL and DKE cases

Table 4.a

State / District	*Trend Equation*	*FirstTrend Break*	*Second Trend Break*
West Bengal	DKL	.32 (5.2*)	-.21 (-2.9*)
Burdwan	DKL	.33 (4.03*)	-.029 (-2.6*)
Bankura	DKL	.36 (4.2*)	-.24 (-2.02**)
Midnapore	DKL	.32 (4.3*)	-.31 (-3.1*)
Hooghly	DKL	.29 (3.4*)	-.25 (-2.2**)
24 Pargana	DKL	.26 (2.8*)	-.29 (-2.2**)
Nadia	DKL	.27 (4.4*)	-.38 (-4.6*)
Murshidabad	DKL	.33 (3.9*)	-.22 (-1.9**)
West Dinajpur	DKL	.29 (5.5*)	-.12 (-1.7**)
Jalpaiguri	DKL	.25 (3.2*)	-.14 (-1.3)
Cooch Behar	DKL	.17 (3.5*)	-.14 (-2.1**)
Birbhum	DKE	.04 (2.67*)	-.035 (-1.6)

Table 4.b

District	*Trend Equation*	*Trend break of the first linear term*	*Trend break of the first quadratic term*	*Trend break of the second linear term*	*Trend break of the second quadratic term*
Howrah	DKP	-.19(-.47)	-.01(-.34)	-3.0(-3.3*)	.10(2.4**)
Malda	DKP	-.34(-1.4)	-.002(-.14)	1.4(2.8*)	-.06(-2.8*)
Darjeeling	DKP	-.67(-1.6)	.059(1.81**)	-.03(-.04)	-.06(-1.36)
Purulia	DKP	-.005(-.01)	-.086(-2.1***)	.17(.16)	.04(.87)

* Significant at 1% Level
** Significant at 5% Level
*** Significant at 10% Level
Figures in the parentheses are the t values.

1983-84 and a sharp decrease in the absolute rate of growth during 1991-92 was found in the above districts and the state as a whole. The district where only the first trend break is significant is Jalpaiguri.As is Birbhum district double kink exponential model is giving best fit with single(first) significant kink, it would imply sharp increase in the relative rate of growth or slope on semi log scale during second sub-period.

Among the double kink parabolic cases in the district of Howrah the second Kink is negatively significant which indicates a fall in the rate of change of rate of absolute growth during 1991-92. Exceptional result is found in the district of Malda where the second trend break is coming positive.

So there is no doubt about the significant improvement in the growth rate of VFP during sub-period II (1980s) over sub-period I (1970s) in West Bengal and its most of the districts. But the performances of sub-period III(1990s) is really alarming. Significant fall in the growth rate of VFP is the main reason of the poor growth rate of VFO during 1990s. The main cause of the high growth rate of VFP during 1980s was institutional reform (Sen and

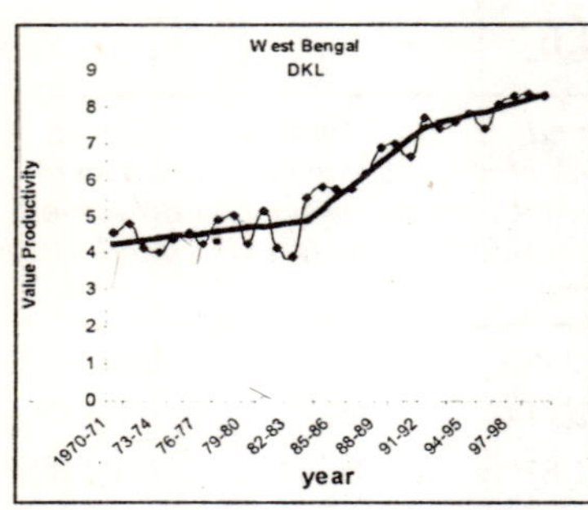

Both significant kink in the DKL case

Only first significant Kink in the DKL case

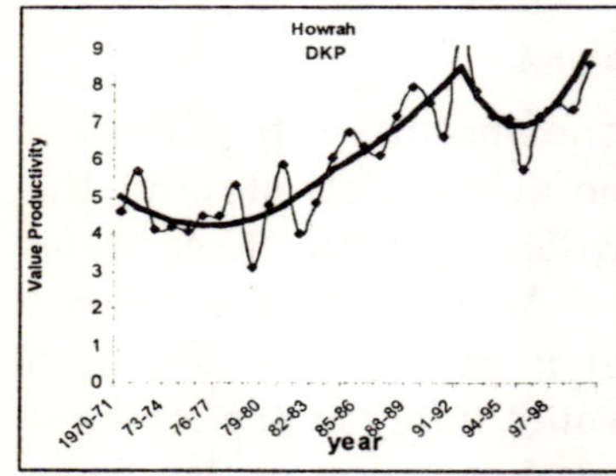

Second significant Kink in the DKP case

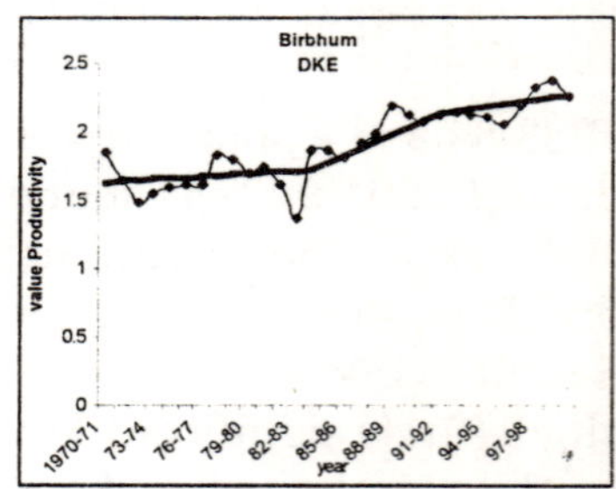

First significant Kink in the DKE case

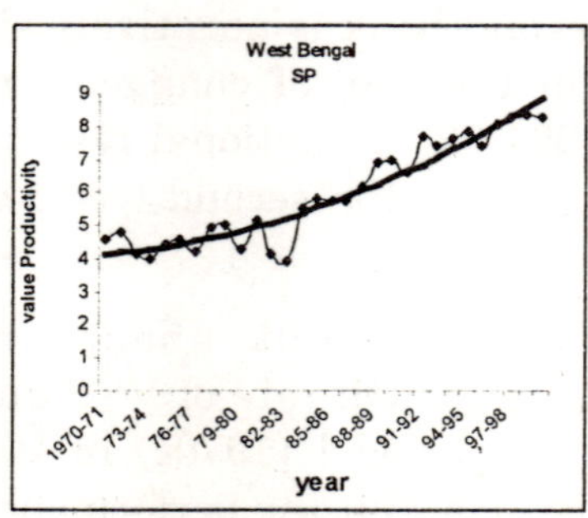

Simple Parabola case

Figure 2: **Graphical representation of some of the selected trend lines.**

Sengupta, 1995; Mukherjee and Mukhapadhyay, 1996) which was started during late 1970s and came in the field in active form during 1980s.Decentralised planning and land reforms are the two important institutional reforms in West Bengal. Decentralized planning is based on a new administrative set up of the three tier Panchayati Raj institutions consisting of village (Gram Panchayat), block (Panchayat Samiti) and district (Zila Parisad). Land reform consists of two types of changes (i). redistribution of ceiling surplus land to the marginal farmers and agricultural labourers and (ii) recording of the names of tenant farmers or bargadars under the auspices of the Panchayats.

Though there has been high growth in VFP in West Bengal during 1980s, there does not seem to have been a commensurate increase in the use of fertilizer and in the adoption of high yielding varieties(HYV) of seeds during 1980s over 1970s. Among the eastern region states only in West Bengal there was a significant trend break in 80s but this trend break could not be explained by inputs. The growth rates of the important inputs like fertilizer, HYV areas, irrigation area ete. were less during 1980s than 1970s (Sen and Sengupta, 1995). The speed of diffusion of HYV seeds between 1980 and 89 was also not significantly different from that of the period 1960 to 1980. Not only that, the speed of diffusion and also the growth rate of the inputs in West Bengal were lowest among the eastern region states. However the yield elasticity with respect to both HYV and fertilizer was higher during 1980s than 1970s and also it was higher than rest of the eastern region states(Saha, 1996). This indicates not the increased use of inputs but the better utilization was responsible for 1980s high growth rate of food grains productivity in West Bengal which happened through the different institutional reforms of 1980s.

There are different arguments about the authenticity of the agricultural date of 1980s in West Bengal as a new sampling design was introduced since mid eighties. May be the high growth of 1980s is owing to the spurious statistical data. But the analysis of Sen and Sengupta(1995) of an independent set of data side by side with official data found almost identical figures during late eighties. The difference was mainly found during 1981-82, 1983-84 and in 1984-85 where the other estimates ie the estimates of cost of production showed much larger yield than the official date. They were of the opinion that even if the new data set was used for the purpose of analysis, still West Bengal would remain as one of the highest rice producing sate of 1980s and the trend break was also remained significant during this period.

The new institutional set up is still continuing, still a sharp fall in the VFP was found in the last decade(third sub-period). Detail study in this field is yet to come. May be the existing reform practice has reached its saturation. There is a limit to any reform practices and it is not possible to sustain the steady growth of productivity unless further technological break through comes. The inter-district variation in productivity growth is also quite prominent in the state. The speed of diffusion of HYV technology in West Bengal has been far less than the other eastern region state (Saha, 1996). Because of the slow diffusion the lagging regions are being more and more left behind. Though the variation in the soil fertility, infrastructure etc are the main cause of the variation in the inter district performance in West Bengal still the uniform distribution of various inputs would minimize the existing level of regional disparities and also improve the growth performance of value food grains productivity in West Bengal.

Conclusion

Following are the main findings that emerged from the present analysis.

1. Growth pattern of food grains productivity in West Bengal and most of its districts are best determined by introducing two kinks in the linear form as compared to any other functional forms with or without kink. In other wards in maximum cases there is the sharp change in the absolute rate of growth in food grains productivity in West Bengal .

2. Both the kinks are statistically significant in most of the cases. In almost all the cases the trend break is positively significant in the year 1983-84. The second significant negative trend break is found in ten districts and also the state as a whole.

3. So far as the growth rate of food grains productivity is concerned in West Bengal and the districts, it was low during the first sub-period(1970-71 to 1982-83) under study. A distinct change was found during the second sub-period in all the districts and the state as a whole. From the first to second sub-period(1983-84 to 1990-91) the state average growth rate was increased from 1.06to 5.2 percent per annum and which again came down to 1.4 percent per annum during third sub-period(1991-92 to 1999-2000).

Both institutional and technological factors are responsible for the high growth rate of food grains productivity during 1980s. Though there was not any improvement in the growth rate of certain important inputs but these were utilized more intensively during 1980s which happened through the different institutional reforms. Thus it can be said that these two factors, institutional and technological, can not be separated out, rather technological factors can be utilized more efficiently through institutional reforms. However despite the continuation of the same systems during 1990s fall in growth rate of food grains productivity has been noticed. The reasons behind is yet to be fully explained. This decline in productivity growth is all the more alarming, because it is the main component of output growth in the state. New institutional and technological changes are very much necessary to give a new dimension to the productivity growth in West Bengal at the dawn of the new millennium.

REFERENCES

1. Basu, A (1998): 'A critique of the progress of rice cultivation in West Bengal', *Bharatiya Samajik Chintan,* Vol. 21, No. 1-2, January- June, pp.45-52.
2. Boyce, Jamse.K (1987): *Agrarian Impasse in Bengal, Institutional Constraint To Technological Change,* Oxford University Press, New York.
3. Chatterjee, Biswajit and Sunanda Roy (1998): 'Growth and Stability of Agricultural production in West Begal and districts, 1970-89- an Economic analysis', in *Regional Dimension of the Indian economy,* Biswajit Chatterjee and Harendranath Sur (eds), Allied Publishers Limited, Calcutta.
4. Chattapadhyay, Manabendu and Gautam Bhattacharya (1986): 'Growth of Indian Agriculture: A reappraisal', *Indian Journal of Agricultural Economics,* Vol.42, No. 1, Jan- Mar.
5. Dey, A.K(1977): 'Green Revolution Contrasts: Rice and Wheat', *Economic and Political Weekly,* Vol-12. No.23, June 4, pp.921-925.
6. Mukherji, B and S Mukhopadhyay (1996): 'impact of institutional Change on Productivity in a small Farm Economy: A case of Rural West Bengal' in *Economy of West Bengal, Problems and Prospect,* D Sarker(eds)(1996), Allied Publishers Limited, Calcutta.
7. Narain, D. (1977): 'Growth and Productivity in Indian Agriculture', *Indian Journal of Agricultural Economics,* vol.32, No.1, January-March.
8. Patel, D.A(1966): 'Growth of Ground nut in Gujarat state' *Indian Journal of Agricultural Economics,* vol.21, No.4, October – December, pp.223-226

9. Rudra, A.(1982): *Indian Agricultural Economics: Myths and Realities*, Allied Publishers, New Delhi.

10. Saha, Anamitra (1996): 'Adoption of Modern Agricultural Technology in Rice cultivation in West Bengal' in *Economy of West Bengal, Problems and Prospect,* D Sarker(eds)(1996), Allied Publishers Limited, Calcutta.

11. Saha, Anamitra and Madhura Swaminathan (1994): 'Agricultural Growth in West Bengal in the 80s: A Disaggregation by District and Crop', E*conomic and Political Weekly*, Vol-29, No.13, March 26.

12. Sau, Ranjit(1983): 'Growth, Stagnation and Fluctuation in Indian Economy', E*conomic and Political Weekly*, Vol-8, No.7, February 12.

13. Sen, Abhijit and Sengupta Ranjai (1995): 'The Recent Growth in Agricultural output in Eastern India, With Special Reference to the case of West Bengal', paper presented at the Workshop on Agricultural Growth and Agrarian Structure in contemporary West Bengal and Bangladesh, Center of Studies for Social Sciences, Calcutta, January 9-12.

14. Srinivasan, T.N (1979): 'trend in Agriculture in India, 1949/50- 2977/78', E*conomic and Political Weekly*, Vol-14, No.30-32, August 28.

15. Swant, S.D (1983): 'Investigation of the Hypothesis of Deceleration in Indian Agriculture', *Indian Journal of Agricultural Economics*, vol. 38, No.13, March 26.

16. Swant, S. D and C.V. Achuthan (1995): 'Agricultural growth Across Crop and Regions: Emerging trend and Pattern', E*conomic and Political Weekly*, Vol. 30, N0. 20, March 25.

17. Vani, B.P and V. Vyasula (1996): 'Growth variability and instability of three major cereals crops in Karnataka: A district level analysis from 1955-56 to 1989-90', E*conomic and Political Weekly*, June 29.

18. DKL è Double Kink Linear DKE è Double Kink Exponential

19. DKP è Double Kink Parabolic DKLQ è Double Kink Log Quadratic

26

Distress Diversification into Non-farm Activities among Poor Rural Female Workers in Pondicherry Region

*V. Nirmala**

*Mogana Soundary***

Section I: Introduction

In most of the developing countries, agricultural transformation is characterized by technological changes and sectoral diversification. More scientific and productive technologies are gradually replacing human labour, besides the sector losing its cultivable areas to the fast expanding industries, housing and commercial activities. As a consequence, there are evidences of a shrinkage in the sector's contributions to gross national product and its share of workforce (Bhadhuri, 1993; Jeemol, 1997; and Parthasarthy, et. al., 1998). The analysis of modern economic growth in the recent developed countries by Simon Kuznets supported this trend in the context of countries that have achieved successful and sustained economic growth. This was partly attributed to the supply-side effects of the improvement not only in the whole economy but in agricultural sector as well, and partly to

* Reader and ** M. Phil. Scholar, Department of Economics, Pondicherry University, Pondicherry-605014.

the demand-side due to the operation of Engel's law resulting in low growth rate in demand for food compared to non-agricultural goods and other services (Chaudhuri, 1993). The process of economic growth has also widened income inequalities, thus compelling the rural workers to diversify into non-farm activities or to migrate from the low-income traditional sector to higher income industrial sector. Besides, the incidence of drought or flood, the seasonal nature of agricultural employment and a rise in educational level have also contributed to a tendency among the rural workers to shift into non-agricultural activities. The increasing supply of casual labour in the Indian rural labour market has been exerting pressure on agricultural and non-agricultural wage employment, thus depressing real wages in the rural sector. This has led to a diversification of wage workers into self-employment activities, which further lowers labour productivity in the sector. This in turn lowers earnings and increases poverty, resulting in a vicious circle with a decline in real wages leading to a decrease in demand for labour and further depressing the wage rates. The slow transfer of labour from farm to non-farm activities, however, indicates the inability of the latter to rapidly create employment opportunities (Jeemol, 1997).

In India, the rural areas bore the burden of workforce restructuring during the 1990s, by acting as the residual sector for the workers who were unable to find non-farm employment either in the rural or urban labour markets. Women workers in the region were the worst affected in the process. The favorable trends of low poverty, real wages and workforce structure of the 1980s reversed during the 1990s, with improved employment elasticities in some of the sub-sectors. However, despite a sharp fall in labour productivity, the post-1990 period witnessed a disturbing new development of delinked trends in rural poverty from the trends in agricultural performance and growth rates in per capita income (Sheila, 1997).

Of late, the increased focus on non-farm sector as an important means of rural income generation in India may be traced back to Vaidyanathan's (1986) seminal work more than a decade ago. He hypothesized that non-farm activities act as a residual sector such that rural workers not fully absorbed by primary sector, spill over into the non-farm sector. Thus, it acts as a sponge for the rural excess labour. This hypothesis was supported by his findings, which revealed a strong positive association between the National Sample Survey (NSS) person day employment rates and the percentage of rural non-agricultural workers. One of the earliest hypotheses postulated on factors affecting the growth of rural non-farm sector was the inter-linkage hypothesis (Mellor, 1976), while the urbanization hypothesis (Kundu, 1991) and equity hypothesis (Samal, 1997) are of more recent origin. The latter stressed on equal distribution of land and rural assets besides the expansion of primary and secondary education, rather than the subsidization of mechanization of agriculture or higher education through consumption expenditure linkages by increasing rural income and achieving a more even distribution of such income.

According to Sheila (1990), two dimensions of growth of non-farm employment emerges in rural labour market which may originate from within or outside the sector. While in the former case, agriculture-led growth may contribute to the diversification of rural workers into non-farm activity, in the latter urbanization and infrastructural development that originate outside the sector leads to it. Under both processes however, rural workers shift into more productive employment in the non-agricultural sector. Further, she identified two types of distress diversification under which non-farm employment acts as a residual labour force absorber: first, wherein supplementary workers with no main occupations take it up as subsidiary activity to supplement their family income; and second, wherein those with main occupations also take it up as a secondary activity.

The VIII Five Year Plan stressed on agricultural diversification as an income augmenting and employment generating strategy (GOI, 1992). As a result, the government poverty alleviation Programmes encouraging non-farm activities have also brought about a change in the Indian rural labour market, due to the greater economic returns from them (Taylor and Yunez-Nande, 1999). Further, due to the more regular employment provided by these activities, they are rather more preferred to the agricultural activities, by the better educated and skilled as well. In fact, the non-farm employment has proved to be an important source and means of raising household income and reducing variability in the southern villages (Walker and Ryon, 1990). Hence, with encouragement from government for non-agricultural self-employment activities, the non-farm labour employment is growing in our country (Visaria and Basant, 1994).

Although the rural women have also been generally benefited by the on-going transformations, their gains have been relatively lower due to their unequal access to opportunities and labour market. This has been aggravated by technological changes and occupational diversification in the region (Rajshri and Lanjouw, 1999). As a result, there is rising feminization of poverty, attributable to their low status, unequal conditions and discriminatory treatment in the labour market. This clearly indicates that the benefits of development have failed to reach women whose choices are generally limited by their low literacy levels and skills. The recent realizations that development should be engendered such that its benefits are shared equally by both women and men, has led most of the developing countries to focus on women's human development. Despite shortage of resources, several schemes and Programmes have been initiated to empower women by investing in their capabilities and bringing about social transformation so as to widen their choices and opportunities. Needless to state that India has not remained untouched by the ongoing structural changes in the development process. With a mere 22.25 per cent female workers in the country, of whom 80 per cent are still concentrated in the agricultural sector (1991 Census), the government efforts have found expression in the launching of specific women development-oriented Programmes like Development of Women and Children in Rural Areas (DWCRA).

The on-going discussions indicate that the analysis of diversification into non-farm activities should be studied within a framework of structure and functioning of labour markets. The economy should be viewed as an integrated one within which farm and non-farm activities, and rural and urban areas are inter-linked. A rise in labour productivity may either increase labour demand or the surplus created within agriculture may be invested in non-farm activities. The additional income thus generated is bound to change consumption demand, which may spill-over to the urban non-farm activity or demand. Hence, non-farm activities are viewed as sponge or residual sector and a potential target for anti-poverty Programmes in rural areas. It is viewed as a sound policy prescription for balanced development, a more equitable distribution of income and poverty alleviation. It needs careful attention and analysis of its interlinkages with employment in agriculture and its poverty alleviation objectives. Against this background, the objectives of the present paper are:- (1) to examine the factors influencing the shifting of rural poor women from farm to non-farm activities in Pondicherry region, (2) to analyze the determinants of non-farm earnings of the sample respondents, and (3) to survey the benefits of shifting into non-farm activities and the problems encountered in the process by the respondents.

The remaining paper is as follows. After the brief introduction, the methodology adopted in the study is outlined in section-II. Section-III discusses the empirical results and the concluding remarks are given in section-IV.

Section II: Methodology

DWCRA is a programme aimed at empowering women through micro-credit and giving them control over income and decision-making power. It was launched in 1985-86 in the Union. Territory of Pondicherry (UTP) as an anti-poverty programme, targeting rural women below poverty line. The present study focuses on diversification of these women from farm to non-farm activities in the Pondicherry region. For the purpose, data were collected from a random sample of 100 poor women using pre-tested schedules during March-May 1999. The methodology used by the paper are simple averages, percentages, ratios, correlation matrix and multiple regressions. The determinants of non-farm employment decision was estimated using Probit and Logit regressions. The estimated equation was of the form:-

$$NFRM = a_0 + a_1 AGER + a_2 EDCN + a_3 SKIL + a_4 DEPR + a_5 CHLD + a_6 ASST + a_7 CRDT + a_8 LSPA + a_9 MAKT + a_{10} FINC + U$$

The ordinary least squares (OLS) regression equation estimated to identify the determinants of beneficiaries' earnings from non-farm employment activity is as given:-

$$ERNG = b_0 + b_1 AGER + b_2 AGSQ\ b_3\ EDCN + b_4 EDSQ + b_5 SKIL + b_6 EXPR + b_7 MARG + b_8 DEPR + b_9 CHLD + b_{10} ASST + b_{11} CRDT + b_{12} NFRM + b_{13} LSPA + b_{14} MRKT + U$$

The description of the variables and their respective expected associations with the dependent variables are shown in Table-1. Correlation matrices were computed in order to examine the possibility of existence of multicollinearity problem in the estimation of the multiple regressions. Further, in order to overcome the emergence of any such problem, step-wise procedure of estimation has been adopted.

Besides, Garret Ranking technique (1969) has been employed to rank the benefits and problems encountered by the sample respondents under non-farm employment. First, the respondents were asked to assign ranks to the listed items on the basis of their significance. Then, the order of priority was converted into ranks by using the following formula.

$$\text{Per cent position} = \frac{100(Rij - 0.5)}{Nj}$$

where,

Rij = rank given to the ith item by the jth respondent; and

Nj = total number of items ranked by the jth respondent.

The per cent position thus obtained was converted into scores using the Garret's table. The scores obtained for each item was added and divided by the number responded. The mean scores were then arranged in descending order and ranked accordingly.

Section III: Empirical Resulst and Discussion

This section discusses the empirical results of the study. Table-1 shows the descriptive statistics along with the expected associations between the dependent and independent variables included in the estimated regressions. The variables are broadly categorized into personal details, family constraints variables and economic factors. As regards the personal details, age of the sample

Table 1: Descriptive Statistics and Expected Association

Sl. No.	Particulars	Means	S.D	Expected Association	
				Non-Farm Employment Functio Function(NFRM)	Earning (ERNG)
A. Personal Detail Variables:					
1	Age in years (AGER)	31.83	7.53	+	+
2	Education in years (EDCN)	5.63	3.91	+	+
3	Skill dummy, taking value 1 if skilled and 0 otherwise(SKIL)	0.70	0.46	+	+
4	Experience under non-farm employment in years (EXPR)	8.22	4.73		+
B. Family Constraint Variables.					
5	Marital status dummy, taking value 1 if married and zero for single, divorced, widowed or separated (MARG)	0.67	0.47		+/-
6	Family size in number (FSIZ)	4.60	1.39		
7	Dependency ratio (DEPR)	1.35	0.86	+/-	+/-
8	Number of children below four years of age (CHLD)	0.20	0.45	-	-

(Table Contd...)

Table 1: (Contd...)

Sl. No.	Particulars	Means	S.D	Expected Association	
				Non-Farm Employment Functio Function(NFRM) (ERNG)	Earning
C. Economic Variables:					
9	Value of land assets in Rs. (ASST)	19950.00	33936.48	-/+	-/+
10	Amount of credit assistance received in Rs. (CRDT)	3936.20	2833.60	+	+
11	Nature of employment dummy, taking value 1 for non-farm activity and 0 for farm activity (NFRM)	0.64	0.48	-	-
12	Non-farm income per annum(ERNG)	5083.20	9613.39	+	
13	Number of days worked per annum (LSPA)	196.70	101.80	+	+
14	Pre NFRM annual family income (FINC)	14238.0	9576.81	-	
15	Post NFRM annual family income (TOTY)	19321.20	10694.84	-	-
16	Market dummy, taking value 1 for regular marketing facility and 0 otherwise (MRKT)	0.39	0.49	+	+

respondents was recorded to be around 32 years during the survey. The mean years of their schooling were up to primary level. On an average, about 70 per cent of them had received work skill under Training Rural Youth for Self-Employment (TRYSEM) scheme or other private vocational training Programmes. They had a mean work experience of around eight years.

The family constraints revealed that about 67 per cent of the respondents were married, while the rest were single, separated, divorced or widowed. The mean size of their family was almost five and the dependency ratio was around one. The average number of children below four in the sample households was only 0.20.

The economic factors showed that the land assets of the sample respondents was worth Rs. 19, 950 on an average. About 64 per cent of them had diversified into non-farm self-employment. The mean amount of credit assistance received was only Rs. 3, 936.20. The average annual earnings of the respondent was only Rs. 5, 083.20, while the number of gainful days of employment was about 197 days in a year. The sample household income before self-employment was Rs. 14, 238 per annum, which rose to Rs. 19, 321.20 after diversification into it. Thus, the household annual income indicates a definite improvement in the economic status of the family which crossed above the poverty line after the respondents took up non-farm activity. The marketing details revealed that only 39 per cent of the respondents had a regular market demand from Anganwadis and Balwadis.

Table 2 present the correlation matrix computed to gain insight into the nature and degree of association between the sets of dependent and independent variables included in the regressions. The results reveal the magnitude and direction of relationship between the paired variables to be satisfying theoretical expectations in almost all cases, thus ruling out the emergence of any severe problem of multicollinearity in the estimation of the two specified functions. Nevertheless, step-wise technique of analysis has been adopted in order to overcome the occurrence of any such problem in the estimation of the regression models.

Table-3 presents the estimated results of non-farm employment decision function using Logit and Probit methods. The estimates of the two methods yielded almost similar results. Alternate models were also estimated to examine the impact of different sets of variables on the dependent variable.. The results clearly indicate that of the included variables, assured marketing facilities and increased number of days of regular employment exercise a positive and significant influence on the decision of taking up non-farm employment in the study area. The effect of the former is highly significant, implying that assured market facility plays a crucial role in the decision, as it contributes to better earnings of the sample women. Further, the increase in number of days of regular employment also has led to their diversification into non-farm activities against the prevailing situations of irregular, low-paid and low farm employment opportunity in the study area. This confirms the distress diversification hypothesis among the poor rural women in Pondicherry region.

The inclusion of other socio-economic variables showed age of the respondents, child below four years of age, value of land holding and family income before diversification into non-farm activity are observed to exercise a positive influence, while their education, skill and credit had a negative effect on their non-farm employment decision. However, all their effects emerged statistically insignificant on the dependent variable. This is because an increase in age led to greater maturity in taking up non-farm self employment among the poor women. The presence of young

Table 2: Non-farm Employment: Logit Function

Sl. No.	Variable	ModelI	ModelII	ModelIII	ModelIV	ModelV	ModelVI	ModelVII
1.	Constant	-0.949(1.14)	-1.347(1.609)	1.323(1.36)	-1.457(1.90)***	-1.428(1.120)	-1.103(1.18)	-1.425(1.85)
2.	AGER	-	-	-	-	-	-	-
4.	EDCN	-	-0.003(0.049)	-	-	-	-	-
5.	SKIL	-	-	-	-	-	-0.248(0.464)	-
6.	DEPR	-0.304(1.119)	-	-	-	-	-	-
7.	CHLD	-	-	-	0.322(0.641)	-	-	-
8.	ASST	-	-	-	-	-	-	0.000003(0.35)
9.	CRDT	-	-	-0.00001(0.07)	-	-	-	-
10.	LSPA	0.004(1.77)***	0.004(1.70)***	0.004(1.67)***	0.004(1.77)***	0.004(1.721)***	0.004(1.52)	0.004(1.75)***
11.	MRKT	1.945(3.39)*	1.884(3.32)*	1.863(2.81)*	1.948(3.39)*	1.885(3.33)*	1.840(3.19)*	1.879(3.33)*
12.	FINC	0.00003(1.187)	0.00003(1.30)	0.00003(1.30)	0.00003(1.22)	0.00003(1.30)	0.00003(1.32)	0.00003(1.29)
	Log-Likelihood	57.560	58.182	58.181	57.974	58.181	58.075	58.119

Note: Figures in parentheses show t-value;
* indicates significance at 1 per cent level,
** indicates significance at 5 per cent level, and
*** indicates significance at 10 per cent level.

Table 3.2: Non-farm Employment: Probit Function

Sl. No.	*Variable*	*ModelI*	*ModelII*	*ModelIII*	*ModelIV*	*ModelV*	*ModelVI*	*ModelVII*
1.	Constant	-0.580(1.17)	-0.825(1.65)***	-0.798(1.39)	-0.891(1.96)***	-0.829(1.08)	-0.637(1.13)	-0.874(1.91)***
2.	AGER	-	-	-	-	-0.0001(0.008)	-	-
3.								
4.	EDCN	-	-0.001(0.025)	-	-	-	-	-
5.	SKIL	-	-	-	-	-	-0.184(0.56)	-
6.	DEPR	-0.183(1.131)	-	-	-	-	-	-
7.	CHLD	-	-	-	0.216(0.692)	-	-	-
8.	ASST	-	-	-	-	-	-	0.000002(0.43)
9.	CRDT	-	-	-0.00001(0.09)	-	-0.00001(0.09)	-	-
10.	LSPA	0.003(1.82)***	0.003(1.75)***	0.003(1.72)***	0.003(1.83)***	0.003(1.77)***	0.002(1.52)	0.003(1.81)**
11.	MRKT	1.171(3.55)*	1.134(3.46)*	1.116(2.91)*	1.178(3.55)*	1.135(3.48)*	1.106(3.33)*	1.133(3.48)*
12.	FINC	0.00002(1.20)	0.00002(1.30)	0.00002(1.31)	0.00002(1.22)	0.00002(1.30)	0.00002(1.33)	0.00002(1.29)
13.	MARG	-	-	-	-	-	-	-
	Log-Likelihood	57.506	58.158	58.154	57.914	58.158	57.998	58.064

Note: Figures in parentheses show t-value;
* indicates significance at 1 per cent level,
** indicates significance at 5 per cent level, and
*** indicates significance at 10 per cent level.

children in the family also did not seem to interfere much with their employment activity owing to their work being home-based. Having own land asset and their earlier family income which was below poverty line encouraged them to take up non-farm activity. On the other hand, their low level of education (i.e., primary school) and low amounts of loans received through DWCRA discouraged them from going in for such ventures. Further, the skill received was found to negatively affect their decision to involve in non-farm activity, mainly because the training many of them had undergone under TRYSEM were different from the activities for which they received equipments under the employment and poverty alleviation scheme. For instance, many women received ordinary sewing machines instead of the embroidery machine in which they were skilled, thus rendering the training undergone unsuitable in such cases and others.

Therefore, the findings clearly indicate that while there are distinct evidences of distress diversification among the rural poor women towards the more remunerative and regular non-farm employment, the absence of required skill and education prevent them from reaping the full benefits from them.

Table 4 shows the estimated results of the respondents' earnings function. The analysis indicates that an increase in the women's age, experience, presence of children below four years of age, credit, labour supply, shift from farm to non-farm employment and assured market facility contribute to their increased earnings in the study area. Of them, the impacts of the nature of employment and labour supply are highly significant, indicating that the encouragement given by government to diversify into more regular and more remunerative employment-generating non-farm activities have succeeded in helping the sample poor women to earn higher incomes.

Table 4: OLS Regression Results: Earning Function

Sl. No.	Variable	*Model1a*	*Model1b*	*Model11a*	*Model11b*	*Model111a*	*Model111b*
1.	Constant	-1776.9(0.46)	-2651.8(0.84)	-12262(2.02)**	-12948(2.23)**	-1700.2(0.44)	-2454.5(0.78)
2.	AGE	60.304(1.19)	61.566(1.30)	803.60)(2.37)**	802.06(2.44)**	56.921(1.13)	59.449(1.26)
3.	AGSQ	-	-	-10.839(2.21)**	-10.977(2.32)**	-	-
4.	EDCN	-146.80(1.60)	-144.05(1.66)***	-158.47(1.76)***	-165.28(1.96)***	-421.80(1.60)	-414.55(1.62)
5.	EDSQ	-	-	-	-	24.380(1.12)	24.056(1.12)
6.	SKIL	-318.15(0.24)	-	-506.67(0.39)	-	-221.95(0.17)	-
7.	EXPN	133.32(0.57)	181.85(0.97)	98.854(0.43)	141.02(0.76)	156.31(0.66)	195.98(1.04)
8.	MARG	-17.703(0.02)	-	-183.92(0.24)	-	33.774(0.04)	-
9.	DEPR	-754.35(1.86)***	-753.60(1.91)***	-974.01(2.38)**	-999.52(2.50)**	-702.53(1.73)***	-697.25(1.75)***
10.	CHLD	357.10(0.47)	-	-476.27(0.64)	-496.82(0.68)	-397.68(0.52)	-
11.	ASST	-0.008(0.78)	-0.008(0.82)	-0.004(0.45)	-	-0.008(0.76)	-0.008(0.80)
12.	CRDT	0.433(1.41)	0.455(1.53)	0.325(1,07)	0.316(1.07)	0.473(1.53)	0.496(1.65)***
13.	NFRM	3371.2(4.64)*	3379.1(4.78)*	3345.7(4.70)*	3372.4(4.88)*	3322.1(4.57)*	3319.2(4.69)*
14.	LSPA	15.285(3.87)*	15.562(4.11)*	13.900(3.55)*	14.475(3.88)*	15.067(3.82)*	15.282(4.03)*
15.	MRKT	1370.3(1.20)	1294.0(1.29)	1315.5(1.18)	1196.2(1.22)	1355.2(1.19)	1303.2(1.30)
	R2	0.359	0.378	0.386	0.404	0.361	0.380
	F-Value	5.616*	7.690*	5.793*	7.719*	5.294*	7.067*

Note: Figures in parentheses show t-value.
* indicates significance at 1 per cent level,
** indicates significance at 5 per cent level,
*** indicates significance at 10 per cent level.

The remaining variables negatively affect the earnings of the women in the region. Of them, the influence of higher education and larger number of dependents in the family are found to be significant. This is because in rural areas, higher education creates a tendency among the workers to seek better employment opportunities in the organized sector or to migrate to urban areas (Taylor and Yunez-Nande, 1999). Meanwhile, the presence of either elder family members or very young ones constrains women's market activities, as domestic work is still their major domain.

The inclusion of age square into the estimated model makes the influence of the two age variables statistically significant and improves the significance level of dependency ratio. The former is attributable to the increased experience age adds to life, thus raising the earning capacities of the sample respondents, whereas a further rise age in negatively affects it due to the constraining effects of the aging process.

The inclusion of education square renders the impact of credit positive and significant; implying that a further increase in the loans made available to the women would raise their earning capacity.

The $\overline{R}^2$ values indicate that about 36 to 40 per cent of the variations in the dependent variable are explained by the included independent variables. The estimated function also emerges statistically significant at one per cent level.

Table 5 presents the ranks assigned to benefits of having shifted to non-farm activities by the 64 sample respondents. Having received new skills and training through government employment-generation and poverty alleviation schemes was assigned the first rank by 47 of them. This was followed by better status and decision-making power (45) and increased income (42). More regular employment was given the fourth rank by 40 sample respondents, which could be mainly due to the kind of activities they had chosen. On the other hand, better access to credit facilities and being able to participate in social services were quoted as the fifth and sixth benefits by less than half of them.

Table 5: Benefits of Non-farm Employment

Sl. No.	*Benefits*	*Number Responded*	*Total Score*	*Mean Score*	*Rank*
1.	Increased income	42	2537	60.40	3
2.	Better access to credit facilities	27	1123	41.59	6
3.	Received new skills and training	47	3044	64.77	1
4.	Better status and decision-making power	45	2815	62.55	2
5.	More regular employment decision making power	40	2208	55.20	4
6.	Participation in social services	30	1556	51.86	5
	Total respondents	64			

The problems encountered by the sample respondents during the course of the non-farm activity are listed and ranked in Table 6. Low profits and low price for their products were quoted as the major problems faced by them. This was followed by marketing problems caused by the distance and inconvenient transport facilities. Work not regular, non-availability of proper work place or godown and competition from better quality products were assigned the subsequent ranks. Capital, transport, raw materials and labour problems were the other constraints experienced by the respondents. Only eight of them quoted high interest rates on loans procured as the last problem.

Section IV: Concluding Remarks

This paper examines the factors influencing the decision of shifting of rural poor women from farm to non-

Table 6: Problems encountered by the Sample Respondents

Sl. No.	*Problems*	*Number Responded*	*Total Score*	*Mean Score*	*Rank*
1.	Low profit	55	4730	86	1
2.	Difficulty in getting raw materials	18	522	29	9
3.	Lack of transport facilities	29	952	32.83	8
4.	Competition from better quality and mechanised products	36	2079	57.76	6
5.	Marketing problems	49	3844	78.45	3
6.	Low price	50	4158	83.16	2
7.	Capital not available on time	31	1519	49	7
8.	High rate of interest on loan	8	122	15.25	11
9.	Labour problems	14	309	22.07	10
10.	Work not regular	45	3195	71	4
11.	Non-availability of proper work place or godown	38	2385	62.76	5
	Total	64			

farm activities, the benefits therein and the problems encountered by them in the occupation. It also analyses the factors that contribute to their earnings in the sector. Data for the study were collected through personal interview during March-May 1999 from a random sample of 100 poor rural women respondents, comprising 64 non-farm sector workers and 36 farm labourers, in Pondicherry region, UTP. The objectives of the study were pursued using simple averages, percentages, ratios, Garret ranking technique, correlations, and OLS, Logit and Probit multiple regressions.

The estimated results of the non-farm employment decision function indicated a clear evidence of distress diversification from farm to non-farm employment amongst the rural poor women in Pondicherry region. This was significantly encouraged by assured market facility and increased number of days of regular employment. These however need to be supported by higher educational level, larger and easy credit, and imparting more suitable skill and training.

The analysis of earnings function revealed that rise in age, diversification into non-farm activities and regular market facilities significantly increased it, while a further rise in age, more years of schooling and the presence of more dependants in the family significantly reduced the respondents' earnings.

A survey of the benefits of non-farm employment showed that the respondents had benefited most from the new skills and training for self-employment obtained under the poverty alleviation and employment-generation schemes. This was followed by better status and employment, increased income and more regular employment. The major problems encountered during the activity was low profits and prices for their products, marketing problems, work not regular, lack of work place, competition from better quality products and non-availability of capital.

The study indicates that employment-generation and poverty alleviation schemes of the Government can reduce rural poverty by providing labour intensive paid work on the one hand, and by providing goods and services that add to social welfare on the other. More and timely credit can help raise the earnings of the poor women and encourage their diversification into non-farm activities by providing more regular employment opportunities. Assured market facilities could be supportive in this direction. Improvement in human capital through higher education and by imparting relevant skills and training could help them further. The living standards of the poor women may thus be improved by employing them in activities which makes optimal utilisation of their skills and training and the local resources.

REFERENCES

1. Bhaduri, Amit (1993), "Structural Adjustment, Labour Market and Employment in India, Asian Regional Team for Employment Promotion Working Papers, ARTEP, International Labour Organisation, New Delhi, December.

2. Bhalla, Sheila (1990), "Labour Use in Rural People", Paper Presented at the Seminar on Agro-Climatic Regional Planning Project, Ahmedabad, March 5-6.

3. ________ (1997), "Trends in Poverty, Wages and Employment in India", *Indian Journal of Labour Economics,* Vol. 40, No.2, April-June, pp. 213-222.

4. Chaudhri, D. P. (1993), "Productivity Trends in Asian Agriculture: 1950-1990", *Indian Journal of Labour Economics*, Vol. 12, No. 2, April-June, pp.89-102.

5. Government of India (1992), Eight Five Year Plan: 1992-97, Vol. 1, Planning Commission, New Delhi.

6. Henry, E. Garret and R. S. Woodworth (1969), *Statistics in Psychology and Education*, Vakils, Feffer and Simons Private Ltd., Bombay.

7. Jayaraman, Rajshri and Peter Lanjouw (1999), "The Evolution of Poverty and Inequality in Indian Villages", *World Bank Research Observer*, Vol. 14, No. 1, February, pp. 1-30.

8. Kaushik, Amar (1993), "Income Generating Effects of Rural Credit: A Case Study of IRDP in Haryana," *Journal of Rural Development,* Vol. 12, No. 1, pp. 89-102.

9. Kundu, Amitabh (1991), "Growth of Non-Agricultural Employment: A Hypothesis on Rural-Urban Linkages", *IASSI Quarterly*, Vol. 10, No. 2, Oct-Dec.

10. Mellor, John W. (1976), The New Economics of Growth: A Strategy for India and Developing World, Ornel University Press, Ithala.

11. Parthasarthy, G., Shameem and B. Sambi Reddy (1998), "Determinants of Rural Non-Agricultural Employment: The Indian Case," *Indian Journal of Agricultural Economics,* Vol. 53, No.2, April-June, pp. 139-154.

12. Registrar General and Census Commissioner, Census of India, Government of India Publication, New Delhi, (Various Issues).

13. Samal, Kishore C. (1997), "Features and Determinants of Rural Non-Farm Sector in India and Orissa: A Survey", *Journal of Indian School of Political Economy,* Vol. 9, No. 1, pp. 65-93.

14. Shukla, Vibhooti (1992), "Rural Non-Farm Employment in India: Issues and Policy", *Economic and Political Weekly,* Vol. 27, No. 28, 11 July, pp. 1477-1488.

15. Taylor, J Edward and Antonio Yunez-Nande (1999), Education, Migration and Productivity: An Analytic Approach and Evidence from Rural Mexico, Development Centre Studies, OECD Publication, France.

16. Unni, Jeemol, (1991), "Regional Variations in Rural Non-Agricultural Employment: An Exploratory Analysis", *Economic and Political Weekly*, Vol., No. 1 Jan 19, pp. 109-122.

17. ________ (1997), "Employment and Wages Among Rural Labourers: Some Recent Trends", *Indian Journal of Agricultural Economics,* Vol. 52, No.1, January-March, pp. 59-72.

18. Vaidyanathan, A. (1986), "Labour Use in Rural India: A Study of Spatial and Temporal Variations", *Economic and Political Weekly,* Vol. 21, No. 52, 27 December, pp. A146.

19. Visaria, Pravin and Rakesh Basant (Eds.) (1994), *Non-Agricultural Employment in India: Trends and Prospects,* Sage Publication, New Delhi.

20. Walker, Thomas S. and James G Rajan (1990), *Village and Household Economies in India's Semi-Arid Tropics*, Johns Hopkins University Press, Baltimore.

27

Comparison Between Government Forestry Projects and Social Forestry Projects

A Case Studies from Orissa

*Dr. Sabita K. Acharya**
*Prof Binayak Rath***

Introduction

Studies on environmental conservation/protection ensuring better quality of life are the urgency and fashion of the modern World in the 21st century. The environmental subjects, e.g., the global climatic changes, green house effect with carbon-dioxide increase in the atmosphere, loss of biological diversity or extinction of animal and plant species, critical conditions of tropical rain forests, etc. are the major problems that are often highlighted in various international forums, academic discussions/debates, and also in the mass media. It is realized that most of these problems are inherited from the loss of forest area due to degradation and deforestation. Thus, forest has a great role in the environmental conservation. In addition to this role forest as a form of renewable natural resource has remarkable contribution in the development of an economy.

* Faculty, Birla Institute of Technology & Science, Pilani, Rajasthan India.

** Professor, Indian Institute of Technology, Kanpur, India.

This means role of forest is complex- at one end it is a source of revenue and hence exploitation is natural; at the other end it is needed for environmental conservation and hence should be properly maintained.

After independence, the Government of India had has been undertaking great care for protecting the environment in terms of plans, programs and policies. In order to solve the problems of forest development, it is argued that to draw proper policies and efficient schemes/program, there should be projection of forest development programs. This argument is based on the premise that in a planned economy like India, where the investment allocations are by and large predetermined at the national level, there is an urgent need to utilize the scarce resources in such a fashion that the targets set in the national plans are fully achieved. Once the overall plan allocation is made, the problem to be tackled is how to maximize the net benefits from investment, which in turn envisages the problem of ranking the alternative projects. Hence, here lies the importance of the Social Benefit-Cost Analysis(SBCA) in a planned economy. The literature on forestry management also portrays the need of SBCA in the forestry sector for establishing their viability. In view of these arguments, in this study we have attempted to evaluate few plantation schemes from a selected region, viz., Orissa. In accomplishing such exercises, we have adopted the approach suggested by the UNIDO Guidelines for project evaluation with proper modifications and some improvements.

Methodology

Method of Sample Selection

By adopting a multi-stage sampling approach[1] the sample units have been selected. We have examined[2] the

1 The first and second step being the choice of the State Orissa and the choice of the district Puri respectively.

2 Acharya S. "Economic Evaluation of various forestry schemes: case studies from Orissa", Ph D. Thesis, IIT Kanpur, 1998.

district level plantation activities through various agents, where it is noted that among the undivided 13 districts of Orissa, Puri district is the one having the maximum plantation activities undertaken by most of the agents. Besides plantations, it is also observed that there are maximum numbers of voluntary organisations involved in increasing environmental awareness in the district. Hence for our study we have selected Puri as our sample district. This study is a modest attempt to compare two types of plantation projects-one purely undertaken and managed by Government and the other undertaken by Government but managed by local people.

The geographical location of the Puri district indicates that Puri is situated at the eastern part of the State of Orissa and it is one of the coastal district. This district is bounded on the east by Bay of Bengal, Boudh-Kandhamal district and part of Ganjam district on the west, Cuttack district on the north and Ganjam district and Bay of Bengal lies on the south side. According to 1991 Census, the population of Puri district was 35.7 lakhs. It is one of the thickly populated district of the State. The density of population is 341 per sq. km. We have covered the following four sample units from two groups in this study:

Group A: Territorial Division, Forest Department, Government of Orissa.

1. Balukhanda Reserved Forest C11, Puri sadar, Puri.
2. Balukhanda Reserved Forest C13, Puri sadar, Puri.

Group B: Directorate of Social Forestry Projects, Forest Department, Government of Orissa

3. Gopalpur VWL, Puri sadar block, Puri.
4. Mundal VWL, Jatani block, Puri.

Method of Data Collection

As our study involves SBCA of various plantation schemes of different agencies, collecting relevant data from the concerned agencies and persons was quite challenging. Since our study needed secondary as well as primary data, we have collected secondary data/information from the files, reports of the authorities and also from the libraries. On the other hand, we gathered the primary data from the concerned field officials and the local people.

Other data like yield rate, local prices of forest products (both minor forest products and timber), people's participation and their remarks for the project have been collected from the local people of sample project areas through direct enquiry by us. Even after tapping all these sources, when some data were still not available, we have resorted to estimate the figures by a method of approximation.

With these sample projects data we move on to the Social Benefit Cost analysis of those units, the very first step being financial analysis followed by economic analysis. In the last step we have attempted to estimate some of the externalities in order to give a complete picture of SBCA.

Application of SBCA in Our Study

To achieve our objectives of evaluating plantation projects, we have adopted the theoretical frame-work that is based on UNIDO Guidelines approach with few modifications. Adhering to the UNIDO approach we have attempted to incorporate the following steps in our study:

1. Calculation of financial profitability at market prices;
2. Introduction of shadow prices of inputs and outputs to arrive at social costs and benefits;

3. Adjustment for the project's impact on saving and investment;
4. Adjustment for the project's impact on income distribution;
5. Adjustment toward merit want promotion;
6. Adjustment for the projects production or use of goods such as luxury consumer goods and basic needs whose social values are less than or greater than their economic values.

In tune with the first step in SBCA we have estimated the financial profitability of all the sample projects at market prices; since our sample projects have different base values, in order to ensure proper comparison we have taken 1990-91 as standard base-year for our analysis. All the prices are changed to the 1990-91 levels with the help of whole- sale price indices. Thus the financial profitability has been estimated at constant market prices. In order to account for the inter-temporal variations, we have discounted the net benefit streams with standard discount rates and have estimated the NPV, BCR, and IRR of the projects.

However, since market is not perfect, financial profitability is not sufficient; hence from step one we have moved to step two where we have estimated the shadow prices of different inputs like land, labour and capital. With these economic prices we have estimated the economic feasibility of the projects in terms of NPV, BCR and IRR at an economic discount rate of 11% as suggested in the literature[3].

The fourth step that concerns with the income distribution aspect implies that the projects should be

3 Sharma, RA and MG Mc Greggor (1991), "Economic Discount and Wage Rates for Social Forestry Projects in India: Estimates and Problems", Project Appraisal.

selected in such a way that the inequality between poor and rich should decrease. Thus, the projects aiming towards upliftment of the socio-economic conditions of the down-trodden class of people in the society should be given more weightage. This aspect has been incorporated in our study assigning due weight to the unskilled labour force through the shadow wage rate. In addition to the income distribution aspect shadow wage rate has taken care of saving investment part of the unskilled labour also.

The other aspect focused in the UNIDO Guidelines is the merit want promotion objective of planning. This aspect is taken care of by the weights used in estimating the shadow prices. The last aspect of luxury goods vs. basic goods could not be incorporated due to lack of data.

Furthermore, to establish the socio-economic viability of our plantation projects, it becomes necessary to quantify the externalities and place a value for them to commensurate with the numeraire of benefits and costs. In this regard some studies (already discussed[4]) have established that material benefits constitute a negligible proportion of the external benefits from the forestry projects. Since forestry is an area that has a lot of positive externalities, the socio-economic evaluation including environmental aspects is a great task. With a view to main-streaming some of those externalities, we have made an attempt in two steps.

In the first step, we have tried to calculate the fuel and fodder benefits of plantation projects, which are generally not marketed, by applying the Contingent Valuation Method (CVM)[5]. To accomplish this objective we have interviewed the beneficiaries directly and elicited the information on what are they willing to pay for the extra

---

4 Ibid.

5 CVM will frequently be the only method of external benefit estimation(Pearce and Markandya, 1984).

fuel they receive from the plantation project. But, the basic assumptions of the CVM methods are (1) individuals fully understand the options that are offered to them and that they are familiar with the good in question, and (2) that it can be relied upon that what people say is really what they would do if a market for the good existed. In this way we have collected the data on the amount of fuel and fodder produced by the project. As far as willingness to pay is concerned, people have generally answered the market price as their willingness to pay. Taking into account these factors we have estimated these external benefits.

As far as ecological benefits are concerned which are, no doubt, associated with our sample projects, we are unable to estimate them as our analysis is based on one-time field survey. As argued in the literature in order to assess the environmental impacts of a project, one has to collect data of different parameters over a long period that is of course time consuming and expensive. Moreover, with inadequacy of scientific knowledge, it will not be proper to quantify those benefits. Simultaneously, it is well argued by environmentalists that without those ecological benefits the socio-economic study will also be incomplete. Hence, we have adopted the estimates of Rath's (1997) study for our estimation. However, the values of these estimates are applied with proper adjustments.

Thus, our approach is an extension of UNIDO Guidelines where we have emphasised the estimation of externalities. The steps followed for the SBCA of plantation projects in our study are as follows:

(a) First, we have estimated the Financial Net Benefit (Financial Benefit-Financial Cost) i.e. at constant market prices;

(b) Second, we have estimated the Economic Net Benefit (Economic Benefits-Economic Cost) after adjusting the market prices with economic prices.

(*c*) Third, we have estimated the Socio-Economic Net Benefits i.e. including indirect benefits (in the form of fuel and fodder) to the economic net benefits.

(*d*) Fourth, we have estimated the Socio-Eco-Environmental Net Benefits i.e. including environmental benefits to the socio-economic net benefits.

All these Net Benefit streams are then discounted at different rates of discount to get the NPV and BCR of the projects. In addition to these at each step the IRRs of the projects are also estimated. As literature shows the NPV is preferable compared to others for decision-making; however, in our study, to compare the projects we felt this is not sufficient as there is a wide gap in the area of the projects. Hence another criterion based on NPV i.e. NPV per hectare is estimated in each case and on that basis we have drawn our conclusion. At the end some policy implication of the study are discussed.

Features of the Sample Projects

Forests of Territorial Division

The Territorial Division, being the most traditional and conventional wing of the Forest Department is actively involved in the plantation activities. It is involved in protection and regeneration of reserved forests, of late, it has started block plantation in order to increase the green coverage. Through our method of sample selection we have selected the two projects, viz. Balukhanda Coup-11(C11) and Coup-13(C13) of district Puri where block plantations of casuarinas are undertaken by the Forest Department of Government of Orissa. These two coups are managed and operated by territorial wing of Forest Department. By taking into account the soil and moisture characteristics that is sandy and saline respectively, the Forest

Department had proposed casuarina plantation that was ideal for the area. Besides casuarina provides good fuel wood to meet the local demand. In fact, the local demand for fuel wood is very high due to the typical system of cooking adopted in the world famous Jagannath temple. It is estimated that the temple needs around 400 quintals of fuel wood daily for its operation. To add to it the Swargadwar requires nearly 40 quintals of wood daily. In order to meet such growing demand, the territorial division have planted 20, 000 casuarina plants in C-11 and 15, 000 plants in C 13. While the area of C-11 is 8 hectare, C-13 covers only 6 hectare. The survival rate in both cases is 70%. Regarding the operation and maintenance of these projects, we have learnt that the territorial division plants the seedlings, takes care till third year of the plants and then tries to protect them through its own staff members. However, when the project attains maturity it is auctioned and generally awarded to OFDC.

Since the projects under consideration, did not completed their life span when the data were collected, the future benefits are estimated on the basis of similar projects that are already harvested. For the analysis of those two projects through SBCA, we have collected the costs and benefits from concerned officials. However, when the required data are not available, we have estimated the figure from our field experience or from concerned officials' statement.

Costs of the Project Balukhanda C11

The important cost components of these projects are land, labour and other materials. Since land is owned by Forest Department, it involves no fixed cost for the financial analysis. Thus, the projects have to pay for labour and materials. The total cost figures for the project C-11 as collected from the concerned office(District Forest Office, Khurda) have been Rs.50, 000/ which include Rs.35, 000/ as labour charge and Rs.15, 000/ as material charge. The other details like components of material are not available. In the first year of operation Rs.10, 000/ is being spent in labour and Rs.3, 000/ in materials; in the second year of operation a higher amount i.e. Rs.12, 000/ is being spent in labour and Rs.7000/ in materials. From 5th year onwards there is no financial cost as such. The maintenance cost is negligible as reported by the concerned officials.

Benefits of the Project Balukhanda C11

The direct benefit of the project is the timber benefit from casuarina trees. The harvest will be done after the maturity of the trees. Since the life-span of these trees are taken as 10 years, only at the end of year 2000 the trees will be harvested and the benefits will be received. But, for our analysis, we have estimated the benefits on the basis of a project which is already harvested in 1996-97. That project was of 21 hectare, the same casuarina plants(2500 per hectare) with the same survival rate of 70% were also there; after the felling 1088 stacks of garinda, 6536 ballaha and 200 stacks of twig and firewood were prepared. At the rate of Rs.180/ per quintal Of garinda, Rs.4/ per ballaha and Rs.70/ per quintal of firewood, the total amount of revenue received was Rs.40, 42, 500/. Thus, per hectare financial benefit was Rs.1, 92, 500/. Taking into account this estimate which has been collected from the DFO, Khurda, we have estimated the direct benefit of both the projects. The total benefits from C11 have been estimated as Rs.1540 thousand.

With these costs and benefits estimates we have moved on to financial evaluation to check profitability and feasibility of the project, which is later followed by economic evaluation and then socio-eco-environmental evaluation.

Plantation Project Balukhanda C-13

Costs and Benefits of Balukhanda C13 Project

The total cost for the project has been estimated as Rs.37, 500/(as collected from the DFO, Khurda) out of which total labour cost is Rs.26, 250/ and total material cost is Rs.11, 250/. In this case also the maintenance cost after fourth year of operation is not included as it is negligible.

In the first year of operation an amount of Rs.8000/ is being spent in labour component and Rs.2000/ in materials; in the second year both the figures are higher and in the consequent years these are less. Finally after 4th year there is virtually no significant cost.

As far as timber benefits which are yet to be harvested are concerned, we have estimated those in the exactly similar manner as has been done for Balukhanda C-11 and accordingly the estimated figure is Rs.1155 thousand.

Forests of Local People

Brief History of GOPALPUR SFP

There was a patch of community land in Gopalpur of Puri sadar block of Puri district which was being used for cultivation of paddy by the people at random intervals. Since it was low lying and sub mergible area, the production had been sub-marginal. In 1984 when the message of Social Forestry reached the village, the villagers thought it wise to utilise the land for plantation with dual purposes, viz.,

- To reduce swampiness of the area, and
- To get better returns from that land.

In view of the interest of the villagers a plantation project was started in Gopalpur in 1985 over 5 hectares of land under the Village Wood Lot (VWL) scheme and it was executed by the Social Forestry Range, Puri. Under the guidance of forest officials, at first instance, 10, 500 plants of four varieties, viz. Casuarina, Eucalyptus, Cashew and Polang, were being planted. The survival rate was nearly 80%. With the assistance of Social Forester of the Puri Range, a Village Forest Committee (VFC) was being constituted with a Chairman from among the villagers and five committee members. It is the VFC who is in charge of the project and after discussion with other members it takes decisions regarding the project. After the maturity of three varieties of plants i.e. casuarina, eucalyptus and Polang (which were mainly used for fuel), it was the VFC with the assistance from officials decided to harvest the trees.

As per the survey undertaken in 1995, finally, there were 2533 existing plants after the 10- year cycle. Except the fruit bearing trees other trees were harvested. After the harvest, the benefits in the form of proceeds were used in these ways: (a) the timber lots were auctioned for cash proceeds and the proceeds went to the VFC; (b) the leaves and small timbers were kept for the fire wood purposes; (c) 1000 seedlings were purchased from the proceed to regenerate woodlots in the area; (d) the rest amount was being used for developmental purposes of the village. Half of the proceeds were kept in the Gramya bank in the name of Village Development Fund. As a result of this large amount of saving, they were entitled to get IRDP loan from that bank. The other half was used for the construction of one village temple, one common room for all villagers meeting purpose and one school building.

The second cycle has started in 1995-96 with active involvement of the people. Accordingly, the villagers have purchased the seedlings and replanted the entire area. But the cashew trees are there as its life span is 40 years. So again after 10 years the other trees will be harvested and once more the plantations will be developed. All these processes will come to an end in 2024-25 only when the cashew plants will mature and then will not give anymore fruits. Thus, the project is expected to operate till continue till 2024-25 and people will get benefit from three sources and those are fuel, fodder and harvest. The harvest is again divided into two parts and those are cashew from 5th year onwards and at the end of each cycle the timber benefits.

Moreover, at the end of 40- year period the other trees along with the cashew trees will be felled and can be used as timber benefits.

However, since our objective has been to analyse the commercial, economic and social viability of the project through the technique of SBCA, it is imperative to draw the profiles of costs and benefits of the project.

Costs of the Gopalpur SFP

To accomplish the objective, we need to estimate the costs and benefits flow of the project. As far as the commercial cost part is concerned we have taken the data provided by Directorate of Social Forestry Projects, Orissa which has fixed per unit(hectare)cost for different schemes like Village Wood Lot (VWL), Reforestation of degraded forests, Institutional plantation etc. However, no data were available on particular project basis. As our concern was with VWL, we would like to discuss the costs for VWL in the next paragraph.

Per Hectare Cost of VWL

The costs of any plantation project comprise of fixed costs and variable costs. The capital cost of the project is the land cost. However, the land used for SFP is mostly government/community land that is very poor in quality. In those cases the land cost is assumed to be zero as there is no payment made for the land. This is also true for Gopalpur VWL, i.e. the land cost component is assumed to be zero.

The variable costs of the project are labour cost, material cost, and maintenance cost. As reported in the SF Handbook for Orissa and also as per our primary information, VWL plantation schemes involve monetary costs from the beginning till fourth year of commencement. For one hectare of VWL plantation, Rs.1, 350/ of labour cost are required for pre-plantation activities like survey and demarcation, clearance of site, burning of debris etc. In the second year Rs.1, 050/ of labour cost are required for carriage of seedlings from nursery to site, scooping of pits, planting operation, intensive soil work, grass cutting and weeding. In the third year Rs.550/ of labour cost are required for post-plantation activities like replacement of casualty, soil working and weeding. In the 4th year Rs.300/ of labour cost are required for deep soil working, weeding, and pruning, etc.

In addition to these labour costs, the project involves material cost till third year of operation. In the first year, the material cost is given to be Rs.50/. It includes cost of stakes, ropes(Rs.5/) and cost of implements(Rs.45/). In the second year of operation, the material cost is Rs.470/ which includes cost of fertiliser (125kg) and insecticide (12.5kg). In the third year the material cost is Rs.230/ which includes cost of fertiliser (75kg) and cost of insecticide (2.5kg). All these labour and material costs are in 1983-84 prices that is the year when the SFPs started in Orissa.

As far as maintenance is concerned, it is very negligible for SFPs as the maintenance as well as watch and ward is undertaken by the local people voluntarily. Thus, in total, for one hectare of plantation, Rs.3250/ of labour cost and Rs.750/ of materials are needed. These general costs estimate norms have been used by us to estimate the cost figures for Gopalpur VWL.

Costs Incurred by Gopalpur SFP

It is already reported earlier that the area of Gopalpur VWL is 5 hectare. Accordingly we have estimated the labour costs and material costs over the life span. However, Gopalpur VWL is a typical project with the life span of 40 years within which there are four cycles of operation. The project started in the year 1985-86; the first cycle has been completed in 1994-95; the second cycle has started in 1995-96 and will be over by 2004-05; the third cycle is expected to start in 2005-06 and the fourth cycle is expected to start in 2015 which will be ended in 2024-25 and then the project will be terminated.

Benefits of Gopalpur SFP

As far as benefits are concerned, the annual direct benefits are being received from cashew and the other trees provide direct benefits after felling, which are being used for fuel purpose. From 5th year onwards the cashew nuts have been harvested. The local price of cashew was Rs.20/ (at 1994-95 prices)as per the primary data and we have estimated the total amount of future production as per local people's experience. According to their calculations, one tree at the peak of its life span would give 2-3 kg of cashew nuts.

Besides cashew, other financial benefits are received from timber. After the completion of one cycle, the matured trees were being felled and the timber was already sold. As the official report shows after the first cycle i.e., at the end of 1994-95, an amount of Rs.4, 10, 000/ was being received from the timber. We have assumed the same amount of timber to be harvested after each cycle. However, these financial benefits are in 1994-95 prices. At the end of the project, i.e. after 40 years cashew trees along with other trees are to be felled. Accordingly, we have estimated that an amount of Rs.4, 20, 000/ would be received from timber at the end of 2024-25.

Economic Evaluation of the Project

The factors which are adjusted in this project are shadow wage rate(which is estimated as 0.4W where W is the market wage rate) and marginal productivity of capital i.e. Economic Discount Rate(EDR) which is also taken as 11%. The opportunity cost of material is taken as the willingness-to-pay; the willingness-to-pay is taken as the cost excluding subsidy. As we have already discussed in the methodology chapter that the willingness-to-pay is taken as 1.35 times higher than the financial cost. With these adjustments, when we estimated the economic costs of Gopalpur VWL, it came to be Rs.77, 561/ (at constant prices at 1990-91) over the four cycles.

While evaluating benefits economically we have considered the willingness to pay price instead of auction price. We have taken the retail price as the willingness to pay price. Generally the retail price is more than the auction price. From our primary data we have checked that the retail price of raw cashew(not so good in quality) is Rs.24/ Rs.25 whereas the auction price is Rs.20/. Since the quality of cashew harvested from Gopalpur VWL is not of so high quality we have taken the willingness to pay or economic price of cashew as 1.2 times the auction price.

So far as timber is concerned the retail price is Rs.220/ whereas auction price is Rs.180/. Hence willingness to pay or economic price of timber is estimated as 1.22 times the auction price. With these adjustments we have estimated the economic/social costs and economic benefits, the net of which gives the net economic benefits.

By introducing these adjustments we found that the total economic benefits comes to Rs.13, 74, 900/ and economic costs as Rs.77, 561/. Hence, the net economic benefit is estimated as Rs.12, 96, 595/ which means the net economic benefit is 1.28 times the financial net benefit. However, when we introduced the inter temporal variations by discounting those at11% EDR, the NPV, BCR and IRR changed significantly.

These above estimates established the economic feasibility of the project. In this context we would like to mention that the BCA of VWL plantation in Korea[6] had

6 FAO(1979), Economic Analysis of Forestry Project: Case Studies, FAO Forestry Paper, 17, 1, Rome.

shown the economic IRR as 17% because the life span of the project was 20 years. And also the costs include supervision and harvesting operation that are excluded in our analysis. On the other hand, the BCA of Kenya saw log ply wood plantation project shows that the economic IRR of the project is 123% for 37- year life span. Of course, there the costs include administration, maintenance, supervision, protection, harvesting, etc. Hence our study lies in between these two studies as its life span is 40 years and it includes labour cost and material cost.

Socio-Economic-Environmental Evaluation of the Project

In order to include the non-marketed benefits we have followed the CVM(already discussed). In evaluating the benefits socio-economically we have considered the fuel and fodder benefits of the project which are the products of plantation. The fuel benefit from leaves and twigs of trees from a 5 hectares plantation project are already estimated[7]. Since the project under consideration is over 5 hectare we have included that amount in the economic benefit stream. However, after the first cycle except cashew trees other trees are already harvested. Since cashew trees are not useful for fuel benefit we have not given any fuel benefit value for these first three years in each cycle. Accordingly, we have estimated that on the 4th year of operation an amount of Rs.900/ is received from fuel; on the 5th year it increases to Rs.1350/ which later increases to Rs.1800/ from 6th year till 10th year. In the next cycle we have assumed the process to remain constant.

In order to estimate other benefits of the project we have made an attempt to estimate the fodder benefit. As per the information collected from the local people, there was no vegetation in the area before plantation. But when plants were raised, grasses started growing which later used for fodder purposes. However, due to lack of actual

---

7 Ibid.

data, we have assumed that nearly Rs.500/ per annum is saved from 4th year onwards. Thus the year-wise benefit figures(from fuel and fodder) are added to the economic net benefit stream resulting in the socio-economic net benefits of the project.

However, till this stage of the analysis we have not completed all the steps of SBCA. The environmental benefits that occupy a significant place for plantation projects are yet to be considered. As already discussed, the standards used in our study for estimating environmental benefits is Rs.56, 880/ per hectare per annum at 1990-91 prices. With the prevailing survival rate of different projects we have estimated the amount differently. For the sampled SFPs since the survival rate has been 80%, the per hectare per annum benefits estimated to be Rs.45, 504/ and hence for Gopalpur project the benefit comes out to be Rs.2, 27, 520/. We have added this amount to the socio-economic net benefit stream from 4th year onwards of each cycle of the project. It is already mentioned that this is a typical project where along with casuarina and eucalyptus, cashew trees are there, the life span of which is 40 years. Hence after each 10 year cycle for next three years the significant environmental benefits are flowing from the cashew trees which are very less in number(90-95). We have assumed that the total area of these trees is maximum around 1 hectare. Accordingly the environmental benefits are estimated (Rs.45, 504/)and are added in the socio-economic net benefit stream resulting in socio-eco-environmental net benefits.

In order to incorporate the inter temporal time preference the socio-economic net benefits are then discounted at 2 % social rate of discount to calculate the NPV, BCR and the IRR of the project.

From the results it is very clear that the Gopalpur project is socially viable in all the cases. While the addition of fuel and fodder benefits increases the NPV to Rs.13, 77, 000/, the addition of environmental benefits further increases the NPV to Rs.81, 38, 000/.

In view of these high and satisfactory NPV, BCR, and IRR results, we have to conclude that in terms of financial feasibility tests, the Gopalpur VWL is proved to be profitable; in economic feasibility tests it is also feasible and from socio-economic point of view it has proved to be socially viable. However, here we will compare it with the territorial projects.

Brief History of the Mundal SFP

Though the SFP in Orissa launched in 1983-84, with the assistance of SIDA, the message of Social Forestry reached the village Mundal (a village under Jatani block in the district Puri) in 1986. The village Mundal with 100 families comprises of two hamlets with 60 families belonging to the backward class, whose economic standard is very low. Most of them are working as agricultural labourers. Fuel scarcity had has been a major problem for them. However, they had no idea how to overcome that problem.

There was a patch of 7 ha. unused Government land which was not useful for any productive purposes. But with the focus on social forestry on degraded land, the SF Range, Bhubaneswar realised that such degraded land can be useful for plantation activities. In order to motivate the people for social forestry, the Forest Department constituted a Village Forest Committee and persuaded the people to go for plantation on the degraded land. In view of these efforts, 17, 500 plants were planted in 1987-88. The plants were of two varieties i.e. Acacia, and Eucalyptus. These two varieties are mainly beneficial for fuel purposes. With a survival rate of 80%, at the end of 10-year cycle, those trees were harvested. In total 3196 trees were felled from which 189 tonnes of firewood and 1632 poles were harvested and a part of it was distributed among the villagers. The rest were sold for Rs.1, 35, 000/ which was received as revenue in the hands of Village Forest Committee. After discussion with the villagers, the Committee decided to replant the area, for which it purchased 50, 000 seedlings from the SFP nursery. The rest of the amount they deposited in the bank in two pass books-one for the village development fund and the other for the village forest development fund. From the first account they are using the money for construction of village temple and one plat form for community use.

The Costs and Benefits of the Project

Like the Gopalpur VWL, we have estimated the costs for the Mundal VWL by taking into account the per hectare plantation cost(fixed by the Directorate of SFP, Bhubaneswar) and total area of the plantation project. As such the total cost is calculated to be Rs.28, 000/ over the life span(unlike the first project here the life span is 10 years) of the project. This includes labour cost of Rs.22, 750/ and material cost of Rs.5, 250/. However, these figures are in 1983-84 prices.

The important benefit they got from the plantation are fuel and the motivation for further plantation. However, these benefits are not priced in the market; hence the only financial benefit is the timber harvest after maturity. As per the primary data collected from the villagers, an amount of Rs.1, 35, 000/ was received in 1996-97 after harvest.

Financial Analysis of Mundal SFP

From the estimated cost and benefit figures we have calculated the net benefit of the project. But since the figures are in different prices (i.e. costs in 1983-84 prices and benefits in 1996-97 prices) we have adjusted them to

1990-91 level. Accordingly, the cost stream is inflated with a factor of 1.677 and the benefit stream is deflated with a factor of 0.576.

Economic Analysis of the Project

To calculate the economic cost we have followed the same procedure as adopted in the Gopalpur SFP. It is clear that at 11% EDR the NPV has improved and the BCR is more than one and IRR is higher than market rate of interest. Hence the project is economically feasible.

But to these economic benefits then we added the indirect benefits flowing from fuel, fodder which are approximated by us. Through CVM we have estimated the standard fuel benefit from 5 hectares of eucalyptus, casuarina plantation. Adhering to the procedures adopted earlier the fuel benefit of Mundal VWL has been Rs.1, 260/ in the 4th year; Rs.1, 890/ in the 5th year which increases to Rs.2, 520/ in the 6th year and onwards.

With a view to include the fodder part of the benefit in the economic analysis (i.e. benefit from 'net resources saved' point) we have estimated that over the years the project would render Rs. 5,500/ by way of fodder supply. This approximation is based on the local price of fodder. But this benefit would flow from the 4th year as prior to that it is very negligible as the area was not suitable for fodder cultivation in the beginning due to degraded soil. We have assumed that the fodder benefit in 4th year to 6th year would be Rs. 500/ per annum and later increased to Rs.1,000/ from 7th year onwards. The addition of these fuel and fodder benefit has raised the net benefits to Rs. 88,990/.

Socio-Economic-Environmental Evaluation of the Project

Furthermore, the environmental benefits are estimated in the same pattern as of the Gopalpur project which is estimated to be Rs.45, 504/ per hectare per annum. Since the area of Mundal project is 7 hectare, the corresponding environmental benefits has been calculated as Rs.3, 18, 528/ per annum. It is already mentioned earlier that we have assumed the environmental benefits to be included from 4th year onwards. Hence the total environmental benefits over the life span becomes Rs.22, 26, 000 which is added to the net benefit stream. Finally, the net socio-economic-environmental benefits has been calculated as Rs.23, 14, 990/ which is 75 times the net financial benefits.

A comparison of the environmental benefits with the total benefits of the project reveals that the environmental benefits of Mundal SFP is 96.15% of the total benefits. This result is at par with other studies like Mathur [8] (1980). In his study Mathur had estimated that the ecological benefits constitute 99.94% of the total benefits of a forestry project.

Observation

The socio-economic and financial analysis of the SFPs, viz., Gopalpur SFP and Mundal SFP have established that the plantations under social forestry programme with people's participation are extremely viable projects. However, to achieve our target we have compared with the territorial projects and the results in table 1.

As we move from financial to economic and to socio-economic, the ordering remains same at 11% and 2% rates of discount respectively, as shown in table 2.

The ordering changes as we move to socio-economic-environmental studies where the externalities are added. In this stage the Gopalpur SFP has the highest NPV which is followed by the territorial projects.

---

8 Mathur, H.N. and Soni P.(1980), "Non-wood Benefits of Forests: An Effort at quantification", 'The Environment' Journal of the Indian Forest college, Dehradun, pp. 5-9.

Table 1: Financial NPV (in thousand rupees) and BCR (in bracket) of projects at different rates of discount

Rate of Discount (%)	*Govt.*		*SFP*	
	C-11	*C-13*	*Gopalpur*	*Mundal*
0	843 (20.27)	632 (20.14)	1011 (8.53)	30.8 (1.65)
2	685 (17.13)	514 (17.2)	617 (7.28)	18.6 (1.41)
5	505 (13.7	378 (13.6)	323 (5.77)	5.09 (1.11)
10	306 (9.5)	229 (9.4)	131 (3.95)	-8.9 (0.76)
12	251 (8.24)	188 (8.13)	95 (3.41)	-13.1 (0.66)

Note: IRR of the projects are 45%, 45%, 30%, and 6% respectively.

1. Taking NPV as a criterion Gopalpur social forestry project has the higher NPV only at 0% rate of discount; otherwise the territorial plantations i.e. C-11 has higher NPV at all rates of discount.

2. Taking BCR as a criterion the territorial plantations have highest BCR at all rates of discount followed by Gopalpur VWL. At 5% rate of discount the BCR of Balukhanda C-11 and Gopalpur VWL are 13.7, and 5.77; at 10% it is 9.5 and 3.95 and at 12% it is 8.24 and 3.41 respectively.

3. Taking IRR as criterion the territorial plantations also have highest IRR followed by Gopalpur project. While the IRR of Balukhanda C-11 is 45%, the IRR of Gopalpur project is 30%.

Table 2: Economic NPV (in thousand rupees) and BCR (in bracket) of the projects

Rate of Discount (%)	*Govt.*		*SFP*	
	C-11	*C-13*	*Gopalpur*	*Mundal*
11	357 (15.8)	268 (15.7)	162 (7.81)	11 (1.52)

Note: IRR of the projects are 56%, 56%, 43% and 17% respectively.

1. With NPV as a criterion the territorial plantations have higher NPV followed by Gopalpur VWL. At 11% EDR the NPV of Balukhanda C-11 is Rs.3, 57, 000/ and that of Gopalpur is Rs.1, 62, 000/.

2. BCR as a criterion shows territorial plantations having maximum BCR at 11% EDR followed by Gopalpur SFP. At 11% EDR Balukhanda C-11 has BCR of 15.8 and that of Gopalpur is 7.81.

3. IRR as a criterion indicates that territorial plantations(56%) having highest IRR followed by Gopalpur VWL(43%).

Table 3: Socio-Economic NPV (in thousand rupees) and BCR (in bracket) of the projects

Rate of Discount (%)	*Govt.*		*SFP*	
	C-11	*C-13*	*Gopalpur*	*Mundal*
2	879 (31.6)	658 (31.4)	855 (16.07)	69.7 (3.67)

Note: IRR of the projects are 58%, 58%, 46% and 22% respectively.

1. At 2% SDR the NPV as a criterion indicates territorial plantations with Rs.8, 79, 000/ is better one compared to Gopalpur project with Rs.8, 55, 000/.(shown in Table 1.3)

2. BCR as a criterion indicates territorial plantations having higher BCR i.e. 31.6 followed by plantations of Gopalpur(16.07).

3. IRR also indicates territorial plantations having highest IRR with 58%; plantations of Gopalpur being second with 46%.

Table 4: Socio-Eco-Environmental NPV (in thousand rupees) of the projects

Rate of Discount (%)	*Govt.*		*SFP*	
	C-11	*C-13*	*Gopalpur*	*Mundal*
2	2821 (99.5)	2110 (98.6)	5336 (95.13)	2009 (78.09)

Note: IRR of the projects are 233%, 230%, 242% and 242% respectively.

1. At 2% SDR the NPV criterion shows Gopalpur project(Rs.53, 36, 000/) is better than the government projects.

2. However, BCR shows territorial plantations having higher BCR(Balukhanda C-11 has 99.5) followed by Gopalpur project with 95.13.

3. But again IRR shows Gopalpur project with 242% is better than the territorial plantation with IRR of 233%.

However, as we have already mentioned that for comparison of all these projects with a wide gap of area of cultivation, these three criteria seem to be insufficient. Hence we have estimated another criterion, which is based on NPV i.e. NPV per hectare. The major findings of this criterion are presented in Table 5.

Table 5: NPV per hectare of the projects at 2% rates of discount

Projects	*Financial*	*Economic*	*Socio-Economic*	*Socio-Economic Environmental*
C –11(Govt.)	85600	107370	109800	352600
C-13(Govt.)	85600	107330	109600	351600
Gopalpur(SFP)	123400	163200	171000	1067200
Mundal(SFP)	2650	7380	9950	287000

1. From financial analysis while Gopalpur VWL has maximum NPV per hectare at 2% discount rate, the territorial plantations is the second one.

2. Economic analysis shows that at 2% discount rate the highest NPV per hectare is obtained from Gopalpur project(Rs.1, 63, 200/) and the second is obtained from C-11.

3. Socio-economic analysis at 2% discount rate also shows highest NPV per hectare from Gopalpur project (Rs.1, 71, 000/) followed by territorial plantation.

4. Socio-eco-environmental analysis at 2% discount rate also confirms the Gopalpur project with Rs.10, 67, 200/ NPV per hectare being the first one.

From the above findings it is observed that while the social forestry plantations are showing higher NPVs, the territorial plantations are always showing high BCR and IRR. The reason behind this is that the costs of territorial plantations are very less compared to benefits. These plantations do not show any kind of maintenance cost whereas for other long life-span projects the share of maintenance cost in the total cost is quite considerable.

Policy Implications

Our study corroborates to other studies like R A Sharma, DPS Verma who have advocated for a socio-economic study of forestry sector as such type of study only depicts the true picture of viability of plantation projects. The ordering changes as we move from the financial analysis to the socio-economic-environmental evaluation. Besides ordering pattern, socio-economic study reveals clearly the wide gap in the viability among all projects. While Gopalpur SFP has NPV per hectare of Rs.1, 23, 400/ at 2% SRD, the territorial projects have Rs.85, 600/.

Here our study also confirms to the hypothesis of Rath(1997) who has expressed his view that since the external benefits of social forestry projects are more prominent than the direct benefits, those benefits should not be neglected in establishing the economic viability of such projects.

Further our study conforms to the idea of Saxena & Agarwal(1997) who have expressed their view that adoption of socio-eco-environmental accounting would help in improving their overall performance. In our study the socio-eco-environmental study confirms the Gopalpur VWL as the most socially viable project through NPV per hectare as criterion.

Thirdly, our study also satisfies to the idea of Blair(1986) according to whom objectives of the social forestry projects should be modified according to the local people's needs; to this we add our view that the social forestry projects should be of mixed variety. This implies that instead of mono cropping patterns in plantations, the policy makers should aim at mixed plantations for higher socio-economic benefits. Moreover, our literature survey also shows that Patel(1987) has called for mixed cropping in social forestry to have better result. Since our sample project Gopalpur VWL has mixed varieties of plants (i.e. casuarina, eucalyptus, and cashew), its profitability is significantly higher than the other social forestry project. Harrison and Sharma(1995) have also found out that 78% of people in Australia planted plots of at least four species, compared with only 5% planting mono cultures. Some land holders have planted together 40 or more species, mostly natives and many of recognised high timber quality. Thus policy makers should keep this in mind while implementing social forestry projects.

From our field observations another point we can add that for plantation projects participation from local people is very much needed for its success. The general remark of the people engaged in social forestry programmes is that the social forestry plantation is their own unlike government plantation. Here we can quote Harrison[9] who is also of the same view: "Often the forests which best meet a variety of objectives are those arising from 'bottom-up' design, that is, involving local community inputs".

On the other hand, the local people of SFPs are very much enthusiastic about their plantations. Both the sample projects fulfil the local needs of fuel, fodder and small timber. The villagers are united for the project. However, as reported earlier that SFPs are successful only where there are homogeneity in castes of the local people. With different classes and castes it is difficult to manage the plantations peacefully. This has been proved from our field experiences also. The Mundal VWL that was established in 1985-86 resulted in division of two hamlets where two different castes are residing. After the maturity harvest the lower caste people are not satisfied with the way the distribution of benefits was undertaken. Now the lower caste people have started another plantation project for which they are very much enthusiastic. Thus, when SFP creates bad relationship, at the same time, it has helped in development of villagers with competitive feeling between the two hamlets.

---

9 Harrison,S.R.(1997), "Recreation and Amenity Values of Reforestation", paper presented in....., Bhubaneswar, Orissa.

REFERENCES

1. Blair, Harry W(1986), "Social Forestry: Time to Modify Goals?", *Economic and Political Weekly*, Vol.21, No.30, July 26, pp. 1317-21.
2. Livingstone, Ian and Tribe M(1995), "Projects with long term Horizons, their economics appraisal and the discount rate", *Project Appraisal*, Vol.10, No.2, June, pp. 66-76.
3. Niskanen, Anssi(1997), "Economic Profitability of afforestation in Thailand and the Philippines", *Project Appraisal*, Vol.12, No.3, Sept., pp.193-203.
4. Patel, V.J.(1987), "Social Forestry: A Farmer's Viewpoint", *Economic and Political Weekly*, August, pp. 1365-1366.
5. Rath B. and S. K .Acharya(1997), "Quantification of External Benefits of Forest Development Programmes", Paper Presented in the 33rd *Indian Econometric Conference*, Hyderabad.
6. Robert, T.Deacon(1995), "Assessing the Relationship between Government Policy and Deforestation", *Journal of Environmental Economics and Management*, Vol.28, No.1, pp. 1-18.
7. Saxena, Rakesh and Rajesh Agrawal(1997), "Socio-Eco-Environmental Accounting: A Proposed Framework For Tree Growers" Co-Operatives With A Case Study", *Working Paper No.110*, Institute of Rural Management, Anand.
8. Sell Axel(1992), "Planning and Evaluation of Projects in countries with high inflation rates", *Project Appraisal*, Vol. 7, No.1, March, pp. 11-20.
9. Sharma, R A and MG Mc Graw(1991), "Economic Discount and Wage Rates for Social Forestry Projects in India: Estimates and Problems." *Project Appraisal*
10. Sharma, R.A(1996), "Analytical Techniques for Social Forestry Evaluation: A Review", *The Indian Forester.*
11. Shukla, Rohit(1992), "Social Forestry in Gujarat Employment and Income", *The Price of Forest*, edt. By Anil Agarwal, Proceedings of a seminar of Centre for Science and Environment.

28

Economic Development through Rural Tourism in India

Challenges and Strategies

*Dr. J. Bala Komaraiah**

Introduction

Basic definitions of tourism ware established at the United Nations (Conference of Tourism and International Travel, Rome 1963) and by the United Nations Commission on Statistics (April 1968). Later on these definitions were revised and updated at the World Tourism Organization (WTO) conference at Ottawa in June 1991 and certain recommendations were formulated. These have been adopted by most of the countries. The W.T.O. distinguishes between three basic forms of tourism:

- *domestic tourism*: involving residents of the given country traveling only within the country
- *inbound tourism*: involving non-residents traveling in another country
- *outbound tourism*: involving residents traveling in another country

* Lecturer, Department of Economics, Faculty of Social Sciences, Banaras Hindu University, Varanasi 221 005 (U.P.).

Tourism has become an integral part of modern life. Tourism works as a force for socio-economic, cultural, educational and environmental changes, and it has had an impact of the same order as the industrial revolution.

Tourism is the world's largest and fast growing export industry, which according to W.T.O generated about US$ 372.6 billion during 1995 by some 567 million tourists worldwide. In the same year travel and tourism is said to have provided direct and indirect employment for 212 million people accounting for 10.7 percent of the global workforce. In 1998, world tourism generated 12 percent of G.N.P.

Domestic tourism is assumed to be nine times greater than international tourism. Thus, tourism provided a major contribution to foreign exchange earnings of several developing and developed countries.

Tourism and economic development

It is generally recognized that tourism stimulates the development of several sectors of the national economy. Tourism:

- creates new local requirements for equipment, food and other supplies fostering new industries and commercial activities and creating a new market for them,
- has a favourable impact upon employment in a country as it increases the opportunities available for work in accommodation, food industries, tour operations and travel agencies, government tourist offices, handicraft and souvenir trades, recreational, amusement and entertainment activities, and various selling outlets,
- increases urbanization through the continuous growth of construction and renovation of tourist facilities. This implies creating and improving

infrastructures and tourist superstructures, particularly in remote and depressed areas,

- helps to increase the state earnings of hard currency necessary for bridging of reducing whatever deficit there is in the balance of payments, and thus fosters the development of the national economy,
- is one of the most effective re-distributive factors in international economic relations. To explain this, one has to admit that travel is a social activity arising from surplus income. Thus the flow of foreign travel is more significant from richer countries to the less privileged. A substantial portion of foreign travel is directed towards developing regions, which are more attractive naturally as they are not yet spoiled by industrialization. Thus tourism redistributes capital between developed and developing countries, and
- activates the economic circuit in country, thus accelerating the multiplier effect.

In developing countries with good tourism potential, tourism may be adopted as an economic activity that could rationalize economic policy, especially through balanced growth brought about by new or additional business production cycles prompted by tourism expansion. Thus tourism can become that cause and the effect of rationalizing economic development, along with the economic production sectors of agriculture and industry.

Tourism's positive contribution to the economic, social, political and environmental advancement of developing countries is contingent upon the able implementation of suitable scientific, technical and technological factors, as well as the appropriate deployment of available resources to maximize benefits and minimize disadvantages. This is not an easy task given that developing countries usually lack of adequate expertise. Such weakness could be surmounted by bilateral assistance from developed countries, as well as international cooperation through international organizations, namely WTO, ILO, the World Bank and Regional Development Banks.

Both proponents and opponents of tourism as a tool of development in developing countries admit that tourism has made influential changes in the structure, value systems, traditions and behavioural patterns of many societies.

Tourism creates a host of multifarious downstream activities, which have the capacity to substantially involve a large number of people. Apart from generating income, being a labour intensive sector, it generates employment mostly self-employment and promotes the overall development of the tourist destinations. Furthermore, with the increase in international tourism, the host country is in a position to earn valuable foreign exchange. This was recognized in the 'Master Plan for Tourism Development, Goa – 1987' by the Indian Government.

Tourism Potential in India

India has an ancient tradition of tourism. The ancient invaders viewed that India as a goldmine with unlimited wealth to plunder, the learned were fascinated by its mystic spiritualism and profound philosophy; the uninitiated saw it as a land of naked fakirs and snake charmers, while the others were simply charmed by the sheer beauty of its natural attractions and amazing variety of its flora and fauma. The lure of show-clad mountains, grandeur of the mighty rivers like the Ganges and the Brahmaputra are inspiring sand dunes of the Thar in Rajasthan, beautiful beaches of Goa along with various medieval forts, architectural grandeur of holy temples and the ageless charm of the legendary Taj Mahal have been beckoning the wonderers since long. The diverse climate conditions too have made it possible for the tourists to visit our country around the year.

These inherent advantages should have made India an ideal tourist destination, but various constraints like Political instability, terrorism and lack of adequate infrastructure have hampered the growth of tourism.

Government Efforts in India

The following are some of the Govt. efforts in promoting and developing tourism in India. The Government of India had established a tourism cell in Ministry of transport in the year 1949 to coordinate activities relating to tourism. To attract foreign tourists, India set-up tourist offices in New York in 1952, London in 1953 and over 20 similar offices were setting across the Globe.

- The first Hotel Management Institute was set up at Mumbai in 1954 to supply manpower resources for tourism development, and the Government entered hotel business by constructing Hotel Ashoka at New Delhi in 1956.
- The tourism cell in the Ministry of Transport was converted into a full-fledged Directorate to Tourism in 1958 to boost tourism activities.
- During the Eighth Plan, tourism was recognized as an Industry with a high potential for employment generation
- Indian Tourism Development Corporation (ITDC) was established in 1996 to develop tourism infrastructure and for promotion of tourism
- Indian Institute of Tourism and Travel Management, an apex institution was established for improving trained manpower in tourism sector.

- The National Committee on Tourism (NCT) was constituted in 1986 to study various issues relating to tourism development and to suggest measure for drawing up a perspective plan for tourism development in the country
- Tourism Finance Corporation (TFC) was set-up in 1989 to make available loans for development of tourism projects.

As a result of the efforts made by the Central and State Governments, tourism industry expanded by the way of increasing allocations for tourism through five-year plans from Rs. 1.59 crore in second Plan to Rs. 364.61 crore in the Eighth Plan. The tourism industry has already become the third biggest export industry after ready made garments and gems and Jewellery and provided employment to over 175 lakh persons in 1994-95 estimated foreign exchanges about Rs. 9, 186 crore in 1995-96.

Rural Tourism

Unfortunately, rural tourism in India has been a neglected area, as the concentration so far has been on urban tourism, based on historical monuments or beach tourism around big cities. It caters to roughly 20 percent of the Indian population and the rest 80 percent living in over 600, 000 villages, remains untouched by the beneficial impact of tourism. A new trend in tourists, both national and international is being noticed, which is their intention to visit rural areas. It is hence important to develop village tourism in order to tap this potential source of income and development.

Research on rural tourism has illustrated an essential element of 'balance' in tourist development. Indeed, much of it has had an implicit cost – benefit calculus. Tourism in rural areas has played a positive role in raising rural incomes and introducing 'growth poles' into backward, low-income agricultural areas, thus preventing or slowing out migration. However, it has had disruptive effects on the rural environment, on local cultures and life styles, on agricultural patterns and even productivity. Consequently, litany of the rural tourism researcher is to call for planning. It is clear that infrastructure development is essential if tourists are to be transported to and accommodated and amused in the rural areas, as this is usually the province of public bodies, then such bodies have a degree of control over access. The key concern is largely that the very thing that rural tourists require a bucolic environment is not destroyed by the sheer weight of tourists. Unique attraction, which exist in an essentially rural environment, such as the cave dwellings of Spain, France and Turkey, and Stonehenge in England, pose particularly difficult problems of balance, access and destruction of the environment.

Due to busy life in urban areas, people in urban areas look for fresh habitat, simplistic ways of life and less stressful environment. International tourists look for cheaper holiday destinations, authentic traditions and culture and original places. Village tourism offers both. Village environment in India is full of fresh air, green pastures and wide range of rural art and handicrafts, folk music, traditional medicines like herbs, yoga, meditation ethnic life style, unique culture and customs. All these need to be marketed as an alternative to mainstream tourism to tourists belongs to local, national and foreign.

Domestic tourism is currently led by religious motivation, which can be expanded to rural areas in order to include the prices of acculturations–inter cultural communication.

Tourism is linked to the development in the areas of economic, social, cultural and ecological. Village tourism can create various self-employment opportunities and informal jobs. It can be advantage in rural areas for farmers who are able to work during off-season and remain in agriculture.

International tourism leads to changes in values, morals, traditions, social hierarchies and affect the ecology. It is up to our planners to preserve the good of the society in our traditions and ignore the bad. Old traditions will get refined and new ones will be created.

The number of international tourist arrivals in India rose from 25 million in 1950 to 183 million in 1970, and average growth rate of more than 10 percent. Since 1973 the effect of rise in oil prices has merely moderated the rate of expansion the number of international tourist arrival was 8, 15, 006 in the year 1994, 8, 42, 842 in 1995 and 9, 31, 458 in 1996 respectively.

Indian Government statement said that foreign tourist arrivals had dropped to 1, 32, 988 in May 2002 from 1, 51, 098 earlier and were down 14.4 percent in May from April 2002 arrivals of 1, 55, 378.

Arrivals in the January to May 2002 period dropped 14.7 percent to 9, 66, 523 from 1.13 million in the year earlier period. The slide in tourism hit foreign exchange earnings in January to May 2002, which fall 14 percent to US$ 1, 182.92 million from the same period last year. This decline is due to the heat of terrorism with the Pakistan and struggled to over come the effects of the September 11 attack in U.S.A.

Poor Infrastructure Facilities

Much smaller countries with far less attractive destinations receive more tourists than India does. This is because access to India has been made so difficult and unpleasant, starting with the complexity of the landing card and extending the absence of the proper airport facilities like no walk on conveyer belts, slow baggage retrieval, inconveniently high X-ray belts, poor facilities for those waiting to receive passengers etc. X-ray machines would catch metal contraband, and sniffer dogs would get to forbidden drugs. There are other many issues to be tackled and the arrival hassles exemplify the problem.

Problems of Rural Tourism

The growth of tourism has its own hurdles; the first is that of land use. Since the much areas of tourist destination are devoted to agriculture, there may be a conflict between demand for tourism and the demand for agriculture. Tourist traffic en route and where it concentrates in particular locations affects the rural environment. Vehicles create congestion on the roads and at sites as well as noise and other forms of pollution. Aircraft noise disturbs the residents and causes damage to wild life. Tourists damage current crops and flora and leave litter behind without tourism the rural environment would have a better chance of being preserved. Italy, Israel and Lebanon have been facing the problems of pollution and effecting the development of tourism industry in these countries.

Guidelines for Sustainable Tourism

Sustainable tourism requires a broad vision, which encompasses larger time, and space frames than what would be traditionally required in normal tourism planning and decision-making. It is not sufficient to implement such general tourism planning principles as, for example, Zoning, clustering, integration between attractions and facilities, interdependence between national and cultural attractions, multiple ways to provide accessibility, elasticity, diversity and complementarities, cost-benefit analysis and applications of carrying capacity.

In addition, certain guidelines have to be followed to achieve sustainable tourism.

- Public awareness of benefits of tourism and how to mitigate its negative impacts should be pursued.
- Local people should be encouraged to assure leadership roles in planning and development with a necessary assistances from Government, business, financial institutions and Universities
- In planning of tourism development projects, primary consideration should be given to the protection of national and cultural assets with due regard to the appropriate social-economic uses and human impacts on physical and built environment.
- Provide samples to other industries of how to conduct business practices that actively contribute towards sustainable development.
- Provide necessary infrastructure in remote areas with tourism potential, to encourage human settlements and other economic activities to grow in harmony with tourism.
- Create socio-economic value for primitive resources including natural beauty, wild life and forests as well as historical and cultural heritage, built heritage and traditional ways of life.
- Use international communication networks to spread messages and practices of sustainable development.

Conclusion

Though, globally India is an important tourist destination, due to tension between the Pakistan and India and after September 11, 2001, (attack on W.T.C. in the U.S.A.) foreign tourist arrival had declined by 12 percent in May 2002. But this is in short run only. We can receive more tourists by strengthening of international cooperation among the countries. We should attract more tourists by our competitive and appropriate tourism policies. In this regard some states like, Goa, Kerala, Tamil Nadu, Karnataka, Rajasthan, Delhi, U.P., Arunachal Pradesh etc. are more ahead in attracting foreign tourists than the other states in India. Government should also give priority to the tourism sector by formulating appropriate policies and allocating adequate funds. Tourism sector can develop only in an environment of peace and stability where the traveler is sure of safety and security, services are prompt and hassle-free and there is no attempt at extortion or cheating and thus India will become one of the most attractive tourism destinations in the near future.

REFERENCES

1. Bishwanath Ghosh "Tourism and Travel Management" Vikash Publishing Home Pvt. Ltd., New Delhi, 1988.
2. Business Standard, A daily News Paper, August 27, 2002; June 4, 2002.
3. Dusmanta K Giri, "Tourism in Rural India" Kurukshetra, Vol. 49, No. 2 Nov. 2000.
4. Francois Villas and Lionel Becheral "International tourism and economic Respective" Macmillan Press Ltd., 1995.
5. Padmashree Santosh Yadav, "Eco-tourism: Problems and Prospects" Employment News, 17-23 August, 2002, New Delhi.
6. Salah Wahab and John J Pigram "Tourism and sustainability Policy considerations" in Salah Wahab and John J.Pigram (ed) *Tourism development and growth: The challenge of sustainability,* Routledge Publication, London. 277-290.
7. Salah Wahab; "Sustainable tourism in the developing world" in Salah Wahab and John J.Pigram (ed) *Tourism development and growth: The challenge of sustainability* Routledge Publication, London.

8. Wahab, S. Elements of state policy on Tourism, Turin: Halgraphica (1974).

9. Wahab, S., "Government's role in strategic planning for tourism, in *VNR's Encyclopedia of Hospitality and tourism*, New York; Van Nostrand Reinhold, (1992) (746-53).

10. World Tourism Organization, "Recommendations on tourism statistics", Madrid, 1998.